THE RESCUE OF DANISH JEWRY

Test of a Democracy

The Rescue
of Danish Jewry

Test of a Democracy

By LENI YAHIL

Translated from the Hebrew by Morris Gradel

The Jewish Publication Society of America

PHILADELPHIA   5730 / 1969

Copyright © 1969 by
The Jewish Publication Society
All rights reserved
First Edition, 1969
Paperback Edition, 1983
Library of Congress Catalog Card Number 69-19039
ISBN 0-8276-0232-4
Designed by Sidney Feinberg
Printed in the United States of America

Contents

Preface to the Paperback edition

October 1983 marks the fortieth anniversary of the events described and analyzed in this book. The many observances of this anniversary indicate that the memory of the Danish Jews' miraculous redemption from the Nazi attempt at annihilation is still cherished by Jews, as by all people of good will, throughout the world.

Forty years, as we know from the Bible, constitutes a distinct and significant historical period. The passage of four decades since the famous rescue of the Jews from Denmark to the protective shores of Sweden thus affords an opportunity to probe once more the web of circumstances that led to this spectacular act of solidarity.

In pondering the matter, three questions come most immediately to mind: Has the historical research of the last fifteen years—since the original publication of this study—unearthed any new evidence which would prompt us to revise our conceptions of the rescue? How has the widespread research of the Holocaust influenced our understanding and estimation of the actions and attitudes of the people of Denmark during the period under consideration? Finally, looking back on the rescue and on the forty years that have elapsed, what is the significance today of the events of October 1943?

In answer to the first question, one may observe that the extensive Danish historical examinations of the period of the war years, along with the published memoirs and biographies of leading personalities of the time, shed light on many aspects of the events in Denmark under the German occupation. Still, to the best of my knowledge, no major divergence from the overall conception that is here set forth has come to the fore, although there have, of course, been welcome additions as well as correction of details.

Regarding the second question, it can be noted that today we know more about the attempts at rescue of the Jews in both eastern and western Europe than we did fifteen years ago. The many failures, the lack of insight and understanding, the lost opportunities, as well as the trials of Jews and non-Jews to save Jewish lives, have been greatly elaborated. We have come to comprehend the complexities of the Jewish struggle for survival prior to the implementation of the "final solution." Indeed, the many studies about the situation of the Jews and the behavior of the governments and peoples in occupied and satellite states show that wherever a government or a political leadership retained its function, it had the equally viable options of joining the Germans in persecuting the Jews and deporting them, or of protecting them and resisting their deportation. Their decisions depended on the character of the regime, its relationship with Germany, and its assumptions concerning the outcome of the war. No less important was the impact of anti-Semitism prevailing in the population or, on the contrary, the latter's spontaneous identification with their Jewish fellow-citizens.

The behavior of the Danes showed no exception to these rules. Their unequivocal identification with their Jewish fellow-citizens was in part an outgrowth of the general war situation of 1943 and their scornful rejection of Germany's violation of the occupation terms. Without this coincidence of factors, the act of rescue would probably have not been so spontaneous and unanimous. A year before, only half of the Jews in Norway had been able to escape to Sweden with the help of the underground movement.

Finally, to answer the third question, regarding the retrospective significance of October 1943: in the years following World War II, the term "genocide" has become accepted as denoting the most severe crime against humanity. The Danes' spontaneous action, together with other similar individual or collective attempts, thus anticipated and demonstrated the most significant salutary development in modern political consciousness. However, in the nuclear age, one is moved to observe, spontaneity may no longer be considered sufficient to safeguard a population—or even mankind.

The Danish rescue operation of October 1943, as I noted in my preface to the earlier edition of this book, "indicates which elements enable a small nation to remain true to itself even under the most trying conditions. It restores to their special honor the humane values, so often distorted and underestimated under the impact of the worldwide struggle for power and predominance." Times and conditions have changed. Nevertheless, even after forty years, this remarkable rescue stands out as a praiseworthy and heroic event—and this is how it ought to be remembered for all time.

L.Y.

Jerusalem
June 1983

L'idée des droits n'est autre chose que l'idée de la vertu introduite dans le monde politique.
—ALEXIS DE TOCQUEVILLE

Introduction

The rescue of Danish Jewry in October 1943 became a legend even as it occurred. The news spread immediately throughout the free world and was greeted with enthusiasm and deep satisfaction. Here was a tiny nation in the grip of an omnipotent conqueror; yet in the very hour when it became stripped of its arms and its democratic rule was violently suspended, it suddenly rose and snatched a handful of Jews out of the very hands of their oppressors and spirited them away to safety in Sweden in an operation often referred to since as "little Dunkirk." In those dark days of the cruel war and the Nazi regime's overpowering deeds of horror, a ray of light appeared. The brotherhood of nations and the dignity of man were turned into rapid and courageous action by two Nordic peoples—conquered Denmark and neutral Sweden. The free world, locked in a bitter war against the enemy of mankind, paused for a moment before this act of salvation which so vividly expressed those principles of humanity under whose banner the Allies had gone forth to battle.

At the time neither the rescuing Danes nor the rescued Jews nor even the secure Swedes had such thoughts in mind. On the contrary, perhaps the most astonishing phenomenon, and the very element in which greatness lay, was the fact that the Danes regarded their deeds as not in the least extraordinary or worthy of praise and admiration. In their opinion they merely did the natural and necessary, and never for a moment considered the possibility of abandoning the Jews to their fate. The Jews, confused and numb with shock as they were, clasped the proffered hand of rescue and let themselves be borne along on the stream of energy which burst forth from the Danish people. Reading their various accounts of those fateful days one is struck by three recurring points: events overwhelmed them as in a nightmare; most of them quickly developed strong instincts of self-preservation and learned rapidly how to adapt themselves to danger and deal with it under the guidance of their rescuers; and the emotion that outlasted the memory of their terror is their feeling of deepest gratitude to the Danes who rescued them and to the Swedes who gave them refuge.

Only at the end of the war, upon their return home to their everyday lives, only when they became fully aware of the catastrophe that had befallen the Jewish people— only then did the Danish Jews begin to understand the extent of the miracle that had happened to them. This feeling was expressed by Jul. Margolinsky in the closing lines of his introduction to Aage Bertelsen's Danish book *October '43:*[1]

The Bible, in the Book of Esther, tells that 2,500 years ago the wicked Haman plotted the annihilation of the Jews of Persia. . . . Had the compilation of the Bible not been concluded so many generations ago, one could well imagine that the story of the events of October '43 would have been included in the Holy Scriptures to be commemorated for generations to come.

These words would appear to have been inspired by two motives. One—perhaps the most essential—was that the rescue action was so wonderful and seemed so miraculous that its equal could be found only in the chronicles of the Bible. The second is the wish to confer on the Danish people the greatest reward a Jew has to offer—to perpetuate the deed and insure the Danes their place in Jewish history.

In examining the relationship between saga and history in light of contemporary scholarship, Martin Buber explains in his book *Moses* that "saga and the writing of history start out from the identical point, the event" and that "it is the saga which in particular preserves historical memories, not of what the consequences show to be 'historical event,' but of that which roused the emotions of the man undergoing the experience."[2] The Jews of Denmark had, it is true, no cloud or pillar of fire to guide them; nor did the sea divide so that they could pass on dry land to the shore of safety; but the spirit of the times found in the noble figure of the old Danish king, Christian X, the symbol of its awakening. This process commenced—long before the actual attempts at deportation or the rescue action—when the attitude of the Danish people deterred the Germans from implementing any of the restrictions or laws normally connected with their attacks on the Jews in other countries, preparatory to the deportation and extermination. This earlier period also gave birth to the legend that the yellow star could not be introduced into Denmark because the king had threatened to don this badge of shame together with his Jewish subjects. After the rescue operation this story became the common property of almost everyone who took an interest in the miraculous rescue of the Danish Jews. No one—raconteur, journalist, writer, politician, not even research scholars—could find a more striking expression of the Danish character and behavior than this story or others of a similar stamp. From the historiographic viewpoint the story cannot be corroborated.[3] Not only stories, but also poems were written about the event.[4] At the time, the emotions found expression also in the words of the Jewish Agency Executive's telegram of thanks sent to the Swedish government and to the speaker of the Riksdag (Parliament) on behalf of the Jews of Palestine:[5] "Our prayer is that you continue the noble work which is one of the few rays of light in the moral darkness which envelops Europe today."

In contrast to the integrational force of legend and its irrational source in "the emotions of man," the force of historical research is analytical and its source rational; "there is no scientific-historic understanding apart from its rational understanding," says Buber in the chapter already quoted.[6] Historiography demands from us to lay bare the details in all their scope and contradictions, to investigate their factual veracity, to compare them, to probe deeply in order to understand them, and then again to collate them in such a way that the true historical picture emerges, illuminating the course of events and their causes.

The Holocaust is an event so vast and so unlike any other known pattern of historical and spiritual experience that it is not surprising that our generation, the generation which witnessed the catastrophe and experienced its horrors, seems to be unable as yet to interpret it fully, to make it comprehensible to ourselves and to coming generations. This generation has found an expression and redemption in *action*—in establishing the State of Israel; it has yet to find its historical and historiographical explanation. All expressions have until now been partial and in some way defective, both in the realm of legend—story and poem—and in the field of research. The evaluations are as numerous as the writers and scholars. Philip Friedmann, himself one of the survivors of the catastrophe and one of the first to realize the historiographic duties of our generation, said in 1957 in his lecture on "Problems of Research on the European Jewish Catastrophe":

We cannot as yet determine what impact this crisis will have upon the trend of thought and upon the spiritual physiognomy of our people in the years to come. It is quite unusual for philosophical and historiosophical systems to spring up overnight, or to develop after a holocaust, because they require a long perspective to come into being and crystallize.[7]

In presenting a comprehensive survey of Holocaust research in those days, its institutions, achievements, problems, and inherent dangers, he stresses the variety and multiplicity of the material and the resulting lack of cohesion. He calls for concentration, collaboration, and cooperation with a view to attaining a uniform and comprehensive research method—and, what is more, a general evaluation. We are still far from such a state of affairs.

All the studies are somehow incomplete in that they are limited in location, in subject, or in approach, or in all of these together. One of the most difficult problems of research into the Holocaust is the enormous scope of the material. This does not merely render a collated presentation difficult—even the complicated problems of classifying, arranging, processing, and publishing source material are still far from being solved satisfactorily.

The technical-scientific problem is not the only one, perhaps not even the most important, of those rendering difficult our attempts to prepare the ground for an effective study of the Holocaust. Friedmann, too, in the above-mentioned lecture, points out the danger of preliminary evaluations and emotional attitudes arising from mental reactions to the terrible experiences being detrimental to scientific study. He names such approaches: the martyrological school, the school which overemphasizes the aspects of revolt and resistance, and the nationalist and the Communist schools.

All these create, in Friedmann's view, new myths and undermine the aim of research by imposing on it emotional patterns. All these schools have one object in common: to avoid recognizing the terrible and depressing fact that a third of our people were slaughtered with virtually no possibility of defending themselves, and with almost no help rendered either by their people in Palestine or the Diaspora, or from the nations of the world. "The knowledge of the facts as they were," said Professor B. Dinur, "with all the horror they evoke is, we believe, the only way to point out this abyss into which Man is capable of plunging."[8]

This objective, difficult as it is, is immeasurably more difficult for the generation which witnessed the catastrophe, since this generation is beset by a feeling of guilt. Hence, attempts are made to gloss over the mass murder by over-emphasizing the supreme heroism of the few, to glorify the Jewish capacity for suffering, or to interpret what cannot be interpreted according to set formulas of nationalistic or socialistic ideologies. All of these, whatever their intentions or philosophies, actually belong to one school whose main purpose is to rationalize what happened in order to save the honor and conscience of the nation. In contrast to this school, another has emerged whose declared aim is to look facts in the face and to show the inertia of the victims toward their murderers—more, to reveal the weakness and corruption of Jewish society, which in their opinion, assisted the process of annihilation. This approach, in its various facets, bases its conclusions actually on psychological analysis, which in effect replaces the role of historical research while not always being based itself on scientific psychology. The fundamental purpose of these "accusers" is diametrically opposed to that of the "apologists," for they want to prove that the Jewish people lost its vitality and its moral force.

Though they oppose one another and their basic motives are antagonistic, these two schools—the apologists and the accusers—are united in their methodological approach, an approach which is completely untenable from a scientific point of view. Both take one single factor—the social, the

national, the psychological, etc.—and turn it into the one
and only factor which caused the catastrophe, thus dis-
torting this complex phenomenon and the conclusions to be
drawn from it. Whether they are guided by the desire to
rationalize the fact that the Jews fell victim to the Nazis
or by the wish to blame them for having done so, in either
case emotional judgments precede the study; the scholar
tries to use the research in order to present his ideology or to
create the myth which suits him. And this, as Friedmann
points out, sabotages the aim of research.

Our inability to free ourselves adequately from our
mental reactions and aspirations is perhaps the main reason
why we have not yet been able to achieve a general and
comprehensive presentation of the events of the Holocaust,
not to mention a general evaluation and formulated conclusion. But this difficulty does not absolve us from the
need to strive toward these ends, to attempt to construct
from the sources as comprehensive, variegated, and objective a picture as possible, using all those methods of research, examination, and criticism which historiography has
developed for examining more distant periods of the past.
Even if our generation will not be privileged to summarize
the facts, realize their full connotations, and impart them
to others, it is its duty to pass on to succeeding generations
the immediate and firsthand knowledge that will perish with
it. The source of our weakness in this study is also the
source of our obligation and our authority to deal with it.
The necessary striving for objectivity will not diminish the
spiritual response of our generation. On the contrary, the
more we eliminate prejudice and generalization, the greater
its worth.

This study of the fate of Danish Jewry during the ca-
tastrophe is one of those partial studies, one of the episodes.
Anyone who has tried to deal with the problems of the
Holocaust as a whole may ask: What is the importance of

this study which deals with one atypical aspect of the terrible fate of European Jewry? When millions died what importance is there in the rescue of seven to eight thousand Jews while less than 2 per cent of the local community—many of them old people—perished? Still, the reaction of the free world to this event, however small in scope, shows that it is not small in significance. The true question is: Why were the Jews of Denmark not exterminated as were millions of their brethren in other occupied countries? What or who prevented the German rulers in this case from implementing their plans for the "final solution"?

The success of the Danish rescue operation is generally attributed to five factors:

(1) The small number of Jews in Denmark.
(2) The special political conditions prevailing in the "model protectorate" of the Germans in Denmark.
(3) The geographical proximity of neutral Sweden.
(4) The date of the persecutions—autumn 1943, after the German defeats at El Alamein and Stalingrad had marked the turning point of the war.
(5) The special character and moral stature of the Danish people and their love of democracy and freedom.

These five factors are true and valid, each in its own right, but it is not enough to list them—the significance of each has to be examined.

(1) Other countries also had small Jewish communities—Luxembourg and Norway, for instance. Before the war there were about three thousand Jews in Luxembourg of whom at least two-thirds perished. In Norway 700 out of 1,700 died.

(2) Norway, like Holland, was controlled by the S.S. under the command of *Reichskommissar* Terboven, assisted by that same Quisling whose name became a synonym for Nazi collaborators. No "quisling government" ever arose in Denmark.

(3) Neutral Sweden was just as close to Denmark before October 1943, but prior to that date illegal passage was a costly and dangerous adventure successfully attempted by only a very few.

(4) The fact that the Germans first persecuted the Jews in Denmark in October 1943 was due to the abolition of the "model protectorate" as late as the preceding August.

The question still remains: Why did the Germans not bother the Jews during the whole time when a sort of working agreement was kept up between them and the Danish authorities? In our opinion the decisive factor was the last: (5) It was the character and political regime of the Danes that made it possible for the other factors to contribute to the rescue.

We should not, however, forget that the Danes were not, fortunately, the only people of whom it might be asked: How was it that so many Jews were saved? But Denmark, together with Finland and Bulgaria, was the only country where the success of the rescuers was so general and complete, and certainly the only country where a widespread, spontaneous, and rapid rescue action was overtly carried out. If we find in the course of this study that this general rescue action was indeed a result of the Danish national culture, as reflected in the country's free social structure and democratic form of government, we shall also throw light on the corresponding question: How was it that the Nazi persecutor was in most other other places able to realize his evil plans to so great a degree?

In the case of Denmark, research opportunities are good from several points of view: documents and primary source material are available for all the participants—the Danes, the Germans, the Swedes, and the Jews—but their quantity does not exceed the limits of a historical study. This restricted scope gives some guarantee that the subject can be examined both in breadth and in depth. Moreover, the central event— the transfer of the Jews from Denmark to Sweden—was also limited in time, since it all took place over two to three weeks. The study is also simpler in emotional terms than in most events of the Holocaust which ended in ways other than rescue. Here is a rare instance where the researcher must be careful not to overdo his enthusiasm for the rescuer, anymore than he should overindulge his hatred for the persecutor.

On the basis of these two assumptions—first, that the fundamental question of the factors which led to the rescue may clarify some small part of the unfathomed elements which brought about the catastrophe; and second, that the practical and psychological conditions are favorable for research—we may hope that an investigation into this limited episode may somehow help this generation's efforts to probe and to comprehend what has befallen it.

But beyond all these considerations, we may share the desire to confer on the Danish people the place of honor they merit in the annals of our people and perhaps in the annals of our time.

Efforts to rescue the "remnants" [wrote Professor B. Dinur] were an integral part of the Jewish struggle. . . . Gentiles, as individuals and groups, engaged in these activities, risking their lives and the lives of their families in an effort to help their Jewish neighbors. Many of them were killed. Their actions recall the ancient saying of our sages: "A little light pushes away much darkness." These "lights from the darkness" strengthened the belief of many desperate men in the enduring dignity of Man.[9]

Our study endeavors to describe this special historical event in all its scope, to bare its roots, to examine its consequences and implications, and—if at all possible—to learn its lessons.

PART ONE

BACKGROUND

I

Outline of the History of the Jews in Denmark

From the Arrival of the Jews in Denmark to the Outbreak of Persecutions in Germany.

The history of the Jews in Denmark is brief when compared to that of the communities in southern and central Europe. Jews reached this northern land for the first time in the 17th century.[1] Early in the Thirty Years' War, in 1622, Christian IV invited Portuguese Jews from Amsterdam and Hamburg to settle in the town of Glückstadt in Holstein; but the town was occupied in the course of the war and never developed into an important commercial center. During this century Jews began to settle in Copenhagen and in a few provincial towns. The Danish kings were only interested in Portuguese Jews, owing to their wealth, general cultural level, and international commercial connections. *Laissez-passers* and letters of safe-conduct were therefore given—if at all—only to Jews of Portuguese origin, some of whom became, as it were, court Jews of the kings of Denmark.[2]

In fact, however, it was not the Portuguese Jews who

felt attracted to Denmark; the majority of those who wished to engage in trade and to live in the country were Ashkenazis (that is, Jews originating for the most part in Germany and European areas other than Oriental or Mediterranean countries). At the end of the 17th century the right of two such Ashkenazis to settle in Copenhagen was officially recognized. These were the goldsmith Israel David and his partner, Meir Goldschmidt (also known as Stadthagen), from Hamburg. They were even granted permission to hold prayers in their home. In her memoirs, Glückel von Hameln tells of the wedding of her son Joseph to one of Meir Stadthagen's daughters and of her journey to Copenhagen to participate in the event.[3] It was in this period that the tiny community acquired land for a cemetery for those Jews who had obtained "citizenship" in Copenhagen. During the 18th century the Copenhagen community grew from 11 households with 19 persons to 270 households with 1,500 persons. To these should be added 62 households (227 persons) in the provincial towns, making a total of about 1,830 persons. The wealthier Jews established a number of new industries, such as tobacco, textiles, and agricultural implements. Similarly, trading houses were set up and financial enterprises developed; but the number of small merchants and craftsmen remained considerable.

Prayers were at first held in private houses. In 1766 the synagogue of the "German-Jewish nation" (Ashkenazi community) was officially opened. That same day Copenhagen celebrated the wedding of the young king (Christian VII), and the well-known writer Hartwig Wessely, who grew up in the city, wrote a Hebrew poem in honor of the dual festivities. This synagogue was destroyed in the great fire of 1795, which laid waste a large part of the town. During the whole of this century the Jews of Denmark, like those elsewhere, were of course subject to all sorts of restrictions and regulations. Their position was nevertheless better than in many other countries. They were never forced to live in any sort of ghetto, their internal affairs were not tampered with, and they were even granted a degree of autonomy in matters of administration, such as marriages, etc.[4] As early as 1758 the first Jew was permitted to enroll as a student of medicine in the University of Copenhagen, though many years were to go by before Jews could obtain an academic degree and work as doctors. But these educated Jews, some of them of Portuguese origin (and among them, for instance, the well-known de Meza family), usually abandoned Judaism within a short time and assimilated in order to attain those positions closed to them as Jews. At the end of the 18th century Jewish children also began to attend Danish schools, while a Jewish school with Danish as one of the subjects was also established. The artisans' cooperatives too were opened to Jewish members.

Against the background of world events at the end of the 18th century and the beginning of the 19th, far-reaching changes also took place in the internal political structure of Denmark and in its status among the sovereign nations. As a result of the Napoleonic Wars, Denmark lost control over Norway and its fleet was destroyed by the English.[5] At the end of the 18th century Denmark underwent a "silent revolution," particularly through agrarian reforms, when the large estates were distributed among numerous small farmers. The increase in agricultural production led to economic prosperity in the provincial towns and to a steady rise in the standard of living of both the peasants and the middle classes. This new development was threatened by the wars of the 19th century's first decade, which brought a grave economic crisis in their wake. The Jews were also affected by these upheavals: the crisis increased social tension but made their economic initiative all the more welcome. On March 29, 1814, Jews were granted full equality, but this was achieved at the expense of the community's administrative autonomy. The community's internal structure was henceforth determined by royal ordinance, though the special needs of the Jews were to some extent taken into consideration. Moreover, they were not yet in possession of full—including electoral—rights. One of the leading figures in the community and an agitator for reform and equality was M. L. Nathanson (1780–1868), businessman and economist and for many years editor of the important newspaper *Berlingske Tidende*. His book, *A Historical Presentation of the Position of the Jews in Denmark, Mainly in Copenhagen*, is one of the first sources of the history of Danish Jewry, and in it he describes and analyzes the royal ordinances.[6] Some of the principal and typical regulations were as follows: In all matters relating to the civil status of the Jews they were to act in accordance with the laws of the country and not the rabbinical law of the Jewish religious authorities; this included matters of administration, schools, and charity to the poor; they must in all official documents, protocols, etc. avail themselves of the Danish or German tongue and write with Gothic or Latin letters; marriage and divorce must be carried out in accordance with Danish law and required the approval of the king; all rabbis (called "priests") were to be appointed by the king, who also determined their salaries; the Chief Rabbi in Copenhagen was to be the head of all the rabbis in Denmark; each synagogue must be recognized by the authorities. Detailed regulations were also given in matters concerning youth, administration, taxation, sojourn of foreign Jews in Denmark, and so forth.

In the meantime, the Jewish population in the growing provincial towns also increased. In 1834 there were 1,607 Jews in 60 provincial towns and villages, compared to 2,465 who were in the capital, i.e., 40 per cent of the Jewish population at the time lived in the provinces. The larger communities established synagogues, and the numerous cemeteries scattered among the Jewish centers of the period bear witness today to Jewish life a hundred years ago.[7]

The internal developments which took place at the time in the other Jewish communities in Europe generally, and in Germany in particular, also left their mark on Copenhagen. A strong movement for reform arose, and religious conversion assumed proportions similar to those affecting upper-class Jewish society in Berlin at the time. As early as the second half of the 18th century various family connections were established with Moses Mendelssohn and his circle.[8] The Copenhagen community became involved in an inner struggle about reform. The authorities forced certain reforms on the Jews. One of the most prominent was the ceremony of confirmation, which was first held in 1817 by order of the authorities.[9] For their part, as early as 1813 the Jews themselves had asked for the names "Jew" and "Jewish nation" to be officially abolished and requested that individuals be described by name and civil status, and their faith as "Mosaic." No new synagogue had as yet been constructed and prayers were held in fifteen different places. As in Germany, there was a marked rise in anti-Jewish tension, which at times erupted openly—in 1813 in the form of a "literary war" and in 1819, following the "Hepp-Hepp" riots in Germany, as a sort of pogrom, when Jewish businesses in the center of the town were destroyed.

Since the community in Copenhagen was small and bereft of any local Jewish tradition, it was obliged to import its rabbis. Abraham Salomon from Mähren is mentioned in 1687 as Copenhagen's first rabbi. The Copenhagen rabbis were opponents of reform and were generally orthodox Jews; Chief Rabbi Abraham ben Gedalia (acted 1793–1828) even opposed the study of Danish. The Jews of Copenhagen were now eager to find a man who would combine Jewish tradition with modern European culture. They found him in the person of the young rabbi Dr. Abraham Alexander Wolff (1801–1891), who was born in Darmstadt, Germany. He was chosen as the Chief Rabbi of Denmark in 1828. In his sixty-two years of office Wolff succeeded in uniting the divided community and in granting it a more or less orderly administrative form and religious image. His first act, which helped him to unite the community in concerted action, was the building of a new synagogue. Wolff launched an appeal and—to his own surprise—raised 27,000 ducats. The remaining sum required was lent by the authorities. On the Friday after Passover 5593 (April 12, 1833) the synagogue was inaugurated with special prayer and ceremony.[10] Throughout his long years of public activity, Rabbi Wolff attempted to find a synthesis between traditional Judaism and modern trends, in theory and in practice, and he devoted to this end a large part of his literary work.[11]

As Denmark progressed toward fulfillment as a modern democratic state based on a constitution, the Jews were also granted full civic equality. The constitution of Denmark was signed on June 5, 1849. The paragraphs which laid down the legal framework for religions outside the official State Church are as follows:

81. Citizens have the right to congregate for the purpose of worshiping God as their views dictate, but nothing shall be studied or said which is contrary to morality or to the public order.
82. No one is obliged to make a financial contribution to any form of worship other than his own; but if anyone does not consider it necessary to be a member of one of the recognized religious communities, he is obliged to pay the legal taxes to the State Church for the benefit of the school system.
83. The administration of communities deviating from the State Church will be laid down in detail by law.
84. No one shall be prevented from exercising his full civil and political rights by virtue of his religious faith, but no one shall be permitted to evade his general civic duties by virtue of this faith.[12]

It goes without saying that together with the Catholic faith and a number of Protestant denominations the Jewish religion was also considered a "recognized religion." Nevertheless, many decades were to pass before the Jews achieved full equality in all respects. As in 1814, official recognition was conditional upon compulsory state inspection of the community's affairs.

The second half of the 19th century was a period of prosperity for the Jews of Denmark. Once again, as at the beginning of the century, the rise of Jews in economic and social life was connected with a national crisis. The defeat of Denmark in the war with Prussia and Austria in 1864 led to a severe crisis both in economic and national terms. The Danish economy had hitherto been largely based on fishing and on the export of corn to other countries in Europe. The war destroyed this structure, which was replaced by agricultural development, mainly in the sphere of dairy farming and pig breeding. The new produce was exported mainly to England. The Jews played a considerable part in this change, which to a certain degree saved the country's economy, and they also helped develop the country's financial resources. Two important private banks—*Landmandsbanken* and *Privatbanken*—were founded by Jews. Isaac Hartvig Glückstadt was for many years director of *Landmandsbanken* and exercised considerable influence on the Danish economy, while he was also president of the Jewish community during a long period. Important in economic affairs were such families as Bing and Hambro—the latter already having branches in Norway and England.[13] The economic influence of the Jews was accompanied by a rise in their cultural level, which not only helped their integration into Danish cultural life but gave rise to many prominent personalities both inside and outside the country.[14] The Jews generally were absorbed into the country's economic and intellectual life and anti-Semitism therefore showed little increase, although the rise of the anti-Semitic movement in Germany at the end of the century also had repercussions in Denmark. Rabbi Wolff himself played an active part in the campaign against anti-Semitism.

Wolff's successor as Chief Rabbi was David Simonsen, who was the first modern rabbi of the Copenhagen community to be born in Denmark. He continued the work of his predecessor and made a name for himself in the Jewish world at large. He collected one of the largest Jewish libraries ever—some 40,000 volumes—which he bequeathed to the Royal Danish Library in Copenhagen, where it forms a special section, the Bibliotheca Simonseniana. It has since grown to 50,000 books.[15]

Generally speaking, the tiny Danish community lived its internal life in considerable isolation from world Jewry, though on a number of occasions Danish Jews contributed to general Jewish activities. In 1744 they took part in the campaign organized by European Jewry to intercede with the empress Maria Theresa on behalf of the Jews of Prague, who were threatened with expulsion.[16]

In the eighties of the 19th century Rabbi Wolff tried on a number of occasions to exploit the family relationship between the Danish royal family and the Russian family of Romanov, with a view to remonstrating on behalf of the Jews of Russia. These efforts, initiated by a number of rabbis in Russia and eastern Germany, bore no fruit. Better results in this sphere were apparently obtained by the efforts of Rabbi Simonsen in 1907.[17] During this period Simonsen felt himself obliged to come to the help of refugees from Russian persecution who also began to arrive in Denmark. The Jewish community in Copenhagen at the time experienced some decline—the number of Jews in Denmark in 1834 had been 4,072 but dropped to 3,476 in 1901 (3.3 per thousand and 1.4 per thousand of the population in the respective years). This was the result of assimilation, mixed marriages and conversion, which were corollaries of the integration and rise of the Jews in the social life of the country. In the years 1894–1903 the percentage of mixed marriages among all Jewish marriages was as high as 45 per cent.[18] The Jewish community was led by the old and wealthy families, and its administrative pattern remained the same as in the first half of the 19th century. These families were not particularly inclined to receive refugees from the pogroms in Russia. That some of these Jews, mostly workers and craftsmen, did find refuge in Copenhagen was due to a considerable degree to the efforts of Simonsen, who by that time was no longer in office as Chief Rabbi. Between 1901 and 1921 this group grew to 3,146 Jews, of whom 2,615 were refugees from the Russian pogroms and 531 refugees from the First World War. They increased the number of Jews in Denmark to 6,000, or 1.8 per thousand of the population.[19]

The newly arrived Russian Jews were different in all respects from their old-established Danish coreligionists. They were poor—among the poorest people in the whole city—while most of the Danish Jews belonged to the upper and middle classes of society; their families were young and blessed with children (45.7 per cent under the age of fifteen and 2.4 per cent above the age of sixty); whereas the families of the Danish Jews included few children and were inclined to be middle-aged or elderly (16.3 per cent under fifteen and 19.8 per cent over sixty). The new arrivals were steeped in Jewish religion and tradition and in Yiddish culture, in contrast to the assimilation which marked the veteran Jewish population.[20] The proportion of mixed marriages among the old families was 51.7 per cent in 1921, while the corresponding figure for the Russian immigrants was 6.1 per cent, which brought the final number for the whole Jewish population to 31.5 per cent.[21]

As a consequence of the general development of the Danish economy and the increased number of large businesses concentrated in Copenhagen, the Jews moved from the provinces to the capital city. In 1901 there remained only 245 Jews in the provincial towns, or 7.1 per cent of the whole Jewish population, compared to 40 per cent in 1834.[22]

At the end of the nineteen-twenties the great majority of the Danish Jews were concentrated in the capital. The leadership of the community remained in the hands of the socially and economically well-established families, and their rise and integration into the Danish social fabric led to assimilation and thus to a constant whittling away of their numbers. On the other hand, the new Jewish population surpassed them numerically but lagged far behind them socially and economically. It had no say in the administration of the community, but benefited from its institutions, aid, and schools. This body was mostly religiously observant, belonged in part to the Jewish Socialist movement (the Bund) and continued to cultivate the Yiddish tongue.[23] Already in 1902 the first Zionist Federation was set up, but its activities were restricted to a small circle. Among its founders was Dr. Louis Frænkel, who also published the first Jewish newspaper of importance.[24] Only with the First World War, when a number of Zionist leaders came to the neutral city of Copenhagen, was there any marked Zionist activity in the city itself, with repercussions beyond its confines. In October 1918, the office set up in Copenhagen by the World Zionist Organization issued the declaration of the Jewish people's objectives—in the Diaspora as well as in Palestine—to be claimed in the coming peace negotiations.

The Danish Jews' attitude toward their social and national status in Denmark was determined by the concepts of reform introduced at the end of the 18th and the beginning of the 19th centuries, and accepted by the authorities. The ordinances of the government converted these ideas from theory to practice. The typical autonomy of the Jewish community before the emancipation, which had been characteristic of the Copenhagen community of the "Jewish nation" as early as the end of the 18th century, was replaced by royal ordinance, which dealt with the affairs of the "Jewish Church." Equality was bought at the price of complete abolition of the traditional Jewish organizational form and by voluntary withdrawal from belief in national Judaism. The only form that remained was the religious one, which the reform movement failed to influence—Nathanson's attempts to this end had been in vain.[25] The traditional religious character—in the somewhat modernized version resulting from the work of Rabbi Wolff—has left its mark on the Copenhagen community and on its synagogue to this very day. However, as against the orthodox and the traditionalists, there were many veteran Danish Jews who surrendered to both opportunistic and idealistic motives and left the Jewish community in order to merge totally into the Danish people and society, and to identify themselves with its religious as well as its spiritual values. This movement was halted by the presence of the Russian Jews— as long as they remained the first or second generation in Denmark. Their very existence prevented the disintegration of the community. At the end of the nineteen-twenties this element was so firmly established in economic and social life as to feel capable of demanding a share in the administration of the Jewish community. This was at the time when the dark clouds of German national socialism were gathering on the horizon.

The Jewish Community in the Thirties

On the 12th of April, 1933, King Christian X took part in the festive service held in the Copenhagen synagogue to celebrate the hundredth anniversary of its existence. There were those among the Jews who thought that the king would cancel his appearance, but Christian X was not the man to change his ways because a boycott against the Jews had been declared in Germany; ". . . The event [the king's presence] was a source of joy and admiration at the very time when our brethren on the other side of the border were being humiliated by their government."²⁶ The occasion was not without symbolism: from the beginning of the Nazi persecutions it was made clear to the Jews of Denmark that the Danish people and its leaders, with the king foremost, were fully and unreservedly on their side.

The character of the community underwent changes in the thirties. Until the end of the twenties, the immigrants from Eastern Europe had still not achieved the right to vote in elections to the executive committee.²⁷ Now, however, their influence in Jewish public life gathered intensity and in 1930 the Jewish Society of 1930 (*Jødisk Forening af 1930*) was founded, with the participation of various elements, including members of the old families who recognized the need for reviving Jewish life, and the newer immigrants who were striving for representation. The change in atmosphere was also reflected in the community's newspaper. From 1930 on, we find in the *Jødisk Familieblad,* apart from news of Jewish activities in general and Danish activities in particular, a good deal of information about Palestine, the Zionist movement, and its personalities; the paper also dealt extensively with subjects related to Hebrew culture, and the number of announcements on these topics or on Hebrew courses and the like was by no means negligible. Yiddish culture also occupied a certain place. Here and there, we come across discussions of the problem of German Jewry in light of the growing Nazi threat.

On February 18, 1931, the *Jødisk Forening* held a public meeting where the author Henri Nathansen lectured on ideological problems, and his words were reported in some of the national papers. According to the version appearing in the *Jødisk Familieblad,* Nathansen attacked the leaders of the community for isolating themselves from reality and for their lack of any contact with the various streams determining the character of Jewish life in the world at large. They neglected, said Nathansen, they even sabotaged, Jewish culture in Denmark itself—for example, the two Jewish schools in Copenhagen had non-Jewish headmasters. "It would be superhuman to ask of these headmasters that they run the schools in a Jewish atmosphere and with the imprint of Jewish culture." In conclusion, states the same report, he asks: "Is it really our duty to cut ourselves off from our own past and our own people? No, and again no. Judaism stands face to face with the question: To be or not to be, renewal or obliteration, life or death."[28]

Nathansen's provocative words aroused lively discussion in the paper over several months, among the participants being the then Chief Rabbi Friediger, Professor Simonsen, and the leader of the Yiddishists. The more tense the situation in Germany became, the fiercer the debate within the Copenhagen community. Nathansen made himself so unpopular with leaders of the community that they ignored him and instead invited the Danish poet Valdemar Rørdam to write a cantata in honor of the synagogue's centenary celebrations. This cantata was sung at the festive service already mentioned. "It was," Margolinsky comments, "the irony of fate—or should we say nemesis—that a few years later Valdemar Rørdam was to reveal himself as an out-and-out Nazi."[29] However, in the elections to the community's executive committee in December 1932, the first Zionist candidate appeared. He was Benjamin Slor, a native of Palestine, who had come to Denmark on the eve of the First World War for training in physical culture and had remained there. His house became the center of Zionist activity in Copenhagen. Participation in the elections was greater than usual, and the rising elements within the community made their official presence felt for the first time.[30]

With the rise of Hitler to power, the community's spokesmen were reserved in their enunciations. There is, in the issues of the monthly paper for February and March 1933,

virtually nothing on events in Germany and their significance for the Jews. Only in April did a leading article on the
subject appear. The position of the writer was similar to
that of the assimilationists in Germany as expressed by the
Central Organization (*Central Verein deutscher Staatsbürger
jüdischen Glaubens,* usually referred to as CV) and its
newspaper. The main argument against Nazi anti-Semitism
in the organ of the Copenhagen community said: "The
whole basis for Nazi persecution of the Jews is faulty," as
though it were possible to disarm Nazi anti-Semitism by
logical argument. There was clearly no inclination to recognize the real nature of the threat to the Jewish people.
Members of the Jewish *Forening* reacted otherwise. They
tried to arouse the public—Jewish and non-Jewish alike—
to the dangers of militant anti-Semitism, and at the end of
November 1934, the *Forening* organized a large public
meeting on the subject "Anti-Semitism and Culture," with
a speaker from each of the four large political parties. These
took a firm stand against anti-Semitism. The main idea
running through the speeches was that anti-Semitism and
culture are irreconcilable contradictions. All the speakers
also emphasized that the Jews of Denmark were an organic
part of the country's economic and cultural life and even
expressed surprise that a meeting of that sort was considered
necessary. One of the speakers, the representative of the
Conservative party, Christmas Møller, declared that he
could not imagine special regulations for the Jews being
introduced into Denmark, though he added: "It must be
said that our society is not in a position to absorb fifty or
a hundred thousand new immigrants but this is not the
problem at the moment." The daily *Dagens Nyheder* of
November 23, 1934, ran the headline JEWS FEEL NEED TO
HAVE THEIR STATUS CONFIRMED.[31] The community's organ of
course attacked the organizers of the meeting; according
to the writer, meetings of this sort were liable to give
prominence to the problem and to undermine the sympathy

and interest of the Danish people for the Jews. The article did, however, also state: ". . . We have a Jewish question which occupies our thoughts, and a Jewish honor which we shall defend with body and soul." The same issue of *Familieblad* also reported a talk by the principal of a Folk High School on the Jews and their place in Danish society. The speaker reached the conclusion that the positive attributes of the Danish Jews outweighed the negative. "We have made our imprint on the Jews and not the reverse." Such an article appears to have been more favorably regarded by the editors of the paper than Jewish initiative.

The Danish authorities were keenly aware of the problem of anti-Semitism in those years and many elements strove to immunize the Danish people against the poison liable to creep in from the south.[32] Among the Jews active in this campaign was Rabbi Dr. Marcus Melchior, whose lectures were well received by the public at large. In 1936 a new Danish edition of the *The Protocols of the Elders of Zion* impelled a number of theologians to come out in a public declaration against anti-Semitic literature in general and the *Protocols* in particular. Public reaction in Denmark reached its height after the "Crystal Night," though not everyone understood the full significance of the events, and there were those who believed stories of "spontaneous outbursts" by the German people which the German authorities, as it were, had tried to restrain.[33] An amendment to the Criminal Law of 1939—stating that anyone who by virtue of false rumors or slander incited hatred against any section of the Danish population by reason of its religion, origin, or citizenship would be subject to fine or imprisonment—may, however, be regarded as a direct result of the happenings in Germany.[34]

In the meantime the character of Jewish community leadership had undergone changes. In a democratic Denmark under Social Democratic control it was no longer possible to apply regulations which barred a large part of the Jewish population from participating in the administration of community affairs. At the end of 1933 a committee was set up whose task was to propose an amendment to the electoral system, and in the summer of 1935 the community's executive suggested to the municipality of Copenhagen and to the Ministry of the Interior changes which would lead to a democratization of the system. The proposals were accepted and ratified in October 1936. In the elections which took place at the end of the year a community council of twenty-one members was elected for the first time, and its members included six Jews who had immigrated from Eastern Europe since the turn of the century. In March 1937 Slor joined the executive committee, which consisted of seven members.[35]

The new and perhaps central problem the community had to face in the thirties was the question of Jewish refugees from Germany. Refugees were classified into two groups in Denmark: political refugees and Jewish refugees (clearly there were also Jews among the political refugees, but these did not usually ask for help from the Jewish community). This division was in fact, if not officially, made by the Danish authorities. The attitude of the authorities to the refugees was reserved. Only the opponents and victims of nazism, such as the Social Democrats and Communists, were recognized as political refugees. For these, the Matteoti Fund was set up by the Social Democratic party under its chairman, Hans Hedtoft. For Jews two committees were set up. One was the Committee for the Support of Intellectual Refugees founded in the autumn of 1933 by Niels and Harald Bohr, with Aage Friis as chairman. The committee's appeal to the public in October 1933 was signed by some fifty of the country's most distinguished intellectuals. The second committee was established by the Jewish community under the name of the Committee of the 4th of May 1933, with the attorney Kai Simonsen as its secretary. The name of this committee was deliberately chosen, its meaningless title being intended to avoid any public admission that its purpose was to help Jewish refugees. In January 1934 the various committees formed a central coordinating body.

The Danish authorities laid down extremely severe criteria for accepting Jewish refugees. Entry permits were given only to those who could prove family relationship with a Danish citizen resident in the country, and whose economic support could be guaranteed in advance. But even those who managed to meet these requirements were not always permitted to enter.[36] Almost none of the refugees, neither those defined as political nor as Jewish, received a work permit. An exception were a few hundred agricultural trainees, who came to Denmark under a special arrangement to work for farmers and fishermen in preparation for their eventual immigration to Palestine (more details are given later in this work). The political refugees, however, settled down much more successfully, due to the help of their colleagues in the leftist parties and the trade unions.

Extremely difficult was the position of refugees without entry permits who crossed the border illegally. Most of them were not in fact expelled, but all sorts of obstacles were placed in their way. These "infiltrators" became the prototype of the political refugee, and Dr. Fritz Bauer[37] relates in his evidence that when he came to Denmark the authorities were unwilling to recognize him as a political refugee, since he had managed to keep his German passport and had entered Denmark legally. Jews who entered the country illegally had particular difficulty in obtaining residence permits.[38] The number of Jews who managed to escape to Denmark from Germany or the first conquered countries (Austria and Czechoslovakia) was relatively small in comparison to those who made their way to Holland, France, and Britain. They numbered about 4,500 men, women, and children from the first persecutions up to the

occupation of Denmark. About 3,000 of them managed to
gain entry into other countries. At the time of the German
conquest there remained in Denmark about 1,500 Jewish
refugees,[39] while the total number of foreign or stateless
residents of the country was approximately 29,000 (compared to 22,000 in 1935). The Jewish refugees constituted
therefore less than 5 per cent of all foreigners; but in fact
they formed some 12 per cent, since the overall figure also
included Swedes, Norwegians, and other overseas nationals,
who together formed 50 per cent of all foreigners. The
Jews have therefore to be sorted out from the remaining
13,000, who included Germans, Dutch, stateless, etc.[40]

The position of the Danish authorities has to be considered in the light of the grave economic problems be-
setting Denmark at the time, not the least being widespread
unemployment. In the pre-occupation period Denmark still
had strong trade connections with Britain, but its economic
dependence on Germany was not unimportant. Of greater
weight was its political dependence on and fear of the mighty
neighbor to the south. However, not only the authorities
but also the public at large regarded the refugees with much
reservation. "Refugee work was not simple and never earned
understanding from the public" was one comment on the
work of the Committee for the Support of Intellectual
Refugees.[41]

As regards refugees in general and Jewish refugees in
particular, Denmark was thus no better than any other
country. It attempted to curb the development of nazism
and of anti-Semitism within and opposed any discrimination against its Jewish citizens and their civil rights, but
was not prepared to make any sacrifice or run any risk for
the sake of the persecuted Jews of Germany. We shall see
that the Danes were to regard the Jewish problem in a
different light when the Nazi menace had penetrated within.
This attitude of the Danes, as of other nations, to the
Jewish refugee problem had, as we know, the most tragic

consequences, for many of those who tried in vain to obtain a visa to freedom were later exterminated as part of the "final solution." We should not, however, forget that at the time no one imagined that the Jews were destined for systematic extermination. It is still difficult to understand how, before the occupation period, people could be sent back to Germany, even though such instances were rare.[42]

With the establishment of the Committee of the 4th of May 1933, the Jewish community endeavored to come to the aid of the refugees. Expenses were covered by special fund-raising appeals. The income from these appeals ranged from 50 to 150,000 Danish kroner a year, and all in all the Jews of Copenhagen in the years 1933 to 1939 raised almost three-quarters of a million kroner.[43] Part of the expenses incurred by the refugees were covered by the Danish Ministry for Social Affairs. The community opened a public kitchen for the refugees run by some of its women members. The money collected by the community was not adequate for transporting refugees to overseas countries, and here help came from the general Jewish organizations—HIAS (Hebrew Immigrant Aid Society), the Joint Distribution Committee, and the Jewish Agency for Palestine. With the help of B'nai B'rith, summer camps for children from Germany were arranged. These did not cater to large groups —the largest number benefiting at any one time was 120 in the summer of 1934. On the eve of the Second World War twenty-four girls who had spent the summer in Denmark returned to Germany (as of 1936 the Germans allowed only boys under ten years of age to leave the country).[44]

A number of activities were initiated in cooperation with the institutions of the Zionist movement. The most important was the training scheme for 1,500 agricultural pioneers who came to Denmark to train for work on the land prior to their emigration to Palestine. The initiative in this case came from Benjamin Slor. Training of this sort was begun on a small scale as early as the twenties, and these experiments formed the basis for a more widespread operation when persecution in Germany began.[45] The scheme was organized under the auspices of the Committee of the 4th of May 1933, and to begin with places were prepared for twenty pioneers. However, at the end of September 1933 there were already places for ninety-two men and twenty-eight women from Germany. In the following years the scheme comprised 200 to 250 places a year. The operation was based on a special agreement between Denmark and a number of other countries through the offices of the Agricultural Travel Company, according to which Denmark agreed to receive agricultural trainees for a period of one year. During this time the trainee received a work permit, food, lodging, and a small amount of pocket money. The condition for his employment was that he would not take any place for which a Danish farm laborer was available. Since the permit was restricted to one year, during which time it was not always possible to obtain an immigration certificate to Palestine, an exchange system was worked out in the course of time with England, Italy, Yugoslavia—which also had training centers—and Sweden, where the scheme was organized by Slor's brother-in-law, Dr. Emil Glück, on lines similar to those in Denmark. A trainee unable to travel to Palestine at the end of the year was transferred to one of these four countries. During all the years the scheme was in operation, Slor was responsible for budget operations and carried out the negotiations with the community's institutions and with Jewish organizations abroad. The technical and secretarial administration was taken over by Jul. Margolinsky, who writes:

A comprehensive aid program for foreigners of this sort naturally required a permanent organizational framework. From the beginning I took it upon myself to organize the training scheme. In June 1933 the first meeting was held in my apartment in the presence of twenty-five young, new arrivals. They chose

a secretariat consisting of representatives for the various pioneer
groups and laid down practical rules for work then and in its
future development. These secretaries all worked on farms, but
they were in touch with me by post and telephone. Only some
years later was a permanent secretariat with its own office
opened in Copenhagen.

Expenses were considerable. They included clothing, organization of cultural activities, and general and particular
social needs. There were no few cases of people who fell
ill or stopped work for other reasons. In the course of time
families were also founded and children born. The community allocated from 20,000 to 50,000 kroner a year as
part of the budget for supporting refugees, but this sum
covered less than half the expenses. The rest came from the
Jewish Agency and the Joint Distribution Committee,[46]
which, as indicated before, also bore the transportation costs
of immigration to Palestine. While discussing the problem
of financing this fare in the executive committee of the
community in August 1933, "the Chairman, C. B. Henriques,
pointed out that further contributions from the committee
were out of the question and that if need be the young
people could be sent back to Germany instead of to Palestine
when they had finished their training."[47] In fact, this step
was never taken; but such a statement appears to us today
as a proposal to hand these young people over to their
murderers. At the time, however, no one foresaw the "final
solution." Henriques's comment nevertheless shows that Slor
and his colleagues had no easy struggle against preformed
ideas and outworn procedure that no longer fitted the needs
of the hour. Hugo Valentin has explained:[48] "The members
of the old families were used to bureaucratic methods and
were opposed to new ideas. Their reputation for honesty
and fairness and the goodwill they enjoyed in the eyes of
the authorities were their great assets."
Before the outbreak of the war 1,000 of the 1,500 pioneers

who had arrived in Denmark since the beginning of the operation in 1933 had left. Of these, 600 emigrated to Palestine, 300 continued their training in other countries, and 50 emigrated to other lands, mainly to the United States.[49] These thousand young men and women formed about a third of the 3,000 refugees who succeeded in leaving Denmark before the occupation. With the fate of the roughly 500 who remained we will deal later. It should not be forgotten that 4,500 refugees—equal to 75 per cent of the Jewish community—were a heavy burden on that body. As for the pioneers, the community was responsible for them toward the authorities.[50]

Other activities of the Jewish Agency were carried out for "Youth Aliya" (emigration of young boys and girls to Palestine). Youth Aliya at the time was organizing aid programs in various countries, where Jews contributed to the maintenance of children in Palestine. The first appeal in Copenhagen in 1934 raised almost 50,000 kroner, which was sufficient to finance the immigration of 30 children. A second appeal in the spring of 1938 brought in only 17,500 kroner. However, after "Crystal Night," Youth Aliya sought, for children who had not yet received immigration certificates to Palestine, places outside Germany where they could await their turn. In cooperation with Danish women's organizations, particularly the Women's League for Peace and Freedom and the Society of Jewish Women, and after drawn-out financial and organizational preparation, the authorities agreed to have Denmark receive children between the ages of thirteen and seventeen. The first of these reached the country in the summer of 1939, and a larger group arrived on the day war broke out. They were distributed to various farmers' homes throughout the country. Some of the children from Germany, Austria, and Czechoslovakia were taken by the Danish women out of concentration camps, where they had been held alone or together with their parents.[51] This operation was led by Mrs. Melanie Oppenhejm of the Society of Jewish Women. The number of "league children," as they were popularly called, was a little above 300. The groups arrived in the early months of the war; 136 children managed to continue their journey and to reach Palestine even after the German conquest of Denmark. They traveled in three separate groups via Sweden and Russia. In October 1943 there were, however, still 174 of these children in Denmark.[52]

In connection with these activities Denmark was visited by various leaders of the Jewish Agency and the Hechalutz (pioneer) movement. These included Enzio Sereni, Adler-Rudel, Dr. Kreuzberger, Norman Bentwich, and others. They took part in the discussions of the community and its committees, appeared at public meetings, and all in all played an important role in activating the Danish Jews toward helping the victims of persecution.[53]

The Jewish population in Denmark at the time of the German invasion was thus small in numbers but consisted of several different elements. The last population census before the occupation was carried out in 1931, but details of religious affiliation appear only in the census of 1921; figures are, however, available from the period of flight and deportation, and with their help certain conclusions may be arrived at. It should be emphasized here that these figures give us some idea of the composition of the Jewish population in Denmark at the time but should not be regarded as exact in all respects. In this stormy period for Denmark, as for all the countries of Europe, people were constantly being moved from place to place and from country to country; deaths were not recorded; attempts at flight succeeded or failed with resulting fatalities without any details registered—all in all, it is possible only to arrive at a reasonable estimate. We feel, however, that we have not gone too far astray from the true position at the time.[54]

The Jewish population, which consisted of the old families and the Russian Jews who arrived in Denmark at the time of the Russian pogroms and the First World War, numbered approximately 5,000 persons, to whom should be added some 1,500 refugees in the country at the time of the occupation. To these 6,500 should also be added about 150 who succeeded in leaving Denmark between the occupation and the outbreak of persecution in October 1943, and the approximately 1,300 Jews—offspring of mixed marriages— who accompanied their Jewish relatives in their flight and thus regarded themselves as Jews or feared that the Germans would so regard them. We therefore reach the conclusion that the total Jewish population in Denmark at the critical hour was about 8,000 persons, i.e., a little under 2 per thousand of the total Danish population. Of these, 2,100 to 2,200 were not Danish subjects, though they included some who had been born in Denmark.[55] Of these 8,000 Jews, 7,220 were registered in the Swedish refugee files and 475 were registered by the Danish government as deported to Theresienstadt; the remaining 300 left Denmark, as stated, during the occupation, perished in one way or another and did not reach either Sweden or Theresienstadt, or remained in the country openly or in hiding. The 7,220 Jews who escaped to Sweden were accompanied by 686 non-Jewish Danes connected with them by family ties, so that the total number of escapees was almost 8,000.[56]

Summary

The characteristics of the Jewish population in Denmark changed considerably during the thirties as a result of the events taking place in the Jewish world beyond its borders. Refugees from Eastern Europe who joined the community during the first two decades of the century now began to climb the economic, social, cultural, and public ladder, and their presence prevented that disintegration of the community which had seemed certain at the end of the preceding century. In consequence, the veteran leaders of the community recognized the need for democratization of its administration and for bringing new representatives into their own ranks. The new elements also caused a cultural and organizational revival among the old families, and the alert members of both groups felt themselves attracted to the Zionist activity that was in the ascendant throughout the world. With the rise of nazism in Germany, these two groups were particularly aware of the two new duties the times had brought with them: to render help to German-Jewish victims of persecution to the extent possible within Denmark, and to immunize the Danish populace against the disease of anti-Semitism. Help to the refugees was subject to the restraining hand of the authorities, but within the permitted framework, the active elements—with the support of international Jewish organizations—succeeded in impelling the whole community together with its leaders toward active cooperation in the enterprise, and toward assumption of the total administrative and financial burden (though this success was achieved only after certain internal struggles).

In addition to the humanitarian assistance given to individual refugees, the Jewish community in Denmark was mobilized together for the first time in a collective venture whose declared objectives were Zionistic and whose initiators and supporters were Zionists from home and abroad. Two operations were carried out: the pioneer scheme and the Youth Aliya enterprise. The leadership of the community was as yet still mainly composed of members of the old families, and these were in fact borne along on the stream of initiative whose source was the Zionist elements on the one hand and the vigilance of the Danish public and authorities on the other—for these groups recognized themselves as responsible for those refugees whose entry was permitted. This vigilance found expression in the establishment of assistance funds, in financial aid from government offices, and in administrative help from organized public bodies, the legal institutions, and the police. It also found expression in the enactment of an amendment to the law aimed at providing the security authorities and the courts with a legal instrument for war against domestic anti-Semitism. This vigilance on the part of the Danish people and authorities inspired the Jews with a feeling of security.

PART TWO

THE PERIOD OF NEGOTIATION

II

Under State Protection

The Occupation and Its Characteristics

The German army invaded Denmark and Norway on April 9, 1940. The Danish people were taken completely by surprise; but the authorities too had largely ignored the many symptoms and warnings of the preceding period. The German attack rendered worthless the German-Danish non-aggression pact of May 30, 1939.[1] The Germans claimed that this step—a clear infringement of the pact—was necessary in view of the threat of an Allied invasion of Norway. The war situation on the northern front at the time was extremely complicated and could be interpreted in various ways, as indeed it was both during and after the war.[2] In any event, the Germans declared to the Danes that the country was threatened by an Anglo-French invasion and that it must therefore be Germany's duty to take the Nordic countries under its protection to prevent the war spreading to them.

The German minister, Cecil von Renthe-Fink, presented to the Danish foreign minister his government's official note, which demanded that the Danish government accept the German occupation with good grace. The note ended as follows: "In keeping with the good relations which have always existed between Germany and Denmark, the Government of the Reich assures the Royal Danish Government that Germany has no intention *now or in the future of encroaching upon the Kingdom of Denmark's territorial integrity or political independence*" (author's italics). The brief reply of the Danish government included its capitulation, and Foreign Minister P. Munch repeated the sentence of the German memorandum emphasized above, while protesting against the violation of Denmark's declared neutrality.[3] This quotation turned the passage from the German note, so to say, into the basis for the German-Danish agreement which regulated the cooperation between the occupier and the occupied. Thus the interpretation of this sentence, given in theory and practice by each of the two partners, served in the coming years as a yardstick for what the Danes called "the policy of negotiation."

During some three and a half years—until August 29, 1943—Danish democratic government continued to function in accordance with the parliamentary system as laid down in the constitution—a government appointed by the king and responsible to the Rigsdag (Danish parliament). The Germans from time to time reaffirmed the special status of the Danish government,[4] but the Danes themselves examined the maintenance or breach of the agreement in the light of certain criteria. Those were the preservation of Danish independence, i.e., noninterference in the affairs of the army, navy, and police; full maintenance of the constitution and normal functioning of the parliamentary institutions and of the courts; freedom of the trade unions and political organizations; and freedom of political expression. The defenders of the policy of negotiation assert that—until the final crisis at any rate—they succeeded in preserving the country's territorial, national, and economic integrity, though they had to make concessions in all these spheres.[5] Their opponents point out, however, that the Germans undermined the democratic and independent Danish regime step by step, and that in fact none of the guarantees given by the Germans at the time of occupation were honored.[6] But there was, and is today, no divergence from the opinion that the main objective was not only to preserve the Danish people and its physical existence but also—and perhaps more important—to preserve its spirit and the basic values of its social and political life. At the time of the occupation it seemed to the nation's leaders that there was no other way of achieving this except by negotiation with the Germans. The majority of the population supported the government's policy, and only a tiny minority were then in favor of resistance. In the course of time, as concessions, infringements, and encroachments increased, internal debate became more critical and active opposition, particularly in 1943, gained in momentum.

Above all differences of opinion, however, the people and its leaders were conscious of a number of basic values, which were not merely subscribed to by everyone, but for which every Dane who associated himself with the essentials of the constitution was prepared to fight. These were the basic principles of freedom, equality, law, and justice. When in August 1943 the Germans demanded from the Danish government that it waive these principles and act against them, the government refused, and parliamentary rule was suspended.[7] Until then, the Danish authorities had conducted a policy of negotiation as the lesser evil and as camouflage for passive resistance. After the war, a pronouncement made at Christmas 1940 by the then prime minister, Thorvald Stauning (who died on May 3, 1942), was made public: "We will be forced to do many things," he said, "for which people will afterward spit at us, if we are to bring Denmark unscathed through this period."[8] It should nevertheless be understood that many Danes and some of the nation's leading figures at the time not only were convinced—as was Stauning himself—that Germany would win the war, but also regarded that country with sympathy. Support for this view may be found in the speeches both of Stauning and—more markedly—of Erik Scavenius, who was foreign minister from the summer of 1940 on.[9]

It was in fact one of the leaders of the Danish resistance movement, Professor Mogens Fog, who pointed out after the war that Denmark, unlike Norway, had no quisling government on one side with an underground movement on the other, and that it was the lawful authorities of the nation who proclaimed an agreement with the Germans and carried out a policy of collaboration.[10] The government could only follow this policy and guide the country through the devious ways of negotiation with the Germans as long as it knew that the majority of the people stood behind it. National unity and agreement were the government's bastion.[11] This striving for unity expressed itself in various arrangements and regulations. The need for internal solidarity was reflected in a sort of domestic armistice, which led in the summer of 1940 to the establishment of a broad coalition government of the five main parties under the Social Democrats, who had directed Danish policy during the ten preceding years. In addition, a new body—a sort of liaison office between the government and the Rigsdag— was set up. This was the Council of Unity (also called the Council of Cooperation and in the course of time referred to as the Council of Nine, after the number of its members). The council contained representatives of the five main parties (Social Democrats, Conservatives, *Venstre*, Radicals, and *Retsforbund*), and its task was to insure the unimpaired maintenance of parliamentary rule, whether the Rigsdag was in session or in recess. It seemed—and this was confirmed by experience—that in conditions of occupation this smaller body would be more apt to reach decisions on internal and external affairs than could the two houses of representatives through public debate. The statement establishing the council stated: "The parties represented in the Rigsdag, in their desire to preserve the existing constitution as the basis of political life, have decided to enact a measure of national Danish cooperation. The parties lay aside all disagreement and will unite to preserve the independence and integrity of our country, which are the principal wish of the people."[12] This body quickly became the central institution of political life. As stated, the council regarded as its primary duty the preservation of the country's national integrity and democratic independence.

This assignment was by no means simple. At the time of the occupation the Danish people were not cast in one mold. During the thirties the country had undergone economic difficulties and unemployment on a scale hitherto unknown.[13] Economic insecurity at home was complemented by the feeling of insecurity caused by the rise of the antidemocratic forces in Europe. The widespread use of force by the Fascists in Italy, in Spain, and of course in Denmark's mighty neighbor, Germany, as a solution for domestic and foreign problems; the failure of the League of Nations; the ineptitude of the democratic powers—all these factors aroused doubts and scepticism in the hearts of many, who wondered whether Denmark had chosen the right path by disarming at the beginning of the thirties and by continuing its traditional system of parliamentary rule and free debate on internal affairs. Nevertheless, Danish Social Democracy continued to gain in strength until, at the end of the decade, the party suggested a change in the constitution to unify the two houses of parliament. However, in the spring election of 1939 the party suffered a setback and the number of its seats in the Rigsdag was reduced. Then war broke out before the reform could be introduced.

Certain antiparliamentary, rather than antidemocratic, trends manifested themselves among the population. As in all periods of crisis, the deficiencies of the democratic system stood out: party differences, fruitless discussions, disunity at the critical moment, lack of decisiveness and action. This encouraged tendencies to seek less conventional methods.

Nazism attracted very few even of the discontented, who abhorred systems of terror, but there were people who, while "not going so far as to abolish democratic rule, often enunciated vague concepts of other forms of government, which though designated as democratic were in reality more or less camouflaged imitations of Fascist regimes."[14] It is clear that a serious threat would arise were these tendencies to flourish when the country fell into Nazi hands —a situation which in itself not only seemed to prove the ineptitude of the Social Democratic parliamentary system but also opened up vistas for help and support from the occupying power, which, after all, wished to incorporate Denmark into its "New Order." It cannot be claimed that attempts in this direction were not made from both the Danish and the German side,[15] but they all failed in the end, and the legal and democratic institutions maintained their authority, with the support of the majority of the people.

Honor for this fact is due to the national spirit and love of freedom of the Danish people, without which the authorities could not have demanded the "preservation of law and order." This national discipline was achieved without any recourse to coercion. It is, however, doubtful whether the country's leaders, parties, and institutions could have united the people so completely had there not existed independent forces which made it their aim to emphasize and consolidate the "bases of Danish freedom."

These forces were to be found inside and outside the parties, among adults and youth, workers and students, the organized and the unorganized. During 1940 and 1941 a large movement sprang up throughout the country, a movement of unity with the aim of preserving "the political, intellectual, and personal freedom of the people and the special cultural character of Denmark."[16] The movement spread from man to man, group to group, organization to organization, town to town, and party to party, and an umbrella organization—The Union of Danish Youth (*Dansk Ungdomssamvirke*)—was set up. It rose from the grass roots, from the young people themselves, assisted by the Council of Elders, a group of older people who helped both intellectually and materially. The movement generally assumed the form of cultural activity, for its own sake and without undertones, and aimed to strengthen the national consciousness by study of the country's nature, people, and history. In the course of time there was a natural transition to political topics, and the courses were also used as channels of communication for messages which the government was unable to bring to the notice of the people by newspaper or radio under the conditions of occupation. The state broadcasting system nevertheless cooperated with the movement by arranging suitable cultural programs, and one of its leading officials was a member of the Council of Elders.

The initiators and organizers of the Union of Danish Youth were true heirs of the celebrated Danish priest N. F. S. Grundtvig (1783–1872) and the Folk High School system which he bequeathed to the people. Even in his youth, and certainly by the 1840's, this unusual man had come to the conclusion that the classical system of education then practiced in Danish schools did not fulfill the needs of the people, and he organized new programs and even experimented with the establishment of a new type of school for adolescents from all sections of the population. During the grave crisis which swept over Denmark following its defeat in 1864, when the national consciousness was shaken to its very core, it was Grundtvig and his disciples who succeeded in giving the people a new cultural and national content. This inmost conclusion, drawn from disaster, and the inner mental and spiritual strength which these same schools gave to the people, without any motives of practical or material advancement, was what consolidated the Danish spirit of democracy and humanity. "Grundtvig had, after the misfortune of 1864, by his bluff Danish manner, strong biblical faith, and manly instinct for freedom, given Denmark a new aim in life, so vital that it influenced the whole of Nordic development. He has now [i.e., under the occupation] been, as it were, rediscovered." These words by the then aide-de-camp to the king[17] sum up a public phenomenon unparalleled as an example of the close connection between education and culture on the one hand and the national spirit of freedom and democracy on the other.

The movement enjoyed the active personal support of the coalition government's minister of education, Jørgen Jørgensen, who was also a member of the Council of Elders. In recognizing that the educational-cultural work in strengthening the "Danish mentality" had to be "a silent task, from man to man," he returned to the "popular-Christian sources which were the old foundation of the Folk High Schools."[18] In one of the early meetings of a small group to discuss these problems, he explained that the ideas of these schools were the basis which now had to be built upon. Similar thoughts were voiced at the time by various groups and sections. Besides the clergy, teachers were prominent among those who played an active role in this cultural-political activity. The movement would, however, possibly never have achieved its wide scope and made such deep inroads among the population had it not had as its leader a man who became within a very short time the symbol of the national conscience. This was the young theologian and professor of church history in the University of Copenhagen, Hal Koch.

Like many others who then took a leading part in the "cells of unity" everywhere, Hal Koch was previously unknown to the public at large and was not connected with any party or organization. He had, however, spent some of his student years in both Italy and Germany and had come to the conclusion that fascism and national socialism were not products of any national culture but were an international conspiracy against democracy. Recognizing that the main danger to the Danish people lurked within and that youth in that hour was in need of a guiding spirit, in the autumn of 1940 he held a series of lectures on Grundtvig as a young man. In an interview published in *Berlingske Tidende* before the lectures started, he said:

I have decided to give these lectures because I feel that we are at present in a state of terrible confusion—from all points of view: national, human, and Christian. . . . The task awaiting students on completion of their studies is not to get a job at a fairly good salary—but to live as Danes capable of building the life of the people. To this end they have to know the truth. Of course, the University should not be exploited for propaganda toward any particular form of life; but I think that it would be useful to present to the students the image of a man who more than others knew the meaning of living as a Dane.[19]

The lectures were open to students of all faculties. At the very first lecture the large auditorium was packed and long queues of students and visitors stood outside, so that the lecturer himself had the greatest difficulty in reaching the podium. In the course of time, Koch was obliged to hold each lecture twice. In his many talks and lectures, held all over the country in the years that followed, Hal Koch warned young Danes not to listen to big talk or imagine that the time had come for vigorous action. He urged self-criticism and self-recognition and tried to arouse the young to an interest in politics, but not to that form which divided into parties and groups, for he was after all the leader of a movement of unity. He wished to convert this same unity of youth into an instrument against Nazi and antidemocratic thought and attitudes. As he said:

The task of the Union of Danish Youth is to politicize youth, that is, to arouse interest and spread knowledge regarding the country and public life until a feeling of responsibility has been created. . . . Politicization and responsibility of this sort are the only bases on which rule of the people can safely rest. . . . Until now there has been a tendency—in academic circles at least—to regard politics as an inferior occupation, and there has generally been little interest in public affairs. If this trend continues, we are destined to have a regime of gangs, be they democratic or dictatorial. The aim is therefore—to arouse interest and responsibility as citizens among the best of our youth, those who will decide our future.[20]

In addition to planning lectures and organizing study groups and other forms of education and explanation, the Union of Danish Youth also issued a monthly *Newsletter to Youth Leaders* (*Lederbladet*), a central organ where Koch summed up his opinions on general and topical questions. In 1942 he even published a booklet called *The Day and the Way* in which he expressed his opinions and observations and attempted to guide Danish youth through the political and moral labyrinth of the period. He stressed the general principles of humanity on which Danish society was based and which formed the foundation of politics. In practical terms, he concluded that the policy of negotiation should be supported, for in it he saw a guarantee of the democratic unity of the people. Although he considered it an error that the Germans had not been actively resisted at the time of the invasion, he opposed underground operations and acts of terror. Since national unity had not been forged in battle against the Germans, he considered it necessary to strengthen it by politico-educational means. He was not unaware of the doubtful, even dangerous, elements inherent in the policy of negotiation. Denmark, he pointed out in his book, though privileged in comparison with other conquered countries, had nevertheless paid a high price—the people no longer controlled their own home. "This has meant that we have said many a Yes and many a No which have not come from our own hearts, and that our talk has taken on a fateful hypocrisy."[21] Even in underground circles which rejected the policy of negotiation, Koch's book was recommended reading.

In every sphere—government, parliamentary life, among adults and youth—the striving for unity and for internal cohesion was paramount. There was an attempt to examine how best to survive the stern test of maintaining a democratic way of life, at a time when the country lay prostrate before the traditional enemy attempting to superimpose a totalitarian regime. Internal unity seemed the best, indeed the only, way of preserving national integrity against the dangers from without and within.

The Jewish Question—a Danish Problem

The principles on which the unity of the Danish people was based found full expression, *inter alia,* in the attitude of the Danes to the Jewish problem; more than that, it was one of the most vivid criteria of the existence of these principles. Until the German conquest, the Jewish question had not engaged the attention of the Danish authorities as a domestic problem of any significance. The few Jews living in the country constituted no problem. The authorities also prevented the arrival of large numbers of Jewish refugees[22] because they were not interested in having such a problem manifest itself in Denmark. This situation, however, changed radically with the occupation, after which the Jewish question became a kind of symbol, a barometer of principle in theory and practice. On this point there was no divergence between the attitudes of Danish officialdom and of the underground movement. There was not the slightest disagreement with the view that the rights and lives of the Jews had to be protected. We shall see in the course of this study what effect this attitude was to have on the fate of the Danes and of the Danish Jews, and what the theoretical and practical consequences were to be for the three groups: the German conqueror, intent on consolidating control and exploiting the Danish economy; the Danes, engaged in a struggle for existence and independence; and the Jews, threatened with deportation and extermination.

It was the opinion not only of the Danes but also of the local German representatives that the Jewish problem was one of the factors which were essential for Danish independence and cooperation. The German minister, Renthe-Fink, sent the following report to his Foreign Ministry on April 15, 1940—i.e., only six days after the occupation:

The Danish authorities are apprehensive as to whether we will, for all that, show too much interest in the internal situation and take steps against Jews, refugees, and extreme leftist groups, and create a special police organ to this end. If we do anything more in this respect than is strictly necessary, this will cause paralysis of or serious disturbances in political and economic life. The importance of the problem should not therefore be underestimated.[23]

In Danish eyes too, police and Jews were two sides of the same coin. In the minutes of a meeting of the Council of Nine on December 15, 1942, we find that the then minister of justice, Thune Jacobsen, said that "it has been possible for two years to preserve the Danish police without any German interference in essential aspects. We have also satisfactorily dealt with the Jewish problem," and that he had given the Germans information on the National Socialists with a view to keeping them in check.[24]

Thune Jacobsen, who was generally considered to be one of the unfaltering protagonists of cooperation with the Germans, was chief of police at the beginning of the occupation. In this capacity, he had a meeting at Copenhagen airport in April 1941 with Himmler, who was en route to Norway. The meeting was held at the request of the *Reichsführer* S.S. According to Jacobsen, Himmler talked about the attitude of the Danish police to the Danish National Socialists and the problem of communism in Denmark and added that there was also a Jewish problem in Denmark. Jacobsen answered that "if the *Reichsführer S.S.* thinks that 5,000 Jews here in Denmark constitute a problem, then of course, we have a problem, but the Danish population does not consider this topic a problem."[25] The Danish attitude was well known to the Germans. In March of that year (1941) there appeared in the official German journal *Die Judenfrage* a leading article under the heading DEN-MARK—A COUNTRY WITHOUT A JEWISH PROBLEM? The author complained that the phrase "Denmark has no Jewish problem" took a form that allowed for no discussion and that preoccupation with racial problems was considered "un-Danish."

Christmas Møller, leader of the Conservative party, was a member of the national government from July to October 1940, but was obliged to resign at the request of the Germans. He was one of the founders and leaders of the resistance movement. In a famous speech on October 16, 1941, to an assembly of young people at Hellerup High School in Copenhagen, he delivered a strong attack against the Germans and maintained that they had not kept their promises of the 9th of April, 1940. He explained the essence of democracy as opposed to that of dictatorship, and stressed that the democratic system was the only one suitable for the national character of the Danish people, as could be understood from the fact that "the treatment of the Jews, as practiced in Germany, is completely unsuitable for the Danish character."[26]

What is significant here is that for the Danes *national consciousness and democratic consciousness are one and the same.* Only as a free citizen in a lawful and democratic state can the Dane behold his patriotism. This view is a principal part of Grundtvig's legacy. Equality, freedom, the rights assured to every Dane, and the duties incumbent upon him as laid down in the constitution are valid for all citizens without exception, and all citizens constitute a mutual guarantee to one another that these principles will be maintained. This national-humanist Danish conception is radically opposed to the concept characteristic of German nationalism even long before Hitler, who only developed it to extreme conclusions. To the same degree as Danish nationalism finds expression in the people's democratic way of life, of which the equal rights of the Jews form an integral part, extreme German nationalism required the Jew as a counterweight and an enemy in order to arrive at national self-consciousness and -realization. Hatred of the Jews was as integral a part of German nationalism as of nazism. For reasons of nationhood and democratic principle, the underlying assumption of Danish life and thought led, under the occupation, to *political identification* with the Jews. The struggle of the Danish people for its national existence during the occupation therefore included the struggle for the equal rights of the Jews, just because it included a struggle for their political and social structure, their way of life.

This principle was most clearly expressed in an article by Hal Koch in *Lederbladet* on the occasion of the New Year in January 1942, under the heading DENMARK AND GERMANY and the subheading "Some Comments for People of Our Time on the Occasion of the New Year." The article dealt with relations between the Danes and the Germans which were at the time in a state of crisis (more details will be given later in this study). In order to explain the very crucial point these relations had reached, Koch expressed his opinion on the Jewish problem, which had just come to the fore. He presumed that the Danish youth organization was attempting to effect cooperation between Germany and Denmark, but said that this was possible only in the presence of certain other assumptions, the most important being the implementation of the promises given by Germany on April 9, 1940, without which the whole situation would disintegrate. If an active anti-Jewish policy were to be initiated in Denmark this would be evidence that these promises had been trampled on.

Certainly [he says] this is a question of right and justice for the Jews, but in addition—and this is something fundamental—justice and freedom in Danish life are at stake. . . . We therefore have to know whether those who say that these promises may be ignored are right [the reference is to the Danish Nazi press, which demanded action against the Jews]. If this is the case, then the way we have gone until now is no way. [That is to say, the policy of negotiation has to be seen as a mistake. Koch concludes his article:] We should not forget that our country's fate will be decided not by the war in the outside world but by the extent to which we are able to maintain truth, justice, and freedom by being ready to pay the price.

Even though the fate of the Jews plays an important role in this article, it is primarily Denmark's fate which is under review. The Jewish problem and the way it is handled indicate precisely the limit which no one in Denmark apart from the Nazis was prepared to exceed, and serves therefore as a yardstick in theory and in practice.

Hal Koch's words were written at a time when the Jewish problem appeared for the first time on the political agenda and the pages of the press. Until this time both the Germans and the Danes had avoided mention of this sore point. However, in the early winter of 1941 general political developments and the increasingly more violent German campaign of extermination of the Jews led to an attempt to accelerate the "solution of the Jewish problem" also in Denmark. The attempt failed, thanks to the firm attitude of the Danish people and its leaders and the perspicacity of the German minister, Renthe-Fink.[27]

It will be seen that throughout the history of the occupation each general and political crisis in relations between Germany and Denmark involved danger to the Jews. Generally the extremist National Socialist elements in the German Foreign Ministry then renewed their attempts to raise the Danish Jewish question. The phenomenon could be observed for the first time with Denmark's participation in the anti-Comintern pact in November 1941.

Immediately after the German invasion of Russia on June 22, 1941, the Danish police began to arrest Communist leaders and active members of the party, including members of the Rigsdag. Three hundred fifty persons were arrested at the time and were at first put in various Danish prisons but later assembled in the detention camp at Horserød.[28] This action was, of course, carried out under intense German pressure. In this instance, the Danes preferred to carry out the arrests themselves in order to prevent action by the German police. Since the Communist party had until then been a legal party, it would not have been difficult for the Germans to make the arrests by themselves. The Danes feared that a larger number of persons would then be arrested and would be deported to concentration camps in Germany.[29] The operation caused, however, a very serious internal crisis, particularly since it was accompanied by the establishment of a "Free Corps" of one thousand Danish volunteers, who were sent to the eastern front.

In spite of opposition, a law was passed on August 28, 1941, forbidding all Communist organizations and activity and giving the minister of justice authority to arrest Communists.[30] This was an infringement of the constitution, which laid down that no Danish citizen could be arrested because of his religious or political opinions. However, this grave encroachment on Denmark's internal independence was only a first step, and in November the Germans forced the Danish government to join the anti-Comintern pact by threatening to annul the agreement of April 1940. More than in the arrest of the Communists, the Danes saw in this development a breach of the German promises given in this same agreement. Scavenius did succeed in adding certain reservations to his signature, but the public correctly evaluated these as worthless. The country reacted strongly and for the first time the students of Copenhagen held demonstrations—with public support—and even addressed a protest to the king. German irritation at these protests was very strong.[31]

And precisely at this time the Jewish problem emerged. Scavenius participated in the anti-Comintern pact ceremony in Berlin on November 25, 1941.[32] While in the German capital, he had talks with Goering and Ribbentrop and was even received by Hitler himself. The Jewish question was raised during his meeting with Goering. At first Goering emphasized that national socialism was not an "export commodity," apparently with a view to mollifying the Danish foreign minister by showing that the Germans had no intention of imposing their regime on Denmark. But he then began to talk about the Jewish problem. Scavenius recalls:[33] ". . . But Denmark, [Goering] said, could not circumvent the Jewish question. To this I replied, as always, that there was no Jewish question in Denmark." At the same time, various German papers wrote that now that Denmark had joined the ranks of those fighting against communism and for a "New Europe," it had also to solve the problem of the Jews, who were, as a people, supporters of communism. A pronouncement in this spirit was also reported by the official Danish news agency on November 28 from government sources in Berlin.[34]

These hints were not chance remarks. Goering's notorious orders to Heydrich to make the necessary preparations for "a general solution of the Jewish problem in Germany's sphere of influence in Europe" were issued on July 31, i.e., shortly after the German invasion of Russia.[35] During fall and early winter the *Reichssicherheitshauptamt* (Administration of the Reich, German security headquarters—RSHA) and Martin Luther's department for Jewish affairs in the German Foreign Office began to plan the big operation. The signing of the anti-Comintern pact was considered a good occasion to carry out at least part of the program.[36] The Wannsee Conference, as is now known, summed up the plan for the "final solution" and communicated it to the departmental heads of the Reich. This fateful meeting was first fixed for December 9 but was postponed following the Japanese attack on Pearl Harbor, and it took place on January 20, 1942. On December 8, 1941, a day before the original date set, Franz Rademacher presented to his superior, Luther, at the latter's request, a memorandum with regard to the proposed meeting, which set out the proposals of the German Foreign Office.[37] Paragraph 7 of this document talks of "influence on remaining European governments to initiate Jewish legislation." The "remaining European governments" are all those not mentioned in the preceding paragraphs (Romania, Slovakia, Croatia, Bulgaria, Hungary) and therefore include Denmark.

The hints dropped in Berlin were quickly understood by the Danish National Socialists, and Frits Clausen, who was considered their leader, asserted in an article aimed at the students that the countries which had joined the anti-Comintern pact could not avoid, sooner or later, taking a stand on the Jewish international question. He added that it was known that a large number of the organizers of the demonstrations against the pact were "our local Jews"[38] (a claim which was doubtless completely unfounded). The National Socialist groups at once attempted to exploit the occasion. As early as November 27, 1941, two days after the pact, the anti-Semitic weekly *Kamptegnet* (*Battle Emblem*), which was modeled on the German *Stürmer,* called for a rally of the Danish Anti-Jewish League.[39] This renewed activity reached a peak December 20, 1941, when an attempt was made to burn the Copenhagen synagogue. Earlier, hooligans had tried to destroy the statue of the Danish-Jewish author Meir Aaron Goldschmidt. The arson attempt failed, and the perpetrator was caught and on February

3, 1942, condemned by the Copenhagen court to three years and twenty days' imprisonment and ordered to pay the costs of the case. The court records describe the crime as follows:

According to the accused's confession, he, on December 20, 1941, at 12:30 A.M., caused a fire in the synagogue, 12 Krystalgade, in that he, with the aid of a ladder, climbed up to a window of the synagogue on the courtyard side, broke a window, poured onto the windowsill an inflammable liquid he had brought with him in a soda-water bottle, and then set fire to it.[40]

No serious damage was caused, and the significance of the event lay in the conclusion that both the Danes and the Jews drew from it.

The Danish politicians were also perfectly aware that the Jewish problem threatened at the time to become a factual political issue. On the day of his return from Berlin, November 26, 1941, Scavenius presented a report to the Council of Nine. Without mentioning the name of Goering, he reported the opinions expressed in Berlin with regard to the Jewish question, and added that no practical proposal had been put forward. Alsing Andersen, chairman of the trade unions and leader of the Social Democrats in the Rigsdag, replied that the question had already been debated in his party and it was their opinion that developments of this sort should be halted from the first moment. This view was supported by Ole Bjørn Kraft, representative of the Conservative Folk party and member of the Rigsdag's foreign policy committee, who demanded outright rejection of any demand of this type. In the course of the discussions in the council and the government following participation in the anti-Comintern pact, it was resolved that on three points Denmark would not give way to German demands. These were joining the Axis (Germany, Italy, Japan); introduction of Jewish legislation; and the dispatch of a regular Danish army to the eastern front.[41]

The minister of religion invited Chief Rabbi Friediger to call on him at this time and assured him that there was no basis to the rumors that the Nuremberg Laws were to be introduced in Denmark. "As long as a Danish government has anything to say in this country," he added, "the Jews have no grounds for fear." The Chief Rabbi passed this message on to his community in a synagogue sermon.[42]

At a conference of clergymen who regarded themselves as disciples of Grundtvig, which took place in December 1941, the participants debated whether to organize petitions from the Rigsdag's electoral districts to demand that members of the Rigsdag vote against any attempt to introduce racial laws. The suggestion was waived in order not to arouse undue publicity on the question. Rabbi Friediger, who reported this discussion, relates that at another meeting of clergymen held at Askov High School the same problem was debated, and one of the participants wrote to him that "for us this is not just a question of Jews and their rights, but for us Danes it must first and foremost be a question of a small nation's right to exist, yes, a question of our entire national attitude and of the fundamentals of popular government: equality and human dignity."[43] Frederik Torm, professor of theology at the University of Copenhagen, was the prime mover of a resolution adopted by the students and faculty of theology to the effect that should persecution of the Jews be instituted, they would give strong public expression to their opposition. This internal decision was implemented during the persecutions of October 1943.[44]

In the article previously mentioned, Hal Koch expressed the public reaction. He too stressed that "We must here from the first moment say a clear No." This clear "no" was not merely due to Hal Koch's attitude to the Jewish problem; it was aimed not only at the German authorities but just as much at the Danish government, to show that he and the Danish youth organizations would not accept further concessions to the Germans. It was assumed that

Jewish legislation was to be the next demand of the German authorities, and this further step on the road of concessions Hal Koch and his supporters wished to prevent.[45] It was precisely this combination of the general political problem and the Jewish problem that showed the extent to which the Jewish problem had become a Danish problem.

Koch's article was published in *Berlingske Tidende* on January 6, 1942, and the Jewish question then became a subject of general public discussion throughout the country. The National Socialist press reacted sharply with articles full of libelous and personal attacks on Hal Koch. Weighty articles appeared in the daily paper *Fædrelandet*, in *Kamptegnet*, and in the paper of the German minority, the *Nordschleswigsche Zeitung*. Here the Danish Nazis tried to explain, according to their own lights, the Jewish problem in Denmark and the relations between Denmark and Germany. Their main assertion was that the people were "led astray" by types like Hal Koch, that they were "struck blind," and that it was therefore impossible "to base the enlightenment of the Danish people on the elements of the racial problem," all the more so since the authorities supported the opponents of national socialism. However, the main problem that engaged Hitler's lackeys in Denmark, and for which the Jewish problem was but a pretext, was the question of Denmark's place within the "European New Order."[46]

During these weeks, the German minister, Renthe-Fink, played a decisive role. He succeeded in removing the question from the agenda and in causing a decision to be reached that Denmark for the time being would not be included in those countries mentioned in the plan of the "final solution," as laid down at the Wannsee Conference. Renthe-Fink explains that Ribbentrop's attitude to Denmark was a divided one. On the one hand, he wished to see quiet and order reign in Denmark—in contrast to Norway, where the S.S. was in control and Ribbentrop's influence was nonexistent.

He was also sensitive to foreign reaction to German behavior. On the other hand, he wished to see national socialism triumph in Denmark and to see the country made *Judenrein*. He feared that if he did not carry this out, the task would be given to his rival, Himmler, and be implemented by the S.S. As long as the National Socialist rulers of Germany believed that they would succeed in bringing the Danish National Socialists to power without using coercive methods, they preferred this solution. However, the extremist elements in the German Foreign Office (mainly Luther, head of the *Deutschland* Department, and his assistant, Rademacher) tried constantly to force the issue. Renthe-Fink, arguing that he wished to prevent both the rise to power of the National Socialists and the emergence of the Jewish problem, tells that he maneuvered between the *Deutschland* Department and Ribbentrop, with the conservative elements in the Foreign Office—mainly the head of the Northern Department, Grundherr, and apparently also the director-general of the Ministry, Weizsäcker—giving him support.[47]

On the whole, Renthe-Fink employed various tactics to avoid a deterioration of the situation. One of these was to play for time. This is transparent from the correspondence between Rademacher and the legation in Copenhagen, which continued over a year and a half. In July 1940 Rademacher sent a circular to all German representatives abroad requesting them to furnish the *Deutschland* Department with accurate information on the Jews in each country. The letter to Copenhagen was sent on July 22, 1940.[48] It contained an extract from a book by one Zander on "Dispersion of Jews in the World," with a brief description of the position of the Jews in Denmark, and requested examination of the accuracy of the text. The letter continued:

It is important for us to know how many Jews there are in the various countries, in which essential large industrial and business enterprises they wield dominating influence, and how big the total Jewish capital is estimated to be. I would ask that these questions be answered quickly, as they may be of importance for the preparation of a peace treaty.

(At that time the Germans still believed that they would finish the war rapidly.)

On January 27, 1941, that is, about a year and a half later, Rademacher requested Copenhagen to furnish an early reply to this circular. A note in the margin of the copy shows that the matter was again taken up for discussion on March 31, 1941.[49] A further letter dated March 4, 1941, shows that prior to this time a telephone conversation took place between Berlin and Copenhagen, in which Renthe-Fink apparently maintained that the original circular could not be found anywhere in the legation, and Berlin announced that a copy would be sent to him. On April 2, a further reminder was dispatched, demanding not only the report but an explanation of the long delay in carrying out the order. This time Renthe-Fink replied as early as April 18.[50] He announced that the material was now being prepared, but since there were no official statistics or other publications, the work was experiencing considerable difficulties. Rademacher decided in a marginal note to return to the matter on June 4. On this date the question was again postponed until September 3, and on September 5 yet another reminder was dispatched. A copy of this note was presented for discussion on November 5, with the result that a new reminder was sent on November 14. Hereafter, as we shall see, the affair entered a new phase.

According to Renthe-Fink, there was complete agreement on the Jewish question between himself and the successive military commanders in Denmark, Generals Kaupisch and Lüdke. In October 1940, certain parts of Jutland were declared zones of military security and identity cards were introduced. The orders of the German High Command were that Jews were forbidden to enter these security areas, but General Lüdke and Renthe-Fink agreed not to take any measures against the Jews, not to remove them from the areas, and not even to mark their identity cards in any special way.[51] Moreover, when on September 1, 1941, the compulsory wearing of the yellow star was officially announced in Germany, Renthe-Fink and the general decided privately not to demand that the Danes introduce any mark of Jewish identification.[52] In a memorandum to Ribbentrop in January 1943, Luther reports that even Frits Clausen was of the opinion that "wearing of the Jewish star would arouse the protest of tens of thousands of Aryan Danes."[53] The matter never came up for official discussion throughout the occupation.

We have seen that Renthe-Fink tried to influence the policy laid down in Berlin. Already in January 1941, in a talk in the Foreign Office in Berlin, he had succeeded in winning Ribbentrop's support for his line against Luther's objections. As the lesser evil, Renthe-Fink then proposed that financial help continue to be given to the Danish National Socialists (whose practical possibilities he correctly estimated as being nil) while Luther asked for a radical upheaval.[54] During the visit of Himmler to Copenhagen mentioned earlier in this chapter, Renthe-Fink held a private talk with him, before the mentioned meeting with Thune Jacobsen. The minister explained that his legation rendered every possible support to the National Socialists and exercised strict control over the Communists and Jews. Their influence, he explained, slight in any case, was on the decline, and direct measures against the Jews should be avoided—in the German interest. The question could first be resolved only with victory. Himmler was particularly impressed by Renthe-Fink's comment that the enrollment of Danish volunteers for the *Waffen S.S.* could not succeed if persecution of the Jews was instituted, as this plan was of particular interest to him.[55]

In concert with Grundherr, Renthe-Fink succeeded in November 1941 in moving Ribbentrop—and through him, Hitler—to reaffirm the moderate political line in Denmark. However, immediately afterward, in the wake of the anti-Comintern pact, the Jewish problem sprang to the fore again. The initiative taken by extremist elements might well have engendered sweeping conclusions and caused a drastic change in the situation.[56] At that very time, i.e., between the 11th and 17th of December 1941, Rademacher visited Copenhagen and used the opportunity to have a talk with Renthe-Fink on the problem of the Jews in Denmark. He asked if it were not possible to frighten the Jews to that extent that they would leave the country of their own free will. To this Renthe-Fink replied that he imagined that the Jews would gladly leave Denmark, since the proximity of Germany aroused their grave fears, but where could they go? And he asked if it were not possible to postpone the solution of this problem until after the war. Rademacher now renewed his demand for the celebrated report. Rademacher, however, did not talk only with Renthe-Fink. To one of the counselors at the legation, G. L. Schaller, he related in strictest confidence the story of the murder of the Jews in the Balkans and his intention of also taking action against the Danish Jews. Schaller passed the information on to his minister.[57] Three days after Rademacher's departure from Copenhagen the synagogue arson attempt took place (there is no proof of any connection between Rademacher's visit and this act, though such a possibility cannot be excluded). In the new year, Hal Koch's article appeared and the Jewish problem became public.[58]

News of the discussion that had flared up in Denmark reached other countries—presumably via Stockholm—and was made public in the press and radio, mainly in England but also in the United States. On the same day that Koch's article appeared in *Berlingske Tidende*, extremely distorted information was given by the Scandinavian broadcasting

service in England and thereafter by the BBC itself.[59] These
broadcasts stated that the Nazis in Denmark were exerting
pressure on the Danish government to introduce the Nuremberg laws and that three ministers, known for their positive
attitude to the Germans,[60] had put forward a proposal in
this spirit to the government and the king. The king, however, had threatened to abdicate if his Jewish subjects were
molested. This news was undoubtedly false.[61] Renthe-Fink,
who apparently realized that same day, January 6, that the
matter could not be kept quiet, raised it in talks with
Foreign Minister Scavenius and Transport Minister Gunnar
Larsen. His idea was to obtain from the two Danes who
were known to have a positive attitude toward Germany
the reply he needed for the cable he wished to send to
Berlin. Scavenius assured him that the king did not intend
to abdicate but, as anticipated, he added that he could
not deny that in the present situation the raising of the
Jewish problem by the Germans would undermine his
policy, which strove to bring Denmark closer to the German
spirit. Renthe-Fink repeated these words to Berlin on the
afternoon of the same day, emphasizing that the rumors
were caused by an announcement in an American newspaper.[62] By means of this telegram, he hoped to scare Ribbentrop, who, as stated, was sensitive to foreign reaction to
events in Denmark and was not interested in causing disturbances within the country. In order to drive his point
home, the following day—January 7—Renthe-Fink sent a detailed memorandum on the same subject.[63] Here he tried
to uncover the background to the rumors, intended, in his
opinion, to make the government unpopular in the eyes of
the people. He then gave the essential content of Hal
Koch's article and some of the counterarguments of the
National Socialists. His recommendation: noninterference.

The reaction of the German Foreign Ministry was not
long in coming. On the day of the telegram, January 6,
Grundherr replied to Renthe-Fink and informed him of the

contents of a broadcast in Norwegian from London on the same subject.[64] However, it would appear that Luther was also worried. On the copy of Renthe-Fink's cable received in his department, somebody wrote on January 7: "Herr Luther wishes to clarify the source of the rumors. To the best of his knowledge no steps have recently been taken regarding the Jewish problem in Denmark."[65] On January 10, the director-general of the Foreign Ministry received the following note, signed by the head of the Minister's Bureau, Franz von Sonnleithner: "The foreign minister requests you to inform him who demanded from the Danes that the Jewish problem be raised, as stated in Minister von Renthe-Fink's telegram No. 18 of January 6." This request reached Luther on the 11th, and on the 15th he presented his reply in a "memorandum to the minister regarding raising of the Jewish problem in Denmark."[66] Luther asserts here that his department had not raised the question either with the Danish legation in Berlin or directly with the Danish government, and that the minister had received no instructions to raise the matter officially.

Renthe-Fink confirms[67] that Luther was correct in this assertion and that he, Renthe-Fink, had raised the question without receiving orders to this effect, intending to bring about an elimination of the danger. He achieved his objective. At the Wannsee Conference on January 20—five days after writing the above memorandum—according to the minutes:

The Deputy Director of the ministry, Luther, stated in this connection [i.e., organization of the "final solution"] that a thorough handling of the problem would reveal difficulties in certain countries, for instance in the north, and that postponement of the operation in those countries was to be recommended for the time being. In consideration of the small number of Jews in those countries this postponement should not be regarded as an important deficiency. On the other hand the Foreign Ministry does not expect great difficulties in the west and southeast.[68]

Renthe-Fink, in accordance with information given to him by Weizsäcker during a private visit to Denmark in the summer of 1942, says that Luther stated what he stated on the express order of Ribbentrop.[69] Be that as it may, there is no doubt that Renthe-Fink at this time succeeded in making it clear to the planners of the "final solution" that an operation against the Jews would harm German interests in Denmark.

In Denmark the debate continued both among politicians and the public at large. Prominent in the political discussions was Scavenius's tendency to refer to the Jewish problem as something that was best served by silence. Talk also drifted around to the anti-Semitic journal *Kamptegnet*, and the foreign minister said: "The paper harms its own objectives."[70] Developments confirmed his words, as we shall see below. Members of the government and others even continued to give public utterance to their energetic opposition to any action against the Jews. Not all of them spoke so clearly and decisively as Hal Koch, but rather expressed their views by insinuation. This method was widespread among the Danes in those years, and words were spoken according to the principle of "reading between the lines."[71]

However, it so happened that February 3, 1942, marked the centenary of the birth of a celebrated Danish literary critic, the Jew Georg Brandes. Opinions on Brandes had always been divided in Denmark, and he had never been regarded as a representative of the Danish spirit in the same way, for example, as Kierkegaard; but his birthday was turned into a demonstration. Memorial meetings were held in various places, and Social Democratic leaders and university professors lectured on Brandes before large assemblies of students and other groups. The event roused the ire of the Germans, culminating in a protest to the Danish government and refusal to allow a broadcast scheduled for February 4.[72] In these lectures the Germans were not attacked directly and could therefore find no other cause for complaint than to accuse the organizers of "Communist propaganda." It is understandable that it was not pleasant for them, for instance, to hear Hartvig Frisch quote from Brandes's letter on Renan's prayer to Athene on the Acropolis: "The world will only be saved by returning to you and thus shaking off the barbarism in which it finds itself."[73]

On that same day, the 3rd of February, sentence was passed on the young man who attempted to set fire to the synagogue.[74] The relatively severe punishment was explained by the accused's two previous though short terms of imprisonment, but no one in Denmark was unaware at the time of the demonstrative significance of the sentence.[75]

Renthe-Fink's summary of the Jewish problem at the time was given on two occasions. On January 16 he dispatched a report summing up the events of the first half of January[76] in which he devoted a short chapter to the Jewish problem. He briefly repeats the upsurge of rumors following the "hostile reports in the press and radio" (meaning abroad). He recalls the discussion in the Danish press and points out that the matter had begun to fade but "the good thing was that the Jewish problem was discussed publicly in Denmark for the first time. How great is the opposition still prevailing in Denmark today against a solution of the Jewish problem I have already explained in my cable of January 6 and my written report of January 7." He sums up his views for the second time in his comprehensive report on the position of the Jews in Denmark which was at long last sent to Berlin on January 21.[77]

This report was compiled by Danish Nazis who had set up an institute for racial research.[78] Renthe-Fink, however, added a sort of introduction, in which he analyzed the situation in light of recent experience. After the usual explanation that the enemies of Germany outside and within had raised the question in order to cause unrest,[79] he repeats and underlines the Danish assertions, as formulated mainly by Hal Koch, that the Danes would consider the introduction of anti-Jewish legislation an infringement of the German guarantees of April 9, 1940, and a destruction of the foundations of independent Danish life. To pacify the National Socialists, he said: "It is hard for us to realize how far large sections of the Danish population lag behind in their attitude to the Jewish problem." Even politicians and public figures, he continues to explain, express the view that in Denmark, fortunately for them, there is no Jewish problem, and they do not—the National Socialists excepted —understand that in the "New Europe" which is to evolve the problem of the Jews must be settled in a uniform manner. He then enumerates the reasons for this apparently strange phenomenon; this analysis, consisting as it does of a mixture of truth and lies, is particularly interesting. Renthe-Fink concludes as follows:

As long as it is desirable for the prosecution of the war and for our general political interests not to disturb peaceful development in Denmark, we should not entertain the idea that a solution of the Jewish problem is possible in Denmark. We are therefore content for the present mainly to persuade the Danish government to keep the Jews out of positions where they can exercise a harmful influence. It is said that the government has decided in future not to appoint Jews to important posts and not to grant Danish citizenship to Jewish emigrants.[80] Moreover, we seize every opportunity to point out to the Danes the importance of the Jewish problem.

Renthe-Fink did not know that he wrote these recommendations on the day of the Wannsee Conference.

If there was indeed an advantage in the fact that the Jewish problem was now being debated publicly for the first time, then there is no doubt that this discussion, more than it drew the Danes closer to the German conception, made the Germans realize that they would not succeed in convincing the Danes in principle or in practice, and that they could not touch upon this sensitive spot without endangering the whole structure of relations as constituted at the beginning of the occupation. Renthe-Fink assumed, and rightly so, that it was not worthwhile even to extreme Nazis to jeopardize these relations because of a few thousand Jews.

It should redound no less to Renthe-Fink's credit that he knew how to exploit the mentality of the Nazi leaders in an effective manner in order to prevent, or at least postpone, an attack on the Jews of Denmark. However, the decisive factor in the whole matter, as he himself maintained, was the firm stand of the Danes, leaders and people as one, on this question. It was this moral-political attitude which made it possible at the time for this German—who was Hitler's official representative yet no anti-Semite, who supported the occupation of Denmark by the Reich yet did not wish to force National Socialism on the Danes—to act in accordance with his understanding and safeguard the Danes and the Jews from upheaval.[81] Renthe-Fink of course wanted first of all to save his policy, the policy of cooperation (the success of which also insured his personal status), but he was keenly aware that persecution of the Jews would mean the failure of the policy of negotiation between Denmark and Germany.

The Legends About the King—Are They True?

"The king is a national symbol on which feelings and thoughts are concentrated. . . . It is clear to all that he watches over Denmark's dignity, that he shows where to draw the line, that his attitude compels respect even among the foreigners in his land. More than once he has been known to indicate a limit beyond which none shall pass." These words by a Swedish professor forcefully express the lofty role played by the Danish king in a period fraught with difficulties. This is the grain of truth around which legends have been woven about King Christian X and his deeds on behalf of his Jewish subjects.[82]

The legends began to grow, it would seem, with the British and American newspaper reports of the king's threat to abdicate should anti-Jewish legislation be introduced. However, most of the stories began to circulate from 1943 on. In January 1943 an article on Denmark[83] was published in the quarterly journal *Foreign Affairs* and contained a description of the king's general attitude toward the Germans, together with the "information" that "at least once after the proposed introduction of anti-Jewish legislation he attended services at the synagogue in Copenhagen." This statement was completely unfounded, the presence of the king at the centenary service of the synagogue in 1933 being confused with his imaginary participation in prayer during the occupation—something which was utterly fictitious. This item is nevertheless stubbornly repeated by almost everyone—writers, journalists, and research students —who has taken an interest in the fate of the Danish Jews during the German occupation.[84]

The second point around which legends flourished was the fact that Danish Jews were not forced to wear the yellow star. This was so fantastic an omission in the eyes of observers that they felt bound to provide some extremely unusual explanation. The legend goes that when the Germans raised the subject of the yellow star, the king threatened that he himself would be the first to wear it, and the Germans thereupon withdrew their demand. In this connection, mention is often made of a saying which the king had indeed uttered, namely, that there was no Jewish problem in Denmark since the Danes had never had inferiority complexes as far as the Jews were concerned.[85]

Few Danes actually fell for this tendency to create legends, though Henrik Kauffmann, who had been ambassador to the United States and had played an important role in the foreign policy of the underground movement, wrote an article after the persecutions of 1943 in which he included all the above stories.[86]

From a purely historiographical point of view, it is clear that there is no basis for most of these stories. But the premise put forward by several people that the king's character was such that he might well have said and done such and such a thing is correct.[87] Moreover, a number of things that the king did in fact do are known to us. In the winter of 1941–42 Rabbi Dr. Marcus Melchior in cooperation with Rabbi Wolf S. Jacobson issued a book of commentaries on the weekly portions of the Torah.[88] Rabbi Melchior presented a copy of this book to the king on the occasion of the New Year, 1942, and the king replied with a letter, written in his own hand, on December 30, 1941. Together with his thanks for the book, the king added: "I have heard with regret of the synagogue fire and am happy that the damage was slight."[89] There is no doubt that this letter was written with a view to expressing the king's solidarity with his Jewish subjects, in those very days when the Danish National Socialists were trying to provoke unrest as a prelude to action against the Jews. In the days of the grave crisis, in the autumn of 1943, the king interceded directly with the Germans on behalf of the Jews, as we shall see below.

The difference between the king's attitude in his letter to Rabbi Melchior and that of Hal Koch and others as regards the Jewish problem is one of form, of opportunity; but there is no essential difference between them. The king embodied and symbolized the national spirit. This became historical truth even though it found its expression in legends, and the frontiers between his real actions and those ascribed to him have been blurred beyond recognition. The profound admiration which all Jews, not only those in Denmark, had for the Danish king was quite exceptional,[90] since the behavior of the Danish people and their successful protection of the Jews among them were exceptional amid the general annihilation. This reveals a frightening aspect of the Holocaust: that behavior which could be considered as natural and self-evident for a civilized people was, it would seem, so exceptional in the eyes of contemporary Jews that they had to have recourse to legends in order to give expression to their excitement.

The Jewish Problem and the "Telegram Crisis"

In the summer of 1942 signs began to appear of a change in the attitude of the Danish population toward the occupying power. German victory in the war did not seem as assured as previously, and the presence of the occupier in the country and the economic consequences of the war became steadily more oppressive. Premier Stauning died in May 1942 and his place was taken by the finance minister, the most prominent figure among the Social Democrats, Vilhelm Buhl. Acts of sabotage were on the upsurge and British help to Danish underground groups was increasing. The Danish population as a whole did not as yet support the underground movement, which had enormous difficulties to contend with, but its operations were more than once greeted by a silence which could well be regarded as sympathetic. Typical of the spirit and behavior of the people is the story on the state funeral of Stauning. It was held in the largest hall then existing in Copenhagen (Forum) with the participation of 12,000 people. The crowd waited for the arrival of the king and, when they discerned a movement near the entrance, rose to its feet. However, it was Renthe-Fink who came in. "It is impossible to describe," writes the historian Hartvig Frisch, "with what speed the people sat down again, and as the hall was large the movement was like a ripple and became a unique demonstration of silence." Upon entering the hall, the king ignored the saluting Germans completely and greeted the crowd, all the time demonstratively turning his back on the Germans.[91]

The flight of Christmas Møller at the end of April 1942 to Sweden and then to England, where he assumed leadership of the Danish Council, acerbated the tensions between the Germans and the government on the one hand and between the country's officially responsible leaders and the underground groups on the other. The Germans now made intensive efforts to insure victory on the field of battle, and in Denmark this resulted in increased emphasis by the Germans on matters of military security. In that summer they demanded the evacuation of all Danish troops from Jutland, where they constructed strong defense works along the coast and enlarged the airfields.[92] In all areas and in all aspects the Germans exhibited more aggressiveness during that summer. Increased efforts were now also made to accelerate the "final solution." *Aktion Reinhard,* named after Reinhard Heydrich, the assassinated head of Reich Security, was set in motion with a view to completing the annihilation of Polish Jewry.[93] Throughout Western Europe the large-scale deportations eastward began in the summer of 1942.

In the wake of the increasing general tension the activity of the Danish National Socialists led by Frits Clausen was intensified. The leading spirit among the Germans in regard to the Danish National Socialists and their struggle for power was the cultural and press attaché in the German legation, Dr. Gustav Meissner, Luther's confidant and a sort of "fifth column" within the legation. He bombarded the authorities in Berlin with reports, among them—according to Renthe-Fink—some which had not been submitted to the minister for approval as required by the regulations.[94] Meissner endeavored to describe the situation in Denmark as influenced by the Communists on the one hand and by the Allied Powers on the other. In keeping with National Socialist propaganda methods, the Jews appeared in the double role of scapegoats for both; they are the initiators and they are the operators.[95]

The Jewish problem, however, played a particularly prominent role in descriptions of the economic situation. The main part of the detailed report presented by Renthe-Fink in January 1942 dealt with the allegedly dominant influence of the Jews on the Danish economy. Assertions of this type were used repeatedly not only in the reports of Meissner but in the report of Clausen himself. The Jewish problem appears in all these as an addendum and corollary to the main problems which the National Socialists sought to resolve in their own way. After it became clear to them that they could not attain power, they demanded as a first step the abolition of the legally elected government and its replacement by a "business government," which they assumed would be more pliant and would fulfill the German demands more willingly.[96] To give his assertions greater weight, Clausen also complained of the great influence of the Jews in administration, cultural life, and the economy—exaggerating it very much. His intentions are transparent from his conclusions: "It is self-evident that the Jew in Denmark can simply not desist from using his power fully and actively against Germany, though he may take certain precautions in the matter. The question is therefore less the concern of the Danish National Socialists than of the German Reich."[97] Clausen then recommended an action against the Jews as of the utmost urgency. His aim was clear: he hoped to overthrow the legal regime step by step and wanted the Germans to do the work for him. He wished them to hurry toward the principle action he anticipated by first initiating an action against the Jews. He himself did not wish to engage directly in persecution of the Jews since this would arouse fierce opposition against him, and he therefore emphasized that the problem was more one for the Reich than for the Danish National Socialists.

Clausen's weighty memorandum was apparently written not only under the influence of Meissner but was also inspired by Germany, more precisely by Himmler and his

entourage. In the latter half of August, two of Himmler's—
not to say Hitler's—confidants visited Denmark. One was
Dr. Wilhelm Stuckart, director-general of the Ministry of
the Interior, whose official mission was to inspect the administrative situation with regard to intensified defense
measures against British attacks. The other was S.S. *Brigadeführer* Otto Ohlendorf, notorious as the commander of the
Einsatzgruppen, engaged in terror operations behind the
advancing German armies in the east. Among other things,
both visitors were interested in examining and activating
measures concerning the Jewish problem. In a joint meeting
of the guests from the Reich and the top local German
officials, sharp criticism was leveled against the general position in Denmark, while Ohlendorf also attacked treatment
of the Jewish question. Before this meeting Ohlendorf had
demanded, in a private talk with Renthe-Fink, that steps
be taken against the Jews. He threatened that if it was not
clear to the Danish government that it had to act, then the
Germans would have to take the necessary measures.[98] In
other words, Ohlendorf threatened that Himmler and his
men would intervene.

Renthe-Fink was well aware of the danger to his Danish
policy in general and the Jewish problem in particular and,
as in January, he feared the commencement of a campaign
to bring the National Socialists to power via activization of
the Jewish question. He succeeded, however, in convincing
Stuckart that it would be a mistake to raise this issue, and
in the report of his visit to Denmark which Stuckart presented to Himmler, the Jewish problem was not mentioned.
This was in itself no little success for Renthe-Fink.[99] In
addition, Renthe-Fink elaborated his viewpoint in his comprehensive memorandum of August 28, 1942.[100] Once again
he brought the Danes into the discussion. A long talk with
Scavenius on August 24 dealt with all the points at variance
between the Germans and the Danes, and even touched
upon the Jewish problem. In light of Ohlendorf's threats,

the German minister was much more aggressive and demanded from the Danish foreign minister the removal of
Jews from all key positions.[101]

On this occasion too Scavenius's reply was quite unequivocal. He maintained that the Danes themselves would
not act against their own citizens and that it was not possible at that time to institute measures against the Jews
"since the Danes would regard this as a denial of their
ideals."[102] Renthe-Fink adds that he emphasized to Scavenius that in the long run Denmark could not continue to
exist as a democratic-parliamentary island in a Europe controlled by the National Socialists. "The process will not
cease simply because Denmark is not prepared to participate." Expressions of this type were often flung equally
at the Danish and the German authorities, in order to
illustrate, as it were, the German minister's National Socialist loyalty, but on this occasion Renthe-Fink became really
frightened and thus he was eager to obtain a concrete
concession to put before Himmler and his circle. This was
confirmed by Renthe-Fink himself:

... it was quite clear that a new anti-Semitic wave from Germany was on the upsurge. I hoped this time too to head off the
storm if I could succeed in getting the Danes to support the
interests of their Jews and, without directly discriminating
against these, nevertheless to take certain measures which would
show that the Danish government wished to keep Jewish influence in public life under control. This gave rise to the caution-
ary talk I had with Foreign Minister Scavenius on 24.8.42
[August 24, 1942].[103]

Renthe-Fink here reached the limits of his understanding
of the Danish position and of his ability to stem the tide
of anti-Semitism which also threatened to engulf Denmark.
He did not understand that the Danish government could
not concede this point without conceding the political
principle on which it was founded. A concession of this

sort for tactical reasons would have negated its moral authority in the eyes of the people, who indeed, as Scavenius said, would have regarded it as a betrayal of their ideals. The incident illustrates clearly the fundamental difference between the Danish conception of the Jewish problem as a test case of the maintenance of the legal order and the mentality of Renthe-Fink, with his desire to preserve German rule in Denmark, though he abhorred militant anti-Semitism and terror. The German minister—unlike the Danes—did not appear to grasp that this sort of surrender to German demands would inevitably bring further concessions in its wake. The moment the Germans were to see that the government's attitude on the Jewish question had slackened they would have increased their demands and rapidly undermined the protected position of the Jews. Renthe-Fink's idea was to use the concession in order to preserve the status quo and the policy of cooperation, whereas the Danish leaders saw in abandonment of the Jews the uttermost limit of cooperation. Not only did Renthe-Fink at that instant reach the limit of his ability to defend the Jews; as a result of the increasing tension in both the Danish camp and among the German leaders, he also reached the limit of his ability to preserve the Danish-German policy of negotiation.

The battle lines were now clearly drawn. On the one side, the Danes with their determination to continue their democratic rule; on the other, the small and powerless group of Danish National Socialists with their dream of seizing power with the help of Dr. Meissner and the extremist German elements with whom he was connected. The Jewish question was to serve as a pretext for reversing the status quo in Denmark. Renthe-Fink tried, as we have seen, to ward off both phases of this threat by attempting to persuade the authorities in Berlin that nothing was to be gained by drastic measures which would lead to open resistance on the part of the Danes and disturb economic relations[104]—and by attempting to persuade the Danes to take some sort of action against the Jews.[105]

Renthe-Fink apparently did not know at the time that the intensified demands for a change in the political line in Denmark, and in particular the renewed efforts of those German leaders interested in pushing events rapidly forward, were connected with increasing persecution of the Jews throughout Europe. On August 21, 1942, Luther presented to Ribbentrop a nineteen-page summary of the development of the Jewish problem and the steps taken with regard to the deportation of European Jews since 1939.[106] This memorandum describes the main stages of the operation and deals in detail with France, Romania, Slovakia, Croatia, and Bulgaria. Hungary is also mentioned and even Italy (in connection with Croatia). It is noteworthy that in these last two countries no practical steps had as yet been effected. Denmark is not mentioned. Luther underlines the close cooperation of his department with the RSHA (mostly IV B 4—Eichmann's section). The memorandum also contains fairly detailed proposals for the future and the steps to be taken. It would seem that Ribbentrop was wary of too eager an initiative by his confident Luther in the Foreign Office and perhaps of too close a cooperation with Himmler's organization. In any case, on August 28 he issued the directive known as the "stop order," designed to restrict Luther's independence, and forbade him to communicate directly with German representatives in the various countries. Luther was to use the regular channels of the Foreign Ministry, that is, his directives and announcements were subject to approval by Director-General Weizsäcker.[107] On that same August 28, Eichmann held a meeting with his envoys in various countries. It was decided to hurry up the transportations before the onset of winter.[108] The events in Denmark should therefore be regarded in light of this intensified activity by the executors of the "final solution."

As stated, Clausen presented his report to Grundherr during the latter's visit to Copenhagen.[109] Grundherr passed it on to Renthe-Fink on August 24 and on September 1 to Rademacher.[110] He maintained that during his stay he sharply criticized the state of affairs and Renthe-Fink in person, and even spoke "with the Danish Foreign Minister Scavenius in a way that could not be misunderstood." As a result of these assertions, Rademacher reached the conclusion that "no real progress can be expected except by moderate but constant pressure whereby Denmark will also be persuaded to take up the Jewish question." All these details are known to us from a memorandum Rademacher attached to Clausen's report when on September 2 he presented it to Luther's private secretary (in order to bring it to Luther's attention). Luther apparently now sensed a convenient opportunity to push forward the Danish Jewish problem in his own manner. According to the "stop order" he was not permitted to act on his own initiative, but he saw an opportunity of harnessing Grundherr to his plans. As was his wont he wrote his comments across the text of Rademacher's memorandum (it was now September 9) in the following words: "Party comrade Rademacher —I am in full agreement with Clausen and yourself that we must at once deal with the Jewish problem in Denmark and solve it radically. Please prepare, together with Minister von Grundherr, a memorandum to the Foreign Minister. Our interests demand that it be 'either-or.' "[111] Rademacher's reply came on September 17 and shows that Grundherr had succeeded in persuading him that "the time has not yet come for this question to be raised in principle with the Danish government." He quotes the moderate policy approved by Ribbentrop which includes, in his view, "moderate but constant pressure," so that there are no grounds for new directives. The intention was clearly to prevent the matter's being put before Ribbentrop.[112]

In the meantime, Renthe-Fink sought to head off a

calamity, and on September 15 he sent a detailed report on the removal of Jews from the Danish economy, which, it will be recalled, was one of the practical demands of the anti-Semites.[113] The letter begins as follows: "After Jewish firms in Denmark have been eliminated as representatives and agents of German firms and after Jewish importers' business connections with German sales organizations have been suspended. . . ."[114] Renthe-Fink then proposes a further step, namely, that the supplying of fuel and coal for Danish enterprises by the Germans would take place only if Jews or their influence were removed from those firms. In a detailed discussion spread over two pages or more he explains the technicalities involved in carrying out this program. Toward the end of the document he lays stress on the political difficulties and supply disturbances liable to arise from such an action, but nevertheless recommends the plan while asking that its preparation be carried out with flexibility and caution. This memorandum is a classic example of the methods of those elements in the Foreign Ministry who wished to avoid extreme actions. Renthe-Fink, like Grundherr, gives the impression of striving for the removal of Jews from the economy (and his positive recommendation impresses the reader as a sign of his personal approval); but he attempts, on the other hand, to gain time and put off any practical measure by suggesting a program whose realization is fraught with complications.[115]

This was not, however, the only step taken by the German leaders in Copenhagen in order to forestall radical upheavals and action against the Jews. On September 18–19, an important member of Renthe-Fink's staff, Paul Ernst Kanstein, was received by Himmler in the latter's field headquarters in the Ukraine.[116] The plan which Kanstein tried to discuss with Himmler regarding the Jewish problem in Denmark had originally seen the light of day during the crisis of January 1942, but only after the death of Heydrich did Kanstein and Renthe-Fink see a reasonable possibility of influencing Himmler in the way they wished. In that same nocturnal conversation, when various matters regarding the interests of the National Socialists in Denmark were discussed, Himmler assured Kanstein that he for his part would institute no measures against the Jews in Denmark. Kanstein's main argument was once more Germany's interests, particularly in Danish agricultural production. He pointed out to Himmler the danger of a general strike which was likely to break out in the event of Jewish persecutions. As we shall see, Renthe-Fink and Kanstein attached too much importance to Himmler's assurances.

On September 24, 1942, Luther informed Weizsäcker in a memorandum of Ribbentrop's order, given—Luther claimed —by telephone, in which the foreign minister enumerated those countries where action against the Jews was to be intensified. "After a short lecture on the deportation of Jews from Slovakia, Croatia, Romania, and the occupied areas, the minister now ordered us to approach the government of Bulgaria, Hungary, and Denmark, with a view to initiating the expulsion of Jews from their countries."[117] It is noteworthy that this new directive was based on Luther's own survey and proposals of August 21. The same countries mentioned there appear once again, with one addition— Denmark. The fact that Denmark was this time included in the plan should be regarded as a result of the renewed efforts of the "activists" in the period from July to September. However, the main reason for Ribbentrop's increased aggressiveness would appear on this occasion to be Hitler himself. Renthe-Fink recounts that on September 23 Hitler flew into one of his celebrated rages and attacked Ribbentrop violently for his failure to make progress in solving the Jewish problem.[118] It is a known fact that Ribbentrop was terrified of Hitler and never stood up to his wrath.

Only a few days were to pass, however, before Hitler turned his ire upon the whole of Denmark. It may be as-

sumed that he had for some time wished to abandon the
moderate approach and apply sharper methods also to
Denmark. The pretext was given to him by none other than
the king. On September 26, 1942, Christian X celebrated
his seventy-second birthday and received greetings from
Hitler. The king replied in a terse and formal telegram:
MY UTMOST THANKS, CHRISTIAN REX.[119] On September 29
Renthe-Fink was ordered by Ribbentrop to deliver a sharp
protest to the Danish government and immediately afterward leave Copenhagen for Berlin. This episode is known
in the history of the occupation period as the "telegram
crisis." The Danish minister in Berlin was also requested to
return home. A month passed following Renthe-Fink's departure, during which negotiations between the Reich and
the Danish government took place through indirect channels
until the arrival of the new minister and plenipotentiary,
Dr. Werner Best. The political struggle between the mod-
erates and the extreme National Socialists among the German leaders, which had been waged throughout the period
of the occupation, not only continued but increased in intensity until the decisive crisis broke almost a year later,
at the end of August 1943. During this time the army,
under a new commander, General Hermann von Hanneken,
joined the ranks of the extremists.

The Jewish problem, which accompanied the telegram
crisis, as it had all the political crises, and was one of its
modes of expression, did not remain quiescent even in the
interregnum between Renthe-Fink and Dr. Werner Best.
Luther apparently reckoned on being able to exploit a
favorable opportunity when it seemed that Denmark was
a free-for-all, and on October 8, 1942, he delivered his
affirmative reply[120] to Renthe-Fink's proposals of the 15th
of September. His move would seem to have been coordinated with the RSHA, for on October 12 Himmler wrote
to Heinrich Müller (Eichmann's immediate superior): "On
September 29 I received a report on the preparation of a

card index of arrests in Denmark. I agree to the arrest of the Jews, members of the community,[121] and of Marxist agents."[122] No mention is made here of the previous assurance given to Kanstein, although it must be stated that Luther's and Müller's projects were also not set in motion. This delay might again have been due to some extent to the Danish government. This time there was no public discussion, but Henning Dalsgaard relates[123] that at the time of the crisis he was sent at the behest of the prime minister, Buhl, to Meissner in the German legation, to find out whether there was any basis for the rumors that persecution of the Jews would take place, and was told to make it quite clear to Meissner that in Buhl's opinion "such a demand would be incompatible with the formation of a new Danish government."[124]

At the end of October, Scavenius was summoned to Berlin for negotiations with Ribbentrop on the formation of a new Danish government. Before his departure the government met in order to lay down lines of policy. Buhl decided—with the support of all the ministers—that Scavenius had to stand firm on three points: a radical change in the structure of the government, anti-Jewish legislation, and implementation of the death penalty.[125] On his return from Berlin, Scavenius reported to a meeting of the government on November 6 that the Jewish problem (and the problem of acts of sabotage) was not raised by Ribbentrop.[126] The new plenipotentiary, Werner Best, arrived in Copenhagen on November 5. He began to negotiate at once on the formation of a new government. After a number of unsuccessful attempts the premiership was offered to Scavenius.[127] The ministers in the outgoing government and the Council of Nine formulated in concert four questions of principle and made their agreement to Scavenius's government conditional on his replies. The second question referred to the Jewish problem. In his reply, given at a meeting of the government on November 7, Scavenius stated that he was opposed to legislation against the Jews but that he was also opposed to the promotion of Jews and to their public appearance, in broadcasts and the like.[128] With Best's assumption of office, the attitude of the decisive political authorities to the Jewish problem was thus as clear as it had been in the days of Renthe-Fink.

Best—in Renthe-Fink's Political Footsteps

The new plenipotentiary, Werner Best, had been a National Socialist from his youth, was prominent even before Hitler's rise to power, and was thereafter one of Himmler's and Heydrich's closest associates.[129] It was expected that he would work hand in hand with the Danish National Socialists—but to the great surprise of the Danes this is not what occurred. From the day of his arrival in Copenhagen he strove for a "policy of understanding," until it became clear in the summer of 1943 that this was doomed to failure. It was natural that these efforts should be accompanied, as in the days of Renthe-Fink, by tactics designed to prevent the emergence of the Jewish problem. Before coming to Denmark, Best spent a week in the company of Renthe-Fink, who accompanied him to Ribbentrop's field headquarters and then to the office of the Führer himself (in Ribbentrop's presence) on October 27, 1942. Notes in Best's appointments book show that during this trip he spent many hours in conversation with Renthe-Fink.[130] Together they composed the memorandum based on the instructions received by Best during the visit to Hitler. The day before Best's arrival in Copenhagen, on November 5, Renthe-Fink wrote him a letter summarizing, it would appear, their joint talks.[131] It may be presumed that the Jewish problem was among the subjects, although it was not raised specifically during the talk with Hitler.[132] It seems as if it was not a good idea at the time to discuss the Danish-Jewish question with Hitler, who apparently agreed by keeping silent.

During these last days, however, Best also held meetings with members of the RSHA, and in the Foreign Ministry with Luther and Rademacher of the *Deutschland* Department.[133] About a month later, Rademacher visited Copenhagen. In a memorandum dated December 23 he reported that during his visit he had discussed with Best "the next steps against the Jews in Denmark." He then states that following these talks Luther decided to wait a month and only then to send new instructions to Copenhagen "to initiate the next moves."[134] In a memorandum of January 20, 1943, Luther stresses that the measures planned for the Scandinavian countries had been delayed for the time being to give Best "the possibility of taking his own steps toward a solution of the Jewish problem in Denmark."[135] Luther presumably had more confidence in Best than in Renthe-Fink and really expected initiative from him on the Jewish question—but at the beginning of February Luther's career came to an end.[136]

Before his disappearance from the political scene, Luther agreed to Best's proposal for a further postponement of the Jewish question in Denmark. On January 6 and 7 Best visited Berlin. Under cross-examination in a Copenhagen prison on August 31, 1945, Best asserted that he had gone to Berlin for consultations in the Foreign Ministry, although the official list of his appointments in Berlin does not show such a visit. Best's own appointments book contained the names of RSHA officials, among them Ohlendorf, who, said Best in his prison statement, was firmly opposed to his moderate political line in Denmark. Best argued that these talks were completely fortuitous. They include, however, a meeting with Eichmann, of which the Danish police report says:[137] "He had a talk with S.S. *Obersturmbannführer* Eichmann of what was called the RSHA's Jewish section.

The discussion concerned a German proposal to set up in Denmark a special camp for prominent European Jews. The prisoner had counseled against this, as it would make a bad impression on the Danes." As in the previous year, discussion of the general political line in Denmark was related to activization of the Jewish problem. It is difficult to say what Eichmann had in mind with the above proposals, but there is no doubt that he wished to include Denmark in his sphere of operations, even if the pretext should be the establishment of a "camp for the distinguished." At the same time, Best also—perhaps primarily—discussed the Jewish question with Luther and Rademacher.

On January 13, 1943, Best wrote a comprehensive memorandum based, as stated in his foreword, on the above talk; it differed little in content from the various memoranda of Renthe-Fink. Best's main assertion was that an attack on the Jews would be regarded by the Danes as the first step in the abolition of their constitution. He adds that the Danish prime minister had announced that he, together with the entire government, would resign in the event of "special measures against the Jews." Should this occur, continues Best, it would not be possible to form a new legal government and he would be obliged to take over the country himself as commissar of the Reich in the same manner as had been done in other countries. This comment shows the difference between the tactics of Best and Renthe-Fink. The latter would never have pointed out such a possibility. Best too had no such step in mind (at the time at least) but he dared to threaten such an outcome, since he was convinced that Ribbentrop was opposed to it, for it would mean that Denmark would be removed from his sphere of influence and come under Himmler's control, as had Norway. Best then proposed the same relatively limited measures previously recommended by Renthe-Fink: removal of Jews from key positions and from Danish-German trade, together with a proposal of his own—the arrest of a few Jews under the pretext of political or criminal offenses (which was very rarely implemented until the crisis broke). Luther forwarded Best's main proposals to the minister in a memorandum dated January 28, 1943, with a request for approval.[138] Ribbentrop indicated his agreement in the margin and on February 1, 1943, Sonnleithner informed the Foreign Ministry of the fact. On February 6, Luther informed Best by cable of the Foreign Ministry's agreements to his proposals.[139] This would appear to have been one of Luther's last acts before his arrest (see Appendix).

Following Luther's dismissal, Ribbentrop carried out a reorganization of the ministry and changed the communication and work methods with a view to insuring his own control over instructions and their implementation.[140] But he himself, as is known, was incapable of taking a firm line and swayed to and fro between moderate and extreme courses of action. In a conversation with the Italian foreign minister, Bastiani, on April 8, he compared the regimes in Norway and Denmark.[141] He explained that with the help of the "extremely energetic Dr. Best" he was trying to use "velvet gloves" in Denmark. In Norway, on the other hand, brutal methods were employed. "The result is that there are no more acts of sabotage in Norway, whereas in Denmark they are on the rise." The Jewish problem was not mentioned, though it was clear that waiving of the "final solution" formed part of the "soft policy" through which he aimed at reaching a compromise with the authorities of the occupied country.[142] Perhaps Ribbentrop's doubts regarding the "soft policy" were among the factors which induced him on April 19 to send a telegram to Best demanding a report summarizing the Jewish problem.[143] Best had to reply to two main questions: (1) To what extent did Jews hold key positions and wield influence in Denmark—in trade with Germany, for instance—? and (2) Was it nevertheless not possible to make certain demands on Scavenius's government pertaining to the Jews without causing it serious difficulties? We now know that Eichmann's department was at the time planning a new attack on the Foreign Ministry in connection with policy toward the Jews in Denmark,[144] but we do not know if threats on this subject were uttered before Ribbentrop's cable to Best or after the latter's reply.

Best answered on April 24 in an extremely detailed memorandum.[145] The first paragraph explains at length the value of the Jewish question as a matter of principle for the Danes. This is in fact an expanded repetition of his former note of January 13. He thus anticipates his reply to Ribbentrop's second question which he apparently considered the decisive one. Paragraph 2 replies to the first question. In brief, Best writes that the importance of the Jews in Denmark both in terms of numbers and of the positions they held was so negligible that "immediate measures against them would appear unmotivated and incomprehensible." To support his statement, Best gives details and data on Jewish participation in the various spheres of Danish public and commercial life.[146] Best not only wishes to show that he has examined the data but also adds in the last note to this paragraph that his research has been so comprehensive that when the time comes, it will be easy to effect a general settlement of the problem. His deeds during the autumn crisis of that year will show us that he not only said these words in order to pacify the protagonists of rapid action but that he took into account that this hour of trial was liable to come.

Paragraph 3 suggests the possibility of immediate steps, namely, to give back to the 1,351 stateless Jews (i.e., refugees) living in Denmark their German nationality in order to set them apart from the Danish Jews. He assumes that all the difficulties involved in action against Jews of Danish nationality will not arise with regard to these refugees. This proposal was examined and rejected by Rademacher's successor in the Foreign Ministry, Ebehard von Thadden. He attached his viewpoint to Best's reply and presented both to Ribbentrop on May 5 with a note asking the minister

whether any action should be taken.[147] Ribbentrop, however, preferred to delay his decision and on May 13 requested that the document be presented to him again in
four weeks' time.[148]

During this interval, however, Himmler aroused himself anew with regard to the Danish Jewish problem. Relations between Best and Himmler at the time were extremely close, Best maintaining them behind Ribbentrop's
back. On May 18, Horst Wagner, Luther's successor and the
liaison man with the RSHA, informed Ribbentrop that
Himmler would like to see Best on his next visit to Berlin.
Among the subjects Himmler wished to discuss, emphasis
was placed on the fact "that personal talks must be held
at some time or other on continued treatment of the Jewish
question in Denmark." Ribbentrop replied through Sonnleithner on May 22 that Himmler had no authority to
decide matters with Best. Decisions regarding those affairs
falling within his jurisdiction rested in the hands of the
foreign minister only. Ribbentrop did, however, agree to
Best's visiting Berlin.[149]

The visit took place in the first week of July.[150] The
Foreign Ministry had, however, already succeeded in wrest-
ing an assurance from Himmler that he would for the present
desist from any action regarding the Jewish problem in
Denmark. On the stages of negotiation which led to this
decision we have contradictory accounts, but there would
seem to be little doubt that an active role was played by
the new director-general of the Foreign Ministry, Gustav A.
Steengracht von Moyland, and by Luther's successor, Horst
Wagner. Announcement of the decision was made by Wagner to the director of the RSHA, E. Kaltenbrunner. Wagner's file also contains the following note dated June 30:[151]
"During a talk with the *Reichsführer* S.S. [Himmler] I
raised the question of the Jewish problem [in Denmark].
The *Reichsführer* instructed me to   inform the Head of
the S.D. [i.e., Kaltenbrunner] that all action regarding the

Jewish problem was to be avoided until new orders from him, provided that the foreign minister is in agreement. The foreign minister willingly acceded to this request."[152] What lay behind Himmler's decision remains unknown, but from now until the eruption of the crisis at the end of August the Jewish problem in Denmark lay quiescent.

Summary

During the whole of the period from the occupation of April 9, 1940, until the outbreak of the crisis on August 28, 1943, the Jewish problem dogged the footsteps of all then active on the Danish political front—Dane and German. It was not the main or central political problem. It did not form the subject of negotiations or the cause of struggle, and —apart from one interval—was not an item of public discussion. Yet all knew that it was there and that it was a yardstick of relations between Germany and Denmark—for the leaders of democratic Denmark, for the German representatives in the occupied country, for the Danish National Socialists dreaming of power, and for the Nazi leaders desirous of incorporating Denmark into the "New Europe" they intended to establish and rule by their own lights. So long as six or seven thousand Jews went about freely in the Danish state everyone knew that free and democratic Denmark had not been conquered, in spite of the presence of Hitler's legions. To the Nazis at home and abroad the situation was a thorn in their flesh. But they could do nothing, because the country's leaders (even those sympathetically inclined to Germany)—public figures of all types, the country's intellectuals, all sections of the population and the king at their head—all these negated the very fundamentals of anti-Semitism. Hal Koch was the first to express publicly what all felt: that this was a vital thread in the Danish fiber.

As long as the Germans, for their own reasons, were interested in honoring the agreement they had forced on the Danes, they could not touch the Danish Jews. This fact was crystal clear to the traditional diplomat Renthe-Fink, and the National Socialist Best inherited his evaluation. Thus the two of them, one after the other, struggled courageously and energetically against the machinations of those who were in a hurry to include the Jews of Denmark in the "final solution."[153] This unique situation affected not only Jews—Danish subjects and stateless—in Denmark itself, but also Danish Jews in other parts of Europe, who were considered not the subjects of a conquered state but the citizens of a neutral country.

All those who have hitherto engaged in studies of the rescue of the Danish Jews have laid most of their emphasis on the period of Werner Best. Renthe-Fink's years of office have not been investigated, but have for the most part been shrouded in legend. Since it is rare, however, that something springs from nothing, the events of October 1943 cannot be understood without a knowledge of what happened, or rather did not happen, from the day of occupation until the summer of 1943—that time which we may call "the period of protection."

This protection was not achieved by political defense alone. This was but one arm of the general struggle of the Danes to preserve the image of their country. Side by side with the diplomatic struggle, a hard internal battle was waged against the local National Socialists. It was in the nature of things that this politico-social fight against the small faction of Danish Nazis should include a struggle against militant anti-Semitism, which here too served as a criterion and a testing ground. It should not be forgotten that this battle, which was crowned with triumph, was waged while Denmark lay prostrate under Hitlerian occupation.

CHAPTER

III

Anti-Semitism in
Occupied Denmark

National Socialism in Occupied Denmark

When Germany occupied Denmark, the Danish National Socialist Workers' party (Danish initials, DNSAP), founded in 1930 and the main National Socialist party in the country, numbered some 6,000 members.[1] In the general election of April 3, 1939, it received over 31,000 votes.[2] Its *Führer* was Frits Clausen. Close to it in ideology was the stronger Farmers' party *(Bondepartiet)*, led by the aristocrat Jørgen Sehested, which obtained almost 51,000 votes in the same election.[3] These two parties together accounted for about 5 per cent of all the votes cast. In addition, there existed seven small Nazi groups, the most interesting being the National Socialist Workers' party (NSAP), founded in 1935 by Aage H. Andersen. This party issued the paper *Kamptegnet* and became the main focus of anti-Semitic activity and propaganda. All these groups and subgroups merged, split, were liquidated, and reestablished several times and in no coherent order.[4] During the occupation their number reached no less than seventeen competing groups, besides the two larger parties already mentioned.[5] For the purposes of this study, the Danish Anti-Jewish League is of primary importance. It was founded in 1941 by Aage H. Andersen after the two largest groups—DNSAP and NSAP—had merged, with a view to waging the war against the Jews more vehemently than could be done within the framework of the DNSAP. Many of the remaining small groups published, over longer or shorter periods, leaflets and bulletins primarily dedicated to attacking one or more of the other factions.

A card index of the members of the DNSAP was found in Frits Clausen's home in Bovrup after the war. These data have been subjected to statistical investigation in light of a number of sociological criteria.[6] The card index contains 22,689 names. The diagram shows the number of new enrollments in the party from the outbreak of the war (September 1939) until its conclusion (April 1945).[7]

Monthly Enrollment of New Members in the DNSAP, 1939–45

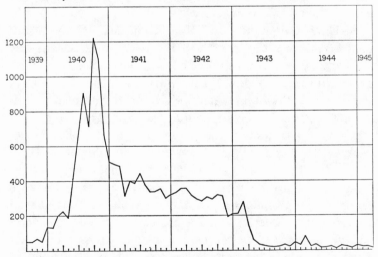

The predominant feature of the chart is the sudden rise between April and October, 1940, followed by an almost equally drastic decline, which continues more slowly until May 1943. From this point on new enrollments are virtually negligible. The diagram corresponds exactly to political developments over the period. "Danish nazism," writes Børge Outze,[8] "was a grave threat in the period April 9, 1940, to November 17, 1940. Thereafter, it disintegrated through internal dissensions and forfeited all opportunity of being helped to power." That same November 17 was set aside by Clausen for the coup through which he hoped to seize power. As camouflage there were to be a meeting, a parade of his "battalions," and the laying of a wreath in memory of the fallen of April 9 (thirteen in number!) near a statue in the center of town. The Germans, however, decided not to give Clausen their support and on the appointed day only the demonstrative part was carried out and this ended in utter fiasco: at the end of the ceremony the angry crowd fell upon the dispersing members of the "battalions." Apart from a few blows nothing happened to them, except that the crowd in a fit of what Frisch called "grim humor" removed their trousers and boots.[9]

In Outze's opinion—and this is confirmed by the sociological research—the growth of the party in 1940 was due to fear and opportunism.[10] Most of the increase was registered in Copenhagen and the provincial towns, as against the prewar situation, when the National Socialist parties were strongest in the agricultural areas.[11] Party members formed 0.6 per cent of the population. In the elections of March 1943 the DNSAP obtained 43,309 votes or 19.1 per cent more than the number of party members (it doubtless included a good many votes from members of the rival factions not participating in the elections) or less than 2 per cent (in Copenhagen, 2.6 per cent) of the total votes cast.[12] *Bondepartiet* dropped to 24,000 votes.[13] The two parties together therefore had more than 67,000 votes (3 per cent) as against 82,000 (5 per cent) in the 1939 elections—a decline of about 16 per cent.[14]

The Anti-Semitic Organ "Kamptegnet"

Among the reasons for the Nazi fiasco in Denmark was the Nazi press's low standard, which could not command the services of any capable journalists. This fact of course accounted for much of the general Danish disgust with the "new winds that blew from the south." The first issue of the DNSAP's daily paper *Fædrelandet (Fatherland)* appeared on September 1, 1939. On November 20, 1940, Renthe-Fink reported that its circulation had risen during that time from 4,000 to 23,000. A popular Danish joke at the time said: "What is a Danish National Socialist? One who sells *Fædrelandet*."[15] In fact, circulation never topped the 10,000 mark. The official organ of the party was the weekly *Nationalsocialisten*, founded in October 1931. In August 1943 the publishers appealed to its readers to make a special effort to increase circulation "since the time is once more ripe to make the organ of the party leaders the true militant organ of Danish national socialism."[16] *Fædrelandet* made itself particularly obnoxious to the public by playing the part of an informer—during the flight of the Jews, for instance. Still, the paper which devoted itself primarily to anti-Semitism was *Kamptegnet*, though attacks on the Jews and their supporters were not lacking in *Fædrelandet*.

On January 10, 1936, a group of leading Danish theologians—three professors and a lecturer at the University of Copenhagen[17] and the Bishop of Copenhagen, Fuglsang-Damgaard—issued a statement attacking an anonymous anti-Semitic pamphlet *The Christian Church as Seen by the Nordic Peoples*, which was based on *The Protocols of the Elders of Zion*. An explanatory article by Professor Frederik Torm revealed the story of the forgery.[18] The affair aroused attention even in Germany, where the *Völkische Beobachter* of January 14, 1936, published a report from its Copenhagen

correspondent under the heading DANISH THEOLOGIANS NERV-
OUS and the subheading "The Jewish Problem Raises Its
Head in Denmark." The report of the then German min-
ister, Richthofen, on January 13, also sees the approach of
the Danish theologians as an attempt to counteract "the
constantly growing understanding of the Jewish problem in
Germany," which he maintains, was evident among the
Danish population.[19]

The German diplomat gives Aage H. Andersen as the
author of the anonymous booklet. Andersen was the leading
anti-Semitic propagandist in Denmark throughout the
period. From the minister's letter we also learn that Andersen had just been expelled from the DNSAP for his "extremist standpoint." At the time of the publication's appearance the Danish minister of justice did not see any possibility of bringing a charge against Andersen. But what
was not done in 1936 was carried out in 1938, when Andersen was sentenced to eighty days' imprisonment and his
writings were confiscated. He informs us of this himself
in a letter written after the German conquest (on July 8,
1940) to his colleague Paul Wurm, a member of *Der Stürmer*'s editorial staff and director of the World Anti-Jewish
League. In this letter he appeals for increased support from
the German anti-Semites and complains bitterly of his continued difficulties in Denmark.[20]

Aage Andersen had begun to publish *Kamptegnet* even
before the war, as early as May 1939, his aim being to
create an organ similar in form and content to *Der Stürmer*.
His party, NSAP, was the official publisher. At first, *Kamptegnet* appeared as a monthly, but then after the outbreak
of war, it began to appear fortnightly on the first and
fifteenth of each month, beginning on October 1, 1939. From
June 28, 1940, it became a weekly, but already on November
1, 1940, it had to close down owing to financial difficulties.
It should be recalled that this was during the first phase of
German rule, when the Danish National Socialist move-

ment was still growing. On August 1, 1940, Luther compiled a report on the internal situation in Denmark, based on a detailed report of July 10, 1940, sent to him from Copenhagen. The information contained in this document was completely distorted. It was written with deep contempt for the legally constituted government and its position and motivated by an idealization of the Danish National Socialist movement in general and Frits Clausen in particular.[21] Thanks to this imaginary presentation, Ribbentrop obtained Hitler's approval for financial support to the Danish National Socialists.[22]

On April 8, 1941 (a year after the occupation began), Renthe-Finke wrote a detailed explanation of why 550,-000 kroner (225,000 marks) were required as a quarterly subsidy for the Danish National Socialists. Luther passed his proposal on to Ribbentrop in summarized form on April 21. Ribbentrop wrote his approval in the margin, but with the comment: "Only for three months at a time."[23] Following this achievement, Renthe-Fink came forward with a new request on May 3, this time to help Aage Andersen reissue his weekly *Kamptegnet*. He explained that Andersen had sought help from *Der Stürmer* and had even thought of publishing his paper under the same name—which Renthe-Fink did not consider a good idea—but the application had failed. Renthe-Fink even sent Meissner to Berlin to find out what had happened.[24] As a result of a talk between Rademacher and Meissner in Berlin on May 21, it was decided that economic assistance to *Kamptegnet* would be given out of the general allocation already approved.

Why did Renthe-Fink support Andersen? The discussion between him and Luther on a National Socialist coup in Denmark will be recalled. Renthe-Fink considered that support of Clausen would be the lesser evil. In line with the same policy he therefore continued to support the Danish Nazis. It will be seen from his letter on Andersen's behalf that the latter was extremely active. If the minister obtained assistance he could insure himself some degree of influence over Andersen's operations and in fact reduce the amount available to Clausen at the same time. It may be assumed also that Renthe-Fink knew only too well that Andersen's paper would never come to exert any real influence on the Danish people, and this was borne out by the failure of the paper during the first year of occupation.

Moreover, all this was at the time when Renthe-Fink was successfully evading an answer to Rademacher's demands for a detailed report on the Danish Jews; and he no doubt reckoned that the appearance of *Kamptegnet* was much less dangerous than the publication of such a report.[25] As on all similar occasions, it is clear that only the firm Danish stand on the Jewish question made such tactics possible. As early as the day after the Rademacher-Meissner meeting, on May 22, 1941, the first issue of the paper appeared in its new form—an exact imitation of *Der Stürmer*. Andersen's party had meanwhile disintegrated, and in its place he established on October 31, 1941, the Danish Anti-Jewish League—a "League for the Advancement of Racial Consciousness"—with *Kamptegnet* considered its official organ. Because of this connection with the anti-Semitic newspaper, the Danish authorities refused to register the league as an official Danish organization.[26] *Kamptegnet* continued to exist until May 27, 1943, when its last number appeared. The paper was finally closed by German order as part of Best's efforts to settle its debts and avoid an official declaration of bankruptcy. The history of *Kamptegnet* up to the day of its demise was characteristic of the behavior of the Danish people, its institutions and its authorities, and the way in which it obliged the Germans to accept its ideas.

There is no place here for a detailed description of the paper, which was an anti-Semitic publication in all respects, except that its editors—in addition to imitating *Der Stürmer* —took the character of the Danish people into consideration and tried to give it the tone of a serious journal, its subjects being examined and presented with alleged scientific accuracy, and its discussions balanced and sensible. Let us take, for example, the number on "reissue day," May 22, 1941. The front page carries an article about a Jew punished two hundred years previously (curiously enough, on April 9, 1740) for having traded without a license in one of the provincial towns. The main discussion was apparently to be found on the inside page with the first of a series of articles by Aage Andersen under the heading IS THERE A JEWISH PROBLEM IN DENMARK? In these articles, whose numbers ran into dozens, Andersen attempts to refute the assertion that the problem did not exist in Denmark, and to prove the strong influence—harmful, of course—wielded by the Jews in all walks of Danish life: trade and industry, finance, culture, journalism and radio, medicine, public administration, and the public institutions.[27] An assertion not without foundation was that "the strongest resistance to National Socialist thought processes is to be found in Danish schools and educational establishments" (September 4, 1941). Among persons attacked were two prominent professors of medicine, Erik Warburg (the king's physician)[28] and L. S. Fridericia, and the Nobel prizewinner Niels Bohr. Attacks of this type on celebrated and respected personalities were often accompanied by their photographs, which usually showed cultured and interesting faces—and the contrast between them and the anti-Semitic drawings and caricatures a la *Stürmer*, which filled the pages of the paper, was vivid. These attacks, far from arousing anti-Semitism, were more apt to arouse opposition to anti-Semitism.[29]

The Copenhagen Jewish community was of course also attacked (July 17, 1941) as a "recognized government institution," as were leading Jewish figures, such as the chairman of the community, C. B. Henriques,[30] Rabbi Dr. Melchior (June 19, 1941), and the author Henri Nathansen (July 3, 1941). The Jews of other countries, particularly of the United States, also came under heavy fire.[31] A particular object of provocation were the refugees, Jewish and political. The paper, for instance, labeled a Social Democratic refugee active in the workers' educational program as "Stauning's Jew" (August 28, 1941). The attacks further included the agricultural trainees working for Danish farmers, complaining among other things that they had "besmirched" the previously Jew-free island of Bornholm by their presence since the eve of the war (May 22, 1941).

In addition, Zionism itself was analyzed and debated (October 16 and 23, 1941), with pictures of Herzl, Weizmann, Jabotinsky, and others. Professor Klausner's book *Jesus of Nazareth* was quoted (May 29, 1941) to prove that Judaism is not just a religion but a national concept and therefore constitutes a foreign body in all other nations. The Jewish settlement in Palestine also came in for its share — "the Jews are abhorrent in Arab eyes" and "the Arabs despise and hate the cowardly Jews who seek to steal their land from them" (June 19, 1941). Special prominence was naturally given to the allegedly large role of the Jews in communism in general and in the internment and labor camps in Russia in particular, which were described in detail and supported by photographic material (August 14, 1941).

Great stress was laid on the subject of mixed marriages. Apart from articles on this subject clothed in pseudo-scientific guise (e.g., THE EUROPEAN RACES AND OUR PEOPLE on June 29, 1941), a weekly column under the heading THE WEEK'S RACIAL INFAMY appeared, with a list of names and sometimes a picture of the young couple. It is interesting that this "condemnation"[32] did not appear to deter anyone from entering into a mixed marriage. Readers were also strongly urged to obtain from the Genealogical Institute "race certificates" similar to those of the Central Bureau of Racial Science in Germany (see, for instance, the issue of May 29, 1941). The *Kamptegnet* of October 2, 1941, called for sterilization of the Jews. From time to time the paper also appealed for final steps to solve the Jewish problem also in Denmark. Thus on September 18, 1941, we find the view that the anti-Communist law was a legal precedent for anti-Jewish legislation. *Kamptegnet's* share in the debate on the Jewish problem following Denmark's joining of the anti-Comintern pact has already been discussed. A year later, after the telegram crisis and the formation of a new government, the paper demanded both the "solution of the Jewish problem" and, in a separate article, the wearing of the yellow star (November 26, 1942).[33]

It is noteworthy that as early as the fall of 1941 the paper talks of the "liquidation of European Jewry" and complains that the situation in Denmark is so different: "While Jews all over Europe await their liquidation, it is interesting to see with what enormous cheek the Jews here at home continue to behave" (October 23, 1941); or "The Jews will make Denmark their international free port" (November 6, 1941). However, *Kamptegnet* surpasses itself on May 7, 1942, with a photograph of three Jews awaiting deportation to the east. Beneath the photograph of three people whose whole beings are stamped with the profoundest despair, we find the caption: "Now they have an opportunity to reflect that one cannot with impunity live from cheating and deception and the exploitation of other human beings." Neither "examples" of this type, nor headings like LET US NOT WASTE OUR MISPLACED SYMPATHY ON THE JEWS (December 11, 1941), nor the joy of the paper at the anti-Jewish law in Pressburg and the yellow star in Slovakia (October 9, 1941) were likely to attract the Danish people to the concept of anti-Semitism; on the contrary, the result was even greater recoil.

The Daell-Wassermann Case

The attitude of the Danish public to anti-Semitism in general and to *Kamptegnet* in particular was reflected in in an important court case brought against the editors of the paper. One of the journal's foremost objectives, to which a good deal of space and energy was devoted, was the attempt to "strip bare" the role of Jews in Danish economic life with a view to their removal from all its spheres. Like the column on mixed marriages, a "weekly list" of businesses groaning under Jewish influence was also published, the provincial towns being no exception.[34] Numerous articles and "studies" were devoted to this subject.

In this connection, the paper began in December 1941 to attack the large Copenhagen department store Daell's Varehus, owned by the brothers Daell. Peter M. Daell had from time to time taken part in public life.[35] During the Finnish winter war against the Soviet Union in 1939–40, he was a member of a committee set up to render Finland effective help.[36] After the outbreak of war between Germany and Russia in June 1941, certain Danish groups sympathetic to the Germans, upon the initiative of Transport Minister Gunnar Larsen, again attempted to organize aid to Finland, this time by raising a brigade of Danish volunteers who would join the German forces fighting in Finland against the Russians.[37] The plan, however, went aground in the Council of Nine and the government, and all that remained was some humanitarian help in the form of food supplies.[38] Peter Daell contributed to the failure of the program in that he had rejected Gunnar Larsen's invitation to join a new organizing committee on the grounds that this time it was a question of help to Germany, which he was not prepared to render.[39] Daell, moreover, got in touch with various politicians, including Christmas Møller, and informed them of Larsen's approach; it would appear that he played a part in awakening opposition to the project in good time.[40] The Danish Nazis did not forget his role in what they regarded as a fiasco.

It will be recalled that the anti-Semites in Denmark awakened to new life in the wake of Denmark's participation in the anti-Comintern pact, and in a long article on December 11, 1941, *Kamptegnet* appealed to Prime Minister Stauning to solve the Jewish problem at once, "without hesitation and without excuses"—for the anti-Comintern pact made such a move obligatory. The heavy Jewish influence that still marked all walks of life, "in spite of the new official Danish attitude to the Jews confirmed by treaty," had to be eliminated. The same issue included the first attack on Daell's Varehus, where "Jewish methods" were employed; side by side with these a marked sympathy for Finland existed. On January 15, 1942, in the same issue which delivered the sharp attack on Hal Koch, we find a frontal assault on Daell. This time he and his Jewish secretary, Ella Wassermann, are accused of intimate relations, which have—according to the paper—resulted in the secretary's complete control over the whole business and its staff. Daell, like Koch, is stamped as a "Jewish lackey," and again the Jewish and Finnish questions are linked together. The article distinguished itself by particularly repulsive language and lewd insinuations.

Both Daell and Wassermann now took the paper to court on a charge of libel. The High Court found the charge substantiated and announced official acceptance of the case on February 2, 1942.[41] *Kamptegnet* retorted sharply in its issue of February 12 in a leading article headed VICTORY FOR JEWISH INTRIGUE which continued: "Our revelations of the reasons [for Daell's withdrawal from the Finnish plan mentioned above] . . . have revived Daell's love for Finland. This renewed affection has found expression in a summons against the editors of *Kamptegnet,* where he demands, among other things, compensation of 10,000 kroner—for the benefit of Finnish children."

The legally responsible editor of the paper at the time was the well-known anti-Semitic author Olga von Eggers. Following the court charge against her, she resigned from the board of the paper and Aage Andersen became the responsible editor in her stead. Andersen continued the same line from February 26 to March 5, 1942; then the debate came to an abrupt end. The reason for this sudden silence may be found in Renthe-Fink's letter of March 9, from which it transpires that the Germans themselves had intervened and ordered Andersen to stop this style of writing. It seems that Renthe-Fink's letter is the result of an anxious inquiry from Berlin. The changes in the editorial board were also the result of German demands.[42] In the meantime, Daell and Wassermann had also issued summonses against Andersen.

The verdict was handed down on May 15, 1942: Olga von Eggers was sentenced to 120 and Andersen to 80 days' imprisonment, and each was fined 3,000 kroner, ordered to cover the costs of the case, and directed to publish the verdict in the daily press.[43] Olga von Eggers was aged sixty-six and tried, without avail, to make use of this fact as an extenuating circumstance. She enjoyed at the time certain financial assistance, given by law to authors. This subsidy was annulled by the government during its meeting on June 13, 1942. In the words of the minutes: "It was agreed that the Minister of Education would suspend the support given to Olga von Eggers under the Finance Law."[44] The Rigsdag ratified the government's decision. Hartvig Frisch adds the commentary that the verdict caused much satisfaction among the population at large.[45]

The Danish Nazis fully realized the government's intention.[46] But the two anti-Semitic writers did not give up and appealed the sentence. Nor did they stop at this. Even before their appeal was laid before the Supreme Court they renewed, in November 1942, their attacks on Peter Daell and Ella Wassermann. During the days of the telegram crisis in October 1942, old issues of *Kamptegnet*—including one filled with the Daell debate—had been handed out in the streets.[47] Moreover, on November 5, 1942, the very day Best arrived in Copenhagen, a new report appeared on the front page under the giant heading SENSATION IN

DAELL-WASSERMANN CASE. The contents and style were the same as in the previous articles. The writers apparently felt that a new era had dawned in Denmark and that S.S. member Dr. Best would invest them with all the privilege and protection they had been denied under Renthe-Fink.[48] Similar articles appeared on November 12 and December 10. However, the opinion of the Supreme Court differed from that of the editors of *Kamptegnet,* and, it transpired later, so did that of Dr. Best. The court handed down its new verdict on March 29, 1943. Not only did it not annul the previous conviction, it added to it. Each of the writers was sentenced to 160 days' imprisonment, and together they were fined 10,000 kroner. This was a time of increasing tension in Denmark compared to the year before, and the more severe sentence was no mere chance.

Best Liquidates "Kamptegnet"

The Danish anti-Semites knew in advance that they would lose the case. Apparently, they also discerned that the new German plenipotentiary would not protect them. Already on February 22, 1943, the administrative director of the Danish Anti-Jewish League, F. Banner-Jansen, asked for assistance from the German parent organization, the World Anti-Jewish League. The letter breathes a spirit of despair. The writer complains:

It has gone so far that more or less any Dane who is in sympathy with Germany cannot bring a civil action. In view of the peculiar attitude of our courts, it is clear that great difficulties are put in the way of Danes who sympathize with Germany. But the difficulties are even greater for those Danes who stand in the front line of the fight against Judaism and for National Socialism.[49]

It asks for German guidance in the future and requests that Aage Andersen, whose further presence in Denmark was impossible, be permitted to join the *Waffen S.S.*

On March 2, 1943, Wurm passed the letter on to Rade-macher for action, together with his own recommendation. A photocopy of the material was sent to Best with a request for his opinion. Best replied in a memorandum dated April 15, 1943,[50] in which he sets out detailed reasons for his proposal to close down *Kamptegnet*. The editors of the paper, he asserts, are themselves responsible for a decline in circulation from 14,000 to only 3–4,000. He firmly rejects the suggestion of saving Andersen by putting him in the *Waffen S.S.* He reports, however, that he has placed at the disposal of the two writers a sum to cover the fine and the costs of the case. He claims that the paper does not justify the large subsidy of 8,000 kroner a month:

Friends of the Germans and many National Socialists among the Danes have for some time opposed the aims of the paper. They point out that this type of propaganda is not suitable to the character of the Danish people and is unlikely in any respect to win understanding for the Jewish problem among wider sections of the population.

According to Best, the readers consist of a small group interested in the paper's pornographic stories, and of Jews who want to read what others say about them. He suggests that the paper be closed down and in its place, as pro-posed by Clausen, space be allocated to anti-Semitic prop-aganda in the weekly *Nationalsocialisten*. This solution will also avoid a public declaration of *Kamptegnet*'s failure. Four days after this memorandum, Best received Ribben-trop's cable requesting fresh information on the Jewish problem in Denmark. We do not know whether Ribbentrop's questions were connected with the court case or with Best's memorandum; in any event Best constantly attempted not only to avoid raising the Jewish question but also to elimin-ate the small groups of extreme anti-Semites.

First of all, he successfully prevented any assistance from reaching Andersen. Anti-Comintern circles and the

Anti-Jewish Action in Berlin suggested sending reinforcements to Copenhagen. Best succeeded in preventing not only the dispatch of a representative of these organizations, but also Andersen's trip to Berlin. He said quite unequivocally that Andersen's presence in Denmark was required for liquidating *Kamptegnet* and that there was no point at the time in beginning negotiations.[51] The anti-Comintern organization owed money to Andersen and suggested sending the money to Copenhagen, but Best objected and suggested instead that the sum be transferred to the Foreign Ministry in place of the 10,000 kroner that he had paid from his funds to cover the fine. His suggestion was accepted.[52]

Wagner laid Best's proposals for the abolition of *Kamptegnet* before Ribbentrop on June 10, 1943. The paper had by then in fact ceased to exist (the last number appeared on May 27), but it transpired that its debts could not be paid. Best maintained that his office was not in a position to settle the deficit of 20,000 kroner and asked that this sum be placed at his disposal in foreign currency, since it was undesirable to make a public declaration of bankruptcy.[53] The approval of the foreign minister was necessary for an allocation of this sort. At first the head of the Northern Department, Grundherr, was asked for his views, and after he had expressed agreement to Best's proposal, Ribbentrop added his "yes" in the margin.[54]

Best meanwhile was apprehensive of the results of his application and on June 28 sent another detailed memorandum on the subject. On July 3 Wagner informed Best by telegram of Ribbentrop's approval.[55] The same telegram indicated that written instructions would follow. These did not, however, appear, and on July 17 Best sent a reminder by cable.[56]

On August 28, at the height of the political crisis, Best suddenly remembered that he had not yet received the money for the final liquidation of the paper, and he again dispatched a telegram. REQUEST TRANSFER URGENTLY, stated the telegram, IN ORDER THAT "KAMPTEGNET" BE FINALLY LIQUIDATED. The money arrived during the peak of the crisis; on September 13 the legation in Copenhagen reported

Quittung

$\mathit{t.\ h.\ 20\,115.- \approx 10.\,\text{svt}\ \text{Run}}$

in Buchstaben: _hundertzwanzigtausend ein hundert und fünf reichsmark_ (Juni 191 ℳ)
für restliche Abwicklung von „Kamptegnet b."
erhalten.

von der Kasse d

whalten zu haben, bescheinigt

Zahlstelle Kopenhagen
der Legationskasse
des Auswärtigen Amts.

Kopenhagen , den ...*1. Sept.* 194*3*

Als Liquidator von Kamptegnet *

DA ____1549____ /143   D 531543

Receipt for the German payment of *Kamptegnet's* debt, received from its Danish liquidator. (*From the files of the German Foreign Office, microfilm Yad Vashem.*)

that the sum had been given to the paper's official receiver, and the receipt, dated September 7, 1943, was attached.[57] The next day, Best sent his well-known telegram suggesting that the Jewish problem in Denmark should now be solved. This strange combination of events, which could hardly be attributed to mere coincidence, calls for an explanation, as does the surprising fact that Best considered the liquidation of *Kamptegnet* as urgent at the very time when his own position in Denmark was in jeopardy. These points will be dealt with later in our discussion of the events themselves.

After *Kamptegnet* had ceased to appear, not only did Best withdraw his objection to Andersen's leaving Denmark, he was even interested in getting rid of him. In the wake of Wurm's approach to the Foreign Ministry, Thadden now proposed, in concert with Best, to allow Andersen to enter Germany. The generally negative opinion of Andersen, reflected in Thadden's memorandum, was underlined in Best's detailed letter of June 28, 1943.[58] Here he accuses Andersen of deriving unreasonable personal gain from the monies given him for the paper and of general disorder in his private affairs. Best's agreement that Andersen be employed by the anti-Comintern was given on condition

that Andersen will not exploit his activity in Berlin to interfere in internal Danish affairs in a manner opposed to the political line I have taken, and that he will not create a mistaken impression of the true situation in Denmark through distorted reports which are not in keeping with actual conditions. I request that the attention of the anti-Comintern be drawn to these points and that their programs on all important matters be checked, if possible by approaching me.

The formal arrangements having been concluded, Best announced on July 19, 1943, that Aage H. Andersen had left Copenhagen on July 15.[59] However, after the removal of the Jews in November 1943, we find Andersen back in Denmark and continuing to work for "racial consciousness."

Best therefore achieved his aim of keeping the Jewish question off the agenda during that period. *Kamptegnet* was closed down, Andersen was removed—at least temporarily —from Denmark, and the concurrence of Ribbentrop and Himmler in letting the Jewish question rest was obtained. These ends were attained with the active assistance of officials of the German Foreign Office: not only Grundherr, who had already helped Renthe-Fink, but also Wagner and Thadden supported Best's policy. He was entitled to think that militant anti-Semitism no longer constituted a danger to his strategy. Best was keenly aware of the sensitivity of the Danish people and authorities to the Jewish problem, and he energetically sought to insure that this source would not give rise to German disturbance or to Danish disquiet and dissatisfaction.

Two and a half months later the whole pot had boiled over, and persecution of the Jews was under way in Denmark. The only question which concerns us here is how did it come about—and this is the riddle in the whole affair— that this same Best was the one who, in the end, took the initiative in the deportation of Jews? What was his motive in turning against them?

The Struggle Against the "Purge"

The removal of the Jews from Danish economic and public life was, as mentioned, the main practical objective of the anti-Semites as long as they could see no possibility of deportation or other sweeping action. *Kamptegnet* was not alone in regarding the "revelation of Jewish influence" as one of its main tasks; the various reports on the subject, written by Germans and Danes, deal in the main with the economic problem. The most comprehensive and thorough of them all was the report presented by Renthe-Fink to Rademacher on January 21, 1942,[60] which earned high praise from the latter in his reply of March 25.[61] It comprises twenty-nine pages and is divided into eight sections. The relative lengths of the sections indicate that particular stress is laid on Jewish influence on the economy and on the problem of assimilation and Danish-Jewish family connections (*Versippung*).

Section 1, the introduction, is a kind of historical survey. As regards the economy, close examination is made of the various branches: banking, trade, real estate, insurance. Figures are given on Jewish capital, and the direct and indirect influence of Jews on firms and economic branches are examined. After dealing with the Jewish role in the arts and sciences, the report states that the Jews hold some capital in newspapers but "as far as editorial matters are concerned the Jews do not wield any decisive influence on the press." The memorandum goes on: "Only a relatively few Jews participate in political events." Family connections between Danes and Jews are also examined with regard to all walks of life.[62] Mention is made of the well-known fact that the number of mixed marriages is greater than the number of all-Jewish marriages, and that "the pro-Semitic aspects . . . should be understood against this background." The report's conclusion also attaches great importance to the fact that Jewish and Danish families, particularly in the higher strata of society, are extremely mixed.

The conclusion drawn is that close and smooth cooperation between Nazi Germany and Denmark will only be possible after the Jewish problem is solved; that this solution is also dependent on the general development of national socialism in Denmark; and that this solution will only come about following the general European solution—until then there is no possibility of taking any effective action against the Jews of Denmark "because of their strong position." The memorandum is naturally replete with distortions and misleading data of various types.

Attempts to harm Jewish commerce, to reduce the share of Jews in all economic branches, and to prevent the activities of Jewish personalities in public life continued nevertheless. The German Chamber of Commerce, founded in 1936, was one of the bodies through which the Germans attempted to penetrate into Denmark by using fifth-column methods;[63] it now engaged in collecting statistical data on "Jewish" business and firms, according to papers found after the war.[64] As early as 1942 Sten Gudme was able to report, in his book *Hitler's Model Protectorate*, published in London, that a year after the occupation the collection of data on the Jews began and that this was the first step toward removing them from economic life. He maintains that in foreign trade, carried on completely under German supervision, difficulties in the supply of goods were placed in the way of Jews. He even cites a "well-known Jewish business" which was obliged to close down for this reason.

It happened, however, that the Germans themselves were not interested in carrying out a total purge of Jews from economic life. On March 12, 1943, the Foreign Ministry passed on to Best by telegram the contents of a letter received from the head of Himmler's intelligence service, Walter Schellenberg. It requested Best to postpone the dismissal of the manager of Danish Standard Electric, who was apparently Jewish, since both the army and Schellenberg were interested in successful negotiations for a general agreement with the firm. Best appears to have willingly carried out this request.[65] Moreover, the general impression is that the Jews were not adversely affected to any marked degree, as is also clear from their financial capacity evinced during and after the flight.

A chapter in itself was the efforts of the Germans to "purge" public posts of Jews. In this they met the most energetic resistance from the Danes. They were often compelled to withdraw their pressure or achieved their aims only after the most strenuous and stubborn efforts. Mention has been made in Chapter II of Renthe-Fink's talk with Scavenius on August 24, 1942,[66] when he demanded the dismissal of the two directors-general, Einar Cohn and Aage Svendsen, on the grounds that they were of Jewish origin. The Germans returned to this question at the beginning of November that year during negotiations on the formation of a new government in connection with Best's arrival. Kanstein then raised the matter twice in talks with the director-general of the Danish Foreign Ministry, Nils Svenningsen, and once with the premier-designate, Scavenius.[67]

Svendsen remained at his post during the whole of the occupation, but Einar Cohn fled to Sweden in the fall of 1943. There he lectured at the Stockholm School of Economics and Commerce and thereafter served as economic counselor to Danish diplomatic representations in Stockholm, London and Washington. In the summer of 1942 Cohn was the cause of a most surprising talk on the Jewish question between Renthe-Fink and Gunnar Larsen. During a "private" lunch at Renthe-Fink's residence on July 10, 1942,[68] the German minister complained to Larsen of a talk Einar Cohn had given on the radio some days previously. He maintained that the Danes should prevent public appearances of this type by Jews (particularly if his name was Cohn and he was the director-general of a ministry), since they aroused attention in Berlin, to whom he had reported the incident—with the result that there was now "a new document preserved in Berlin on the Jewish problem in Denmark." He went on to point out that occurrences of this sort were undoubtedly regarded in Berlin as provocation. According to Gunnar Larsen,

Renthe-Fink went on to say that he could not understand why the Jews in Denmark were not as still as mice; in that way the raising of the problem could best be avoided—also in the long run. Neither did he understand why those Danish Jews who had had the opportunity had not, for their own sake, long since departed.

It was presumably talks of this type which led Scavenius, when forming his government, to take the stand that Jews in public posts should not be too conspicuous.

The struggle of the Danes to preserve their political form and democratic values was reflected, *inter alia,* in the unceasing fight of the Danish press for independence and freedom of expression.[69] It was actively supported in this campaign by the Foreign Ministry's Press Office, led by Karl J. Eskelund who strove to defend the press, as much as was possible, against German attacks and demands. Among the newspapers which formed the object of these onslaughts was the Conservative journal *Nationaltidende.* The paper held out for fourteen months against the German demand to have the managing editor, Aage Schoch, removed, until he was finally compelled to resign at the end of February 1942.[70] In their first attack, the Germans claimed that he was a Jew. *Pressen Under Besættelsen* informs us that Eskelund could have proved that this assertion was unfounded "but he naturally did not allow himself to be involved in a discussion on this plane."[71] This was typical: the Danes were prepared to argue with the Germans on the point at issue but not as to whether someone whom the Germans did not like was Jewish or not. Two Jews did, however, work for the paper—a reporter, Bertel Bing, and the administrative director, Holger Cohen. The Germans demanded the dismissal of these two together with the managing editor.[72] Bertel Bing's sphere of activity was reduced but the combined opposition of all journalists forced the Germans to withdraw their demands for his dismissal.[73] They returned to the attack, however, after the exit of Aage Schoch.

On March 7, 1942, the counselor at the German legation renewed the demand to Director-General Svenningsen of the Foreign Ministry. The latter replied that his ministry could not intervene in the administrative organization of the newspaper. On May 28, 1942, the German press attaché, Schröder,[74] raised the matter again and received the same answer. Finally, *Fædrelandet* and *Kamptegnet* came to the aid of the Germans. On June 2, 1942, the commander of the Danish Free Corps, C. F. von Schalburg, was killed on the eastern front.[75] Cohen refused, for "political reasons" to publish in *Nationaltidende* the obituary notice requested by Frits Clausen. The two Nazi newspapers now attacked Cohen vehemently and thereafter, on June 20, the Germans announced that their patience was exhausted and that if Cohen were not removed from the paper he would be arrested and deported to Germany. After a meeting with the paper's management board and with members of the government, led by Prime Minister Buhl, Cohen announced that he denied the charge of incitement against Germany, as the Germans had asserted, but if the alternatives open to him were resignation or captivity in Germany, then he preferred to resign. The Germans were not satisfied, and in October they made attempts to stop all contact between Cohen and the paper, but Eskelund refused to take up the matter. The extent to which the Danes regarded matters of this sort as matters of principle is shown by the fact that the incident was raised by Ole Bjørn Kraft in the Council of Nine. He first protested on April 23, 1941, against the German demand to remove Børge Outze and Bing from *Nationaltidende;* then, according to the minutes, he added: ". . . when the removal of two members of *Nationaltidende*'s staff is demanded . . . of the one simply because he is a Jew, then the situation is far gone."[76] On the second occasion, Kraft asked Foreign Minister Scavenius for an explanation of the resignation of Holger Cohen. During the discussion that followed, he said that "it would no doubt have been wise to accept the announcement, but the fact that he was informed that he would be deported to Germany if he did not resign must give rise to consternation. They have no right. . . ." (according to the agreement of April 9, 1940).[77]

Summary

The Danes were sensitive to any encroachment on the legal status of the individual, his right to freedom, his security. A person's Jewish origin was important to them insofar as it constituted a pretext for the Germans to break the law and use arbitrary force. This was the meaning of Kraft's statement that "the situation is far gone" if a man's dismissal could be demanded solely because he was a Jew. The struggle of the Danes with the Germans for the maintenance of law as they understood it was their daily war throughout the occupation. They fought to maintain the orderly operation of their democratic institutions in general, but they also fought a small and bitter war for the maintenance of law in a thousand isolated instances; in this they saw a guarantee for continuation of their independent existence. They regarded their defense of the Jews as an essential link in the chain of their own struggle for survival. They felt that they were defending themselves when they were defending the Jews, and they thus carried out this policy both within the framework of their general political relations with the Germans and within the limited framework of everyday problems.

On September 2, 1942, on the eve of the telegram crisis, the then prime minister and leader of the Social Democrats, Vilhelm Buhl, broadcast to the nation. He appealed to the Danish people to abstain from acts of sabotage and to maintain "law and order" and added:

Far the greater part of the population knows that the avoidance of unrest is of fundamental importance for Danish society during the occupation and for the preservation of our popular and national values. And the people's constantly correct behavior has thus also been the decisive prerequisite for conditions in this country to develop in keeping with the line laid down on the 9th of April, 1940, and whose starting point is the assurance then given from the German side.[78]

However, in the same measure as the authorities strove for the maintenance of law and order even in conditions of occupation, the members of the resistance movement claimed that the law had been broken and that a struggle with all means available was essential for its reinstatement. In a speech for students by Mogens Fog, which was illegally distributed in the summer of 1943,[79] he enumerated one by one those values which constituted the basis of Danish life, and which were doubtless identical with those hinted at by Buhl: respect for the individual—the primary element of democracy; love of freedom; love of peace; and faith in the final triumph of the spirit. Those values, he asserted, were now in danger and it was the duty of everyone to revitalize them and go forth in their defense. In their name he called upon youth to join the movement of active resistance against the Nazis. His conclusions are the reverse of Buhl's, though they spring from devotion to the same values. This essentially uniform approach to basic values brought together in the hour of need official Denmark and clandestine Denmark in spontaneous and complete cooperation in the task of rescuing the Jews.

PART THREE

THE HOUR OF CRISIS

IV

The Political Crisis and Jewish Persecution

The Policy of Negotiation and Its Breakdown in August 1943

Dr. Best was the central figure in the singularly dramatic clash between anti-Semitic nazism and Danish democracy which convulsed Denmark in the first days of October 1943. Here was a man with two faces, all his actions replete with double meanings and contradictions. Prominent as these characteristics were in Best's behavior toward Denmark and its affairs in general, they were nothing compared to his enigmatic manipulations round and about the fate of the Danish Jews. In the midst of the crisis, with the state of emergency in force, he suddenly proposed that the Jews be persecuted and driven from Denmark—but at the same time, at enormous risk to himself, he supported a counteraction designed to prevent the persecutions and enable the Danes to save the lives and property of their Jewish fellow citizens. His whole behavior, it would appear, is an inexplicable riddle.

Double-dealing was one of the ingredients of Nazi rule,

engaged in everywhere as much by its leaders and operators as by its victims. It is characteristic of all dictatorships, but the Nazis nurtured it deliberately, seeing in it an extremely effective political weapon in political and social relationships. Deception was practiced toward the Jews to mislead them as to their fate, but this was only one of its many applications. Treaties were signed in order to facilitate a later assault on the enemy; promises, given in order to create a sense of false security, were broken; threats and false accusations, outbursts of frenzied rage and pseudomoral sermonizing, approbation and castigation, lies of every size and variety—all these were daily fare. Everywhere this psychological warfare paved the way for conquest, servitude, and murder, and then served as their justification. The oppressed and the enslaved learned to fight with the same weapons. Prime ministers as well as concentration camp inmates used them, for in the struggle for survival the price of honesty was death. This atmosphere also dominated the internal relationships of the Nazis. Since it was forbidden to criticize a superior, adverse opinions were passed on in devious ways. The men at the top played off their subordinates against one another and divided up authority in order to insure for each of themselves as dominant a position as possible.

Events in Denmark will show us many of these tactics in action. The destruction of trust between man and man and between nation and nation and the sowing of seeds of constant suspicion were perhaps the Nazis' most terrible bequest to our world, outside the Communist realm which follows similar devices. The application and methods of double-dealing varied in keeping with circumstances and the character of people and nations, but the feature in itself was the same everywhere. It was so used in full measure both by the Danish collaborators and by the resistance movement.[1] The pressures of occupation also invested the Danish official policy of the period with a strong element of double-dealing, and the Danes were well aware of this.[2]

It was not surprising therefore that Best played a double game, as had his predecessor, Renthe-Fink—though to a lesser degree. Best had been a Nazi from his early youth and had had a thorough apprenticeship in the political and human ideology and practice of nazism. To be two-faced became his second nature.[3] Nevertheless, something strange happened to him, something perhaps unique among the top Nazis to whom he had belonged at the beginning of his career: he had doubts about some of the theoretical and practical conclusions of nazism. This attitude complicated, not to say almost sabotaged, his rise to the highest levels of the regime and had a profound effect on his actions in Denmark, where he waged a constant fight for his position and authority. His behavior and deeds in regard to the Jewish question cannot be understood without some knowledge of his personal as well as his political background.[4]

Among the special files found in Ribbentrop's Chancellery (*Dienststelle* Ribbentrop) was a secret report on a conversation between Churchill and a Swedish diplomat. When the talk came around to Hitler's mild treatment of Denmark, Churchill remarked that even the most brutal dictator has his pet parrot.[5] The story actually originated in Copenhagen[6] and is still heard today when occupied Denmark is discussed. However, anyone who wants to know the truth as to why Hitler and his followers treated Denmark differently from other occupied countries—so differently that they long desisted from interfering with the internal form of government, or disarming the defense forces, or persecuting the Jews—will find a fully convincing answer hard to come by. It is not our task here to attempt a comprehensive reply to this complicated question. It is, on the other hand, impossible to understand the fate of the Danish Jews in general and in the hour of crisis in particular without indicating the background and nature of the relations between the Germans and the Danes. Their developments along certain lines may be deduced from the march of events.[7]

The political line of April 9, 1940, molded the policy of the government until the crisis of August 1943, and in certain respects even beyond.[8] An active resistance leader such as Mogens Fog has admitted that "the course was maintained with the full support of Danish leaders in political, organizational, economic, and administrative life. And what is more—to begin with—with the support of the Danish people."[9] The support of the people for the policy of negotiation was in fact quite evident right up to the early summer of 1943.

This line necessitated no small degree of double-dealing. Most of the country's leaders were first and foremost interested in preventing foreign or domestic Nazis from taking over control of government and administration.[10] As Mogens Fog rightly indicates, this policy also imposed a difficult task on each individual citizen, who was faced with the practical problem of deciding day after day the crucial question: whether to oppose the Germans and maintain an independent Danish position—as the country's leaders secretly wished; or to cooperate with the Germans—as demanded by the government's declared policy.[11] Frits Clausen was thus not so wrong in his repeated assertions to the Germans that all "cooperation" by the government was mere lip service and that all action was in reality directed against the Germans.[12]

We have already mentioned that there were many leaders and ordinary citizens, particularly in the first two years, who believed that the Germans would win the war,[13] and this belief guided their behavior. But even these people endeavored above all to preserve the individuality of the Danish people, the "Danish line" as they called it, and not to submit to German nazism, as much because it was nazism as because it was German. This basic stand explains why that same Scavenius who was regarded by everyone (and of course by his opponents in particular) as the chief representative of collaboration with the Germans, and who was called to the premiership with German support,[14] in the hour of crisis did not hesitate to take his place at the head of the nation's representatives and its government—and severed, himself, the cord of cooperation. True, he acted under pressure from his insurgent people, but the fact that the country's leaders of all shades of opinion denounced at that moment all possibility of compromise was what preserved the integrity and spirit of the nation in this hour of trial.[15]

The moderate attitude of the Germans toward the Danes is usually explained by the economic benefits that could be reaped from Denmark—and only from a tranquil Denmark whose internal affairs operated without disturbance.[16] The Danes were therefore allowed to continue their standard of living, and though they were obliged to introduce price controls and rationing, they were the only people among all the occupied areas whose standard of living was higher than that of the Germans themselves—even in the first years of the war.[17] The reason did not lie in German affection for the Danes but in their awareness that "surplus production in so decentralized a system as Danish agriculture, with its large number of independent farms, would evaporate completely"[18] if there did not exist what the Germans called *Lieferungsfreude* ("willingness to supply"). In May 1942 Meissner also attributed the failure of the Danish National Socialists to the fact that the Germans were interested in working with the national government in order to insure economic cooperation.[19] S. Hartogsohn (one of the few Jews who remained openly in Denmark after October 1943 and continued, with German knowledge, to work as secretary of the National Bank[20]) stressed that the agricultural output the Danes were able to place at the disposal of the Germans far surpassed the calculations and assumptions of the Germans prior to the occupation. According to Danish calculations, 3.6 million Germans received their meat, pork, and butter rations from Denmark in 1942, 4.6 million in 1943, and 8.4 million in 1944.[21] At the height of the crisis in August–September 1943, the German Food Ministry explained to the Foreign Ministry that it was not interested in exploiting the situation to make greater demands; on the contrary, it would put up with the temporary upheavals in the hope that the plenipotentiary of the Reich would soon succeed in restoring the arrangements in Denmark to their former proportions.[22] The degree to which this policy bore fruit may be seen from the statistics given above, though account should also be taken of the fact that German rations were reduced.

The year 1943 became the year of destiny in German-Danish relations. We have seen in preceding chapters how the various crises led in the fall of 1942 to the replacement of the leading German representatives: Instead of the relatively moderate General Lüdke, came the coarse and ambitious General Hanneken, and the career diplomat Renthe-Fink was exchanged for the National Socialist Best. We know from a memorandum by Grundherr[23] the precise instructions received by Hanneken from Hitler on October 1, 1942, the day before the general's arrival in Copenhagen. According to this document, Hitler was then of the opinion that the course of the war had rendered null and void the German assurances of April 9, 1940, which formed the basis of Danish-German relations. In the long run, in a Europe controlled by Germany, it would be impossible for a country with a democratic government and a monarchy to exist. The aim was to convert Denmark into a German province. The blame for developments was not to be placed on former German representatives who had acted under instructions; but from now on it would be necessary to act in accordance with new directives. As plenipotentiary there would be a National Socialist who would rule with a mailed fist. German behavior must not be as toward a friendly country but as toward an enemy country.

When Best received his instructions from Hitler on October 27, he was told things of a similar nature, except that Hitler added that he was interested in negotiating with a legally constituted government. Best afterward seized upon this latter remark to justify his attempts at a policy of cooperation.[24] Hitler's relatively moderate comments were apparently the result of discussions which had meanwhile taken place with Himmler, in which Himmler strove to maintain the former situation. This is clear from Himmler's note preparatory to his talk of October 22[25] and from a letter he wrote to Berger on October 25.[26] This letter shows that Himmler knew very well that the Danish National Socialists under the leadership of Frits Clausen did not constitute a force which could obtain control of the country for him.

It may be assumed that Best was conversant with Himmler's stand and therefore knew, when he set up the government of Scavenius a few days after coming to Copenhagen, that he had acted in accordance not only with the wishes of Ribbentrop, who was not interested in a deterioration of relations with Denmark, but also with those of Himmler. We know that Best, who was formally subordinated to Ribbentrop, also regarded himself as no less responsible to Himmler. (When Best entered the Foreign Ministry in 1942 he wrote to Himmler that he would endeavor to carry out his new duties as a mission entrusted to him by Himmler.[27]) Best, however, had his own aims, tendencies, and ambitions, which for the time being seemed to be at one with Himmler's. His responsibility toward two authorities meant that throughout his service he had to resort to constant manipulation to preserve the confidence of both his masters and to avoid any conflict between them or between himself and one of them. Particularly when his policy was not approved by one or both of them, Best was necessarily compelled to clash or arrive at a dead end. Grundherr also pointed out that Best in fact fell between two stools.[28] Since the Jewish question served as a kind of seismograph of Danish developments, the conflict often emerged in this connection.

Best's most dangerous opponent, however, was Hanneken, who was determined to carry out Hitler's instructions to the letter. His practical intention was to disband the Danish army and set up military rule in Denmark. This is not the place to dwell on all stages of this internal German rivalry,[29] but a few significant points may be mentioned.

The Danes were surprised to see Best take up the policy of negotiation.[30] He made his intentions clear in a speech delivered at Arhus on February 9, 1943: "I understand the nature and attitude of the Danes," he said, "and in the policy I have carried out in these three months there is evidence that I have learned a chapter of the Danish mentality. I have used this knowledge to advance the co-operation between Denmark and Germany."[31] At first his efforts were recognized, and on February 24 Berlin again officially confirmed the special position of Denmark and its government:

The orders of the chancellor of the Reich, Hitler, regarding the mobilization of Europe for total war do not apply to Denmark. Denmark is regarded as are the neutral countries. It is emphasized that Denmark occupies a special place among the conquered countries and in this case too no encroachments will be made on Denmark's sovereignty. Denmark was conquered by the German army out of military necessity but Germany does not interfere in the administration of the country and Denmark will continue to be an independent state among the other nations.[32]

Best also supported the legal Danish government on the home front. The National Socialists were, as stated, sharply divided—Best has claimed that he added to these internal dissensions in order to reduce the strength of the Danish

Nazi organizations[33]—and among the population at large they did not enjoy any support. Still, an attempt was made to set up an organization on the lines of the S.S. The initiative, however, came from Germany, and the Schalburg Corps was established on February 2, 1943.[34] The corps thereafter played a provocative role in acerbating relations and increasing tensions in the summer of 1943.

In the elections to the Rigsdag held on March 23, 1943, the National Socialists suffered a decisive defeat and the government won an overwhelming victory. The very fact that the elections took place—and with German approval —marked a political and moral triumph for the government of Scavenius, to whose credit, it is generally agreed, this success must be ascribed.[35] These elections had one central aim: to unite the people around its government and to demonstrate its loyalty to the political system and, as a corollary, its opposition to the German occupier. The joint declaration of the five coalition parties, which called upon the people to express its opinion by participation in the elections, said, *inter alia*:

The election of March 23 is different from all other elections. It does not concern the usual party divergences. It has a longer perspective. The election should confirm the will of the people to defend that freedom which is our thousand-year legacy, and that popular rule Danish men and women refuse to give up. In this way, the election will be a confirmation of faith in Denmark and its future.

This aim was fully achieved.[36] The increased sentence in the Daell-Wassermann case should also be understood against this background, as should Best's efforts in the spring and early summer of 1943 not only to prevent any anti-Jewish action but also to quell and annul the sources of anti-Semitic propaganda.

The great unity of the people, as demonstrated by the elections, also underlined its unwavering determination to resist German political or ideological pressure. The elections gave the population a feeling of internal cohesion and made it conscious of the fact that it was by no means powerless toward the enemy—in contrast to what it had apparently felt during the first years of the occupation. The elections were quiet and orderly, as is the case in Scandinavia, but they in fact served as the starting point for a growing resistance movement of the people against the conqueror. Acts of sabotage increased from month to month all over the country and were followed by a wave of political strikes. Neither the Danish authorities nor Best anticipated results of this sort. The government, the Rigsdag, the king himself, and the trade unions—all of whom attempted to halt this popular uprising—stood powerless before it.[37]

The inner feeling of strength inspired by the elections was consolidated by the knowledge that the run of victories of the seemingly invincible conqueror had been broken. The defeat at Stalingrad, prior to the elections, was followed in the early summer by the end of the campaign in Africa, the Allied landings in Italy, and the fall of that country's Fascist regime. At the beginning of August 1943 neutral Sweden, which had also given way indirectly to German demands, canceled the right to transit to German troops. To the Danish people and its small yet stubborn resistance movement these were encouraging omens heralding the sure and rapid termination of vile foreign rule.[38] British air raids, even on Copenhagen itself, aroused no protest despite the loss of life involved.[39]

In August acts of sabotage reached a peak, both in number and scope, and clashes even occurred between the population and the occupying troops. In Odense a German officer was badly beaten up by an angry crowd.[40] The sharp German reprisals were countered by strikes.[41] It was clear that political initiative had slipped from the hands of the Danish authorities into the grasp of the underground movement.

The two sides—the German army and the resistance movement—added fuel to the flames.[42] From the beginning of the month Best had demanded that the Danish government take sharper action against acts of sabotage. In reply, Scavenius suggested resigning, but Best firmly rejected the offer. He was still trying to save his policy.

At the beginning of July, during his visit to Himmler, Best achieved full recognition of his policy, not only by the Foreign Ministry, but also by Himmler. During the whole period he kept in touch with Himmler and secretly sent him his official reports to the Foreign Ministry. At times he was threatened by dangerous complications as a result of these measures but managed to avoid any real conflict.[43] His relations with Himmler were not merely correct but even breathed a certain cordiality. This is shown in a letter from Himmler dated January 19, 1943: "Formalities mean nothing. You should always act as if you had the full powers mentioned. What I can do to support you, especially in your wish that there be no disturbing outside interference in your rule, I shall do always."[44] In reply to a report which Best sent to him in May, he praised him for his achievements in Denmark and informed him that he had asked Ribbentrop's permission for Best to visit him (Himmler) and expressed his wish to visit Denmark "in a private capacity." The letter concluded in his own handwriting: "Cordially yours."[45]

This situation should be understood in light of the misleading descriptions of affairs in Denmark appearing in Best's reports. How great Best's success was in this report may be seen from a letter written by Himmler to Berger on July 15, 1943, (after Best's visit) as follows:

Please inform S.S. *Gruppenführer* Dr. Best that the other day I reported to the Führer on the situation in Denmark and informed him that from the point of view of security policy and the sabotage problem, this is at present the best country. I also hinted shrewdly to the Führer the difficulties existing with regard to General-Lieutenant von Hanneken.[46]

Best himself says in his defense statement that by then
this description no longer fit the actual situation. On August
22 he asked the Danish government to restore quiet at any
price, even by using the Danish army.

Best was now apparently convinced that he could not
continue his previous policy. From a letter to Himmler on
the same day we learn that "in view of developments I am
taking into account the possibility that we must alter the
way we administer Denmark." He suggests that in the
event of failure by the Scavenius government he take the
country under his own control and run it with the help of
a nonpolitical Danish administration. These proposals, which
he put before the Foreign Ministry as early as August 18,
1943, were agreed upon in coordination with Hanneken,
who in turn passed them on to the General Staff (OKW).[47]
Best requests Himmler's support for his, Best's, proposals in
the event that a suggestion for military rule in Denmark
is put forward and asks him to make available, should the
need arise, the S.S. and police forces required for bringing
the situation under control. He suggests that Himmler
waste no time in issuing the relevant instructions to the
bodies concerned—the RSHA, *Hauptamt Ordnungspolizei*,
and the S.S. *Führungsamt*—in order that they be ready to
give him assistance the instant it is needed.[48]

But Hanneken had been faster on the uptake. On the
24th of August Best was called to the General Staff, where
—through the medium of Ribbentrop—the Führer's wrath
was poured upon him,[49] and on his return to Copenhagen
on the 27th he brought with him extremely stringent instructions, in accordance with which he presented the Danish government with an ultimatum on August 28. This
consisted of two parts: one referred to the situation in
general, while the second demanded special action against
the town of Odense, which had especially aroused Hitler's
anger. The general ultimatum demanded that a state of
emergency be proclaimed throughout the country, strikes

and meetings be forbidden, and the following measures be introduced: a curfew, a ban on the holding of weapons, and the establishment of courts-martial, the death penalty for acts of sabotage and carrying of arms, and press censorship under German control.[50]

On August 29 a large meeting of trade union officials led by Alsing Andersen and Vilhelm Buhl was held in Copenhagen. Buhl declared:

If the Germans make demands contrary to the honor of the people, then we are ready for the decisive crisis, which would mean military dictatorship. Let us not, however, cause the abolition of the Rigsdag and the government through internal dissension.

To this he added a warning as to the probable consequences of suspension of legal rule for the inhabitants of southern Jutland and for "our *Jewish fellow citizens*" (author's italics).[51] At a joint meeting of the government and the Council of Nine, Buhl's resolution to reject the whole ultimatum was seconded by the Conservative Ole Bjørn Kraft, and was carried. The politicians then consulted the king and obtained his assent.

That same evening, August 29, telephone communications with Sweden were cut, and it was clear that the state of emergency had begun. During the night the German army entered Copenhagen. The royal palace was blockaded, and the king remained a German prisoner throughout the state of emergency.[52] The Germans disarmed the Danish army and interned officers and other ranks. Danish naval personnel, however, succeeded in sabotaging most of the ships at anchor in the port of Copenhagen, while some escaped to Swedish ports.[53] Hanneken took power into his hands in a proclamation containing most of the points of the ultimatum, while the king was informed that the authority of the Danish government was thereby annulled.[54] For his part,

Christian X assembled the directors of the various ministries and enjoined them to continue normal administrative functions. To avoid a constitutional vacuum, the Danish government submitted its official resignation to the king but this was not accepted, and the situation remained, as it were, in midair. The king, as stated, formally requested the civil service to continue exercising its functions, and thus gave legal validity to the country's administrative operations and ordinances.[55]

August 29, 1943, stands out as the turning point of the occupation. Best's policy of understanding and Scavenius's policy of cooperation (which was in effect a policy of passive resistance) had both failed. It may be assumed that the fact that Denmark reached its crisis at a relatively late hour saved it from catastrophe, casualties, and destruction on a large scale. The productive and organizational mechanism of the country remained intact throughout the war.[56] No quisling government arose in Denmark (the little strength the Danish National Socialists had was nullified before the crisis) and "even those horrible actions—first and foremost against the Jews—which occurred between August 29 and the end of the war were but a small part of what would doubtless have happened had 'the Norwegian situation' arisen at a earlier time."[57]

Who Initiated the Persecutions?

The crisis exploded in August. September was devoted to efforts to overcome it and restore a stable situation. The state of emergency was lifted on October 6. Danish soldiers, and later their officers, were demobilized into civilian life and the Danish army went underground.[58] No new Danish government was formed and the parliamentary institutions remained idle; but directors of ministries continued to carry out their administrative duties. Politicians and parties operated only behind the scenes.[59] However, on October 1, in the midst of the crisis and on the eve of the persecutions, the Danes signed a new agreement with the Germans on the supply of agricultural produce during the coming year— an agreement which promised Germany greater supplies than had the previous agreement, which expired on September 30.[60]

In the middle of that month negotiations were also begun between Kanstein, who had been appointed as head of administration,[61] and the Danish Ministry of Justice regarding the operational scope of the Danish police. These talks were about to be terminated by an agreement when, on the night of October 1–2, the Germans carried out their manhunt of Jews.[62] In many areas such as these just mentioned cooperation or pseudocooperation continued; but at the same time there was no pause in acts of sabotage by the underground movement. In the economic and administrative spheres, the two sides continued to act in coordination with one another, and in this factual respect those who claimed that no practical change took place after August 29 were doubtless right.[63] A decisive upheaval had nevertheless taken place—and the persecution of the Jews, with its aftermath, was one of its symptoms.

Why did the Germans begin these persecutions and who initiated them? This question has engaged students of the occupation period[64] and it engaged the judges trying Best after the war.[65] It is not clear why Best, on the 8th of September, sent telegram No. 1032,[66] in which he suggested that the favorable opportunity presented by the state of emergency be exploited to finish with "the Jews and the Freemasons." There had indeed been many indications that Best had no wish to initiate persecutions. Had he not written all those memoranda to persuade Berlin that it was both undesirable and unworthwhile to persecute the Jews of Denmark? Had he not himself told Duckwitz of the telegram, so that the latter had tried by all means to prevent its consequences and had finally informed the Danes?[67]

Was it not common knowledge that this intelligent man, who had now been forced to yield to Hanneken's brutality and lust for power, was not an anti-Semite and in fact considered persecution of the Jews to be stupid and useless?[68]

Responsibility for the attack on the Danish Jews has been placed on various persons, and it is known that the final order was given by Hitler himself; so what choice had Best but to yield? On grounds such as these, Best has not been held responsible for the operation.[69] It is our intention in this chapter, however, to show that it may be assumed that Best, and Best alone, was responsible for setting the persecution of the Jews in motion, and that this act—which seems to be devoid of any motivation—was of fateful significance for Best politically and personally and also had a decisive effect on the interplay of political forces.[70]

It should first be pointed out that all of Best's own pronouncements and statements of evidence on the affair are of little value, since they all had one aim—to shift the blame onto someone else. Since September 1943 Best has adapted his explanations to the nature of the questioner and the question in each case. The Danish government, in its memorandum to the Nuremberg trials, claims that it does not know exactly who initiated the persecutions, but it is clear that the initiative came from Berlin. This view is based on the explanations of Best himself, who asserted that the initiative came from the RSHA and from the Nazi party; and here he recalled "in particular the name of Rosenberg."[71] At Nuremberg, Best replied to a question of the Gestapo's defense counsel, Merkel, that "the persecution of the Jews was apparently ordered by Hitler himself"; he, Best, opposed the action, but when the Foreign Ministry gave him the order, he had demanded that it be carried out while the state of emergency and military rule were still in force.[72]

S.S. *Standartenführer* Dr. Rudolf Mildner, in his declaration of June 22, 1945, laid the blame on Ribbentrop. He too relies on the opinion of Best, who explained Ribbentrop's alleged motives to him in a talk held in September 1943 during which they both agreed that it was not wise to persecute the Jews of Denmark.[73] In a statement dated June 28, 1946,[74] Best, now interested in defending Ribbentrop, denied that he had said any such thing. He stressed, however, his own opposition to the persecutions and his agreement with Ribbentrop on this point, and laid the blame on Himmler. Best's telegram of September 8 is not mentioned throughout the document. He describes Mildner's evidence as being based on a misunderstanding.[75] In the court in Copenhagen he afterward claimed that his proposal in telegram No. 1032 was put forward after news had leaked out to him from Ribbentrop's office that on Hitler's orders Jewish pogroms would now be instituted in Denmark. He thereafter stuck to this version.[76]

In other words, to Mildner of the S.S., Best explained at the time that the foreign minister had initiated the persecutions; when he thought it necessary to defend Ribbentrop he accused Himmler. When asked to explain his telegram, he went back to the story he had first told Duckwitz[77] immediately after its dispatch and here again named Hitler himself as the initiator. Best had earlier hinted to the Danish government that Rosenberg was among those responsible. Sir David Maxwell Fyfe, the British prosecutor at Nuremberg, pointed out that Best, the oppressor of Denmark, had given evidence for the Gestapo. After the court had seen the documents presented under cross-examination,[78] could it believe a word of what Best had said? The same opinion was expressed the following day by the Russian prosecutor, Rudenko.[79]

On different occasions during the crisis period and in his statements of evidence after the war Best admitted that developments in Denmark in August 1943 marked his own political failure. In one of his memoranda he states: "If one means by policy the practical realization of certain principles, then my policy in Denmark ceased on August 29, 1943." Not only had his policy of cooperation and understanding failed but he had also suffered a personal political defeat.[80] His entry into the Foreign Ministry and his mission to Denmark were not merely designed to restore his former luster in the eyes of the S.S. and Reich leaders but also to prove the wisdom of his own policies. On August 30 he again wrote to Himmler in an effort to save what he could: "Well, what Lieutenant-General von Hanneken has striven for from the first has happened, and what has been done cannot be undone." He goes on to say that he does not know what will now happen in Denmark or even what his own fate will be. If he should remain at his post he would first of all need considerable police forces, as he had already pointed out in his letter of August 22, for the Danish police were not anymore to be relied upon. He would also require German officials and, he adds, his office is already investigating this matter. However, if he should be dismissed, he would like to return to Himmler's service and not remain in the Foreign Ministry. The whole tone of this letter is one of self-justification and self-defense.[81]

Confused though he was, Best in fact recovered quickly and at once began an attempt to win back his lost authority and then consolidate it even further. His objectives in those hectic days would seem to have been as follows:

(a) To insure reaffirmation from the central authorities of his position as the chief representative of the Reich.

(b) To prevent the return of democratic rule to Denmark and in the future to govern the country and cooperate with the Danes with the aid of a civil administration.

(c) To prevent the various National Socialists and quislings from taking advantage of the situation.

(d) To create an administrative and judicial system in Denmark which would be responsible to him alone.

(e) To set up a police force under his personal command to constitute a counterweight to the army, and with its help—and, if possible, with the cooperation of the Danish people—to wield control over the country.

The two decisive points were the first and the last, and he successfully attained both of them. His authority was reaffirmed and German rule in Denmark was now based on police strength; only Best did not succeed in achieving exclusive command. The French prosecutor at the Nuremberg trials, M. Faure, could sum up as follows:

The German police force in Denmark was thus set up a few days after the crisis I have just described. . . . During the whole period referred to [i.e., after the crisis] this force carried out the most important task of the three arms of German authority [civil administration, army, police] and was the main instrument by which the Germans exercised their sovereign authority. We can therefore say that while Norway and Holland were examples of civil control and Belgium and France of military control, Denmark was a typical example of police control. [M. Faure continues:] The seizure of power by the German police in Denmark in the period September 1943 until the liberation was the cause of an unusually large number of criminal acts.[82]

The German police force in Denmark was thus established in September 1943 on the initiative of Best. Its establishment was closely related to the Jewish persecutions, either as a result of Best's own initiative or someone else's which he exploited for his own ends.

Establishment of the Police Force

When Dr. Best, after only a few months in office, realized that he was unable to defeat Hanneken and that the general's aims constituted a threat to his position and policy, he sought to establish some sort of counterweight. His career had taken him through the police forces, the S.S.

and the S.D.; thus Best sought to base his rule on the police. In all his postwar statements regarding the police force in Denmark, Best emphasized that upon his arrival in Copenhagen there were only a few German policemen, and these worked in liaison with the Danish police. These few policemen were under his command. Only in the fall of 1943, he asserts, was a German police force in fact set up in Denmark and G. Pancke appointed as its commander. Pancke was—contrary to what Best at first understood—independent in all police matters, and this with Himmler's support.[83] Best thus elegantly glosses over everything that had happened throughout a whole year (from his own assumption of office on November 5, 1942, until Pancke's arrival on November 1, 1943). By this omission Best managed to divert attention from the fact that he himself was the one who brought German police to Denmark. True, his main object—to be the sole commander of these same police—was frustrated by Himmler, who instead sent a "Higher S.S.- and *Polizeiführer*" to be "the third player in the Skat game"[84] together with Hanneken and Best. Himmler himself informed Best of the move in a letter which was meant to be cordial, written in October, after the events to be described in this and the following chapter.[85]

The German Foreign Ministry archives house a whole file devoted to Best's efforts to obtain his own police force.[86] He began this action precisely on the day of the Danish elections, March 23, 1943. He explained the need for a police battalion for purposes of defense against paratroop-supported acts of sabotage and for protection of firms working for the Germans.[87] After some negotiations, an order was issued on April 23 to transfer a battalion from ill-fated Cholm in Poland to Copenhagen,[88] together with Ribbentrop's explicit proviso that "in normal times the battalion would be subordinate to the Reich's plenipotentiary, Dr. Best, or his substitute." With the help of Kurt Daluege, Best tried to regulate the relationship between his police and

Hanneken's army.[89] In the following period Best of course reported with alacrity all his big successes in the war against sabotage, but this did not prevent his demanding, on May 11, 1943, fifteen more S.D. men in addition to the thirty he already had. After much pressure twelve S.D. constables arrived in July.[90]

We have seen that Best was aware a week before the crisis broke that police reinforcements were needed, and in a letter he wrote to Himmler immediately after the state of emergency was declared, on August 30, he saw the consolidation of his position by German police forces as one of two alternatives, the second being his resignation and departure from Denmark. After the war Best asserted that he had on several occasions offered to resign but continued in office each time at the request of Ribbentrop.[91] In light of Best's letter to Himmler these claims should not perhaps be taken too seriously, although Ribbentrop was undoubtedly interested in his ministry's maintaining its control over Denmark. Best knew this well and exploited it for his own ends, but in the matter of standing firm against Hanneken, Ribbentrop was a shaky pillar of support. Best knew that only a real operational force at his disposal in Denmark itself could form a counterweight against the army. He was aware of this fact early on, as we have seen, and was naturally all the more convinced of it the moment that practical control of Denmark passed into Hanneken's hands.

At the same time (August 30) that he put forward his proposals to Himmler, he also presented similar suggestions to Ribbentrop. The exchange of telegrams between Best and Ribbentrop on August 30 and September 1 shows clear attempts by Ribbentrop to leave political power and a determination of the future form of control in Best's hands.[92] In a telegram dated August 31 which reached Copenhagen on September 1, Ribbentrop informed Best that "IN ACCORDANCE WITH THE DECISION OF THE FÜHRER, YOU, AS PLENIPOTENTIARY OF THE REICH, ARE ALSO POLITICALLY RESPONSIBLE

FOR DENMARK DURING THE STATE OF EMERGENCY." He then laid down Best's powers, which included the establishment of a new Danish authority which was to receive from him directives concerning relations with the royal house, press affairs, radio, and Danish economic affairs. However, in all matters of military security and problems concerning the state of emergency Best was to come to an understanding with the military commander. In the event of differences of opinion, the decision was to rest with the Foreign Ministry.

Best would not appear to have had unlimited confidence in the Foreign Ministry's power of decision. Even before receipt of the telegram of August 31 he himself sent a telegram—Number 1001. Because of its important bearing on the events of September, it will be given here in full:[93]

TO THE FOREIGN MINISTER PERSONALLY:

I HAVE RECEIVED THE INSTRUCTIONS TO PREPARE A NEW ORDER IN DENMARK IN ACCORDANCE WITH THE FIRST OF THE TWO POSSI-BILITIES EXPLAINED IN MY TELEGRAM NO. 995 OF 8/30/43 AND HAVE INITIATED THE NECESSARY MEASURES. I WILL REPORT REGU-LARLY ON FURTHER DEVELOPMENTS.

BEFORE A GOVERNMENT IS SET UP AND THE STATE OF EMERGENCY TERMINATED, ADEQUATE GERMAN POLICE FORCES MUST BE SET UP IN DENMARK. JUST AS THAT POLICY BEGUN IN 1942, NAMELY, TO DIRECT DENMARK WITH THE HELP OF THE COUNTRY'S OWN POLITICAL FACTORS, HAS HITHERTO BEEN CONSISTENTLY CARRIED OUT, SO TOO IT IS NOW NECESSARY TO APPLY WITH THE SEVEREST CONSISTENCY THE POLICY OF THE MAILED FIST AND DEMONSTRATION OF GERMAN MIGHT INTRODUCED ON 8/29/43. THE RESISTANCE MOVEMENT MUST NOT IN THE FUTURE BE FOUGHT WITH THE AID OF DANISH FORCES. THE DANISH POLICE WOULD NOT REFUSE ORDERS (AS DID PART OF THE NORWEGIAN POLICE) BUT THESE ORDERS WOULD NOT LEAD TO ANY RESULTS. THE DIRECTORS OR MINISTRIES CONCERNED HAVE ALSO EXPRESSED THE VIEW THAT IN THE FUTURE GERMAN COURTS SHOULD DEAL WITH ATTACKS ON GERMAN INTERESTS, SINCE THEY THEM-SELVES CANNOT BE RESPONSIBLE FOR THE MEANS AT THEIR DISPOSAL BEING APPLIED WITH SUFFICIENT EFFECTIVENESS. (WITH THIS CON-

CESSION THE DANISH STRUGGLE OF 3½ YEARS FOR EXCLUSIVE JURIS-
DICTION OVER THEIR CITIZENS HAS IN FACT COME TO AN END.)

IN MY OPINION, IT IS NECESSARY BEFORE TERMINATION OF THE
STATE OF EMERGENCY TO TAKE THE FOLLOWING STEPS:

1. THE ESTABLISHMENT OF SOME 25 GERMAN POLICE STATIONS,
COMPOSED AS FOLLOWS: ONE-THIRD GERMAN SECURITY POLICE AND
TWO-THIRDS ORDINARY GERMAN POLICE (TOGETHER WITH DANISH
ASSISTANTS); TO THIS END TWO ADDITIONAL POLICE BATTALIONS AND
300 SECURITY POLICE ARE NEEDED.

2. THE ESTABLISHMENT OF A SPECIAL COURT UNDER THE PRESI-
DENCY OF THE PLENIPOTENTIARY. THE JURIDICAL BASIS FOR SUCH
A COURT MAY BE FOUND IN THE DIRECTIVES CONCERNING S.S. AND
POLICE COURTS.

3. IN ORDER TO PREVENT COMPETITION BETWEEN THE GERMAN
POLICE AND FIELD INTELLIGENCE AN AGREEMENT SHOULD BE DRAWN
UP WITH THE OKW (AS IN FRANCE) WHEREBY FIELD INTELLIGENCE
FORMS PART OF THE CIVIL POLICE SYSTEM, WHICH WILL THEN ALSO
CARRY OUT THE OPERATIONAL TASKS OF MILITARY INTELLIGENCE.

4. CANCELLATION OF THE NEW SALARY REGULATIONS FOR GERMAN
OFFICIALS (DIRECTIVE NR. PERS. B 10203 OF 8/11/43), WHICH ARE
NOT ADEQUATE FOR THE SUBSISTENCE OF THOSE GERMAN POLICEMEN
IN WHOSE HANDS GERMAN INTERESTS IN DENMARK WILL IN THE
FUTURE LIE.

5. ALLOCATION OF FINANCIAL MEANS FOR MAINTAINING ALL
SECURITY OPERATIONS, ESPECIALLY THE ESTABLISHMENT OF A WIDE-
SPREAD INTELLIGENCE SERVICE (TWO MILLION KRONER ARE NEEDED
AT ONCE).

BEFORE FULFILLING THESE NEEDS IT WOULD, IN MY OPINION, BE
IRRESPONSIBLE TO TERMINATE THE STATE OF EMERGENCY.

                                                    BEST

This telegram sums up all Best's efforts: an increase in
the police force which would of course be under his command; establishment of special courts under his presidency;
inclusion of military intelligence in police intelligence, under
him; the placing of money on a large scale at his sole disposal. Nowhere else, it seems, are his ambitions so explictly

expressed. It is also clear that these objectives, including even control over a sphere under military command (intelligence and security services) were at complete variance with the actual state of affairs in Denmark at the time. Best is trying here to force through a drastic upheaval and to immobilize Hanneken as the general had tried to immobilize him. In his reports throughout this period Best attempts to show that Hanneken is incapable of evaluating the situation correctly, that he encroaches upon Best's preserves, and that his actions do not bring any closer a solution of the problems that have arisen.[94]

In the meantime, Best awaited a reply to his telegram, and when it failed to come (Best was, in those days, used to receiving Ribbentrop's replies even within a few hours) he sent another cable on September 3, as follows:

IN REFERENCE TO MY TELEGRAM NO. 1001 OF 9/1/43, I REQUEST THAT THE COMMANDER OF THE SECURITY POLICE, WHO WILL BE UNDER MY ORDERS, BE SENT AS SOON AS POSSIBLE IN ORDER TO PREPARE THE ESTABLISHMENT OF THE NEW POLICE STATIONS AND TO TAKE ALL THE OTHER NECESSARY STEPS.[95]

Again there was no reply, no reaction. On September 6 Best sent Ribbentrop another telegram in which he discusses the general situation in Denmark, the political problems involved in setting up a new Danish government, and so forth.[96] He does not mention his previous telegram but says in the last paragraph: "SINCE NORMALIZATION OF THE SITUATION AND TERMINATION OF THE STATE OF EMERGENCY MAY BE ATTAINED ONLY *after the establishment of an adequate police force*, THERE IS NOW A FURTHER OPPORTUNITY TO WAIT FOR NEW DANISH PROPOSALS [regarding the question of setting up a new government] TO BE PUT FORWARD" (italics added). However, once again Best was to receive no reply to this, his main question.

We know from Best's letter to Himmler of August 22 that

his conception was to rule in Denmark with the help of a "Danish civil but nonpolitical administration," with the German police under his command preserving order. The telegram of August 30[97] contains two suggestions to Ribbentrop: to set up, within the legal Danish framework, either "a nonpolitical cabinet," or, without the participation of the king or the Rigsdag, an "administrative committee." Ribbentrop chose the first alternative[98]—it may be assumed to Best's surprise and disappointment. Thereafter Best attempted to prevent any rapid decisions on Danish rule (see the above quotation) in order to play for time and maneuver developments in the direction he wanted. The Danes too were uninterested, in the circumstances, in setting up a legal government.[99] In the end Best obtained what he was after, and the arrangement made upon the outbreak of the crisis (namely, the concentration of administration in the hands of the directors of ministries) also continued after the end of the state of emergency and right up to the end of the war. In his efforts to prevent the formation of a government, as favored by Ribbentrop, and to convince the latter of its impossibility, Best on September 20 also used the pretext that the persecution of the Jews would preclude the setting up of a constitutional government.[100]

On September 7 two things happened which were completely unrelated to one another, but both of which may have affected Best's consequent actions. The first was that he received the receipt for the money owed by *Kamptegnet,* indicating that it had been finally liquidated.[101] The danger that the extreme anti-Semites in Denmark would raise their heads now vanished. The second event was the murder, on that evening, in the center of Copenhagen, of a sergeant in the Cholm police battalion, that battalion which had come to Denmark in May at Best's request. This incident caused much agitation among the German authorities and may have been the motive for Best's decision that he had to have police reinforcements at any price.

Best's Responsibility

On September 8, Dr. Best dispatched his celebrated telegram No. 1032, in which he suggested that persecution of the Jews be carried out. The cable ran as follows:[102]

I REQUEST THAT THE FOLLOWING INFORMATION BE PASSED ON TO THE FOREIGN MINISTER:

WITH REFERENCE TO YOUR TELEGRAM NO. 537 OF 4/19/43 AND MY REPORT OF 4/24/43—II C 102/43—I HEREBY BEG, IN LIGHT OF THE NEW SITUATION, TO REPORT ON THE JEWISH PROBLEM IN DENMARK AS FOLLOWS: IN ACCORDANCE WITH THE CONSISTENT APPLICATION OF THE NEW POLICY IN DENMARK, IT IS MY OPINION THAT MEASURES SHOULD NOW BE TAKEN TOWARD A SOLUTION OF THE PROBLEMS OF THE JEWS AND THE FREEMASONS. THE NECESSARY STEPS SHOULD BE TAKEN AS LONG AS THE PRESENT STATE OF EMERGENCY EXISTS, FOR AFTERWARD THEY WILL BE LIABLE TO CAUSE REACTION IN THE COUNTRY, WHICH IN TURN MAY LEAD TO A REIMPOSITION OF A GENERAL STATE OF EMERGENCY UNDER CONDITIONS WHICH WILL PRESUMABLY BE LESS CONVENIENT THAN THOSE OF TODAY. IN PARTICULAR, AS I HAVE BEEN INFORMED FROM MANY SOURCES, THE CONSTITUTIONAL GOVERNMENT—SHOULD IT EXIST— WOULD RESIGN. THE KING AND THE RIGSDAG WOULD ALSO CEASE THEIR PARTICIPATION IN GOVERNMENT OF THE COUNTRY. IT MAY BE ASSUMED, MOREOVER, THAT IN SUCH AN EVENT A GENERAL STRIKE WOULD BREAK OUT, FOR THE TRADE UNIONS WOULD CEASE THEIR ACTIVITIES AND THEIR RESTRAINING INFLUENCE ON THE WORKERS WOULD BE REMOVED. IF MEASURES ARE TAKEN DURING THE PRESENT STATE OF EMERGENCY, IT MAY BE THAT THE FORMATION OF A LEGALLY CONSTITUTED GOVERNMENT WILL BE RENDERED IMPOSSIBLE AND IT WILL BE NECESSARY TO SET UP AN ADMINISTRATIVE COUNCIL UNDER MY LEADERSHIP. I WOULD THEN HAVE TO LEGISLATE BY MEANS OF DECREE. IN ORDER TO ARREST AND DEPORT SOME 6,000 JEWS (INCLUDING WOMEN AND CHILDREN) AT ONE SWEEP IT IS NECESSARY TO HAVE THE POLICE FORCES I REQUESTED IN MY TELEGRAM NO. 1001 OF 9/1. ALMOST ALL OF THEM SHOULD BE PUT TO WORK IN GREATER COPENHAGEN WHERE THE MAJORITY OF THE

LOCAL JEWS LIVE. SUPPLEMENTARY FORCES SHOULD BE PROVIDED BY
THE GERMAN MILITARY COMMANDER IN DENMARK. FOR TRANSPOR-
TATION, SHIPS MUST BE CONSIDERED A PRIME NECESSITY AND
SHOULD BE ORDERED IN TIME. AS REGARDS THE FREEMASONS, A POS-
SIBLE SOLUTION IS THE FORMAL CLOSURE OF ALL THEIR LODGES (TO
WHICH ALL THE LEADING PERSONALITIES OF THE COUNTRY BELONG)
AND THE TEMPORARY ARREST OF THE MOST PROMINENT FREEMASONS
AND CONFISCATION OF LODGE PROPERTY. TO THIS END STRONG OPER-
ATIONAL FORCES ARE ALSO NECESSARY. I BEG TO REQUEST A DECISION
AS TO THE STEPS I SHOULD TAKE OR WHAT I HAVE TO PREPARE IN
CONNECTION WITH THE JEWISH AND FREEMASON PROBLEMS.

DR. BEST

We have seen above that Best laid the blame for the
initiation of the persecutions on a variety of people and
stubbornly denied that the thought sprang from his own
head. His last version, which he repeated several times, was
that he was informed by telephone from Ribbentrop's office
that Hitler had decided that the persecutions in Denmark
be carried out at once but that it was forbidden to reveal
this terrible secret to anyone. In order to head off disaster,
Best claimed, he sent off this telegram of September 8 with
a double motive in mind: to point out once again all the
difficulties that such an action would bring, but at the same
time—after he had learned that this was the irrevocable
order of the Führer—he asked that the action be carried out
as long as the state of emergency in Denmark was maintained. Nevertheless, he asserts, he took upon himself the
hazardous task of undoing the implementation of the persecutions.[103]

Let us examine the telegram in the light of Best's assertions and the facts as they are known to us. The telegram
was sent to Ribbentrop but was not restricted to him personally, as were a number of other telegrams Best sent at
that time.[104] It is signed "Dr. Best." In his Nuremberg statement Best explained[105] that he usually signed in this way
telegrams intended for the Foreign Ministry only; whereas

telegrams which he intended for or assumed would be sent to Hitler were signed simply "Best." We find, indeed, both versions on telegrams. (The main telegram, 1001, is in fact signed just "Best.") Two conclusions may be drawn here: telegram 1032 was intended for Ribbentrop, for the Foreign Ministry, but not especially for Hitler. We find in it all those factors which Best was interested in achieving at that particular time:

(1) Constitutional government in Denmark would definitely come to an end and the king and the Rigsdag cease to be decisive political factors; instead, an administrative council under Best would be set up and his decrees would have the force of law.

(2) Rapid transfer of the police forces requested in telegram 1001, for carrying out the operation on that allegedly favorable occasion, would occur.

(3) Hanneken would have to place some of his forces at Best's disposal, and this would be a sort of demonstration that control had returned to Best.

Best's explanation that he sent the telegram with a view to postponing the persecutions for as long as possible was mainly developed in his statements from 1948 on.[106] We have seen how the German Foreign Ministry's "veteran diplomats" developed a system of writing long reports apparently in support of proposals put forward by the Nazi leaders but in fact intended to contradict and reject them.[107] In his defense statement—presumably his last formulation of this sort—Best also dwells at length on this form of reporting, which arose out of the conditions of dictatorial rule.[108]

With regard to the telegram, its main emphasis is not put on the difficulties but on the mode of action. Further, it is surprising that Best cannot remember the exact details; he does not know whether the information was given to him on the 7th or the 8th of September or who gave it to him.[109] That he should forget the latter can only be regarded as extremely strange. It may be plausible that a person cannot remember the time he received such sensational news, as Best claims it was in the afternoon or the next morning; but it is difficult to believe that he cannot remember the source. However, in the summer of 1949 this problem was explained by F. von Sonnleithner, who worked in Ribbentrop's office at headquarters in the period under review. On June 23, 1949, he gave evidence in the Copenhagen District Court (*Østre Landsret*) and it was his "clarification" of various complicated points which led to Best's eventual acquittal.[110] Sonnleithner was aware of the City Court's verdict on Best, which had been translated for him by Best's German advocate.[111] This same advocate had gone through all the material of the case and had had the opportunity of talking to Best himself. Sonnleithner states that he read telegram No. 1032 when he was a witness at the *Wilhelmstrasse* (Foreign Ministry) trial in Nuremberg. He adds that the cable at once impressed him as a "typical example of the method one had to use when one wished to prevent something."[112] Moreover, he added, even Ribbentrop used the same method toward Hitler when necessary. He states further that he himself was informed "a day or two before the telegram was sent that Hitler had decided, upon the initiative of another party—not the Foreign Ministry—to deport the Jews from Denmark."

Since he knew that Ribbentrop was in favor of preserving the status quo in Denmark, Sonnleithner informed Best by telephone "that the matter will now take place in Denmark too and the Jewish problem also be solved there." He was afraid that the line was being tapped and thus did not use the word "Jew," but merely said that that which Best feared would happen, and he possibly also added the figure six thousand. As far as he could judge from Best's reaction he was sure that Best understood him. He also interpreted Best's reaction as meaning that he had already received a warning from someone else in the minister's office. (This comment was apparently intended to fit in with Best's

citation of several persons who had given him the information; one of the persons Best had mentioned was safely far
away in South Africa at the time of the investigation.[113])

There is no doubt that during the crisis period Best held
frequent telephone conversations with the minister's office
and received many pieces of information later confirmed by
official dispatches to him. Sonnleithner adds that in order
to cover himself he also sent a written message to Berlin
officially informing the Foreign Ministry of the Führer's
order. He assumed that this announcement was to be found
among the documents assembled in Nuremberg, though he
had not himself seen it. The note does in fact exist.[114] It
was sent on September 18, 1943.

If we accept Sonnleithner's words at their face value,
then he waited ten days before attempting to cover up for
the telephone conversation. The story would therefore appear to be all dressed up, since if there was any point in
covering himself it had to be done immediately—as in fact
it was. The decision regarding the persecution of the Danish
Jews was not taken before September 16. On the 17th Best
received from the Foreign Minister the telegram informing
him of the decision to carry out the deportation.[115] It may
therefore be assumed that the telephone conversation, if it
took place at all, occurred on September 16 or 17, after
Hitler's decision, and not on September 7 or 8.

Other documents may be found in the Inl. II files of the
German Foreign Ministry which refute Best's statements.
On September 9, Thadden passed Best's telegram No. 1032
on to the Minister's Bureau with "a request to inform Inl. II
of the minister's instructions."[116] In a letter of October 12 to
Müller of the RSHA, in which Thadden explains developments in the light of the operation's failure, he writes:

In view of the particularly delicate nature of the matter I desisted from taking an immediate stand and merely verified first
of all by telephone that the telegram from Copenhagen was

given to the minister by his staff, and I also requested, again
without taking a personal stand, that I be informed of the
minister's instructions.[117]

On September 13 the Minister's Bureau wrote to Thadden
requesting the Inl. II Department to express an opinion
regarding a solution to the problem of the Jews and Freemasons in Denmark. Thadden replied on the 14th:

The Inl. II Department, in conformity with the views of the
relevant persons in the RSHA, is of the opinion that the present
time is the only one possible, if we wish to impose a solution
of the Jewish and Freemason problem in the near future. With
regard to the serious political considerations which, according
to the Political Department, weigh against an imposed solution,
we would refer to the expression of opinion of Minister von
Grundherr, a copy of which is attached herewith.[118]

Unfortunately, this statement of Grundherr's has not been
found.[119] The state of affairs is, however, fairly clear: not
only Thadden but also Ribbentrop was surprised by Best's
proposal.

To test reactions, Ribbentrop asked the opinion of the
department concerned; had a prior order from Hitler already
existed there would have been no point to such a question.
Sonnleithner stated that the news of Hitler's decision was
given to him "either by Ribbentrop himself or by Hewel—
the Foreign Ministry's liaison officer with Hitler."[120] Moreover, Thadden writes that the RSHA—meaning here the
department of Müller-Eichmann—was also in agreement
with him. The tone of the letter does not indicate that the
initiative came from that department. Further proof lies
in the fact that Himmler's notes contain no mention of
persecution of the Danish Jews before September 20.[121] If
we conclude therefore that Hitler made his decision on
September 16 and that it was previously known neither to
Ribbentrop nor Himmler, then no "other party" in initiating
the persecutions remains than Best himself.[122]

Best informs us in his defense statement that the leading circles had a poor opinion of him and that they laid the blame for the serious state of affairs in Denmark on his shoulders.[123] In his diary entry for September 8, Goebbels expresses his displeasure with Best, though he believes that now, after the declaration of the state of emergency, everything will be all right.[124] Elsewhere in his diary he describes Hitler's opinion of Seyss-Inquart (positive), of Terboven (negative) and of Best, "who knows only the velvet glove."[125] There is no doubt that in those days of critical failure all Best's enemies hastened to talk ill of him, and their words even reached his ears. He states this in a letter written to Himmler on September 10. He sends him here a memorandum on the events leading up to the state of emergency, since "I am aware that the true position is not known in Berlin." Copies were sent to Kaltenbrunner and Berger. In these communications too Best tries to show how little Hanneken understands the political problems and how he hopes to perpetuate the present state of affairs (i.e., to give Denmark military rule).[126]

Best thus had every reason to demonstrate that he was a loyal National Socialist and a strong man, who would at one blow turn the situation in Denmark to his own advantage. Whether the idea was his own brainchild or was suggested by someone else is of little importance, although we have seen that it was improbable that it came from Hitler's headquarters or from any other leading Nazi.[127] What is clear is that Best used the situation as leverage in his struggle for power in Denmark.

It cannot be irrefutably proved that the additional police battalions requested by Best in telegram No. 1001, which arrived in Denmark in the middle of September, were dispatched in the wake of his proposal to institute persecutions of the Jews, though there are indications that this was the case. The battalions began to arrive even before the crucial decision of September 16. We have seen that on September 3

Best requested that a police officer be sent at once to prepare for the arrival of the battalions. It will also be recalled that he received no reply to his telegram No. 1001.[128]

The first to arrive, on September 14, was Gestapo agent Karl Heinz Hoffmann.[129] Dr. Rudolf Mildner was appointed commander. On the telegram form dated September 3 one of the deputies in the Inl. II Department, Geiger, noted on September 8: "Head of Inl. II says to await orders." There follows an unsigned note dated the 16th to the effect that Mildner in Kattowitz was assigned to Copenhagen "three days ago."[130] To this Geiger adds on the 18th that the order was supposed to have been given but it has not yet reached him. Mildner arrived in Copenhagen on the 16th.[131] It is not out of the question therefore that the rapid action between the 8th, when orders were awaited, and the 13th or 14th was the result of Best's telegram on the persecution of the Jews.[132] Only in his last, the defense statement, does Best tell that the additional police battalions came to Copenhagen in September "for war against the resistance movement and acts of sabotage."[133] The police battalions and officials of the S.D. arrived between September 15 and 30—on the very eve of the persecutions. On the latter date the last battalion arrived from Norway.[134]

All in all it can thus be said that the plan for persecuting the Jews—whether presented to Best from outside or initiated by himself, as is our view—was well suited to serve as a leverage with whose help Best could concentrate in his hands the practical implements for taking Denmark under his personal tutelage. Moreover, this rule, based on the presence of German police troops, would have assumed the form planned and proposed by him even before Hanneken brought about the state of emergency.

Failure in Denmark would mean the end of Best's career; it would mean that his star would fall still farther in the S.S. firmament and above all in the eyes of Himmler himself. He doubtless recalled his "exile" in France and his desperate efforts to regain the favor of the S.S. leaders.[135] He was assuredly prepared to cling to any driftwood to save himself from the sea of oblivion, and in his view the suggestion to persecute the Jews was such driftwood. There were persons in his entourage who interpreted the plan in this light.[136]

If Best was indeed driven by inner contradictions—by the struggle between ambition and understanding, between connivance and conscience—at that time the ambitions and the connivance were at any rate in the ascendant. In the further course of the German occupation of Denmark similar situations recurred. Best's status in the eyes of his leaders continued to be mediocre, and he was alternatively the subject of deception and deceit. In his defense statement he himself talks of "the war on two fronts."

At this moment [the rejection of the ultimatum by the Danish government], the last phase of the occupation period in Denmark began. For the plenipotentiary, Dr. Best, this phrase was one of hard and ceaseless war on two fronts. On the one hand, he endeavored to defend German interests, as he understood them, against the increasing assaults of the enemy—through partisan actions and unsettling political maneuvers. On the other hand, he strove to prevent, or at least to minimize, the growing intervention in Danish affairs of the Führer's general staff and other German authorities . . . insofar as this intervention clashed with true German interests.[137]

The main factor in this campaign on two fronts was Best's fierce determination to preserve his own position. This two-fronted and two-faced policy involved him in complicated tactics in all spheres, but its implementation became especially obvious when, on the one hand, he suggested that the Jews be persecuted and, on the other, worked toward the frustration of that very persecution.

V

Operation Failure

In his relations with the Danes, Dr. Best's maneuvers in his "war on two fronts" forced him to conceal the origin of the Jewish persecutions but also to do all he could to hamper their performance. He was convinced that he could not maintain his position in Denmark or appear before the German authorities as a confidant of the Danes if the latter were to find out that he had been the instigator of the pogrom. Opponent of persecution in theory and in practice —this had to be his public image. Were the order to intern thousands of Jews to be ascribed to him, he would forfeit all chance of maintaining himself in power, for even with his three police battalions he could not rule Denmark by force. Cooperation and goodwill on the part of the Danish administration were essential to him.

Best therefore employed various tactics to nullify the effects of the misfortune he had himself brought about:

(1) He maneuvered others into protesting to the central German authorities against the persecutions.

(2) He tried to implicate the army. Under the state of emergency, the army was responsible for the general situation. If the army were to avoid the population's hostility, it too had to oppose the persecutions. Best,

however, was interested in precisely the reverse
process: if the action could take place under the
military aegis the army would be blamed, while Best
could pose as the decent fellow to whom such operations were distasteful.

(3) He had to create the general impression that the
persecution of the Jews was by Hitler's personal
order, while Best—though he had no choice but to
obey—was in fact opposed to it.

(4) Every opportunity had to be granted the Jews to
escape and the Danes to help them do so.

The basic assumption underlying all these machinations
was the attitude of the Danes. No German then in the
country, soldier or civilian, could doubt that persecution of
the Jews would arouse the energetic opposition of the whole
population. The manipulations of the Germans in occupied
Denmark should not be allowed to cloud the fact that the
real credit for German efforts to prevent anti-Jewish
action was due to the Danes and to the Danes alone. It was
they who enabled the moderate (and impelled the im-
moderate) Germans to contribute in one way or another
to the rescue of the Jews.

Attempts at Prevention

It was Best himself who brought about the first attempt
to prevent the operation by informing G. F. Duckwitz on
September 11 of his notorious telegram No. 1032.[1] A good
deal has already been written on Duckwitz,[2] and the main
points are well known. On September 28 Duckwitz had a
secret meeting with the Danish Social Democratic leaders
where he informed them of the imminent onslaught on the
Jews. This was not the first meeting with Danish leaders.
Contact had been established at the end of 1942 through the
offices of the counselor at the Swedish legation, Nils Eric
Ekblad.[3] Evidence since given by Hedtoft, H. C. Hansen,

Buhl, and Alsing Anderson confirms that on that same day, September 28, Duckwitz telephoned to Hedtoft that he had most urgent news and the meeting with Danish leaders was therefore arranged at a place where the Danes already had a secret appointment with Ekblad. This very fact shows the degree of confidence the Danes had in Duckwitz.

Duckwitz knew Denmark well. He had worked in the country before the war as a business representative and he spoke Danish. He had been a National Socialist in his youth[4] but had later drifted away from the movement. During the occupation he served as shipping attaché in the German legation. His main contact man among the Danes was Hedtoft; with Duckwitz's help the Danes received important information on developments in leading German circles, a good deal of which was passed on to British intelligence. Duckwitz was also the first to inform the Danes of Best's confrontation with Hitler on August 24. Nevertheless, he kept in close touch with Best. It is difficult to say whether Best was aware of the scope of Duckwitz's Danish connections, though he presumably knew that they existed.[5]

According to Duckwitz, Best possessed sound political judgment and was open to any reasonable suggestion regarding the Jewish problem. In several talks Duckwitz had with him on the subject, he became convinced that Best was firmly opposed to any action against the Jews in Denmark.[6] It was his view that Best did not give the start signal with malice but that he sent the telegram in all sincerity and naïveté in order to prevent the operation. Duckwitz considered Best's step a tragic miscalculation.[7] He describes how Best explained to him on September 11 that he was sure that both the Foreign Ministry and the RSHA were opposed to the deportation of the Danish Jews. Best also presumed that the army would resist the measure, particularly during the state of emergency when it would be held responsible for all incidents in Denmark. Duckwitz too is at a loss to identify the persons surrounding Hitler who apparently suggested that the deportation be carried out at precisely that moment.

Duckwitz relates how he reacted sharply against the proposal, and the vigorous discussion with Best that followed ended in his threat to resign. That same evening or the next morning Best summoned him for a further talk. It now seemed to Duckwitz that Best had in the meantime realized the grave consequences his initiative was liable to produce. He nevertheless asserted that his telegram was of only academic interest and that its dispatch was the surest way to bring about a negative decision, once and for all, regarding the troublesome Jewish question. Duckwitz, however, could not share Best's optimism and claimed that certain parties in Berlin would willingly seize upon this opportunity presented to them by the plenipotentiary of the Reich in Denmark—especially since his former opposition to Jewish persecution had now been replaced by his personal recommendation of it. He expressed his readiness to leave at once for Berlin to try and prevent the transfer of the unfortunate telegram to headquarters and other parties. Best himself, continues Duckwitz, was now eager for someone to explain his true intentions to the Foreign Ministry. On September 13 Duckwitz flew to Berlin.[8]

As it happened, Duckwitz came too late, for that same day Ribbentrop's response had arrived at the Foreign Ministry.[9] When, after the war, Best defended his telegram, he no longer claimed that he thought to prevent the persecutions by sending the cable, but that he would have the operation—which he considered inevitable—carried out under the state of emergency. On the basis of his impressions of the events of those days, Duckwitz himself entertained no doubts that it was in fact Best's telegram which set off the action. Best even claimed after the war that Duckwitz did what he did upon his, Best's, initiative.[10]

Duckwitz saw what he rightly called "Berlin's reply," the telegram dated September 17, on the 19th. That same day he wrote in his diary, "I know what I have to do."[11] Best may have been sure that Duckwitz knew what he had to do, but he presumably did not tell him so explicitly. No evidence to this effect is available from Duckwitz himself, and none of the Danes involved recall that Duckwitz said anything about acting at Best's behest.[12] After the failure in Berlin Duckwitz tried to get the Swedes to act. On the pretext of an official journey to Stockholm on September 22, a meeting was arranged for him with the Swedish prime minister, Per Albin Hansson, through the mediation of Ekblad.[13] Duckwitz proposed that the neutral Swedish government intervene to prevent the deportation of the Danish Jews. At Hansson's suggestion, Ekblad returned with Duckwitz to Denmark, and since the Germans would not grant him an entry permit, Duckwitz smuggled him through.[14] Already during his trip to Stockholm Duckwitz had raised the possibility of transferring the Jews to Sweden, and he drew up a code with his friend and counterpart in Stockholm, Dr. Riensberg, whereby they could communicate on the subject. According to Duckwitz, this scheme was to prove extremely useful.

The second man persuaded by Best to attempt postponement of the action was *Dr. Mildner*, commander of the police battalions ordered by Best to Denmark. S.S. *Standartenführer* Mildner came, as stated, from Kattowitz, where he served as S.S. area commander. His duties included chairmanship of the political committee at Auschwitz and he sat as judge in the local S.S. court. He was thoroughly acquainted with the camp to which he sent Jews from his area.[15] He had met Best as early as 1938 in connection with the organization of Jewish deportations.

Mildner's various statements at the Nuremberg trial have been mentioned above.[16] As in most utterances of the kind, truth and lies are interwoven. Mildner asserts that the plenipotentiary of the Reich received an order from Himmler to deport the Jews. No such order has been discovered. All Best's instructions came through the Foreign Ministry. Mildner also claims that as commander of the police battalions he was subordinate to Best. "Since I was opposed to the persecution of the Jews both personally and for practical reasons, I asked Dr. Best the reason for his order."[17] There are no grounds for believing that Mildner "personally" opposed the persecution of the Jews, though there were indeed practical grounds. He further describes the already-mentioned talk with Best where he explained that Ribbentrop was the instigator of the action against the Jews. Best also mentioned to Mildner that he was forced—against his will—to carry out the order. Mildner relates that he at once sent a cable to the head of RSHA Department IV, Müller, asking that the action be cancelled. His reasons were those of Best: the opposition of the Danes, the deterioration of relations, the effect on foreign countries. To these he added the probable disruption of contact and cooperation with the Danish police.[18] Mildner states that he received a reply from Kaltenbrunner repeating and confirming Himmler's order to deport the Jews. He then flew to Berlin on September 25 to present his views to Kaltenbrunner or Himmler personally,[19] but spoke instead with Müller, who immediately cabled again to Himmler. However, shortly after Mildner's return to Copenhagen, Himmler sent his final order: "The action against the Jews is to be carried out at once." So much for Mildner.

Kanstein learned of the plan to persecute the Jews only after receipt of Hitler's order on September 17. He states that he consulted with Minister Barandon, Best's deputy, with Duckwitz, with the head of military intelligence, Oberst von Engelmann, and with others on ways of preventing the operation. All were agreed that the action was contrary to German interests in Denmark. They supported

Kanstein's suggestion that he go to Berlin and lay their petitions before the Ministries of Foreign Affairs, Interior, Trade, and Agriculture. Kanstein also suggested this move to Hanneken, as his superior during the state of emergency, and even the general gave his agreement.[20] Kanstein also spoke of this journey to Best. He knew that Best had in the past been opposed to persecution of the Danish Jews and expected that now too he would express his disapproval to his superiors. According to Kanstein, however, Best avoided the issue, though he did not oppose Kanstein's trip. Kanstein flew to Berlin and claims that in all the ministries and in personal talks he found understanding for his view that it was not wise to attack the Jews of Denmark. He was everywhere promised that the report would be passed on to higher levels. He returned to Copenhagen just as Mildner flew to Berlin.

The opponents of Jewish persecutions were now joined by *the army*. Best informed Hanneken of Hitler's order only on the 20th and the general at once cabled his reservations to General Staff headquarters, as follows:

DR. BEST'S TELEGRAM ON AN EARLY SOLUTION TO THE JEWISH PROBLEM IN DENMARK HAS BEEN APPROVED IN PRINCIPLE BY THE FÜHRER.

AT BEST'S SUGGESTION, THE DEPORTATION WILL BE CARRIED OUT DURING THE MILITARY STATE OF EMERGENCY.

IT IS NOT YET CLEAR WHETHER POLICE STRENGTH WILL BE ADE-QUATE FOR SEIZURE OF THE JEWS AND THEIR FAMILIES—ABOUT 6,000 PERSONS, LIVING MAINLY IN COPENHAGEN. THE OPERATION WILL PLACE A HEAVY BURDEN ON THE ARMY WHICH WILL NOT BE ABLE TO ACT VIGOROUSLY, PARTICULARLY SINCE IT WILL BE NECES-SARY IN COPENHAGEN AND ON THE ISLAND OF FYN TO USE NEW RECRUITS. THE BENEFITS OF THE DEPORTATION STRIKE ME AS DOUBT-FUL. NO COOPERATION CAN BE EXPECTED AFTERWARD FROM THE CIVIL ADMINISTRATION OR FROM THE DANISH POLICE. THE SUPPLY

OF FOOD WILL BE ADVERSELY AFFECTED. THE "WILLINGNESS TO SUP-
PLY" OF THE ARMAMENTS INDUSTRY WILL BE UNDERMINED. DIS-
TURBANCES REQUIRING USE OF MILITARY FORCE MUST BE EXPECTED.[21]

Reitlinger, who uses approximately the same sources, points out that there did not appear to be anyone in Denmark willing to persecute the Jews.[22] The next day the OKW requested an explanation from the Foreign Ministry. In the margin there is a note to the effect that the matter has already been put before the Führer, that the deportation is to be carried out during the state of emergency, and that termination of the state of emergency should be postponed for the time being. This reply, signed by Jodl, was dispatched to Copenhagen on September 22.[23] All therefore tried to prevent the action: Duckwitz, Mildner, Kanstein, and the army. All cabled or flew to Berlin, or did both. The only one who did not bring his reservations on the persecutions to the notice of the central authorities was Best. In the meantime, however, new complications arose.

The State of Emergency and Its Problems

The officers and men of the Danish army were interned by the Germans on August 29. The problem of their release and the lifting of the state of emergency occupied Best and Hanneken from the beginning of September.[24] The original intention was apparently to keep the length of the state of emergency short, even less than a month. Best, however, was not interested in its termination before his authority was assured. On September 14, in a proclamation to the population, Hanneken hinted at the possibility of alleviation or even cancellation of the state of emergency should the population show opposition to the acts of sabotage.[25] The OKW's telegram of September 16 to headquarters in Denmark stated that the release of the Danish soldiers who were held in confinement should be carried out in stages up to November 15.[26] That same day Hanneken proposed that the state of emergency be lifted "toward the end of next week," that is, within seven days.[27]

Best at once employed every possible means to prevent the termination of the state of emergency so long as the powers he had requested were not assured him. The same day he began to bombard the Foreign Ministry with telegrams requesting a reply to the remaining items of his telegram No. 1001. His main assertion was that together with the arrival of the police forces—his main demand— his other requests should also be fulfilled in order to consolidate German rule.[28]

In cable No. 1081 of September 17, Best asks that the state of emergency be maintained until at least the 26th, the king's birthday. He states that he has promised Hanneken his agreement to lift the state of emergency provided that "there be placed at my disposal the means necessary to preserve future German interests in Denmark." In his view, a solution of the problems can be expected by the suggested date—a day or two after the king's birthday. At the end of the telegram he gives details of his conditions for the termination of the state of emergency. In this connection, he mentions telegrams No. 1001 of September 1 (containing his basic claims for consolidating his authority), No. 1032 of September 8 (demanding the deportation of the Jews), and No. 1051 of September 13 (specifying the sums needed, in his view, to run the country in its new form). Here before us are those very points which Best considered as essential for the consolidation of his own authority and the prevention of any continuation of military rule by Hanneken in "normal" times. These points, in one bundle, are his basic claims, the problem of financing the regime, and the question of Jewish deportation, which had been turned by telegram 1032 into an integral part of his policy during that month (just as the prevention of Jewish deportation had been an integral part of his "policy of understanding" *before* the hour of crisis).

On the day Best sent telegram No. 1081 he received the official notification of Hitler's decision in principle to carry out the action against the Jews. (That is, he received the reply to his telegram No. 1032.[29] It is thus natural to assume that he sent the above telegram before he received this reply.) The next day, September 18, Best replied to the deportation order. He states that the operation can be prepared in nine or ten days. In the same cable he tries to impress on his superiors the need for the prolonged stay of the police force by again pointing out the negative political consequences of the persecutions. The last paragraph of the telegram states:

POLITICALLY SPEAKING, DEPORTATION OF THE JEWS WILL UNDOUBT-EDLY CAUSE A SHARP DETERIORATION OF THE SITUATION IN DEN-MARK. THERE WILL BE NO FUTHER POSSIBILITY OF FORMING A LEGAL GOVERNMENT. INSIDE THE COUNTRY THERE MAY BE UNREST AND EVEN PERHAPS A GENERAL STRIKE. I ASK THEREFORE THAT THE POLICE FORCES AVAILABLE FOR CARRYING OUT THE ACTION REMAIN AT MY DISPOSAL TO OVERCOME POSSIBLE DIFFICULTIES AFTER THE ACTION ALSO.[30]

Yet now, with the police forces arriving, Best was not interested in carrying out the deportation order, most of his attempts to prevent the action were concentrated in this ten-day preparatory period.

The reply to Best's proposal to lift the state of emergency after the king's birthday came on September 20. On the same day the OKW announced that the Führer agreed in principle to terminating the state of emergency on condition that the military commander, in concert with the plenipotentiary of the Reich, considered the situation sufficiently secure. The final decision was to be given in a few days, after the Foreign Ministry had expressed its opinion.[31] Only now, after receipt of this message, did Best inform Hanneken of the plan to deport the Jews, which led, as we have seen, to the army's attempt at prevention. This attempt, like all the others, was of no avail. Perhaps it might have been possible to avert the dire decree had not Himmler himself intervened on that very day, September 20 (apparently for the first time), and taken the initiative. We know that among the subjects discussed that day by Himmler in his talks with Hitler was the question of obtaining troops from the interned Danish army.[32] The contents of the discussion are evident from a telegram sent to Best by Sonnleithner on behalf of Ribbentrop on September 22.[33] This telegram states:

ON 9/21/43, DURING DISCUSSIONS ON THE GENERAL SITUATION [daily meetings usually held in Hitler's office in the evening[34]] THE QUESTION WAS ASKED AS TO WHAT SHOULD BE DONE WITH THE INTERNED DANISH TROOPS. . . . THE REICHSFÜHRER S.S. REQUESTED FROM THE FÜHRER THAT THE 4,000 YOUNG SOLDIERS BE TRANSFERRED TO HIM. HE INTENDS TO TRANSFER THEM TO GERMANY AND HOLD THEM NEAR THE GERMAN DIVISION, IN THE HOPE THAT A LARGE NUMBER OF THEM WILL BE ATTRACTED TO THE S.S. . . . THE FÜHRER AGREED. ANOTHER ORDER OF THE FÜHRER GIVEN A FEW DAYS AGO [reference is to termination of the state of emergency] IS HEREBY CANCELLED. THE FOREIGN MINISTER HAS INSTRUCTED ME TO PASS THE ABOVE ON TO YOU FOR YOUR PERSONAL INFORMATION ONLY.[35]

It may be assumed that this news struck Best like a thunderbolt. He was keenly aware that there was almost nothing so calculated to incite the Danes as the transfer of Danish citizens to Germany. They had resisted this move in every case in which an underground fighter had been caught and tried, and every single instance of this sort had caused unrest and anger among the population. The thought that four thousand young soldiers, guilty of no offense, who had been interned in defiance of the agreement signed at the time between Germany and Denmark, would be transferred to Germany so that they might be coerced into the S.S.—such an eventuality spelled the destruction of any chance of arriving at some sort of settlement with the Danes. The combination of this measure and the persecution of the Jews would mean the establishment of a regime of force in Denmark like those in the other occupied countries. From this point on, all Best's efforts were devoted to canceling both these decrees, and they are always referred to in conjunction with one another. It must be said to Best's credit that he succeeded in frustrating both of them—and it was not the simplest thing in the world to frustrate a project of Himmler's.[36]

The military commander received the same orders in Jodl's well-known telegram of September 22, which stated:

(1) REICHSFÜHRER S.S. HAS RECEIVED PERMISSION TO RECRUIT VOL- UNTEERS FROM AMONG FORMER MEMBERS OF THE DANISH ARMY AND TO TRANSFER UP TO 4,000 OF THE YOUNGER AGE GROUPS TO S.S. CAMPS IN THE REICH; (2) THE DEPORTATION OF THE JEWS WILL BE CARRIED OUT BY THE REICHSFÜHRER S.S. WHO HAS TRANSFERRED TWO POLICE BATTALIONS TO DENMARK FOR THIS PURPOSE; (3) THE MILITARY STATE OF EMERGENCY WILL CONTINUE AT LEAST UNTIL THE COMPLETION OF THE OPERATIONS REFERRED TO IN PARAGRAPHS (1) AND (2). A SPECIAL ORDER WILL BE ISSUED WITH REGARD TO ITS TERMINATION. (4) THE PLENIPOTENTIARY OF THE REICH HAS RE- CEIVED A NOTICE IN SIMILAR VEIN FROM THE FOREIGN MINISTRY.[37]

On that same day Himmler had a talk with Keitel on these problems, and it may be assumed that Jodl sent the telegram following this talk.[38] In reaction to this order headquarters in Denmark telephoned to OKW and tried to have the edict revoked.[39] The arguments of the com- mander in Denmark were as follows:

(1) Annulment of the demobilization order would be re- garded by the Danes as a broken promise (wortbruch). This fact would complicate relations with the civil administration and the Danish police. (At the side of this paragraph

Keitel wrote "must find pretext for breaking promise.")

(2) Deportation of the Jews during the state of emergency would harm the public prestige of the army. Instead of the order given, headquarters in Denmark suggested that the deportation be carried out after the state of emergency was lifted, and on the sole responsibility of the Reich chargé d'affaires, since "as this is a political matter, participation of the army is not beneficial." (The reader of this report drew a heavy line through the part about prestige and wrote in the margin, "Nonsense, there are only practical necessities."

The report goes on to say that if operations 1 and 2 of Jodl's telegram are insisted upon, suspension of meat and fat supplies to the Reich must be reckoned with. Keitel wrote on the paper on September 23 "No change!" On the same day he sent a telegram to headquarters in Denmark, with copies to the foreign minister and to Himmler.[40] The same telegram, which is the official answer to the telephone conversation, states that the operations are to be carried out as outlined in Jodl's telegram. The pretext to be given the Danes for postponement of demobilization will be acts of sabotage—until Himmler has enrolled his four thousand recruits. The Danes are to be told that the recruits are being taken to Germany for an explanatory course on the destructive propaganda of the Communists and the dangers inherent in bolshevism. The deportation of the Jews is to be carried out by Berger, Himmler's confidant.

In fact Berger was only given the task of getting the four thousand recruits. Since he was unable to travel to Copenhagen personally he sent two of his men. Best was able to persuade them that the operation was undesirable and together with him they drafted the letter which convinced Berger that the implementation of Himmler's proposal was not even to his own advantage. One of the main arguments was that all the young recruits were farmers' sons and that the whole operation was liable to have immediate negative

results on the supply situation, for the agricultural population would at once rise up in protest.[41] Both the army and
Best expressed their opposition to the drafting of "volunteers" directly to their respective superiors.[42] As a result of
all these efforts Himmler finally gave up the idea, though
the problem did not fade out completely until the end of
the state of emergency following the Jewish persecutions.

The Final Decision

During the days when the German military command in
Denmark was attempting to prevent the enrollment of recruits to the S.S., Ribbentrop sought to impede implementation of the anti-Jewish action. On September 23 he presented a "note to the Führer"[43] with the intention of raising
doubts as to the desirability of the deportation and, should
Hitler refuse to budge, insuring that the operation would
take place during the state of emergency. Ribbentrop used
the arguments developed by Best in his telegrams, mainly
in No. 1032 and No. 1094 (on September 18).[44] At the
same time, Ribbentrop presented Hitler with Best's reply
on the practical methods of action, as given in telegram
1032. This note of Ribbentrop's is one of the two documents
responsible for Best's exoneration from blame for the Jewish deportations, which he obtained in his appeal to the
District Court in Copenhagen. The court was of the opinion
that the note proved that Hitler had not previously seen
Best's telegram and that it could not therefore have been
Best who sparked the persecutions.[45]

It would appear that Ribbentrop was genuinely anxious
and feared the probable political consequences of persecution of the Danish Jews. He was also doubtless aware of the
threat inherent in the transfer of troops to Himmler in
Germany. It was not unlikely that he feared the loss of his
control over Denmark. The persecution of the Jews might
mean that the center of gravity would shift to Himmler

and to the subordinates who would carry it out.[46] This danger was also evident from a discussion at that time on the appointment of a commander for the police battalions which were then arriving in Denmark. As we have seen, Best's expectations were not fulfilled and Pancke was appointed instead. Himmler did not want the battalions to be subordinated to Best and he apparently obtained Hitler's immediate approval of Pancke's appointment.[47] Ribbentrop, who had no choice in the matter, afterward pretended that he too was against having the battalions under Best's command.[48] Whatever Ribbentrop's motives were, the conclusion should not be drawn that the contents of the celebrated telegram were not previously known to Hitler. The constant repetition of arguments is, after all, a well-known method of persuasion.

Hitler at any rate was not impressed by Ribbentrop's arguments and on the same day decided that the deportations would take place as planned. He was not convinced that deportation of the Jews would lead to a worsening of the political situation in Denmark. He did, however, agree that the persecutions should be carried out during the state of emergency (see comments in margin of Ribbentrop's note). Ribbentrop's anxiety was also evident in the order sent to the Foreign Ministry in his name on September 25 which states that the deportations are to be carried out "in accordance with the Führer's orders" but that every effort should be made to prevent unnecessary incitement of the Danish population. Thadden passed this order on to Müller of the RSHA on September 28 and added that the operation was to be carried out in close cooperation with the plenipotentiary of the Reich.[49] The same day Best received the final order to implement the action and to announce "when the transfer can begin."[50]

Duckwitz relates that Best was on that day extremely depressed and even let slip a remark that he would like to build a bridge over the Sound by which the Jews could

Jul ō 2A45g

Notiz für den Führer.

Betr.: Judenaktion in Dänemark. *soll, wie be-
fohlen durchgeführt werden.*

Gemäss der Weisung des Führers, dass der Abtrans-
port der Juden aus Dänemark durchgeführt werden soll,
wurde Dr.Best zunächst ersucht, über die Art der
Durchführung des Abtransports der Juden sowie über die
Zahl der für die Aktion erforderlichen zusätzlichen
Polizeikräfte genaue Angaben zu machen.

Dr.Best hat berichtet, dass er zur Durchführung
der Judenaktion zusätzlich 50 Beamte der Sicherheitspolizei benötige. Eine Vermehrung der Ordnungspolizei
sei nicht erforderlich, da bereits Verstärkungen vorge-
sehen seien. Für den Abtransport der Juden aus Gross-
Kopenhagen werde ein Schiff benötigt, dass mindestens
5.000 Personen fassen müsse. Im übrigen könne der Abtransport der restlichen 2.000 Juden in Eisenbahnzügen
erfolgen.   K211115

Dr.Best hat noch darauf hingewiesen, dass die
Durchführung der Judenaktion die politische Lage in
Dänemark wesentlich verschärfen werde. Man dürfe dann
nicht mehr damit rechnen, eine verfassungsmässige
Regierung in nächster Zeit bilden zu können. Es könn-

H322364   te

                                 D 524771

- 2 -

te zu Unruhen und gegebenenfalls zum Generalstreik
kommen. Möglicherweise würde der König und der Reichstag ihre weitere Mitwirkung an der Regierung des Lan-
des einstellen, vielleicht danke der König auch ganz
ab.

   Im Hinblick auf die Bedenken des Reichsver-
treters in Dänemark bitte ich um Weisung, ob der Führer die Judenaktion jetzt durchgeführt zu sehen
wünscht. Bejahendenfalls wäre es dann richtig, die
Aktion noch während des Ausnahmezustandes vorzu-
nehmen.

Westfalen, den 23.September 1943.

K211116

H322365

D 524772

Ribbentrop's note to Hitler emphasizing the dangers involved in the action
against the Jews. (*From the files of the German Foreign Office, microfilm
Yad Vashem.*)

escape to Sweden.[51] Ekblad—also with Duckwitz as the source—adds that Best even contemplated suicide. He says that Best returned that day from another visit to Hitler, where the Führer vented his spleen on him because of non-implementation of the action against the Jews. No other source, not even Best's diary, mentions this second journey and it is doubtful whether it ever took place.[52] In any case, it is certain that Best's position at the time was almost hopeless: not only did the order to transfer four thousand soldiers to Germany threaten the whole future of his rule in Denmark, but it was now also his mission to carry out an immediate deportation of the Jews. In order to implement both projects he and Hanneken had to inform the Danes officially that lifting of the state of emergency and demobilization of the troops had been postponed for the time being owing to "railway sabotage." This resulted in great disappointment and indignation throughout Denmark.[53]

It was feared that both actions might lead to disturbances, and it was doubtful whether the Danish authorities, under the leadership of the ministerial officials on the one hand and the German police at Best's disposal on the other, could keep the situation under control. In a telegram dated September 29[54] Best writes: "THE ANGER OF THE POPULATION WILL EXPRESS ITSELF IN A WAY THAT WILL OBLIGE US TO USE STRONGER GERMAN FORCES. I ESTIMATE THAT IT WILL BE NECESSARY TO TREBLE THE POLICE FORCE PUT AT MY DISPOSAL."[55]

To all these troubles was added the friction between Best and Hanneken. As stated, the army was also opposed to the two operations. German naval headquarters in Denmark was particularly unenthusiastic. It hoped to enroll volunteers for the German navy from among the Danish soldiers interned on August 29. After receiving the information and orders regarding deportation of the Jews, it seemed to the German admiralty in Denmark that this action would nullify any such possibility. On September 24 the daily orders of naval headquarters contained the following:

The head of naval warfare reports from "Admiral Denmark" that the release of the Danish army—which was the prerequisite for the enrollment of volunteers for the navy and was fixed for September 27—has been postponed for the time being, since the plenipotentiary of the Reich has suddenly raised the question of the deportation of Jews from Denmark. [Notice is then given of Hitler's decision regarding four thousand troops for Himmler.] For the navy this means the necessity over a long period of supplying German crews to the coastal patrol fleet of the Big Belt. Minesweeping in the North Sea and off the coast of Jutland, which will be of the utmost importance with the advent of the autumn storms, will thus not be carried out on the scale required. Productivity in Danish shipyards will decrease more and more.[56]

On the same subject we find an announcement dated September 26 to the effect that it will only be possible to recruit the five or six hundred men needed for the navy after early release and demobilization and after a certain period of calm. Moreover, "any further political tension will lead to an indefinite postponement of the enrollment of volunteers." So much for the navy. General headquarters adds that the military commander in Denmark has in the meantime expressed his agreement with the views of the navy but that a decision has to be awaited from the OKW.[57] It has been seen that the army wished to postpone the pogrom until after the state of emergency was over, in order to lay the responsibility on Best. Moreover, on the eve of the projected deportations an open quarrel erupted between Best and the army, with repercussions reaching as far as Hitler.

Dr. Best's plan at the beginning of the month included a proposal that field intelligence should be attached to the police battalions under his command. In his statement on deportation of the Jews Best also pointed out that military participation would be necessary. Under pressure from Best the Foreign Ministry began on September 19 to investigate the possibility of transferring field intelligence to his authority.[58] Even before any decision was reached, Best demanded that the army place field intelligence and other forces at his disposal in order to carry out the deportations —but the army refused. Best complained of this to Ribbentrop on September 29 in a telegram signed simply "Best."[59]

The complaint did indeed reach Hitler, as Best had intended, and Keitel was at once questioned on the matter, but he of course denied the allegation and talked of a misunderstanding. Ribbentrop reported this to Best on September 30.[60] Best complied with the minister's request to clarify the source of the misunderstanding and replied in telegram No. 1175 dated October 1.[61] He based his response on information from Oberst von Engelmann, head of German intelligence in Denmark, who had at first received an order from OKW not to take part in the action against the Jews. However, afterward—on October 1—this order was canceled and replaced by new instructions to the effect that the military police and field intelligence were to support the security police.

On the day (September 30) that the matter was brought before Hitler, Thadden rushed off an "express letter" to Eichmann (whose deputy, Rolf Günther, was in Copenhagen planning the operation) requesting him also to use his influence and persuade the OKW to lift its veto and support the police action.[62] All that Hanneken eventually did was to send fifty troops to seal off the section of the port from which the ship *Wartheland* was supposed, on October 2, to transport the deportees to Stettin. Best failed therefore in his efforts to lay the responsibility for the deportation on the army or even to have it participate to any important degree; nor was he able to exploit the situation to gain control of field intelligence. The Jewish operation was in fact—and the Danish people regarded it as such—an operation of the security police battalions called to Denmark for this purpose.

Developments can thus be summed up as follows: On September 17 Best received the official and affirmative reply to his telegram No. 1032, in which he proposed deportation of the Jews. At the same time the army suggested that the state of emergency be lifted within seven days. Best, however, requested postponement of this step since he had not managed to prepare and consolidate his authority in Denmark: the police battalions were only beginning to arrive; the other powers he considered essential had not yet been approved; the nature of the regime after the state of emergency also had not been determined. Best was not even sure that it would consist (as he hoped) of the concentration of administration in the hands of the ministerial department heads—led by Svenningsen—and not of some sort of political regime (such as Social Democrats or, even worse, Nazis, who would receive their orders directly from Himmler). And then the last motive: if the deportation of the Jews were inevitable it must be pushed through under the state of emergency, so that the army would participate and take upon itself the main measure of reprobation.

Attempts to prevent the deportations followed fast on one another, some upon Best's initiative and others with his approval. The participants in these efforts were all those responsible for German rule in Denmark: the Gestapo head (Mildner), the civil director (Kanstein), the army commander (Hanneken), and of course Duckwitz, acting on his own authority but in fact above all else with Best's direct encouragement. These attempts met with complete refusal by the central authorities, and even Ribbentrop himself, who had been among those trying to prevent the action, could do nothing.

It now seems that Himmler was the center of this opposition. He was interested in the Danish complications and wished to exploit them for his own ends. He wished to take under his wing four thousand young Danish recruits, now interned, and transfer them to Germany instead of demobilizing them. Then Best and the army united in an attempt to head off this new calamity, though this did not prevent their conflict over the deportation of the Jews, for which the army—correctly—held Best responsible. The armed forces in Denmark (in particular the navy) were firmly opposed to the action against the Jews and endeavored to avoid participating in it. Only Best's intrigue, which had brought the matter to Hitler's attention, forced the OKW to order Hanneken to take part. The general, however, made sure that this part was as restricted as he could make it.

On September 28, the final order to carry out both "assignments"—deportation of the Jews and transfer of the recruits—arrived in Copenhagen. The same day it was announced that the lifting of the state of emergency and the release of the Danish troops had been postponed for the time being. And the same afternoon Duckwitz informed the Social Democratic leaders of the planned deportation of the Jews and of its practical details.

Deportation—A Plan Goes Wrong

In reply to the telegram informing him of the final decision Best indicated on that same September 28 that the deportations could be effected "during this week—probably between October 1 and 2."[63] The exact date depended upon the arrival of the ship that had been ordered. It was intended to complete the action in the course of one night. What is interesting about this telegram is that Best writes as if on behalf of the chief of security police, Mildner, and merely gives the date on which the latter will carry out the deportation order. Best further emphasizes that Mildner

is acting on orders received from the head of the central
security police. Clearly Best wishes to show that he is not
directly involved. After the war he again tried in his various
statements of evidence to prove that he was merely an outside observer.[64] Yet as already mentioned, on the next day
(September 29) he intervened actively to insure the participation of the army. In general, however, his intervention was largely designed to sabotage the action, as we
shall see below.

Immediately after proclamation of the state of emergency,
on August 31, the minutes of the Jewish community's executive committee were confiscated from the office of the secretary, the attorney Arthur Henriques.[65] Svenningsen, who
visited Best that evening, asked him about the incident.
He replied that the minutes contained membership lists of
the Jewish community and that the action had caused consternation among the Jews, who regarded it as the prelude
to further measures against themselves. Svenningsen relates
further that Best denied knowing anything of all this and
said that he had not occupied himself at all with the Jewish
problem. The Germans afterward claimed that the action
was carried out by Danish Nazis.[66] The confiscation of the
lists was not the only anti-Jewish act perpetrated at that
time. Among those interned at the outbreak of the crisis
were a few Jews, among them the Chief Rabbi, Dr. Friediger, and the chairman of the synagogue, Axel Margolinsky.
They were taken to the internment camp at Horserød,
where they remained until the raids of October 1, and were
later among those deported to Theresienstadt.[67]

An operation of wider scope was carried out on September 17, the day after the deportation decision at Hitler's
headquarters. This time it was the German police who appeared early in the morning with a huge truck outside the
community center in Ny Kongensgade. They had first seized
the librarian of the community, Josef Fischer, at prayer in
the synagogue, and taken him with them to the community

offices. Fischer states in his evidence[68] that the German police searched quite openly for lists of members of the community, but in fact took with them only an old card index; they happened not to open a safe which contained the most up-to-date card index.[69] According to Svenningsen's report, he immediately made an inquiry to the authorities. The Germans again furnished an evasive and, as it were, reassuring reply. They admitted that the action was carried out by the German police but stated that it had no connection whatsoever with the Jewish problem, that the investigation did not concern the Jewish community as such but was directed at finding material on anti-German activity; and no action against the Jews was planned.

It may be assumed that the incident and its timing were no mere coincidences. We know that the Germans had long since prepared material on the Jewish population.[70] Evidence on this point was also given during the Copenhagen investigation by one Hans Karl Ingver Hermannsen, as follows:

After September 15, when the Gestapo and security police had been established in Copenhagen, the witness [Hermannsen] was head of the Gestapo's department 1A, where his duties included action against communism, Marxism, extremist movements, and hostile propaganda. Up to that time the witness was in charge of a comprehensive card index which included, among other things, the names and addresses of the Jews in Denmark. Under the new arrangement, however, the Jewish cards were removed and transferred to Criminal Advisor Bunke in department B4.[71]

Practical preparations for the action against the Jews were therefore begun on the 15th after Hoffmann's arrival. His statement about his first activities in Copenhagen[72] includes the following:

A day or two afterward he was called to Best who informed him that an action against the Jews of Denmark would now be carried out and that he and his staff were to prepare the ground by drawing up lists of Jews to be deported. Best said that the basic material for such lists was to be found in Hermannsen's department.

Why then did the Germans pay their visit to the offices of the community? Let us even assume that they needed to complement or correct the lists (it would appear that they previously had card indexes and only now did they prepare lists); still, it should have been obvious that a sudden invasion of the community offices would serve as a warning to both the Jews and the Danes. It is well known that the Germans in their searches for Jews everywhere were particularly careful to employ reassuring and diversionary tactics, and a fortnight before the Jews were rounded up, the Nazis everywhere would have avoided any public confiscation of community lists. There is no doubt that the likes of Best and Hoffmann were conversant with the tactics used on such occasions. Among the reasons Best afterward gave for the failure of the action was that for a whole month rumors were rife among the population that the Germans were planning to deport the Jews, who thus had an opportunity to escape.[73] The possibility should not be discarded that this action—like many actions of Best's in that period—had a double objective: to attain further or complementary material on the Jews but also, and perhaps mainly, to warn both the Danes and the Jews. The action did serve as a warning, at any rate.

In this connection it is interesting that Best himself included in his personal defense material the assertion that his wish to carry out, during the state of emergency, the deportations he had been unable to prevent was motivated by the consideration that the new police forces which had recently arrived would not be sufficiently familiar with Danish conditions to act in an effective manner.[74] It may be that on the one hand he used the police battalions to in-

sure his own status and on the other took the above possibility into account. It will be recalled that Mildner's attempts to have the decision reversed were unsuccessful.
Hoffmann states that Mildner told him after his return from
Berlin that "Müller took up a neutral stand and did not
support Mildner."[75] Moreover, a short while after Mildner's
return and about a week before the persecutions Rolf
Günther, Eichmann's deputy, and two assistants arrived in
Copenhagen to organize the operation.[76] It was apparently
feared in the RSHA that after Mildner had tried to prevent
the action, he would not organize the operation with the
devotion required, and one of the "specialists" in this type
of work was therefore called in.[77]

A particularly interesting chapter is the story of the
manipulations through which the Germans in Denmark,
led by Best and Mildner, succeeded in undermining Günther's efforts. The latter shut himself in a special office for
the purpose of planning the action with the help of the
material previously prepared. Finally the operational plan
was submitted to Mildner for approval at a special meeting.
Here we are confronted with the unique situation of
Eichmann's agents having to work not only without any
support from the local population and authorities, including
the police—all of whom were known as determined opponents of the persecutions—but also meeting passive resistance
from the various German authorities. One of the decisive
tactics of this sort was the resolution carried by Mildner
and Hoffmann at the above-mentioned meeting. This stated
that the German police were forbidden to open the apartments of the Jews by force, since such violent entry and
the thefts that were liable to follow would disgrace the
Germans in the eyes of the Danes.[78] This order was to have
far-reaching effects. One Jewish family, for instance, only
heard about the night's happenings from Danish neighbors
the following morning, since they had not heard the door-

bell ring when the Gestapo came to arrest them during the night of October 1–2.[79]

If Best really intended to warn the Jewish and the Danish populations by confiscating the papers in the community office on September 17, then he achieved his object. From then on rumors of approaching persecution of the Jews increased constantly.[80] There were also some Jews who began to leave their homes during that time. Best himself stated that this was confirmed by the cross-examination of Jews seized.[81] One Jew relates that he fled on the 23rd and hid in the home of Danish acquaintances where he was captured, apparently through an informer. In his cross-examination by the Gestapo he was asked the source of rumors of the deportations, what he knew about the escape routes to Sweden, and similar questions.[82] Together with the rash of rumors, the word went round by word of mouth that Best was not interested in deporting the Jews but that he might be forced to do so against his will.[83]

In his official contacts with the Danes, Best of course denied any knowledge of this project and stated that in no circumstances would such an action take place. To the Bishop of Copenhagen, Fuglsang-Damgaard, who expressed his anxiety at the rumors, Best declared that persecution of the Jews in Denmark would take place only over his dead body.[84] Similar reassuring statements were made by him and by Kanstein to the Danish authorities. These promises were so convincing that Svenningsen felt himself entitled to tell the chairman of the Jewish community, C. B. Henriques, who approached him on the 25th, that there was no foundation to the rumors. This assurance was in turn so convincing that Henriques, as is well known, did not at first believe that the politicians were speaking the truth when they came to warn him and through him the whole community.[85] Duckwitz, however, did not stop at the warning he gave to the Danish statesmen on the

28th. On the next day he went to the Danish Foreign Ministry and asked to see Svenningsen. Svenningsen was not available, so Duckwitz gave the information to the head of the political department, Frants Hvass.[86] Svenningsen himself received the news from Henriques who relates: "The next day [September 29] I of course went to the Foreign Ministry and informed Director Svenningsen of the warning. He was astounded at the news and said that he would have to call a meeting of departmental heads at once to see what could be done."

Now the authorities became indeed convinced of the true state of affairs and as a result of Svenningsen's meeting with the other department heads,[87] he and the director of the Ministry of Justice, Eivind Larsen, visited Best on the afternoon of the 29th. This meeting was described by Best in a telegram sent that same day, which is reproduced in full here, since it throws light on his tactics at the time. The cable ran as follows:[88]

I HAVE JUST [5 P.M. on September 29, 1943] HAD A VISIT FROM THE DIRECTOR OF THE DANISH FOREIGN MINISTRY, SVENNINGSEN, AND THE DIRECTOR OF THE MINISTRY OF JUSTICE, EIVIND LARSEN. SVENNINGSEN ASKED IF THE GERMANS INTEND TO DEPORT THE JEWS FROM DENMARK. THEY CLAIM THAT THE CITY OF COPENHAGEN IS FULL OF RUMORS OF A MOST CONCRETE NATURE, AND THE NIGHT OF OCTOBER 1–2 IS MENTIONED AS THE TIME OF THE ACTION. THEY ALSO CLAIM THAT SHIPS TO DEPORT THE JEWS HAVE ALREADY ARRIVED AT THE PORT OF COPENHAGEN. THESE RUMORS, THEY STATE, ARE LIABLE TO CAUSE CONSIDERABLE UNREST AMONG THE DANISH POPULATION. THE FULFILLMENT OF THE ACTION AGAINST THE JEWS WILL STRIKE AT THE MOST SENSITIVE POINT OF THE DANISH CONCEPTION OF JUSTICE AND WILL HAVE UNPREDICTABLE CONSEQUENCES. SVENNINGSEN THEREFORE WISHES TO KNOW IF THE GERMANS INDEED INTEND TO DEPORT THE JEWS. A DENIAL, WHICH HE WILL OF COURSE NOT PUBLISH, WILL UNDOUBTEDLY REASSURE AND FACILITATE THE WORK OF THE DANISH ADMINISTRATION.

I REPLIED THAT THE DENIAL REQUESTED ENTAILS A POLITICAL OB-

LIGATION WHICH I AM NOT AUTHORIZED TO UNDERTAKE WITHOUT
INSTRUCTIONS FROM THE GOVERNMENT OF THE REICH. I PROMISED
TO REPORT THE TALK TO BERLIN AND TO GIVE THEM A REPLY LATER.

THE FACT IS THAT SINCE THE PROCLAMATION OF A STATE OF
EMERGENCY AND PARTICULARLY DURING THE LAST FEW DAYS AN
ATTACK ON THE JEWS IS ANTICIPATED IN COPENHAGEN AND PEOPLE
ARE DISCUSSING IT. HOW IT IS THAT CORRECT DETAILS (DATE OF THE
ACTION AND ARRIVAL OF THE SHIP) HAVE LEAKED OUT, IT IS IM-
POSSIBLE TO SAY. WHEN I WAS FACED WITH LACK OF CAUTION (SUCH
AS TALK BY MEMBERS OF THE POLICE BATTALION THAT THEY HAD
BEEN TRANSFERRED FROM NORWAY FOR ACTION AGAINST THE JEWS)
I PUT A STOP TO IT AT ONCE.

Transparent here is Best's desire to stress once again the
dangers inherent in the deportation action and to prepare
excuses for himself and cover for anticipated failure. Svenningsen also refers to the meeting in his notes. His report
confirms the content of Best's reply as repeated in the telegram. Nevertheless, it would seem that the two Danish
officials had the impression from Best's replies that the
rumors were true and that the persecutions were planned.
They thought, however, that Best would make another
effort to prevent the action.[89] Best thus succeeded in making
the desired impression on the Danes that he was doing
everything possible to prevent the calamity.

During all this time the questions of the release of the
Danish soldiers and the cancellation of the state of emergency continued to be the subjects of talks and telegrams.
Interesting in this connection was the approach to Best of
the chairman of the Red Cross in Denmark, Helmer Rosting,
who proposed a sort of "barter arrangement," namely, to
release the Danish troops a few at a time and in their
place to arrest the Jews and intern them in camps. Best
reported on this suggestion at length and laid special emphasis on Rosting's prediction that the farmers' sons would
be bitterly disappointed if they were not released now, as
had been promised them a few days previously.[90] The pro-

posal was rejected by Ribbentrop on the grounds that the deportation of the Jews had to be carried out in one swoop and not gradually.[91] The personality of Rosting (who originally came from Danzig) was quite shadowy. It is not surprising that in Denmark there should be someone capable of suggesting such a plan, but it is surprising that he should be the representative of the Red Cross. The notion of interning the Jews in a camp in Denmark was discussed that same September 29th by the directors of the ministries, as we shall see below.

Yet it would appear that Rosting's plan suggested to Best a way of insuring the release of the Danish troops and of annulling the state of emergency. On October 1 he sent a cable to Ribbentrop announcing that:

(1) The arrest of the Jews would take place on the night of October 1–2 and they would be sent from Seeland by boat and from the rest of the country by special train.

(2) He would not announce the operation in the press or radio.

(3) Failing other instructions he would leave Jewish property intact in order to avoid accusations that the object of the operation was plunder.

The fourth point in the telegram runs as follows:

THE NEGATIVE EFFECTS OF THE ANTI-JEWISH ACTION CAN BE RADICALLY MOLLIFIED IF IT IS ANNOUNCED TOMORROW, 10/2/43, IN THE PRESS AND RADIO THAT THE INTERNED DANISH SOLDIERS WILL BE RELEASED GRADUALLY IN THE NEXT FEW DAYS. THIS WILL SHOW THAT THE GERMANS DO NOT—AS HAS BEEN SAID HERE IN RECENT DAYS—DEAL WITH THE JEWS AS THEY DO WITH THE FARMERS' SONS BY DEPORTING BOTH GROUPS EQUALLY; THE RESPONSIBILITY FOR THE DIFFICULTIES CREATED IN DENMARK SHOULD BE PLACED FIRST AND FOREMOST ON THE JEWS WHO WILL HAVE BEEN DEALT WITH ACCORDINGLY. I THEREFORE REQUEST, SUBJECT TO THE AGREEMENT OF THE MILITARY COMMANDER IN DENMARK, PERMISSION TO ANNOUNCE HERE TOMORROW IN THE PRESS AND RADIO THAT THE RELEASE OF

THE DANISH SOLDIERS (THERE IS NO NEED FOR THE PRESENT TO MEN-
TION THE OFFICERS) WILL BEGIN IN THE NEXT FEW DAYS.

A similar telegram was sent to OKW by Hanneken with
the additional comment "I AGREE ENTIRELY WITH DR. BEST'S
SUGGESTION IN PARAGRAPH 4." On Hanneken's cable form
these notes appear in the margin: "Does the *Reichsführer*
S.S. know?" and the reply "*Reichsführer* S.S. knows and
agrees" and below them "The Führer agrees," signed "J"
(apparently Jodl).[92]

In his defense statement Best claimed that he exploited
the Jewish operation to bring about the demobilization of
the Danish army, and in view of the documents mentioned
above this would appear to be correct. The plan for transferring the four thousand troops was abandoned.[93] In his
Nuremberg declaration Best explained that it was Hitler
who demanded that the release of the troops be coupled
with the action against the Jews.[94] Here, as with the proposal to carry out the persecutions, the final decision did
indeed come from Hitler, but again the initiative was Best's;
he himself linked the two subjects, as we have seen above.
This was the background of the idiotic announcement broadcast on the day after the night of persecutions:

As a result of measures taken by the German authorities, the
Jews have been removed from public life and prevented from
continuing to poison the atmosphere, for it is they who have to a
considerable degree been responsible for the deterioration of the
situation in Denmark through anti-German incitement and moral
and material support for acts of terror and sabotage. In the next
few days, in response to the inquiries of large sections of the
Danish population, release of the interned Danish soldiers will
begin and will continue at a rate corresponding to the technical
possibilities.[95]

This announcement aroused a storm no less violent than
the deportation itself. The interned Danish military and

naval commanders announced that they and their troops refused to be released at the expense of the Jews and regarded the suggestion as a slur on their honor. Everyone in Denmark knew that the announcement was a lie; to the injury of the Jewish persecutions had been added the insult that the Danes were expected to believe that the Jews were responsible for the situation.[96] At that time the Danes did not understand that this announcement was mainly intended not for their ears but for the ears of Hitler and Himmler. This is made clear from a telegram[97] sent by Best on that critical October 2 which stated: "SO FAR, THE FIRST DAY AFTER THE ACTION AGAINST THE JEWS HAS SHOWN THAT THE ANNOUNCEMENT ON THE EARLY RELEASE OF THE INTERNED DANISH TROOPS HAS INDEED TOTALLY SILENCED ALL THE UNDESIRABLE REACTIONS OF THE DANISH POPULATION AGAINST THE JEWISH OPERATION. COMPLETE QUIET REIGNS IN THE COUNTRY." Best was no doubt fully aware that this was just as much a lie as his official announcement given above, both of which were aimed mainly at Hitler. Best was the prisoner of the regime he served and of his own tactics.[98]

The opposition of the Danish people to the deportation of the Jews was clearly expressed even before the action itself, and the protests of the public, organizations, and well-known personalities began to reach Best one after the other. Best reported two of them to the Foreign Ministry. One was from the king and the other came from the chairman of the central economic organizations; they presented their protests on September 30.[99] This latter protest was of special importance since, as we have seen, negotiations were then in progress on the renewal of Danish supplies to Germany, and supply was of central significance: to the Germans because they needed it and to the Danes because they knew the Germans needed it.

During the fateful days after September 20 (on the 22nd,

to be precise), Best telephoned to Berlin with a view to expediting the preparations for renewal of the agreement which was due to expire on the 30th of the month. Though it so happened that this was the date of expiration, it was no coincidence that Best devoted so much time to the problem amid all the many other urgent developments. He was keenly conscious of the fact that possibly no greater weapon of persuasion was at hand in his efforts to mold the situation in Denmark to his liking than the successful conclusion of talks on the new agreement. The need for maintaining supplies from Denmark runs like a thread through all the reports, telegrams, and arguments of those decisive days—not only of Best but also of the army and of Himmler's representatives. Negotiations were concluded on October 1, on the eve of the action against the Jews, and the agreement was signed the next morning, following the roundup during the night. Best reported the success in the last paragraph of telegram 1191 in which he told of the complete quiet that reigned in Denmark after the action.[100] On October 3 he sent Ribbentrop a special memorandum in which he pointed out how much Danish supplies would increase on the basis of the agreement just signed. "The figures again show how important the maintenance of an intact Danish economy is to German food supplies."[101] All this was of course designed to blunt the assault that was bound to come from leading German circles in the wake of the failure of the Jewish deportation. It is quite possible that Best also wanted the Jewish action postponed until the economic negotiations had been terminated.

The head of the German economic mission was O. van Scherpenberg.[102] He, and indeed the other members of the delegation, were not Nazis and belonged to that broad stratum of officials who worked in the German ministries with certain internal reservations as to the Nazis and their practices. This attitude was known not only to Best but also to the Danes, and it was no mere chance that both

Best and Svenningsen felt they had to talk to Scherpenberg about the Jewish action planned to take place at the same time as the economic negotiations. Best strove to appear before the delegation as an opponent of the persecutions,[103] and Svenningsen wished to express the reaction of the Danish authorities to the persecutions and their evaluation of the situation.[104] Best spoke with the members of the delegation before the deportation, in order to prove that he shared their views but that he was forced to carry out Hitler's orders. Svenningsen, on the other hand, spoke to Scherpenberg after the successful conclusion of the talks in order to take advantage of the opportunity of explaining the Danish protest to a German known not to be a Nazi.

Scherpenberg even relates that most of the Germans he met in Copenhagen were deeply depressed (the incorrigible Nazis excepted).

Without knowing what to expect they talked openly of the danger involved in the persecution of the Jews, and the bolder among them were so free in their pronouncements that I afterward often wondered whether those Jews who were seized in Denmark were not themselves to blame, for there could not have been one Jew left who did not know that he had to go into hiding.

This evaluation was doubtless exaggerated, and seeks to attach some of the blame to the Jews, but it was typical of the general atmosphere that prevailed at the time.

The Action and Its Failure

Many of the Jews indeed took the warning to heart and began to seek means of protecting their lives and property. One of them recalls:[105]

During September the rumors increased and became more and more concrete. On Monday, September 27, I felt it necessary to inform the personnel of my firm that we might have to leave the country. "Personally, I do not believe the rumors," I said, "but should it nevertheless be necessary, I would ask you to remain at your posts and carry on business as usual." I added that should they be in doubt as to how to act they should merely look at my empty chair, and after so many years of cooperation they would have no doubt as to my opinion in the matter.

On Tuesday the 28th my wife phoned and asked me to come home. L. L. was there on a visit. He had heard from a reliable source that on Friday evening the action against the Jews would take place. L. L. said he had heard this from a friendly German whose information was usually correct.

(This story shows—as do many others—that Duckwitz was not the only German who felt obliged to warn the Danes so that they could warn the Jews.)

The account goes on to say that through an acquaintance of an acquaintance Kanstein was approached as to the true position. At first he denied that the Jews were in any danger and that the whole affair had any interest for the Germans at the time. However, on the same evening he informed the man that the situation was now extremely grave.[106] The rumors were confirmed the next day. The Jew approached a Swedish priest who had always shown an interest in his family. The latter advised him to leave Denmark as quickly as possible and to try to obtain for this purpose a temporary Swedish passport; he promised personally to discuss the matter with the Swedish minister. "Pastor B. was quite extraordinary; his honest character was shaken by all the injustice being perpetrated and he boiled with rage. He worked tirelessly to help Jews as much as he could, and did not spare himself. We and many others are grateful to him for his support during our misfortune and his untiring help in those fateful days."

The pastor accompanied the family to the Swedish minister, who promised to do everything in his power and asked them to come back again at two o'clock. He also advised them not to sleep at home on Friday night. When they returned they found the office full of people asking, like themselves, for Swedish passports. Among other preparations our witness made on that day, he drew up a power of attorney making a Danish lawyer responsible for all his affairs. He and his family received their passports and now tried to obtain the German exit permit. In the meantime they were visited by friends and acquaintances, mostly Danes, who came to warn them or to say good-bye. They then journeyed to one of the suburbs of Copenhagen to sleep in a house put at their disposal by friends. With the help of Danish friends, they had packed their possessions, most of which were removed from the apartment for safekeeping. They made sure, however, that the apartment would not stand empty and left simple furniture behind, some of which was loaned by friends. To their intense disappointment they found they could not obtain the German permit. This was a deliberate step taken by Best, who apparently was not eager to help with "building a bridge to Sweden."[107] Their suitcases were packed, and they had thought to leave the country that same evening but they were now obliged to postpone their departure. Neither could they leave on the following day (October 1).

A number of precautionary measures were taken—the man decided not to walk anywhere but only to travel by car, and they also considered not using the phone. In fact, however, amid the general excitement these rules were not kept. The family, with their friends and acquaintances, held a gathering, people came and went, and there was a ceaseless arrival and departure of vehicles in front of the house. Everyone wanted to help or to say good-bye. Our witness recalls how people everywhere stood in the street and openly discussed the possibilities of leaving Denmark.

After all legal ways of reaching Sweden had been exhausted, the family returned to the suburban house on Friday evening. A new plan, whereby a Danish police car was to take them to the coast for embarkation to Sweden, was canceled since the deportation action had begun and German police cars were patrolling the streets. The son and daughter-in-law, who joined them later in the evening, had run into a German police patrol looking for Jews, but had managed to hide. Next day a call was put through—for safety's sake from a public telephone box—to their apartment to hear what had happened. The housemaid, who had remained, informed them that the Germans had been in the house but had not entered their apartment. That day they heard various stories about people who had been seized and taken to a ship anchored in the port. Their daughter and her husband, who had hidden elsewhere, were saved by a miracle. The Germans came to the house and questioned the owner about his Jewish wife. When he replied that she had died over a year previously, they said: "Anyone can say that," and refused to believe him until he showed them the receipt for payment of the burial expenses. They nevertheless searched the house and looked into various rooms, but somehow did not enter that very room where the couple, paralyzed with fright, were hiding. Our witness relates how he was so nervous that "I couldn't even read," and dared not even talk on the telephone. For several days further efforts were made to find a way of crossing to Sweden and friends continued to visit them and offer assistance. The escape was finally organized and they reached Sweden safely.

This description, given here in brief, is typical of many. The same or similar events occurred to thousands of people that night and in the days preceding and following it. Movement in the streets, telephone conversations—all these were more or less overt. Of course, some people were seized or betrayed. But those who did not run right into a German patrol engaged in searching for Jews were usually not captured.

Erling Foss has given an unequaled description of the night of persecutions.[108]

On the night of October 1, at ten o'clock, [he recalls] all telephone connections were cut off—the action would no doubt

begin shortly. Everywhere where there were doorplates with
Jewish names, the German police troops appeared. In villa
quarters they surrounded the houses. They did not take the sick
and even released those who could prove they were half-Jews.
Also those who were married to non-Jews were released. The
expression in the eyes of people brought aboard the two ships
was heartrending, according to reports from town. . . . It was the
Jewish Holy Days, the New Year for Jews, which were chosen,
when the orthodox Jewish families gathered together [the New
Year festival actually took place on Thursday, September 30
and Friday, October 1, and was followed at sunset by the Sab-
bath]. From the various assembly points police vans proceeded to
take up their position at certain spots, from where the arresting
columns were sent out. At the same time the telephone services
were completely suspended, so completely that even the flight
service and "emergency" were not functioning. Ritzau's Bureau
[the official Danish news agency] was occupied to insure that the
teleprinter was not used. . . . The roundup was carried out in
various ways—it is difficult to give a clear picture. Some patrols
were content merely to ring and to go away again if the door
was not opened. Elsewhere, and this occurred often, they
smashed in the door and woke up the whole house to cross-
examine people in the other apartments as to the whereabouts
of the Jews. . . . Danish-speaking people accompanied each
patrol. The most frightful scenes were played out, with whole
families being dragged away, and these produced anger among
the population deeper and more heartfelt than that aroused by
any previous action. People as old as ninety-two and babies two
months old were seized and put on board ship. Mrs. Texière,
the 102-year-old mother of the actor Jakob Texière, was among
those deported.

The old-age home next to the synagogue in Krystalgade was
surrounded by 150 men, and all the inmates, aged from sixty to
ninety, were taken away. The Germans behaved here with
incredible brutality. They burst into the room of an old lady
who was paralyzed and had been bedridden for eleven years,
and since she could not get up they bound her with leather
straps and dragged her to the synagogue, where all the old
people were assembled. Here they were cross-examined as to

their acquaintance with this or that saboteur and since it was only natural that they did not know any, they were beaten and kicked. From the synagogue, as from all the rooms, the Germans stole any valuables they could lay their hands on; and the German police troops relieved themselves in the synagogue.[109]

During the entire afternoon of that October 1 Svenningsen attempted in vain to see Best. The protest of the king had, however, been presented that day and Best hastened to pass it on to Berlin.[110] But this did not prevent the Germans from informing the Danes that "during the night they would arrest elements hostile to the Reich." Only close to midnight, when the operation was already fully under way, was Best ready to talk to Svenningsen, who was again accompanied by Eivind Larsen. In this meeting Best confirmed that the "elements hostile to the Reich" were the Jews and that they would be transferred to camps in Germany the next day. Svenningsen tried to prevent the deportation and gain time; he presented Best with a letter, written previously by hand, in which he suggested that the Jews caught be interned in Denmark by the Danish authorities.[111] Best replied that he could not make a decision but that he would pass on the proposal to Berlin. He also explained that the operation was directed only against "full Jews," and that half-Jews or Jews married to non-Jews would not be deported. Best also informed Svenningsen that the "problem of the interned soldiers would find its solution in connection with the action against the Jews." The order to delay their release would be rescinded and the army released gradually in the next few days. In keeping with this promise to Svenningsen, Best reported on the talk to Berlin by cable that same night,[112] and he added: "I convey Director-General Svenningsen's application and indicate in this connection that the boat will leave Copenhagen at 10 A.M. and the train from Aalborg at 11 A.M. For my part I will make no change in these transport arrangements." He was well aware that he would receive no counterorder from Berlin. The next morning at seven Best dispatched the telegram containing the text of the official communiqué.[113] In it he also:

(1) States that the action against the Jews was carried out without disturbance.

(2) Says that "As of today it will be possible to say that Denmark is free of Jews, since no Jew will be able to remain or operate here legally." We shall see below how Best afterward used this formulation to calm the storm that arose in Berlin after the failure of the action.

(3) Suggests a special regulation aimed apparently at insuring continuation of the operation and seizure of Jews who succeeded in escaping during the night. This ordinance was not published, and Best claimed later that this was due to Hanneken and Mildner.[114]

(4) Announces that in concert with the military commander an announcement will be published assuring the release of the Danish troops. He then gives the text of the announcement already quoted but adds that "care should be taken to exploit the propaganda value of the steps taken in the spirit expressed here."

According to Best, 202 persons were seized in Copenhagen during that night. This was clearly inadequate to fill a ship or the train assigned to take the Jews from the provinces to Germany. At noon on October 23 Best sent a telegram in Mildner's name intended for Eichmann's department in the RSHA.[115] Here he endeavored to correct somewhat the bad impression the failure was liable to make by pointing out that the Chief Rabbi was among those seized (he had in fact been under arrest since August 29) and that the vacant space on board ship had been filled by 150 Danish Communists who had been held in the Horserød camp since the beginning of the action against the Communists in the summer of 1941. With regard to the train, he sent a notice to Berlin in Hoffmann's name in which, "Since the results of the arrest action do not justify the dispatch of a train to the concentration camp Theresienstadt," he asks that the Jews sent by train be delayed at Kiel and be transferred to their destination at a favorable opportunity.[116] This train apparently contained 82 Jews, for the total number seized during the night was 284.[117]

To round out the picture, one more episode may be mentioned here, even though it had no direct impact on the events in Denmark. Helmuth von Moltke, one of the leaders of the German resistance movement,[118] heard of the imminent action in Denmark in his place of work, the German War Ministry. He found a pretext to travel to the Scandinavian countries and reached Copenhagen on October 1. There he contacted M. B., a woman who, together with her brother, was an old acquaintance of his. His plan was to warn the Danes of what was about to happen. On the morning after the night of the persecutions he went to her brother's house and said with radiant face: "I congratulate you on the wonderful result. He wanted six thousand and he got only a few hundred."[119] Obviously his warning, even if it had been the only one, would have come too late. What is important is that he knew that if the Danes were informed in advance they would do everything to save the Jews.

Excuses for the Fiasco

On October 3 official orders were received from OKW regarding the release of the Danish army and the lifting of the state of emergency on October 6.[120] The naval announcements of that day state that after the demobilization, attempts should be made to enroll Danes in the Schalburg Corps and for naval and military guard duties. It is noted, however, that "It is doubtful whether such recruitment has any chance of success after what has happened in the meantime."[121] For his part, Best added to the telegram in which he announced annulment of the state of emergency on

October 6: "I HAVE INFORMED BY WORD OF MOUTH THE
CENTRAL DANISH ADMINISTRATION, REPRESENTED BY THE DI-
RECTOR OF THE FOREIGN MINISTRY, SVENNINGSEN, THAT UPON
THE TERMINATION OF THE MILITARY EMERGENCY ALL GERMAN
INTERESTS IN DENMARK WITHOUT EXCEPTION WILL AGAIN BE
CONCENTRATED IN MY HANDS." To this he added his own
interpretations on his right to issue decrees.[122] From that
day, therefore, Best considered himself once more as the
sole governor of Denmark. From his struggle with Hanneken he had emerged triumphant. But restriction of his
authority now came from an apparently unexpected source
—from Himmler. Here he paid for his failure in the action
against the Jews—which had insured his position in the eyes
of the Danes. Best was quickly aware of the danger and he
did all that was possible to explain away the fiasco con-
vincingly.

The rumor about the failure of the action appears to
have spread very rapidly in leading German circles. Best
claimed that the orders had been given to inform only the
RSHA of the exact number of deportees,[123] "since it ordered
the action against the Jews." From various sources it was
reported that upon his hearing the results of the action
Hitler was seized by one of his paroxysms of rage.[124]
Whether this was the case or not, there is no doubt that
Eichmann and his deputy, Günther, who was formally
responsible for the operation, were all the more enraged
since they were powerless to do anything.[125] Something
unusual had happened to them: the Jews had slipped from
their very grasp and disappeared, so to speak, behind a
living wall raised by the Danish people in the space of one
night. Even at his trial Eichmann could not forget Best and
this failure of his.[126] In an interview with the journalist
Stassen, he said bluntly: "Denmark caused us more difficulties than anything else."[127] Thadden declared in his evidence that he had sought to warn Best of the gathering
storm.[128] Best replied to the telegram of warning on October

5 with telegram No. 1208 in which he summed up all his defense arguments, as follows:

(1) Dr. Mildner, "who gave all the orders," was responsible for the action.

(2) The apartments were not forced (this was one of the main complaints of the RSHA) because it was known that most of the Jews were not at home and "bursting into empty apartments would have made an undesirable impression and given rise to looting, for which we would have been blamed."

(3) His suggested ordinance had not been published.

(4) The small number seized (284) was the result of the night of the hunt only. In the following days additional Jews were captured.[129]

(5) Both the head of the S.D. and he, Best, had foreseen that only a few would be seized, and in support he refers to his telegrams wherein he stated this before the operation. He points out that the Jews had a whole month to prepare for flight "until the police forces arrived and it was possible to carry out the operation." Moreover, there were in Denmark inadequate police and military forces to keep watch on the coast, which stretches for hundreds of kilometers, and the German navy had neither sufficient boats nor coastguardsmen.

(6) He repeats the assertion made immediately after the action: "Since the practical object of the action against the Jews in Denmark was to cleanse the country of Jews and not to engage in headhunting to the greatest possible degree, it may be said that the operation achieved its goal. Denmark is purged of Jews [*Judenrein*], since no Jew affected by the regulations can remain or work here openly."

In other words, Mildner and not Best was responsible for the fiasco. It would appear that Himmler agreed, for Mildner was removed from Denmark three months later as a result of this failure.[130] It should, however, be remembered that he was not punished in any way but continued to work in the RSHA.[131] Further, Best was not to blame if the Jews had been given an opportunity to escape; or to put it differently, he had asked for police forces at the beginning of *September*. (This is an additional indication that in Best's eyes too the arrival of the police and the implementation of the pogrom were connected and interdependent.) Similarly, it was not Best's fault if the special regulation proposed by him "had not been published and not been carried out." Moreover, the military and civil authorities in Denmark did not have the manpower necessary for effective guard duties. And then finally—the object has been achieved for all that. The fact that it was not achieved exactly as Hitler wished nor as Himmler wished was no doubt obvious to Best.

Himmler's reaction was not slow in coming. It should be pointed out, however, that no serious measures were taken against Best and it would seem that not even an investigation—as Eichmann intended—was made. The reasons are to be found in the internal discussion that took place after the action. It will be recalled that Thadden wrote to Müller on October 12, 1943[132] and therein expressed his reaction to Best's proposal in telegram 1032. This letter had a sequel in the talk held between the two on October 16. Thadden reports that in this meeting Müller said to him: "Operations are ordered from above and are carried out as far as possible. The opportunity of implementing a decisive action will not return since the police forces required are not available."[133] We find an echo of these words in Eichmann's talks with Stassen where he claimed that "it was clear to me that I as a German could not demand the Jews from the Hungarians—we had had too much trouble of that sort in Denmark. I therefore left the whole affair to the Hungarian authorities."[134] Although his claim is not correct since he in fact did "demand the Jews from the Hungarians" (that is, he simply took them), the remark shows that

Denmark taught the Germans a lesson: it was not easy to implement the "final solution" against the opposition of the people among whom the Jews lived.

The conclusion of the debate may be seen in a memorandum written by Otto Six of the German Foreign Ministry on October 25.[135] It transpires that the failure of the persecutions had formed the subject of talk in a number of the regular morning meetings in the Foreign Ministry. Six writes his report on the basis of a talk held with Best in Copenhagen, and this may therefore be regarded as a summing up of Best's own assertions. Here is also to be found the first allusion to illegal transportation and its importance for the Danish underground movement. As will be seen below, this transportation was developed in the wake of the Jewish flight.

Himmler's reaction to Best's opposition to the persecution of the Jews and the recruitment of volunteers also found expression in the fact that Pancke was appointed as Best's peer and was not subordinated to him; Himmler also took pains to give his higher S.S.- and police-*Führer* a special status. It is interesting that in the two letters we know Best wrote to Himmler during the crisis period, he did not even mention the deportation of the Jews[136] (it may of course be that these were not the only letters written during that time). Best received two replies: the letter we know of, in which Himmler informed Best of Pancke's appointment,[137] and an invitation to take part in the notorious meeting of Himmler with all the S.S. commanders in Europe, fixed for October 4 in Poznan, where Himmler delivered the celebrated speech on the extermination of the Jews.

In a telegram dated September 29[138] Best asks permission to travel to the meeting in his official capacity. It is not known whether such permission was granted, but in any case he did not go.[139] The invitation meant that at that time, on the eve of the action in Denmark, Himmler considered Best a partner in the extermination of the Jews. After the failure of the operation, he would seem to have changed his mind. It may, however, be assumed that the decision regarding Pancke had already been taken during the period of emergency. During the whole of October the Foreign Ministry and Best nevertheless struggled to insure the latter's position and to prevent control of Denmark from passing into the hands of Himmler's men.[140] On November 7 a talk took place between Kaltenbrunner and Steengracht, and the general discussion of the problem of authority also included Denmark.[141] A month later, on December 6, Pancke officially took office with a clear order from Hitler that he was "attached" to the plenipotentiary of the Reich.[142] Ribbentrop tried to insure that the chief of police would at least receive his "political instructions" from a member of the Foreign Ministry, and Himmler agreed to this in principle[143] although it was not always adhered to in practice.

Best, however, was obliged to explain the persecution of the Jews not only to the central German authorities but also to the Danes. Here of course he was not forced to prove that he was not responsible for the failure of the action but, on the contrary, that he was not to blame for the fact that Jews were deported. On October 4 a meeting took place between him and Svenningsen at which the Danish official informed him of the unfortunate impression made by the combined announcement on the deportation and the release of the interned Danish troops. He emphasized the profound indignation felt by both the population and the administration. The talk in general was concerned with the termination of the state of emergency and the future form of government in Denmark.[144] As for the Jews, Best assured Svenningsen that there was no intention of deporting half-Jews or partners of mixed marriages. The next day he confirmed in writing to Svenningsen the procedure then still in force in the Reich on this question.[145] In further talks[146] Best claimed that had there been a Danish government, it could have prevented the deportation by threatening to resign, but it was the

Danes themselves who did not wish to set up a government. He also stressed that the Germans had carried out the action once and had done no more, that is, they had left property intact and had not continued to search for Jews who had fled. Nor had they proclaimed any special regulations for Jews, such as racial laws (perhaps he also meant the unpublished directive). In other words, Best said to the Danes: *I did everything I could and if I did not succeed in preventing the deportation then the fault is yours, because you did not form a government.*[147]

Summary

Just as it is impossible to understand the proposal for a pogrom, as laid down in telegram 1032, without reference to the general crisis in Denmark, so it must be realized that the action and its failure were interwoven with the manipulations, maneuvers, and general problems that marked the march of events in Denmark during the month of September.

Four factors affected developments: Best and the army, who were engaged in a struggle for power in Denmark;[148] the Danes, who sought to preserve their freedom and independence to the greatest degree possible; and the central German authorities, also rent by dissension according to the various interests at stake. Part—and no negligible part—of this struggle between and inside the various parties found its expression in the battle over the fate of the Jews in Denmark. More than on any previous occasion, the Jewish problem became the touchstone of political ambitions. We have seen that there was not one problem demanding solution with which the Jewish problem did not come to be connected or on which it did not exercise its influence, directly or indirectly, during that month.

victorious. With the end of the state of emergency, Han-

    In the struggle with the army, Best in fact emerged

neken returned to the same status, if not a lesser one, he held before the crisis broke. But Faure's definition remained correct—that Denmark after the period of emergency was a typical example of a police state (though this was only true in practice when Pancke actively assumed office in December). It is not our task in this study to examine the far-reaching changes that took place in Denmark after the establishment of this regime, but it is our duty to emphasize that it was established upon the initiative of Best, who exploited the Jewish problem to this end. His decisive act during the period was thus the importation of the police battalions. Here, however, he met his main defeat: the general command over this regime was not given to him, as he undoubtedly intended it should be.[149] This failure was the result of two factors: the internal rivalry between Himmler and Ribbentrop, and the "weakness" Best had revealed in the eyes of Himmler and of Hitler. The failure of the action against the Jews contributed greatly to the creation of this opinion, though the annulment of the troop transfers to Germany certainly annoyed Himmler no less.[150] Nevertheless, Best succeeded in carving a position for himself, and he remained a decisive factor in Denmark right up to the end of the war.[151] From the crisis on, Best rightly considered the officials of the Foreign Ministry under Steengracht as his main support within the Reich.[152] His attempts and strivings to regain his place in the S.S. on the basis of his achievements had failed.

It will be recalled that from the beginning of September (in fact from the middle of August) Best demanded that his regime be set up on new foundations in all spheres. The establishment of police control was to be accompanied by suitable arrangements in administration and in judicial affairs. But the problem of legal jurisdiction was not resolved and the struggle around it continued over a long period. As to the civil administration, the problem was solved by continuing the arrangements with the ministerial department heads. However, fortunately for the Danes, Best did not succeed in establishing any German control of Danish administration. Best's status therefore remained very delicate, and he was aware that he needed the cooperation of the Danes to maintain his rule even within the framework of the new civil administration. He therefore could not dare to incite the population against him. Best knew that the deportation of the Jews, if it were carried through as planned, would cause an uprising—and he therefore allowed the action to fail, even though he cautiously refrained from becoming involved in the rescue actions. Moreover, the Danish spirit affected not only Best but all the local German authorities, until there hardly remained in the country one German who was prepared to implement the action in the generally accepted Nazi manner. Even Mildner, who had only recently arrived, was quickly convinced that the deportation could not be effected with the forces at his disposal so long as the people were in opposition.

The true victor was thus the Danish people whose moral and political attitude triumphed over nazism and created a situation in which Eichmann's agents were rendered impotent. Moreover, as we shall see shortly in this study, the active resistance of the Danes to the deportation of the Jews had far-reaching consequences in the internal political situation and opened a new era in the dramatic history of occupied Denmark.

CHAPTER

VI

The Jewish Community During the Crisis

The First Phase of the Occupation

It was clear that the feeling of security enjoyed by the Jews in Denmark was profoundly disturbed by the German occupation of the country, and more frightened than any were those who had fled from Nazi Germany to Denmark. On the face of things, however, the position of the refugees changed but little. Twenty-three of them, mainly political refugees, were arrested at the request of the Germans and interned in the Danish camp at Horserød set up at the time, but some were quickly released. The Danes themselves arrested those refugees in order to prevent their seizure by the Germans. The same system was again used in June 1941 with the arrest of the Communists.[1] As we have also seen, attempts were made to repeat the procedure when deportation threatened the Jews—but this time unsuccessfully.

On April 22, 1940, the Germans arrested the secretary of the United Danish Emigrant Aid Committee, Georg Breit-

scheid.[2] On the day of the occupation, the Germans confiscated the card index of refugees in the office of the Social
Democratic party, which included the names of those receiving aid from the Matteoti Fund.[3] In June 1940, Renthe-Fink
requested and received a card index of all foreigners in Denmark. On the basis of this material the German minister
reported that there were 4,384 stateless persons, "among
them 600 former Germans, of whom about 200 are Jews."
According to the statistics available there is no doubt that
this figure was much smaller than the number of Jewish
refugees who were living in Denmark at the time.[4] With
the help of this card index additional refugees were arrested
between July and September. In the course of the year the
number arrested reached 127, but of these 24 were released
(one of the latter was Fritz Bauer). In 42 cases the Germans
demanded that they be handed over to the frontier police
at Flensburg, and the Danish authorities complied.

This information was given in a comprehensive report
published by the Ministry of Justice in July 1947 at the request of the Parliamentary Committee of Investigation.
The subject of the report was the activity of the State Attorney for Special Affairs in connection with German demands during the occupation, particularly with regard to
the arrest of Communists. The report's letter of presentation
was signed by Per Federspiel, at that time Minister for
Special Affairs.[5] The handing over of the refugees to the
Germans is explained in the report by the fact that these
were Germans who had entered Denmark illegally and were
unable to support themselves, and who would in any event
have been expelled from the country. In addition, the report
asserts that after the occupation Denmark was unable to
continue giving asylum to foreign subjects (to Britons, for
example), and particularly not to Germans or stateless ex-
Germans. "It was possible to assume that Germany would
respect Denmark's sovereignty with regard to *Danish* citi-

zens but there were insufficient grounds for protesting against the handing over of the occupying power's own citizens in the occupied area."[6]

In 1941, sixty-three more refugees were detained, mainly during the arrest of Communists, but forty of them were afterward released. Of all the refugees held in Horserød camp another eighty were handed over to the Germans at that time.[7] There are no exact figures available as to how many of these were Jews—apparently not many.

In the list of Communists arrested after June 22, 1941, a few Jewish names appear. Four of the eight were members of the community but the others were also known as Jews.[8] Most of them were released after a short time. One who was an active member of the Communist party was deported, together with the Communists who were added to the Jews on October 2, 1943. He was taken to Stutthof and, after this camp was evacuated, to Nawitz camp, where he died on February 16, 1945.[9]

During 1942 and 1943 a total of nineteen refugees were arrested, sixteen of whom were handed over to Germany, the other three being released.

Aid to the refugees continued in the meantime, but on December 23, 1940, the attorney-general was summoned to a meeting with Kanstein and was asked for precise information on the Matteoti Fund, the Committee of the 4th of May, 1933, and the Committee for the Support of Intellectual Refugees. The Germans demanded the reports of these committees and the closing of their bank accounts. The official explanation was that the committees were suspected of being centers of illegal propaganda against the Reich. The Ministry of Justice complied with the demand. The committees were liquidated and their archives confiscated and handed over to the German authorities "for perusal." They were of course never returned. The Germans demanded that the bank accounts be frozen but an agreement was drawn up whereby the funds were transferred to the state for safekeeping. The committees formally ceased their activities on April 1, 1941, and the remaining sums were deposited in a savings account for refugee emigration expenses.[10]

After the occupation, a few Palestinian Jews remained in Denmark, some of them emissaries and some students at the state college for physical training. They received exit permits to Sweden and from there succeeded in returning to Palestine via Russia and Turkey.[11] A group of Youth Aliya members and a number of agricultural trainees also managed to reach Palestine via Siberia. Others among the agricultural pioneers succeeded in obtaining visas to the United States, and they too were permitted to travel via Sweden.[12] Greater difficulties were encountered by those who had entry visas to other overseas countries and were required to sail from Lisbon. On August 7, 1941, Renthe-Fink presented to the German Foreign Ministry a list of eight Jewish refugees who had visas to the United States and to Chile and who had requested permission to travel via Germany to Lisbon. They were in possession of temporary Danish passports (*Hilfspässe*). The Foreign Ministry transferred the request to the RSHA and on August 23, 1941, Eichmann gave his negative reply: "In reply to your letter of August 19, 1941, we beg to inform you that in our opinion and in view of the final solution of the Jewish problem in Europe now being planned, the emigration of Jews from our occupied areas should be prevented."[13] The official motive given was that the emigration of Jews from the occupied countries would reduce the emigration possibilities of Jews from Germany, Austria, and Bohemia. There is no need to point out that this pretext was utterly false.

In reply to this refusal, Renthe-Fink suggested in October 1941 that a section on racial affiliation be incorporated in the application form for an exit visa. What impelled Renthe-Fink to make this suggestion—which was so contrary to his general behavior on the Jewish question—has not been explained. The idea found favor in the eyes of the RSHA but the administrative procedure took a long time. On August 25, 1942, the affirmative reply was received together with approval of the new questionnaire, which was now introduced for the whole of Europe, including Turkey. There were doubtless many instances where people could have escaped had it not been for this item. It may also be presumed that at the time he suggested this innovation Renthe-Fink did not know the true significance of the phrase "final solution," since we know that he first heard about the mass murders in December 1941. The final confirmation of the new procedure reached Copenhagen only in October 1942, after Renthe-Fink had already left Denmark.

It has been pointed out earlier in this study that Renthe-Fink constantly advised that the Jews should not take a prominent part in Danish public life, and the Danish authorities also accepted this view. It is against this background that the policy of the community and the behavior of the Jews during that period is to be understood. In a talk between the chairman of the community, C. B. Henriques, the vice-chairman, Karl Lachmann, and Svenningsen on September 25, 1943, the Jewish leaders asked him explicitly if he did not think that the time had come for them to change their policy of preventing the flight of the Jews and the transfer of their capital from Denmark. Svenningsen replied in the negative. He was of the opinion that the old line should be followed in order not to arouse the wrath of the Germans and give them a pretext for attacking the Jews.[14] This discussion shows how the policy of the community was coordinated with that of the authorities. The Danes considered themselves as responsible for the safety of the Jews. Since they saw in the safety of the Jews a guarantee of the maintenance of law and internal autonomy in Denmark, they were opposed to any Jewish move which might undermine this position. The Jews also knew that the Danish statesmen and heads of government, one after the other, had made the security of the Jews a *conditio sine qua non* for the maintenance of a constitutional Danish government. The safety of the community was therefore conditional upon the existence of law and order in Denmark, and the Jews were thus afraid to take any step, big or small, which might be interpreted as a breach of the law. This view was shared by all who took an active part in Jewish or refugee affairs. For instance, in the summer of 1943 Niels Bohr was invited by the British government—through underground channels—to flee Denmark and come to England. He refused to do so on the grounds that his flight might have catastrophic consequences for those refugees from Germany who worked in his institute, and perhaps for the whole Jewish community.[15]

Considerations of this sort determined the relationship of the community's leaders with the underground movement in general and even resulted in opposition to the flight of Jews. They were apprehensive not only of German wrath but of Danish indignation at the fact that these Jews, who were willing enough to live with them in normal times, deserted in the hour of trial. They feared too that any Jew seized as a saboteur might well serve as the pretext for an onslaught on the entire community. They therefore opposed not only flight but also any Jewish participation whatsoever in the underground movement, acts of sabotage, and the like.[16] What is more, they even refused to hide the card index of the community or to take other precautionary measures to protect the documents and property of the community, so that in the hour of investigation the community would not be accused of illegal activity.[17] The community's organ ceased publication. The Committee of the 4th of May, 1933 also wound up its activities immediately after the occupation, long before the Germans demanded its liquidation. One of the reasons for this step was that financial support of the activities of the committee, given until then by the international Jewish organizations, was automatically suspended.

On October 30, 1940, we may read in the minutes of the community: "The chairman declared . . . that the collection that was going to be made among the members of the community has not taken place [reference is to the annual collection for refugees]. . . . An arrangement has been made whereby help to the refugees will now be given through the social welfare offices, while the community will undertake to look after the Youth Aliya organization and the agricultural trainees." On the other hand, the agricultural pioneer organization together with its secretary continued its work as usual, with no interference from the Germans until the outbreak of the persecutions.[18]

At the beginning of 1943, the executive committee of the community discussed the question of whether preparations should be made for an eventual flight of the Jews, should German persecution occur. At this time rumors had reached Denmark of the extermination of the Jews in Poland, and the Germans even felt obliged to issue a denial. The members of the committee were all agreed that no flight should be planned for this reason: it was impossible to hide six or seven thousand Jews except with the help of all the non-Jewish inhabitants of the country. It was impossible to approach the Danes with such a request or to expect that it would be met. It did not seem likely at the time that very many could escape to Sweden. An "inner flight" within Denmark would, in the view of the community leaders, merely cause panic among the Jewish population, which was nervous and anxious in any case, and would provide the Germans with an excuse for taking action. It was asked whether any special plans should be made for saving the children, but the reply here was also negative.

Rabbi Melchior has presented all these arguments in a comprehensive article on the period, in which he asserts that such a rescue action could only succeed if it were spontaneous and that it could not possibly have been planned in advance under the circumstances then prevailing.[19] He replies here to the criticism leveled after the war against the stand of the community leaders. However, this policy of relying entirely on the Danish authorities meant that not even the majority of the community as individuals took any precautionary measures. Even those who were convinced from the very beginning of the occupation that the Danish Jews would not come through unscathed took no steps whatsoever to save themselves. Some bought poison with a view to avoiding capture by the Germans when that time came,[20] and one woman knitted sweaters for her children so that they would not be left without warm clothes. Her family also transferred the contents of its safe to that of a Danish friend.[21] Very few fled immediately after the occupation, and further flight was blocked by the attitude of the community. The only group which became stirred and tried to find a way out of the trap were the agricultural trainees of Hechalutz, and even here the really active were few in number.

The most reasonable escape route seemed of course to be that to Sweden, but prior to October 1943 this was by no means a simple matter. Flight across the Sound was a daring and complicated venture. Danish fishermen and seamen were not at that time very enthusiastic about smuggling people over. Some fishermen who had agreed in April 1940 to take Jews over to Sweden had been arrested by the Germans on their return to Denmark.[22] Moreover, the minefields and the German patrol vessels turned this illegal crossing into a highly dangerous operation. To all these were added the difficulties awaiting the escapees on the other side of the Sound. The Swedes were at the time most uninterested in encouraging an escape movement from Denmark which was liable to complicate their relations with the Germans.[23] Moreover, account should also be taken of the general atmosphere in Denmark prior to the summer of 1943 when the underground movement was small in numbers and unsupported by the population at large. It was a grave problem to find hiding places for their own resistance fighters, let alone to smuggle them over to Sweden. There were no few cases where resistance fighters who were forced to disappear wandered from place to place for months on end amid great hardships, and with no possibility of crossing the Sound.[24]

All these difficulties did not, however, discourage the Hechalutz trainees from finding a way out of Denmark. Uri Yaari (today a member of kibbutz Neot Mordechai but then still known as Hermann Waldmann) was one of these pioneers who could not sit by and wait patiently for the Germans to act. He wanted to fight. However, he and his friends did not think in terms of Sweden, from where there seemed to exist no way out to the front, but sought instead routes through the Balkans to Turkey and thereafter to Palestine. Their plan was to ride concealed under railroad cars bound for Germany with a view to reaching the shores of the Black Sea. Uri Yaari has related the stories of these attempts[25] which all failed, even though one person got as far as Munich and another to Sofia (only to be seized in Hamburg on the way back). Five persons lost their lives in these attempts. The group trained and experimented with various escape systems for over two years, but after repeated failure the forty members disbanded. The Danish police began to keep watch on Uri Yaari, and the Jewish community also felt duty-bound to intervene in a matter it considered dangerous both to the pioneers and to itself.[26]

The whole question was openly debated between the Hechalutz members and the community in the spring of 1943. At about the same time, a group of ten fishing trainees succeeded in stealing a boat from the island of Bornholm and reaching Sweden after a hazardous journey in a stormy sea. News of the incident reached the Germans, who delivered a sharp warning to the Danish authorities. Eivind Larsen and the attorney-general categorically demanded of the community that such activity cease.[27] Benjamin Slor personally talked with the Hechalutz secretariat and requested that no further escape attempts be made. In connection with the Passover festival, Margolinsky sent a circular to all the trainees based on the precept, "This year we are here, next year in the Land of Israel."[28] The letter goes on: "We are sorry to say that the past ten years have not led to much understanding of the obligations members should feel toward the public and the institutions which have made their stay in this country possible and which bear responsibility for them." He further explains that until now nothing has been said about various activities of trainees in view of their lack of experience and their youth (the reference is apparently to the efforts of Uri Yaari and his group), but that in the present situation local interests cannot be ignored.

Our members, like all other residents of Denmark, have first of all to preserve peace and order, particularly since there has until now been no reason to introduce any changes in the position of the agricultural training scheme in Denmark or its members, unless they themselves cause such a change by their behavior. Everyone has a duty to take care that peace and order are not violated, be it out of a lack of responsibility toward society or a lust for adventure or mistaken convictions. . . . [In conclusion, the circular asks for understanding of the concept of freedom through responsibility.] Freedom is not, and cannot be, identical with a striving for modes of life or ideals without reference to the comprehensive responsibility owed to the greater whole.

Today, after the passage of many years, Uri Yaari in effect has reached similar conclusions to those of Margolinsky. "The plan was fantastic and apart from loss of life led to no results," he writes in his story. However, had the Jews of Denmark not been saved in the way they were—and no one could then have known what fate held in store—then the attempts of those young men would not have been considered as "fantastic" or "adventurous" but as acts of supreme heroism on a par with the deeds of their comrades in the ghettos of Poland. This tragic episode and the varying evaluations of it in later years show how difficult it is to judge how the Jews and their leaders should have acted, or not acted, in the ghettos or in any other place under German rule.

Within the restricted framework laid down by the policy of the community—which was also the declared policy of the authorities—the Jews protected their interest and their honor. We have already seen how they enjoyed the greatest possible support from the Danish people and authorities. For their part, the Jews generally avoided any public activity which might attract undue attention. Jewish youth organizations, however, kept watch on the synagogue. It will be recalled that an unsuccessful attempt was made to set fire to it in 1941, and during 1942 various attempts at desecration also occurred—from the drawing of swastikas on the walls to the casting of pigs' feet into the building during the Shabbath morning prayers. Grating was installed outside the windows in addition to the tall iron railings surrounding the building. But the main activity was the implementation of guard duties from the autumn of 1942 until the state of emergency. These were organized with the support of the Danish police, with whom the Jewish youth serving as watchmen were connected by direct telephone. They also bore an official armband and were equipped with truncheons.[29]

No pioneer youth movement existed in Denmark. The only Zionist youth organization was that of Bnai Akiva but during those years, as a result of external pressures, the organizational and cultural activity of Jewish youth and its internal solidarity increased. In line with the Danish youth organizations they too set aside all ideological differences.[30]

The Hour of Crisis

C. B. Henriques himself relates in his statement of evidence that while he was still carrying out the policy agreed upon in concert with the authorities, the rank and file of the community began to leave town. Not only Svenningsen, however, was deceived by Best and believed his assurances that the Jews stood in no danger; Bishop Fuglsang-Damgaard also came to the community office (on September 28 at 3 P.M.) in order to calm the Jewish leaders and to tell them that he had it from most reliable sources that there was no real foundation to the rumors.[31] Henriques clung to all these comforting announcements and wanted very much to believe that his evaluation was correct. This is the explanation—and the one he himself gives—for the fact that when the Social Democratic leaders came to him that evening to deliver their warning he refused at first to believe them.

He was not, however, the only Jewish leader warned on that Tuesday, the 28th of September. Alsing Andersen's secretary, Inga Bardfeld, was married to a member of Hechalutz. She told Margolinsky that the news was bad, and he sent her straight to Rabbi Melchior.[32] Her warning had two consequences: one was that the next day, the eve of the Jewish New Year, Rabbi Melchior announced at the morning service that the Jews should hide or flee and that the New Year prayers would not be held.[33] Second, Margolinsky at once organized a messenger service to all the training centers to warn the Hechalutz members. These two acts were the only acts of warning organized by the Jewish institutions as such—all the other warnings were the work of individual Jews and of Danes, both individuals and organizations.

The members of the community's executive committee met the next day, September 29, at 10 A.M. in Henriques's office. The chairman passed the information on to the members and requested them to circulate it among other Jews. He called a new meeting for three o'clock that afternoon, with the participation of the attorney H. H. Bruun, who would, it had been agreed upon during September, represent the interests of the community and administer its affairs should the need arise. It was agreed that each committee member would warn his friends and acquaintances. In other words, no warning activities were organized, just as no plan of escape had been prepared. At 11 A.M. Henriques, Lachmann (the vice-chairman), and a third member of the committee were received by Svenningsen, to whom they reported the news. On the spot Svenningsen called the other departmental heads to a meeting at two o'clock that afternoon.

Already during their previous meeting on September 25 Henriques had asked Svenningsen if the administrative heads would follow the example of the Danish government and resign should the rumors prove to be true and the Germans act against the Jews. Svenningsen confirms in his evidence that he replied that he did not think such a step was feasible.[34] Henriques, however, asked further whether it could be presumed that the directors-general would continue to govern Denmark and that a constitutional government would not be set up. To this Svenningsen replied that the situation had continued thus for a month and he did not have the feeling that any change would take place.[35] Henriques presumably asked this question because he understood that a Danish government would probably protect the Jews as it had done in the past, while no such reaction was to be anticipated from the administrative heads. Now that the question of resignation in the event of persecutions had become a practical issue, he repeated the question. It was also raised afterward in the internal discussions of the departmental heads, who replied negatively.[36]

This change in attitude indicates the radical changes that had taken place in Denmark since the collapse of the policy of negotiation. With the removal of the government and the absence of the parliamentary institutions a vacuum was created, and no one was officially responsible toward the people. This vacuum was filled by the underground movement, which set up its own public institution. We have already pointed out that the first proclamation of the Freedom Council called upon the population to help the Jews. It will thus be seen that in those days of crisis also the Jewish problem served as a barometer of Danish policy, as it had done from the beginning of the occupation. The council of departmental heads was not capable of demonstrating openly in favor of the Jews, but the Freedom Council did not hesitate to call upon the people to defend the lives of Jewish citizens.

During the meeting on the morning of September 29 in his office, Henriques also asked whether an approach to the king was possible. Svenningsen replied that such a step would be of no use since the king was actually a prisoner and unable to intervene. At the afternoon meeting, however, with the participation, at Svenningsen's request, of the king's political secretary, Gunnar Bardenfleth, the question was again raised. This time the king's secretary thought that the king would be prepared to express his support of the Jews. And, as we have seen, Christian X did indeed send a letter of protest to Best.[37]

This afternoon meeting of the departmental heads was one of several held during those days of crisis at which the Danish administrative heads debated the problem of the persecutions.[38] According to one version, Henriques took part in the meeting mentioned above, and according to another version, he talked with Svenningsen, Eivind Larsen, and the king's secretary but left the Foreign Ministry when the other officials arrived.[39] The question of whether Henriques was present all the time is important, since later in the meeting the suggestion was put forward that the Danes intern the Jews in a camp in Denmark to prevent their delivery to the Germans. It would appear that in making

their suggestion the administrative heads were not aware
how radically things had changed since the summer of 1941,
when the precedent of Communist arrests by the Danish
authorities had taken place. At that time Denmark's political life had been still normal. It was no coincidence that
now underground circles at once leveled sharp criticism
against the proposal,[40] and pointed out that the lesson had
been learned that German assurances could not be relied
on and that the arrest of persons by the Danes was no
guarantee of their safety. A second proposal connected to
the one for setting up a Danish camp for Jews suggested
that the Jews pay the Germans ransom money.

The question of whether Henriques took part in the meeting is important insofar as it was claimed that both the
suggestions had been made by the Jews themselves.[41] That
this was not so may be seen from the following part of the
official minutes of the meeting:[42]

The question was: Can we do anything and how? Director-

General Eivind Larsen raised the idea of making the Germans
a counterproposal to intern the Jews here in Denmark in order
to avoid their deportation. The idea was also mooted that a
large sum should be given by the Jews as a guarantee. The
Jewish representatives expressed to the department heads their
opinion that in the circumstances they would regard any such
step as welcome.

However, Arthur Henriques's version has a slightly different
connotation. It runs as follows:

The chairman of the community expressed the opinion that
internment in Denmark was naturally better than imprisonment in Germany, and that ransom money was also preferable
to this, but [asked] how it was possible to think of arresting
Danish citizens and what the crime was for which ransom money
should be paid. The reply given was that the suggestions were
intended to bribe the Germans and mitigate the punishment.

The chairman then asked if it was intended to accuse the Jewish citizens of sabotage. To this Eivind Larsen replied: "No, not under any circumstances." The chairman thereupon answered that in that case he did not understand what motives could be given for internment or ransom money. The reply was that these suggestions should be at hand in a meeting with Dr. Best, if he were not otherwise willing to negotiate. The chairman then stated that it would perhaps be best if the department heads would refuse to continue their functions if action against the Jews was in fact implemented. They considered this as unthinkable, as complete chaos would result.[43]

Henriques was therefore extremely consistent: during the whole period of occupation the Jews had placed their trust in the government and the king. Since the government no longer existed, he asked that the council of administrative heads fulfill instead its function as regards the Jews. But in their view (and also in the view of the responsible politicians) the administrative heads could not resign. The only hope left therefore was that the king would intervene on their behalf. The king indeed agreed to this request but his intervention had no practical effect. This conception of Henriques's was unrealistic, although it should be understood in the light of the Jewish relationship to the king as the symbol of protection and of the true spirit of the Danish people. The whole attitude of the chairman of the community found its expression in his opposition to the no doubt well-meant proposal of the departmental heads who wished to alleviate the situation. But those among the officials who thought that this method would save the Jews also erred in their evaluation of the true position. Here the insight of the underground movement was undoubtedly more correct. It is strange to note how at the twelfth hour the Danish authorities, of all people, seized upon proposals typical of the lifesaving efforts made by the Jews in various episodes of persecution and pogrom. Unlike the leading Danish politicians up to August 29, 1943, the departmental heads did not understand the political significance of the situation. According to Haestrup they looked upon the question of the Jews' deportation only as a human calamity, and some of these officials argued that "one was not confronted with any political problem but with a purely humanitarian task."[44] It seems that even the fact that the detained Communists were deported together with the Jews did not change their view.

Conscious of his rights as a Danish citizen, Henriques revolted against the said proposals and defended the honor of the Jews. He did not argue "It will not help." He asserted "It is unjust." He defended—and defended with honor—the great achievement of the Jewish community in Denmark: equal citizen rights. But in this defense there was also inherent a protest against the fact that the hand of Jewish destiny had been laid upon his community. As we know, it was decided at the meeting that Svenningsen would approach Best and find out from him the intention of the Germans. Only when the persecutions had already begun did Svenningsen suggest the internment of Jews in Denmark. Ransom money was never proposed.

When Henriques, on September 29, returned from the Foreign Ministry he met with members of the community executive, as arranged that morning. It was by now 3 P.M. There were present at the meeting only three of the seven members of the committee—the rest having already fled. The Danish attorney was also present and the administrative, financial, and other affairs of the community were formally transferred to him. Thus ended the rescue activity of the community. The committee deliberately organized no systematic operation to save lives. Everything was left to the individual, his initiative and his luck. Every single person warned his relatives and acquaintances, escaped with his own resources, or accepted the help offered him. This help was at first given by friends and acquaintances or by ordinary citizens, and afterward by the underground organizations. The community, which had deliberately throughout the period avoided the planning of flight, was, when the crisis broke, incapable of organizing any such operation. Even the fate of its institutions, such as old-age homes, was left—in accordance with the rule laid down—to family and friends to decide. This is the explanation for the fact that some thirty of the old people in the home next to the synagogue were trapped. One old lady committed suicide.[45] All the Danish reports on the persecutions relate that these old people and the poorer Jews were the main victims of the deportation. This fact must be mainly attributed to lack of organization and attention on the part of the community.[46] Still, all the inmates of another and smaller old-age home succeeded in escaping.[47]

The victims were mainly of two categories: (a) those who were unable to help themselves because of physical incapacity to do so, such as old people; and (b) those who did not have the necessary connections with Danish circles or the sums of money required for the organization of their flight (that is, the poorer sections of the community). The leaders of the community had in concert and in advance taken precautions for the security of its money and property. This was something that could be done legally. On the other hand, no organizational measures were taken to protect human lives, for this could only be done outside the framework of the law—and for this the community was not prepared, either mentally or practically.[48] The community as an organization, an association of human beings, a society sharing a common fate, disintegrated. Only the family unit remained intact.

An exception to all this was the organization of pioneers under Slor and Margolinsky. As mentioned, Margolinsky and the Hechalutz secretariat organized a written and oral warning system to members. As a result, 329 adults and 26 children, out of a total of 360 adults and 29 children, afterward reached Sweden. In other words, 31 adults and

3 children—less than 10 per cent—were seized. For the children of Youth Aliya no warning system was organized, and of the 174 still in Denmark, 38—or more than 20 per cent—were deported to Theresienstadt. The remainder managed somehow to escape to Sweden.[49]

David Sompolinsky has given the following description of how events unfolded in those days.[50]

It is difficult today [he recalls] to explain why, when the Germans took the card index [from the community office on September 17] in order to prepare a hunt against us, we did not understand the situation. Despite all the indications of an imminent action against the Jews, we continued to be sceptical. This was the country I had grown up in, where I had no quarrel with anyone; I had had no form of contact with German soldiers, and it was unreasonable to suppose that they would without reason, without a trace of moral justification, seize, arrest, and deport citizens of the country. But theoretically we knew that it was possible and that it had happened in other countries; but we could not get used to the idea that it could happen to us. Inhumanity, brutality, the absence of any consideration for human feelings and of any sense of justice—it was incredible that people could be capable of all this. We had over the years become accustomed to seeing the "green" soldiers in the streets, where they almost seemed to behave like human beings. Was it conceivable that by order they could overnight turn into the most terrible beasts of prey?

In 1943 the Jewish New Year fell on Thursday and Friday (September 30 and October 1). The day before the holiday the rumors increased that the German action against the Jews would definitely come. According to Hedtoft (in the foreword to Aage Bertelsen's well-known book), Henriques was supposed to inform all the Jews when they gathered in the synagogue for New Year prayers [this version does not correspond fully with Hedtoft's report and must be attributed to Sompolinsky alone], but in fact no clear message was given with the authorization of the eommunity's leaders. At the morning service on the day before New Year it was announced that the New Year service would not be held and that Jews should not congregate. But this information was only received by those who visited the synagogue on a weekday. There were hardly more than a score of Jews present.[51] In any case, many families decided to leave home and spend the holy days in the country. At the time this required considerable means or good connections with non-Jews in the country. Some attempted to flee to Sweden. This illegal passage then cost 4,000–5,000 kroner per person—a considerable sum which most Jews could not raise at short notice. . . . The evening before the holiday was marked by confusion. While some left home, others thought they should keep together. They thought that if the Germans really planned an action they would be ashamed to make an open attack on the Jews, for they would not want to attract the attention of the Danish population. They could certainly seize Jews singly or secretly, but if several families were assembled together—this was unthinkable.

The synagogues were closed but some people organized services in their homes, among them my father, blessed be his memory. . . . Toward the end of the service a young Dane came into the room without ringing. I had seen him before among workers in the street. He began to explain quietly that we should break up and leave the apartment at once, for the Germans were going to attack the Jews, and this might well occur within a few hours. All those present had already heard numerous rumors, so his words did not make much of an impression on them, and they began to discuss the matter among themselves. But fortunately for us a surprising change then took place in the young man's behavior. With choking voice he asked us to leave the house. He explained that he had been instructed by the local branch of the Social Democrats to inform all Jews in the district. He begged us to believe him and left the house with tears in his eyes.

Sompolinsky goes on to describe how his family left the city and he remained alone in Copenhagen, for he possessed the uniform of an inspector in the civil defense which enabled him to appear in the street even during a curfew.

We shall see later how he took an active part in the Danish action to rescue the Jews.

This story is characteristic of the behavior of both the Jews and the Danes. Many of the Jews did not even want to believe the announcements of the Danes. One of them recalls:

Since Mr. Staffeldt had many Jewish friends, he set out immediately to warn them. Most of them did not believe him in the beginning, and he had the difficult task of undermining their confidence and their false feelings of security in terms of "it can't happen here in good old Denmark." In order to do so he returned to them several times, even three or four, during the following days, but only after the news was confirmed from different sources and brought and pressed on the reluctant people from various directions were they ready to draw the implied and necessary conclusions.[52]

From the evidence of the Jews themselves it is possible to conclude that the nearer anyone was to the authorities, the less he believed that any danger really threatened the Jews. This was especially true not only of Henriques but of all who went to departmental heads and listened to the reassuring announcements.[53] There were nevertheless some Jews who during the month of September began to take serious measures, such as the accumulation of a large sum of money, or the real or fictional transfer of ownership of their businesses, houses, and so forth to Danish friends. It happened more than once that in mixed marriages it was the Danish partner who was the more alive to the danger. Of fifty-nine eyewitness accounts by Danish Jews, it transpires from seven that the people themselves realized during the month of September that the danger was real and even began to draw practical conclusions—mainly following the confiscation of material from the community office on September 17.

Even after they had accepted flight as a fact many did

not at first think of escape to Sweden but thought they could merely go into hiding and after a short while return home as if nothing had happened.[54] This attitude was also encouraged by the authorities, who considered that the Germans would be content with the night of persecutions and would not thereafter continue persecution or deportation. Best's own behavior seemed to lend itself to an interpretation of this sort. At first therefore most of the evacuees and their helpers sought temporary places of refuge in the country or in hospitals. It was a minority which at once found a way of escaping to Sweden. This situation changed radically within a few days for two reasons: first, it was soon evident that all those people could not be hidden over a longer period, and second, on October 2 the Swedish radio announced officially that Sweden had tried to intercede with the Germans and was prepared to receive the Jews.

Here is the description of one of the Jews:[55]

The events of 1943 were a violent shock to me. Of course I was well aware that I was a Jew, but as a member of an old Jewish family, which had lived in Denmark for over 200 years, I had always felt first and foremost Danish, and the Jewish problem had in fact never existed for me. In school, among my fellow students, and afterward as a lawyer, I had never been regarded as different from any other Dane. My Judaism seemed to me a sort of family tradition which for me was extremely important but which had never constituted any barrier between me and non-Jewish citizens. It was one of my greatest and finest experiences when it became clear during those days of destiny that not only I regarded Denmark as my home but that this was also the opinion of all the Danes who showed such admirable willingness to help in the hour of danger.

Even after the Germans conquered Denmark in 1940 the thought did not enter my mind—naïve as I was—that I was living in danger. My non-Jewish wife told me afterward that from that moment on April 9, 1940, when she saw and heard the German planes circling over Copenhagen, fear seized her and never left her. But I, as stated, went about somewhat as if I was wearing blinkers. I continued to work and I lived like everyone else under the mental pressure caused by the German occupation and in constant hope that Hitler would be quickly defeated. Only on August 29, 1943, did I realize the gravity of the situation. A number of Jewish acquaintances, leaders of the community, were arrested at that time together with other Danish notables who were known as opponents of the Germans. It was clear that special attention had now been concentrated on the Jews. At the same time I heard of the German search at the offices of the community when lists of the names and addresses of members of the community had been confiscated [reference is to the first action of August 31]. On the assumption that our turn would now come we fled a few days later and hid with good friends. But we calmed down again. Life had to go on and we returned to our apartment. We thought no more about flight. I had a few days' holiday coming to me, and at the end of September we spent them with my wife's parents in the town of N——. During our stay there we received letters from my parents and from other relatives couched in strange terms and not entirely comprehensible, but in any case we had the impression that Copenhagen was rife with rumors of an impending action against the Jews. On one of the last days of September we were playing bridge with friends. Of the four couples present, three represented mixed marriages.

During the game the hostess was called to the phone. I still recall it as if it were today, that feeling of impending tragedy that struck us when our hostess, herself Jewish, told us that the call was from her mother-in-law in Copenhagen, who had said that an action against the Jews would take place on October 2 and that she (our hostess) must leave her house at once together with her children and travel to friends in the country. The danger this time was thus serious. We discussed the situation and made our plans. We did not speak of flight abroad. At the time we did not know whether such a possibility existed. The result of the discussion was that my sister, who was also present at the bridge party, would travel the next day with her two children and myself to A——, a provincial town where her brother-in-law was pastor. We felt we would be safe there. My wife remained for the time being in N——. There in the pastor's house I heard the Danish radio broadcast on the action against the Jews and that they had been "removed" from the population. At the sound of these fateful words it seemed to me as if the whole world had collapsed. My first thoughts were for my parents and my numerous family. I naturally assumed that the worst had happened and that they had all been seized by the Germans, but it transpired afterward that all my relatives had been saved and had reached Sweden safely. . . . At the pastor's house I heard on the Swedish radio that the Bohr brothers had fled to Sweden by boat and that the Danish Jews were being cordially received. I was still unaware that the "flight" had been organized, though this became rapidly clear.

Summary

The conquest of Denmark by the Germans found the Jews naturally frightened, but they quickly calmed down when they saw that the Danish authorities stood firm in their defense. They believed in the power of the government and in the great prestige of the king and therefore consciously adopted a policy in keeping with that declared by the government. As in most cases of this type, they were more meticulous in preserving the legal position than the Danish leaders themselves. The Danes played—some more, some less—a double game. But not so the Jews. The preservation of law and order was their main preoccupation.

Since the emancipation at the beginning of the 19th century the life of the community had been based on the laws and regulations laid down by the authorities. For almost 150 years the Jews of Denmark had made no political decisions and taken no administrative action without the supervision or even the instruction of the Danish authorities—and certainly never without their approval. The Danish law had granted them equal rights, had preserved their freedom, their property, their honor. The leadership of the community identified itself with the law and with the authorities that applied the law. As a group the Jews of

Denmark had no other source and no other basis for its existence than the law. Its leaders were incapable of taking any steps to insure the existence of the Jews that was outside the framework of the law, and they could not anticipate to what extent the Danish people would identify itself with them beyond the confines of the law. The members of the executive committee felt in the spring of 1943 that the foundations of the law were about to crumble beneath the feet of all Danes, and they were in the dark as to the people's attitude toward them in the absence of a stable rule of law. They knew no other way than to continue to cling with all their might to that same law and to place their trust in the "preservation of law and order." The attitude of the Danish people in the hour of the persecutions was a revelation to them all, the fulfillment of a hope, and an experience perhaps no less profound than the very persecutions themselves.

When the rule of democratic institutions was annulled in Denmark, protection of the Jews, which was one of the hallmarks of the legal situation, was in fact also annulled. The heads of the community learned that the administrative leaders were incapable of fulfilling the function toward the Jews formerly undertaken by the government and that they were even prepared—in a desperate attempt to save the Jews—to undermine their status as citizens protected by law. It was Henriques who did not agree here to bend the knee of his community and to waive the honor of the Jews as citizens. Still, the Jews, seeing the reed of their support broken, were able to think and act in an independent and organized manner only in the economic sphere, where they were used to operating—in accordance with the law—on their own initiative: they insured the property of the community. But the violent shock that afflicted the leadership of the community, with the collapse of its status as a body protected by the law, paralyzed its capacity for organized public action. The members of the committee deliberately

abandoned the community to each individual's own initiative. For this situation no organizational tools had been
prepared. Not all were completely bereft of instinct and perception; the vice-chairman of the community, Lachmann,
for instance, gave evidence that from the beginning of the
occupation he had expected a German action against the
Jews and had replied to questions immediately after the
meeting with Svenningsen that had he had small children
he would flee. He said this at a time when the director
of the Foreign Ministry still held the view that the Jews
must not use any illegal methods of flight. When the persecutions erupted the leaders of the community recognized
that the Danish authorities had not only been mistaken but
that they were also incapable of rendering the Jews any
assistance. Henriques states in his evidence that he was
under the impression that the departmental heads were at
a loss, and the reports of their meetings confirm this impression.

The shock received by the leaders also affected the community at large. Those in touch with the authorities and
deeply involved in Danish life were generally furthest removed from all sense of reality. The rank and file, however,
began to flee when the rumors erupted[56] until Henriques
felt himself obliged to ask Svenningsen for his evaluation.
When, however, Lachmann asked if the time had not come
to change the community's legalistic policy and organize
a flight plan, the answer was in the negative, that the community was incapable of reaching so revolutionary a decision by itself. When it became clear to Henriques that the
revolutionary situation existed, he at first refused to accept
the facts.

And yet the physical and even mental state of the Danish
Jews when the Germans attempted to arrest and deport
them was of a special category. Thanks to the policy of the
government and its firm protection of its Jewish citizens,
the Germans in Denmark did not take any of the prepara-

tory steps used in implementing the "final solution" in all the other places under their rule. The Jews in Denmark led until the very moment of the persecutions a normal civil life. They bore no mark of identification such as the yellow badge, they were not removed from their homes and assembled in ghettos, they were not deprived of their property, and they did not suffer from hunger. Restrictions and disturbances were virtually negligible. Their feeling of insecurity and anxiety was not so very different from that of the whole population with which they identified themselves. All this resulted in an exceptionally rude shock when the crisis broke. But it did not strike at people whose body and spirit had been broken—they had hardly even been dented. Organizational activity came to an abrupt standstill, but the individual in most cases recovered quickly, particularly since he was helped so actively by the Danish population.

The Danes also suffered shock and were faced, in the course of one night, with a new and cruel reality. They had never been led step by step to regard the Jews as outlaws and outcasts; now this was demanded of them on the spot. But hard reality did not paralyze the initiative of the people —it stimulated it. If the administration was at a loss, the people were not and they went forth to deeds unparalleled in the history of the Holocaust.

VII

Operation Rescue

"It is, indeed, really this cooperation on the part of the active, sound, and moral forces of the people which gives the conception of democracy meaning in a progressive and highly civilized society such as ours." The sentence is quoted from the foreword to Erling Foss's book in which he describes the transition from latent passive resistance to active struggle.[1] This active collaboration of widespread sections of the Danish people came for the first time fully to the fore during the operations for Jewish rescue. "The anger in Denmark over what had happened," says Hartvig Frisch,[2] "was without bounds. Nothing that the Germans had previously perpetrated in Denmark had aroused the population to such an extent." He then explains that the Danes were stirred up not merely by the human tragedy involved, but also by the fact that this was simply an act of savagery without any military importance. Though ignorant of the innermost workings of the minds of the German authorities, the people nevertheless sensed the ruthlessness which had motivated Best. He did in fact expect that his action would arouse strong popular opposition and even envisaged the possibility of a general strike. He did not, however, foresee— nor could he have foreseen—the abrupt transition of the population from passive and latent resistance to active and open struggle. "Courage and initiative were the stamp of the Danish people. It has never . . . acted more worthily and nobly than in those days."[3]

Underground Cells Prior to August 29

Best, lacking as he did a basic understanding of democracy, was unable to envision the spontaneous reaction of a citizen originating from a feeling of responsibility to the population as a whole. The Nazis themselves had in fact completely distorted the notion of civic spontaneity by using it as a cover for their organized crimes. Moreover, the behavior of the Danes, both of the authorities and the general population, prior to this emergency, gave Best—who had never fully understood the Danish mentality—no grounds for suspecting that this people could revolt. Until the very hour of crisis "the preservation of peace and order" was the primary general objective of the Danes. The underground groups were, for their part, small and virtually isolated. The motto of the people was "What's the use?"[4] Erling Foss describes how before August 29 an underground existence was almost an unknown phenomenon. Living under an assumed name or having a false address was actually nonexistent. People were wary of putting their houses at the disposal of the underground movement or of supporting it in any other way. They avoided all contact with these "dangerous" people, and with "the English agents."[5]

Writing about this problem more than ten years after the war, Foss pointed out that since even members of the underground still only with difficulty grasped the mentality of the general population in those days, the postwar generation would be hard put to it to understand the precrisis attitude. A long process of fermentation was necessary to convert the peace-loving, law-abiding, neutralist Danes into active underground fighters. We should also bear these facts in mind if we wish to understand the behavior of the Jews at that time. Frode Jakobsen, one of the few who had created the kernel of an organized underground movement, wrote on the 30th of September, 1943, to Christmas Møller:

For me the main thing is the struggle for the soul of the people. The essential aim is to get the people to fight. . . . One cannot in all conscience totally reject the assertion that it is not the Danish people but small "gangs" which are fighting. . . . In my opinion "how to draw the masses into the war" is more important than "how to cause the greatest practical damage to the Germans." . . . I am in no doubt that we must work toward this broader popular rising. Whether this will succeed and how it is to be done—well, I must admit I can't see quite clearly at the moment.[6]

Best, Himmler, and Hitler then came to Frode Jakobsen's aid, and the persecution of the Jews created the popular base of the Danish underground toward which he and his friends had striven.

It should, however, be pointed out that under the surface the will to active resistance had stiffened even before the advent of the crisis—otherwise the crisis would not have come. In 1943 one of Jakobsen's group conducted a survey on the attitude of the population to anti-German acts of sabotage. This showed that public approval of sabotage had increased considerably. Of 900 replies examined, 70 per cent of the men and 50 per cent of the women unconditionally supported such acts. In the days of crisis, the general hatred toward the Germans increased, though the masses preserved their customary silence. "What the 29th of August failed to do in this respect," say Hæstrup, "was completed by the action of the Germans against the Jews at the beginning of October."[7]

In these circumstances, the underground was from the beginning a collection of groups and not a centrally organized movement. Each such group usually acted at its own discretion and in keeping with local conditions. To the extent that contact was maintained with the English, more systematic work was carried out. Chance and improvisation played a large part. "Here, as with all illegal organizations, many heads directed and many hands carried out."[8]

In June 1943, Mogens Fog had explained that what were asked for were the small actions:[9] anti-Nazi propaganda wherever possible, disturbance of trade relations with and supply to the Germans, neutralization of the antidemocratic German laws forced on the Danes, support for the victims of Nazi persecutions and for the underground movement, distribution of illegal newspapers, provision of meeting places, and organization of communications and hiding places should the need arise.

The architect of this internal organization and training of the people was Frode Jakobsen. From the beginning of the occupation he was convinced that it was essential to resist the Germans actively, and he set about creating an organization in preparation for the time of need. As of 1941, he devoted all his energies to this end,[10] and gathered about him a number of people with similar views, namely, that action was essential even if the population as a whole was opposed. One of his collaborators was Christmas Møller, who organized the Danish resistance activities in London following his flight in May 1942.[11] To begin with, Jakobsen dubbed the founder groups of the Danish resistance movement "the study circle," which was abbreviated in the course of time to "the circle" or "the ring." In Copenhagen, such circles were organized along professional lines—architects, engineers, doctors, teachers, clergymen, civil servants, trade unionists. Throughout Denmark the organization was based on the principle of electoral districts.[12] "The object was to activate as large a part of the Danish people as possible and not to create a clearly defined organization."[13] The tasks laid down were:

(1) establishing contact and distributing information
(2) providing economic support for victims
(3) forming a general organization to cover the whole country
(4) choosing individuals who would be ready to carry out especially dangerous assignments, such as illegal radio broadcasts, acts of sabotage, etc.

In 1942 the organization consisted of 10,000 members; in autumn 1943, of 20,000; and then later, of 30,000. The establishment of contacts and passing on of information was organized in such a way that each individual was only acquainted with a very restricted group of people.

As for financing, it was decided that each member of this organization would contribute 1 per cent of his salary to a common fund for the relief of families of Nazi victims. These professional groups afterward played decisive roles in the Jewish rescue operation, and particularly prominent among them were the doctors and the clergy.[14] In the trade unions, small cells of key people from the rank and file were set up. Political and trade union leaders were not active in the underground and some were even opposed to it. Jakobsen relates how in 1942, an attempt was made to establish contact with the Danish prime minister, Buhl, but even he said to them: "When you wish to do illegal work it is not particularly wise to apply to the prime minister."[15]

The doctors were among the first who were aroused to resistance as a large group. When in 1942 rumors were rife that the Germans might apply the Nuremberg laws in Denmark, the doctors presented a petition with over 500 signatures to the Ministry of the Interior and pointed out the dangers to Danish democracy inherent in anti-Jewish discrimination.[16] Under the leadership of Professor Husfeldt, the doctors joined "the ring." These organized doctors comprised 75 per cent of the entire medical profession—the highest percentage of medical membership in a European underground movement in the Second World War. No less important than the doctors were the clergymen. They too set up their own organization, to which no fewer than 90 per cent of all priests belonged.[17] English pilots who parachuted supplies to the underground were given instructions that in the event of their having to land or bail out, they were to find their way to the nearest church and contact the priest.[18]

Considerable influence in creating a spirit of resistance was exercised by the illegal press. Prior to August 1943 this was restricted, as was the whole resistance movement, but it likewise underwent internal reorganization and prepared itself for a wider scope of activities. Thus, when the crisis erupted, illegal newspapers swamped the country.[19]

The Freedom Council and the Popular Uprising

During the month of September 1943, the Danish people in general and its leaders in particular were engaged in an inner struggle over the country's political structure and over the form that leadership would assume under the new conditions. On September 2, Alsing Andersen sent to all the trade unions a circular sharply condemning the acts of sabotage of "Communists and chauvinists."[20] Underground circles for their part leveled severe criticism at the fact that the permanent undersecretaries continued to collaborate with the Germans.[21] It seemed that the people, who were used to guidance from parliamentary institutions, had been left without representation, without means of expressing public opinion, and without the possibility of acting in accordance with it. This danger was averted by the establishment of the Danish Freedom Council. This council united the leaders of the underground movement and its various independent groups, and these achieved through it cooperation and unity of action, if not always consensus of opinion.[22] The idea of the council was first mooted by Erling Foss as early as May 1943, and the council was in fact established on September 16, 1943.[23] The proclamation setting up the Danish Freedom Council was already formulated in September,[24] but was first published throughout the illegal press at the beginning of October, and was followed by a declaration on the subject of the persecution of the Jews.[25]

The main problem which the council had to solve at its inception was its status—internal and external. It was not at first assured of the authority in the eyes of the people which was essential for its operation. Moreover, the politicians—who were regarded as the leaders of the people— remained outside the council.[26] In rallying immediately to the side of the Jews, the Freedom Council represented the people's spirit of revolt and thus the fact that it placed itself at the head of the rescue operation contributed decisively toward consolidating its position within the country. The proclamation on the Jewish persecutions ran as follows:

The Danish Freedom Council sharply condemns the pogroms the Germans have set in motion against the Jews in our country. Among the Danish people the Jews do not constitute a special class but are citizens to exactly the same degree as all other Danes. With the implementation of anti-Jewish pogroms the Germans have carried to its conclusion the systematic destruction of Danish law and order; as a result all contact between Danish and German activity must be terminated. In consequence hereof we urge every member of the Danish administration and police force to reject all cooperation with the Germans and each Danish worker to deny, delay, or restrict all deliveries to the occupying power. The Council declares that the Germans, as is their custom, have accused the Jews of being behind the sabotage and unrest, but have not attempted to present the slightest proof for this assertion. We Danes know that the whole population stands behind resistance to the German oppressors. The Council calls on the Danish population to help in every way possible those Jewish fellow citizens who have not yet succeeded in escaping abroad. Every Dane who renders help to the Germans in their persecution of human beings is a traitor and will be punished as such when Germany is defeated.[27]

This appeal was followed at the end of the month by a call for acts of sabotage, and in November the council published a detailed program for the rehabilitation of liberated Denmark after the war, under the name "When Denmark Is Free Again." During the short interval between these two declarations and the publication of the program embodying the goals of their struggle, thousands of Danes from all walks of life who had taken part in the Jewish rescue joined the ranks of the underground movement; a new financial basis for operations was set up, and escape routes to free Sweden were initiated. The rescue operation of the Danish people was undoubtedly spontaneous. "If it had ever been thought that the 9th of April [1940] had revealed a people incapable of action when the country was in danger, the days of October [1943] showed that virtually the whole population suddenly and without warning was prepared to take up the fight."[28] For the Danes themselves this was a great experience which liberated them from the depression they had borne for years. The underground movement was keenly aware that it had been presented with a great opportunity to convert the people into a fighting people. And they knew how to take advantage of it.

A wave of protest engulfed the country. There was scarcely an organized body which did not express its profound indignation, until Best notified the Danish authorities of his objection to the many protests streaming into his office and threatened that if they did not cease, he would take recourse to actions.[29] As stated, the protests began to arrive even before the actual start of the persecutions. The most important were the protests of the king, the economic and business organizations, and the Church. Following the night of persecutions, at least forty protests were sent by organizations and associations of all kinds in all parts of the country: from the institutions of higher learning, from judges, lawyers, teachers, engineers, officials, police, the army and the navy, libraries and museums, social organizations and church associations.[30] To these should be added a protest of the Supreme Court and of the interned members of the army, who protested at their release being connected with persecution of the Jews.[31] Protests came in from the trade unions, from the Union of Danish Youth organization.

A week later, the five main parties affiliated with the Council of Nine issued an official statement saying, "The Danish Jews are a living part of the people, and the whole nation is therefore profoundly affected by the measures which have been taken and which must be regarded as an infringement of the Danish conception of justice."[32] The politicians at first hesitated, for they feared that a protest would cause a deterioration in the attitude of the Germans toward them, but public opinion forced them in the end to join openly in the protests. The parties outside the recognized political leadership—the opposition, as it were—also protested. Here it became clear for the first time that the political leadership had in fact passed into the hands of the underground movement; the official and recognized parties were obliged to toe the line laid down by the Freedom Council. As stated, Best finally objected to the protests, and his sharp reaction led to the controversial decision of the Copenhagen City Council to refrain from actually sending the protest it had resolved upon after long discussions.[33]

The press and the radio successfully resisted attempts to introduce anti-Semitic propaganda. Immediately after the declaration of the state of emergency new regulations were promulgated, but the press continued adamantly to refuse anti-Semitic articles, although it was forced to agree to print articles written by Germans. However, papers not only insisted on indicating clearly in each case that the source of the article was German, but they also demanded that in these articles too no anti-Semitic propaganda be introduced. They explained that "it was extremely important that no point of view be expressed . . . which would cause direct resentment among readers; e.g., expressions on the Jewish question from the German point of view would cause great difficulty."[34] The radio yielded on one point only—that in the future no Jews would come to the microphone.

Even during the state of emergency it was the anti-Semites who felt themselves persecuted and in need of protection. One of the anti-Semitic agitators claimed in a note at the end of his book that Danish anti-Semitic literature was forced to fight for freedom of expression. If freedom of expression was indeed regarded as valuable, he maintained, then it was necessary to change the situation then existing whereby the Jews in Denmark prevented all forms of free expression against them. It was impossible in Denmark, he complained, to talk of Jewish encroachment in the same way it had once been possible to talk of the encroachment of the Germans, English, or French.[35] Erling Foss tells of two members of the Gestapo who in the street attacked two people with Jewish features. A crowd at once gathered and became so angry that the Germans escaped only with the greatest difficulty to the nearest subway station.[36]

However, the main reaction of the population was the positive one of giving help. David Sompolinsky relates:[37]

In train, tram or simply in the street, unknown Danes turned to us and offered their help or gave us money. Once someone gave me a gold ring and once in the train a man took off his coat and asked if I'd take it. . . . I could not refuse. Many Danes who were not active in the rescue operation felt obliged to do something or other. I remember one day that the tram conductor refused to accept my fare. I threw the money into his bag. When I got off he said to me in all sincerity, "I am ashamed."

The two groups which organized the strongest public demonstration against the German action were the university and the Church. The student committee of Copenhagen University decided on October 2 to demand the suspension of studies. They condemned the "weak attitude" taken by the senate and threatened to strike. That same day the senate met and voted almost unanimously (but for one vote) to shut down classes for a week (from October 3 to October 10). On October 3 the provincial University of Arhus was also closed.[39] Following in the footsteps of the universities, the secondary schools also closed their doors. The fact that studies in institutions of higher learning throughout the country did not take place that week enabled the students in particular to take part in the rescue operations in exceptionally large numbers. In this way the resolutions voted at the time of the discussion on the Jewish question in the winter of 1941–1942 were put into effect.[40]

The struggle of the Church against nazism in general and anti-Semitism in particular is a chapter in itself. We have already seen how the priests organized themselves within the underground movement even before the crisis broke out. But they did not hesitate throughout the entire occupation to express their views publicly and from the pulpit. Kaj Munk said in one of his sermons that in the event of the Germans trying to behave toward the Danish Jews as they had behaved toward the Norwegian Jews (who had been persecuted and deported), the Christian citizens of Denmark would not limit themselves to bearing a yellow star of David on their sleeves, but would publicly declare that the Nazis had thereby canceled all rights and turned the social order into chaos.[41]

Many of the priests also found a way to express their views in articles published in newspapers or in the ecclesiastical press. In one such article pastor Johannes Nordentoft called for an active struggle against anti-Semitism. He wrote that to stand aside was the same as participating in anti-Semitic activities.[42] These articles were usually so outspoken that in October 1942 the Ministry of Religion found it necessary to issue a warning against the line taken in church newspapers.[43] In January 1943 the Bishop of Copenhagen, H. Fuglsang-Damgaard, issued a public warning against racial hatred and on August 31, immediately after the declaration of the state of emergency, he wrote in a circular letter that a priest must not give up "truth, right, and justice."[44] It is clear that the anti-Semitic press foamed with rage against the Church. In the *Fædrelandet* of January 3, 1943, the well-known anti-Semite Frits Heide wrote, in an article on the Church called "The Jewish Poison in the Danish Spirit," "It is quite impossible to understand how it has come about that this poison has penetrated so deeply into the Church; nothing in any of our social institutions is fought for with such fanaticism as this cause of 'the safety and freedom of the Jews.'" One of the large newspapers (*Nationaltidende*) ran every Sunday a church column usually containing a verse from the Old or the New Testament, the commentary on which generally referred in unmistakable terms to a topical subject. On October 25, 1943, the column quoted the 137th Psalm ("By the Waters of Babylon"). It was clear that this referred to the Danish Jews who had been forced, as it were, into "exile" and from there longed for their Danish homeland. The editor of this column was Professor Flemming Hvidberg, one of those who had at the time protested against the publication in Danish of *The Protocols of the Elders of Zion*.[45]

During the whole of September and particularly when rumors about the persecutions grew rife, Bishop Fuglsang-Damgaard was filled with anxiety for the fate of the Jews, especially after he learned that the Chief Rabbi, Dr. Friediger, had been arrested on August 29. He negotiated with the Ministry of Religion to insure that the weddings and funerals of the Jewish community would take place with full ritual correctness.[46] Toward the end of the month he tried to obtain reliable information on the rumors; we have already seen that he was misled, since his source of information was the Ministry of Foreign Affairs.[47] On the morning of the 29th of September, the bishop was informed by the secretary of the Jewish community of the bad news received the evening before. After the information had been confirmed by Svenningsen, Fuglsang-Damgaard suggested to the director-general of the Ministry of Religion that a letter of protest be written to Best in the name of the Church. (This letter had already been prepared previously. Following the confiscation of material in the office of the community, the bishop on September 23 sent a letter to other bishops in which he informed them of what the Germans had told Svenningsen, namely, that the small-scale searching of houses was not to be interpreted as a prelude to persecution of the Jews. Nevertheless, he decided at once that in the event of the persecutions taking place, the Church, with the bishops at its head, would have to raise its voice in protest. This protest was now sent to the Foreign Ministry for Svenningsen to pass on to Best.[48])

The text of the protest was at the same time sent out by express letter to all the bishops in Denmark with the suggestion that it be read out from the pulpits of all the churches should the rumors prove to be true. This instruction was carried out on Sunday, October 3, in all Danish churches. The protest consisted of three parts. The first part developed the theme that Jesus had after all been born in Bethlehem and was a son of the people of Israel. The second part condemned the persecutions as irreconcilable with the humanitarian concept and the Christian love of neighbor. The third part contained the words:

We understand by freedom of religion the right to exercise our faith in God in accordance with vocation and conscience, and in such a way that race and religion can never in themselves be a reason for depriving a man of his rights, freedom, or property. Despite different religious views, we shall therefore struggle to insure the continued guarantee to our Jewish brothers and sisters of the same freedom we ourselves treasure more than life itself. The leaders of the Danish Church have a clear understanding of the duty to be law-abiding citizens and would never revolt needlessly against those who exercise the functions of authority over us—but our conscience obliges us at the same time to maintain the law and to protest against any violation of rights. We will therefore unambiguously declare our allegiance to the doctrine that bids us obey God more than man.[49]

Erling Foss tells how in one Copenhagen church the bishop began his sermon of that same Sunday with the story of the night of persecutions and expressed his opinion in no uncertain manner. Finally, when he had read out the text of the protest letter, the whole congregation rose spontaneously to its feet, confirming its agreement with "Amen."[50]

The declaration of the Church implies the spiritual and moral foundation on which the Danish State was built. Every Dane felt at the time that this foundation, the basis of the life of the people and of the individual, was in danger. As one man they rose to defend it. A Jewish woman says, in her story of the flight of her family and its rescue, that the Danes did what they did not for the sake of the Jews as Jews, but in defense of right and justice.[51] In many trials of war criminals conducted after the war, a new legal principle was proclaimed, namely, that a man is obliged to rise against his superiors if they order him to perform a deed contrary to public and private moral law. This rule was accepted in defiance of most German war criminals' assertions that they did what they did because they were bound to carry out the orders of their superiors. This latter claim, as is known, also played a central role in the argument for the defense in the Eichmann trial. The declaration of the Danish Church in fact already expressed the principle of personal responsibility, and there is perhaps nothing which illustrates more clearly the basic difference between Danish and German mentality than these different interpretations of the duty and obedience that the citizen owes to the State. Here we find the cornerstone of true democracy. The Danish approach to the basic problems of political life was thus radically different from that of the Germans, and it was this that prevented the Germans from understanding, let alone foreseeing, the reaction of the Danish people to the persecution of the Jews and other acts of terror.

The Operation

In his memoirs, published after the war, one of the doctors who took part in the rescue action divides the operation into four phases: establishing contact with the Jews; finding hiding places near the coast; obtaining the necessary money; and acquiring boats.[52]

The first phase may be said to have begun with the warnings. A woman who worked in a government office relates:

I had made no plans for possible flight. On September 15, 1943, I returned to Copenhagen after having spent some time in the country and a few days later a very good friend of mine, now head of a government department, rang me up. . . . She asked me if I could not pay a short visit to her office and, she added, bring a reasonable amount of money with me. I had at the time heard certain rumors, and therefore could imagine what she wanted of me.

[At her office] she suggested two alternatives: I could either move into her apartment in Copenhagen, which she was not using at the time since she was living with her mother in Holte (outside the capital), or I could come and live with her there. On the basis of what she had heard she did not think that I would any longer be safe in my own home. She then gave me the key to her apartment in Copenhagen—and with cordial thanks and a promise to make a decision, I left her. . . .

A few days later I visited her again, this time to thank her and return her key, and to inform her that I had it from the best sources that the danger had passed and that I would therefore remain at home. She had, she told me, also received similar information; but she added that her offer was of course still valid if I wished to avail myself of it at a later date.

About a week later—I think it was the 28th of September—I came home late in the afternoon and at about five o'clock the telephone rang. A voice I did not recognize said that he was ringing from *Politiken* (one of the large newspapers) and asked me to come to the newspaper office as soon as possible, as they wanted to talk to me. I asked to whom I should go and was told that I would find out when I came. As I occasionally did a little typing work for *Politiken,* I asked whether I should bring my shorthand notebook. The reply was negative, and I then realized what it was all about. I went up to *Politiken* and was at once received by —— whom I had known for many years, and who asked me, "Would you like to go to Sweden?"

"No, certainly not," I replied, "I too have heard certain rumors——"

"They are no longer rumors, but extremely grave facts," he broke in, "and in any case you must promise me not to be at home on the night of October 1."

"I am not accustomed to giving promises of that sort," I replied.

"Well," he said, "you will not leave here until you have promised me."

Only then did I think that I understood. "But if things are like that," I continued, "then there are lots of people I must warn."

"You should only think about your nearest relatives," was his reply, "since measures will be taken to have everybody informed."

I promised to leave my house and, shaken to the core, I left my acquaintance, whom I was not to meet again until May 1945.

I had only just returned from the newspaper office when one of my colleagues (also a Jewess) who lived nearby, came to warn me. *Folketing* [Parliament] member Alsing Andersen [the head of the trade union movement] had visited her personally to inform her of the danger and had requested that she also

inform me; otherwise he would do it himself—but there were
so many he had to go round to.[53]

After the announcement by Duckwitz, the Social Democratic leaders mobilized all the resources at their disposal—
the trade union movement and the party—in order to warn
as many people as possible. Frisch also relates that "arrangements were immediately made to warn Jewish fellow citizens. Two days before the action, a meeting of Social
Democratic chairmen in the capital was held and the imminent danger announced. The great majority of Jews were
successfully warned."[54]

Not only Alsing Andersen, but also Hedtoft, Buhl, H. C.
Hansen, Frisch, and others were on the move day and night
warning as many Jews as possible. Most of the Jews were
warned from various quarters and several times over. Apart
from the politicians and journalists, those who delivered
warnings also included members of the manufacturers' association,[55] civil servants, and members of all the free professions—and of course the priests.[56] Other participants were
the staff of the Swedish Embassy and—in a few isolated
instances—even Germans.

As we have already seen, the work of delivering warnings
was not always easy. However, most of the Jews left their
homes within a few hours and also passed on the news to
one another. From the moment that people were convinced
that there was no choice but to run and go into hiding, they
generally adapted themselves rapidly to the situation, also
helped by acquaintances, friends, and even strangers. Many
recall that they managed in the space of a few hours to
make arrangements for their property. One of them tells:

Before I left Copenhagen on the 11th of October, 1943, I gave
a power of attorney to a neighbor . . . authorizing him to take
any steps he thought necessary with regard to all property
owned by my wife and myself. Our house was immediately
cleared of all furniture and was let to a Danish family. All the

furniture was stored at another neighbor's house. . . . These friends likewise took it upon themselves to insure that the house was once more furnished and ready to receive us, upon our happy return home on July 15, 1945.[57]

People transferred their businesses, houses, valuables, cash deposits, and so forth. A large and well-known businessman, for instance, transferred the right of signature, and his firm —under another name—continued to operate until its owner returned from Sweden; the four "directors" then went back to their former jobs and the business reappeared under its original name.[58] In certain instances housekeepers remained to look after absentee homes, or lawyers kept an eye on property. Clearly, all these cases refer to people of means, whose friends and neighbors came from the same milieu. Not everyone found his home and business in this admirable condition upon his return—and this point will be dealt with later.[59]

The first problem was to find hiding places. A Danish proverb says: "Where there is room in the heart, there is room in the house." And there was room in abundance. The means were varied and variegated, depending on the individual's temperament, his social relationships, economic conditions, degree of initiative, and surroundings. Some simply moved to their summer houses or to those of their friends. In no few instances Jews received invitations for days and sometimes weeks before the outbreak of the persecutions. Even where the request came from the Jews themselves, these were never refused. Occasionally, it is true, the owner of a house became worried about the situation. In such cases attempts were made to move as quickly as possible—but these were isolated examples. People flung open their doors and accommodated whole families until the houses were sometimes ready to burst. All found a place to sleep and were given food; offers of payment were usually refused. A doctor who was one of the organizers of the action tells[60] how at first his wife prepared all the food herself, but in the course of the operation this proved to be too heavy a burden and arrangements were then made with a nearby restaurant. Although the food was of course paid for, cutlery and crockery were supplied free of charge. Moreover, when the lodgers were poor Jews, the presentation of a bill was often forgotten. It should be recalled that at the time there was rationing in Denmark and essential products could be obtained only with food coupons.

There were many cases of complete strangers going up to Jews in the street and offering them the keys to their houses.[61] It is clear that this type of help gave the Danes themselves profound satisfaction. Here was an opportunity —acceptable to all and not questionable like acts of sabotage —of demonstrating resistance to the Germans. One of the heads of the resistance movement among the clergy tells of the peace of mind he felt and how it remained unaffected by the dangers involved in the rescue operation. It would seem that many Danes had a similar feeling and that this motivated their actions. In this connection one participant writes:[62] "In the midst of all the tragedy we underwent a great experience, for we saw how that same population which had hitherto said to itself, in awe of German power, 'What can we do?'—how this same population suddenly rose as one man against the Germans and rendered active help to their innocent brethren."

Institutions also opened their doors. For short stays schools were placed at the disposal of the refugees, but it was clearly impossible to keep many people in them for any length of time without attracting undesirable attention. Among other institutions which took in refugees were the hospitals. A special role was played by one of the large Copenhagen hospitals, Bispebjerg, which rapidly became an assembly center for large numbers of refugees on their way to Sweden. The central figure in this action was a surgeon, Dr. Køster. The rescue operation of the doctors in greater

Copenhagen and its branches throughout the country was in the hands of the eye specialist Dr. Steffen Lund of the Copenhagen *Kommunehospital*.[63]

From the beginning of the occupation the hospitals of Copenhagen succeeded in blocking German penetration. In various ways, by using all the means at their disposal—administrative difficulties, Danish-German relations, and clever exploitation of German interests—they succeeded in preventing German interference in the internal administration and affairs of the hospitals. Even before the state of emergency, the hospitals treated wounded members of the underground as the need arose, and their preparedness and alertness was of course stepped up after August 29. Large-scale action first began, however, with the flight of the Jews.

All the hospitals in Copenhagen were connected with the central classification office *(Visitationen)*, where patients in need of hospitalization were distributed to the various hospitals. This office was situated in the *Kommunehospital*, where there was a doctor on duty day and night, and it became a center of the rescue operation. When the persecution began it was decided to join the hospitals to the rescue activity—"It was a natural task for hospitals to open their doors and try to hide [the Jews]."[64] At first the Jews were sent to the different hospitals, given fictitious pure Danish names, and then dispersed among the various departments, so that the whole action aroused no particular attention even inside the hospitals. It was therefore virtually impossible for the Germans to find the Jews. Hospitals were also chosen as hiding places for security reasons. The leaders of the operation relied on the assumption that in a large hospital it would be impossible to pin down any one person as responsible. The doctors also insured the safety of their operation by exploiting the numbers involved. They knew that the Germans would not admit publicly that several thousand persons had been smuggled over to Sweden by an organization that numbered hundreds and thousands of participants, particularly since they could not bring the whole country's medical service to a standstill. Doctors therefore received instructions that in the event of their being caught during the operation, they should confess that they had taken part in the rescue of the Jews and say that all the country's doctors had collaborated with them. The ends justified the means; during the flight of the Jews not once did the Germans penetrate the hospitals and very few doctors were arrested. (This situation was to change later on in the course of their work for the Danish underground movement.)

During the first few days the number of Jews hidden in hospitals was still relatively small, and the organization for transferring them to Sweden was as yet operating on a restricted scale. It soon became clear, however, that one of the difficulties was to locate those Jews who had left Copenhagen and stayed in the woods and other hiding places outside the town, but who were unable by themselves to organize an escape to Sweden. Most of these Jews were working people without means. The doctors' organization looked for them, rounded them up, returned them to Copenhagen, hid them in hospitals, and from there organized their transfer to Sweden. For this search not only were the general country practitioners, who knew the area and its people, recruited, but also members of the Academic Rifle and Sports Club (*Akademisk Skytteforenings Terrainsports-afdeling*). This organization was well trained in field sports, and its members, mostly students and young people, combed the woods and succeeded in locating the Jews who had taken refuge there, many of them for many days without adequate food.

The plan of the operation was laid down at an early meeting attended by leading doctors from all the hospitals. The operation was directed by a small staff which met each morning at nine o'clock in the library of the *Kommune-hospital*, discussed the events of the day before, and drew up plans. This arrangement insured united and coordinated leadership of the operation. In the course of time the staff was joined by a shipping expert who took upon himself the organization of sea transport. A doctor sums up:

In this way the whole of the Copenhagen medical profession was implicated in the rescue action, from the medical director right down to the youngest intern. It would have been very difficult for the Gestapo to stop this activity without compromising itself in Berlin's eyes. . . . It was therefore possible in the course of a relatively few days to create an organization which could locate the refugees, transport them to a fairly safe place until they could be taken to Sweden, transfer them to the embarkation point, and then finally take them over the last and often the most difficult stage—across the sea.[65]

It is estimated by the leaders of the operation that about 2,000 persons passed through Bispebjerg Hospital.

The operation reached large-scale proportions only in the second week in October, when a start was made in bringing the scattered Jews back to Copenhagen. When the people first arrived, they were accommodated for the night in the little funeral chapel. Later they were transferred to the medical lecture hall in the cellar of one of the buildings; but since this place was also not considered sufficiently safe, they were then taken to the nurses' quarters, which were right next to but not inside the hospital. The nurses placed their small apartments of one or two rooms—about 130 of them—at the disposal of the fugitives and accommodated entire families in these rooms, while they themselves stayed awake or slept in the kitchen. An office was also set up under the direction of two senior nurses to look after the refugees and to keep in touch with other persons involved, such as taxi drivers, police, fishermen, messengers, etc. They also took charge of the considerable sums of money which were needed for the operation (this was kept in a bag for shoe-cleaning material!). The refugees were not of course registered under their real names, which were not even known to their rescuers. The office also decided the order in which they would travel to Sweden.

The operation could not, by its very nature, proceed according to a prearranged plan, and every trip to and from the hospital therefore involved the risk that the many taxis, ambulances, and even furniture removal vans which were used would be seized by the Germans. One night, for example, relates Dr. Lund,[66]

. . . we received information that Bispebjerg Hospital was surrounded by Germans. We therefore drove there to examine the situation from close quarters and found that the Germans had indeed stationed police guards and members of the Schalburg Corps, who examined all the ambulances entering and leaving the hospital. Moreover, there were also German guards on all the staircases. Since there were two hundred refugees in the hospital that night, it cannot be said that the situation was particularly encouraging. Because of the guards we could not remove the Jews from the hospital but we took them all to the nurses' quarters, since we thought that this was the safest place should the Germans carry out a search during the night. We thought it likely that such a search would be carried out in view of the stationing of guards around the hospital over a period of several hours. After this watch had continued for some time without anything happening, we came to the conclusion that no search order had been given by a higher authority. Only such a higher authority had the power to order a large-scale action such as searching the hospital. We knew that the authorities in *Dagmarhus* (the Gestapo headquarters) would only come to their offices in the morning and that we had to move the people quickly, before anything happened. Thus it was that at nine o'clock in the morning a funeral cortege left the chapel. The procession consisted of twenty to thirty taxis all filled with refugees. The operation succeeded and the refugees, who knew nothing of the danger they were in, had all slept well in the nurses' apartments placed at their disposal. But the nurses themselves did not sleep much that night.

In this or similar ways, solutions were found to extremely complicated problems. Here, as in many other places, it was noteworthy that an alert appraisal of the situation, together with a realistic evaluation of German psychology and habits, helped greatly to prevent mishaps and even more to overcome them. The operation was thus thought up and carried out by an organization that sprang up in the course of one night. Voluntary participation in the action was spontaneous, though numerous unforeseen situations remained and these required bold improvisation. However, it was precisely this combination of the two factors—systematic organization on the one hand and flexibility and initiative on the other—which insured the success of the complicated operation.

In retrospect, writers—and even the organizers of the action—have been inclined to emphasize these spontaneous and improvised aspects.[67] If systematic organization is to be understood, not as a routine and schematic operation, but as an operation planned and thought out in light of the circumstances, then it was due to the outstanding and varied organizational ability of the Danes—so much superior to that of the Germans—that the rescue operation was successfully carried out. Moreover, were it not for the fact that the overwhelming majority of the Danish people remained separate from the Germans during the occupation, both spiritually and organizationally, it is doubtful whether the operation of October 1943 could have been implemented, and the example of the hospitals which consciously prevented German penetration throughout the whole period provides the proof.

An outstanding role in the rescue work was played by Richard and Vibeke Ege. The house of the professor of biochemistry and theory of nutrition, situated near the Institute of Biochemistry, became a teeming center of activity for tens of fugitives on their way to the coast. Professor Ege was a close friend of Professor Husfeldt, who was a member of the Freedom Council and leader of the doctors' organization. Many of the threads of the operation were woven in Ege's flat, and the whole plan was profoundly influenced by the personality of Ege and his wife. All who came into contact with them during those days and weeks are full of admiration for the work of this man, who continued to engage in rescue operations on a large scale right up to the end of the war.[68] The doctors were, it would seem, the largest of the professional groups belonging to "the ring." In the teachers' group, the work of Bertelsen, a district leader of "the ring," was particularly well known, and he too devotes part of his book to the story of his cooperation with Professor Ege.[69]

However, other groups both large and small were also set up. In many cases a kernel was already in existence and was expanded and consolidated as a result of the rescue operation. An example is the group of students who called themselves The Student Intelligence Service (*Studenternes Efterretningstjeneste*). In continuation of the operation they set up an escape route and were extremely active in all rescue work.[70] Another underground group, which called itself after the legendary hero Holger Danske and which dealt in sabotage, broke up after August 29, but was revived, under the leadership of Jens Lillelund, in connection with the rescue of the Jews, and thereafter returned to its sabotage activities. One of its members was Mogens Staffeldt, whose bookshop became also a center of operations and a starting point for the coast and the boats.[71] Even before the outbreak of persecution and the flight of the Jews, Mogens Staffeldt was active in smuggling British pilots to Sweden and also helped a number of Jews, who felt themselves to be in particular danger, to get across the straits. Among these was Professor Stephan Hurwitz who afterward became head of the Danish refugee office in Stockholm (on this occasion Staffeldt got in touch with a leading member of the Danish intelligence service, and this was of particular significance both to intelligence and the underground, since both sides began to exchange information). Staffeldt began to participate in the rescue operation in order to save his Jewish friends, but the activity soon expanded.[72] Also among the underground organizations which played a part in the rescue of the Jews was the Communist body "Bopa."

A special chapter in the story was the relationship of the police to the underground in general and to the rescue of Jews in particular. Before August 29, there were a few individual policemen who were connected with the resistance movement and even aided it.[73] But the force as a whole took the legalistic line of "keeping law and order," and more than once even showed rather exaggerated zeal in apprehending members of the underground. The situation changed after the resignation of the government. With this breach in the legal framework of the State, the police felt far less obliged to fight against the underground. Moreover, during the month of September the German police battalions requested by Best arrived, and their presence naturally aroused a good deal of suspicion and opposition within the Danish police. This was not at first clear to the Germans. "It took a long time before it dawned on the authority-minded Germans that the Danish police could deviate from laws and regulations and act on their own initiative, guided by their conviction alone," says one of the resistance fighters who cooperated with the police.[74]

As already stated, the Germans were at that time negotiating a new agreement with the Danish police, and it was symbolic that this negotiation was interrupted by the persecution of the Jews.[75] One of the Jewish witnesses relates that when rumors were at their height, he went up to the deputy commissioner of police, with whom he was acquainted, and asked his opinion of the situation. The officer's reply reflected in no small degree the transitional period in the attitude of the police force. He said that he did not think that the Jews were in any danger if they only kept quiet; he pointed out, however, that many Gestapo members had arrived, though he did not suppose that they could do much, since the Danish police would not collaborate.[76] A directive in this spirit was issued by the commissioner of police on October 1,[77] and upon the outbreak of the persecutions the police force at once ranged itself alongside the underground movement. The coastguardsmen, for instance, argued that they were unable to prevent illegal sailings since they did not have the necessary patrol boats.[78] The police, however, did not content itself with such passive resistance but in fact rendered untiring help to the rescue organization. In the wake of the action an escape route was even set up which was completely organized by the police. This turning point was one of those which led to far-reaching repercussions for the underground movement and for Denmark, and eventually for the police force itself. Many stories bear witness to the activities of the policemen and their cordial and sympathetic attitude to the rescue work—not only did they ignore the open activity in the fishing villages and turn a blind eye to the boats leaving the shore, but they put their own patrol boats (which, it will be recalled, were not "adequate" for coast guard duties!) at the disposal of refugee transport to Sweden. We meet police in all the various stages of activity as organizers, guards, escorts, and passenger carriers. But we shall return to this point later.

Escape Routes

A mass flight of this type which occurs all at once cannot possibly be orderly, and perhaps Rabbi Melchior is right in his assertion that only as a spontaneous action could it have succeeded. In any event, the beginning of the operation was marked by a general lack of experience and organization. Each individual, each group, each family, each circle of

friends—all twisted and turned to find a way out of the
dilemma. From eyewitness accounts we learn of many attempts at escape, including a considerable number of futile
ones, made by Jews and their helpers. It was often difficult
for the individual to choose from among the different suggestions put before him. Some paid extremely large sums of
money to fishermen who were ready to transport them.
Some were prepared to flee to Sweden immediately after
leaving their homes. The majority, however, intended (as
we have seen) merely to go into hiding "until the storm
blew over." But it rapidly became clear that the storm would
not blow over so soon and that the road back was closed.
Only the way forward therefore remained. This fact was
recognized as much by the Jews, who wished to relieve
their hosts of a burden which grew heavier and more
dangerous all the time, as it was by their helpers.

Hæstrup says:[79]

The resistance movement was not created by directives and
orders from above, but grew organically out of constant activity
from below. This activity was then met by a unifying, guiding
effort from above, from all the upper echelons of the movement,
and through this meeting between movement from below and
direction from above the whole structure gradually took shape.

This meeting between the movement below and the
guiding hand above first crystallized on a large scale in the
days of the Jewish rescue operation. The scale was large in
geographical and in social terms, for the movement embraced nearly all parts of the country and all sections of the
population. The relatively small organized cells of this varied
and variegated resistance movement became operational
centers. These active groups had two parallel objectives:
help and rescue on the one hand, and exploitation of this
judicious moment for expanding and consolidating the resistance movement on the other.

We have seen that transportation to Sweden was at first

beset by many problems. As the need for flight grew more urgent following the state of emergency, escape to Sweden during September also increased; but the individuals involved were still few and far between. In his evidence, Per Federspiel has pointed out that from the beginning of the flight it became clear to him that this was an irrevocable opportunity for the resistance movement to expand its activities, to assure itself of financial support, and to organize a transport system to Sweden. He reached these conclusions long before facts confirmed his evaluation. Federspiel realized the pressing need for transport to Sweden during his work of financing the underground movement, a task in which he had been engaged from early days, in cooperation with the English. He also explains that it was impossible to organize in Denmark a mass appeal for contributions to the underground movement, so long as the police regarded opposition to the resistance movement as their duty. Indeed, only in the very hour of rescuing the Jews did the underground movement first receive large sums from broad segments of the population.[80] Until then the resistance movement had striven not only against the Germans but also against the great majority of the Danes, and the forces "organized from above" had not found the forces of the people coming to meet them "from below." We may again recall the words of Frode Jakobsen that the resistance cells had to smash through the wall of isolation and "conquer the soul of the people" in order that a resistance movement should arise in Denmark. This wall was breached decisively at the time of the persecution and rescue of the Jews.[81]

Federspiel points out the well-known fact that only now were fishermen in large numbers ready to endanger themselves and their boats in rescue operations—though this readiness was generally accompanied by considerable monetary demands. However, it was now possible to find the necessary sums, large though they were, whereas formerly there had been almost no fishermen ready to endanger

themselves and their livelihood even for money, nor funds
to pay them with. "It was strange to see," says Hæstrup,
"that as late as July 1943—only three months before the great
stream of refugees to Sweden was in full flow—no one either
in Sweden or in Denmark dreamed as yet of such a development." At that time, in his opinion, perception of the problem was as yet quite inadequate. He continues:

The story of the rescue organization is one of the strangest and
most incredible in the history of the resistance movement. It
abounds with reports of imagination and boldness, impudence
and improvisation and the instinct for attaining the simple and
self-evident solution. In the hour of bitter need, it became clear
that these and many other qualities were abundantly present
in the idealists who set up the great rescue organizations and
found the solution in an operation plan that matched the
demands of a desperate situation. Thus did they inscribe their
names indelibly in Danish history.[82]

And we may be allowed to add that they have also inscribed their names and that of the Danish people in the
history of the people of Israel.

The first spontaneous operations—usually due to private
initiative—were independent, merged only by chance, and
sometimes hindered one another. The rescue action was as
yet amateurish. The operational centers arose later, as if of
themselves, and began to direct activities with growing
order and method. As the organization of rescue progressed
so did the organizational strength of the underground movement. Frode Jakobsen recalls that in the rescue of the Jews
the Freedom Council played the role of liaison officer,
broker, and coordinator.[83] But it was precisely due to this
that the context of the action grew wider. Within this context various centers operated, each usually with its own
branches. Some have already been mentioned; one more
may be added here, since it was highly significant from an
organizational point of view.

In a collection of articles in which various people tell how they came to be involved in the resistance movement, Børge Outze tells of the activity of one particular center.[84] It was set up in the editorial office of the newspaper *National-tidende*, which had previously acted as an illegal clearing-house for the intelligence service.[85] Its members maintained contact with various underground groups with a view to collecting information from them, while also keeping in touch with various other bodies—from the fire brigade to the police force. At the time of the persecutions and the rescue operation, information began to flow in from all quarters and was passed on to those who could use it; the editorial office thus soon became the center of a sort of "barter trade." Outze tells how the word "potatoes" was used as a code to represent persecuted human beings. For instance, "So-and-so many sacks have been sold." "How many potatoes I sold today to Mrs. Ege and to the owner of Mikkelsen's restaurant!" "How many we sold today through middlemen to Lyngby!" (Bertelsen's area of activity). "It would be good for the potatoes to get some fresh air or to be transferred to another place," and so forth.[86] All this represented the work of coordination being carried out. It meant that this or that group would leave from this or that fishing harbor, in north or south Copenhagen. Contact was maintained with places along the coast, means of transport were obtained, escorts provided, and meetings with the boats planned. If there was a surplus of people or not enough to fill this or that boat, the question was referred to the center. Any organizer of a group of Jews who had no clear idea of how to smuggle them to the coast and from there to Sweden would apply to the *Nationaltidende* office. This work of coordination did not hinder locally organized and spontaneous action. On the contrary, this was necessary each time unforeseen circumstances arose: the appearance of a German patrol, the breakdown of a boat, lack of in-structions to refugees or to a boat—in short, all those complex situations which the Danes knew how to tackle with the same admirable instinct of which Hæstrup speaks.

But the importance of the guiding hand grew as the scope of the action increased. Another activity was added: many of the refugees handed to their rescuers the keys of their homes. The resistance movement had from the very beginning suffered from a shortage of hiding places for its members. Now they took over the empty apartments of the Jews, put ordinary Danish families into them, and hid resistance fighters in the vacated homes of the latter. The existence of the center was soon fairly common knowledge; not only information and telephone conversations from Copenhagen and scores of other places along the coast reached it, but also refugees seeking an escape route; and the editorial office swarmed with people. Although there were occasional infiltrations by enemy agents, the Germans never interfered, and this despite the fact that the editorial office of *National-tidende* had long been suspected of underground activity.

Very few Jews were themselves active in the rescue work. One of these was Mrs. Ina Haxen, half-Jewish and of Swedish extraction, who was married to a Dane and became one of the assistants of Professor Ege and his wife.[87] There was also David Sompolinsky, who was engaged in hiding Jews from the very beginning. As a medical student he had also come in contact with the rescue work of Bispebjerg hospital and took part in the first stages of this operation. In the course of his search for temporary shelter for Jews, he came across the secondary school in Lyngby (one of the suburbs of Copenhagen) whose headmaster he knew personally. The latter put him in touch with "reliable teachers," including Aage Bertelsen who became, in Sompolinsky's words, "the uncrowned king of the Lyngby group" and whose home quickly became known to both Jews and non-Jews as an office for Jewish rescue. The house was open day and night, and from it some seven hundred Jews were sent to Sweden, but after three weeks the center was liquidated by the Gestapo.[88] Aage Bertelsen describes in his book how David Sompolinsky continued to work with the group until he too was forced to flee to Sweden.

Also among the active Jews was Uri Yaari, who has already been mentioned in connection with the attempt of agricultural pioneers to find their way to Palestine.[89] Despairing of escaping from Denmark, Yaari decided to join the underground movement. Yet only after he had proved (by a dangerous mission carried out alone) that he was indeed sincere was he accepted by an underground group in the provincial town of Odense. When the persecutions of the Jews started, he began—together with one of his friends—to plan their rescue, and in the course of this activity he was betrayed to the Gestapo by an informer. He succeeded in hiding his Jewish identity and was at first sent, for being a Danish saboteur, to the concentration camp in Sachsenhausen; but later he was transferred to Auschwitz.

Professor Walter Berendson, a well-known expert on Scandinavian literature, who had himself come to Denmark as a refugee, gives an example in his book of the way operations were carried out in the early days. Referring to his own flight on September 25,[90] he tells how that night an advanced party of a dozen people set out in a number of rowboats, each commanded by a "captain." There were four people in Berendson's boat. The leader, an experienced seaman, took the oars and set out to sea. It soon transpired that the boat was far from seaworthy: one of the oarlocks broke and was lashed down by rope, a hole was discovered in the side of the boat and plugged with a coat, and since the scoop for bailing out water had been left ashore the professor's hat was pressed into service. Berendson himself was a man of sixty-seven, and the two others proved to be incapable of taking over the oars. The wind, the waves, and the currents tossed the tiny boat hither and thither, and it proved impossible to keep to the route. After nine hours of unrelieved rowing by the leader, the boat reached the Swedish island of Ven in the middle of the Sound. The use of small boats was in fact stopped shortly afterward, for on October 1, the Germans issued a regulation ordering all small boats and sports craft to be concentrated in specific anchorages "in view of the approaching winter."[91] The flight of refugees in such small boats was of course known to the Germans, and it may be assumed that this ordinance was intended to close the breach. Thereafter, fishing boats were mainly used.

Of the many stories of flight by sea, one of the most interesting is that of Erling Kiær, a bookbinder and a lieutenant in the reserve, who organized an escape route at the narrowest point of the Sound between Helsingborg in Sweden and Helsingnor in Denmark. The two countries are connected here by ferries and train ferries, the journey taking twenty minutes. Kiær opens his story on the 1st and 2nd of October, as follows:[92]

A few days previously many Jews had come to Helsingnor to try and get across to Sweden. They were despondent and deeply afraid, and their attempt to cross the straits was panicky and unplanned. They tried to contact fishermen or sail across by themselves. By day and night they fled in all sorts of craft they had bought, borrowed, or rented. Mass flight began. . . . Afterward the rescue operation was organized by collecting the Jews in various private houses in the coastal towns and villages. We ourselves arranged the crossing, and then and only then did we bring the refugees from the hiding places they had previously been forbidden to leave.

This system was fraught with many dangers and one day Kiær bought a small boat with a rather weak engine. This was the beginning of the "Kiær Line." He was at that time very far from being an expert seaman, and he relates how he bought a large quantity of tablets to prevent seasickness for his own use. He established good contacts in Sweden, and in Denmark was helped by a group which included a lawyer, a journalist, and a policeman. He had the cooperation of the police on both sides of the Sound. He continues:

I was in constant touch with Denmark [he himself lived on the Swedish side] through a young policeman who guarded the ferry. From him I received instructions about when to anchor off the Danish shore and when to arrive. . . . I always sailed to bathing jetties. . . . We used about fifty of them—with or without the owner's permission. Some people were even kind enough to lend us their houses so that we could hide people there prior to sailing. These hiding places were relatively safe and people could get food and sleep. . . . Sometimes the crossing of the straits was difficult. Whatever the weather or the degree of darkness, the passengers were usually nervous and tense. During the first half of the journey to Sweden it was forbidden to speak or smoke. If anyone pulled out a cigarette or matches, these were thrown overboard without a word. The light of a burning cigarette could be seen from afar, but the Germans did not seem to be aware of this, as we ourselves were often warned of their presence by the glow of a cigarette.

Kiær took both mail and passengers back with him to Denmark. He also helped the Swedish police to get rid of unwelcome visitors without fail, and even transported spies to Denmark. After the end of the Jewish rescue operation, he continued to ferry members of the underground movement, Danish officers, and others who could not or did not want to use the official routes. From here on his account forms part of the more general story of the establishment of an underground route to Sweden.[93] Gersfelt says of him that "he was without doubt the man who made the greatest personal effort in the transportation of refugees."[94]

Kiær was unusual in that most other rescue organizers worked with the help of fishermen and all kinds of boats. As the flight of Jews increased, so did the scope of the illegal transportation across the straits. Large groups of tens and sometimes hundreds of Jews were assembled and divided up among various vessels. Whole flotillas of fishing boats filled with refugees set out from the fishing ports from time to time, even in broad daylight. Some fishermen made the trip three times a day. Fishing anchorages north of Helsingnor became agreed-on sailing points with the Danish coastguardsmen, insuring the safety of the operation. Once a large expedition was caught in one of these harbors as a result of information given to the enemy (this will be referred to again below). However, the very next day, tens of people once more set out from this harbor. Where possible, larger vessels, mainly cargo boats whose holds could conceal hundreds of people, were used.

In addition to the boats chartered specifically for transporting refugees, regular means were also employed. Danish vessels sailing to German ports concealed refugees, usually twenty to thirty in number, among their cargoes. The boats would stray slightly off course, approach the Swedish shore and transfer their passengers to Swedish boats at prearranged places. This system of meetings at sea was also developed by fishing boats as the operation continued. A particular role was played by the passenger boat which plied the route from Copenhagen to the Danish island of Bornholm. Its route lay through a canal on the south Swedish peninsula of Falsterbo. In anticipation of the German inspection prior to sailing, the escapees were hidden in the holds, but as the boat made its way slowly through the canal, they jumped overboard and swam ashore. This system was also improved on in time until there was no need to leap into the sea.

One woman writes:[95]

A man came and gave the signal to start. We were taken by taxi to the beach near a little fishing harbor. Each of the four passengers and the organizer were then hidden under a bush by the shore. The plan was that at a certain time we were to crawl along the beach to the harbor, where there was a watchtower manned by Germans. We lay a whole day waiting for darkness. Up on the road we could hear cars drive by and we shivered with fright. Once a truck stopped right opposite our hiding place, but luckily it contained underground fighters who comforted us with the news that there were armed resistance fighters in the nearby ditches. As far as we knew, the Germans in the watchtower had been bribed to turn a blind eye. At seven o'clock in the evening, a strange sight revealed itself. From the bushes along the beach human forms crawled out on their stomachs. We discovered that these were other passengers of whose presence we had been completely unaware. After awhile we reached the fishing boat without mishap and were herded into the hold, like herrings in a barrel. As there was not enough space down below, a few passengers were wrapped in fishing nets and in sacks on the deck. Owing to mines, a considerable detour had to be made and there was also a danger of running aground—soundings had to be constantly taken. The fishermen had been informed that we would pass by two German patrol boats, equipped with searchlights. We had a crew of two and twenty-one refugees, who in fact did not see one another until next day. At eight o'clock the boat sailed after we had said good-bye to our various helpers, among whom was a well-known freedom fighter, whose name or cover name we did not know—all we knew was that he was probably a schoolteacher, and later in Sweden we heard that he had been killed by the Germans. Shortly after our sailing, a wind blew up and many became seasick and were forced to come up on deck and retch, as they could not bear to be in the smelly hold. Then we saw the searchlight of the German patrol boat. The engine was immediately stopped and we were ordered to stand stiff and still around the wheelhouse, whose weak light could have given us away. We made our way slowly and with as little noise as possible. Everyone thought his last hour had come and was ready to jump overboard and drown, rather than be taken by the Germans. Dramatic scenes took place—someone lit a lamp on the masthead and the others trembled with rage, quarrels broke out, nervousness spread and actually, we could very easily have been discovered. Tension on board was extreme, though we were happy that freedom and rescue lay before us on the horizon. However, the passengers calmed down after the initial danger had passed and made every effort to stay calm, though every muscle was tense for fear of discovery.

The little boat had in the meantime gone off course because of the gale, and twenty-one lives lay in the hands of two fishermen. Gradually it began to grow light, but we had no idea of the boat's position. Would we land on Bornholm? Would we ever be saved? At seven in the morning, land was sighted, but what land? Dared we hope that it was the Swedish coast—our goal was Trelleborg. The boat approached the coast; we hoped that liberty was at hand. We were really in Swedish territorial waters. The Danish flag was raised and people threw their arms around one another and cried for joy. We were saved at last. The harbor we had sailed into was full of Swedish warships on whose decks sailors waved and shouted "Välkommen" ("Welcome").

Let us also hear the story of an easier voyage:[96]

When we reached the harbor they put me in a storeroom used for fishing equipment. It had no windows, but the door remained open and I could see the whole harbor. The Danish police guarded the entrance to the harbor and a Danish policeman walked up and down on the pier. After about an hour and a half we saw a German patrol boat near the north end of the harbor exit, and after it had disappeared, the policeman on the pier made a sign, whereupon the order was given to hurry down to the fishing boat whose engine had already been started. We comprised a total of ten refugees—Danish Jews and foreigners. I was pushed down on the deck and covered with planks. We sailed. The sea was completely calm, there was no wind. I tried to peep through the planks but was ordered to stay covered, as there were planes above us. However, we approached Swedish territorial waters without incident. Now we could all go out into the fresh air. Shortly before we reached the shore a Swedish boat met us, and when it became known that we were Danish refugees they cried out one word only: "Välkommen." In my opinion the Swedish tongue is beautiful, but never before had it sounded so beautiful as when I heard that word of greeting from the Swedish police boat.

Financing

One of the main problems facing the rescue organization was to acquire the money needed for the operation. At first, when transportation was largely carried out on a private basis, the cost ranged from 1,000 to 10,000 kroner per person.[97] This meant only the more affluent could afford to escape; the others—and they were most of the Jewish population—were forced to sell possessions in order to obtain money,[98] and those who had nothing to sell simply ran and, as we have seen, hid as best they could. Here and there a rich Jew willingly helped others, but usually it was the underground movement and the other Danish rescue organizations which collected and allocated money; they also succeeded in lowering the price of the journey. At the beginning of the operation the average price was estimated at 2,000 kroner per person, but after some reorganization this figure fell to 500.[99]

All the accounts of the operation mention the problem of financing and the desperate situations which arose from time to time. There are also stories, however, of the remarkable—and often unexpected—help received from many quarters. But the various rescue organizations, such as those initiated by the hospital personnel, realized quickly that a comprehensive and systematic solution to the monetary problem was essential. They therefore created funds, one of the main ones being that established by the employers' and manufacturers' associations. One piece of evidence includes the story of one woman's efforts to collect money: "She related that the money was at first obtained from friends and acquaintances. The first contribution was that of the businessman A. A., who paid 10,000 kroner as 'conscience money,' since he had not previously believed her stories about Germany, even in the years immediately prior to the war." During October A. A. paid 40–50,000 kroner. The brother of this same woman put her in touch with the Industrial Fund. "Thus began the utilization of this fund, not only for the flight of the Jews but also for other activities of this section of the resistance movement."[100] Dr. Lund relates:[101]

It was very often the financial difficulties which were the most troublesome. In order to coordinate the various aspects, including the financial, the medical association embarked on broad measures of cooperation, including contact with an unofficial committee which met a couple of times a week. This committee included representatives of various social groups—a lawyer, an industrialist, a civil servant, and so forth. In addition, contact was maintained with politicians and trade union leaders.

These various connections contributed toward the general coordination of organizational matters, particularly of financial matters. When considerable amounts were involved, the problem of covering up arose, since it was obviously impractical to give receipts. In certain cases, receipts were written for contributions to "the war against latent want in Copenhagen." The main treasurer was a lawyer who collected the money and allocated it to various operational centers. He explains in this connection that the money was partly from private and partly from organizational sources. Among the private donors was the chairman of the Jewish community, C. B. Henriques, who gave several hundred thousand kroner.[102] Those Jews who could afford it paid the fishermen cash, but the then treasurer was quite sure that no one was ever left behind for lack of money—and indeed no such case had ever been recorded. Dr. Gersfelt tells how particular trouble was taken to balance the number of poor and rich Jews so that the latter would cover total expenses, in most cases without being aware of it. He adds:

"However much we tried to make up groups of richer and poorer people, it almost always happened that in the evening we were left with a certain number of the poorest whom we had not managed to send."[103]

About a fortnight after the beginning of the operation the money in the central fund ran out and an appeal was made to the Board of Trustees of the Jewish community, who were already in Sweden, to allow the community's assets (which were, as stated, then being administered by the lawyer Bruun) to serve as collateral for a large loan. A loan of 750,000 kroner was then arranged for, and this was paid back by the community after the war.

In discussions on the events of those times both Jews and non-Jews usually justify the monetary demands of the fishermen. However, there were quite a few cases of embezzlement and exorbitant prices.[104] On the other hand, there were also fishermen who transported refugees free of charge or refused any extra payment over and above "what was due" to them.

Estimates of the sum involved in the flight of the Jews vary. The treasurer maintains that during the month of October about 3 million kroner passed through his hands. One of the doctors points out that the medical association alone collected more than a million kroner.[105] Obviously the total sum expended by the rescue organization was greater than the sum of these two figures—about three times as much, or about 12 million kroner (which, at an exchange rate of $1 = 20.29 kr, was a little less than $600,000).[106]

In a sociological survey of the composition of the Danish refugee population in Sweden, Jul. Margolinsky arrived at the following conclusions:[107] 7,220 Jews came to Sweden from Denmark, together with 686 non-Jewish relatives (most of the latter came after the main Jewish flight was finished). Margolinsky distinguishes between four groups of Jews: the Danish Jews who had lived in Denmark for several generations, the Jews who came to Denmark as refugees after pogroms in Russia at the beginning of the century and during the First World War, half-Jews (i.e., children of mixed marriages), and refugees from Hitler. These were distributed as follows:

Old-established families	1,431	persons
20th-century immigrants	3,112	"
Half-Jews	1,301	"
Refugees	1,376	"
Total	7,220	persons

The more prosperous were to be found among the old-established families and the half-Jews and mixed couples (2,732 persons), while those who arrived in the 20th century were usually craftsmen, small businessmen, or workers—all usually poor, as were the refugees from Hitler (these two groups together made up 4,488 persons).

The better-off Jews were, as stated, usually the first to leave, while the poorer ones hid to begin with, and were rescued afterward by the underground organization. Fifty-six pieces of evidence which were checked as to the date of their flight (with or without their families) revealed the following:[108]

Fled before October 1	8
Fled from October 1–7	31
Fled from October 8–14	11
Fled after October 15	4
Remained in Denmark	2
Total	56

In other words, just about 70 per cent of these witnesses reached Sweden before the end of the first week. This would appar to be typical, since most of them were people who were able to pay their own way. They also gave evidence of the sums of money paid out. The figures here are not entirely accurate, since the data were not always carefully presented, but they may be taken as an example. They include the flight of 175 persons who paid a total of 370,000 kroner. The average outlay per person was therefore 2,125 kroner.

On the basis of these estimates, which are of course all very general, it may be assumed that the affluent groups paid about 5.5 million kroner, to cover the cost of their own flight. To these would be added 750,000 kroner returned by the community after the war and a certain sum paid by the richer Jews for the poorer ones. The Jews themselves therefore paid between 6.5 and 7 million kroner. The flight of the poorer refugees was mainly organized during the second week, and thanks to the rescue organization, prices then dropped to 500 kroner per person. Thus, it may be assumed that the organized flight cost approximately another 5 million, which was mainly collected from non-Jewish Danes. Since the population of Denmark was about 4 million, this means that each Dane paid 1.25 kroner for the rescue of the Jews, and each such rescue cost about 1,650 kroner or about 80 dollars. This calculation did not include transportation expenses on land or maintenance expenses of persons at the assembly points or in hiding. These expenditures were mostly covered by the Danish organizations.

Dangers and Mishaps

We have seen that the doctors regarded the mass nature of the operation as a safety factor. This consideration was no doubt justified as regards so vital a service as the health organization in the capital, whose workers were involved in the rescue operation almost to a man. The situation was, however, different in small and faraway places. It was impossible to hide the rescue operation of thousands of people from the eyes and ears of the population, and in the small towns along the shore, every child knew what was going on in certain houses and in the port. Here too there was a certain element of security in the general nature of the activity; a local resident, even if he were inclined to be pro-German, would certainly hesitate to call down upon himself the wrath of the overwhelming majority of the population who supported the rescue operation. This would seem to explain the fact that there were so few informers.[109] Gersfelt tells of "three stages of warning" in such cases: first, informers would be sent a funeral wreath; if this did not help, they were sent a card on which was drawn a cross of the type engraved on tombstones; then they were sent a tiny model of a coffin. If none of these warnings helped, retribution was carried out, particularly against agents who posed as refugees. The bogus refugee received a "half ticket": when the boat was halfway across the Sound he was thrown into the sea. (This system was changed when the Swedes later agreed to imprison these offenders.)[110] Another safety factor was the fact that the spiritual elite of the country took part in the rescue campaign and they devoted to its planning and operation the best of their intellectual powers. In contrast, the German soldiers and policemen and the Gestapo agents and their Danish colleagues were mainly crude people whose level of intelligence was not of the highest. Another factor was the blind superiority complex of the conqueror, convinced of his irresistible might. A last, but certainly not least, reason was that the life of the Germans in Denmark was generally very comfortable, and after four years of war they were not enthusiastic about disturbing its even tenor. Moreover, the Germans were incapable of foreseeing that a population of millions would rise, almost as one man, to defend a few thousand Jews.

There are several stories illustrating that the Germans were not only prepared to accept bribes, but also occasionally showed compassion and allowed vehicles full of refugees to pass.[111] The general opinion is that the Danish Nazis—

few though they were—were more dangerous than the Germans themselves. A student relates:

The medical association used to supply its agents with large sums of cash, so that we could use it to give bribes if we were arrested. It was not usually difficult to bribe the German soldiers, and it was also possible to come to an agreement with the Gestapo, though this was not always certain. On the other hand, there was very little chance of bribing the members of the Schalburg Corps.

There are innumerable stories about the trains—which were full of Germans—carrying Jews from Copenhagen to the coastal towns. The Germans always pretended that they saw nothing at all. Not one case of an arrest on such a train has been recorded. One witness recalls: "That evening there were at least as many Germans as Jews on the train, but having looked each other over, each side pretended that the other did not exist." Sompolinsky describes how the Danish passengers mingled thoroughly with the Jews so that the Germans would not be able to identify the latter. There were also scattered instances of German soldiers taking advantage of such opportunities to desert to Sweden.[112]

There is no doubt that the attitude of the Germans to the flight of the Jews was conditioned by the atmosphere prevailing among the leading German authorities,[113] who were well aware of what was happening. For instance, the watch on Jewish houses continued even after the night of the persecutions. The keys were officially handed over to the police or the local authorities.[114] Duckwitz in his memoirs lays particular emphasis on the courageous action of the German commander of the port of Copenhagen, who saw to it that the coastal patrol vessels of the German fleet were in need of repairs precisely at that time and were therefore unable to put to sea. For some time the Germans even allowed official and legal emigration and issued a number of exit visas for Sweden. This arrangement was canceled after an act of sabotage in one of the restaurants frequented by the Germans.[115]

On the official level the task of guarding the coast and of "preventing illegal exit" remained in the hands of the Danish coast guard. Not only that, but the majority of those caught during the rescue operation—that is, those caught by the Germans—were handed over to the Danish police for trials in Danish courts. As a result, many of the prisoners were released without a trial or received short sentences (and many of these were often abbreviated later on).[116] It was an open secret that the Germans deliberately abstained from interfering with the flight of the Jews. The German minister in Stockholm, Thomsen, writes in his report of October 10, 1943,[117] that the Swedish press estimated the number of refugees who had arrived up to that time as five to six thousand, and he adds: "The paper points out that it may be assumed that the transportation of the refugees is being carried out with German connivance." That the mild attitude of the Germans toward the rescue of the Jews was not mere chance is shown by the fact that at the end of the operation the difficulties and dangers increased and the Gestapo attacked illegal transportation to Sweden with much greater severity. In the meantime, however, the underground organization had acquired so much experience that they usually knew how to effect such transportation without undue hindrance.

Despite all this, it did of course happen that refugees and their helpers were caught. It occasionally occurred, as it did to the family of the author Ralph Oppenhejm, that the Danish captain who had taken them on board after their own boat had broken down handed them straight over to the Germans; they were afterward taken to Theresienstadt.[118] Usually an odd person here and there or a small group was captured, but only rarely was a whole transport taken. Such a tragic event took place at Gilleleje, a fishing

Danish Nazis hold a public rally in a Copenhagen square shortly after the German occupation.

Grateful acknowledgement is extended to the Danish Information Office for its kind assistance in providing illustrations for this volume.

All photographs are courtesy of the Royal Danish Ministry for Foreign Affairs.

Danish Foreign Minister Erik Scavenius (left) escorts the German plenipotentiary, Werner Best, to an audience with the Danish royal family.

A few days after the German occupation, King Christian X resumed his daily rides through the streets of Copenhagen with no special protection.

Jewish refugees coming out of hiding as their vessel enters Swedish waters. Note Danish flag at upper right.

A fishing boat with Jews on board, having set out during the night from Frederikshavn, Denmark, makes its way into Gothenberg harbor, Sweden.

Escapees being helped out of their hiding places on transport which has reached Swedish waters. Through the cooperation and mobilization of the greater part of the Danish populace, 18,000 persons, including some 7,000 Jews, were smuggled through German patrol lines to Sweden.

With supplies running low, the resistance resorted to disarming German soldiers in broad daylight.

Underground newspapers were vital builders of morale during the occupation. Shown here is one of 225 makeshift presses and editorial offices that operated throughout Denmark.

On March 21, 1945, the Gestapo headquarters in Copenhagen was destroyed in a British low-level air attack. Most of the hostages kept on the
upper floors managed to escape. A major objective of the resistance in
requesting this attack was to destroy Gestapo records which would be
used in persecuting Jews as well as members of the underground.

Minerva/Hansen

Dr. Fritz Clausen, the Danish Nazi leader, in Frøslov Prison Camp after the war. Photograph may have been posed; note empty wheelbarrow and Clausen's attire.

פליטים מדניה מתקבלים ב
התשד

Ernst Saxtorph Jorgensen

Harold Eisenstein at work on his relief sculpture at the site of the Denmark School, Jerusalem. With him are Sven Sechusen (left), former member of the Danish resistance, and Ambassador Herlitz of Israel. The caption at the foot of the sculpture reads, "Danish refugees being greeted in Sweden 5704."

harbor north of Helsingnor, which was one of the transportation centers. A local committee dealt with the housing of the refugees, who were brought into the town by the tens and hundreds in the early days of October; the committee also allocated boats and ships. Nearly all the rescue organizations were connected with this center, and the story of the tragedy therefore appears in all the descriptions. Some of the refugees waiting to sail were lodged in a small hotel near the shore. There was a girl—apparently not local—working in this hotel, and she was in love with a German soldier. Upon his transfer to the Russian front, she thought she could have him brought back to Denmark if she informed the Germans of the smuggling out of Jews. She therefore got in touch with the notorious Gestapo agent in nearby Helsingnor. The results were not long in coming. Between October 5 and October 7, the town was full of hundreds of refugees, and additional groups were on their way there. Apart from the fishing boats involved, cargo boats had also been specially chartered. On the evening of the 5th when the boats were about to sail, the Gestapo suddenly appeared, and tens of Jews were seized. The Germans failed that evening to discover the many other refugees hidden in houses. The next day more than two hundred of them succeeded in escaping to Sweden in broad daylight, but most of the others were forced to wait until nightfall, and again the Gestapo made an appearance. The Jews were hidden in every possible nook and cranny. Nevertheless, 110 refugees were seized, 90 of them in the attic of a church.[119]

These actions were reported by Best by telegram on October 7 and 8; according to him, the number of refugees captured amounted to 170.[120] The action was clearly expedient for Best, particularly at a time when Berlin's attacks on him were increasing. This failure remained, however, an isolated one. On all other occasions large groups in danger of being captured were successfully hidden and spirited away. In a few cases, where a larger number of refugees fell into German hands, it afterward transpired that most of them were half-Jews and—in keeping with Best's policy—they were released. In one instance Best reported to Berlin that during one such action a half-Jew "who had no reason to escape" was killed.[121]

The principal of an agricultural school—which was used for a short time at the beginning of the operation as a base of departure—gives a vivid description of the stratagems employed to deceive the Germans.[122]

October 7 was our most dramatic day. . . . Sailing time was set for eight o'clock in the evening. At 7:30 the pupils were sent to keep a watch on the whole area, all of them near telephones so we could be warned. At 7:50 the guard at the sailing point reported that all was well. "Yes," I said, "but there are still ten minutes left. Go to the corner and see that no undesirable vehicles travel near G——" (the sailing point). At 7:58 one of the guards came running: "A truck without lights is traveling toward G——. There were people in it, but in the darkness we could not see who they were." We were at a loss. Precisely at that moment a car with refugees was due from the south. We had no time to stop it, and meanwhile the Germans had apparently surrounded the school. . . . At that moment the vehicle, cautiously and with lights out, entered the courtyard. Just when we were racking our brains as to how to help them, the driver thought it might be a good idea to enter the school and ask if everything was all right. . . . Another vehicle was already on its way to G——. Overtaken by what he guessed to be a German truck, the driver of the latter vehicle stopped at once, turned around, and drove into a farm a few hundred yards away. A moment later the German truck returned with lights ablaze to investigate the vehicle it had just passed. However, by then the Jews were already ensconced in the shuttered farm, and the Germans continued on their way to G——.

He then tells how two persons, one of them a doctor and leader of the group, went out to patrol the area and were seized by the Germans. Claiming they were pupils of the school, they said they were looking for thirty horses which had gone astray. This was, however, the second time they had been caught that evening and had told the same story. The Germans were now unwilling to release them. Meanwhile, a few drivers and those Jews who had not continued to G—— were gathered in the school. When they were all sitting and drinking coffee, the Germans appeared.

We heard the hobnailed boots on the steps, and upon our "Come in" there they stood, in full warpaint, with pistols and flash bombs, and the look on their faces was not particularly attractive—to put it mildly. "Are you the principal?"

"Yes."

"There are two of your pupils who for the second time tonight say they are looking for horses. The first time I sent them home and ordered them to stay indoors. What's going on?"

I moved a step toward the German, looked him straight in the eye and said, "As head of this institution I am accustomed to my young wards carrying out the orders they are given."

"Yes, of course," said the German officer, almost clicking his heels. "Then it's true that they went out to look for the horses?"

"We have here thirty horses of a particularly distinguished strain. During the day they are free, but at night we put them in the stable. You disturbed this work at the beginning of the evening and I had to send my boys out again later on."

"Well, if that's the case, then it's all right, but who are these visitors?"

"Personal friends of ours." I answered in the same quiet tone, while the Jewish refugees who sat around the table confirmed this with a nod of their heads.

"What sort of a vehicle is that in the yard?"

"That is the car our guests came in."

"Good." He clicked his heels and maneuvered himself through the door. I followed after him. The Germans opened the door of the car and lifted up the seats. "Everything in order." (The Jews had removed everything which could have betrayed their presence.) The German then came up to me and said in a friendly voice: "I have to tell you that we were told that Jews were sent from here via G—— and that's why we came."

"Is that so?" I said, "They talk so much in Denmark these days; but it's usually all lies."

"You haven't hidden any Jews here?"

"Done what?" I asked in the greatest astonishment. He repeated the question. "No," I said, "we don't dabble in that sort of thing."

"Gut," he said. A short pause. "Even if none of your youngsters were outside to spy in one way or another, then they come home very late."

"When there are sixty to seventy young people in the house, I can't guarantee that they all go to bed at the same time. It happens in Denmark that a boy becomes interested in a girl, and then it also happens that they come home a little late, usually arm in arm. Something like this," I said, and squeezed his arm slightly in order to illustrate my remark.

A broad smile lit up his face, "Yes, of course," he said loudly and full of understanding, "that's quite natural." He thought no doubt that "die dummen Dänen" (the stupid Danes) had told the whole truth and that they (the representatives of the master race) could quietly return to G——, and that is what they did.

One of the important—and perhaps the most decisive—factors which insured the success of the operation despite German patrols was cooperation from the police. We have already noted that after a transitional period the police force clearly decided to support the rescue operation, and in the wake of this collaboration became attached to the resistance movement. The very night of the persecutions, the Danish police commissioner still dutifully sent out to all police stations the official announcement received from the Germans.[123] From the moment, however, that it became known that the Germans were releasing half-Jews and people of mixed marriage, the police commissioner ordered reports to be drawn up on the persons arrested, with a view to ascertaining whether they might belong to one of these categories.[124] From here on the police in fact took the side of the persecuted. The activities of central headquarters were supplemented by those of hundreds of individual policemen who did not wait for orders and instructions but acted in accordance with what they considered to be the need of the moment. David Sompolinsky relates:[125] "Perhaps the law stopped being the law the moment the Germans placed themselves above all moral laws. I know that agricultural pioneering trainees who had been brought to the police station in Helsingnor the day after the roundup were saved by the police arranging their illegal journey to Sweden." The police were on the whole playing a dangerous game. For the sake of the Germans they pretended to apply the law and pursue refugees at sea, while in fact their boats acted as escorts; they then issued false reports so that the attention of the Germans would be diverted from the embarkation points along the coast. Once, when a German navy unit approached a refugee vessel the police succeeded in arriving first and arresting the escapees. The police refused to hand them over to the Germans on the pretext that they had broken Danish law by leaving the country without permission and by smuggling out money. They therefore had to be put on trial in a Danish court, and only after serving their sentence could they be handed over to the German military authorities. The police continued this line and supported the Danish underground movement until, in September 1944, the Germans carried out a mass arrest action against the police. Some of the policemen managed to escape. Those who were caught were taken to different concentration camps in Germany and released toward the end of the war. At the time of the Jewish flight, the Germans did nothing to the police but usually only gave them a reprimand and a warning.

In those days [says Bertelsen] even those who were responsible for its application infringed the law. The police were ready to arrest people without a preliminary hearing and released criminals from prison against the rules of law and order; priests and doctors issued false certificates; and pharmacists issued prescriptions without adhering to the standing instructions.[126]

The Danes showed great aptitude in exploiting the psychological weaknesses of the Germans: their blind faith in every piece of paper with an official stamp on it; their haughtiness, of which the Danes made use by intrigues in which they made themselves out as fools; their love of money and their enthusiasm for Danish delicatessen, beer, etc.; the remnants of conscience left in them and the need even of Gestapo agents to appear as decent people in Danish eyes. As a result of this psychological perception the "stupid Danes" carried out the most daring and dangerous operations, and often a long time went by before the Germans realized that they had been hoodwinked. Then of course their anger knew no bounds and they did not rest until they had carried out their revenge.[127] Audacity springing from coolness and realistic imagination guided by alert observation—these were the hallmarks of the Danish underground fighters; and it first became clear in October 1943 that these qualities were the preserve of many Danes among all sections of the population. The professor and the fisherman, the doctor and the taxi driver, the priest and the policeman—all understood each other without as much as saying a word.

However, while many people were extricated from the most critical situations, some 275 were captured in trying to escape. Of these, about 80 half-Jews or persons married to Danish non-Jews were released. In addition to the 284 Jews sent to Theresienstadt on October 2, another 190 afterward joined them. These latter were sent in two batches, both by train—one on October 13 (170 persons) and one on November 21 (about 20 persons). Of the 275 only about 200 were seized in the harbors or on the way to them. The rest, including a considerable number of agricultural trainees and Youth Aliya members, were arrested at home after the first night of the roundup. The 80 who were freed were mainly those who had been caught in flight by the Gestapo.[128] In effect, therefore, while 7,220 Jews succeeded in reaching Sweden, only 120 were actually caught in flight—i.e., about 1.6 per cent. Even if we take into account the total number of Jews whom the Nazis were able to add to the internees in Theresienstadt (190), the proportion is still very small (about 2.3 per cent). And if we assume—as we may undoubtedly, in keeping with the opinion of the majority of Danish commentators—that the Germans were not especially interested in seizing the escaping Jews, it should not be forgotten that the action was carried out by a population without means of security and defense, with its army dispersed and, at first, under a state of emergency. Here and there armed cover was given to the action by the underground or the police, but generally this was an uprising mainly borne along by the force of the spirit, while the Germans had at their disposal all the might of a conquering army and of the Gestapo.

The difficulties of the action were many. The rescuers had to contend with, in addition to the Germans, lack of experience, difficulties of transport and communication, technical hitches, and last but not least, the weather. Of fifty-six witnesses who were also asked about this, twenty-five, or almost 50 per cent, told of one or two and sometimes even more breakdowns before the final sailing. Among these twenty-five, there were only three cases of arrest. These failures resulted from all the factors we have mentioned: the boat or the fishermen were not ready for the journey because of technical hitches; a boat was late in coming; it was impossible to embark because of the weather; a boat broke down, with all sorts of resulting complications—and all these in addition to the constant threat of the German police and patrol boats, minefields, and informers. Only a united people, from whose ranks arose leaders unknown a day or two before, only a people who was determined to prevent the Germans from carrying out their evil plans, only the whole nation—volunteers in body, soul, and money—could overcome all the difficulties and succeed in a mass rescue operation.

However, not all the boats reached Sweden safely. On stormy nights some capsized and refugees were drowned. People were also drowned while being transferred from Danish to Swedish ships on the open sea. No exact figures are available on the numbers of these victims but they may be estimated at about thirty.[129] On the night of October 5–6, two boats sank, one with nine people on board. In another instance on the same night, the fishermen wished to return to the Danish coast because of the storm, but the Jews did not agree—they preferred drowning to falling into German hands; however, they reached Sweden safely.

About the same number as those lost at sea despaired and committed suicide.[130] Many Jews carried poison in case of need, but most of them did not take it even in the hour of danger, and if they were caught the poison was of course taken away from them by the Germans.[131] A particularly tragic and much-mentioned case was that of a German Jewish refugee who abandoned all hope of flight and murdered his wife and two children. He did not succeed in committing suicide and was taken to a mental hospital.[132] Among the suicides was the celebrated author Henri Nathansen, but he took his life when already in Sweden, apparently as a result of profound emotional shock.[133]

A good deal is told about the behavior of the Jews. Many of them were very nervous and the need for sedatives was not limited to their small children. The drugs did not always have the desired effect, especially on the children, and the problem of babies crying was a very serious one[134] (as it was with the Jewish underground movement everywhere,

since it mostly consisted of complete families). Some Jews
were excessively frightened and some lightheaded and lacking in self-control. Such a time of danger usually strips bare
the character of a man—for good and for bad—and this was
also the case with the Jews. Presence of mind and extraordinary calmness and readiness to help others were found
side by side with hysteria and extreme egoism. There were
informers among the Danes and there were informers among
the Jews. Erling Foss recalls two incidents which endangered the lives of two Danes engaged in underground
activity: one of them was Federspiel;[135] the other lost his
two sons during the ensuing flight.

Summary

Was there really no anti-Semitism in Denmark except
among the handful of people who followed nazism? The
king's aide-de-camp writes: "Of course there was a certain
degree of anti-Semitism. Aside from a few outstanding exceptions, the Jews were not accepted by the country's old
and distinguished families."[136] He goes on to emphasize
that the persecution of the Jews constituted in Danish eyes
a serious German encroachment upon Danish internal affairs.
We do find here and there hints of what is sometimes called
"petty anti-Semitism."[137] A considerable number of Danes
undoubtedly took part in the rescue operation in protest
against German infringement of the law and the moral
order rather than from any positive attitude toward the
Jews. It should be recalled, however, that many Danes were
married to Jews or maintained with them close business and
personal relationships. This human element played a decisive role in the rescue action, at least in its early days. As
the operation moved on to a more organized plane, the
personal element naturally decreased. It may be said that
prior to the occupation and even during its early years, the
Danes were unaware of any specific Jewish problem, and

their repeated statements to the Germans to this effect were undoubtedly sincere. The persecutions and the rescue action, however, made the Danes as a whole realize that here indeed was a group of people somehow distinct from the rest of the population. For the first time this group appeared before Danish eyes as a compact and different body, by virtue of its looks, customs, qualities, and defects.[138] The Danes nevertheless rebelled against the Nazi thesis that this people had to be separated from humanity as a whole and earmarked for annihilation. At the same time, Hitler forced the Danes against their inclination and practice to see the Jews as a distinct entity with an unusual destiny. This fact had other consequences in the course of time, and we shall return to it below.

With few exceptions, the Jews were the object and not the subject of the operation, though they bore a large share of its expense. The great majority reacted to the identification of the Danish people with their cause with feelings of profound gratitude. Despite former signs of such solidarity by the people, the authorities, and the leaders throughout the occupation, the rescue operation nevertheless came as a surprise—no one could have foreseen that in the hour of need the mass of the nation would give this identification the full force of action. No other example had ever been known. The rumors of extermination which also found their way to Denmark told of no such story.

The Germans stood astounded and to some degree helpless before this strange phenomenon. They did not grasp the profound motives which had led the Danish people to its energetic deed, nor did they understand the way in which it was carried out. How could this calm, pleasant, and easygoing nation have changed its nature overnight? They could not comprehend what was clear to each and every Dane, from the simplest to the most brilliant intellect—that now was the time to act in obedience to a profound and basic call more powerful than any law, be it laid down by their own leaders or by the foreign conqueror. German abolition of Danish law in the state of emergency helped to brush aside the barriers of habit, and each individual suddenly came face to face with his own conscience, and his own conscience alone. The persecution of the Jews was the signal and the Germans themselves had given it. "The somber night of October," says Bertelsen, "was for me a ray of light. From here on, there was no room for doubt or hesitation."[139] The inner conflict Mogens Fog spoke of—which each day caused each Dane to ask himself: "to obey or to resist?"—was resolved overnight. The majority of men and women sided with resistance.

The Germans in Denmark did not, with some few exceptions, understand the meaning of freedom of conscience and its strength and therefore could not grasp what was happening. The means they had generally employed in imposing their will somehow failed to work. They tried to put the actions and behavior of the Danes in a ridiculous light— from Best, who stormed at "this ridiculous little country," right down to the Gestapo agent who asserted that the Danes were a ridiculous people for, unlike the heroic Germans willing to die for Hitler, they were unwilling to die for their king.[140] How then was one to understand that this "ridiculous people" could risk itself for the sake of a few thousand Jews? How then could the Germans understand that in defending the Jews the "stupid Danes" were saving their own souls? And indeed, was it only the Germans who failed to understand that this was the essential problem to be grasped from the tragic fate of the Jewish people in the Second World War?

Frode Jakobsen notes two results of the persecution of the Jews which were significant for the resistance movement: "(1) People who had previously been passive were now spurred into action in the mass; and (2) the Council and the resistance movement as a whole now came to control a fixed route to Sweden. This latter result meant assured and rapid communication with England."[141] To these may be added two more points: the change of police attitude to the resistance movement and the disclosure within Denmark itself of new sources of financing.

The true victor of October 1943 was the resistance movement: the wrath of the people and its passive resistance flared into open activity. The movement gathered up all segments of the population and harnessed them to active resistance. In March of that year the people had expressed its opposition to the conqueror by confirming its electoral support of the government through the elections—now, with all legal power gone, there was no point in silent demonstrations of this sort. The survey which "the ring" had carried out had shown how deeply committed was the will of the people to take part in active resistance. But this will had not yet found an outlet in action or an answer to the hesitation and doubts, as the appeal of Alsing Andersen to the trade unions proved. The doubts and inhibitions crumbled in the hour of persecution. The rescue operation freed the Danish people from its inner bonds and at once placed at the disposal of the resistance movement wider and newer means of strategy. This same Alsing Andersen now called upon the unions to join in the work of warning the Jews and himself went from house to house, secure in the conviction that this was the paramount need of the hour. He himself thus opened those very sluice gates he had tried so hard to dam—and this was most typical and symbolic of the about-face of the whole people.

Moreover, isolation and internal separation are distinct characteristics of all totalitarian regimes and dictatorships. Cooperation between man and man, common responsibilities, are systematically destroyed and terror takes their place. A wedge is driven between man and wife, parents and children, between one citizen and another in all work and social relationships. Suspicion and fear impress their stamp upon all human contacts. Democracy—and this is one of its hallmarks—can only exist in an atmosphere of willing cooperation. Occupation also has an isolating effect, particularly if the occupying power is totalitarian. The Danes had successfully defended their internal and political image and had fully preserved their own way of life, institutions, and social values. But this self-defense was hidden and concealed beneath the general urge to "preserve peace and order." The rescue action unveiled not only rebellion but also a remarkable measure of mutual cooperation; it became a revelation of freedom, of renewed personal self-consciousness, even of happiness. A priest active in "the ring" writes: "The priests were extremely active in all the help rendered by practically the whole population and were happy to be partners in the growing activity of the people."[142] To this feeling of release from passivity was added a self-respect, a release from a no longer bearable yoke of degradation.

The days of October 1943 marked a turning point in the history of the occupation, a brief interlude unlike the days that had passed or were to come, but which contained the transition "from passive resistance to active resistance." The phrase was so significant and so representative of the period that Erling Foss chose it as the title of his documentary on the German occupation and the resistance movement.

The soul of the people was won for the movement of liberation and resistance in those days of transition. From then on the moral and public authority of the Freedom Council was no longer in doubt. Resistance to the Nazi conqueror was not due to the Jews, nor did the underground movement fight for them. It fought for the day "when Denmark would again be free." The internal reorganization and the girding of the resistance movement for planned and systematic struggle, which marked the last months of 1943, profited from the mass support of the people gained during the days of Jewish tribulation, and from the admiration of the free world that the Danish people earned in the days of Jewish rescue.

PART FOUR

DEPORTATION AND RESCUE:
AFTERMATH

VIII

In Defense of Deportee Life and Refugee Property

The Danish people, led by the underground movement, had succeeded in transferring most of its Jewish population to Sweden. The direct and active part played by the authorities in this action was small; the policy of the Danish administrative leaders before and during the crisis had deprived them of any possible role as rescuers. But this did not mean that, having failed to delay the deportation, they abandoned the Jews or evaded all responsibility for their lives and property. The reverse was true.

One point must be emphasized: the protests against the deportations, the relief of the deportees' suffering, and the struggle to have them returned—these questions were constantly in the mind of the Danish administration. It was in this sphere that the disappointments were most painful—and the joy greatest when the persistent attempts bore fruit. It was also in this sphere that no failure or difficulty was allowed to lead to any relaxation of effort or any dilution of the Danish demands.[1]

This activity had a number of practical objectives:
(1) Determination of deportees' identity, examination of

their family structure to see which of them could be exempted from deportation according to Best's criteria, and the demand for the return from Theresienstadt of those persons deported "in error."

(2) Alleviation of the plight of the deportees and care for their well-being to the extent possible. This work was carried out with three main aims: to prevent the deportees from being transferred to other camps, mainly to Auschwitz; to enable Danish representatives to visit the camps; and to send parcels to the internees.

(3) Protection of the property both of the deportees and of the refugees in Sweden and assistance to those of their non-Jewish relatives who had remained in Denmark.

(4) Quick removal of Danish citizens from the deteriorating Reich and transferal to Sweden (these efforts succeeded toward the end of the war). This operation is generally associated with the name of Folke Bernadotte, although the active share of the Danes in its planning and implementation was much greater than is generally realized.

It is evident from the character of these tasks that they inevitably overlapped one another. This chapter will attempt to deal with each of them separately.

Danish Help to Victims of the Occupation

Official assistance to the victims of the occupation did not begin with the crisis of 1943. The problem first emerged after the arrest of the Communists by the Danish authorities themselves in June 1941.[2] The Communist leader and Rigsdag member Martin Nielsen, who was among those interned, requested the authorities to support the dependents of those seized.[3] The government agreed and sought ways and means of authorizing the matter within the framework of existing social welfare regulations, without having to introduce new legislation and arouse public discussion and attention. It found a solution in paragraph 281 of the Social Welfare Law, which provided for special assistance to the families of national servicemen retained in the army over and above the normal period. According to amendments introduced after the crisis (October 25, 1943) in the form of a new subparagraph 281a, it was laid down that families of the following persons were entitled to assistance: those arrested by the German authorities; those deported to camps in Germany; and those forced to change their place of residence or work as a result of operations of war or sabotage. The object of this assistance was to insure a standard of living for the dependents equivalent to that existing prior to the war or arrest. The allowance, which was linked to the wage index, was granted for purposes of rent, tax payments, etc. and for special expenses such as dental treatment and occupational training. In the course of time subsidies were also given for food and clothing. The allowance also covered such expenses as visiting relatives in the camp at Horserød. The local authorities responsible for the allowances were in fact required to pay only 10 per cent, the remaining 90 per cent (and sometimes the whole amount) being provided by the Ministry of Social Welfare and by national insurance. The Treasury allocated to these departments a special sum for coverage of these allowances. Only during and after the crisis did this activity reach its full scope; it then came to embrace all the Danish deportees, including the Jews.

Apart from dispatch of parcels to all the Danes under arrest in Germany, special attention was paid to the problems of the apartments, businesses, and property of the Jews. The Danish authorities had taken steps to protect Jewish homes in the midst of the crisis, and the police prevented burglary and looting of the abandoned apartments. However, not only the apartments were guarded. On October 3, a secret operation was carried out under the supervision of the Copenhagen municipality to remove the Torah scrolls from the synagogue to a safe place in one of the city's churches. The Ministry of Social Welfare requested the Social Welfare Department of the municipality of Copenhagen to take upon itself responsibility for the abandoned homes. The addresses of absentee Jews were collected from official and private sources, and the workers of the department entered the apartments, if necessary by force. They made an inventory of valuables and furniture. Cash, savings books, and the like were deposited in a municipal safe. In certain cases the rental contract was annulled, and in others arrangements were made for the rent to be paid. Furniture and other possessions were packed and placed in storerooms. A trustee or director, as the case might be, was appointed for businesses. The social welfare services also took care of payments for purchase agreements, insurance, and other debts, in order to prevent the nullification of contracts or any other adverse effects liable to redound to the disadvantage of the absent deportees and refugees. The Social Welfare Department of Copenhagen took charge of the affairs of 1,970 Jewish families in one way or another.[4]

Another branch of the administration—the Foreign Ministry—directed its activities at the German authorities. Its officials demanded precise lists of the deportees and information on their whereabouts. Strenuous efforts were made to maintain a close check on all the various deportees and to follow the fate of each one personally, to the extent that this was possible. According to a report dated November 1, 1945, 6,104 men and women were deported from Denmark; of these, 4,978 returned.[5]

The Deportees

Those Jews who were not deported in the first batch on October 2 but were seized later during flight were, as is

known, assembled in the camp at Horserød. Some 275 men,
women, and children were brought there in the early days
of October. The attitude of the German camp authorities
was good and even courteous, in contrast to the behavior
of the Gestapo in Copenhagen's central prison. Valdemar
Koppel relates this[6] and adds that the German camp commander appointed one of the internees to be responsible
for the Jews there, "one who was most suitable for the
task," he adds ironically. The man was a former circus
acrobat, who had traveled widely in Germany and knew the
language well. He carried out his functions in a reasonable
and mature way, with great zeal and showing a strong
sense of justice. His assistant was a former cabaret singer
possessed of a profound sense of humor.[7] Koppel points out
the strong feeling of mutual help prevailing among the
Jewish internees and recalls in particular the lawyer Oppenhejm (the father of the author Ralph Oppenhejm). He and
his "warmhearted and energetic wife"[8] were both "full
Jews" and therefore had no chance of being released from
the camp; but he encouraged all who had any hope of being
recognized as a half- or quarter-Jew or who had Aryan relatives to present applications for release, and he helped to
formulate them.

On their arrival at the camp, they found there Rabbi
Friediger and Professor Erik Warburg, the king's physician,
who had been among those arrested on August 29.[9] According to Koppel, Warburg won the affection of the Danes and
the admiration of the Germans, and even gave orders to
German soldiers while they stood at attention before him.
Twice a day a long queue formed in front of the clinic, and
Warburg not only treated the physical maladies of the
internees but gave them comfort and consolation.

As already indicated, four batches of deportees were sent
—two at the beginning of the operation (one by ship, the
other by train) and two more on October 13 and November 23. While the first three batches consisted mainly of

Jews, they comprised only about half of the last group of 31 persons. Of the latter, three young Jews succeeded in jumping from the train and escaping. On arriving in Germany, the women and children were sent to Ravensbrück and the men to Sachsenhausen, where one Jew died and the professional know-how of another was exploited for the printing of counterfeit money. The remaining Jews were later transferred to Theresienstadt, ten of them arriving there in January 1944. Transportation conditions were the well-known ones: people were conveyed in closed cattle wagons, virtually without food or water; and here, as in all such horror trains, some died or went mad.[10] Among the Communists dispatched together with the Jews on October 2 was Martin Nielsen. After the war he told[11] of the disembarkation of the Jews from the ship in Swinemünde. In later years, he indicates, at the camp in Stutthof and in the death march at the end of the war he saw incidents at least as horrible, but none remained so sharply embedded in his memory as the brutality with which the Germans pushed and ejected the old Jews from the ship.

Upon their arrival in Theresienstadt, a difference could be discerned in the treatment of the Danes compared to that of the other deportees, though the Danes themselves were probably unaware of this at the time. When they arrived on October 5, an "official reception" was held in the presence of the camp commander and senior S.S. officers. The head of the "independent Jewish administration," Dr. Paul Epstein, was obliged to make a speech of welcome, as it were, to the new residents, while Rabbi Friediger, who acted as the head of the Danish group, saw no choice but to move a vote of thanks. Apart from this "ceremony," the reception of the Danes did not differ from that of any others in the camp—all their belongings, apart from the clothes they stood up in, were taken from them. The Danes grasped the situation and managed in various ways to destroy the cash they had with them.

It is difficult to determine the exact number of Jews sent to Theresienstadt. The numbers quoted vary from 470 to 475. Most sources, however, confirm that there were in fact 464 Danish Jews in the camp.[12] The discrepancy may perhaps be explained by the fact that not all the Jews deported in fact reached their destination, as we have seen above. Five persons who were returned to Denmark from Theresienstadt in January were apparently not included in the 464. In any case, the picture would seem to be as follows:

Two batches on October 2		284
Two batches on October 13 and November 23		190
	Total	474
Missing or returned		10
Number of Jews from Denmark in Theresienstadt		464

This figure includes 40 children of Youth Aliya and 28 agricultural pioneers (plus 3 children born to the pioneers in Denmark)—i.e., 71 from Zionist organizations and another 35 refugees of various kinds, making 106 refugees, together with 358 Danish Jews. In addition, some Jews were dispatched singly to various concentration camps. These included Communists seized as resistance fighters, persons not identified by the Germans as Jews, and a few captured after attempts to escape at a later date; but all in all there could not have been more than 5 or 6 persons involved.[13]

In the beginning the Danish internees at Theresienstadt suffered the same lot as the other inmates, whose stories have been described in the many existing accounts of that camp.

Parcels

Efforts to dispatch parcels of food and clothing to ghettos and internment camps were made in various places. Requests for such parcels reached both Sweden and Denmark as early as 1942.[14] The International Red Cross attempted as of the summer of 1942 to organize the dispatch of parcels, particularly to Theresienstadt. Both individual and general packets were prepared. Negotiations with the German authorities, through the German Red Cross, were extremely difficult, and only in the summer of 1943 were a few scattered successes achieved. Among the first parcels permitted were those containing drugs and medicine. The struggle was intensified thereafter and the situation became easier—on the surface at any rate—when the Germans decided in 1944 to make Theresienstadt a "model camp."[15]

On October 22, 1943, the deputy head of the German Foreign Ministry's political department, Erdmannsdorff, announced that the chargé d'affaires of the Danish government in Berlin had addressed two requests to him: (1) to allow a member of the legation staff or a representative of the Danish Red Cross to visit the Jewish deportees; and (2) to publish at an early date the addresses of the deportees, so that their relatives might send them food parcels in any way considered feasible.[16] The Danish diplomat also stated that it had come to his notice that permission had also been given to send parcels to Jews of other nationalities (reference is apparently to the permission given to the International Red Cross). This application by the Danish authorities was carried out in coordination with a group of people organized and led, in this instance too, by Professor and Mrs. Ege.[17] A systematic operation was planned on the basis of a list of deportees, preliminary and incomplete though this was. Professor Ege and his helpers contacted the Ministry of Social Welfare or the social welfare services of the city of Copenhagen and with their assistance prepared parcels consisting of the deportees' own clothes. The dispatch of these parcels was organized through the offices of the Danish Red Cross and with the knowledge of the Germans, who gave their permission in November 1943, though they refused to allow the dispatch of food parcels.[18]

The sending of letters was also permitted. The organizers managed to add some medicine to these parcels. Moreover, Professor Ege was an expert in nutrition, and under his guidance several pharmaceutical firms produced large quantities of multivitamin pills. The total amount was sufficient for five hundred persons for a year. As stated, the Germans officially forbade the dispatch of food and medicine. The head of the Danish Red Cross, Helmer Rosting (whose doubtful activities prior to the deportation have been touched upon[19]) was a boyhood friend of Professor Ege, who succeeded in convincing him that vitamin pills were not forbidden by the German orders, since they were neither food nor drugs. Receipt of the parcels was acknowledged by special cards on which the deportees succeeded, by hints incomprehensible to the Germans, in emphasizing the need for food parcels. Regards were sent, for example, to a well-known grocer in Copenhagen or to a sausage factory. Repeated requests to the Gestapo in Copenhagen to allow food parcels were refused; nor was the approach of the Danish chargé d'affaires to the German Foreign Ministry any more successful.

Professor Ege and his friends, however, did not despair and sought means of circumventing the German ban. The Fund of 1944 was set up with the support of several parties, in particular the clergy's underground movement. With the help of this fund the dispatch was begun of apparently private and unofficial food parcels. Since the number of the deportees' relatives remaining in Denmark was quite small, a group of people was organized to act as consignors for the parcels. Many of these "patrons" were priests. A large number of them were prepared to cover the cost of the parcels themselves and even requested to do so. In all instances, however, where expenses were not adequately covered, the director-general of the Ministry of Social Welfare and National Insurance, H. H. Koch, undertook to make up the difference from the Fund of 1944.[20]

Professor Ege established a special card index of addressors and addressees, together with the age of the deportees and their addresses in Denmark. In certain cases note was also made of the location of belongings and furniture or of the people through whom such information could be ascertained. The card index contained only details of clothes and requests for food parcels, and the dates terminate with the year 1943. It should be remembered, however, that the dispatch of food parcels was "private" and therefore could not be indicated openly on the cards. In some cases, the address of the sender is given as Sweden, while in Denmark the network embraced the whole country.[21] With the help of this card index seven hundred parcels were sent off regularly every month. Since it was generally whole families that were deported, the parcels were sent to each member in turn, and in this way the whole family was constantly supplied with parcels. Since the card index was incomplete, the deportees indicated those omitted by signing the names of the latter instead of their own as the recipients of the parcels.[22]

The organizers of the operation were naturally very uncertain at first as to whether the parcels would in fact reach their destinations, and even acknowledgment of receipt was no proof that the deportees had indeed consumed the food sent to them. It transpired, however, that the pedantic bureaucracy of the Germans lived up to its reputation—the railway and postal authorities, having apparently received no notification of the Gestapo's ban, religiously fulfilled their functions even inside Theresienstadt. It is doubtful, on the other hand, that the Germans were really "unaware" that parcels were being received by the Danish Jews in the ghetto; it would appear more probable that they preferred to turn a blind eye to what was going on. Proof of the success of the operation was the return of a number of parcels marked "unknown" (these had not been sent to Theresienstadt but to one of the extermination camps). This activity continued until the visit of the official delegation to Theresienstadt in June 1944, after which it was organized officially by the Red Cross. It was part of widespread Danish activity in the dispatch of parcels to all the Danish inmates of the internment camps.[23]

There is no doubt that these food parcels saved the lives and the health of most of the Danish internees in Theresienstadt as in other camps. The first parcels were received in Theresienstadt at the end of February 1944. During the five preceding months twenty-four of the Danish inmates died, while in the almost fourteen months until liberation only twenty-seven more perished—that is, mortality dropped by more than 50 per cent. No less important, however, than the nutritional value of the parcels was their psychological effect, for they were vivid proof of the bonds between the prisoners and their homeland and of the fact that they had not been given up for dead.

All the psychic well-being that accompanied the better food [writes Dr. Friediger] was just as important as the physical, and the mind was fortified by the wonderful realization that at home they were thinking of us and working for us. For—so we thought—when those at home take care that we shall not starve to death, then they will also find ways and means of delivering us from this hell.[24]

The food brought benefits not only for the Danish deportees. The goods were in great demand in Theresienstadt both by the Jewish prisoners and the German and Czech camp staff, with whom the contents could occasionally be used as a means of bribery.[25] The privileged material situation of the group earned for it a special status in the camp and naturally also aroused jealousy. In certain cases the Danish Jews also obtained food parcels for individuals from other countries. Rabbi Friediger also relates that surplus vitamin pills were given to the hospitals. Adler accuses the Danes of "disgraceful greediness" but nevertheless stresses that they maintained good relations with the other groups, particularly with the Czechs.[26] A different opinion is held by Ze'ev Shek. He belonged to the Zionist youth movement, and the members of Hechalutz deported from Denmark shared their parcels with comrades from other lands, according to the general habit of the organization. Shek also relates that the older people "created for themselves a reputation of selfishness."[27]

Individual Releases

From the very beginning of the pogrom, the Danish authorities seized upon Best's interpretation of the deportation order—namely, that it did not apply to the offspring or partners of mixed marriages. As early as midday of October 2, the Danish police commissioner, as we have seen, sent instructions to all police stations to pay particular attention to this point and to find out who was and who was not eligible for release under Best's ruling. It has already been noted that the Germans themselves released from deportation no small number of half-Jews and partners in mixed marriages. There remained, however, others in these categories among the deportees. The Danish authorities and in particular the Foreign Ministry in the person of Frants Hvass, head of the political department, instituted efforts from the beginning of October 1943 to have such persons returned to Denmark. On October 6, the Danish legation in Berlin presented Grundherr with a memorandum on this subject with full details of twelve such cases.[28] The next day Thadden passed the note on to Eichmann with the following message: "In order to contribute to a more tranquil atmosphere in Denmark, the Foreign Ministry would be grateful if an investigation is carried out as early as possible and the necessary arrangements made, should there prove to have been illegal arrests."[29]

The RSHA replied on October 12 in a letter signed by

Eichmann's deputy, Günther. He claimed that all the persons mentioned in the Danish note were full Jews, apart from one Jewess who had been married to an Aryan, but since he was dead the Jewish laws now applied to her. Her two daughters had declared that they preferred to remain with their mother. "For these reasons too—apart from reasons of security which oppose such a move—their return to Denmark is thus out of the question."[30] He then goes on at length to claim that all the cases concerned have been repeatedly and thoroughly examined, that a number of persons had even been released before the deportation, and that there are therefore no grounds for complaint.

The Foreign Ministry approached Best on this matter on the same day. In his telegram of reply on October 13[31] he pointed out that he had in fact not promised the return of persons deported in error, but his position and that of the chief of security police (Mildner) vis-à-vis the Danish authorities would be most disagreeable if these people were not returned. In addition, he raised the question of the release of aged persons with the comment:

The chief of security police is in full agreement with me that the arrest and deportation of Jews of such advanced years is superfluous, since they can no longer cause any harm, politically or racially. The sympathetic feelings of the Danes would be satisfied could these old people be exempted from the action against the Jews.

He refers here to two specific instances: the retired headmistress Hanna Adler[32] and the 102-year-old Mrs. Texière, Copenhagen's oldest inhabitant. This latter case is referred to constantly in the two-month-long discussion on the return of the persons from Theresienstadt.

In the meantime, on October 14, the Danish legation presented Thadden with two additional names deported, it claimed, in error.[33] In view of the RSHA's refusal to act,

Inl. II now addressed itself to Ribbentrop and asked him to make a decision regarding the cases in question. The note to the minister of October 14[34] asked:

(1) Should aged Jews be exempted from future arrest? On this point the department accepted Best's viewpoint.

(2) Should children be exempted from arrest? Here the department corroborated the assertion of the RSHA that exemption of children "would contradict the basic aim of our Jewish policy."

(3) Should the aged Jews already arrested and deported be released? The department did not support the Danish demand.

(4) Should the *Reichsführer S.S.* be approached with a view to obtaining the release of half-Jews and partners of mixed marriages? The department points out that such an arrangement could be made only on the basis of a talk with the *Reichsführer S.S.*, since the relevant officials in the RSHA were opposed to it.

The department recommended the release of "at least a few outstanding cases" and stated that the political department of the Foreign Ministry (i.e., Deputy Director-General Hencke) also recommended such releases. Ribbentrop complied with the request to make an early decision by replying the next day, October 15;[35] he accepted Best's arguments and "decided in principle in favor of a more flexible handling of the Jewish problem in Denmark." This was announced both to Best and the RSHA.[36] But no practical decision had in fact yet been reached, and the Danish legation in Berlin continued in the meantime to add names of "errors," the number of which now amounted to twenty.[37] A further comprehensive note was presented on October 29 with reference to the same cases which Günther had rejected as eligible for release, and further evidence was brought to show that they did in fact belong to the eligible category.[38]

More important, however, than this material with its

individual details was a memorandum the Danes presented to the German Foreign Ministry on October 25. Here all the claims regarding the deported Jews were assembled for the first time: a list of all the deportees for purposes of examining errors and preparing the dispatch of parcels by relatives; a request for the return of children and old people and persons deported in error; and a request for permission for an official of the Danish legation or a representative of the Danish Red Cross to visit the deported Danish subjects. The tone of the document is fairly sharp, particularly if account is taken of the fact that it was presented by the authorities of a conquered country to the conquerors.[39] It is evident that Günther's assertions had caused the Danes no little irritation, and they countered with Best's assurance of October 5, according to which partners in mixed marriages and their children were exempt from deportation.[40]

In the meantime, on October 25 Ribbentrop had again been asked for a decision on all the points raised in the earlier Danish note. The memorandum pointed out that the foreign minister had not yet laid down a ruling with regard to the release of persons from Theresienstadt. Sonnleithner replied to this (on October 28) that the minister would like to discuss the matter again with the RSHA, that he felt that it should be necessary to deport only young and dangerous persons, and that "the Jewess aged 102 can no longer cause any harm in Denmark, and her deportation would only serve as propaganda against us." He also opposes the deportation of half-Jews and asks that a list of the children be forwarded to him.[41]

This directive from Ribbentrop led to an additional thorough examination of the situation by the Gestapo head, Müller, himself and by the Foreign Office. As a result, Eichmann was sent to Copenhagen to investigate the situation and to negotiate with Best on the various unsettled questions. Wagner informed Best of this in a telegram dated October 30.[42] A second telegram that day informed Best of

the names of the persons whose deportation to Theresienstadt had been questioned by the Danish authorities.[43]

Eichmann visited Copenhagen on November 2, a month
after the commencement of the deportations. Best cabled
the results of the talks the next day; he had reached agreement with Eichmann on the following points:

(1) Jews over sixty would not be arrested or deported.

(2) Half-Jews and Jews living in a mixed marriage would
    be released and returned to Denmark.

(3) All the Jews deported from Denmark to Theresien-
    stadt would remain there and not be transferred to
    other camps (that is, Auschwitz), and the repre-
    sentatives of the Danish administration and the
    Danish Red Cross would pay a visit to the camp in
    the near future.

At the end of the telegram Best asks if the RSHA will
"act in accordance with Eichmann's proposals."[44] In accordance with Best's request, the Foreign Ministry held
consultations with Eichmann on the day of his return to
Berlin—November 4. At this or another meeting the problem
of the visit to Theresienstadt was also discussed with the
German Red Cross, and the same day Eichmann's reply
was transferred by telegram to Best as follows:

RSHA OBERSTURMBANNFÜHRER EICHMANN HAS PROMISED THE IM-
PLEMENTATION OF THE PROPOSALS IN THE ABOVE TELEGRAM [of
Best]. IT IS EMPHASIZED THAT PARAGRAPH 1 REFERS ONLY TO THE
FUTURE. AS REGARDS PARAGRAPH 2, EACH CASE WILL BE THOROUGHLY
INVESTIGATED,AND ONLY WHEN IT IS CLEAR BEYOND A SHADOW OF
DOUBT THAT AN ERROR HAS OCCURRED WILL THE DEPORTEES BE
RETURNED. AS REGARDS PARAGRAPH 3, THE RSHA AGREES IN PRINCIPLE
TO THE PROPOSED VISIT, BUT THIS SHOULD NOT TAKE PLACE BEFORE
THE SPRING OF 1944. THE JEWS IN THERESIENSTADT WILL BE
ALLOWED TO WRITE TO DENMARK, BUT THE DISPATCH OF FOOD
PARCELS IS STILL UNDESIRABLE.[45]

It is finally pointed out that the Jewess Texière may remain
in Denmark—"Eichmann himself states that her whereabouts

are unknown. . . . She is presumably in hiding in Denmark." His supposition was correct.[46]

These decisions were passed on to the Danish legation orally or in writing,[47] but in the meantime the Danes continued to present the German Foreign Ministry with new names and at the same time attached material to prove the correctness of their former demands for the return of deportees. Without mentioning Günther's refusal to recognize such people as "mixed," the Danes attempted in each case to add factual and moral weight to their arguments.[48] These constant representations impelled a new letter from Thadden to Eichmann on December 16, in which he asks for examination of the possibility of immediate release of a group of five or six persons among the Jews "as proof of the implementation of the assurances given by *Obersturmbannführer* Eichmann in Copenhagen."[49]

Eichmann complied. On January 4, 1944, Thadden announced the agreement of the RSHA to the release of five persons during the coming week—their names are given in the memorandum.[50] As to investigation of the other cases it was claimed that this could not be carried out since a large part of the files had been destroyed in air raids. The RSHA also refused to provide a list of the deported Jews and suggested that the Danes be given the excuse of destroyed files. A decision regarding parcels had still not been made. Hencke informed the Danish minister, Mohr, of all these points when the latter visited him on January 5.[51] Mohr also made various demands designed to verify the fate of those deported during the winter from Denmark to concentration camps in Germany. With regard to parcels, Hencke explained the ban by saying that they were superfluous, since the Jews and the Danes in Theresienstadt received the same rations as the German population and— so he claimed—it was impossible to improve the situation of the Danish Jews for disciplinary reasons. As we know, the Danes did not accept this refusal and did not believe all these reassuring statements; they sought and found a way of circumventing the ban on the dispatch of parcels.

On January 19 Thadden noted the names of the five liberated half-Jews *(freigelassene Mischlinge)*.[52] However, the Danish authorities still refused to keep quiet. On that same day the legation presented Thadden with copies of all the material and correspondance the Danes had submitted since the beginning of October 1943.[53] This was their reply to the assertion that it was impossible to carry out any further examination of the personal status of deportees because the files had been lost. But these efforts were no more successful. The German tactics of partly complying with Danish claims in order to blunt the latter's initiative were successful to some extent. Hereafter the Danes concentrated their efforts mainly on the demand to allow a visit to Theresienstadt.

Together with these central activities, the Danish authorities also endeavored to determine the fate of individuals who had disappeared or whose fate inside Theresienstadt was not clear. In most cases their courteous but stubborn questions usually elicited some reply at last, especially after the visit in June 1944.[54]

The Visit to Theresienstadt

We have mentioned that as early as October 1943 the Danes requested permission for a member of the legation staff or a representative of the Danish Red Cross to visit the deported Jews, and it was agreed in the talks of November 4, following Eichmann's visit to Copenhagen, that such a visit would take place "in the spring."[55]

The parties interested in the visit and involved in the negotiations from the very beginning were the International Red Cross in Geneva, represented in Berlin by Dr. Marti; the Foreign Relations Department of the German Red Cross, led by one Hartmann; and, on the Danish side, the Foreign

Ministry and the Danish Red Cross. The visit to Theresienstadt was one of the links in a chain of activities planned
by Eichmann's department, which included not only a visit
to the "model ghetto" but also to the work camp of the
inmates of Theresienstadt at Birkenau—and preparations for
both visits in the form of transfers to the gas chambers at
Auschwitz. The visits themselves were designed to calm the
fears of the world regarding the fate of the Jews and to
prove that the rash of rumors was false. The addition of the
Danes to the representatives of the International Red Cross
especially served the interests of the RSHA. The Danes were
the privileged group at Theresienstadt and, thanks to the
parcels they received, were well-fed and -clothed. By involving the Danes in the visit, Eichmann would not only
comply with their request to visit the camp, but would also
show the Red Cross—and through it the whole world—the
one group out of all the masses that populated the ghettos
and concentration camps which was in relatively good
physical and spiritual condition. Moreover, the Danes would
see that their efforts on behalf of the internees were being
made within the framework of international activity, as it
were. It was this combination which rounded out the deception.

On November 19 Best announced in a cable to Berlin
that Helmer Rosting had informed him of the request of
the Danish Red Cross to the presidium of the German Red
Cross to be allowed to visit, in their present quarters, the
Jews and Communists deported from Denmark. At the same
time, said Best, he had received a similar request from the
head of the Political Department of the Danish Foreign
Ministry, Frants Hvass. Best points out that the visits would
probably set Danish minds at rest.[56] This request was also
passed on by Thadden to the Minister's Bureau and to the
RSHA on November 22.[57] In both cases Thadden mentions
the decisions made during Eichmann's visit to Copenhagen
and even asks that the Danish requests be answered and

that the visit be arranged at an earlier date. The RSHA's negative reply was given on December 14 by Eichmann himself.[58]

On February 18 the Danish minister, Mohr, again visited Hencke and repeated his request for the return to Denmark of those Jews deported in error; he also reminded Hencke of the assurance given that a visit to Theresienstadt would be permitted. Hencke noted in his report on the meeting that he knew that such an assurance had been given several months previously by the RSHA, but that it was clear that such a visit was not desirable.[59] He informed Inland II of the talk. Following Hencke's note, Thadden apparently talked to Eichmann, who informed him that the visit was "not desirable before May." In a letter to the RSHA he states:

With regard to the visit to the Theresienstadt camp, the Foreign Ministry intends to delay its reply to the Danish minister until about May, since according to a *verbal pronouncement* by Ober-sturmbannführer Eichmann a visit before that time would be undesirable. [Italics are author's.][60]

Both Hvass and Rosting, however, again approached Best on the question of the visit: they received the reply that the visit could presumably take place during the second half of May.[61] In the meantime, Best and Thadden debated whether it was a good idea for two important Danes such as Hvass and Rosting to visit Theresienstadt. Best claimed that Hvass should be allowed to come since he was the official in charge of these matters and "he is therefore in a position to spread reassuring news and thus achieve the political objectives at which the visit is aimed."[62] On April 6 Thadden passed both requests on to the RSHA; he asked that a final date for the visit be fixed during the second half of May and also gave details of the discussion between the Foreign Ministry and Best as to who the visitors should be. A similar correspondence on the visit was in progress between the German Red Cross and the RSHA.[63]

In April Hvass himself paid a visit to Berlin. He apparently went straight to the RSHA and there got in touch with Mildner, with whom he had conferred about the same problems during the latter's tour of duty as chief of security police in Denmark.[64] Mildner confirmed this in a declaration at Nuremberg.[65] He asserted there that when he was still in Denmark he promised officials of the Danish Foreign Ministry that he would obtain permission for Danes to visit Theresienstadt. He also claimed that he sent such a request to the RSHA and even asked Müller personally to authorize the visit. He further related that Hvass visited him in April and asked him to make another attempt in the matter. Hvass confirmed this and stated that he visited Berlin in this connection a number of times and on one occasion was even received by Müller himself.[66] On May 12 Hvass was again in Berlin and this time also made a call on Hencke;[67] this may have been the occasion when he also met Müller, since four days later, on May 16, Mildner replied to Thadden's letter of April 6 that "the *Reichsführer S.S.* has given permission for a visit to the Theresienstadt ghetto by the representatives of Denmark and Sweden mentioned in the above letter." The date of the visit was indicated as "the beginning of June."[68] The Danes continued to exert pressure on the Germans to inform them of the exact date of the visit. Their constant inquiries kept the German Foreign Ministry busy, and Hencke apparently felt so uncomfortable that at a meeting of the leading officials of the Ministry he asked Director-General Steengracht to clarify the matter with Kaltenbrunner.[69]

The date of the visit was finally fixed for June 23, 1944, in an announcement by Müller both to Thadden and to the Red Cross on June 13.[70] On June 17 Wagner informed Best that the visit would take place on the date arranged, at twelve noon. In an internal memorandum Thadden stated that he himself would accompany the visitors, and on June 20 he requested the necessary permits for Hvass, Rosting, a member of the Danish legation staff in Berlin (but no such person in fact participated), and the representative of the International Red Cross in Berlin, Dr. M. Rossel.[71]

Immediately after the visit of this commission on June 23 three reports were written: one by Hvass, one by Dr. Juel Henningsen (who went instead of Rosting), and one by Dr. Rossel. The Danish reports have not as yet been released for publication but are accessible for perusal. A summary of Rossel's report is given by Adler in his book *Die Verheimlichte Wahrheit*. The two Danish reports and his experience as an internee in the camp formed the basis for Adler's comprehensive description of the visit which appears in his book *Theresienstadt*.[72]

All three reports are similarly constructed: the factual data of the camp are given on the basis of a survey by the "elder of the Jews," Paul Epstein, who lectured at the beginning of the visit on the structure and administration of the ghetto (the use of this term was forbidden—it was called instead *Jüdisches Siedlungsgebiet*, "the Jewish settlement area").[73] A description of the actual progress of the visit (which lasted eight hours) follows. Each report then contains a summary stating that the town was clean, the people looked healthy, and their clothes were tidy and even "better than the normal dress of the Germans at the time."[74] The sanitary and health arrangements were excellent; housing conditions were not easy but were humanly bearable. All three visitors are full of admiration for the apparent achievements of the autonomous Jewish administration *(Jüdische Selbstverwaltung)*. There are slight differences in tone between the three reports, in style and in the presentation of facts or alleged facts. Dr. Henningsen was the most sceptical and Dr. Rossel the most positive.[75]

How did it come about that the visitors, particularly the

Danes, were so deceived by the German tricks that, in Cilla Cohn's words, "even the great Potemkin would have been green with envy at the sight of so much ingenuity"?[76] In order to understand the matter it is necessary to review briefly the events preceding this visit.

In his report of June 7[77] Thadden wrote that it had been necessary to postpone the visit until the spring of 1944 "since the RSHA considered that for visual reasons the visit would be possible only after 'the trees in leaf had made the landscape more beautiful.'" But Eichmann and his assistants did not rely exclusively on the spring scenery. The visit was postponed so long because several months of work were needed to give the ghetto the appearance desirable in the eyes of the visitors. The streets were cleaned, the houses painted, greenery planted. This work was directed by one of Epstein's assistants and afterward his successor, Rabbi Dr. Benjamin Murmelstein.[78] The beautification program was at any rate fully successful, and Henningsen noted in his report that the town made a "bright and friendly impression." The preparations also included deportations from Theresienstadt to Birkenau which "relieved" the population density in the ghetto.[79]

On the eve of the visit, some of the Danes were transferred to new and better living quarters and, all in all, the rooms were decorated and refurnished to the extent of lampshades and even of flowers and plants. However, this amelioration was applied only to the ground floor, while in the upper floors nothing was changed—on the contrary, all the people evacuated from the lower floor to create a more spacious impression were crammed into the top floors. On June 22, the camp commander, Rahm, assembled all the Danish Jews, and Epstein presented them with severe orders as to how to behave during the visit. First of all he forbade any expression of criticism of the state of the town. If they were asked the reasons for the death of relatives or husband or wife they were strictly forbidden to talk of malnutrition, typhus, dysentery, and the like. If the results of the visit did not satisfy the Germans, the dispatch of food would be suspended and all the Danes would at once be deported from the camp. Those Danish Jews who the Germans feared would not adhere to these instructions were sent the next morning to a place outside the camp. Also removed were all the aged and sick and all the shabbily dressed. Tubercular patients and various others were hidden and locked up. The Czech gendarmes were also removed from the camp; only some fifteen S.S. men remained.

The visit did indeed satisfy the Germans. All reports confirm that the Danish Jews, with Rabbi Friediger at their head, uttered no complaints, nor did they apparently give any hints as to the farce being performed. They merely complained of the hard psychic stress and requested that food parcels continue to be sent and that books be added. The visitors were generally permitted to talk with the internees only in the presence of the Germans and an interpreter. Hvass, however, reported that he had a private talk with an acquaintance, now one of Dr. Friediger's assistants, the engineer Ove Meyer; but Meyer too gave no information beyond the generally proffered.[80] The German threats of the preceding day had doubtless had their effect. The fact that the visit took place at all, the presence of official Danish representatives in this place of exile, the greetings from the king and from Bishop Fuglsang-Damgaard (brought by Hvass to Friediger), the strenuous German efforts to normalize the town's appearance, the fact that the S.S. men that day were dressed in mufti, the removal of S.S. headquarters from the center of town, the improvement in food rations that day, and the ameliorated living quarters—all these factors clearly left a deep impression on the Danish Jews and encouraged them to believe that better times had come. The author Ralph Oppenhejm describes the morale of the inmates immediately after the visit as "hectic optimism."

These high spirits were little evident, however, in a letter sent by Friediger to Hvass and Henningsen immediately after the visit, which seems to have been written for predominantly practical reasons.[81] However, the optimism was shared not only by the Danes but by the whole ghetto. Adler talks of this with much bitterness, and Oppenhejm also points out that disillusionment was not long in coming, when month followed month with no marked change in the situation.[82] When, in particular, the large transfers of inmates from Theresienstadt to Auschwitz began that fall, in many cases hope turned to despair.

It should be noted, nevertheless, that not all the improvements were canceled. The children's playground vanished, and food was not distributed in the dining hall as it had been on the day of the visit, but the rations remained larger. Those Danes who had been moved prior to the visit remained in their improved living quarters. The S.S. office did not return to the town, and the workshops, which had been replaced by lawns, were not reestablished. The visit itself, the forlorn appearance of the S.S. in badly fitting clothes, the opportunity to behave more freely—exploited in particular by the children—all these seemed to relax somewhat the iron grip around the prisoners' necks. Ze'ev Shek, in dealing with the visit and an evaluation of it, says:

The difference here does not lie in the facts, which are correct in themselves, but in their evaluation. In my view, that optimism, exaggerated and mistaken though it may have been, prevented frustration, stimulated the spirit of resistance, and strengthened the will to live—and thanks to this people held out. The nimbus surrounding the S.S. was dispelled and self-confidence and faith in the final collapse of the Germans grew—at least among the young. True, among elder people depression was widespread after the visit, and this of course affected us too; but the Hechalutz leaders exploited the visit as an encouraging development, for more dangerous than the Germans was the feeling of self-despair within the ghetto.[83]

Another view, however, is given by Rabbi Dr. Leo Baeck, who described the day of the visit as one of the worst in the ghetto's history, worse even than that cursed November 11, 1943, when all the inmates were kept on parade outside the ghetto throughout the entire day.

They [the commission] appeared to be completely taken in by the false front put up for their benefit. Many of the houses were so overcrowded that a tour through one of them would quickly have revealed the real state of things. . . . The commission never bothered to climb one flight of stairs. Perhaps they knew the real conditions—but it looked as if they did not want to know the truth. The effect on our morale was devastating. We felt forgotten and forsaken.[84]

In any case, the Germans undoubtedly achieved their object. Not only did Rossel thank the German Foreign Ministry in cordial terms for the opportunity given the commission to visit Theresienstadt, but also the Danish authorities expressed their appreciation to the director-general, Steengracht.[85] In Denmark Hvass summed up his positive impressions, and his words were quoted by Best in a telegram dated August 2. The summary in general corresponds to the tone of his report and Hvass confirmed that these were indeed his impressions.[86] The Germans learned a lesson and continued to keep up the town's physical appearance. They even made a documentary film on Theresienstadt. For all that, the S.S. refused to accede to the Danish requests to release the remaining half-Jews and partners in mixed marriages, their explanation being that in this way positive impressions of the camp would be undermined.

The visit had consequences which reflected both its positive and its negative aspects. The Germans again announced that the Danes would not be deported from Theresienstadt, and unlike previous assurances, this was of a formal and official nature. The dispatch of parcels was officially permitted and was thereafter organized by the Red Cross, which also took over the postal services. The internees even received a large consignment of books, as requested. As to the names of the deportees, the Germans replied now, in a way, to the repeated Danish requests, but the step was largely illusory. After repeated failure to obtain such a list, during the visit Hvass presented the Germans with list of names corresponding more or less to Professor Ege's card index. It contained 481 names.[87] The number of Jews from Denmark at the time of the visit was estimated at 427. On June 27 Günther returned Hvass's list together with a letter and comments. The general trend in Günther's note was to reduce the number of deportees and deceased and to gloss over the "missing."[88]

One consequence of the visit laid quite bare the trap of deception into which the Danes had fallen. During the visit they had been shown stores for clothing and other items, where the internees could buy (so it would seem) whatever they desired. The Danish Red Cross accordingly on four occasions sent money to the deported Jews—10 marks per person (on the basis of the 427 in the Danish list). This money never reached the deportees, and it was, in any event, impossible to buy anything in the camp. The Danish internees were nevertheless forced to acknowledge to the Danish Red Cross receipt of the money, which was in fact frozen in a "special account" (*Sonderkonto*) in a bank in Prague; the Red Cross continued to send its contributions until they amounted in time to about $5,000.[89]

Even during the war, but more particularly afterward, severe criticism was leveled against the commission for failing to realize the true situation and letting itself be duped by the Germans. The question was also raised in the Danish parliamentary commission, where Hvass explained:[90]

Dr. Juel Henningsen and myself were naturally aware that many of the arrangements we saw in Theresienstadt had been made solely in connection with the visit. What we paid particular attention to, however, was not these measures but the state of health of the Danish Jews, their clothing, and their housing conditions. [With regard to the latter, Hvass stressed that they could] by no means be compared with those their coreligionists lived in in the real concentration camps. . . .The Danes had an image of Theresienstadt as an extremely primitive concentration camp, full of *Mussulman* who collapsed and died en masse in the street. The impressions of the visit, which were quite different, were the basis of the report's positive tone.[91]

It also transpires from Hvass's words that the Danes saw examination of the state of the Jews from Denmark as their task and ignored—consciously or unconsciously—the state of the camp as a whole. This would account for the disappointment of people such as Rabbi Leo Baeck, who sensed this fact.[92] The general state of the camp interested the visitors only insofar as it formed a background for the state of the Danish Jews. This is also evident, for example, from their taking no notice of the fact that Theresienstadt was not—as the Germans had informed them—a "final station" but in fact served as a "transit camp" from which people in the thousands were sent further, to extermination in Auschwitz. The Danish visitors emphasized the assurance given to them that no *Danish* Jew would be sent. Nor did they grasp any of the hints which were apparently made to them in this respect.[93]

It should be understood that the Danes, who had fought so long and so determinedly to achieve this visit, saw in its very realization a humane and a political achievement. Nor may this evaluation be doubted. It is true that the representatives of the German Red Cross, who had visited Theresienstadt a year previously, were not deceived to the same extent.[94] On the other hand, they also achieved nothing, since the Nazis saw no need to make any efforts for their benefit of the kind that were later made for the Danes.

It is very difficult here, as with most questions which involve an evaluation of human behavior in the years of the Holocaust, to reach any decisive conclusion as to whether the Danish visitors acted well or badly. Adler, in any event, does not condemn them but accepts their arguments. And, as we have seen, Ze'ev Shek also lays his main weight on the positive aspects of the visit. There is no doubt that the Danish Jews regarded it as a guarantee of their redemption. Denmark was a conquered country engaged at that time in a most bitter struggle for its economic and political existence,[95] and in light of these facts the achievements of the visit must be regarded as remarkable and unique in the whole history of the Jewish calamity. It was neither in the power of the Danes to free all the inmates of Theresienstadt, nor could this have been their objective. There are those who claim that the large number of deportations to Auschwitz from Theresienstadt in the fall were due to the visit—as though the Germans wished to eliminate the impression made by the event—but there is no evidence that this was so. The Danes, in any case, once more demonstrated by their behavior and its results what characterized their policy toward the Jews during the occupation: they succeeded in safeguarding their Jewish citizens, in checking the frenzied rage of nazism, and within their own sphere of operation in damming the terrible stream which swept the Jews of Europe toward destruction.

The Way Back

During the whole period from October 1943 until the end of the war the Danes regarded the problem of the deported Jews from two points of view: as part of the general problem of Danes interned in German camps and as a special problem in itself. The other prisoners were usually Danes sentenced by the Germans for acts of sabotage, espionage, and the like—they had in any event been arrested while engaged in anti-German activity. Although the Danish authorities strove unceasingly to prevent the deportation of such persons to Germany, it was nevertheless difficult for them to oppose German arguments of "self-defense." More

serious in Danish eyes was the deportation of some two
thousand Danish policemen, who were arrested and taken
to concentration camps in Germany when the Gestapo decided in September 1944 to abolish the independent Danish
police force. Nevertheless, women, children, and old people
were not arrested and deported without reason—only men
(and occasionally women) considered dangerous to German
rule. Their acts were regarded as acts of war, whereas the
deportation of the Jews appeared to be purposeless savagery.
This point was also recognized by Best who confirmed, to
the German authorities at least, that the Jews engaged in
neither sabotage nor espionage.[96]

In distinguishing between the "guilty" and the "innocent"
the Danes negotiated with growing persistence from the
fall of 1944 on, with a view to obtaining the early release
of prisoners from the concentration camps. As a result, the
Germans agreed on December 1, 1944, to release those internees who did not belong to the most dangerous categories
(active underground fighters, assassins, Communist functionaries, spies) and to return them to a camp in Denmark
(an internment camp under Danish direction at Frøslev,
near the German border). In the wake of this agreement a
fleet of Danish cars left for Buchenwald on December 5,
1944, and returned a week later with almost two hundred
policemen.[97] This operation was no chance happening. Since
the winter of 1943–44 the Danes and Norwegians had debated the possibility of having their prisoners and internees
returned from Germany. The chief planners of this rescue
operation were a Danish resistance fighter, Rear Admiral
Carl Hammerich, and his Norwegian wife and the Norwegian N. C. Ditleff,[98] who worked in Stockholm on behalf
of Norwegian civilian prisoners. Hammerich approached
the Ministry of Social Welfare and in cooperation with the
Foreign Ministry began to plan the campaign. Large food
supplies were stored in the Danish legation in Berlin and
in a number of consulates throughout Germany; even
vehicles which could go to the aid of the captives upon the

collapse of the Reich were acquired. Similar preparations were made within Denmark itself.

Direct diplomatic negotiations with Germany began only in the fall of 1944. The following winter Hvass spent several weeks in Germany negotiating this question with various German authorities. Small Danish convoys also traveled to various camps in North Germany in January and February 1945 to bring back prisoners. The operation only reached large proportions, however, with the celebrated Swedish rescue action known as "the Bernadotte action," which began in the second half of February 1945. In the first stage the Germans—more precisely Himmler—agreed to a proposal to concentrate all the Scandinavians in the camp at Neuengamme, near Hamburg. The sponsors of this program were the Norwegians and the Danes[99] and it was carried out under the supervision of Bernadotte. For the purpose of transporting the prisoners the Danes placed at Bernadotte's disposal two convoys totaling sixty-two vehicles (including fuel supplies), and later at least one hundred Danish vehicles were engaged in the conveyance of internees from Neuengamme to Denmark or to Sweden via Denmark. Near the frontier and inside the country, the Ministry of Social Welfare organized exemplary reception services, which took care of all the hygienic, medical, and social problems. All these services in "the Bernadotte action" functioned in cooperation with the Swedish Red Cross.[100] The Danish rescue operation was almost complete when it managed to include even the release of the Jews in Theresienstadt. At the same time, Himmler agreed to the transfer of the released captives to Sweden, and the Jews were sent there directly from Theresienstadt.

Liberation came as a complete surprise to the Danes in the camp.

On Friday, April 13, in the morning I went to my office as usual, [recalls Dr. Friediger] and at eleven o'clock a Czech girl burst into my room and cried: "There is a Danish car in front of headquarters!" I thought she was making fun of me. You see, I had told her several times that I had dreamt of our return home and that they would come to fetch us either by plane or with thirty or forty buses from Copenhagen.[101]

Many people that morning saw the Danish vehicle in front of headquarters, but it disappeared, and for several hours people thought that it might have been a hallucination. Only in the afternoon was the rabbi called to headquarters, where he found the medical officer of the Danish legation in Berlin, Dr. Johannes Holm, who informed him that Folke Bernadotte's buses would take the Danish Jews to Sweden. Dr. Holm must be given credit for the agreement of the RSHA for the Danish Jews to return from Theresienstadt. With the help of Dr. Rennau, the German liaison officer with Bernadotte's headquarters in Friedrichsruh, Dr. Holm succeeded by intrepid personal intervention in foiling the plans of Gestapo men and obtaining the necessary permits. A prominent role in the success of these manipulations was played by cases full of food and Danish *snaps*.[102]

I imagine [says Dr. Friediger] that even if the heavens had opened before me at that moment, the splendor I would have seen would not have been greater than the effect this announcement had on me. I sat as if frozen in my seat, and my expression was apparently so strange that Dr. Holm repeated his message and the camp commander confirmed, in a more courteous tone than usual, its authenticity.

The Danes were told to pack their belongings. The excitement that seized them is almost indescribable. Friediger relates that a few hours later he walked through the Danish quarters to see how things were going and found, for example, one family of parents and two children sitting in tears amid their belongings, incapable of packing. Everyone assembled that evening in one of the barracks, but the buses only arrived the next night, and on Sunday, April 15, early in the morning, they left on their journey north. On their way through the ghetto the remaining inmates lined both sides of the street in the thousands, crying and waving to the Danes. In the central square a band was playing. Discipline broke down even more than on the day of the commission's visit. For the first time, people dared to smoke openly the cigarettes brought by the bus drivers and by the accompanying officials. Together with the hope that the end of the war was near, fear lurked in many of their hearts: the Danes were going—now they were abandoned. The Swedish Red Cross team was deeply moved by the great difference between Theresienstadt and the other camps from which they had previously brought prisoners to Neuengamme. The luggage of the released Jews was so copious that there was barely room in the buses.[103] But the main thing was they were free. "We approached the gate of the ghetto," relates Friediger, "the gate was opened—and we were free men. No one said a word. We simply could not utter a sound."

Boldly and swiftly the Swedes maneuvered their thirty-five buses between the Russian and the American front lines. They passed through gutted Dresden and through Potsdam, whose ruins still burned after the raids of the previous night. The nights were spent in the open. Two days later, on April 17 at seven in the morning, they crossed the Danish frontier.[104]

In Haderslev the returning Danes met a tumultuous welcome: flags were waved, songs were sung, and the schoolchildren and the whole population lined the streets and showered them with flowers, sweets, and cigarettes. Cilla Cohn describes how people were beside themselves with joy.[105] The liberated found it difficult to grasp that all this joy was directed at them. The Germans, however, reacted with stern orders and with threats, and thereafter the buses were led silently and through side roads to the free port of Copenhagen (Frihavnen); here ferries carried them to safety in Sweden.

Summary and Statistics

Four hundred and twenty-five Jews went to Sweden from Theresienstadt:[106]

Deportees from Denmark	417
Children born in the ghetto	3
Czech women who married Danish Jews in the ghetto	4
One Danish-born person who joined the group in Theresienstadt	1
Total	425

According to Dr. Friediger's notes, a total of 53 persons died in the ghetto and one person was, in spite of everything, sent to Auschwitz. Two of the dead were stillborn babies. If we take 464 as the basic number of Danish prisoners in the camp, 51 or 11 per cent perished. The distribution of inmates by age group was as follows:[107]

Age in years	0–18	19–34	35–59	Over 60	Total
Deportees					
By numbers	53	156	137	118	464
In percentages	11.4	33.6	29.5	25.5	100.0
Died in ghetto					
By numbers		1	9	41	51
In percentages		2.0	17.6	80.4	100.0
Percentage of dead in each age group		0.6	6.5	35.7	
Percentage of dead among all deportees		0.2	2.0	8.8	11.0
Total percentage of deaths among Danish inmates in concentration camps					19.0

It will be seen that the aged constituted about 25 per cent of the Danish deportees in the ghetto, but about 80 per cent of all the deceased among the Danish Jews. More than a third of this age group died, while in other age groups the percentage of mortality was much lower. Nevertheless, the proportion of Jews who died in the camp was lower than that among all Danish deportees. Of the 464 deportees, 243 were men and 221 women. Of those who died, 22 were men and 29 women.

No exact details are available on the other persons who perished as a result of the persecutions. It may, however, be assumed that about 60 died altogether in camps and a similar number during flight or through suicide.[108] We reach a figure, therefore, of some 120 Danish Jewish victims of Hitler, a large proportion of whom were old people. The number of Jews living in Denmark in the fall of 1943 may be estimated at about 7,700. Thus those who died formed about 1.6 per cent. The figures do not include those who continued to live in Denmark throughout the occupation, some in hiding and some openly. Margolinsky has estimated their number as being between 50 and 100.[109] One of the prominent examples of the latter was Hartogsohn, secretary of Denmark's national bank. He tried at first to escape like everyone else but got into difficulties. However, since his whole family, who lived in the provincial town of Randers, had been taken to Theresienstadt (although he had tried to warn them) he decided that he could not leave Denmark, in case he might be able to do something to obtain their release. He continued his work at the bank and traveled there daily by tram from his suburban apartment. The Germans knew where he was, but they left him alone and he himself had no contact with them. His wife was non-Jewish.[110] He thus belonged to that category of Jews who were officially exempt from deportation, but his case and that of Professor Warburg were quite exceptional in that they continued to fulfill their important public functions. Yet these exceptions proved the rule—that the Danish people and its authorities had succeeded in obtaining for the Jews within their borders a protected status.

IX

Sweden—Near yet Far

Neutral Sweden

The Danish rescue operation could not have succeeded without Sweden's support, that of its people as well as its authorities. It has been pointed out above that such support was virtually nonexistent prior to the autumn of 1943, and a mass flight across the Sound seemed thus out of the question.[1] Neither Sweden's reserved attitude toward underground Denmark prior to October 1943 nor the considerable help it rendered thereafter were chance occurrences, but a consequence of Sweden's peculiar position during the Second World War. Neutral Sweden stood between the eastern and western fronts. It alone among the Scandinavian countries was able to pursue the policy determined upon before the war. During the thirties Sweden had attempted to unite the northern countries in a defense pact, particularly when the Abyssinian War proved that the League of Nations was incapable of defending small and neutral nations. These efforts, however, ended in failure in 1937. Responsible for this failure were Norway, which did not recognize the danger, and especially Denmark, which despaired in advance of being able to defend itself against its neighbor to the south.² Sweden therefore drew the conclusion that it had to pursue a policy of "absolute neutrality," and this line was also accepted by the other Nordic countries (including Finland) at a meeting of the four foreign ministers in Oslo in April 1938. In a broadcast on the Swedish radio two days before the meeting of ministers, the Swedish foreign minister, Sandler, said:

There can be only one course for a united Scandinavian policy. It is, if a conflict arises between the Great Powers, to assert our right to pursue a policy which will keep all the states of Scandinavia out of the war. . . . The strengthening of Scandinavia has one significance only: do not disturb the peace of Scandinavia!³

As a result of this attitude, Sweden in the spring of 1939 rejected Hitler's offer of a nonaggression pact; Denmark, however, accepted it.⁴

In the winter war between Russia and Finland, Sweden adopted a policy which came to be called "nonbelligerent interventionism." On the eve of the war Sweden rendered Finland diplomatic support and after the war broke out placed at that country's disposal practical, though unofficial, help in the form of money, arms, and ammunition. Moreover, nine thousand fully-equipped Swedish volunteers joined in the battle. It is estimated that the value of this help amounted to some 400 million Swedish kronor (about $80 million). Sweden also permitted the transit of Allied war matériel to Finland but refused to allow the transit of an army or to offer open military assistance.

In the midst of these developments, a change took place in Sweden's internal policy. The foreign minister, Rickard Sandler, was compelled in December 1939 to resign in view of his overt anti-German attitude, and the Social Democratic government was replaced by a broad coalition, the Foreign Ministry being given to the career diplomat Ernst Christian Günther. Swedish neutrality now took the form of inclining

toward Hitler's interests. The new foreign minister expressed the opinion that "it must be a national duty for each
and every one of us in our words and deeds to take care not
to render the government's work more dangerous." The
objective was, in other words, not to anger or incite him or
his supporters by any action that might serve the Allied
cause, including any open criticism in the press.[5] This policy
was intensified following the German attack on Russia, and
its peak coincided with that of German military success. On
hearing the disquieting news of German troop concentrations along the Baltic coast in April 1940, the Swedish chief
of staff requested general mobilization, but Günther, with
the government's support, refused. When Denmark and
Norway were attacked, talks were held between Germany
and Sweden in which Hitler demanded that Sweden preserve "absolute neutrality"; this meant allowing the transport through Sweden of German troops and equipment. The
Swedes for their part saw no choice but to agree and in the
summer of 1940 finally permitted the transit of German
troops and war matériel. Swedish concessions reached their
peak when a complete German division crossed into Finland
from Norway during the second Finnish war (following the
attack on Russia in the summer of 1941). The Germans also
used Swedish territorial waters and air space.

Swedish policy was motivated by both internal and external considerations. First of all, it should be recalled that
everyone—the belligerent and the occupied countries alike—
were in favor of a neutral Sweden. This view was expressed
by Molotov on April 9, 1940, demanded by Hitler, and
mentioned on various occasions by Allied spokesmen. Even
the Norwegians, whose bitter grudge against the Swedes
lasted even beyond the war, admitted that a neutral Sweden
was more important to them than a belligerent one. And
this was also the Danish view.[6]

To this interest in Swedish neutrality by all those engaged
in hostilities should be added internal Swedish reasons for

it. Sweden, like the other Scandinavian countries, was un-
prepared for war. During the war it not only strengthened
its army but also put its industry on a war footing. The war
nevertheless caused Sweden serious economic problems.
The Germans, with utter disregard for Swedish neutrality,
wreaked havoc with the country's merchant fleet on the
grounds (not entirely unfounded) that it served Allied interests. Up to the spring of 1941 Sweden had lost 400,000
tons of shipping. Moreover, the country was forced to import not only flour, oils, fruit, cotton, and other goods, but
also coal. The Germans were prepared to supply Sweden
with coal in return for iron ore. Sweden, like any country
at war, was obliged to ration food and supplies throughout
these years.

As in Denmark, Swedish policy during the first years of
the war was based on the assumption that Germany would
be victorious. It has been pointed out that the Swedish
politicians were not impelled by their convictions, which
they kept to themselves, but by what they considered to be
politically realistic and by their duty to their country.[7] It
may of course be claimed that necessity dictated their
policy; but they converted this obligatory neutrality into
an ideology of allegedly loftier moral value than participation in the war. Thulstrup notes in this connection that
"very early an unhealthy and unreal neutralist ideology was
developed, which claimed that the war did not in fact concern us and that the neutrals were morally superior to the
powers engaged in war. . . . In reality it was the armed
victory of the Allies which gave Sweden back its freedom. . . ."[8]

Sweden's political problems and attitude were also reflected in the refugee question. At the beginning of the
persecutions in Germany, Sweden distinguished, as did
Denmark, between political refugees and Jewish refugees.[9]
Even a man like Sandler was not keen before the war on
receiving Jewish refugees.[10] In the second half of the thirties,

Sweden had begun to recover from the economic crisis and grave unemployment which had afflicted the country, like the whole of Europe, since the late twenties. It is clear therefore that wide sections of the population objected to the admission of refugees. One prominent example was the demonstration of University of Uppsala students against the readiness of the authorities to issue entry permits to eleven Jewish doctors, some of them of world repute. As a result, permission to enter Sweden was not granted.[11]

After Munich, in the fall of 1938, Sweden abolished the regulation allowing an unconditional residence of three months in the country. Thereafter residence permits were granted only on conditions even more stringent than those operating in Denmark. People who tried to enter without a permit were often forcibly returned.[12] The archives of the Jewish community in Stockholm contain thousands of files with unfulfilled requests for permission to enter Sweden. An agricultural training scheme was, however, introduced, though on a smaller scale than in Denmark, and several hundred children were also brought to the country (mainly in the years 1938 and 1939) to await the further emigration overseas of their parents. There was likewise a certain movement of "transmigrants"—persons who waited in Sweden for visas to other countries. Between 1938 and 1942 some 1,100 such persons passed through, while at the end of 1942 there were in Sweden some 3,000 Jewish refugees (in addition to the 900 Norwegian Jews who came at the end of 1942 and the beginning of 1943). Such achievements were due to the initiative and support of certain elements among the Swedish public. In Stockholm alone there were seven aid committees (including one from the Jewish community), and to these should be added various public committees under the aegis of the workers' movements, the Red Cross, and so forth.[13]

On the other hand, Sweden also contained active pro-German and anti-Semitic groups, whose influence was discernible in both government offices and the police.[14] The government's policy in the first years of the war, and in particular the pressure brought to bear on the press, encouraged these elements. There were, however, also active and stubborn opponents of these tendencies. Special mention must be made of the author and member of the Riksdag Ture Nerman, whose journal *Trots Allt (Despite Everything)* became the central platform of opposition to nazism in Sweden.[15] No less energetic or persistent, though of another type, was the editor of the newspaper *Göteborgs Handels- och Sjöfartstidning,* Torgny Segerstedt.[16] The paper was suspended from time to time by the authorities because of its descriptions of German cruelty and terror in Norway and its persistent attacks on Nazi Germany.

The Turning Point

Swedish policy during the war may be divided into two parts—before and after the battle of El Alamein;[17] however, only from the spring of 1943 on (that is, after Stalingrad) was any marked change discernible. Symbolic was the fact that from that time on Torgny Segerstedt's paper, mentioned above, appeared regularly. The change in attitude led in June 1943 to annulment of the German transit right through Sweden. This demonstration of opposition, against which the Germans were powerless, also had a positive effect on the fighting morale of the Danish people.[18] Just as the persecution and flight of the Jews in Denmark stimulated the Danish resistance movement, so did these events impel the Swedes to take the first public steps indicative of the changed line. They declared their readiness to help the Jews and offered them refuge. While the Norwegian refugees—non-Jews and Jews alike—had been received with a resounding silence, the flight from Denmark reversed the whole Swedish policy regarding refugees. From then on Sweden took upon itself a new role and became at the end of the war an overt place of refuge for the persecuted in their thousands. Moreover, Sweden did not stop at humanitarian action but cooperated, if in a camouflaged manner, with the Danish resistance movement and enabled it to set up a bridge to the free world on Swedish soil.

The acclaim with which Sweden's action of October 1943 was received throughout the free world consolidated the new line and encouraged its continuation. The Swedish politicians were probably also aware that they were thus earning for their country an honored place in the world that would arise after the approaching eclipse of Hitler. In Sweden, as in Denmark, the popular action was spontaneous and broad sections of the population felt, as did the Danes, relief and satisfaction. Still, this turning point in the behavior of the Swedish authorities and people did not come about entirely of its own volition. That same energy which accumulated within the Danish underground movement and became an attribute of the people in the days of the Jewish persecution expressed itself in the Swedish initiative at the beginning of October 1943.

Ebbe Munck, a young journalist, was the liaison officer of the Danish resistance movement in Stockholm. He had gone there with this task in mind as early as the fall of 1940. From that time until the end of the war he was the central figure in the Danish resistance organization in Stockholm and was involved in everything there that was remotely connected with Denmark's struggle for liberation. Hæstrup says of him:

Through his work, he had earlier and more forcefully than anybody else striven to extract Denmark from that neutrality which, in the face of a movement such as nazism, seemed to him a national, political, and ethical impossibility.[19]

Munck points out that only after August 29, 1943, did his work take on a comprehensive and systematic form. As long as the Danish legation in Sweden represented the official Danish government, his work was, he states, almost as illegal as the activities of the Danish underground movement.[20] On December 9, 1943, the Freedom Council appointed Munck its official representative in Stockholm.[21] In early October the flight of the Jews became the central task in Stockholm as in Denmark itself. At the same time, there came to Munck's assistance one of the most prominent Danish personalities of the era: Professor Niels Bohr.

Bohr's mother was, of course, a Jewess.[22] Mention has also been made of the fact that Professor Bohr was among the Danes who offered help to the German refugees,[23] and a not insignificant number of them found work in his institute. It is interesting that until the fall of 1943 the Germans not only made no attempt to disturb his work but—and this is confirmed by the evidence of both Renthe-Fink and Best—they even afforded him a kind of special protection.[24] Bohr was alive to this fact. In a talk with Ebbe Munck in Stockholm on October 6, 1943, he said: "It was with the highest German protection that I have been allowed in the last few years to continue my work in Copenhagen, and only now am I aware to what degree my work was the object of espionage and counterespionage." This remark is a clear indication that the German "protection" was not altogether motivated by humanitarian considerations.[25]

It will be recalled that in the summer of 1943 Bohr was invited, through underground channels, to go to England, and that he rejected the offer on the grounds that his flight might endanger the lives of his colleagues, the refugees, and perhaps of all the Danish Jews.[26] In early September he was warned by the Swedish minister in Copenhagen, Dardell, that the refugees working with him were in danger.[27] Bohr contacted the underground movement, which arranged for their transfer to Sweden. Then at the end of September he learned that in connection with the deportation of the

Jews it was intended to arrest him too. In 1958 Bohr said that it was the Swedish minister who had warned him on September 29, but immediately after his flight to Stockholm he related that the informant was a German woman working for the Gestapo who had seen the papers affecting him.[28] It is quite possible that he was warned twice, as was often the case during those days. At the last moment he and his family were assigned to a boat which was to take one of his friends, a German refugee, the professor of neurophysiology Dr. Buchtal, to Sweden. Bohr himself had put the professor in touch with the underground movement. They reached Sweden on Thursday, September 30, and Bohr at once continued to Stockholm. Bohr states that upon arrival in Sweden one thought was constantly in his mind: "If the Swedish government renders active assistance, then it must be possible to find a way to help the Danish Jews."[29] He added that until then he had never engaged in politics. The day after his arrival in Stockholm he went to the Foreign Ministry, and in the course of his talk with the head of the Political Department, Boheman, learned that the Swedes had already begun to take action.

News of the imminent pogrom in Denmark apparently reached Sweden by various routes. It was natural that one of the main sources of information was the Swedish minister in Copenhagen. Dardell had reported to his Foreign Ministry on the Jewish problem in Denmark as early as September 6, when he announced that although it did not seem as if danger was imminent, it "was hovering in the air." On the afternoon of September 29 the Swedish Foreign Office received a telegram stating that on the morning of October 1 or 2 six thousand Jews were expected to be arrested and then deported to Germany by ship.[30] An additional point should be mentioned here. Together with the previously mentioned message of October 6, Dardell stated that the Jewish community had asked him whether, in the event of German steps being taken against the Jews of

Denmark, the Swedish government would announce at once that it was prepared to receive the Jews.[31] However, as far as we know, Dardell was not the only one who warned the Swedish government, since it will be recalled that Duckwitz visited Sweden and in his talk with Per Albin Hansson suggested to the premier that Sweden should intervene.[32]

In any event, the Swedish Foreign Office that same day, September 29, and again the next day, contacted the Swedish minister in Berlin, A. Richert, with a view to instructing him to approach the German Foreign Ministry. It was decided that Richert would ask the Germans whether there was any foundation to the rumors of the deportation of the Jews from Denmark and that he would stress that a deportation of this kind would arouse great indignation in Sweden. In addition, the minister was to suggest the transfer of all the Jews to Sweden, where they would be placed in a camp; the Swedish government was to be responsible that there "they would not engage in any activity liable to harm Germany."[33] It is known that Richert visited Steengracht on October 1 after telephoned instructions from Stockholm. The order was apparently given following a request made by Svenningsen, via Dardell, to the Swedish government. The subject of the talk was jotted down by Steengracht and was also forwarded to Best. The Swedish minister presented his government's warning, as stated, and added (no doubt according to instructions) that Foreign Minister Günther had taken this step only because he feared that an action against the Jews on such a scale would arouse a strong reaction among the Swedish population. The German played innocent and replied that there was a state of emergency in Denmark and that he did not know what measures the army, which was responsible for the maintenance of order, might consider necessary for security reasons; nor did he know anything about a planned action against the Jews. In his report he requests that the conversation be reported immediately to the foreign minister.[34]

This story was related to Niels Bohr by Boheman.[35] It appears that the Swedes had no intention of taking any further steps. Bohr and Ebbe Munck and his colleagues, however, had other ideas. It transpires from Munck's diary and from his letters to Christmas Møller in London that it was the Danish group, with the active support of well-known Swedish elements, which was responsible for the publication by the Swedish government of its announcement to the Germans. The day after the action in Denmark (i.e., on October 2) Bohr saw Foreign Minister Günther. It would seem that the day before, the Danes had tried to persuade the Swedes to make public their note to the Germans, in the hope that this move might prevent the deportation. Since this was not done, Bohr asked the Swedish foreign minister to approach the Germans again and propose that the ships carrying the Jews be diverted to Sweden instead of to Germany. Günther made this suggestion to the German minister, Thomsen, who visited him that same day at noon.[36] No reply to the proposal was ever received.

Through the offices of the Danish minister in Stockholm, J. C. W. Kruse, and with the active cooperation of Professor Stephan Hurwitz,[37] an appointment was made for Bohr to see the king that same afternoon. In their talk Bohr suggested to the king that an announcement be made of the Swedish approach to the Germans. The king made no reply, but at the end of the audience the foreign minister was called to him. That same evening the Swedish radio broadcast news of the Swedish intervention in Berlin and emphasized the fact that the minister had declared in the name of his government that Sweden was prepared to receive all the Danish Jews. As we have seen, it was this announcement which impelled both the Jews and their Danish helpers to organize the mass flight. In a letter to Christmas Møller dated October 12[38] Munck relates that the Swedish government agreed to make the announcement public only after the archbishop, some professors, and other well-known personalities had declared their willingness to sign an open letter to the government on the subject. On October 4 the Swedish minister in Berlin again approached Steengracht and offered in the name of the Swedish government to receive the children of internees, whose deportation had in the meantime become a fact.[39] This time Steengracht reacted rudely, replying to Richert that Sweden had no right to intervene in Danish affairs; he also reproached the Swedish diplomat for the sharp reaction of the Swedish press.

The Swedish move had far-reaching repercussions. On October 3 the Foreign Office spokesman informed foreign journalists officially of the announcement broadcast the previous evening.[40] Both announcements were given wide coverage in the Swedish and world press. The Swedish newspapers, almost without exception, delivered a strong attack against the Germans and thus aroused German wrath. Moreover, the news was passed on rapidly from Stockholm to the whole of the free world and could be found in British, American, Swiss, and of course Palestinian Jewish newspapers; it was also broadcast on both side of the Atlantic and even by the French radio in Brazzaville.[41] The correspondents of the world's press bureaus in Stockholm generally passed on what they read in Swedish newspapers, which were full of stories both real and fictitious; thus the heroic acts of the Danish people reached the world in legendary form.[42] There were, however, some newspapers which interpreted events more or less correctly.[43]

The main reaction of the Swedes was nevertheless not verbal but practical—absorption of the refugees who reached the Swedish shores by the thousands. The German news agency and the German minister in Stockholm flooded the Foreign Ministry in Berlin with news of the reaction of the Swedish public and press.[44] Their reports describe the meetings and the public prayers (in the Stockholm concert hall a large meeting took place, with the participation of members of the royal family, the bishop, and others) and give details of the arrangements made for the refugees, the collection of funds, and so forth. A particular ground for German anxiety was that their friends among the Swedes also made public their opposition to the deportation of the Danish Jews.[45] The Swedish press exploited the opportunity to present general surveys and articles on the Germans. In view of this world reaction, the Germans felt obliged to explain the Danish action, a task that was assigned to the deputy-director of the press office, while the *Völkische Beobachter* poured out its wrath on the Swedes.[46] This was the first time a public clash of this sort had taken place between Sweden and Germany—that is, for the first time Sweden revealed that she had taken a stand against Nazi Germany; this was a public declaration, as it were, that it belonged to the free and democratic world.

No less sharp than the reaction of neutral Sweden was that of Finland, Germany's "ally." The German minister in Finland, Blücher, also bombarded his Foreign Ministry with long and detailed telegrams on the negative reaction of the Finns to the persecution of the Jews in Denmark. One of his objects was to prevent any similar action in Finland.[47] He too stressed that friends of Germany were among those protesting against the action in Denmark. On October 4 he reported a talk with the foreign minister in which the latter discreetly but seriously referred to the matter. "The German actions against the Jews," asserts the envoy, "are a subject on which public opinion is united against us." Karl August Fagerholm[48] wrote, "Finland must not hesitate to express her participation in Denmark's sorrow—this is not the way in which the occupying power will win the sympathy of Finland."

It is superfluous to point out that the Jewish population in Palestine was extremely alive to the events taking place in Northern Europe. *Davar* expressed fear for the fate of Danish Jewry as early as September 6. The Danish stand against anti-Semitism was well known, but in view of the changes in occupational rule the paper asked, "Is there still a way to save them?" (i.e., the Jews of Denmark). *Davar* was also the first paper in Palestine which, on October 3, published the Swedish announcement. In the course of time the country's newspapers published reports both true and distorted on events in Scandinavia, as did all the world's press.[49] *Hatsofeh* published on October 8 the declaration of the Chief Rabbis to the Swedish consul in Palestine, in which thanks were expressed not only to the Swedish king, government, and people, but also to the archbishop and other religious personalities who had raised their voices "against the barbaric eruption." Sweden had given, the message continued, an example to the entire world.

In the meantime the Swedish Foreign Office did not confine itself to diplomatic activity. One of the problems occupying the Danish underground movement at the beginning of October was the difficulty in discovering the Jews still in hiding in Denmark. The search for them was aided by lists of missing Jews compiled by Danish Jews already in Sweden. These lists were at first passed on to the underground movement by means of the Swedish diplomatic courier and the Swedish legation in Copenhagen.[50] (Later on the resistance movement used its own channels.) Moreover, the Swedish authorities made strenuous efforts to grant Swedish nationality to as many Jews as possible, to enable them to come to Sweden legally. These efforts were only partly successful. The Swedish legation in Copenhagen also tried to assist in the matter of safeguarding Jewish property, but the Swedish authorities refused to allow the transfer of money and valuables.[51]

The Start of Illegal Transportation

In those first days of October Ebbe Munck saw it as his primary duty to organize matters on the Swedish coast so that the Danish Jews could come across quickly and safely.[52]

As mentioned, the illegal connection between Denmark and Sweden was until then extremely restricted in scope, and Ebbe Munck had neither boats, crews, nor even money. Two factors solved these problems for the Danish underground fighters in Sweden: the willingness of the Swedes—officials and public alike—to take part in the illegal rescue operation; and the initiative of a number of Jews in Sweden. Over the years a group of people had formed within the Jewish community in Stockholm who considered it their primary task to render help to the victims of Nazi persecution. These were the same people who had endeavored in vain to obtain entry permits for Hitlerian refugees, had set up training facilities for agricultural pioneers, and—in brief —engaged in any activity designed to help those in danger.[53] These efforts were increased with the advent of war. The community in Stockholm kept in constant touch with the international Jewish organizations, which helped it to maintain the refugees and especially to finance their emigration overseas.

Adler-Rudel, who was responsible for the Jewish Agency's European Department, which had its office in London, arrived in Sweden in the spring of 1943. At the time of the Bermuda Conference[54] he suggested to the agency a work program for neutral countries of refuge, mainly Sweden and Portugal. He himself traveled to Sweden to try and organize any help he could for the Jews of Europe.[55] He asked the Swedish government to suggest to Germany that twenty thousand Jewish children be released and allowed to come to Sweden. Although the Swedish government did not reject the request, it never really reached the stage of an earnest attempt.[56] During a talk on this subject with the minister for social affairs, Gustav Möller, Adler-Rudel also raised the question of the future of the Danish Jews. He claimed that in his opinion it was not unlikely that the day would come when the Jews of Denmark would be forced to flee; indeed it was desirable that they begin to leave Denmark as early as possible. This was when a number of agricultural pioneers fled, thus arousing the ire of the Germans.⁵⁷ Gustav Möller replied that he would see to it that every Jew who reached Swedish shores would be well received, and if the serious situation envisaged by Adler-Rudel came to pass, then Sweden would do everything in its power to help. As we have seen, Gustav Möller kept his word.

Adler-Rudel, however, did not rest content with this assurance but took steps to purchase a boat which could convey pioneers and other Jews from Denmark to Sweden. He and a number of Zionists among the community in Stockholm raised—by special appeal—the 30,000 kronor ($6,000) required to buy the boat *Julius*, which was legally registered in midsummer 1943 and presented to Hechalutz.⁵⁸

During this time a "committee of cooperation" was set up at Adler-Rudel's initiative in the office of Fritz Hollander, a partner in one of Sweden's largest Jewish firms, and to it were affiliated nearly all the Jewish organizations in Stockholm and its help be sought in planning possible of rescue. One of Hollander's employees⁵⁹ proposed to him and to his partner, Norbert Masur,⁶⁰ that contact be established with members of the Danish underground movement in Stockholm and its help be sought in planning possible escape routes for the Danish Jews. Such contact was duly effected between Hollander, Masur, and Ebbe Munck. The first meeting took place about the end of August or the beginning of September. Here it was made known to the two Swedish Jews that the Danish resistance movement had made no preparations for organizing any large-scale rescue and had no technical or financial means at its disposal. Ebbe Munck, however, put the two in touch with two young architects, Ole Helweg and Bent Kalby, who were prepared to operate a rescue service between Denmark and Sweden, if a fast motorboat were placed at their disposal.

The operation required money. Masur approached the

chairman of the Jewish community, Gunnar Josephson, who was prepared to help but suggested that the community itself be kept out of illegal activity. Instead he directed Masur to one of the prominent members of the community, the attorney Ivar Philipson, with whom Masur had a meeting on October 3. During that evening and the next day Philipson collected more than 100,000 Swedish kronor.[61] It should be noted that Philipson's appeal to the Jews of Sweden took place on the day after the pogrom in Denmark and the official Swedish declaration that the Danish Jews would be given asylum. These two factors probably removed the inhibitions of Jews as regards participation in illegal activity. Ebbe Munck noted in his diary that on October 4 at eleven A.M. Masur and Philipson visited him and suggested buying a boat for transporting the Jews. They also related that the *Julius* had crossed to the Danish coast four times but had not succeeded in finding the people it was supposed to rescue. This failure was not surprising, since the communications between Denmark and Sweden necessary for the successful organization of such crossings simply did not exist. Most of the Danish Jews were thus transferred by the organization set up on the Danish coast.[62]

In the meanwhile both Hollander and Philipson traveled to Malmö, where they engaged in planning the operation and in buying an additional boat. The organization of the rescue service was handed over on October 9 to the journalist Leif B. Hendil, who had been forced to flee to Sweden after having been engaged in similar work on the Danish side.[63] Hendil set up his office in Malmö. He was assisted by a Danish Jew, the wholesaler Jørgen Polack, who was mainly concerned with administrative and financial matters. The amount of working capital at first was 164,000 kronor, collected by Philipson, who also participated in the operation of the route. The action depended on the acquisition of not only suitable boats and crews but also all sorts of equipment such as fuel, spare parts, fishermen's clothing, extra rations, and the like. All these items were obtainable in Sweden only with ration coupons.[64] The Danish underground had no direct channel of approach to the Swedish authorities, and Philipson, with wide government, industrial, and commercial connections, served as a faithful agent of the illegal transport system. Moreover, the boats could only be purchased by a Swedish citizen, and most of them were bought and insured in his name. Currency conversion and other banking transactions were also carried out by him. His files include some four hundred incoming and outgoing letters, dealing mainly with all these technical problems, which were a prerequisite for the route's smooth operation. His letters are remarkable not only for their concise style but also for their simplicity and the way in which he directed his requests to all the institutions as something to be taken for granted.[65]

The authorities generally approved the requests put before them. This was not entirely because of Philipson's work, since relevant instructions in the matter had been given by the government. The first fuel allocations of 1500 liters had even been decided upon in a government session held on October 8, 1943.[66]

This, however, was not all. The local authorities in Malmö were prepared to assist Hendil to the best of their ability, but the police commissioner, Richard Hansen, demanded relevant instructions from a higher authority to cover himself—otherwise he could not cooperate.[67] The members of the organization had easy access to the government, since Helweg was married to a relative of Foreign Minister Günther. On October 12 he handed Günther a memorandum[68] which served as the basis for the whole illegal Danish transportation service. The boats were to sail under the Swedish flag.

What we require now [ran the memorandum, following a brief explanation of the scope of the service] is that the foreign minister know that the operation is purely humanitarian and that he announce as soon as possible to the head of security that there is no opposition to this Danish-Swedish effort, whose aim is to help refugees in trouble. And it may be assumed that as long as the occupation of Germany continues and becomes more severe, there will always be refugees who wish to cross the straits. The boats have been registered and all the formal arrangements made in full accordance with the law . . . but approval of the above will of course be important in the present situation, as we wish to operate in full agreement with Sweden.

The note then repeats and emphasizes that no politics are involved. Günther gave his affirmative reply and three days later, on October 15, Richard Hansen appeared in Hendil's office and announced that he had received the notice of approval.

It transpired from the letter [Hendil wrote to Munck that same day [69]] that a senior official of the Foreign Ministry announced Günther's approval and the matter was passed on to the head of security services, who also agreed. The local authorities thus received backing and Richard Hansen was wreathed in smiles.

The next day a meeting was fixed with the police and the naval authorities.

As a result of this meeting Hendil was allowed to use the Malmö sailing club as a hiding place and port of departure, and he writes thus to Munck on October 16: "It is only possible to reach it after sailing through both the police and the navy—a better hiding place cannot be found." Similar arrangements were also made with the customs authorities.

Among the first operations carried out—in cooperation with the fleet—were routine patrols of the coast by ten to twenty hired fishing vessels, whose duty was to meet the Danish vessels and guide them safely to a suitable port.[70] Hendil was now in a position to operate his own boats—and the *Julius* also entered upon the scene.

The boat was skippered by a former pioneer and fishery apprentice, Erich Marx, and he was assisted by two other young pioneers. Hendil drew up an agreement with them on a charter basis.[71] In a report he wrote in Stockholm on January 21, 1944, he said:

With the help of the boats acquired by Ivar Philipson and with the help of the *Julius* our organization in Malmö, in close cooperation with a parallel organization on the Danish coast, maintained an almost regular service from the middle of October to the middle of December. To this end about 35,000 kronor were spent. We conveyed in our boats 302 persons, whose names may be found in special lists and among whom were 8 condemned to death, 2 severely wounded by the Gestapo, an old and paralyzed woman, and so on and so forth. The boats of the Danish organization transported 239 persons, so that our organization all in all helped 541 people to cross the Sound.[72]

It transpires that most of the work from the Swedish side at the time was carried out by the *Julius*.

With the development of regular transportation, new assignments were given the line, such as first of all the dispatch of unofficial mail—in both directions—and the transfer of informative and even propaganda material. The skippers were also assigned general missions by the underground movement and private ones by the refugees. For these and for its routine work, the line needed an organization in Copenhagen parallel to that in Malmö and on October 22 Hendil traveled to Copenhagen to help set it up. The *Julius* faithfully carried out all the duties imposed on it, and Hendil pointed out in the letter already quoted that the boat conveyed "thousands of letters and carried out hundreds of missions."

However, on December 11 a mishap occurred (due, it was claimed later, to the work of an informer). The boat crossed to Denmark to bring back a large group of refugees. Its crew that day consisted of Marx, Helweg, and naval lieutenant Stærmose.[73] On approaching the meeting place on the Danish shore at eight o'clock in the evening, they suddenly saw before them, at a distance of some 800 meters, a boat which was quickly identified as a German patrol vessel armed with cannon. They tried to flee but the Germans opened fire and they were forced to stop. The Germans boarded the *Julius,* searched the boat, and found a bag of mail and some hand grenades; they ordered the crew to follow them to a Danish port. From there the three "Swedish fishermen" were taken to Gestapo headquarters in Copenhagen for cross-examination.

Mailbags usually contained mostly lists and addresses. There was a standing order that in the event of seizure the bags were to be sunk in the sea with the help of a lead weight previously placed inside. Marx and Helweg worked inside the boat and attempted to burn or otherwise destroy anything incriminating and directed Stærmose to throw the bag overboard. For reasons that were never completely clarified this was not done and Marx, who discovered this at the last moment before the Germans boarded the boat, attempted to hide it (since throwing it overboard was now impossible); but, as may be imagined, it was discovered by the Germans without difficulty. The three "fishermen" were thus forced under examination to explain the suspicious circumstances: why they had entered Danish territorial waters, how they came to have the mailbag, and what was the object and the origin of the hand grenades. In the waiting period at the port of arrival the three succeeded in agreeing upon tactics and in smuggling out a warning to their comrades. They decided to say that only Helweg understood German, while Stærmose would pose as a dumb idiot, since it was feared that he would reveal his language as Danish and not Swedish. Marx, who appeared as chief fisherman, had had some experience of the Gestapo and its methods of interrogation, for prior to his arrival in Denmark he had spent a year in a concentration camp. They related to the Germans—Marx always with the help of a translator, which gave him time to think up his reply—that they had reached the Danish shore as a result of engine trouble (they had managed to prepare the necessary "evidence"). The mailbag had been given to them, so they said, by an unknown man who paid them 200 kroner. They manipulated their replies with such skill and agility that they not only convinced the Germans of the truth of their story, but the Gestapo also suggested to Marx that he engage in espionage in Sweden on their behalf. He accepted the offer with alacrity.

The seizure of the boat by the Germans became known to Hendil and his colleagues on December 14. Munck at once consulted with Philipson and Hollander and these immediately contacted Foreign Minister Günther (and Helweg's family). Günther also called Dardell, who happened to be in Stockholm. The latter returned at once to Copenhagen and considered approaching Best and requesting the release of the fishermen.[74] On the 15th, however, Hendil's staff, who feared for the future of the captured men and the whole organization, were astonished to see the boat making its way quietly into Malmö harbor. The Germans no doubt then realized that they had been tricked, and the liaison officer who was supposed to meet the "spies" in Malmö failed to appear. The twenty-five refugees who should have come with the *Julius* were taken to another place and from there were safely transferred to Sweden.

Even after the safe return of the three men, the transport route was in danger, since the mail seized by the Germans contained mostly addresses. A number of persons were indeed obliged to flee Denmark following the incident. Moreover, it was necessary to remove the *Julius* from service.

A few words are in place here on the boat and the members of its crew. It was not an ordinary fishing vessel, like those generally used in the Sound, but a large boat capable of entering the open sea. After the mishap it began at first to operate as a normal fishing vessel, and Philipson worked hard to acquire for it the necessary equipment and permits. But this work did not apparently satisfy Marx, and he decided to make an attempt to take the boat to England. On May 25, 1944, Munck informed Christmas Møller that two Jewish fishermen, Erich Marx and Erich Helmuth Julius, were about to sail from the Swedish west coast for England.

The two men, who are stateless, have lived in Denmark for many years; they have been active in the transport of refugees and have saved over three hundred. The English authorities have been informed about them and perhaps you can also help them if the voyage is successful. They deserve all the help they can get.[75]

Two days later Hendil informed Munck that Marx and Julius had sailed at four A.M. On June 16 Munck noted in his diary that these two men had reached England safely on June 3 after having successfully overcome all dangers and obstacles.

The *Julius* and its crew were not the only ones to leave the organization during the early months. The two architects Helwig and Kalby also resigned,[76] while Stærmose was removed by the organization.[77] After the work had gotten under way, Hollander and Masur also left its operation in the hands of Hendil and his associates.[78] The only one of the initiators who remained until the end of the war, therefore, was Philipson. Relations between him and Hendil grew steadily more cordial. This transpires from the following letter dated October 4, 1944:

Dear Leif:
   In these days I have realized that a year has passed since we began our joint work. . . . It is almost certain that we shall meet on October 9 [the anniversary of Hendil's association with the project]. I was very pleased with your and your colleagues' kind regards on the occasion of the anniversary of our work and I

thank you very much for the year that has passed. Cooperation has always been perfect, and I am sure that you will understand me when I say that I hope it will soon be over.

With kindest regards.

The wish expressed here was to be fulfilled seven months later.

Organization and Financing

The first phase of the transport operation may be said to have ended with the *Julius* mishap. On December 18 Hendil wrote to Philipson:

All routes have been closed as of this morning, following a German protest that Swedish fishing boats are transporting illegal mail to Denmark. How the future of the routes will be organized no one can know. This evening I am sending Helweg up to G. [i.e., to Günther in Stockholm] with a memorandum, a copy of which I attach here.[79] . . . They [the people sent to Sweden] include members of various social classes and nationalities. There were both single persons and whole families, both of Jewish origin and so-called Aryans, and children whose parents had been forced to leave them behind in Denmark. They included workers, officers, students, policemen, teachers, doctors, etc. who were threatened by a death sentence or some other serious punishment. Many were wounded or sick. In some of these cases such shocking details were revealed that we who are connected with the route were grateful for having had the opportunity of carrying out this work.

Hendil goes on to describe the additional tasks such as carrying mail and other freight, but promises that this part will be restricted and that emphasis will be on help to human beings. The service was operated without profit and was therefore cheaper than others; its advantage was that it was set up by an organization operating on both sides of the Sound. It had a permanent staff and its own boats. Between ten and thirty refugees were reaching Sweden each day, and an organization that could save many was needed, in view of the deteriorating situation in Denmark.

Helweg was received by Günther on December 20.[80] According to Munck, "His Excellency was not in the best of moods during this talk, but thawed in the course of it, and it may be assumed that we shall obtain approval to continue, if pressure is brought to bear from other quarters."[81] Approval was indeed given, and in the early days of January Munck held meetings to discuss the organization of the routes.

The underground movement apparently now realized that the service required a clearer and more permanent organizational form, and on January 11 a meeting was held in Malmö, where the efforts of the previous three months were examined and summed up and policy lines laid down for all the routes. In the summary of discussions and decisions "transport organization" appears for the first time as a comprehensive term. The meeting was attended not only by the personnel of the transport service on both sides of the Sound but also by representatives of the Swedish fleet.[82]

The minutes of the meeting open with an introduction explaining organizational principles, based mainly on two apparently contradictory factors but which here complement one another: decentralization on the one hand and central control on the other. The various routes operated within separate and independent organizational frameworks. This fact insured that in the event of one route's being destroyed, the others would continue to function. At the same time, there existed operational centers—one in Denmark and one in Sweden—engaged in coordination, distribution of assignments, and mutual aid.

Above all the independent organizations, [the report goes on] there are several persons who do not participate directly in the work of the organization but are fully conversant with the routes, points of departure, and work methods, and are therefore capable of transferring passengers from an overloaded to a less utilized route. [This form of organization was in fact born during the Jewish rescue action.] . . . At that time some 5,000 persons were brought over in two or three weeks, that is, an average of 250–350 a day. Between October 15 and November 15 the number dropped markedly, so that the average for the second half of November and for December was 10–15 passengers daily—a little more at the beginning of the period and some 5–8 daily toward its close.

This number, the report states, would seem to be more or less constant. It was clear that the reduction in the number of refugees also meant changes in the methods of operation. In this connection, another factor had also to be taken into account.

Ebbe Munck foresaw the possibility of a routine transportation service as early as the end of October, with the cessation of the mass flight. On October 25 he wrote to Christmas Møller: "I will try to continue and consolidate this route [Hendil's] even after the problem of the Jews is solved." (At the time the search for missing and hidden Jews was still going on, and this subject appears repeatedly in correspondence during the whole month of November.) However, in the same letter Munck points out that stricter German control over the sea routes is discernible. The reduced number of refugees on the one hand and the more serious security problems on the other created conditions for the operation of illegal transportation different from those existing during the Jewish flight.

The success of the operation was now entirely dependent on a rapid and accurate intelligence service from coast to coast. Here the underground movement was aided by all the legal bodies which continued to maintain official communications between Sweden and Denmark. "The telegram route," as it came to be called, operated by means of ferries which plied between Copenhagen and Malmö and Helsignor and Helsingborg, with the help of civil aircraft continuing to fly between the two countries and even with the assistance of the telephone. At a later date special code words were also used on the Swedish radio to indicate places and dates of assembly, announcements, and the like. The times and places of meeting, on the Danish shore and on the open sea, were determined in this way with astonishing accuracy. Without it, it would have been impossible to maintain the service, as was clear from the first fruitless voyages of the *Julius.*

Under the name of the Danish Help Service a transport route between Gothenburg and Jutland was introduced in the spring of 1944. It was operated in close cooperation with Hendil's route and benefited directly from the monies collected by Philipson. It was headed by a former radio dealer in Copenhagen, Werner Gyberg. He was active in the underground movement and had been arrested by the Germans in 1942, but had succeeded at the beginning of September 1943 in escaping to Sweden with Hendil's assistance. Officially, Gyberg was a clerk in the Danish consulate in Gothenburg, with an entry permit to the port.

The Gothenburg boats in fact engaged in fishing, then met Danish fishing vessels on the open sea and exchanged their catch for refugees, so that the Danes could return home with fish on board. At first Danish saboteurs worked as fishermen, but they were later replaced by professional fishermen, who were Danes sailing under the Swedish flag and with Swedish papers. Not one man was lost during the whole period. The meetings were arranged with the assistance of the Danish radio set up in Stockholm to serve the Danish refugees in Sweden. The first boat began operating in the spring of 1944 and by the end of the war the route possessed three large vessels, each equipped with a hiding place for twenty-one refugees. Three to five crew members worked on each boat.

The organizational principles for illegal transportation as laid down in the meeting at Malmö were implemented in the course of time on all the routes and may be summed up—decentralization and centralization, intelligence services, and official help—in the map and organizational diagram.

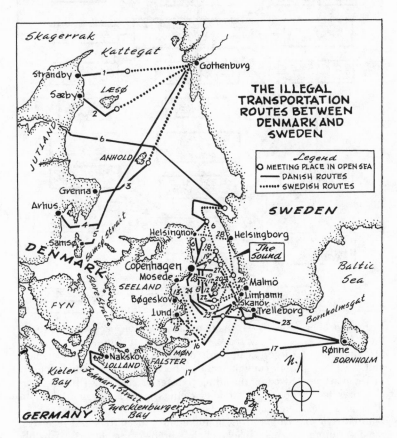

Danish Help Service (Gothenburg): Nos. 1, 2, 3, 4, 5; Speditor (Denmark): Nos. 6, 7, 8, 9, 21; Danish-Swedish Refugee Service (Hendil-Malmö): Nos. 6, 10, 11, 12, 13, 14, 15, 16, 17; Students' Intelligence Service: Nos. 6, 18, 19, 20, 21, 22, 23, 24, 25, 26; normal steamship route to Bornholm: No. 27; Kiær Line: No. 28.

This map is exhibited in the Freedom Museum (*Frihedsmuseet*) in Copenhagen. Most of the Danish routes start from Copenhagen, while Malmö and environs are the starting points for most of the Swedish routes. Different organizations sometimes used the same sea routes, with the result that some numbers appear for more than one route.

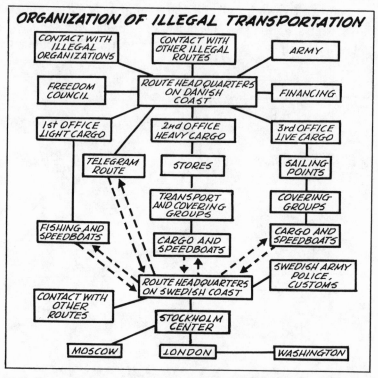

ORGANIZATION OF ILLEGAL TRANSPORTATION

Unbroken lines (————) show organization on each coast; broken lines (— — — —) show sea contact from both sides.

1st office, light cargo: dealt with military intelligence in Denmark and Sweden; postal communications between underground centers in Denmark and Sweden, including transfer of currency (mainly from Denmark to Sweden); private mail (letters, parcels, luggage) in both directions, including transfer of money to refugees in Sweden.

2nd office, heavy cargo: arms, ammunition, transmitters and receivers, movie equipment, mobile field clinics, propaganda material (mainly from Sweden to Denmark).

3rd office, live cargo: refugees, couriers, intelligence agents, politicians.

(Diagram courtesy of V. la Cour. *Danmark Under Besaettelsen,* III. Copenhagen: Westermann, 1946)

The spontaneity that had marked the period of the mass Jewish flight and the establishment of the first transport routes on the Swedish coast were thus replaced by a systematic and planned organization. The memorandum of January 11, 1944, deals with all the transportation problems (organization, financing, security, etc.) methodically, point by point.

Hendil's route was only one of many transport organizations, but it was one of the most important, largest, and most consistent. It was moreover the first route to be based on the Swedish coast, and through it the Swedish government was connected to this activity of the Danish underground movement. "The first route started on Swedish soil was the Danish-Swedish Refugee Service, whose work methods became the model for later routes."[83] This route is of special interest because of the large role played by the Jewish rescue in its establishment and maintenance.[84] From October 1943 up to the end of the war on May 5, 1945, the service transported 1,888 persons on 361 trips and made more than 500 crossings with mail, intelligence material, and the like.[85] In the report of the route written in Malmö on January 18, 1944, it was stated:

In order to establish and expand cooperation between the Danish and the Swedish coasts Hendil was called over to Denmark on October 22 and here, in the course of a week, he set up the organization—including telegram service, signal system, "passenger" assembly, financing on the Danish side, etc.—which formed the structure on which the Danish-Swedish Refugee Service was organized in its final form and served as the basis for its functioning.[86]

The chief liaison officer in Denmark was Gyberg's partner, Robert Jensen, known to the whole underground movement by the name of Tom.[87]

Since Ebbe Munck, and apparently Hendil also, had at the end of October begun to think about continuation of the service and its expansion, it had been clear that the 164,000 kronor collected for them by Philipson would not be adequate to finance operations for much longer than three months. Polack's bookkeeping was meticulous, and each week he sent to Stockholm financial reports which included details of salaries and all the other expenses, from stamps to equipment and operational costs.[88] On the basis of a financial summary drawn up in Stockholm on January 21, 1944, the service had spent 120,000 kronor up to the end of 1943.[89] In addition to the income of 160,000 kronor, 600 Danish kroner had been collected in Denmark, making a total of about 165,000 Swedish kronor. In place of the *Julius* two new boats had been acquired, and the costs for the next three months were estimated at about 72,000 kronor. A deficit of over 20,000 kronor was therefore anticipated. The service itself had transported 541 persons at a cost of about 250 kronor per person.[90] In the course of time this figure was reduced, but it became necessary to seek new sources of financing.

As early as the beginning of November the route had begun to carry out that operation which the official Swedish authorities had refused to permit: currency transfers. The Jewish refugees included many persons of means who wished to transfer their money to Sweden. This service was carried out by the route, which collected a certain percentage in fees from the persons concerned. At first 15 per cent was taken but after a short while this was reduced—presumably by the underground movement—to 10 per cent. This fee was not taken from each and every one, and at first a distinction was made between those who could and those who could not pay. Other routes also provided a similar service, but Hendil was apparently one of the main agents.[91]

Arne Sejr[92] states that in this way a total of 2 million Danish kroner were transferred to Sweden, including 175,000 for underground purposes for which no fee was charged. It would seem, however, that the actual total was larger— perhaps 3 million kroner. The fees trickled into the funds of the route only in hundreds, occasionally in thousands, of kroner;[93] moreover, half this income was allocated to the

Danish resistance movement. Yet the newly developing organization needed greater amounts, particularly for the acquisition and equipping of boats and the establishment of required operational procedures.

At this point an idea was born—so obvious in its conception that it emerged in two places simultaneously. Philipson's correspondence includes a letter from Hollander and Masur dated November 19, 1943, in which they present details of expenses which amounted to 10,000 Swedish kronor in value (though part of the sum was Danish currency). And the letter continues:

An attempt must be made to obtain the Danish kroner needed . . . through contributions from the Danish Jews now in Sweden, who can arrange for payment to be made by their trustees in Copenhagen. To this end talks should at once be held with Professor Hurwitz and with attorney R.[94]

The letter goes on to talk of the urgent need for finding the addresses of Jews still in hiding in Denmark and suggests various ways of locating them. In other words, two functions are proposed, still as part of the primary Jewish rescue effort: to find and transport the Jews still remaining in Denmark; and to finance this operation with the contributions of Danish Jews already in Sweden. The second point is the new idea.

The same suggestion was discussed in a completely different connection in a letter written on November 30, 1943, by one of Hendil's contact men in Denmark.[95] He writes:

I would now like to discuss the problem of financing the transportation. We cannot close our eyes to the fact that the great majority of the passengers today are *completely without means* [emphasized in the original] though they have worked faithfully. In this connection, it seems to me worthwhile trying to obtain some contributions from the Danish Jews. The money could be paid here. I am thinking, among others, of our common acquaintance . . . who paid for his son and himself a sum which is ridiculous in view of his circumstances. Let us not forget, and the Jewish gentlemen should also know it, that many people have given enormous sums in order to help them. The Jews escaped. These people have paid so much that they cannot help much more without causing themselves considerable harm. Had the Jews financed their own flight, it would be simple today to obtain money for others. When I talk to people about this problem, I do not say the above explicitly—nor should you do so. The Swedish Jews can also make it clear to the Danish Jews that it is now their turn to participate in the game. Before, when they lived here, it was understandable that because of the racial problem they did not want to take part in anything illegal, in order to avoid calamities. But now when they are all safe, they do not have to remain outside. They need to do it for their own sakes, for it will cause bitterness in many circles if it becomes known that they are not interested in supporting anything except themselves. Well, you doubtless know how to play this card much better than I do.

The idea here is the same except that it does not aim at financing the transfer of Jews still in Denmark (there were very few of these left at that time) but at helping the work of the resistance movement in keeping up the illegal routes. We will not dwell here on the undercurrent of bitterness in this letter, a point which will be discussed later.

From the material known to us, it does not appear that the suggestion of Hollander and Masur was put forward by Philipson for discussion. Hendil, however, was at once impressed not only by the proposal but also by the spirit of the letter quoted above, and he wrote to Ebbe Munck on December 3 that he thought it justified to demand 15 per cent of the transferred money (instead of only 10 per cent) "among other reasons out of the healthy thought that the Danish Jews whom we Aryans [sic!] helped should now assist in the transfer of people unable to pay, as these are either poor Jews or political refugees."[96] The same day he also replied to his contact man: "I will put forward your views on the Danish Jews at a meeting in Stockholm with representatives of the escaped Jews."

The man whom Hendil contacted on this matter was a member of the Henriques family, president of the old-established family bank in Denmark. Carl Otto Henriques was a banker of repute and an adviser to the Danish Treasury. At the time of the persecutions he lay in a hospital but did not consider flight, since his wife was non-Jewish. However, he was informed by underground channels that the Germans had included him in a list of people they intended to kill in revenge for the slaying of Germans by the resistance movement. Despite this situation the former minister of finance succeeded in obtaining for Henriques an exit permit and a visa to Sweden. This was apparently during that very short period when the Germans allowed legal exit, and he crossed over to Sweden with the regular means of transport. In Sweden he was consulted by all the Danish parties, from the legation to the underground movement. He also had close connections with the Swedish banks, a fact which promised to be an advantage in the financial arrangements. Following Hendil's approach, Henriques agreed to launch an appeal and himself contributed the first 15,000 kroner.[97] The attorney Kai Simonsen undertook to administer the project.

Among the active collaborators in the rescue work forced to flee Denmark, following the discovery of the mailbag in the *Julius,* was Henrik Kraft, head of the publicity department of the well-known Tuborg Brewery. He at once joined the central staff of underground workers in Stockholm, and from Munck's diary we learn that on January 3 and 4, 1944, he took part, together with Philipson and others, in talks on the financial arrangements for Hendil's route. Kraft was assigned to represent the Danish central organization in matters connected with the appeal. After consultations with Minister Kruse and Stephan Hurwitz[98] the technical procedure was agreed upon: the Jews signed promissory notes

—small pieces of paper representing an obligation to pay a certain sum of money to Denmark's National Bank upon the return of the refugees to Denmark—on the assumption that their property would not be affected in the meanwhile. These notes were deposited with the Danish minister, who in return handed over the corresponding sum in Swedish kronor. On returning to Denmark the Jews paid their debts and the notes were destroyed.

In approaching potential donors the organizers of the appeal presented them with a leaflet describing the work of the Danish-Swedish Refugee Service and explaining the tasks for which the money would be required. In part this sheet was a repetition of the various reports, from the memorandum to Foreign Minister Günther on December 18, 1943, to the financial summary of January 21, 1944.[99] In part too the explanatory sheet was based on the letter quoted above. It stated, for instance, that many institutions and private individuals in Denmark had, as of October 1943, contributed large sums for the rescue of the persecuted and that it was harder to collect money in Denmark now than it had been previously.[100] It also emphasized that the economic circumstances of the refugees now arriving were much more straitened than those helped in October and November.

The spirit of comradeship created during the latter months of the past year would also be endangered were refugees in the future to be inadequately assisted. The Danish-Swedish Refugee Service has therefore decided to approach a number of Danes now safe and secure, and request them to support the work with a contribution—the aim being to create a fund which will insure operations for six to nine months.

It further stated that the money would be transferred to the Swedish and Danish organization and that administration of the account would be entrusted to that same man

who had from the beginning represented the Swedish con-
tributors—the reference of course being to Philipson. Nowhere in the leaflet is it stated that the appeal was directed
to Jews and only Jews. "Danes" is the only word mentioned.[101]

On January 29 Ebbe Munck wrote to Christmas Møller
about the appeal and pointed out that the first 100,000
kronor had been promised. On March 6 he noted in his
diary that the appeal had passed the 300,000 mark; on
April 1 he wrote that he had met with Henriques in order
to examine the possibility of realizing, through the legation
in Stockholm, the obligations of the Danish Jews in Sweden,
which came to about half a million kronor ($100,000),
almost double the originally estimated amount.[102] Kai Simonsen pointed out after the war[103] that the Danish Jews re-
sponded willingly to the appeal, since all were grateful
to the Danish people for their rescue. The operation of the
route was insured by this financing and by the income
(which continually increased) from currency transfers.

In the summer of 1944, however, the route suffered a
severe setback. Once more a mailbag fell into the hands
of the Gestapo and this time the calamity was greater than
before, since the Germans located "Tom," and when they
came to arrest him on July 24, he and a colleague were
killed while attempting to escape. Weeks, even months,
passed before the route recovered from this blow. Precautions were intensified. Only toward the end of the year was
the system perfected and implemented. In the meantime the
route was suffering from a lack of money, and it was therefore decided at the beginning of 1945 to launch a new
appeal. The result was a sum much smaller than the one
raised by the previous appeal—about 250,000 kronor.[104]
Altogether the Danish and Swedish appeals and the service
fees for currency transfers placed at the disposal of the
Refuge Service 1¼ million kronor.[105] The Danish Jews alone
had contributed over a million kronor. To this sum of at

least one million kroner should be added the 6.5–7 million kroner the Jews themselves are estimated to have paid for their flight. All in all, therefore, the eight thousand Danish Jews paid close to 8 million kroner for their rescue.

According to Hendil, only 375,000 kroner were used for operating the route on both sides of the Sound, the rest of the money being devoted to other purposes: support of other routes,[106] assistance to resistance fighters and their families, illegal newspapers, intelligence services, the Freedom Council, and various other underground activities, such as preparation of false papers.

Among the refugees transported were 150 foreign subjects, 40 of them Allied pilots who had bailed out over Denmark.[107] Among the Danes carried over were underground leaders, ministers, senior officials, officers, and resistance fighters from all social groups, together with 150 children of varying ages. Also carried out were special missions, such as the transport of sick and aged people accompanied by a doctor. In addition to the transport of mail, propaganda material, arms, and ammunition, the route brought over 14,000 textbooks for Danish refugee schools in Sweden and 40,000 scientific and other volumes from the free world to the underground movement and to scientific research workers in Denmark. Most of the money, Hendil claimed, was not spent on the route itself or used in Sweden but was placed at the disposal of the resistance movement in Denmark.

The Jews Among the Refugees in Sweden

On October 12, 1943, Ebbe Munck wrote to Christmas Møller: "The enormous stream [of refugees] has naturally overwhelmed all absorption facilities, and it must be assumed that some time will pass before an organized procedure is under way. This is, however, a matter for the legation, the Swedish authorities, and the Jews themselves." Munck was right on both counts: some time passed before the temporary and spontaneous absorption arrangements assumed a fixed form, and those who dealt with such arrangements were primarily the Swedish authorities and the Danish mission, and to some extent the Jewish communities as well.

On October 16 the lieutenant-governor of the Malmö district informed the head of the Juridical Department of the Foreign Ministry that between the 4th and the 16th of October 6,670 refugees had reached southern Sweden, 90 to 95 per cent of them Jews.[108] The number of arrivals increased daily, amounting to 1,400 on the 9th, but the next day it dropped to 410 and finally settled at less than 200 a day. By the end of November 7,600 persons had arrived.[109]

Preliminary arrangements included lodging, food, clothing, registration of the refugees, examination of papers, customs, etc. After the first few days the Swedish police were helped by a number of Danish policemen, since both sides were interested in thorough security checks. Apart from the problems connected with any flow of refugees, the illegal transport system had to be protected against espionage and care taken not to disrupt the relations of neutral Sweden with Germany. A special problem in this connection was the wide press publicity given to the flight. The letters of Munck and Hendil, in particular, during those October days again stress the importance of secrecy. Only in the middle of the month did they succeed in stopping the publication of detailed information by the press. As for absorption of the refugees, the Swedish authorities were opposed to large urban concentrations, and camps were therefore set up in places relatively far from the main centers. This policy did not help in the long run, however, and many, particularly among the Jews, managed to give the guarantee of self-sufficiency required by the authorities for anyone wishing to live in one of the cities—this was possible because the Danish Jews had relatives or acquaintances among the Swedish Jews and even non-Jews, and these people assisted them to settle in the towns.

The authorities made every effort to alleviate the lot of the refugees. Not only was free medical treatment given— including on occasion hospitalization lasting several months —but attempts were made to make the technical arrangements easier. In Malmö, for instance, the banks opened for a few hours even on Sunday in order to enable people to convert their Danish money into Swedish kronor.[110]

The settlement of refugees and their families naturally required large sums of money. This problem was at first alleviated, though not solved, by a spontaneous action by organizations and individuals which collected and contributed money.[111] The Swedish authorities were prepared to undertake the financial burden, but their intention was to have the Ministry for Social Affairs exercise central control. The aims of the Danes themselves were, however, different. The active elements, especially the officers who had fled to Sweden after August 29, were interested in an independent organization. A small Danish refugee office already existed and could now be reorganized on a broader basis.[112] Following various negotiations on this subject, Stephan Hurwitz was called on October 20 to Minister Kruse, who suggested that he take charge of the future Danish Refugee Office.[113]

Ebbe Munck's letters reveal, during the weeks and even the months following, details on the development and consolidation of the office.[114] Unexpected financial help was received by the organizers from the Danish minister in Washington, Kauffmann. He placed at the disposal of the refugee aid authorities Danish funds that had remained in the legation in Washington. To these sums were added $50,000 presented to him by Jewish organizations in the United States to help Jewish refugees in Sweden.[115] All these amounts together were nevertheless insufficient to provide help for the refugees or maintain the administration required for this purpose. The Swedish government placed at the disposal of the Danish Refugee Office a loan which at first amounted to 5 million kronor, and increased the sum over a period of time until at the end of the war it amounted to 30 millions[116] (the Swedes afterward waived the repayment of loans granted to the Danes and Norwegians during the war). After the municipality of Stockholm had also placed an office at the disposal of the organization in the center of town, it began at the end of October to operate on an official basis. According to Stephan Hurwitz, this "state in miniature" dealt with three main problems: employment, arrangements for students, and the establishment of "police authority."[117] In fact, however, it engaged in many other spheres of activity, such as care of the aged, the sick, and children (even providing specially built schools, in which not only the majority of the pupils but also many teachers were Jews).

The Jewish refugees, who arrived in Sweden after a journey usually replete with fears and hazards, drifted numbly through the preliminary procedures. One of them describes how, after landing, the refugees were brought to their first reception station:

At the head of the procession there marched a police constable, and several others marched at our side. It was peculiar to wander as refugees under guard through a strange city, and it was difficult to realize that it was not a bad dream but harsh reality.

Naturally, everyone also stressed the feeling of relief and joy at having been saved. Indeed, as already mentioned, most of them had relatives or acquaintances, and with the aid of these many refugees quickly found work and an apartment and began to lead more or less normal lives. Such aid was given both privately and in organized form by the communities. The first who hastened to assist were naturally the Jewish communities in the port towns of Malmö, Helsingborg, and even Gothenburg; Stockholm's community—the largest and most affluent of them all—also took an active part. The latter also launched a special appeal in which 215,000 kronor were raised. A sum almost as large was given by international Jewish aid organizations. With these funds the Stockholm Jews rendered support to the absorbing communities in the south, to the members of Hechalutz who had fled to Sweden, to children of Youth Aliya, and even to private individuals.[118]

Margolinsky pointed out that as of November 1, 1944, the expenses of the Refugee Office amounted to 12,300,000 kronor and estimated that some 5,000,000 kronor had been used on behalf of Jewish refugees, of which 300,000 went for exclusively Jewish purposes.[119]

Friends and relatives in Denmark sent the refugees their belongings through the normal postal channels, and mention has already been made of the sums of money transferred. To the camps went those Jews who had no personal connections—mainly poor people, many of them religious. Care was taken to provide the latter with kosher food, and their special needs were taken into account as far as possible.[120]

As stated, non-Jewish Danish refugees also arrived in the wake of their Jewish compatriots. This flow was slower but steady, and by the end of the war the number of these refugees amounted to nine thousand, compared to about eight thousand Jews. The total number of Danish refugees in Sweden at the end of the war was therefore about seventeen thousand.[121] The non-Jews were, as stated, young resistance fighters, mostly simple people without means, most of whom came alone while their families remained in Denmark. It was natural, therefore, that it was precisely these who were sent not only to camps but to distant regions, where the Swedes provided hard pioneer work for the Danish and Norwegian refugees. They worked in the northern forests, built roads, were employed in agriculture; their lives were obviously much tougher than those of the Jews who had settled down in cities. Not only the Jews, however, managed to find a niche in cities. According to Margolinsky's survey there were 2,750 refugees—Jews and non-Jews—in the camps on January 1, 1944; by September 15 the number had dropped to 825 and presumably did not increase thereafter. Thus only 5 per cent of the refugees remained in the camps.[122]

An additional factor affected the status of the Danish Jews in Sweden. With the establishment of the Refugee Office a need arose for a staff proficient in administration, and people with these qualifications were found among the Jews. At least 50 per cent of the employees at the central and branch offices were therefore Jews, many of them in leading positions.[123] It should be emphasized, however, that not all the Jews were members of the liberal professions and the like; the data of the Refugee Office showed that out of 5,600 wage earners arriving up to the end of November, 49 per cent were salaried employees; these consisted of 20 per cent metal workers and 29 per cent textile workers.[124]

The strange situation was therefore created that the same young man who had perhaps in the hour of need smuggled the persecuted Jews from Denmark to Sweden, sometimes at the risk of his life, now found himself in the Refugee Office with the Jew he had saved sitting on the other side of the table and determining his fate as a refugee in Sweden. Moreover, Jews and non-Jews were often to be found together in the camps, and as Margolinsky points out: "It was not surprising that a meeting of Jews and non-Jews in the camps would, in view of the differences in social, cultural, and ideological background, lead to friction and arguments."[125]

To these sociological and psychological facts must be added a factor which particularly exacerbated relations. The

Danes saw as one of their primary tasks the raising of a Danish military force that could actively intervene on behalf of Denmark in the decisive hour at the end of the war. This force was at first set up—as was the parallel Norwegian force—under the guise of a police battalion, but was in fact a purely military body, which underwent commando training and which toward the end of the war came to be officially known as "the Danish Brigade." Enrollment in this brigade was on a volunteer basis. Margolinsky points out that owing to the age composition of the Jewish refugees, they included a much lower proportion of young men of military age than did the non-Jewish Danes.[126] It would appear, however, that at first Jews volunteered for the brigade in numbers even smaller than was consistent with this proportion and that the numbers rose only in the last months of the war (a characteristic shared by non-Jews also—such volunteers were known as "latter-day saints"). The brigade finally numbered about five thousand men. A number of Jewish women were among the initiators and officers of the women's auxiliary corps. A more than proportionately large number of middle-aged Jews joined the service branches. All in all, the number of volunteers of Jewish origin amounted to 750 or 15 per cent.[127] But the impression made at the beginning, together with other factors mentioned above, led to an unexpected phenomenon— anti-Semitism emerged among the Danish refugees. Few of the Danes were prepared to admit this openly, but it was undoubtedly true and affected to some extent even central figures in the resistance movement.[128] One of the organizers of the rescue action, Mogens Staffeldt, who was also forced to flee to Sweden, states that after arriving there and realizing this situation he became very depressed.[129] This phenomenon among a people who did more than most other nationalities to save the Jews requires an explanation.

Early in this study it was stated that the attitude of the Danes to the Jews was due more to love of freedom than it was to love of the Jews. It has been pointed out that "the strong reaction of the freedom-loving Danes against the 'removal of the Jews from Danish society' was more a general reaction against the encroachments of the common enemy than a special measure of assistance to the Jews."[130] Moreover, it should be understood that when the people reached Sweden the danger and threat on the part of the Germans vanished, while at the same time these refugees— Jews as well as non-Jews—were removed from their normal form of life under the protection of their own democratic regime. From then on other sociological and psychological factors began to operate, factors which were not only unexpected but probably also unconscious. The opposition and bitterness which the Jews aroused would have been aroused by any group in a better material and social position than the later Danish refugees. This is a well-known phenomenon wherever there are errant groups—refugees or migrants. In the Danish literature describing this period, the psychological symptom known as the "psychosis of refugees" is often mentioned; it is that sensitive and exceptionally tense mental state among people whose normal way of life has been shattered and who have been forced to run for their lives.[131]

The problem of the attitude toward the Jews was complicated, oddly enough, by the good intentions of the institutions. In accordance with their democratic principles, the Danes did not wish to stress the difference between Jews and non-Jews. In the central card index of the refugee office no mention was made of anyone's being a Jew or a non-Jew. Moreover, those Jews who worked in close cooperation with the Danes were particularly concerned with emphasing their equality with other Danish citizens and in glossing over any differences.[132] To the extent that any difference was officially recognized, it was recognized only as a difference in religion. In this latter sphere the Jews were given all facilities, and Rabbi Melchior was appointed officially as the rabbi of the refugees; accompanied by a cantor, he traveled from place to place holding prayers, giving lectures, and meeting people.

This post was parallel to that of the Protestant chaplain, Poul Borchsenius, who worked in close cooperation with Melchior. Of all who were then in official positions in Sweden, he is the only one who admitted the presence of anti-Semitism, tried to interpret and explain it, and—more important—attempted to combat it. After describing the psychological state of the resistance fighter who comes as a refugee to Sweden and finds the Jews well established "on the other side of the counter," Borchsenius adds:

Anti-Semitic propaganda has always taken advantage of the psychological factor in generalization—if a Jew was boastful or pompous, then all Jews were so. If a Jew was too adept in money matters, then all Jews were usurers. As if there are not the same number of Christians with the same bad characteristics. But one does not say that all Christians are the same.

In addition, he describes in his book[133] how he met Rabbi Melchior and learned at close hand the way of life of religious Jews. He tries to make this way of life comprehensible to the many Danes who for the first time had come across the Jews as a distinct group and who had been taken aback at the sight of the orthodox among them.

However, it was not altogether adequate to recognize Judaism only as a special religion and at the same time continue deliberately to ignore the distinct status of the Jews as an ethnic and cultural group—and that at a time when the hate of the Nazis had assigned such a prominent place to the Jews in the great struggle being waged on the battlefields of the Second World War. This was particularly the case since religion does not play an important or decisive role in the lives of the assimilating Danish Jews, who form the majority of Denmark's Jewish population. The leading

Danish Jews apparently did not adequately evaluate the signs of the times, when the fate of humanity was being decided on the battlefield. The important contribution of money to the underground movement should have been augmented by the volunteering of personnel. Had the young Jews—many of them students at the universities—joined the Danish Brigade in greater numbers, and thus given concrete evidence of their active participation in the Danish people's struggle for freedom, they would have renounced the status of victims and thereby established a clearer and firmer basis for that identification with the Danish people which they themselves attempted to gain. One young Danish Jew, Hugo Hurwitz, chose an extreme path not open to many: he returned secretly to Denmark, joined one of the underground groups, and took part in the most daring acts of sabotage.[134] Had the administrative heads of the refugees publicly encouraged volunteering for the brigade and not been content with "working discreetly for an improvement of the situation,"[135] they would have served the Jewish public more truly.

On October 10, 1943, the leaders of the Copenhagen community met in Sweden for consultations and there laid down that their authority was also valid in Sweden, but said that religious questions were the responsibility of the Swedish communities and that refugee affairs were the concern of the general Danish refugee organization. Rabbi Melchior, for example, was appointed by the Refugee Office. Meetings of this type took place five times during the stay of the Jews in Sweden, and matters related to the situation and later to the return home were discussed. Prior to their return to Denmark the assembled leaders of the Copenhagen community sent Christian X a telegram of thanks and greetings:

The representatives of the Jewish community in Copenhagen assembled in Falkenberg [near Gothenburg] send to Their

Majesties their cordial greetings on the liberation of Denmark, together with the expression of our profound thanks for the unforgettable efforts of Their Majesties on behalf of the Jews of Denmark.

The king's reply was: "We give you our heartfelt thanks. Au revoir."[136]

It is clear therefore that the heads of the community continued the same line they had followed on the eve of the persecutions, placing their trust exclusively in the official national institutions. To the extent that the Jews participated in the work of aiding the refugees, they did so not as members of the community and as Jews, but as private Danish citizens.

Summary

The flight of the Danish Jews, made possible by the spontaneous help of the Danish people, led to a radical and widespread change in Sweden's attitude toward the struggle of the Danish resistance movement. This change must be considered in the light of developments on the battlefield—here the Allies were increasingly in the ascendant, and not only underground Denmark but also neutral Sweden wished therefore to insure itself a place of honor in the free world. The Swedish authorities were supported in these aims by the Swedish people and press, who seized the opportunity to give spontaneous and clear expression to their revulsion against nazism and their faith in the basic human values of their own society. Profound significance was attached to the fact that a figure such as Niels Bohr, in conjunction with resistance fighters and with active elements among the Swedes, made so vital a contribution to Sweden's change of policy.

Those Swedish Jews who took the initiative in these matters did not anticipate far-reaching political repercussions; they aimed merely at rescuing the persecuted Jews of Denmark. But the results of their action spread beyond these narrow confines, due to the correct evaluation by the Danish resistance leaders on both sides of the Sound of the needs of the hour and the advantages to be gained. The Swedish Jews, and the Danish Jews in their wake, did not lag behind, and their contribution to the illegal transportation enterprise was considerable, both in financial and organizational terms. With the help of these routes, direct communications were established between the resistance movement and the Allied Powers, and with their help too the Danish leaders were able to cross to Sweden for purposes of political contact, for arms negotiations, and—when the need arose—to save lives.

The Jewish refugees from Denmark did not on the whole find their way into the ranks of the resistance movement and its active struggle in Sweden anymore than they had done in Denmark, where they refrained from doing so in accordance with their own and the Danish authorities' policy and strategy. Few at first ventured beyond financial help (willingly given though it was) to the point of personal involvement. However, the Jews doubtless made a valuable contribution to the administration of refugee affairs.

Among the non-Jewish refugees in Denmark the world was somewhat topsy-turvy. The active resistance fighter of yesterday, who had struggled for the freedom of his people and defended the lives of his Jewish fellow citizens, and the Jewish refugee of yesterday, who had been saved from persecution—these, as it were, changed roles. Neither side was capable of evaluating the situation correctly. Not all the young Danes in Sweden volunteered for the brigade solely out of idealistic motives; many joined also out of pure necessity or in order to escape other hardships. Not all the stories told by them of their share in the rescue of the Jews and in sabotage activities were authentic. Still, the fact remains that, certainly at first, the proportion of the Jews prepared to participate actively in Denmark's liberation fell below that of the non-Jews; this exacerbated other existing factors and adversely affected the relations between the two groups. The bulk of the Jews, however, had families and the old and the infirm to take care of, and had little choice but to await the end of the war longing for their return to the homeland.

X

The Jews in Liberated Denmark

Denmark's day of liberation, May 5, 1945, is imprinted forever in the memory of the refugees. Together with the whole Swedish people, they celebrated the end of the war and the fall of the Third Reich. A month (and sometimes more) was to go by, however, before the Jews could return to Denmark and to their homes. Immediate repatriates were the members of the Danish Brigade. Though they were not required to do any fighting, security assignments awaited them in Denmark.

On the very day of liberation a Danish government was formed. It consisted of eighteen members, chosen not on the basis of relative party strength but from those elements which had been active during the war years. Half the ministers were professional politicians, with Prime Minister Buhl at their head, and the other half were members of the underground movement who had in effect directed Danish policy since September 1943.[1] The moment the German army capitulated, the Danish resistance fighters came out into the open with a view to insuring their hold on the country. Lists of Danish collaborators with the Germans had already been drawn up and mass arrests were now carried out.[2] Some of the Danish Nazis resisted by force, and in those first days of peace victims on both sides still fell, including Leib Hirsch Zneider, a Jewish volunteer in the brigade. In general, however, the resistance fighters gained control of the situation, and on May 9, King Christian X drove in an open car through the streets of Copenhagen to open the Rigsdag, with resistance fighters and soldiers of the brigade lining the streets from the royal palace to the Parliament building. The German army left Denmark on May 7. A short time after, German refugees from the east started streaming into Denmark, an additional problem to the many facing the State, which had to reorganize itself after liberation.

As with all the occupied countries, Denmark found itself, in that first postwar period, confused and troubled. The country was torn between the need to restore life to its normal tenor and to its political and economic equilibrium, on the one hand, and the burning demand of many to pass sentence on the collaborators, on the other. The Rigsdag then enacted a special law enabling collaborators to stand trial promptly, a law which—contrary to previous custom in Denmark—also made provision for the death sentence. The debate on this question was sharp, and there erupted now all the conflicting elements which had joined hands against the common enemy.[3]

Side by side with these internal discussions emerged the problems of foreign policy and the desire to insure for Denmark its place among the nations. Here relations with Sweden were an important factor.[4] In a speech before the Swedish workers' organizations, in Stockholm's stadium on May 24, Hedtoft explained in detail the policy of Denmark —the official and the underground—during the war. He expressed the view that a Sweden at war would not have played the important role for Norway and Denmark that a Sweden at peace had done. He pointed out the importance to the Danish economy of Sweden's help during the war and, even more significant, its aid to the resistance struggle,

particularly after the establishment of the illegal transportation routes. Nor did he omit to mention the asylum given by
Sweden "when the Nazis unleashed their criminal action
against our Jewish fellow citizens." He described in glowing
terms the operation of the Swedish Red Cross, under
Bernadotte's guidance, in removing the inmates of the
concentration camps. Hedtoft's speech, which was printed
prominently in the Danish *Social-Demokraten* the following
day, was a kind of comprehensive report on Danish policy
during the war and even laid down the party's future principles. The speech made clear the tension inherent in the
transition from war to peace.

Not only the leading politicians, however, but also many
other prominent Danes felt the urge to explain to the
people what had occurred during the occupation, and the
Danish press in the first few months after the war was full
of articles on the occupation and the resistance movement.
Clearly, much of this material was intended for purposes of
publicity or self-justification, but many of the articles also
contained authentic information on the events just concluded. Among the writers was Hendil, who was, it will be
recalled, a journalist by profession. As early as May 13 he
held an exhibition of his boats, together with widespread
publicity material in the press, where he gave many details
of the route's activity and mentioned the names of his
principal helpers.[5]

The press was, however, not the only medium recounting
the events of the occupation and the problems they had
brought in their wake. There is perhaps no other country in
the world where so much literature on the occupation years
has appeared as in Denmark. Documentary collections,
historiography, and memoirs all underline the need that was
felt to relate the story of the period. The central and most
reliable enterprise of all—inaugurated by the authorities
with a view to examining the events of the occupation
years, describing the facts, clarifying the motives, and con-

sidering the political and ethical aspects—were those commissions of inquiry appointed one after the other by the Rigsdag. Between 1945 and 1950 these commissions studied the actions of those who were responsible for Danish policy during the fateful years of the war, and their findings were published openly.[6]

Among the problems facing the Danish authorities in that summer of 1945 were the difficulties which arose in connection with the return home of the deportees and the refugees. On May 16, 1945, a Central Office for Special Affairs was set up to deal with these matters, with Dr. Melchior representing the Jewish community. This body occupied itself with the problems created by the return of thousands of people, including the payment of "refugee compensation," which was given to those in need and included, for example, compensation to the Theresienstadt internees after their return. The Rigsdag passed a law in this connection at the end of 1945.[7]

A large number of Jews found their apartments ready for occupation, and it has already been mentioned that in many cases relatives and friends had seen to it that everything was in order before the owners returned.[8] Not everyone, however, was in this fortunate position. Some had lost their furniture, and some of the apartments rented out in the meantime were not vacated. As in most places after the war, Copenhagen suffered from a severe housing shortage, and it was found necessary to arrange temporary accommodation for the homeless in schools and similar buildings; 1,300 persons were housed in this way, but in September 1945 the number had dropped to only 400 and by April 1, 1946, to 75.[9]

A more serious problem arose with regard to employment. Many positions had been filled in the meantime and could not be vacated. Small businessmen and craftsmen in particular no longer found what they had left behind in the hour of escape. Some of those who had formally transferred their businesses to the names of acquaintances found that the new "owners" were not prepared to admit the fictitious nature of the arrangement but adhered to the letter of the law.[10] The authorities and the community endeavored to render assistance to the best of their ability, but nevertheless for many the first years after the war were hard and bitter.

A particularly difficult problem was constituted by the stateless who had come to Denmark before the war. According to a letter written on December 11, 1945, to the Ministry of Justice by the United Danish Committees for Refugee Aid,[11] the number of such refugees and their families (many had married Danish women) was 2,169 (including over 200 still in Sweden, many of them former pioneers or Youth Aliya wards). Of those in Denmark of working age, 578 were "normal" refugees, 144 were pioneers, and 71 were Youth Aliya "children." On behalf of these people the committees requested a temporary residence permit such as that given to foreign citizens staying in the country; a work permit unrestricted as to place or occupation; the usual social welfare benefits to the old, the sick, and invalids; absence of pressure on the stateless to leave the country (unless they were socially undesirable cases); and the granting of an identity card for all the refugees, valid in the eyes of the authorities, employers, etc. This letter was signed by Aage Friis, Niels and Harald Bohr, Frederik Torm, Hans Hedtoft, and other distinguished Danes and by the leaders of the Jewish community, C. B. Henriques and Karl Lachmann. The reply of the Ministry of Justice was given on March 14, 1946. The requests were on the whole agreed to, and those refugees who remained in Denmark received Danish citizenship in the course of time.[12]

To these problems should be added that of repayment of debts. Though in many cases these were settled by the Ministry of Social Welfare,[13] both the Jewish community and private individuals were obliged to redeem the notes given on behalf of the resistance movement. The organizers of the Appeal for the Danish-Swedish Refugee Service, as it was now officially called, sent a letter on July 20, 1945, to all those who had signed promissory notes at the time of rescue. The letter included a description of the operation of the route, the objectives for which the money was contributed, and an appeal to pay the sums owed to attorney Kai Simonsen. In addition to underground leaders such as Niels Andersen and Erling Foss, the letter was signed by Ebbe Munck, Hendil, Kraft, Philipson, Polack, and Simonsen. It would seem that all in all most people fulfilled their obligations.

In the days following the end of the war certain psychological symptoms began to manifest themselves among the Danish people. These were a reaction to the years of suffering and the direct effects of the profound changes and abnormal acts that the struggle for life and death had brought about. Many of the resistance fighters were disappointed at not being given adequate opportunity to settle accounts with the collaborators or at the lack of adequate personal recognition of their achievements and the risks they had run. The many economic difficulties which beset Denmark after the war also added to the bitterness, disillusion, and fatigue of many sections of the population when the protracted tension was suddenly relaxed.[14] It is against this background that note should be taken of the social and psychological symptoms that had already come to the fore while the refugees were still in Sweden, namely, signs of anti-Semitism, which increased in Denmark in the immediate postwar years. In the electric atmosphere of the transition period, when people had not yet adjusted themselves to the renewed patterns of free social and political life, the seeds of anti-Semitism sown by the Nazis, in Denmark as elsewhere, now germinated, although in the years of the war they had fallen on barren ground.

How did this increased anti-Semitism find expression in

Denmark at the time? It was a part of that same tense atmosphere mentioned above, when so many hearts were filled with bitterness and disappointment. There was nothing remarkable in this in itself, for it is typical of anti-Semitism and all other forms of phobia against a minority. What was surprising was that it occurred in that same Denmark where the whole people had arisen to protect and deliver the Jews. Now the word "Jew" became a term of abuse used openly and frequently. In an article entitled "Anti-Semitism in Denmark—Despite Everything,"[15] Rabbi Melchior writes:

If one happens to tread on someone's toes in a bus one is a "damned Jew." On Strøget [Copenhagen's main shopping street] the cry "Jew" is heard more than one cares to think, not only toward Jews who are disliked but toward anyone with whom there is a score to settle. Moreover, many Jewish children suffer from this situation in the public schools, where it is no longer a question of anti-Semitism in its more "delicate" form but a transition to something far more serious and dangerous.

In a later article Dr. Melchior gives examples of anti-Semitic undertones even in the paper Social-Demokraten and relates from his experiences in the work of the Central Office how many homeowners refused to have Jewish tenants.[16]

It is to Dr. Melchior's credit that he aired this problem publicly. His first article mentioned above was written in response to an important article by Paul Henningsen in the Communist paper Land og Folk of January 15, 1946, ("Anti-Semitism After the War"). Dr. Melchior's reply, as it were, was also given in what had formerly been an organ of the underground movement, Frit Danmark. Discussion of the problem did not occupy the pages of the general press but was to be found mainly in church, youth, and former resistance periodicals.[17] Dr. Melchior's articles were opposed to the policy of "hushing things up" that was typical of most Jews and of the Danish public at large. In his article Henningsen wrote:

Between man and man, when no Jews are present, the problem is vigorously debated, but in public it is considered tactless to mention it. Such a situation is intolerable, and I take the liberty of raising the issue although I know that many people of Jewish origin consider silence more suitable. The character of the Danish people is the concern of us all, and heaven forbid that the satanic germ sown by the Nazis be allowed to grow quietly. When millions have died in recent years it would be naïve to ignore the existence of the problem.

This is an expression of the principle expounded by Hal Koch—a man belonging to the Church, to an entirely different group—as early as 1942, namely, that the Jewish problem is important for the Danes themselves.[18] The writer reaches the conclusion that the behavior of the Jews themselves is conditioned by the terms that the environment in which they live dictates to them, and, adapting a well-known proverb, he states: "Tell me how the Jews behave in your country and I will tell you who you are." Moreover, in the section already quoted, it is clear that the extermination of the Jews of Europe and the persecutions in Denmark revealed to the Danes that an objective Jewish problem existed and, to their surprise, existed also in Denmark, although they had ignored it so successfully in their contacts with the Germans. The fear that impelled Henningsen to raise the question, despite the opposition of both Jews and non-Jews, concerned the fate of Danish society and its democratic form more than it concerned the fate of the Jews, and can be summed up thus: "God forbid that now that nazism has been defeated it will enter our house through the back door of anti-Semitism."

The assertions made against the Jews were, in effect, the same as those made during their stay in Sweden. In September 1944 interesting talks were held between the

Hechalutz office in Sweden and the associates of Hendil's route (mainly with Hendil himself and with Philipson), following Marx's departure for England.[19] In this context Hendil wrote to Philipson:[20]

I pointed out to W. [a member of the Hechalutz office in Sweden] that when we come home, it will be very important if we can show what a couple of fine, courageous Jewish boys have done to save Danes from German persecution. Your help will be of great value—as is the economic assistance which, with C. O. Henriques's aid, we are trying to distribute most effectively; for both facts contradict the general opinion, now dominant in Denmark, that the Jews have simply fled in order to be able to live here in luxury and security, while they have neither before nor now done anything for the common cause.

It must also be admitted that after his return to Denmark Hendil did indeed publish in the press the most important parts of Marx's story.[21]

In replying to these statements, Dr. Melchior asserted that there were of course Jews in Sweden who did not know how to behave, but were all the Jews to be judged on the basis of those examples? Were the Danish people judged according to the traitors in their ranks? He points out that there were also Danes who abused Jewish trust and quotes the case of those returning refugees who found neither their apartments nor furniture, their businesses nor their work tools.

The same subject is discussed in the Jewish literature of the period, which describes the trials and fears of the Jews in the days of persecution, the few Danes who did not care and the many who surpassed themselves in their efforts to save the Jews, the flight with its dangers—and the fishermen who sought to turn the situation to their advantage. A prominent place in these works is occupied by accounts of the life of the Jewish refugees in Sweden, its joy and its sorrow. Descriptions may also be found of the bitter destiny of the returning refugee who discovered that the fruits of his struggles over many years had vanished.[22]

The first development within the Jewish population that gave rise to public discussion was the fact that a not inconsiderable number of people, including prominent personalities, left the community in the year after liberation. Not only the Danes were tired, the Jews were also tired— and they were "tired of being Jews."[23] Among the Danes themselves there were those who had become persuaded by the Nazi persecutions, and by recognition of the existence of a Jewish problem, that the Danish Jews should assimilate and assimilate completely—that is, remove the problem once and for all.[24] In opposition to this viewpoint and, even more, in opposition to secession from the community, Dr. Melchior wrote a sharp article in the *Jødisk Samfund* of April 5, 1946, under the headline I ANNOUNCE MY WITH-DRAWAL. This frontal attack on the "deserters" introduced a lively discussion in the pages of the paper over several weeks, concluding with a contribution from Lachmann, who was now chairman of the community. His main point was that withdrawal from the community would not help. "We are born Jews," he states, "and no one cares whether we withdraw from the community or not; even if we embrace Christianity, we will remain Jews in the eyes of the world." He too therefore emphasizes that the objective factors of inheritance and environment, not our subjective wishes, are predominant. The same argument, though slightly different in form, was put forward by Paul Henningsen in the article quoted above, when he states that the conditions created by the Christians were what taught the Jews that money is the only thing that counts. "It is a part of Jewish upbringing to always act with the hidden thought in mind that catastrophe can occur." And he goes on: "Might it not well be said that if a number of Jews had money to take with them to Sweden to support themselves it is because we of the noble

Aryan race have taught them that this is important for the preservation of life?"

The attention of the Danish Jews—and even of the Danes themselves—was turning increasingly toward events in Palestine. Emphasis changed from the internal struggle to the struggle between Jews and Arabs and Jews and Englishmen.[25] The main summing-up was given by Dr. Melchior in his article "Some Jewish Problems," which appeared in the Christian paper *Kirkens Front* on September 26, 1946 (part of these ideas and formulations were also used by him in his only article on this subject in the *Jødisk Samfund,* October 15). His starting point is the situation of the Jews of Europe after the war and the fact that the path of the Jews from the camps of destruction in Germany to Palestine was blocked by the English, and he includes as part of this general problem the question of anti-Semitism in Denmark. "Can the Jews be assimilated among the nations?" he asks. He reaches the conclusion that individuals can but *the whole cannot.* No nation commits suicide. A nation with a past as rich as that of the Jews will not abandon hope for the future. Moreover, the particular characteristics of the Jews can enrich and vary the culture of the country in which they live. The Jewish enterprise in Palestine will also bring honor to the Jews in the world at large. As for Denmark, he points out that the Jewish problem which has arisen is imaginary and artificial, a sign of the cultural decline caused by the war. Dr. Melchior concludes his article thus: "A people's culture is measured by its attitude to this problem, and Denmark must return to that high peak on which it formerly stood." The article is accompanied by photographs from Palestine and of refugees on their way to reach that country's shores.

Pinches Welner, who in 1953 published the most pessimistic book on the occupation and the postwar period written by a Jewish author, had in 1946 written a booklet by the name of *The War Against the Jews*,[26] which dealt with the current problems of Palestine. He concludes as follows:

This time the Jews will also have something to say on the solution of the Jewish problem solved recently by the Germans in their fashion. What they [the Jews] ask for is simply a piece of territory—and this can only be Palestine—where they make the decisions and where Jews, leaving their country of origin under stress or of their free will, can seek and find safety.

Few of the Danish Jews, however, in fact took such a step and emigrated to the State of Israel.

The Danish Jews who returned to their motherland are to this very day deeply and sensibly grateful to the Danish people. They also came to realize very quickly that what had happened to them was quite exceptional amid the calamity that struck at European Jewry.[27] Upon their return some went round and personally thanked all those who had helped them. Others wrote of the days of persecution out of a feeling that these were exceptional historical events whose memory had to be preserved. "A few days after I came to Sweden," writes one of them, "when I had calmed down a little, I realized that I had taken part in a historical event, and I decided to write down my experiences."[28] The second development which left its mark on the Jewish mind was that all sections of the population were in the same boat.

There were babies and senile oldsters and sick people who could not stay in the hospital. There were patchwork shoemakers and big directors, working-class wives and middle-class matrons —and all these seven thousand children of mankind were for the first time in Denmark's history enveloped by the same fate and had the same hope of being able to wriggle their way over to the other side, to Sweden, freedom's and redemption's land.[29]

After a short while the desire to return to a normal, routine, traditional existence increased its hold on the

Danish people. Within a year nearly all the resistance members had left the government. Hardly any of them remained in political life, the great majority returning to their former occupations. Not only the leaders, but all sections of the population strove to return to quieter ways. The more such normalization won ground, the less anti-Semitism reared its head. This fact supported the thesis of Rabbi Melchior that this anti-Semitism of the immediate postwar period was a transitory phenomenon, created by temporary sociological and psychological conditions.

One of the Jews wrote in his evidence:

When all the tragic aspects of these events have gradually faded, there remains the glowing experience of all the love and helpfulness we met both here and in Sweden—among friends and among strangers; this has again shown us—more clearly than ever before—what it means to have friends; it has shown us how virtually all our countrymen reacted against this meaningless injustice and brutality, and how the staunch solidarity of all Danes found its most brilliant expression.

Conclusion

The Danish people are a normal people; a small people, whose land bestows no special favors; a people who have to work hard to win bread from earth containing no special resources. They are dependent on others greater and richer than themselves for the raw materials they need and for the marketing of their agricultural and industrial products. The world recognizes the quality of their meat and dairy products, and the good taste which marks their design of man's everyday utensils. They are held in affection for their affability and for their capacity to enjoy life, to see the lighter side of things, and to imbue others with their spirit of cheerfulness. Danish society has succeeded in liberating its members from many fears, thanks to its economic structure and its social security, and its democratic parliamentary system guarantees the freedom of the individual and the rule of law. Denmark's national day is the day on which the constitution (Grundlov) was granted. The Danes are known as individualists, and it is true that the dignity of the individual is held dear. Every effort is made to insure him not only his political and social rights and his daily bread, but also a good education and upbringing. At the same time, the country's leaders depend to a large extent on the common sense, spirit of freedom, and sense of humor of the individual Dane.

More than in any other period of history the Danish leaders during the occupation relied on the individual— man and woman, the aged and the young, farmer, worker, fisherman, businessman and member of the liberal professions, policeman, and soldier. They relied upon his knowing how to comport himself, keep a cool head, and respect the basic values of his society. For this was the main problem of the Danes: to preserve themselves, their country, and their principles of government. Opinions varied as to how all this should be achieved: through accord with the Germans or through rebellion. While the first viewpoint was in the ascendant during the early years, the tendency toward resistance increased as German strength diminished. The Dane is neither unimaginative nor cowardly, but his circumstances demand that he be a realist without being an opportunist; the Nazi minority in the country was in fact always isolated. Both alternatives—cooperation or resistance —demanded a considerable degree of pretense, of wordless understanding between man and man, of rapid reaction, agility, and ingenuity. The Danish approach to underground activity, as first expressed in prominent form during the rescue of the Jews, united and integrated local independence and initiative with guidance and coordination by the central leadership. This system demands of each individual a large measure of self-discipline and responsibility. Thanks to these organizational methods, the resistance movement succeeded in combining planning with spontaneous action.

The protection of the Jews by the Danes was an organic part of the protection of the country's image. Moreover, in addition to identification with the Jews from motives of political principle and social philosophy, there were many Danes, especially in the upper classes, who had personal connections with the Jews through their work, through friendship, and even through family ties. Within the framework of the policy of negotiation the Danish defense of the Jews was a part of the defense of the whole nation. Thus the abstention of the Jews from any underground activity caused no adverse comment; on the contrary, this was precisely what the Danish authorities wanted of them in order to deprive the Germans of any pretext for attack. Furthermore, this was also the demand of the Germans so long as they were not interested in raising the issue.

The situation changed radically, however, when the rescue of the Jews and their removal to Sweden was carried out, not by the authorities who were supposed to be protecting them, but by the people under the guidance of the resistance movement. This produced a basic change of protector, as well as a change in the way help and rescue were provided. Moreover, the departure of the Jews also meant a basic change in their very situation, which previously had evoked the full identification of the Danish people with their fate. Now the lives of the Jews were no longer in danger, and the attitude of the Germans toward them had thus no longer any principal and general meaning. The German attempt at deportation of the Jews in the midst of the fateful crisis in their relations with the Danes proved indeed that the position of the Jews was a barometer of these relations. But with the radical change in the position of the Jews and in the internal situation in Denmark (through the transfer of political authority to the Freedom Council), the Danish attitude toward the Jews no longer had the same political and fundamental significance. Thereafter there were other criteria.

Thus for the people who remained in occupied Denmark, where the conqueror's oppression and terror constantly increased, the full identification with the fate of the Jews automatically came to an end, since it no longer served as a symbol of the fate of the Danish people. Furthermore, those Danes who were also forced to flee across the Sound found the Jews there not only generally better established than themselves but in many instances the arbiters of the fate of their rescuers. The anti-Jewish sentiment, which could be found here and there even during the rescue operation, now seemed to spread. It was as if the barrier holding out the anti-Semitic propaganda of the Nazis had suddenly been removed; or as if this propaganda was a sort of germ which could hibernate over a long period but return to life when conditions were suitable for it. The epidemic, though not dangerous, spread rapidly.

The serious crisis in relations came only with liberation. Only then did the Danes lose some of their sense of proportion. Gradually, as the Danes returned to their normal state of equilibrium, they shook off these anti-Jewish symptoms. It should be stressed, however, that the possibility of discussion and argument was never absent, and it may be assumed that debate on this issue played its part in quickly terminating the crisis between the Danes and their Jewish fellow countrymen.

The Germans under the Third Reich did not behave like a normal people. They perpetrated deeds and created situations which were not only outside accepted usage but beyond previous conceptions of humanity. The normal man's instinctive shrinking from murder was replaced by the suppression of this abhorrence as the desirable end. This image of man dragged from the dark recesses of the soul, these forces of destruction given unbridled license, found an echo in certain elements in almost every nation. Denmark was one of the few countries where they failed to gain a foothold; there was no framework to absorb them, despite the encouragement the policy of cooperation might have given them. This fact had a surprising consequence: it engendered something like normality in German behavior. Those among the occupiers who were not already beyond the pale of human decency found a pillar of support in the Danes; others simply retreated. It was clear to the Germans that in Denmark the Jews were to be left alone. Moreover, rational considerations of economic benefit and common sense meant something in Denmark and acted as forces of restraint.

Even when the crisis broke, the Germans were unable to abandon the principle of self-interest. Eichmann himself admitted that in Denmark he could not do as he wished and that it was impossible to implement the "final solution" against the will of the people. In the midst of the state of emergency, negotiations took place on a new commercial agreement and on the supply of Danish agricultural and industrial products to Germany—as if everything was normal. The Danes were well aware that here lay their strength in German eyes.

The personal complications Best maneuvered himself into were, from a historical point of view, accidental. Their factual consequences, however, had nothing of chance about them but showed how much the man's actions were conditioned by the behavior of the Danes. He did not import the police battalions in order to deport the Jews; he imported them—on the pretext of the Jews' deportation—in order to consolidate his own rule in Denmark. However, owing to the attitude of the Danes he was not able to carry out the deportation in the normal Nazi manner. After he had been compelled to permit the Danes to smuggle the Jews over to Sweden, he was restrained by Himmler from using the police battalions for his own ends. His whole operation was a failure. He did not exploit the Danish situation—the Danish situation exploited him, and he found himself between the hammer of Danish society and the anvil of the Nazi central authorities.

The efforts of the Danes to apply their methods beyond the borders of their country to cover their citizens in concentration camps were less successful. Thus in Theresienstadt the Germans beat them at their own game: they presented a façade of apparently normal conditions, and the Danes were drawn into the web of deception.

The Jewish people are not, by virtue of their very existence, a normal people. During their long history of dispersion among the nations, they willingly accepted this fact as long as they regarded themselves as the people chosen by God to be His witness by virtue of their existence. This singularity was the axis around which the Jewish people revolved in their manifold and variegated social, economic, and cultural relationships with the nations among whom they dwelt. Since the dawn of modern times, when the ghetto walls crumbled and the Jews were, so it seemed, freed from their isolation, the inner force of their religious singularity had been fading, confronted, as it were, with the aspiration to be "like all the nations." This inner urge toward normality was supported by the striving for equality which, according to Tocqueville, characterizes the basic situation of modern society. It seemed at first as if the emancipation, which gave the Jews legal equality though usually no full social equality, would achieve the aims of normalization. However, when it transpired in the 19th century, particularly toward its close, that this goal had not been reached, the despondency of the Western Jews and the tribulations of the Jewish masses in Eastern Europe led to the founding of the Zionist movement, with its aim of creating normal conditions of national life in Palestine, that country for which the Jewish people had never ceased to yearn.

From then on the Jews were divided into two camps: those who sought normalization through adaptation to the life of the peoples among whom they dwelt; and those who sought to build a normal national life in Palestine. Emancipation in Europe generally led, by its very nature, to assimilation. Precisely where this was achieved, the dividing line between Jew and non-Jew and the national peculiarities of the Jewish people in the social, cultural, organizational, and political spheres became blurred. There remained the religious way of life. But this too was deteriorating, so that all that remained were some inherited characteristics of the Jewish image. The war of life and death which Hitler and the majority of the German people declared on the Jews seemed to bring home to the Jews in those very countries where they had achieved the greatest measure of emancipation and normality the fact that the process had failed.

The small Jewish community in Denmark is a classic example of normalization within the absorbing nation, so advanced and thorough that some degree of separation from world Jewry could be discerned. At the beginning of the 20th century, this group was in fact well on the way to gradual self-elimination, a development delayed by the arrival in Denmark before and after the First World War of a tiny tributary of that stream of Jewish refugees flowing from east to west. This increment of Eastern Jews prevented the disintegration of the Jewish community in Denmark and brought it new facets; but it did not succeed in changing its basic character, and little time was to pass before the new immigrants had integrated into the life pattern of the veteran Danish Jews.

The rise to power of Hitler placed the Jews of Denmark in a new situation: they were asked to help. They did help, they made financial and organizational efforts, but they were restricted by the regulations on absorption of refugees laid down by the authorities. They were now obliged to weigh their responsibility to the Jewish people as a whole, in its dire straits, against their responsibility to the country whose laws had granted them rights and demanded of them obligations. This conflict was described by a Jew from

Sweden (where a similar situation existed) as "double loyalty."

With the conquest of Denmark by the Germans the whole situation changed radically. Two things now became clear. The first was that the Danish people stood firm. They knew that freedom and equality were indivisible and that in defending the Jews they were in fact defending their own freedom. The second was that it was this very defense which made the situation of the Danish Jews abnormal. They were deprived, due to the situation, of the possibility for independent political decision. They were not given the choice open to every single Dane: to support the policy of negotiation or to join the underground. Only within a very narrow but legal sphere were they permitted—by the Danes—to defend their rights, as illustrated by the watch on the synagogue under Danish police protection. All in all, the Jews in Denmark were and remained an object: an object of persecution and an object of rescue, an object of the political decisions of others—now the Germans, now the Danes. Even Henriques's proud reply to the departmental heads does not change this fact, but merely shows that his only support at that moment was the law and that the concepts of the law were all he could cling to. But the law could not save anyone. In the hour of crisis the Jews were the passive indicator of the balance of power.

Apart from a few Jews who fled on April 9, 1940, the only individuals among the Jews in Denmark who refused to be mere objects and attempted to act independently were those pioneers who tried to escape from the trap. The plan for escaping by hiding under railway wagons crossing Germany was no doubt doomed to failure and stamped with the mark of immaturity, but the germ of independence and will to escape were healthy symptoms. Those concerned, together with the young men who fled in a stolen boat to Sweden and roused the wrath of the Germans, broke out of the framework allocated to the Jews, for which the Danish authorities were responsible. Nevertheless it was these pioneers who found the way to the underground. The spirit of revolt among the Danes, as among these Jews, united them in their action. This is the background of the work of the boat *Julius*. In this brief cooperation between Hechalutz and the underground, Hendil saw a factor likely to dispel the anti-Jewish resentment that had arisen. Hechalutz for its part did not consider it its special duty to save the honor of the Danish Jews; its eyes were on the Land of Israel.

Those Swedish Jews who took the first measures to save the Jews of Denmark were also Zionists. The others followed in their footsteps. Just as the rescue of the Jews by the Danes was a passing phenomenon which nevertheless cleared the way for the establishment of the illegal transportation system, so the initiative of these Zionists was a transient phase which nevertheless led to the setting up of a bridgehead. It is no mere chance that the Zionists Hollander and Masur afterward felt that Hendil's route was none of their concern, while Philipson, the non-Zionist Jew steeped in Swedish life, did what other Swedes did—made the illegal transport work his personal affair.

The protection of the Jews by the Danish authorities reached its close during the crisis, but the passivity of the Jews as a public body continued even while the Danes themselves were moving from "passive to active resistance." The Jews were not aware of the schism that had arisen between them and the Danish people as a result of the change in their own objective situation, on the one hand, and the change in the Danish attitude toward the occupying power, on the other. They had just been given proof of how strong Danish solidarity with their cause had been; when they suddenly felt the new and hostile winds that began to blow, they were incapable of grasping what had happened. As refugees in Sweden, the Jewish community of Denmark clearly did not become conscious of any social or political responsibility of its own which would compel it to make decisions in public affairs. On the contrary, the Jewish leaders denied the existence of any such separate and autonomous responsibility and wanted to be regarded as Danes only. Therefore those of them heading the Refugee Office were as a matter of principle uninterested in knowing how many Jews there were in Sweden. The fact that the leaders of the Danish Jewish community were not conscious of the need to solve special Jewish social political problems also made it possible for them to disregard the need to arrive at a collective decision in such a highly political problem as the enrollment for the brigade. At first this decision was left to the individual. Only gradually and timidly, under the impact of the critical voices, did the leadership change this atttude.

The Danes, on the other hand, by virtue of the events, recognized the Jews as a separate entity, with its special destiny, living among them. They too, however, were unwilling to admit this fact which was so much at variance also with their own basic conception. Therefore there arose a kind of silent conspiracy to hush things up. This consciousness of the Jewish situation on the part of the Danes having been held in check, it then found other less pleasant ways of expression. All the more important was the fact that the air again became cleared with the help of the public discussion that developed in the year after the liberation.

These developments indicate that assimilation alone did not lead the Danish Jews to normality. The Danish people crossed over from "passive to active resistance," but the Jews were slow to make the corresponding transition from passivity (out of coercion) to activity (out of choice).

Those Jews who after the war broke away from the community took a logical step from their point of view. There were doubtless many among them who had simply grown tired of being Jews and sought the solution of individual assimilation. But there were also those among them who left the community not because they were—in Dr. Melchior's words—deserters, but because they regarded the Jews as having evaded their duty. However, they might well have been asked: Why did you not try to change the situation? Why do you accuse Jewish officialdom, since you did not attribute to it any responsibility and authority in general public issues?

However, the truth is that there are no real grounds for accusations or counteraccusations. The Danish Jews had trod this path since they had been granted civil equality. At the time, this had been given at the price of renouncing all Jewish cultural, social, and administrative autonomy. The experience of the occupation intensified the dependence on the formal law: it was this law which defended the Jews and which prevented them from venturing beyond its official bounds. The paradox was that it was precisely an illegal act, an act beyond these bounds, by which the Danish people saved the Jews; while the authorities responsible for the law felt themselves compelled to suggest their— illegal—internment, in the forlorn hope that they might thus be protected. The Jews did not realize that these facts obligated them too. In the hour of liberation the leaders of the community sent their telegram of greetings and thanks to the Danish king, the symbol of law and order. It did not apparently enter their minds also to send greetings and thanks to the Freedom Council, the representative body of the people in their fateful hour of danger, which had guided the underground groups and the spontaneous supporters in the rescue action.

It is understandable that Jews did not integrate completely and immediately in Denmark after the liberation, since the country still bore the imprint of the time it had spent "outside the law." The anti-Semitic symptoms which emerged were doubtless the fruits of Hitlerian seeds, although the problem was not as imaginary as Dr. Melchior claimed. But the general return to a normal pattern of life also enabled the Jews to be absorbed once more into the Danish society, based on the law before which all men are equal. In the meantime, however, the State of Israel arose and with it a new problem of double loyalty.

The Danish story teaches us that the possibility of influencing the Germans and their treatment of the Jews existed. The prerequisite was conscious identification of the whole population with its Jewish citizens. Only where there was true equality was there a true defense of the Jews. But recognition was not enough. The decisive act of the Danish people was an act of spontaneity, arising neither from consideration nor reflected decision. It was clear to each and every one that this was the thing to do—and no words were necessary. An instinctive response of this sort can spring only from an education so profound that it reaches the very roots of man's basic evaluations and reactions. The path followed by the Danes both in their passive and their active resistance can only lead to success if people act on the basis of personal initiative and political maturity, two criteria which were demonstrated by the Danish underground organization.

Danish individualism proved itself to be firmly rooted in the responsibility of the individual to all his fellows, in mutual responsibility between man and man: personal responsibility and conscious responsibility. It was this responsibility that in the hour of need motivated violation of the law—as expressed by the leaders of the Church in their pastoral letter on the persecution of the Jews. Shirer relates in his book on Scandinavia (p. 240) that during a courtesy visit to one of the mayors in Copenhagen, General Kaupisch looked out of the window and saw, on the very day of occupation—April 9, 1940—how people went quietly about their business as on any ordinary day. "What discipline!" he exclaimed in admiration. "No discipline," his Danish host corrected, "but culture." The secret of this culture lies in the union of national consciousness and social aspirations, in the all-embracing conception of the place of man in his people and his society. This is what creates a balance between the individual and society.

The Danish story also teaches us, however, that a Jewish group with firmly established rights can—when the fine balance of the people amid whom it lives is disturbed—suddenly find itself faced with hostility; it happened even in that Denmark which at the risk of life and limb had defended the Jews. The system has not yet been found which will insure the Jew living in the Diaspora the complete normalization of his situation as a part of society and as an individual.

In the Hitlerian period this was a question of life and death. Fortunately for us, his insane solution was not implemented in full, owing to the fact that the world rose against him and defeated him and that there were nations and individuals who regarded genocide as a negation of human culture.

The Holocaust was a catastrophe in the life of the nations no less than it was a catastrophe in the life of the Jewish people. It did not happen in a vacuum; it happened within the very heart of the peoples of Europe and thus cast into grave doubt the value of that human culture which Europe had created. This culture has two main roots: the ancient culture of Greece and Rome, and Christianity. Its modern social-political embodiment is what we call Western democracy. In most countries of Europe this culture did not stand the test of the Holocaust. Yet the Danish experience shows that it was possible to preserve cultural values in theory and in practice, and in so doing prevent the implementation of barbaric extermination. Moreover, even the Germans in Denmark woke up to a recognition of the values of that culture to whose creation Germany itself had contributed in the course of many centuries.

Just as the civilized world has good reason to reflect on the reasons for the catastrophe which overwhelmed it in the period of the "final solution," so too should it benefit from the lessons of those instances where tragedy was averted. Amid these the rescue of the Jews of Denmark shines with greatest luster, for it was here that humane democracy stood its test.

APPENDIXES

I

The German Foreign Ministry Under Ribbentrop

The German Foreign Ministry passed into Ribbentrop's hands on February 4, 1938, when Hitler carried out a reshuffle of top posts as part of his organizational preparation for war (see Shirer, *The Rise and Fall of the Third Reich*, pp. 318 ff.).

In May 1940 the *Deutschland* Department was set up within the Ministry. This was a new and special organization formed out of two earlier departments. The original *Deutschland* Department had been set up in the days of the Weimar Republic to maintain contact between the Ministry and the Reichstag and attempt to coordinate foreign and domestic policy. The department was then quite small. As early as December 1938, Ribbentrop had established a new and parallel *Partei* Department under his henchman Martin Luther. He had brought Luther from his own special bureau, *Dienststelle* Ribbentrop, which had been his personal office in Berlin before he became foreign minister. The new department undertook liaison with the *Nationalsozialistische Deutsche Arbeiterpartei* (NSDAP) and its various branches. In 1940, as stated, the two Foreign Ministry departments were fused under the name *Deutschland* Department (its files were marked with the letter "D") and divided into six sub-departments:

(1) The *Partei* section, led by Luther personally.

(2) A section which maintained regular contact with Himmler and the RSHA (including the Gestapo) and also undertook the

international liaison work of the police and other international contacts. This section was headed by Likus.

(3) The *Deutschland* section, heir to the original department of the same name. Led by Franz Rademacher, it kept missions abroad informed of important internal affairs and also dealt with matters relevant to the Jewish problem.

The remaining three subdepartments are unimportant for the purposes of this study.

In 1942 the operational spheres of the three sections above were extended on the following lines:

Partei laid down policy for all party activity abroad.

The second subdepartment set up a liaison unit with Sipo (security police) and the S.D. (security service) of the S.S.

The *Deutschland* section dealt with national movements abroad, instructed all German ministries and other parties regarding Jewish questions, negotiated with foreign governments on uniform treatment of the Jewish question, and in general occupied itself with such matters as confiscation of Jewish property, problems arising from deportations, appointment of advisers on the Jewish question in the occupied countries, keeping an eye on Jews, and implementing anti-Jewish legislation, Freemason questions, and racial policy in general.

Luther was directly subordinate to Ribbentrop. He often interfered in other departmental matters (the number of departments was expanded to twelve in 1942). Everything to do with Jews—and such questions were usually classified as secret—was first put before him. At the Nuremberg trial Weizsäcker gave evidence on Luther's department:

Only under Herr Luther's leadership did this section become a large department, a completely alien element in the Foreign Ministry. At Ribbentrop's behest and with his help this department endeavored to win control over the remaining departments. Subdepartments were set up for matters which had nothing whatever to do with the operational sphere of the Foreign Ministry, such as race policy, Jewish affairs, police matters, etc. Connections were also made with the S.S. and the RSHA and to the *Deutsche Arbeitsfront*. . . . This department transformed itself into an instrument or agency which could interfere in anything it pleased [TWC XII, p. 439].

Even as far as location was concerned, *Deutschland* was outside the Foreign Ministry's normal area, since it was housed in a special building several miles from Wilhelmstrasse.

Weizsäcker gives several illustrations of Luther's direct daily contact with Ribbentrop and how he made direct contact with missions abroad without even informing Weizsäcker. From time to time he promised to forward the material in question, but he usually failed to do so, even when it was noted on the documents that they had been forwarded to the director-general.

Hilberg, who was the first to present a systematic description of the Foreign Ministry's structure and its activity on the Jewish question (pp. 349–55), explains how Luther usually took care to involve the heads of the political departments in his activities. This is also confirmed by the cooperation between Grundherr and Rademacher described in Chapter II of this book. Hilberg's statement that by the summer of 1942 Ribbentrop was already convinced of the need to stop Luther's exaggeratedly independent mode of operation has also been confirmed. Luther for his part was not prepared to accept any alteration in his status and tried in fact, in the winter of 1942–43, to clip Ribbentrop's wings. The interpreter Paul Otto Schmidt gave evidence at Nuremberg that Luther attempted to conspire with Himmler against Ribbentrop (it was said that he even wanted to propose Dr. Best as foreign minister—see Chapter II, note 136). The result was that Luther was dismissed in February 1943 and sent to a concentration camp. After being transferred from camp to camp, he was released shortly before the fall of Berlin, but he died shortly afterward. Ribbentrop should in fact have known that Luther was not out of the top drawer—to get him into the Foreign Ministry in 1938 he had first had to rescue him from trial before the party tribunal on a charge of embezzlement.

Luther's dismissal was the signal for widespread personnel changes in the Foreign Ministry. The *Deutschland* Department was disbanded and replaced by two new bodies: Inland I and Inland II. Luther's henchmen were removed from the ministry. Rademacher was "released" for military service. Instead, Horst Wagner, one of Ribbentrop's assistants from the *Dienststelle* period, was promoted. He was appointed head of Inland II with its four subdepartments. The first two subdepartments (A and B) maintained liaison with Himmler and the RSHA on matters concerning Jews, Freemasons, loss of citizenship, contacts with the security police and S.D., foreign police questions, sabotage, and the like. Eberhardt von Thadden joined the department in April 1943 and was later particularly active in a specially established section called *Informationsstelle* XIV, led by Rudolf Schleier. This body sent out propaganda material, organized manpower for anti-Jewish operations, and carried out RSHA instructions on the deportation of Jews. Thadden had been in the ministry since 1937 and had worked in the political department, with the Soviet Union, Poland, and Danzig within its sphere of interest.

The reorganization of Inland, which remained under Ribbentrop's direct authority, was accompanied by the introduction of a new filing system. Material from the *Deutschland* Department, if not destroyed, was transferred to the new departments. Jewish affairs, which had hitherto been marked "D III" were now indicated by "Inland II (*geheim*)" and "Inland II A/B."

Liaison between Inland and RSHA underwent alterations and lost its intimate nature; the two organizations no longer worked in such smooth cooperation as in Luther's time. Rademacher had not only been used to ringing Eichmann and receiving his instructions (even in Luther's presence), he had also, for example, planned his trip with Eichmann in the fall of 1943 to Belgrade to sort out a complicated situation that had arisen over the Jews of Yugoslavia (in the end, Eichmann did not go but sent two of his colleagues instead). All this took place without Weizsäcker's being informed and without his even receiving a report after the event. Eichmann, on the other hand, treated Thadden with simulated respect, and in general he gave the Foreign Ministry greater consideration after the changes that had taken place within it. This is clear, for example, in the discussions of the two bodies on the repatriation of foreign Jews. Ribbentrop did not stop at changes in the *Deutschland* Departments but in May 1943 also replaced Weizsäcker with Adolf Freiherr Steengracht von Moyland, an arrangement which appeared more convenient to him.

It is not surprising that Ribbentrop wished to set up in the Foreign Ministry a nucleus of dyed-in-the-wool National Socialists who were also unconditionally loyal to him personally. Nor is it surprising that these constituted an alien element in the ministry, which had to some extent preserved its structure from the time of the Weimar Republic. It is further quite comprehensible that the ministry contained persons of Thadden's ilk who openly and consciously—and sometimes perhaps unconsciously—cooperated with the Nazis and closed their eyes to the crimes of the latter. What is surprising, however, is the number of "veterans" in the ministry—in the main respectable and enlightened persons steeped in tradition and culture —who faithfully served Hitler's interests. This phenomenon was not peculiar to the Foreign Ministry; it was characteristic of the whole political and administrative system and to a great extent of the military in the Third Reich.

It is not within the province of this study to investigate the full implications of this problem, which is common to any treatment of Nazi actions within Germany. However, in examining the Jewish question in Denmark under the German occupation it transpires that some of these officials played a considerable role in the rescue of the Jews. Credit should be given to such as Renthe-Fink and Grundherr that the Danish Jews were not subjected to restrictions of any sort and that persecution did not rear its head until the fall of 1943. In the line they followed in this respect, they relied completely on the Danes. Without this support from the outside, these Germans could clearly not have acted as they did. This exceptional example, however, gives us some insight into the mental and practical complications in which the veterans found themselves enmeshed and from which they usually found no escape. They never succeeded in recognizing the strength they could have manifested had they been prepared to take action and been capable of doing so. In a conversation with the author, on this subject among others, Grundherr pointed out that the veterans formed 95 per cent of the personnel of the Foreign Ministry, and he came to the conclusion that "we did not know how to make a revolution—we had not been taught this at school" (this does not appear in the notes of the talk filed in Yad Vashem 027/14, where, on the contrary, it is stated that during the war it was forbidden to resign or volunteer for the army).

How little these officials—even the best of them—were capable of understanding the Nazis and the essence of their actions and political methods is clear from Renthe-Fink's own utterances. He himself relates (Memo I, p. 3; see also Chapter II, p. 54) that in a talk on the National Socialists and the Jews in Denmark he said to Himmler, *inter alia:*

"The Danish bourgeoisie is against National Socialism. The final German victory will, however, arouse greater readiness in Denmark." I was shocked when Himmler replied: "One bribes the middle class, terrorizes them if they cannot be bribed," as if this were the most natural thing in the world.

The fact that the minister was so much taken by surprise seems to be more astounding than Himmler's words, because even in 1941 he was not yet aware that this was for Himmler really "the most natural thing in the world." After all it was exactly that method by which the Nazis had overwhelmed the middle class in Germany itself, and not only them for that matter. That the Danish people could not be influenced either by bribery or by terror—this was the new lesson the Germans learned in Denmark.

The Nazis had in fact also bludgeoned most of the officials of the Foreign Ministry with these twin instruments, and Renthe-Fink's words merely show that these veterans had never looked these facts in the face. Grundherr explained in the above-mentioned talk how they attempted to blunt the edge of the Nazi knife to "prevent steps which had their roots in the uninhibited foreign policy of the Nazi rulers and which were, in the opinion of the veterans, meaningless and harmful for Germany." At the same time he admitted that they failed to exercise any influence whatsoever. They cherished the illusion that methods of democratic rule and of the Nazis could work together "to Germany's advantage." The price of this illusion was paid by many peoples, and most of all by the Jews.

Many of the German diplomats who had continued to serve under Hitler wrote their memoirs after the war (the best-known being those of Weizsäcker and Erich Kordt). The same theme, with some variations, dominates them all: coercion and suppression by the regime; absence of any ability to act and the initiative which would have been essential for organizing internal opposition; and the anticipation of salvation from outside (in Kordt's version, from England). The Danish situation was one of the few where such outside help was forthcoming and where it also led to results.

Grundherr also describes in some detail the methods employed from within to counteract Nazi intentions. The following extract is taken from that part of the talk with him that dealt with this subject:

Herr von Grundherr related how, despite Gestapo control, he and Blücher [the German minister of Finland] made each other's views understood with the help of certain code words and figures in telegrams and telephone conversations. Their aim was to arouse such reaction to the reports as could influence decisions by the minister or by Hitler.

These reports were drawn up in such a way that they appeared at first to be in accord with steps ordered or proposed from above—for opposition or counterproposals were impossible in the Third Reich—and then set forth all the difficulties and undesirable consequences which might be expected, concluding once again, as it were, with agreement to the project. Provided they were interpreted intelligently and care taken that they reached the right person at the right time, such reports in many instances resulted in the foiling of potentially harmful plans.

These tactics were used especially in the Danish affair by Minister von Renthe-Fink, who in long reports described the excellence of the situation, the results achieved, and the bright outlook—all of which influenced Hitler and his henchmen in desisting from energetic intervention. Grundherr recalled how he had from time to time issued warnings that "more froth should now be whipped up" in order to prevent interference in this or that matter.

These methods were also widely employed in the Jewish question. Here too Renthe-Fink and Grundherr endeavored to prevent an action or at least to achieve its postponement for as long as possible. Grundherr stated that he was aware that such action was inevitable in the long run. According to a phrase of Minister Blücher's, this would have been like trying to stop a flow of lava with a kitchen pot. The diplomats concerned therefore attempted over and over again to have the matters postponed, by minimizing the importance of an action against the Jews on the one hand and describing the serious consequences and extreme complications likely to arise on the other. In this way, no action whatever took place against the Jews of Finland [p. 2 of notes on the talk; see also Blücher's *Gesandter wischen Diktatur und Demokratie*].

Chapter II of the present study has attempted to describe how the veteran diplomats achieved varying results in their attempt to influence the march of events, and some of the reports are quoted.

However, Dr. Best's telegram on the Jewish question (Chapter IV, BEST'S RESPONSIBILITY) shows how difficult it is to distinguish between the overt and the latent aims in this report, which was from the first intended to satisfy interpretations in both directions. Only when the document is considered in connection with Best's other actions is it possible to divine what he was really after: what he stated at the beginning and end of the report or what he so brilliantly advocated in its middle. Mention has already been made of double-dealing as a characteristic of Nazi-connected activity, and it is understandable that very few managed to keep up their inner integrity. With most, double-dealing became their second nature, even when the original intention had been to ward off injustice or calamity. It is precisely the Danish case which shows how an unequivocal stand such as the Danes' could fortify those who did not wish to be carried away by the Nazi stream; but it also shows the limitations of the system, which had perforce to break down in the long run.

These questions are discussed here in order to emphasize how complicated they are and how much caution must be employed in analyzing the documents of that time, if their true meaning and content are to be revealed. Not every expression of agreement is a proof of collaboration and not every reservation a proof of noncollaboration.

In addition to the references given in the text of this study, the following sources have been used: P. Seabury, *The Wilhelmstrasse* (Berkeley and Los Angeles: 1954), pp. 72 ff., 131 ff., and 136 ff.; a letter dated 7/20/60 from the Institut für Zeitgeschichte in Munich to the director of Yad Vashem's Archives, Dr. Kermisz; documents T 874, T 880, T 881, T 882, and T 883 presented in the Eichmann trial; Rademacher's statement under oath, T 875; Thadden's statement in TWC No. 2, document 906–984; and Steengracht's defense, TWC No. 11, document 806–816 (the last two were not presented in the Eichmann trial).

II

Best's Pre-Danish Period

An attempt at a factual, ideological, and psychological analysis

Biographical Sketch

Karl Rudolf Werner Best was born in Darmstadt, Hessen, on July 10, 1903. His father, a senior official in the post office, died in October 1914 from wounds received on the western front, where he served as an officer in the reserve. According to Best's own evidence,[1] his father's "heroic death" and Germany's defeat made an ineradicable impression on him. At any rate, as a sixteen-year-old high school pupil he had already clashed with the Allied forces (in 1919, during their occupation of the Ruhr and Rhineland). He founded the *Nationaler Jugendbund* (National Youth Union) and participated in the establishment of the *Deutsch-Völkischer Schutz-und Trutzbund* (German National Defense Union). He also engaged in sabotage activities and in 1924 was sentenced by a French military tribunal to three years' imprisonment and a fine of 1000 francs; for some reason he did not serve his sentence but spent only two short periods in jail. In 1925 he took a leading part in an attempt to unite the various nationalist organizations in Hessen into a "national bloc." At the same time, he pursued his legal studies and in 1927 received the degree of Dr. Jur. in Heidelberg and his state certificate the following year in Darmstadt. As early as 1929, when he was only twenty-six years old, he was a judge in the Hessen judicial system.

He had in 1927 left the *Deutschnationale Volkspartei* and at the end of 1930 he joined the NSDAP, becoming a member of the S.S. in 1931. He rapidly became a district leader (*Kreisleiter*) and head of the party's legal department in Hessen. In 1931 he became a *Sturmführer* and in 1935 an *Obersturmführer* in the S.S. When the Nazis won a big victory in the Hessen State Assembly on November 15, 1931 (winning twenty-seven seats out of a total of seventy, as against one previously), Best was among the new members. Ten days later, however, one of his personal rivals revealed the existence of the so-called Boxheimer Documents, named after a hotel, Boxheimer Hof, near Worms, where Best and other local party leaders had met. The documents described a plan, prepared mainly by Best, who also signed it, giving steps for taking power by force in the event of a Communist election victory. The charge of high treason was not pressed against him in the German Supreme Court for formal reasons, but he was barred from public service in Hessen, where he had, after the election, been appointed as a judge in the district high court. Hitler and the party's central leadership officially dissociated themselves from the project, but it may be assumed that it nevertheless cleared Best's path to the high posts he was to occupy after the Nazi seizure of power.[2]

In March 1933 he was appointed special commissar on police matters in Hessen with the rank of governmental counselor (*Regierungsrat*). In July of that year he became general police commissioner, but the following October he had to quit because of inner Nazi rivalry; however he was called by Himmler to Munich. Here the foundations were being laid of that S.S. state through which Hitler later acquired unlimited power in Germany and in the occupied countries. At that time the S.D. (*Sicherheitsdienst* or Security Service) was also being set up; it later became the central organ of the S.S. The whole country was divided into S.D. areas (*Oberabscnitte*). The southwest area, with its center in Stuttgart, was given to Best, who also assumed the post of Heydrich's deputy.[3] He served in this capacity until he was posted to Berlin, together with Heydrich, when Himmler became head of the Gestapo in 1935. At the time of the Röhm *putsch* on June 30, 1934, Best was therefore S.D. chief for an important part of southern Germany (cf. Sauer, p. 954 ff.; Kogon, p. 25). In the Gestapo Best took over the Personnel and Legal Departments. He now served his two masters, Himmler and Heydrich, in two respects—practical and theoretical. During his trial in Jerusalem, Eichmann said: "Best was the architect, I would say, who brought things into line in a juridical manner" (Eichmann trial, session 106, 7/21/61). Best furnished a theoretical justification for the new legal approach and tried to put it into practice in the police departments under his jurisdiction. In October 1936 he was appointed a member of the German legal academy and became chairman of the *Polizeirechtsausschuss* (Police Legal Commission). He developed his own legal theories and those of the Nazis in various articles, and the peak of his literary career was a book, *The German Police*, which became a manual for the S.S. and police and a central source of information after the fall of the Nazi regime (see Nuremberg trial, Eichmann trial, etc.).[4]

In June 1936 Himmler achieved his goal: he was made chief of the German police, and the Ministry of the Interior, to which the police belonged, fell into his lap. Together with Heydrich, who became chief of security police, Best also moved into the ministry. He was given the rank of ministerial counselor (*Ministerialrat*). Only with the outbreak of war was the RSHA set up in its final form (Hilberg, p. 182). In the interim period Best was considered as one of the regime's top men, having the ear of Heydrich and of Himmler himself. It was at about this time that the conversation mentioned by Friedrich Hielscher in *50 Jahre unter Deutschen* presumably took place.[5]

In June 1940 Best was promoted to the rank of *Ministerialdirektor* and appointed head of the occupation forces' military administration in Paris. On August 10, 1942, he entered the Foreign Service, learning the work processes in the various departments until on October 27, 1942, he was confirmed, in a talk with Hitler, as Reich plenipotentiary in Denmark. He arrived in Copenhagen on the following 5th of November.

Best's Struggle for His Position

What motivated Best in 1940 to leave his central and responsible position for a post under military control in France? And what led him two years later to change again and move to the Foreign Ministry and thereby to Himmler's rival, Ribbentrop?

Relations between Best and Heydrich and Best and Himmler had deteriorated over the years, and in fact Best admitted this frankly in his statement of evidence in Copenhagen.

The situation is most extensively dealt with, however, in the letters which Best, between November 1941 and May 1942, wrote to S.S. *Obergruppenführer* Karl Wolff, who was Himmler's adjutant and head of his personal bureau, and to Heydrich himself (Best file, Document Center). The background may be discerned here to some extent. According to these letters, the relationship between Best and Heydrich had deteriorated for purely personal reasons and was due to the difference in their characters. They realized finally that they could not continue to work together, and the respectable solution was then found of promoting Best and transferring him to the military administration in Paris. The conflict was, however, not only of a personal nature, even though the letters make it quite clear that there were profound personal and psychological antipathies. These complications merely made more acute existing disagreements on policy. Various witnesses point out that Best belonged to the group inside the S.S. described as "moderate and sensible": "Dr. Best was, in the Gestapo and in the RSHA, the spokesman for a quietly implemented police strategy, and this brought him into growing conflict with the executive and with Heydrich, leading to Best's departure from the RSHA in 1940," says Victor Hermann Brack (statement under oath, Nuremberg, 1/25/47: Till Extr. IV til Hovedextr. A bil. 6, p. 18).

Another statement under oath (of 1/10/48, *ibid.*, p. 25) illustrates the antagonism that had arisen between Best and Heydrich:

I, Heinz Jost, former S.S. *Brigadeführer*, declared under oath: I recall that in 1939, after the establishment of the Protectorate of Böhmen-Mähren, Best composed a memorandum in which he sharply attacked this move. In it he explained that oppression of the Czech people was opposed to the popular principle he regarded as a cornerstone of nationalism and which demanded respect for every nationality as an independent entity. He delivered a warning that this infringement of a basic principle in national philosophy, to which Germany had hitherto adhered, would have catastrophic repercussions were the mistake not quickly rectified. Dr. Best passed this memorandum on to me in my capacity as head of Department III, which dealt with foreign affairs, and I sent it on, with the author's name, to Heydrich and Himmler. This overt criticism of Hitler's policy widened the gulf between Dr. Best and Heydrich.[6]

Best himself later claimed that only in France did he come to realize that it was not permissible to oppress the peoples of the occupied countries. In his comprehensive statement of defense, "Die Deutsche Politik in Dänemark Während der Letzten 2½ Kriegsjahre," written after the war, he states under the heading THE NEW REICH PLENIPOTENTIARY that from the beginning of August 1940 until the end of July 1942 he had been employed as *Kriegsverwaltungschef* in the *Militärbefehlshaber in Frankreich* and qualified therefore as an expert in the administration of occupied territories. He had indeed become so during his two years of activity in France. But he had also come to recognize the errors made by the occupying power in an occupied country. . . . He had voiced his own opinions and this had rendered the situation "uncomfortable" and led to a reorganization in Paris which had made him superfluous in the military administration; he had therefore placed himself at the disposal of the Foreign Ministry at the suggestion of the foreign minister, Ribbentrop.

It was not quite like that. Ribbentrop was interested in strengthening his ministerial position by appointing S.S. people as diplomatic representatives. In this connection S.S.-*Personalhauptamt* in 1941 put forward to the personnel director of the Foreign Ministry the name of Dr. Best as one of two candidates (Tgb. Nr. 34/41, 4/3/41, Document Center). The suggestion came from the above-mentioned *Obergruppenführer* Karl Wolff in Himmler's bureau, and he also promised Himmler's personal support. In an informal letter of November 5, 1941—Wolff and Best had already known each other in Hessen—Wolff, after a talk with Ribbentrop, advised Best to apply to the latter for admission to the Foreign Service. Instead of giving a direct reply Best countered, in a letter of the 15th of November, with what he himself called an "emotional outburst" and a "written cry of desperation." He recounts in this letter the whole story of his position inside the RSHA in an unmistakable tone of self-pity. He is in fact disappointed with his political career to the point of abandonment. It should be clearly understood that this career was his primary concern. He is thus not very much inclined to act upon the suggestion and asks that Ribbentrop at least first approach him; he will then be receptive to the proposal. Wolff did not answer this letter. Himmler and Heydrich, who did not apparently believe that Best would carry out their plans in France, dispatched a *Höherer S.S.-und Polizei-führer* to that country.

Best now felt himself to be superfluous and on April 5, 1942, he wrote and asked Heydrich directly why Himmler had opposed his candidacy to a post with *Reichsstatthalter* Ritter von Epp in Munich. He pointed out that he was interested in colonial problems and considered himself suited to the post in question. This approach to Heydrich was not likely to engender the most favorable consequences for Best. Himmler's confidant and right-hand man, head of S.S. *Hauptamt*, Berger, stated under oath on April 27, 1948 (Hovedrapp. *ibid.*, Bil. 24):

During the war—in about 1942—I was twice a witness at Himmler's field quarters to discussions concerning Dr. Werner Best's appointment to a government post. . . . It was known to me that in 1940 Dr. Best had left his former post as head of the Department for Administration and Legal Affairs in the German security police because sharp differences of opinion had arisen between him and the security police chief, Reinhardt Heydrich. In the above-mentioned discussions, Heydrich—and at his urging also Himmler—set themselves up strongly against Best, with the result that Himmler declared that he would not tolerate Dr. Best's appointment to the posts mentioned.

During Heydrich's visit to Paris in the first half of May 1942, Best made desperate efforts to have a personal talk with him to "clarify" their relationship, but Heydrich, who in the meantime had read Best's correspondence with Wolff, showed himself unwilling. The flow of letters in which Best tried to right wrongs and correct the bad impression he had made on Heydrich and Himmler was interrupted by Heydrich's sudden death.[7] The attack on Heydrich took place on May 26, 1942, and he died on June 4. On June 6 Ribbentrop wrote a fairly long letter to Himmler on various matters and toward the end returned to the question of a prominent S.S. man's entering the Foreign Ministry. He spoke of the "good cooperation between the ministry and the S.S." (the reference presumably being to Luther's department) and considered it regrettable that the S.S. did not take up its place in the ministry (the letter ends, "In cordial friendship, Ever yours. . . ." NG 3648).

On August 10 Best entered the Foreign Ministry. The good relations with Himmler were reestablished. Kogon points out that it was typical of Himmler to reject people only to proffer them his grace later on, and even to show them more confidence than before their falling into disfavor (p. 356). This was apparently the case with Best also. In his letters to Wolff, Best complained that he had as yet had no opportunity of personal contact with Himmler. After his unsuccessful attempt to meet with Heydrich, he begged Wolff, in a letter dated May 13, 1942, to arrange for him to be received by Himmler. This meeting took place a fortnight after Heydrich's demise. On June 27, 1942, the whole of Best's correspondence with Wolff and Heydrich was transferred to the files with Himmler's mark on every letter, the covering note stating that Himmler had talked with Best and clarified the matter with him (Document Center).

Best, who had on May 6 written to Wolff, "Believe me, I felt myself abandoned by all the good spirits of friendship and just leadership," addressed the following handwritten communication to Himmler after entering the Foreign Ministry:

Berlin
10.8.42.

Reichsführer!

On my return to Berlin I have found your kind greetings on my birthday and the beautiful picture (whose representation of a weaning mother made my wife particularly glad, in view of her similar activities) and I send you my heartfelt thanks. May I take this opportunity of reporting that I have today begun my information work in the Foreign Ministry, and I would like once again to thank you, Reichsführer, for entrusting me with a new assignment which I shall carry out in your spirit.

Heil Hitler!

Yours,
Werner Best

This is not the place to give a psychological analysis of this short letter, nor of the preceding written outpourings, though such an analysis might well contribute to an understanding of the emotional life of these men.

On October 28, 1942, Best wrote to Himmler that he had been appointed plenipotentiary of the Reich in Denmark, had received his instructions from Hitler, and wished to report to Himmler thereon (Document Center; see also Chapter IV).

Concept and Motivation

How was it that Best so interpreted the problems of the National Socialist regime as to bring him into sharp conflict with such leading Nazis as Himmler and Heydrich? What was the criticism that aroused their wrath against him? Part of the answer may be found in the articles he wrote on the problems of German rule over other peoples, where he deals with the so-called "greater territorial order" (*Grossraumordnung*). Of these, three are of particular interest: (1) "Grossraumordnung," *Festgabe für Heinrich Himmler* (C.C. Wittich Verlag: 1941); (2) "Grossraumordnung und Grossraumverwaltung," *Zeitschrift für Politik*, June 1942; (3) "Herrenschicht oder Führungsvolk." Reich, Volksordnung, Lebensraum, *Zeitschrift für Völkische Verfassung und Verwaltung*, III, Band 1942, pp. 122–41 (this article appeared in July).

The first of these articles is written in the involved and pompous style typical of the National Socialists,[8] and Best here expounds his juridical view that the Führer's will is the basis of all law. This is the right of the strong to impose his will on the weak. "National order is decided by the will of the individual, whom we designate as Führer. In the national order the stronger impose their will on the weaker" (quoted in Poliakov and Wulff, *Das Dritte Reich und Seine Denker,* p. 480).

Personal and international law in their earlier form were "mechanical" and had outlived their usefulness. In the liberal era, says Best, concepts of law and justice were based on a system of subjective rights and obligations and on contracts. As against and instead of these there was now emerging a somewhat foggy notion which he calls "the laws of life." What is in accord with these will survive and what is in conflict with them will perish. So far there is no difference between Best's views and those of other interpreters of Nazi theory who wish to eliminate the notions of morals and law prevalent in the democratic system. He even went a step further and asserted that genocide does not conflict with "the laws of life" provided that that it is total: "Elimination and displacement of foreign peoples do not, in the light of historic experience, contradict the laws of life, when they are total" (*Zeitschrift für Politik,* as above, article 2, p. 407).

Here he in fact advocates genocide. But—and this is the theoretical and practical difference between him and his colleagues—he is against *oppression* of foreign peoples. In his opinion the principle of nationality is valid for all peoples, and in keeping with the laws of life even a small and weak nation has the right to develop its own life form. He thus in effect opposes the view that a stronger occupying power engaged in establishing a greater territorial order should introduce oppressive measures. In each succeeding article he rejects in ever sharper terms the oppression and enslavement of other peoples, and it is perhaps not sheer coincidence that these views are most clearly stated in the last article, which appears to have been written after Heydrich's death. This article is by far the most interesting of them all. It was published anonymously in the journal concerned, of which Best was one of the editors. Its motto was taken from *Mein Kampf* and served as a sort of seal of approval. The added editorial note to the effect that the views given are those of the author alone is characteristic of an editorial board which cannot reject an article because of the author's position, although it disagrees with the content. On the basis of historical examples from the Roman Empire, Best attempts to prove that when one people attempts to dominate another by enslavement, it will not be able to maintain its domination for very long. He develops these arguments in the last part of the article under the subheading THE PRIMEVAL AND

ETERNAL TRUTHS (Die Urewigen Wahrheiten), which is taken from *Mein Kampf*. He says (p. 137) that when "the greatest external power" takes the leadership of other peoples into its hands, it should remember these immortal truths if it is to avoid mistakes. Such errors may be in two directions: as regards the people leading and as regards the people led. In the latter case the error, in Best's presentation, amounts to the same—oppression and exploitation:

The attitude of the leading people toward the other peoples in the greater territorial order must take account of the fact that in the long run leadership cannot be exercised without or against the will of those led. If it is thought, however, that the national character of the subjected people can be eradicated and their human substance alone be made to serve those who form a ruling stratum [*Herrenschicht*], this will lead to consequences exemplified in the Roman Empire and elsewhere [p. 140. And the article concludes:] As the strongest nation in the group, the creation of a greater territorial order . . . is the highest degree of the fulfillment of the object of its existence, which strives to maintain and develop itself, because it guarantees continued existence within the framework of the laws of life instead of *decline, which inevitably follows a brief period of "Herrenvolk" phantom* [author's italics].

In light of this article many of Best's replies at the Nuremberg trial appear to be genuine original interpretations and not merely attempts to win the favor of the court. In the judicial inquiries on the S.S., Gestapo, etc., where Best's book on the police was a principal source of information, he gave evidence, and was asked by Merkel: "You said in your book that it was not a question of law but a question of fate that the head of State was setting up the proper law?" Best replied:

No. In that passage of my book, I meant to give a political warning to the State leadership, that is, that this tremendous amount of power to set law arbitrarily—at that time we could not foresee an International Military Tribunal—would be subject to the verdict of fate, and that anyone transgressing against the fundamental human rights of the individual and of nations would be punished by fate. I am sorry to say that I was quite right in my warning [IMT XX, p. 138].

The main point in this discussion is not so much that publication of such opinions—frank or insinuatory, signed or anonymous—in Hitler's Germany showed no little measure of courage. More important here are the inner contradictions which emerge in Best's words and observations. He justifies the Germans' making themselves masters of other nations; but he wishes to preserve the particular national character of such peoples. He rejects the fundamental concepts of personal and international law, dismissing them as "mechanical," but asserts the existence of "the laws of life," valid for individuals and even more so for nations, whose infringement leads to punishment at the hands of "fate." His opinions placed him between the hammer of Nazi theory and the anvil of his own convictions, which were influenced by other spiritual sources;[9] his intelligence attempted—not very successfully—to bridge the gap between the two parts.

A corresponding dichotomy existed in his actions and motivations. Kogon claims: "It was, nevertheless, undoubtedly a striving for power that characterized a Himmler, Heydrich, Best, Kaltenbrunner, Müller" (p. 356). Inclusion of Best in this group would certainly appear justified, as witness his own words, cited by Hielscher, where his lust for power was quite clearly expressed. In a quite early article ("Der Krieg und das Recht" in Ernst Jünger's *Krieg und Krieger*) Best identifies the will to power with the life force. He calls this (as he assumes) new approach "heroic realism."[10] However, the various statements of evidence and the conflict with Heydrich show that other motives were also present. His conscience—to the extent that it functioned in the way generally understood—came into contradiction with the ambitions that drove him, as they did all the other persons in that category. It is worth quoting Kogon once more:

If one looks closely at the psychological setup, it will be seen that S.S. motives were never many-sided, that means of a truly cultural quality, but were always confined to the wishes and strivings of the persons concerned. . . . Both individually and collectively their whole behavior was geared toward domination—and behind this lay more emotions than objective purposes. . . . This hodgepodge of instincts was never purified or moderated by a system of moral values [p. 355].

Aronson emphasizes the important role intellectuals like Best played in bridging the gap between the traditional authoritative thinking and the complete new evaluations of a Himmler (p. 310). "The Bests . . . opened, to simple gangsters of Heydrich's kind and race-fanatics of Himmler's type, the way to power" (p. 317).

Best, who had since his youth trod the path of national socialism and violence, was incapable of divorcing himself from the power group he had associated himself with. When both his inhibitions

and his ambitions brought him into open conflict with them, he felt
himself "abandoned by all the good spirits," and his only positive
aspiration was to return and be received once more into the same
circle, to be able to occupy a position of power once again. He
dreamt of administering a colony, as he wrote to Heydrich[11] (and
that at a time when Germany had no colonies!)—apparently he dared
not dream of a position of power in Europe. And then "fate," in
which he believed so much, came to his assistance: Heydrich was
assassinated, Himmler allowed his grace once more to shine on Best,
and soon after his entry into the Foreign Service a top German
position fell vacant in Denmark. Denmark, where the Germans had
more or less maintained their rule in accordance with his own views
on cooperation between "the leaders" and "the led" in "the greater
territorial order"—it was here that he would be allowed to show
what he was worth. He had previously shown an interest in the
Nordic countries and had visited them during his service in Paris.
This was the opportunity he had awaited for so long: a chance to
show his colleagues and his superiors that an occupied country could
be ruled with understanding and goodwill and that Germany's interests could be best served by these methods. It appeared that the
forces that struggled within him—on the one side the S.S. man's
ambition and thirst for power and on the other the restraints of
conscience and intellect—could now be united in constructive endeavor. Ten months later he was to realize that the experiment had
failed.

Best and Militant Anti-Semitism

Was Best an anti-Semite? Was he an active anti-Semite? Duckwitz
and Kanstein, who first got to know him in Denmark, say that he
was not; his deputy, Barandon, a career Foreign Office man, says
that he was (Beretning, bilag XIII, 1. bind, p. 222). Under cross-
examination in both Copenhagen and Nuremberg Best stressed that
"in regard to the Jewish question I have personally always held the
view that the Jewish national existence (*Volkstum*) should be respected like any other people's" (statement under oath of 6/28/46,
IMT, XLI, p. 165). Jews, he maintained, should be dealt with in
keeping with the policy rules for minorities and with deference
to minority laws; he had therefore set himself against the deportation
of Jews in the form carried out during the war, not to mention
extermination. (This statement appears among the documents in
Frisch, I, p. 401). Doubt, however, is cast on the sincerity of these

THE RESCUE OF DANISH JEWRY

words when Best's actions on the Jewish question come to be examined.

As early as 1931 the Boxheimer Documents state that Jews must not take part in the labor service to which German citizens were subject. At the same time, the plan proposed that receipt of a ration card depend on participation in the labor scheme. This meant that in his younger days Best (who signed these documents) regarded Jews as inferior, quite the contrary of the views quoted above.

The Gestapo report on the 19th Zionist Congress in Lucerne in 1935 is signed by Dr. Best (Political department "Poland," 9/27/35, JM/2241).

Late in 1936 he sent to various ministries, including the Foreign Ministry, information on the illegal emigration of Polish Jews to France and Belgium via Germany (he was at that time the head of the security department of the police [*Abwehrpolizei*]).

His most important action in regard to the Jews, however, he performed in 1938 when he was in charge of the Ministry of the Interior's Legal Department and, as he admitted himself, was responsible for the issue of passports (in Copenhagen he explained that upon his transfer to this ministry he was given a number of assignments and "was thus in charge of issuing passports"). He was thus among the signers of the notorious German-Swiss agreement of September 29, 1938, whereby Jewish passports had to be stamped "J" (NG 3366, printed in Poliakov, *Das Dritte Reich und Seine Diener*, p. 94). The accord assumed legitimacy with the publication of the ordinance over Best's signature in the *Reichsgesetzblatt*, No. 1342, of 10/7/38. Two days previously Best had informed the Foreign Ministry of the new regulations and added: "In addition, I would refer to the repeated discussions between the experts of both ministries." To what extent he was personally responsible for this fateful ordinance is difficult to determine (see also Hilberg, pp. 118 ff.), but it is clear that his contribution cannot be said to fall under "adherence to minority law."

Certain facts are, however, discernible on the scope of his activity regarding the forced return of Polish Jews to Poland in October–November 1938. He visited the camps on the Polish border and participated in the deliberations as to whether the Jews should be driven into Poland or whether it was better to desist, for fear of Polish reprisals against Germans in Poland. It was Best who proposed that these Jews be put into concentration camps near the border, though the suggestion was rejected (NG 2012, 2654, and 2896; see also Hilberg, p. 258).

As is well known, "Crystal Night" (November 9, 1938) was in part an indirect result of the expulsion of the Polish Jews. We learn from Best's diary that he was among those who took part in the organizational work of the Nazis after Crystal Night. Usually the diary mentions only whom he talked with, or where a meeting was held, with no reference to the subject of discussion. For some reason he deviated from this pattern where Jews were concerned. It is of course by no means certain that he noted all the talks and meetings on the Jewish question in which he took part. A more or less complete record of his activities, though not necessarily continuous, is available for the period from April 1, 1935, to October 1, 1942. To this may be added the extracts from the diary used at Nuremberg, which include his stay in Copenhagen up to the end of 1943, together with his statements under investigation in Copenhagen (August 1, 1945, bil. A 35, p. 27). There is also a provisional survey for the year 1944. The first note on Jews appears on February 18, 1937, and concerns a meeting in the Ministry of Finance on special taxation of Jews. But it is in November 1938 that we encounter a whole series of meetings in which Best participated, as follows:

11/17/38: Conference in Heydrich's office on Jewish questions. Conference on the Jewish emigration office.
12/ 6 /38: Meeting at Goering's with the Gauleiters on the Jewish question. Lunch with Freiherr von Eberstein and Heydrich. Conference with Heydrich, Albert, Schellenberg, Ward, Hermanns. Drive to Munich.
12/ 9 /38: Meeting with party judge Schneider. Conference at Heydrich's with Schneider and Müller. Work meeting with judges of Gau courts and state police leaders in *Haus der Flieger* on Jewish questions.
12/13/38: Conference with R. Mildner. Lecture in Vienna. Inspection of the confiscated works of art.
12/16/38: Lecture in Rehnitz. Berth, Bermuth, Eichmann, A. Stahlecker. Dinner in Kaiserhof.

Even these fragmentary notes point to Heydrich's systematic activities during these weeks. It is also clear from them that Best in 1938 met not only Eichmann but also Mildner. (The diary is in the Danish State Archives.)

On September 21, 1939, after the outbreak of war, Best took part in a meeting with the leaders of the *Einsatzgruppen* under Heydrich's chairmanship. The subjects discussed were general topics, politics in the eastern regions, displacement of population, including Jews, and German colonization. The deportation of Jews from Germany to the Cracow area was also discussed (Eichmann trial, T 164; see also Kempner, pp. 67 ff.).

We then hear of Best's involvement with the Jewish problem in France. This cannot be dealt with in detail here, and the topic has been discussed by others to some extent.[12] What is clear is that Best was well acquainted with the whole question and much interested in it. This is borne out, for instance, by the fact that when he was already in Copenhagen Best placed at the disposal of Foreign Ministry Director Weizsäcker documents on treatment of the Jewish problem in France during his period of office in that country (Beretning XIII, 6. bind, pp. 945–97). It transpires from the various collections of documents that Dr. Best's signature is to be found under numerous ordinances and regulations connected with the Jews in France; it is also evident that he chaired meetings or wrote minutes of discussions on this subject. His activity increased in the year that Xavier Vallat was appointed "general commissar on the Jewish question." It is true that Best tried constantly to have the whole matter taken over by the French themselves, and it may or may not be that he did so in order to keep the S.S. away.

In connection with Vallat, Best took part in a meeting with the military governor of France, General Stülpennagel (who was later one of the conspirators of July 20, 1944). This meeting took place on April 5, 1941, on which occasion Vallat received his instructions. The minutes of the meeting were composed and signed by Best. In reply to Vallat's question as to which German authority he was to address himself to on Jewish matters, the general said that this was to be exclusively the military administration (i.e., to *Ministerialdirektor* Best). His authority having been thus affirmed, Best directed Vallat's attention to paragraph 3 of a document which he, Best, had drawn up in preparation for the meeting. The paragraph dealt with a plan of action concerning the Jews in France and is based on the ideas of the "final solution," stating, *inter alia*, that "the German interest is the gradual liberation of Europe's countries from Judaism, and the goal is a complete purge of the Jews from Europe."

It is indeed a bold assertion to say that such a statement is suitable for a man who recognizes the right of the Jews to exist and who opposes their deportation. While paragraph 2 of the document in fact refers to Jews of foreign nationality in France, paragraph 3 (whose significance Best took especial pains to point out) deals with the French Jews themselves. Best recommends that their deportation should be planned "with prewar German policy as a precedent." As is clear from his diaries, Best had himself taken part in the planning of this same policy. During the large-scale action against the Jews of Paris on June 15 and 16, 1942, Best was still in charge of the local military administration.

Best had thus over many years participated in the planning and organization of Jewish persecutions and had engaged in oppression and deportation to the extent that these were part of his duties.[13] It is possible that in theory he was opposed to physical extermination —at any rate there is no positive expression of his being in favor of it. But even if he did recognize the right of all peoples to exist, he recognized this right for the Jews sometimes in theory but not in practice. His open opposition to Jewish persecutions in Denmark (as expressed in his reports and his whole handling of the affair during the year 1943 up to the great crisis) was, as we have seen in Chapter II, a legacy taken over from Renthe-Fink and an integral part of his policy of· understanding toward the Danes. He realized that this was an absolute condition demanded by the Danes. The crisis came when the whole policy broke down, when his position and future hung by a thread, and when he again saw himself on the point of being "abandoned by all the good spirits." How he reacted to this crisis, from which he seemed to have had no escape, has been described in Chapters IV and V.

III

Sources

The source material may be divided into four main categories:

A. *Original contemporary documents:*

1. German documents from the German Foreign Ministry, the German army, and the S.S.
2. Danish and Swedish documents from the Foreign Ministries (sparse—see note below) and the archives of the resistance movement.
3. Jewish documents (sparse—see note below).

B. *Trials of war criminals,* including documents, statements, evidence, cross-examination:

1. The Nuremberg trials.
2. Best's trial in Copenhagen.
3. The Eichmann trial.
4. Investigations of parliamentary commissions.

C. *Statements of evidence,* including written statements and interviews summarized in written form and signed by the interviewee:

1. Evidence of Jews.
2. Evidence of Danes.
3. Evidence of Germans.

D. *The press:*

1. Danish daily papers and general periodicals.

2. Jewish daily papers and general periodicals (including those of Palestine and Israel).

3. Daily papers and general periodicals of other nations, especially Sweden.

It should be noted with regard to the above sources:

A. *The files of the German Foreign Ministry* are freely accessible to research students. Those sections not included in the large microfilm collection at Yad Vashem in Jerusalem may be found in the German archives. No small part of the documents may be found in war trial material. Military and S.S. files saved from destruction and the files from the former "Document Center" in Berlin may today mostly be found in the German State Archives at Coblenz. For this work the large and well-cataloged collections of films and photocopies in the State Archives in Copenhagen were mainly used.

Access to the *archives of the Scandinavian Foreign Ministries* is almost impossible to get. The law in these countries forbids the opening of files for research for fifty years. In both countries officials were prepared to answer some (but not all) questions on the basis of archive material, and in Sweden the author was able to see a collection of documents not classified as top secret.

The situation is different with regard to the *files of the Danish underground movement.* These were collated by the Danish historian Dr. Hæstrup and presented to the State Archives in Copenhagen. Questions of access are decided by the original owners of the material and not by the Archives. The files of the Stockholm lawyer who cooperated with the Danish resistance movement, Philipson, have been presented in their entirety to Yad Vashem.

There are almost no *Jewish documents.* Some help was received from private collections.

B. To the extent that *material relating to trials and investigations* has been published, it will be found in the bibliography given in this work under the heading "Documentary Literature" (or in relevant footnotes).

Files of the Best trial in Copenhagen were placed at the author's disposal—with the agreement of the Danish Ministry of Justice—by the Hessen District Court at Frankfurt, where they were assembled by the late state prosecutor, Dr. Fritz Bauer, for use in trials of war criminals.

C. About fifty *statements of evidence by Jews* rescued in October 1943 were collected by Jul. Margolinsky and Ole Barfoed. Barfoed intended at the time to carry out research on the illegal transportation between Denmark and Sweden. The author was kindly allowed to copy the statements. To them other *evidence by Jews and resistance fighters* has been added—68 statements in all. Most of the statements of the Jews were not published by name, but that permission has been granted.

Statements of evidence by Germans were also used, and new ones even collected when it seemed that such statements might be of value to scientific research (details in text and notes).

D. The *Danish and Israeli newspapers and journals* of the period have been scrutinized. As regards *world and Swedish papers*, clippings were used. Wherever possible the original source of quotations was examined.

SPECIFIC ARCHIVAL SOURCES

a. *Material from the archives of the German Foreign Ministry* (material in the Yad Vashem archives in the form of microfilms are marked JM, photocopies and original documents are marked YVS):

Dienststelle Ribbentrop:
Vertrauliche militärische und politische Berichte, June 1941–July 1942, JM/2477.
Führerberichte 5/16/40–3/18/43, JM/2479.
Luther, Handakten:
December 1939–1942, JM/2498.
Schriftwerkehr, JM/2502.
Büro des Staatssekretärs (A.A. St. S.):
Akten betreffend Dänemark, 5/22/43–10/31/43, JM/2470.
Inland (Inl.) II A/B:
54/1 Auswanderung über Sibirien, JM/2470
63/1 Dänemark: Judenfragen 11/24/34–1943, JM/2503
63/2 Juden in Dänemark October 1943–December 1944, YVS 027/10
303/1 Dänemark: Interventionen, 1/1/34–5/6/35, JM/2281
Inland (Inl.) IIg:
53/1 Endlösung der Judenfrage 1939–1943, JM/2490
54/8 Juden in Dänemark 1942–43, JM/2216
78 Sabotagebekämpfung in Dänemark. Abstellung eines Polizeibataillon 1942–1944, YVS 027/11
351 Berichte und Meldungen zur Entwicklung der Lage in Dänemark 1940–1942, YVS 027/10 Pol. IV, Norden
20/7 PO I Dänemark: Judenfragen December 1933, JM/2430

Pol. VI, Judenfrage VI 2 No. 6 Dänemark 1937–1944, JM/2221
Besprechungen zwischen deutschen und dänischen Regierungskommissionen 1940–1944, JM/2492.

b. *German documents from other sources:*

1. Documents from the Nuremburg trials, unpublished and bearing the designations NG, NO, OKW, PS.
2. Documents of the German army and navy, copied from the copies in the Danish State Archives. Designations on the copies are for Oberkommando West (Norden): NOKW; and for Seekriegsleitung: SKL (YVS 027/12).
3. S.S. documents in the Danish State Archives were originally in the following categories: SS-Hauptamt; SS-Führungsamt; Rasse und Siedlungsamt; Volksdeutsche Mittelstelle; Reichsführer-SS (PK. 442 and 443; in Yad Vashem, JM/2216–2217); Terminkalender Best (microfilm).
4. Akt Best, Document Center (DC); JM/2212.
5. Best: "Die deutsche Politik in Dänemark während der letzten 2½ Kriegsjahre"; YVS 027/15 and JM/2614.
6. Himmler Files, roll 7, folder 56, Dänemark 1941–45.

c. *Trials:*

1. The Eichmann trial, from which minutes are quoted according to date and number of session; documents are marked T, or 06 if they have not been submitted to the court.
2. The trial concerning Dr. Werner Best (Sagen vedrørende Dr. Werner Best), Tillægsekstrakt til Hovedekstrakt A, Ad Forhold II; Hovedrapporter vedrørende Werner Best, bil. A, 1–28; JM/2613.

d. *Archives of the Danish resistance movement and Swedish archives:*

1. Philipson's archive, YVS 027/1–7.
2. A selection of resistance movement documents from the Danish State Archives, JM/1967, 1–2.

e. *Statements of evidence:*

1. Evidence of Jews (limited access), YVS 027/13 and JM/1968–2.
2. Evidence of Danish non-Jews, YVS 027/13.
3. Evidence of Germans, YVS 027/14.

f. *Various Danish documents:*

Details are given in the relevant footnotes; YVS 027/8, 027/9, 027/16, 027/17, and JM/1968–2.

g. A selection of documents from the Swedish Foreign Ministry, JM/1219.

NOTES

Notes

INTRODUCTION   *(For full references see Bibliography)*

1. Introduction to Aage Bertelsen, *October 43*, Aarhus, 1952 (1st edition).
2. M. Buber, *Moses*, East West Library, Oxford, 1946, p. 14.
3. This point will be dealt with more fully in Chapter II.
4. N. Alterman, "The Swedish Tongue" (Hebrew), in the newspaper *Davar*, Tel Aviv, 10/8/43; also, *The Seventh Column*, Am Oved, Tel Aviv, 1945, p. 142; H. Friedberg, "We Will Not Forget the King," Helsinki, 1947. The poem was published privately, in Hebrew and Yiddish, after Christian X's death in May 1947.
5. As published in the newspaper *Hatsofeh*, Tel Aviv, 10/10/43.
6. Buber, *op. cit.*, p. 17.
7. Lecture delivered at the Second World Congress of Jewish Studies, Jerusalem, August 1957, *Yad Vashem Studies*, III, 1957, p. 25. About the problems of the Holocaust historiography, see also L. Yahil, "Holocaust Research Problems" (Hebrew), *Yalkut Moreshet*, Vol. 2, No. 3, 1964, pp. 155–61; "Historians of the Holocaust," *The Wiener Library Bulletin*, Vol. XXII, No. 1., 1967–8, pp. 2–5; "The Holocaust in Jewish Historiography," *Yad Vashem Studies*, VII, 1968, pp. 57–73.
8. B. Dinur, *Guide to Jewish History Under Nazi Impact*, introduction, p. xviii.
9. *Ibid.*

CHAPTER I

1. This short survey deals with the history of the Jews in Denmark until the occupation of the country by the Germans. It is not an

integral part of our study but serves as a general outline of the background to the historical events occurring in occupied Denmark. Most of the literature used may be found in the Bibliography at the end of this book under the heading "History of the Jews in Denmark." The notes will refer only to subjects of special significance. Sources are given only insofar as they do not appear in the Bibliography or as quotation references.

2. Among the names in this connection were Albert Dionys, a rich Jew from Hamburg, Don Manuel Texiera, and Samuel de Lima, and also two doctors—Benjamin ben Emanuel Musfia (Dionys's brother) and Andreas de Castro.

3. *Erinnerungen der Frau Glückel von Hameln aus den Jahren 5407 bis 5479* (Pressburg–Frankfurt-am-Main, 1896), pp. 246–48.

4. An original Danish list of leading members of the community and its administration in 1787 may be found in J. Fischer, *Mindeskrift i Anledningen af Hundredaarsdagen for Anordningen af 29. Marts 1814*, pp. 7–8.

5. In 1801 the English bombarded the port and fleet and in 1807 the city of Copenhagen itself. Traces of the second bombardment may still be seen in the old Jewish cemetery.

6. A more detailed and systematic description of the historical development of laws and ordinances relating to the Jews may be found in A. D. Cohen, *De mosaiske Troesbekjenderes Stilling i Danmark forhen og nu* (Odense, 1837). The Copenhagen community is not particularly endowed with older Jewish source material and documents, as these were destroyed in the fires of 1728 and 1795 and the bombardment of 1807. See also J. Fischer, *Jøderne i København i det 17de Aarhundrede*.

7. The most important places with communities at the time and where Jewish cemeteries exist are: Fredericia, Horsens, Odense, Faaborg, Assens, Nakskov, Randers, Slagelse, Aalborg, and Arhus (Margolinsky, *Gravpladserne*).

8. In addition to Wessely, two of Mendelssohn's brothers-in-law lived in Copenhagen: Moses Fürst, leader of the reform movement, and Josef Guggenheim, who at the beginning of the century sought conversion to Christianity, though he later gave up the idea. Cf. R. Edelmann, "David Simonsen," in *Ved 150 Aars-Dagen for Anordningen af 29 Marts 1814*, p. 103 f.

9. The reform was practiced by the well-known teacher and preacher Isak Noa Mannheimer, who was born in Copenhagen but was later active in Austria. A year later the confirmation ceremony was also introduced into Berlin. The ordinance is described in detail in M. L. Nathanson's book. See also Margolinsky's article in *Jødisk Samfund*, April 1959, "Omkring den første Konfirmation i København i 1817."

431   NOTES FOR PAGES 8 TO 11

10. See *Feier der Einweihung des Israelitischen Gotteshauses zu Kopenhagen am Tage nach dem Pessachfeste 5593, den 12ten April 1833, nebst Predigt und Gebete, welche dabei gehalten wurden,* hrsg. von Dr. Abraham Alexander Wolff, Kopenhagen.
11. On his personality and literary activity, see R. Edelmann's article on Abraham Wolff in *Dansk Biografisk Leksikon,* bd. 26, pp. 242–47.
12. The translation given here is based on the text in B. Balslev, *De danske Jøders Historie* (Lohse: København, 1932), p. 85. In later versions of the constitution the paragraph enumeration is different.
13. With the help of the Hambro family, Denmark received large loans from England in 1850 and 1864 (Balslev, *op. cit.,* p. 60). Another Jewish family, Heymann, were in the forefront of agricultural export to England and founded the well-known Tuborg Brewery. As late as 1914 its produce was popularly known as "Judenbier." See *ibid.,* pp. 109–10.
14. See Jul. Margolinsky, *Les Juifs au Danemark* (B'nai B'rith: Paris, 1942) and Balslev, *op. cit.*
15. See R. Edelmann, "David Simonsen," pp. 104–31.
16. D. Simonsen, "Dänemark und die Juden in Prag 1745," in *Festschrift Adolf Schwartz sum 70. Geburtstag,* pp., 509–18. See also B. Mevorach, "Jewish Diplomatic Activities to Prevent the Expulsion of Jews from Bohemia and Moravia, 1744–45," *Zion,* XXVIII, 3–4 (1963), pp. 125–64 (English Summary, pp. I–II).
17. The sister of the Danish king, Frederik VIII, was the wife of Alexander III and the mother of Nicholas II. At the repeated insistence of the most respected elder of the community, Moses Melchior, the king cabled to his sister on the matter. The pogroms feared did not materialize. See also Israel Halperin's article "The Danish Royal House and the Persecutions of the Jews in Czarist Russia" (Hebrew), *Tarbitz,* 34th Year, Vol. B, 5725 (1964–65), pp. 183–93, and D. Simonsen, "Da Pogromerne i Foraaret 1907 blev standsede," *Tidskrift for jødisk Historie og Litteratur,* I (1918), pp. 188 ff.
18. Balslev gives statistics in *op. cit.,* appendix, p. 133.
19. Margolinsky's article in *Det jødiske Folketal ved 150 Aars-Dagen,* pp. 202 ff.
20. Interesting data on age structure, births and deaths, size of family, mixed marriages, and religious affiliation of children of such marriages are given for each section of the Jewish population in Cordt Trap, *Russiske Jøder i København efter Folketællingen 1921,* and—particularly from a social point of view—in Colding Jørgensen, *Jøderne i Danmark omkring 1931.* The latter

presents detailed data on Jewish occupational structure. Of interest is the following comparison between Jewish and general incomes in Copenhagen:

Income (*in Danish kroner*)	Jews %	Copenhagen %
Under 3,000	42.1	42.7
3,000–10,000	37.8	52.4
Over 10,000	20.1	4.9

Jørgensen drew the conclusion that every tenth tailor in the city was a Jew and that Jews were to be found among workers and small craftsmen, whose economic situation was extremely poor (p. 14).

21. Margolinsky, *op. cit.*, pp. 205–6.
22. See p. 6 above. Today this percentage has dropped to 1 per cent (Margolinsky, *Det jødiske Folketal* . . . , pp. 200–02, and *Les Juifs au Danemark*).
23. The typesetter Josef Litischewsky founded the first Yiddish newspaper in Scandinavia. *Dos Vochenblat* first appeared in May 1911, and together with other Jewish newspapers continued to be published during and after the First World War.
24. *Jødisk Tidskrift*, a fortnightly paper, appeared from April 1907 to September 1908. It was followed by various newspapers until the appearance of the community's official organ *Jødisk Familieblad*, in September 1928. This paper closed down upon the German occupation in April 1940, and after the war *Jødisk Samfund* appeared instead. As of January 1966 its name was changed to *Jødisk Orientering*.
25. See an article by Professor L. S. Fridericia on the occasion of the 150th anniversary of Nathanson's birth, *Jødisk Familieblad*, December 1930.
26. Margolinsky, *Danmark Loge*, p. 64. See also *Jødisk Familieblad*'s special issue of 4/21/33.
27. As early as 1918 Vladimir Grossman issued an appeal in Danish and Yiddish for representation and equal rights in community affairs for the recent arrivals.
28. *Jødisk Familieblad*, March 1931.
29. From an unpublished manuscript on the history of Danish Jewry.
30. See *Jødisk Familieblad*, December 1932 and January 1933. Slor was born in Petah-Tikva in 1892 and was one of the founders of "Maccabi" in Palestine. In Denmark he established a wine (mainly Palestinian) business. As a result of his initiative, many sports teachers came from Israel for professional training. See also Margolinsky, "De tyske-jødiske landbrugspionerers uddannelse," Yad Vashem, 027/13, p. 2.
31. Christmas Møller was later one of the foremost opponents of nazism and anti-Semitism (see Chapter II). The German min-

ister, Richthofen, reported the meeting in detail (AA-Inl. II A/B 63/1).

32. Another example of refutation of anti-Semitism was a talk by the young Conservative leader P. Gudme in the spring of 1935. This was published in *Jødespørgesmaalet i Danmark*, Gyldendal.

33. Leading article in *Berlingske Tidende*, 11/11/38, whose moderate tone stood in sharp contrast to the more alert views of the Social Democrats. The German News Agency commented on 11/14: "*Social-Demokraten* feels itself called upon to describe the ordinances in Berlin as outrageous measures and as worse and more inhuman than the persecutions of the Middle Ages, and similarly talks of the cruel revenge on innocent people for the stupid act of murder by a young lunatic in Paris. With the same impertinence the Marxist paper calls the fine on the Jews a particularly good financial operation for an otherwise non-affluent country." (Pol. VI Judenfrage AA-JM/2221).

34. Rothenberg in *Ved 150 Aars-Dagen* . . . , pp. 139–40.

35. *Ibid.*, pp. 133–57.

36. Dr. B. Simonsen's evidence, Vad Vashem, 027/13. Margolinsky relates in *Danmark Loge*, p. 65, that applications of German members of B'nai B'rith to come to Denmark had usually to be rejected "since the applicants had no previous natural connections with the country and the Lodge was therefore unable to take any action in the matter."

37. Former state attorney-general in Hessen, West Germany, died 1967; Yad Vashem 027/13.

38. See also Cilla Cohn, *En Jødisk Families Historie*, p. 109, on people who slipped over the border because they had been refused a visa—despite family connections in Denmark. Not even the right of residence was granted them, but they finally managed to emigrate to Israel. Cf. H. Horwitz, *En Sabotørs Erindringer*, 1964, p. 9.

39. According to Margolinsky—see note 54. Cf. also H. Valentin, *Rescue and Relief Activities*.

40. *Beretning til Folketinget* (hereafter *Beretning*), VII, bilag. I, p. 187; cf. also Valentin, *op. cit.*, pp. 225–29, and Moritzen in *Contemporary Jewish Record*, May–June 1940, p. 280.

41. Vilhelm Slomann, "Erindringer fra møder med Niels Bohr," *Politiken's Kronik*, 10/7/55, and Bauer: "One could hardly talk of Danish willingness to accept the refugees." He relates that he was not merely refused permission to work but was also barred from completing his doctoral studies in law at the university (evidence, Yad Vashem, 027/13).

42. In 1936 a law was enacted providing for the deportation of "undesirable" foreigners. In October 1938, for example, two

Jewish refugees were handed over to the German police by the Danes. The community paid their fares to the border in order to avoid police escort (from the minutes of the community and a letter from Margolinsky to the author on 1/8/62).

43. This calculation is based mainly on figures in the financial reports of the community. Since those the author saw were incomplete, it is difficult to determine the exact sum. Further, no material was available on the work of the Committee of the 4th of May 1933, and it may possibly now be nonexistent, since part was confiscated by the Germans and part perhaps otherwise removed. Cf. also Rothenberg, *loc. cit.*

44. Margolinsky, *Danmark Loge*, p. 66.

45. Based on Margolinsky, "De tysk-jødiske landbrugspionerers uddannelse," Yad Vashem, 027/13; see also Valentin, *op. cit.*, p. 228.

46. From a letter by the coordinator of the Hechalutz (pioneer) movement in Denmark to members on 1/13/41 (from material collected by the then member of the secretariat Ernst Laske, now a member of kibbutz Neot Mordechai in Israel): "As you know, our finances prior to April 9 were assured, in that aid organizations abroad had allocated about 20 kroner monthly for each member under training. To this was added a subsidy of 30–35,000 a year from the community here and to the secretariat from abroad of 500 kroner monthly. These sums together formed a good basis for the financing of the work here, both for the essential needs of the members and for a widespread cultural activity, the secretariat's official journeys, etc." See also Margolinsky, ". . . landbrugspionerers . . . ," p. 5.

47. Minutes of the community, 8/30/33.

48. Valentin, *op. cit.*, p. 244.

49. Margolinsky, ". . . landbrugspionerers. . . ."

50. For the number of Jews in Denmark at this time, see the end of this chapter. In addition to the activity described here, the Jews of Copenhagen, upon the initiative of B'nai B'rith, contributed 100,000 kroner to the purchase of land for an experimental farm, with a view to cultivating more land and alleviating the unemployment problem. The campaign was initiated in honor of Christian X's jubilee in 1937. All in all, however, the plan failed (Margolinsky, *Danmark Loge*, pp. 70–73).

51. Similar work was carried out by Swedish women, who were particularly active in Austria.

52. According to Margolinsky (letter to author, 12/15/62), three batches were sent: 1/19/40 (50 children); 12/5/40 (44); 3/4/41 (42)—a total of 136. See also Margolinsky, *Danmark Loge*, pp. 67–8, and ". . . landbrugspionerer. . . ."

53. In his report on the agricultural trainees, Margolinsky relates

that he and Adler-Rudel in 1938 also traveled to Oslo with a view to setting up a training scheme there, but their mission was unsuccessful.

54. The statistical data on the Danish Jews is based mainly on the work of Jul. Margolinsky and in particular on the research he carried out during the refugee period in Sweden with the help of the Refugee Office's card index—*Statistiske Undersøgelser over Fordelingen paa Alder og Køn m.m. blandt Flygtninge fra Danmark i Sverige*, Stockholm, 1945 (hereafter Margolinsky, *Statistiske Undersøgelser*). Other sources—government, Germans, etc.—will be dealt with under the flight of the Jews (Chapter VII) and their deportation (Chapter VIII).

55. Margolinsky, *Statistiske Undersøgelser*, gives 2,078 stateless among the refugees in Sweden, to whom should be added a few dozen deported to Theresienstadt.

56. Various figures have been given for the number of Jews in Denmark during the period. According to a German source of 1937 there were 6,000 (Zander, *Die Verbreitung der Juden in der Welt*). R. Hilberg, *The Destruction of the European Jews*, p. 357, gives 6,500 while Tennenbaum, *Race and Reich*, p. 289, talks of 8,000 Jews. None of these authors give details nor do they usually quote the source of the figures.

CHAPTER II

1. The pact stated: "The Kingdom of Denmark and the German Reich will in no case resort to war or any other use of force against each other. In case any third power should take action of the nature described in the first paragraph against either contracting party, the other party will not in any way render support to such action" (cited in R. Lemkin, *Axis Rule in Occupied Europe*, p. 157, notes 1, 2). Cf. also the memorandum of the Danish government: IMT XXXVIII 901-RF, p. 61.

2. In the winter of 1939–40 both the Allies and the Germans planned an invasion of Norway. The Germans were first for two reasons: (1) Decision, planning, and implementation were more rapid than they were under the cumbersome procedure of the Allies, and (2) complete disdain for the declared neutral rights of the Scandinavian countries. See Royal Institute for International Affairs, *Hitler's Europe—The Scandinavian States and Finland;* Th. K. Derry, *The Campaign in Norway;* W. Hubatsch, *Die deutsche Besetzung von Dänemark und Norwegen 1940;* Winston Churchill, *The Second World War*, I, p. 999.

3. Memorandum of the German Reich to the government of Denmark, 4/9/40—see *Beretning*, bilag IV, pp. 14–18, 21; the

German commander-in-chief's proclamation to the Danish army and people, *ibid.*, p. 13; and Lemkin, *op. cit.*, p. 377.

4. For example, on 12/20/40 the director of the German Foreign Ministry, Weizsäcker, explained to the head of the Reich Chancellery, Lammers, that in view of Denmark's special status, the plenipotentiary of the Reich only fulfilled the duties of a minister, as distinct from the tasks of the commissars in Norway and Holland: "He must carry out his duties through diplomatic methods." *Beretning*, bilag XIII, I, p. 25; also *Hitler's Europe*, II, pp. 213–14.

5. Anders Vigen, *Erik Scavenius*, pp. 23–4.

6. La Cour, *Danmark under Besættelsen*, I, p. 245.

7. For fuller details, see Chapter IV.

8. Evidence of Henning Dalsgaard, who was one of the "mediators" between the German authorities and the Danish government. He was accused of collaboration after the war but was acquitted. *Beretning*, bilag VIII, p. 147.

9. Stauning's speeches in *Frit Danmarks Hvidbog* (hereafter *Hvidbog*), I, pp. 96, 105, 107, 108; Scavenius's speeches in *Besættelsestidens Fakta* (hereafter *Fakta*), I, pp. 320, 654.

10. Introduction to *Hvidbog*, p. 10.

11. See S. H. Nissen and H. Poulsen, *Paa dansk Frihedsgrund*, p. 240.

12. Hartvig Frisch, *Danmark besat og befriet*, I, p. 361. It is natural that in the weighty Danish literature on the occupation period, varying conceptions and explanations are to be found, in accordance with the views and experiences of each author. It is not intended here to intervene in this internal Danish discussion which is still in progress. Great effort is being made in Denmark to clarify the history of the occupation period with the help of the considerable documentary material in the Danish and German archives. See also the author's bibliography, *Denmark Under the Occupation*, WLB XVL, No. 4.

13. See W. Shirer, *The Challenge of Scandinavia, passim;* and Haim Yahil, *Scandinavian Socialism in Its Implementation* (Hebrew) Hakibbutz Hameuchad, Tel Aviv, 1966, *passim.*

14. Nissen and Poulsen, *op. cit.*, p. 35.

15. See below, Chapter III, note 35.

16. Nissen and Poulsen, *op. cit.*, p. 76.

17. Th. Thaulow, *Konge og Folk gennem Brændingen*, p. 187.

18. Nissen and Poulsen, *op. cit.*, pp. 54–5.

19. *Ibid.*, p. 130.

20. *Ibid.*, pp. 136–7.

21. Hal Koch, *Dagen og Vejen*, p. 7. On the problem of hypocrisy see the introduction to Chapter IV below.

22. Cf. Chapter I, p. 19 ff.

23. *Beretning*, bilag XII, p. 216.

24. *Ibid.*, bilag IV, p. 757. The change from third person singular to first person plural and back again is in the original. Vigen, *op. cit.*, p. 5, says that as long as the policy of negotiation continued "nothing had happened either to the Jewish citizens or to the police."

25. Thune Jacobsen's report of that date, *Beretning*, bilag VII, I, p. 709, and III, columns 33–34. See also Thune Jacobsen, *Paa Urias Post*, pp. 161, 165.

26. The speech was given on 10/14/41 in the "discussion group" at Hellerup High School, Copenhagen. These groups developed into underground cells and were set up for young people opposed to the policy of negotiation (see Chapter VII). The speech, which was not supposed to be written down, was given in full to the Germans and passed on to Berlin by Renthe-Fink; it was printed in German translation in *Beretning*, bilag IV, pp. 145–48.

27. In this part of our study, which deals with the commencement of the struggle for the fate of the Danish Jews, we have relied mainly on two types of source material: official documents, both of the Danes and of the German Foreign Ministry; and the detailed replies of Renthe-Fink to the questions posed by the author. A study of German Foreign Ministry files—long before I met the man personally—showed that on the Jewish question he systematically sabotaged the efforts of the *Deutschland* Department (for details, see below). After further information about him was obtained, personal contact was made with him in the spring of 1962. He wrote three memoranda to the author. The first, on 6/16/62, is most detailed and contains many references (Memo A). The second, on 8/1/62, includes additional clarifications and answers to ' questions arising from Memo A (Memo B). The third, on 12/10/62, adds further details (Memo C). He included personal information and also points elicited from Paul Ernst Kanstein, one of the senior officials who had worked with him in Denmark and who will also be mentioned further in the course of this study. The author tried to get in touch with Kanstein as early as 1959 on the recommendation of G. F. Duckwitz, but without result. Renthe-Fink also suggested a number of documents not previously considered by the author and pointed out various facts and background data which increased understanding of the period. Duckwitz is mentioned below; he presented Yad Vashem with some of his memoirs relating to the events described in this study. The author met with him in 1957–58 when he was German ambassador to Denmark.

Renthe-Fink was one of the "veteran officials" of the Foreign Ministry. An Appendix to this work attempts to describe the internal structure and work system in the German Foreign

Ministry under Ribbentrop. Within the limits of this study there is no justification for a comprehensive description of the general activity of Renthe-Fink in Denmark. It is sufficient to peruse the twelve columns devoted to him and his work in Denmark in the index of *Beretning* in order to understand that our problem was only one of scores he dealt with. But this problem—to some extent morally as well as practically and politically—was one of the most significant of the period of Danish occupation. Renthe-Fink died in the summer of 1964. Evidence of his relationship to the Jews was given in personal letters by Professor Edgar Salin, Basle; Frau Professor A. Marchionini, Munich; Professor Werner Heisenberg, Max Planck Institut; and Herr H. Arnold, Genf.

28. The camp was situated on the island of Seeland, north of Copenhagen. On the establishment of the camp immediately after the occupation and its administration by the Danes themselves, see the discussion below on the problem of refugees in Denmark at the time of the occupation, Chapter VI, THE FIRST PHASE OF THE OCCUPATION.

29. Frisch, *op. cit.*, I, pp. 165–67; *Danmark under Verdenskrig og Besættelsen* (hereafter *Danmark under Verdenskrig*), III, p. 75.

30. *Fakta*, I, p. 39.

31. Frisch, *op. cit.*, I, pp. 202 ff.; J. Barfoed and E. Kruchow, *Danmark under 2. verdenskrig, kilder og tekster*, I, pp. 91 ff; H. Hansen, *Besættelsens fem onde aar*, pp. 88–90.

32. In addition to Denmark the anti-Comintern pact was signed by Finland, Bulgaria, Romania, Slovakia, and Croatia, while the Nanking government, Japan, Italy, Spain, Hungary, and Manchuria confirmed their membership. The main proviso of the pact was an undertaking to fight communism. The German demand to Denmark to join was presented on 11/20 and less than three days were allowed for a decision to be made.

33. E. Scavenius, *Forhandlingspolitiken*, p. 142.

34. Some publicity was also given to the words of Ribbentrop to the Bulgarian foreign minister, Popoff. See Tennenbaum, *op. cit.*, pp. 263 ff; cf. also Heydrich's statement on 11/29—PS 709 or TWC XIV, p. 644; Frisch, I, p. 208; and *Danmark under Verdenskrig*, II, p. 53.

35. IMT, PS 710; printed in R. Kempner, *Eichmann*, p. 98.

36. See Luther's memorandum of 12/4/41 to the minister (TWC XIII, pp. 195–96; NG–4667); and the opinions of the legal experts which led to the shelving of the plan (TWC XIV, p. 479); Luther's memorandum is translated in Tennenbaum, *op. cit.*, p. 512, note 14.

37. NG–2586–F. Cf. Heydrich's invitation to Luther, passed on to Rademacher on 12/4 with the request that it be accepted in his name "and to prepare for me a memorandum for the meeting

on our requests and suggestions." Reprinted in Kempner, *op. cit.*, pp. 127–28, together with (pp. 126–29) further information on the organization of the conference. On Luther, Rademacher, and the *Deutschland* Department see Appendix below on the German Foreign Ministry.

38. *Fakta*, I, p. 491; also Nissen and Poulsen, *op. cit.*, p. 181.
39. See Chapter III.
40. Udskrift af Dombogen for Københavns Byrets Afdeling for særlige Sager, BB. Nr. 673.
41. *Beretning*, bilag IV, pp. 456, 627–28. Details of the discussion in T. Taaning (p. 567) and H. Hansen (pp. 91 ff.) in *Danmarks Frihedskamp*, II.
42. Dr. M. Friediger, "De danske Jøder under Besættelsen" in *Dansk Udsyn*, XXV, 1945, p. 307.
43. *Ibid.*
44. On him and his colleagues see Chapters III and VII.
45. See Nissen and Poulsen, *op. cit.*, pp. 182 ff. and 217 ff.
46. *Fædrelandet*, front page, 1/7/42: DENMARK, GERMANY AND THE JEWS, with the subtitle: "No Jew in Denmark Can Be Positively Inclined Toward Cooperation Between Our Country and Germany. An Open Letter to Professor Hal Koch Who Has Made the Question of Jewish Legislation Topical." Together with this article, which consisted of some 1300 words, another article of about the same length appeared on page two under the headline: ANTI-COMINTERN PACT AND AN ACTIVE ANTI-SEMITIC POLICY. *Kamptegnet* published on 1/15/42 a leading article entitled: THE JEWISH LACKEY HAL KOCH, with the subtitle "The Church Works for the Comintern," together with an idealized drawing of a pure Aryan Danish woman. *Nordschleswigsche Zeitung* carried on 1/8/42 an article called PROFESSOR HAL KOCH AND THE JEWISH PROBLEM.
47. Memo A, pp. 1–2. Cf. Appendix on the German Foreign Ministry.
48. Inl. II A/B 63/I–JM/2258, which also includes a list of the places where information of this type could be obtained. The documents mentioned below in this connection are all from this file.
49. The German instruction for resubmission of a document is *wiedervorlegen*, usually abbreviated to "w.v." together with the date required.
50. The reminder is printed in *Beretning*, bilag XIII, p. 136. Renthe-Fink's reply—Inl. II A/B 63/I.
51. Renthe-Fink, Memo A, p. 2. It should be pointed out that the number of Jews living in Jutland was small, and the agricultural trainees working in the area had previously been transferred by the Jewish institutions to other districts.
52. *Ibid.*, p. 3. The ordinance on the yellow star was published in

the *Reichsgesetzblatt* (the German official gazette) of the same date, part I, p. 547. For preparations and instructions, see Eichmann trial documents T/682, T/684, T/685; cf. Hilberg, *op. cit.*, pp. 120–21.

53. Inl. IIg 54/8–JM/2216 and see below note 138. With regard to the legends on this subject concerning the king, see the next section in this chapter. In other West European countries the yellow badge was introduced in 1942.

54. Memo A, p. 2 states: "It was my intention to suggest the continuation of the subsidy as the lesser of two evils on the grounds that the anti-Semitic Danish National Socialists could not for a long time be considered in connection with taking power. I was completely surprised when Luther, before I could say anything, declared that in his opinion the Danish National Socialists were adequately prepared and should at once be brought to power. . . . I was no little disturbed at this treacherous attack, but kept myself in check and replied that there must be a misunderstanding. I was convinced that an assumption of power would be hasty and lead to chaos in Denmark, and this was unthinkable. I could give assurances that the commander of the German troops in Denmark shared my view. I was extremely relieved when Ribbentrop intervened and decided the matter by saying that since von Renthe-Fink, who knew conditions best, thought that the time was not yet ripe, then it was best to let everything remain as it was, and the money was at once paid out. This in effect also meant that the Jewish question was postponed." Cf. also Grundherr's memorandum to the foreign minister of 11/4/41, Rademacher's of 11/7/41, and Renthe-Fink's letter to Luther of 11/9/41—*Beretning*, bilag XIII, bind 2, pp. 544–47.

55. Renthe-Fink, Memo A, p. 3.

56. Hitler's approval was given on 11/17/41—see *Beretning*, bilag XIII, bind 2, p. 350. Renthe-Fink and Grundherr knew the dangers threatening their approach. See Renthe-Fink's telegram of 1/4/42, *Beretning* as above, p. 556 and Grundherr's memorandum to the minister of 1/6/42, *ibid.*, p. 557.

57. Renthe-Fink, Memo A, p. 4; Memo B, p. 2; Memo C, p. 1. The date of Rademacher's visit was determined with the help of his personal file in the German Foreign Ministry, according to which he visited Copenhagen in 1941 as follows: 4/5–4/9, 6/10–6/14, 12/14–12/17; in 1942: 3/24, 6/16–6/21, 12/8–12/16. In this connection the speech of the prosecutor at Nuremberg, Kempner, is of special interest—see his book, p. 294.

58. At the end of December, before the appearance of the article, Renthe-Fink announced to the Danish press via press attaché Meissner that "the Jewish problem is no longer topical and

will be solved throughout Europe only after the end of the war": J. Brøndsted and K. Gedde, *De fem lange Aar*, I, p. 296.

59. Renthe-Fink himself, in a telegram dated 1/6/42 (see below), reports on the publication of the announcement in the *Chicago Daily News*. In England it appeared in nearly all the papers on 1/6/42—see, for example, *Manchester Guardian* and *Daily Express* of that date.

60. These three were Foreign Minister Scavenius, Transport Minister Gunnar Larsen, and Minister of Justice Thune Jacobsen.

61. In his monthly report for January 1942 (one of the secret Danish reports sent by him via the resistance movement to England) Erling Foss condemns these reports as "false information" liable merely to undermine the population's confidence in the government. These reports to the free world, which became the principal source of information on behalf of the underground movement, were published by their author after the war in a book called *Fra Passiv til Aktiv Modstand*. This work is one of the most important sources for the events of the period. Erling Foss, an engineer by profession and a member of the Conservative party, became in time one of the prominent figures of the resistance movement. *Berlingske Tidende* (on 1/8) and *Social-Demokraten* (on 1/9) clearly dissociated themselves from the rumors.

62. Telegram No. 18; NG–3931; reprinted in *Beretning*, bilag XIII, bind 3, pp. 1367–68.

63. Inl. II A/B 63/I.

64. NG–3931, p. 1.

65. *Ibid.*, p. 3.

66. Sonnleithner's announcement, *ibid.*, p. 4; Luther's reply, *ibid.*, p. 5; reprinted in *Beretning*, as in note 61, p. 1368.

67. Memo B, p. 5.

68. NG–2586; TWC, Case XI, XIII, pp. 212, 214, and elsewhere.

69. Memo A, p. 6; Memo B, p. 8. In the memorandum itself Luther admits that Rademacher asked Renthe-Fink to point out, in the course of a talk with the Danes, the need to solve the Jewish question. This sentence was underlined by the reader and in the margin of the document is written *nicht insistieren* (don't insist).

70. For discussion in the government, see *Beretning*, bilag IV, p. 632. Scavenius also expressed his views on the anti-Semitic paper to members of Himmler's coterie, as transpires from the report of a conversation, an unsigned copy of which was found in Himmler's personal files, and marked by him with the date 3/29/42 (Himmler Files, Roll 7, Folder 56; and Rigsarkiv, Sp. 67162–67164).

71. For example, the minister of the interior, Knud Christensen, a

Liberal and also a member of the Council of Elders, spoke in this vein at a public meeting in Aalborg on 1/8/42. In connection with problems arising from cooperation with the Germans he said that these were not merely a case of practical daily matters but of popular rule as such, "to which so many of life's great values are attached: press freedom, religious freedom, freedom of assembly, freedom of trade, etc." *Fakta*, I, p. 196.

72. Frisch, I, p. 210; *Beretning*, bilag IV, p. 641.

73. The subject of the lecture was "Georg Brandes and Antiquity"; it was published in Frisch's book *Tænkt og talt under Krigen*, pp. 23–27.

74. His name was Helge Viggo Stærke. Another man involved was the spy and informer Hammeken, whom the Germans smuggled to Germany with a promise that he would not be returned to Denmark. However, he returned in 1944 and continued to work for the Germans. *Hvidbog*, II, pp. 67, 92.

75. That the sentence was regarded as demonstrative was also shown by the violent attack delivered on 2/4/42 in *Kamptegnet*. The government discussed the events of 2/3 in its meeting of 2/6 (*Beretning*, bilag IV, pp. 459 ff.).

76. Inl. II A/B, 63/1.

77. *Loc. cit.;* written on 1/20/42. According to the lists attached to the file, Hal Koch had by then been placed by the Germans on the blacklist.

78. Memo A, pp. 5–6; Memo B, p. 6. On the institution, see below, Chapter III.

79. In the meantime news items continued to appear in the press—for example, in Switzerland: DIE JUDENFRAGE IN DÄNEMARK, *Israelitisches Wochenblatt*, Zurich, 1/16/42; EINFÜHRUNG DER JUDENGESETZE IN DÄNEMARK BEABSICHTIGT? *Basler National-Zeitung*, 1/11/42.

80. The last assertion was not practical—see Chapters III and VI for a discussion of these problems. The report is typical of a certain system prevalent in the German Foreign Ministry at that time; see the Appendix on the ministry in this book.

81. Renthe-Fink himself confirmed this interpretation (Memo B, p. 7): "It must undoubtedly be ascribed to the uncompromising attitude of the Danes that the Jews in Denmark did not come to share the fate of the Jews in most of the occupied countries."

82. Quoted in Sten Gudme, *Hitler's Model Protectorate*, p. 117. The book was published in London in 1942 and aimed at explaining and justifying to the Allies the special position and behavior of the Danes. On the role of the king, cf. also Hæstrup, *From Occupied to Ally*, pp. 6–7.

83. Gunnar Leistikow, "Denmark Under the Nazi Heel," *Foreign Affairs*, XXI (January 1943), p. 352.

84. See Chapter I, p. 13.
85. Thaulow, *op. cit.*, p. 174.
86. "Denmark and the Jews," *Jewish Ledger*, Springfield, Mass., V.S.H.J., 11/12/43. Aage Bertelsen quotes the stories as facts in the introduction to the American and German editions of his book *October 43*. The Danes generally avoid much mention of this point. Margolinsky points out that the Danish translation of Leon Uris's *Exodus* omits the story of the king's appearing in the English original.
87. The author asked Bertelsen about the source of his information. He replied in a letter on 9/11/60: "I regret not being in a position to give you a source for the story on King Christian X and the yellow star of David. I do not think there is any source: the story was on everybody's lips in October 1943. Before I wrote the foreword to the English edition, I asked the same question as you did (to which I also attach some importance) to someone in Copenhagen who I presumed could answer it. As far as I recall, it was the late king's secretary. His reply was that no one knew exactly if it was true in the word's historic sense—but it suited well enough the old king's character! You see, I do not remember the man for certain but I am sure that I have not distorted his answer."

    To a similar question, Renthe-Fink replied in Memo C, p. 7: "In my opinion, the anecdotes and myths contain a mixture of fantasy and truth. The king also took his duties to his Jewish subjects very seriously and would hardly have given his approval to any discrimination. An utterance to the effect that he would wear the Jewish star, should this be introduced into Denmark, could decidedly be believed of him, but was doubtless first and foremost of symbolic significance. Through abdication he would only have done Hitler a favor, since the king stood in the way of Hitler's plans for a New Order."
88. Wolf S. Jacobson and Marcus Melchior, *Glimt af Jødedommen*, København, 1941.
89. Photostatically reproduced in Sabile, *Lueurs dans la Tourmente*.
90. See Introduction, p. xiii, and Lazar Samson, "Ruhm Dir Dänemark."
91. On the period see Frisch, I, pp. 231 ff; *Beretning*, bilag IV, pp. 151–62, 203–13; Hæstrup, *Kontakt med England*, pp. 150–72.
92. See La Cour, I, p. 379, and Scavenius, p. 145.
93. See A. Eisenbach, "Operation Reinhard, Mass Extermination of the Jewish Population in Poland," *Polish Western Affairs*, III, 1962, pp. 80–129.
94. He sent these latter mainly to Luther and even to Ribbentrop himself. Renthe-Fink tells (Memo A, p. 9) of his attempts to obstruct Meissner's initiative. However, the memoranda of both

Meissner and Renthe-Fink and their evidence and that of many Danes, including Scavenius, before the parliamentary commission, show that in this matter, as in many others, Renthe-Fink tried to play on both sides. The documents were published in *Beretning*, bilag XIII, 1. og 2. bind, *passim*, and afhøringer, bilag I, pp. 416–65. See also Duckwitz's memoirs, p. 5, which states that Meissner caused a deterioration of relations.

95. On 7/28/42 Luther's department passed on to Grundherr a report by an anonymous author dated 7/18/42 (*Beretning*, bilag XIII, bind 2, pp. 635 ff.). Its style suggested the authorship or inspiration of Meissner. It describes the morale and the situation in Denmark as influenced by propaganda common both to the Communists and the West. The Jews help the government which is in fact working against the Germans—cf. Meissner's report of 6/27/42 on the influence of Western literature, whose main agent, according to him, is a Jew by the name of David Greenbaum (Inl. II, A/B 63/1). Also see the memorandum of 9/26/42 (Inl. IIg, 54/8), written in the very days of the crisis during a visit to Berlin, in which he begins with a description of the alleged cooperation between the Social Democratic leaders and the Communists and goes on to say: "A thorough investigation of the activity of the Communist forces referred to will easily prove the close connection between them and influential Jewish circles." He also states that since the establishment of the Communist party in Denmark most of its supporters are members of the Jewish community, and mainly Eastern Jews who came after 1900. He exploits here the fact that Jewish workers included members of the "Bund" (see Chapter I). Among the members of the community at the time only a few were known to be active Communists (see Chapter VI).

96. On this point cf. Nissen and Poulsen, pp. 88, 96.

97. This memorandum was written in the form of a letter to Grundherr following a talk with him during the visit of the latter to Denmark. The date of the letter was 8/19/42. See also note attached to its publication in *Beretning*, bilag XIII, bind 2, pp. 642 ff. He also sent a copy to Rademacher (see below).

98. See Meissner's memorandum to Renthe-Fink of 8/22/42 (*Beretning, ibid.*, pp. 645–49; NG–3419), in which he again suggests —following a long analysis of the situation—a "transition government" and asserts that a clear decision should be requested from Ribbentrop on the political line in Denmark. Renthe-Fink says that at this meeting Ohlendorf poured his wrath on Meissner but in fact meant it for himself (Renthe-Fink)—Memo A, p. 7.

99. A copy of the report was given on 9/1/42 to Weizsäcker by Stuckart (reprinted in *Beretning, ibid.*, pp. 670–73).

100. *Beretning, ibid.,* pp. 656–69. A thorough analysis of the memorandum will give a broad idea of the policy, methods and achievements of Renthe-Fink, and also of his mistaken evaluations, particularly with regard to the character and mode of reaction of the Danes.

101. Renthe-Fink's report of that day (*Beretning, ibid.,* pp. 650–53). The reference here is to the director of the Government Statistical Department, Einar Cohn, and the director of the Ministry of Justice, Aage Svendsen, who was also of Jewish origin. For details of this affair, see Chapter III.

102. *Beretning, ibid.,* p. 653.

103. Memo A, p. 7.

104. The economic factor was emphasized not only in the report of Renthe-Fink himself but also in that of Stuckart, who asserted that the Danish claims for independence "which still existed on the face of things" should be taken into account, since it was this which would guarantee the quiet required for industrial— and even more, agricultural—production, which was of such importance for Germany. On this problem see Chapters IV and V and Renthe-Fink, Memo A, p. 6.

105. This tendency was revealed by Renthe-Fink already in his talk with Transport Minister Gunnar Larsen on 7/10/43, i.e., before the visit of Stuckart and Ohlendorf. (Memorandum 7/14/42, *Beretning,* bilag IV, pp. 199 ff.) This talk will be referred to in detail in Chapter III.

106. Inl. IIg 53/1–JM/2216; Inl. IIg 60/3; NG–2586J; Eichmann trial, T/196, in Kempner, *op. cit.,* pp. 222 ff.

107. NG–2586, pp. 58–9. The order was given in Ribbentrop's name by Rintelen, head of his personal bureau. Cf. Hilberg, p. 350, note 12.

108. NG–1965; quoted in Kempner, pp. 219–222. Among other things the problem was raised of Jews in the occupied areas holding foreign nationality should their governments, for various reasons, inquire about their fate. This problem was later extensively dealt with and affected also Denmark.

109. Cf. note 97.

110. This copy of Clausen's letter exists—Inl. IIg 54/8.

111. *Ibid.*

112. Inl. II A/B 63/1. One of the mysteries of the German filing system is the fact that Rademacher's memorandum with Luther's comment and Rademacher's reply are in different files. This is not the only instance of this type. Moreover, Rademacher apparently prepared a draft of the memorandum requested by Luther and this is to be found close to our document; its contents are based mainly on the big report of January 1942 (see Chapter III, THE STRUGGLE AGAINST THE "PURGE"). Grundherr would seem to have succeeded in persuading Rademacher

not to present this memorandum of his. The draft has no heading and no file number, but is dated by Rademacher 9/12.
(Inl. II 54/8). See the Appendix on the German Foreign Office
in this work and the author's report of her talk with Grundherr
—Yad Vashem 027/14.

113. Inl. IIg 54/8.

114. This problem and this argument appear from time to time in
the National Socialist assertions, but they also appear in the
memoirs of Duckwitz, who states that there were Danish businessmen who exploited the occasion to overcome competition
and insure for themselves business with the Germans. Duckwitz's memoirs, pp. 2–3.

115. On this system and others of a similar nature see the Appendix
on the German Foreign Ministry; the subject will be dealt with
again in the course of this study.

116. Evidence of a meeting on the date mentioned (and of another
on 10/1 after the crisis broke) is given by the entry in
Himmler's appointments book (*Terminkalender*) kept by his
secretary, Dr. Brandt (the book is apparently today in the
State Archives of West Germany in Coblenz). The talk itself,
which took place at night, does not appear in the book. Kanstein has, however, recalled it in an interview with a Danish
journalist (see article in *Berlingske Tidende* of 1/15/53–"Den
anstændige tysker i den sorte SS-uniform"). Renthe-Fink also
recalls the talk from memory and on the basis of correspondence and talks with Kanstein in 1962 (Memo A, p. 5; Memo B,
p. 7; Memo C, p. 2). Duckwitz also vouches for Kanstein.
Kanstein was in touch with resistance elements in Germany
and was arrested after the attempt on Hitler's life in July 1944
but was released after personal intervention by Himmler. Due
to Danish evidence on his behalf he was not put on trial by the
Allied Powers. Danish evidence (Dalsgaard) on his above talk
with Himmler is given in *Beretning*, bilag VIII, p. 144. After
proclamation of the state of emergency on 8/29/43, Kanstein
asked to be allowed to leave Denmark, as he did not wish to be
a party to developments. At the beginning of October he was
transferred to Italy. On his role in September's events, see
Chapters IV and V.

117. This document appears on various occasions: NG–5119; NG–
1517 in Weizsäcker's trial; TWC XIII, p. 255; in cross-examination of Ribbentrop, IMT, X, pp. 397–8; reprinted in *Beretning*,
bilag XIII, bind 3, p. 1369. See also Kempner, p. 236.

118. Renthe-Fink states that this became known to him, after he had
left Denmark, from a member of Ribbentrop's closest entourage
(Memo B, pp. 8–9; Memo A, p. 10; Memo C, p. 3).

119. The actual wording of the telegram—in German: "SPRECHE
MEINEN BESTEN DANK AUS"—was no different in fact from that of

previous years. See comparison in *Beretning,* bilag XIII, bind 2, p. 685.

120. NG–5121; Inl. IIg 54/8; the main subject of the letter is the return of Jews—Danish citizens—from the Reich and occupied countries. The date was marked by two of Luther's officials, Rademacher and Klingenfuss.

121. The distinction between *Glaubensjuden* (Jews by religious persuasion) and *Rassejuden* (Jews by race) is that between members of the community and Jews by race, including baptized "Jews."

122. NG–4275; NG–3202.

123. See notes 8, 115, *Beretning,* bilag VIII, p. 143.

124. Cf. *Hitler's Ten-Year War . . . ,* p. 221; it seems, however, that there is overlapping here of Renthe-Fink's talk with Scavenius on 9/24/42 and the feelers put out in October.

125. *Beretning,* bilag IV, p. 192. The introduction of capital punishment was demanded by Renthe-Fink as early as the summer of that year but this was rejected by the Danish government. See memorandum of 9/18/43, *Beretning,* bilag XIII, bind 2, p. 933.

126. *Beretning, ibid.,* p. 193.

127. Best quickly gave up the formation of a government in accordance with the list he brought with him from Berlin (with the character of a business administration, as previously suggested by the National Socialists). He made do with the replacement of three ministers, one of them Premier Buhl. See also discussion in Chapter IV.

128. *Beretning, ibid.,* p. 197. On the whole affair see Frisch, I, Chapter 18, on the government crisis in November 1942, pp. 271 ff.

129. See Appendix on life of Best.

130. Renthe-Fink and Best traveled to Warsaw on 10/24; on 10/25–26 they stayed at the field quarters of Ribbentrop where Best had talks with the minister and his officials, some of them in the presence of Renthe-Fink; on 10/27 they reached Hitler's headquarters. Besides the talk with him, which lasted half an hour and which mainly consisted of a lecture by Hitler, Best had talks with all the top Nazis, including General Jodl and Martin Bormann. On 10/29 Best and Renthe-Fink returned together to Berlin. Notes and microfilms of the diary are to be found in the Rigsarkiv in Copenhagen, but the author was permitted only to take notes and not to make copies.

131. A summary dated 10/27/42 exists in the Rosenberg archive and is reproduced in *Beretning,* bilag XIII, bind 2, pp. 747–8. It is extremely interesting in itself and shows, among other things, that Best received explicit instructions not to encourage the Danish Nazis too much. Renthe-Fink's letter appears in *Beretning, ibid.,* p. 759.

132. Renthe-Fink in Memo A, p. 11: "I am therefore certain that the Jewish question was not discussed during my stay in the Führer's headquarters. It dealt much more with Best's attitude to the king and the formation of a new government."
133. Best's appointments book shows for 10/30–11/4 two talks with Luther, a talk with Rademacher and a talk with Ohlendorf, besides various talks in the Foreign Ministry (a meeting with Stuckart is also mentioned). Luther accompanied him to the airport on his departure.
134. Inl. IIg, 54/8.
135. Luther to the deputy director-general, Gauss, who was the legal adviser of the German Foreign Ministry. Inl. II geh. 53/1.
136. On the removal of Luther see the Appendix on the German Foreign Ministry. An interesting point was made by the British prosecutor at Nuremberg, Sir David Maxwell Fyfe (now the Earl of Kailmuir), who maintained that Luther was planning Ribbentrop's removal and his replacement by Best. He did not, however, give the source of this odd piece of information (IMT X, p. 213).
137. Hovedrapporter vedrørende Werner Best, bilag 35A, p. 141.
138. The memorandum consisted of an original and two copies—Inl. IIg, 54/8; summary of Luther's "memorandum to the minister," loc. cit. See also Hilberg, p. 358; NG–5121.
139. Inl. IIg 54/8; NG–5121.
140. See Appendix on the German Foreign Ministry.
141. IMT XXXV, Doc. 740–D, p. 453.
142. It is noteworthy that Scavenius in his talk with Ribbentrop on 11/4/42, the eve of Best's arrival in Denmark, uses the same expression himself and talks of "die weiche Methode" (the soft method), in contradistinction to the "path of suppression" followed in Norway. With reference to Denmark he explicitly recommends that the soft method be used (summary of the talk by interpreter Schmidt; reprinted in Beretning, bilag XIII, bind 2, p. 758).
143. Printed in Beretning, bilag XIII, bind 3, pp. 1372–73; NG–5121.
144. Thadden's declaration under oath—TWC, Case XI, Steengracht, Def. Exh. Nr. 35; cf. Hilberg, p. 355; Eichmann trial T/584. Thadden's comment is as follows: "I know that the Foreign Ministry approved of Herr Best's arguments and declared the RSHA's request for an immediate deportation of the Jews to be politically untenable. RSHA seemed, however, to be unwilling to accept this stand, since the man responsible for the desk in Eichmann's department ironically informed me that the Foreign Ministry would soon be obliged to revise its attitude."
145. NG–5121; original and two copies in Inl. IIg 54/8.

146. According to this, 345 Jews engaged in business. Photographs prepared by the Danes from German documents include a list of Jewish shops in Copenhagen in 1940 ("Nichtarische Geschäfte des Kleinhandels in Kopenhagen"). This is divided into two parts, textiles and food, and includes 216 names, according to alphabetical order of streets (Rigsarkiv, Sp. 10, 13398–401). The list is doubtless incomplete. On the basis of statistical data from 1931, businesses and financial enterprises numbered 428 men and women, 315 of whom were regarded as wholesalers and only 93 as retailers (see Chapter I, note 20). Cf. Hilberg, p. 358; H. C. Jørgensen, p. 8.

147. Inl. IIg 54/8. Hilberg, who also refers to this matter, relies on NG–5121 and states that the document bears no date. In many cases this or other details were omitted in the copying process, due to lack of understanding of their significance and this happened here with the date. It is generally preferable to use original documents of photographs rather than the collection of the Nuremberg trials. For the discussion on the refugee problem, see Chapter VI.

148. Submitted to him again on 6/11 (Inl. IIg 54/8). It is interesting that about that time, on 5/4/43, the Jewish problem was again raised for discussion in the Danish government by Scavenius himself (Beretning, bilag IV, p. 492).

149. NG–4807. The problem of the relations between Himmler and Ribbentrop and between their organizations is too complicated to be dealt with here except in specific instances relevant to our subject.

150. Best stayed in Germany between July 1 and 7. On the basis of a summary drawn up in Nuremberg on the basis of his diary (in the Rigsarkiv) he spent the first two days in talks with the RSHA in Berlin (Kaltenbrunner, Müller and Ohlendorf are named) and then journeyed east. At Himmler's field headquarters on the 4th and 5th he talked with Himmler and his staff and with the Mufti of Jerusalem. He then returned to Berlin, where he again met mainly with RSHA functionaries before returning to Copenhagen.

151. Both documents in Inl. IIg 54/8.

152. According to Wagner's evidence (TWC, Case XI, Steengracht, Def. Exh. No. 34–Eichmann trial 817–06), it was Steengracht who took the initiative toward Himmler, though it would seem that Wagner here acted on his own initiative. This transpires from Thadden's declaration (see note 144) and also from Wagner's statement that he was severely rebuked by the minister for his initiative and forbidden to negotiate independently with Himmler.

153. Duckwitz names four factors that were responsible for the

postponement of the action against the Jews in Denmark: (1) the German desire to prove the reality of the "model protectorate"; (2) the influence of the German Ministry of Food (see below, Chapters IV and V); (3) consideration for the Danish Nazis so long as they were regarded as potential candidates for assumption of power and so long as they asserted that they were unable to accept responsibility if they were burdened with the persecution of the Jews; and (4) the shrewd tactics of Renthe-Fink, which Best tried to continue—in Duckwitz's opinion less successfully.

CHAPTER III

1. Knud Brix and Erik Hansen, *Dansk Nazisme under Besættelsen*, p. 21.
2. Børge Outze, *Vore hjemlige Nazister;* La Cour, II, p. 453.
3. La Cour, *loc. cit.; Hvem-Hvad-Hvor*, Politikens Aarbog 1940.
4. Description of National Socialism in Denmark in a memorandum of the Danish government submitted at Nuremberg—IMT 901–RF XXXVIII, pp. 607–8; IMT VI, pp. 500–02.
5. La Cour, *loc. cit.* Data on membership numbers of these groups could not, unfortunately, be found. Since members moved from one organization to the other it is extremely difficult to arrive at accurate statistical data.
6. See note 1. The study was carried out at the initiative of sociologists from Denmark, Sweden, Norway, and Finland; pp. 19, 70.
7. *Ibid.*, p. 24.
8. La Cour, *op. cit.*, pp. 450, 473.
9. Frisch, I, p. 127; La Cour II, pp. 450, 465–66.
10. Brix and Hansen, *op. cit.*, p. 31. This view is also supported by the fact that only 19 per cent of the party members were women (*ibid.*, p. 51). In this connection it should be pointed out that in November 1943, when the number joining was in any case negligible, the party suspended the enrollment of new members except where there was no doubt "that the candidate understands our idea and knows what obligations he takes upon himself as a member of DNSAP" (*Fakta*, I, p. 419).
11. Brix and Hansen, *op. cit.*, pp. 25, 33. The share of the party in rural areas was then 50 per cent; now it dropped to 30 per cent. Formerly there had been 25 per cent in Copenhagen and the provincial towns; now there were 40 per cent in Copenhagen and 30 per cent in the provincial towns. The occupational breakdown was as follows: agriculture 23 per cent, industry (workers and clerks) 65 per cent (!), civil servants 8 per cent, liberal professions 3 per cent, others 1 per cent.

12. *Ibid.*, pp. 44, 48, 58.
13. Frisch, I, p. 304.
14. Since participation in these elections reached a record 90 per cent (over 2 million votes) compared to a little under 80 per cent in the elections of 1939 (almost 1,700,000 votes) the percentage of votes received by the two Nazi parties dropped from almost 5 per cent to 3 per cent. The government parties, on the other hand, won 94 per cent of the votes (Frisch, *ibid.*).
15. Renthe-Fink: Dienststelle Ribbentrop, Führerberichte, JM/2479. The joke was used by Frisch in a speech to the Rigsdag (*Fakta,* II, p. 1442).
16. *Fakta,* I, p. 409.
17. Frederik Torm, Aage Bentzen, Joh. Petersen, Fleming Hvidberg.
18. The article appeared in *Berlingske Tidende* under the heading GROSS LITERARY FORGERIES and the subheading "Renowned Danish Theologians Protest Against the Anti-Semitic Publications of the Danish National Socialist Party."
19. Inl. A/B 63/1. This report of the German minister in Copenhagen was, on 1/23/36, sent to all the German diplomatic missions: "To all missions and consulates for information and with the request to observe and report on the development of the Jewish question in the areas concerned as well as on corresponding steps in the National Socialist Jewish policy and Jewish countermeasures—as soon as the situation can be evaluated. [Signed] von Bülow-Schwente."
20. *Ibid.* Wurm passed Andersen's letter on to the German Foreign Ministry, which requested the legation in Copenhagen to explain the matter. The legation's reply was given on 8/7/40. From this letter it transpires that Andersen was found guilty in 1938 of attacks on the government. The contact with Wurm had existed since 1934, as he himself points out in a letter dated 6/16/43.
21. Dienststelle Ribbentrop, as in note 15.
22. This is clear from a memorandum submitted by Luther to Grundherr, Wörmann, and Weizsäcker on 8/5/40 (*Ibid.,* II, 14).
23. *Ibid.* Until the end of 1941 the German subsidy to the DNSAP amounted to $3\frac{1}{2}$ million kroner. See memorandum of Ribbentrop to Hitler on 11/11/41 (*Beretning*, bilag XIII, bind 2, p. 549).
24. *Ibid.*, II, 14.
25. At the head of the letter is written: "with reference to circulars of 22/7/40" (July 22, 1940).
26. *Fakta,* I, pp. 575 ff.
27. For example, see *Kamptegnet:* 5/29/41; 6/5/41; 6/12/41; 7/31/41; 8/21/41; 9/4/41; 1/15/42; 1/22/42.

28. Professor Erik Warburg (see Chapter VII) was often the object of anti-Semitic attacks, e.g., in *Kamptegnet* 10/25/40.

29. See Scavenius's comment at the government meeting on 1/13/42, p. 58.

30. His name appears extremely often, since he was not only chairman of the community and an attorney of the high court, but was also actively engaged in economic and public life in Denmark. See, for example, the issues of 1/22/41; 6/12/41; 7/31/41.

31. For instance, Bernard Baruch was singled out for an attack of this type (7/10/41).

32. For example, 6/12/41; 7/4/41; 9/4/41; 10/2/41.

33. See above, Chapter II, BEST—IN RENTHE-FINK'S POLITICAL FOOTSTEPS. A similar article appeared on 11/27/42 in *Fædrelandet* suggesting that the new Scavenius government "should use the privilege of enacting Jewish legislation." Was Denmark assured no freedom in its internal affairs? It had to use it for this end. . . .

34. The town of Randers was, for instance, often cited in this connection (8/7/41).

35. In addition to the matters mentioned here, Daell had been involved in the attempts of the so-called *Danmarkskredsen* ("Denmark circle") in 1940 to find a solution to the country's problems outside the context of parties and their representation in Parliament. The protagonists of this plan were not necessarily pro-German or of Fascist tendencies. The attempt failed and the circle rapidly dissolved. See *Beretning*, IX, pp. 9–25, and bilag IX, pp. 26, 59, 91, etc.; also Nissen and Poulsen, pp. 71 ff.

36. *Beretning*, bilag IX, minutes, p. 157.

37. This was the period when the Swedes allowed the transit of a German army from Norway to Finland—see below, Chapter IX, NEUTRAL SWEDEN.

38. *Beretning*, bilag IV, pp. 443, 584, etc.; X, p. 44, etc.

39. See F. L. Bindsløv, *Pressen under Besættelsen*, p. 147.

40. These details transpire from the trial of Gunnar Larsen held after the war; *Beretning*, bilag X, pp. 470 ff. and protocol, pp. 132 ff., 157. It emerges from the documents that a small group of volunteers did after all travel to Finland "in a private capacity," but even the Germans were not interested in the project. Rademacher wrote on 6/23/41 that he was opposed to the plan since he was not interested in strengthening "Scandinavian solidarity," and he asserted that Danes wishing to fight communism could do this on the eastern front (memorandum to Luther, NG–3105). Daell was afterward active in the underground movement.

41. All details of the trial are taken from approved copies of the court records placed at the author's disposal. Since this in-

volved a good deal of trouble, I wish to express my thanks to Chief Rabbi Melchior for his assistance in the matter.

42. Inl. II A/B 63/1.
43. Summary of the trial by the Germans dated 5/16/42, *loc. cit.*
44. *Beretning*, bilag IV, p. 469. On 6/25/42 the minister of education informed the Council of Nine of the matter.
45. Frisch, I, p. 241.
46. The Nazi weekly *Nationalsocialisten* published on 7/2/42 an article attacking the government for not implementing the law against the communists. "What use is the law?" it asks. "Here again we have an outstanding example of how affiliation to the anti-Comintern pact is carried out in practice: by stopping the subsidy payments to the authoress Olga Eggers." Quoted in the report of the Ministry of Justice to the Parliamentary Committee of Investigation, *Beretning*, bilag VII, bind I, p. 202.
47. According to the copy of the court proceedings mentioned in note 41. It appears that at the same time a judicial inquiry was instigated. *Fædrelandet* announced on 10/30/42 that a printer called A. O. Hanneken had given evidence in the Daell case on 10/29 that he had printed and distributed thousands of anti-Semitic leaflets.
48. In this connection see an article of 11/26/42 calling for "a solution of the Jewish problem."
49. Inl. II A/B 63/1.
50. *Ibid.* The request carries the date 3/6/43 but from various indications on the document it would appear that the material was not sent to Copenhagen before the end of the month, and possibly arrived there only after sentence had been handed down.
51. Note of Thadden of 4/30/43 and his letter to Best of 4/4/43; Best's reply in telegram No. 601, *ibid.*
52. Letter to the Foreign Ministry dated 5/17/43; this is Best's reply to Thadden's letter of 5/8/43, *ibid.*, and Thadden's letter to Best of 5/28/43, *ibid.*
53. Memorandum to the minister, *ibid.* The fact that the paper had already closed down is not mentioned here—only that the number of its readers has dropped again, this time to, it is said, 1,800.
54. Letter of the Minister's Bureau to Grundherr, 6/20/43—Grundherr's memorandum of 6/22/43; among other things, it says: "The *Stürmer*-imitated anti-Jewish paper *Kamptegnet* has, from my observations in Copenhagen, done us more harm than good. Educated Danes often describe it as repulsive pornography." Explicit instructions were given by the Minister's Bureau on 6/24/43, *ibid.*
55. *Ibid.* This is the same week that Best spent in Berlin and in Himmler's field quarters; cf. Chapter II, note 150.
56. Telegram No. 853.

57. Telegram No. 985 (all the correspondence—Inl. II A/B 63/1). See photostat of the receipt, this page.
58. *Ibid.*
59. *Ibid.* On 7/28/43 Thadden informed Wurm of this.
60. See above, Chapter II, THE JEWISH QUESTION—A DANISH PROBLEM; Inl. II A/B 63/1.
61. *Ibid.* The letter quotes an extremely positive opinion by the State Institute for the History of New Germany (*Reichsinstitut für Geschichte des neuen Deutschland*). From various notes, it transpires that the report was also submitted to Eichmann and to the Foreign Department of the German Nazi party.
62. These genealogical investigations were mainly carried out by two Danish Nazis—Otto Branner and Paul Hennig (see Melchior in La Cour, I, p. 360).
63. See Danish government memorandum to Nuremberg trials: 901–RF, IMT XXXVIII, p. 605.
64. See *Fakta*, II, p. 652; and Chapter II, note 142.
65. Inl. IIg 352, "Berichte und Meldungen zur Entwicklung der Lage in Dänemark"; Best's reply, telegram No. 350 of 3/18/43 (Yad Vashem 027/11), as follows: WITH REGARD TO FIRMS WHICH CARRY OUT IMPORTANT WAR PRODUCTION IN WHICH WAREHOUSE PROCEDURE IS INVOLVED, WILL THE DEFENSE ECONOMY IN THOSE CASES WHERE JEWS ARE IN MANAGEMENT EXPEDITE CURRENT ORDERS IN THE INTEREST OF THE WAR ECONOMY. WHEN NEW ORDERS ARE PLACED, JEWISH INFLUENCE WILL BE EXCLUDED AS FAR AS POSSIBLE. IN THE CASE OF STANDARD ELECTRIC, I AGREE WITH THE MEASURES WHICH MAKE POSSIBLE A SMOOTH CONTINUATION OF PRESENT PRODUCTION.
66. See above, p. 68.
67. *Beretning*, bilag IV, pp. 223, 227, 235. The aim of the Germans at first was to impose a Nazi minister of justice on the Danes. When they saw that they would not succeed, they requested that their candidate be appointed director-general. In Svenningsen's statement to the parliamentary commission he said: "We continually rejected this as something which seemed to us as radically wrong and utterly out of the question" (*ibid.*, protocol, p. 75).
68. Gunnar Larsen's report of 7/14/42 (*Beretning*, bilag IV, p. 199).
69. The reference here is to the overt press, as distinct from the underground press which played a decisive role in forging active Danish public resistance to the Germans. For details of the courageous, stubborn, and disciplined struggle of the overt press see Bindsløv, *op. cit.*
70. *Ibid.*, pp. 149 ff. The German apprehensions regarding Schoch were not unfounded—he was one of the key figures of the resistance movement. See Hæstrup, *Hemmelig Alliance, passim.*

71. Bindsløv, Chapter 4, note 14.
72. *Ibid.*, p. 150.
73. Gudme also gives evidence of this, *op. cit.*, p. 32.
74. Jürgen Schröder replaced Meissner a year later in the spring of 1943. Meissner was apparently a victim of the Foreign Ministry's purge of Luther's friends. He returned to Germany in April 1943 and from there was sent to the front (see on Rademacher in the Foreign Ministry Appendix below). Gudme, *op. cit.*, p. 36.
75. The Schalburg Corps formed a year later as a Danish S.S. force was named after him. See Chapter IV.
76. *Beretning*, bilag IV, p. 565.
77. *Ibid.* pp. 692–93.
78. This speech was apparently considered of such importance that it was published in full in *Fakta* (I, p. 205) and also by Frisch (I, pp. 381–83).
79. Fog, *Danmark Frit*, pp. 29–33. The speech was recorded, sent to England and broadcast from there on August 29.

CHAPTER IV

1. Cf. Hannah Arendt, *The Origins of Totalitarianism*, pp. 382, 452.
2. Cf. Chapter II, THE OCCUPATION AND ITS CHARACTERISTICS.
3. Flemming Muus, the British General Staff's representative in Denmark, tells in a book dedicated to his mother-in-law (who was seized while working for the resistance movement) of an incident demonstrating Best's suggestiveness while telling obvious lies and giving false arguments (Muus, *Monica Wichfeld*, pp. 145–46). Grundherr said of Best that "he lied courageously" when he reported Danish affairs to his superiors, and the comment was meant as a compliment and a sign of resistance to meaningless orders. See minutes of the talk, Yad Vashem 027/14.
4. See Appendix on Best's life below.
5. The bird is generally transformed into a canary. See P. Møller, *Kanariefuglen og Hitler;* David Lampe, *The Savage Canary;* Leistikow, *Foreign Affairs*, January 1943, p. 395.
6. Vertraulicher Bericht, 5/11/43, JM/2477.
7. Cf. Chapter II, THE OCCUPATION AND ITS CHARACTERISTICS.
8. H. R. Martinsen, "Da regering og Rigsdag sagde nej til tyskerne," *Det stod ikke i avisen*, p. 72.
9. Introduction to *Hvidbog*, p. 11.
10. Cf. Chapter II, THE OCCUPATION AND ITS CHARACTERISTICS. Hæstrup mentions this point in various places: "Let not the situation be misunderstood. The government was decidedly anti-Nazi. It acted out of opportunism, defeatism, and a sincere

wish to save the people from more suffering than necessary"
(*Exposé, European Resistance Movements*, p. 15). See also
Deutschland und der Norden, p. 7).

11. Hvidbog, p. 10.
12. In the various reports. Cf. Chapter II, notes 95, 97.
13. See Chapter II, THE OCCUPATION AND ITS CHARACTERISTICS.
14. See Chapter II, THE JEWISH QUESTION AND THE "TELEGRAM
    CRISIS" and BEST—IN RENTHE-FINK'S POLITICAL FOOTSTEPS.
15. "There were in fact no divergencies from the opinion that it
    would one day be impossible to avoid open resistance to Ger-
    many and that both from a moral and a political point of view
    it was desirable that the Danish people should take upon itself
    a large part of the burden of liberation. Opinions varied only
    as to the time and the form" (Peter Tabor, "Den Danske Presse
    under Besættelsen" in Frisch, II, p. 293).
16. The explanation of the French prosecutor at Nuremberg, Faure,
    that the behavior of the Germans in the first period was due to
    international considerations and to the hope of "Germanizing"
    Denmark from within through Nazi propaganda (IMT VI,
    p. 500) does not appear sufficiently plausible, though it was true
    that Ribbentrop was sensitive to international reaction to events
    in Denmark (see Chapter II, THE JEWISH QUESTION—A DANISH
    PROBLEM). Even less convincing is his view that the crisis of
    August 1943 was caused by "the disappointment of the Germans
    at the economic effort of the Danes" (*ibid.*, p. 506).
17. See RIIA, *Europe under Hitler*, p. 39.
18. Frisch, II, p. 24 (Jens Otto Krag, "Byerhvervene of krigsø-
    konomien").
19. Letter of Meissner to Luther, 5/12/42 (*Beretning*, bilag XIII,
    bind 2, p. 579): ". . . but it [i.e., Danish national socialism]
    lacks the great propelling impulse, which cannot be created as
    long as on the German side one is interested in insuring the
    economic cooperation between Denmark and Germany im-
    portant for us through cooperation with the coalition govern-
    ment."
20. Evidence, summary of talk, Yad Vashem 027/13.
21. Krag, *op. cit.*, p. 46, note 18. According to Gudme, *Denmark*,
    p. 153, Danish agriculture was, under normal conditions, cap-
    able of supporting an additional twelve million persons. Leistikow
    (*op. cit.*, pp. 349–50) emphasizes the damage caused to Danish
    agriculture by the loss of trade to England on the one hand
    and German exploitation on the other.
22. "Herr Backe [director of the Ministry of Food] has with this
    decision assumed that maintenance of Danish agriculture's
    production willingness and capacity is of such vital importance
    for Germany that everything in this sphere should be avoided

which might cause lasting damage and make difficult the efforts of the Reich plenipotentiary to reestablish orderly conditions" —AA.ST.S. Akten betreffend Dänemark vom 24.3.43 bis 31.10; 43, Bd.4, JM/2470. The role of the director of the German Food Ministry at the height of the crisis will be referred to again in this work.

23. NG–3918, reprinted in *Beretning*, bilag XIII, bind 2, pp. 702–03, and translated into English in *Documents on International Affairs*, Vol. II, *Hitler's Europe*, "Denmark," pp. 219–21.

24. Best himself summed up the duties assigned to him in a six-month report (NO–1722). Reprinted in part in *Beretning, ibid.*, pp. 817 ff. and in Best's defense statement: "Die Deutsche Politik in Dänemark während der letzten 2½ Kriegsjahre," p. 11, Yad Vashem, 027/15 (photocopy)—hereafter "Die Deutsche Politik. . . ."

25. These were handwritten notes of Himmler in preparation for his talks with Hitler. They were found in the Document Center in Berlin and have in the meantime apparently been removed to the archives in Coblenz. They are also registered in the State Archives in Copenhagen. The note mentioned here is from 10/22/42 and is only partly relevant to our subject as follows: "Note for the Führer . . . conditions in Denmark (in meantime do not suggest anything)." The Danish registration is 7771 DC APO 742A, Rigsarkiv, Pk. 443, Box 19, Dan 195.

26. Berger was the head of the *S.S.-Hauptamt*. The letter was from Himmler's field headquarters, marked "Secret," and made out in two copies. The text ran as follows:

"Dear Berger:
  "After discussing the matter with the Führer, I can say on the situation in Denmark that no acute changes in any direction should be reckoned with. The main thesis is that the Danish government be allowed to continue to commit its sins. I ask you to keep this strictly secret. Clausen may unhesitatingly be informed that I am very little pleased with his political attitude toward Lieutenant-General Gørtz with the departure of the Danish Free Corps. One cannot exercise politics through impulses and atmosphere, one must also do something with one's head. As for the new plenipotentiary, I think that there is nothing to say as yet. I consider it best that no one with full powers come at all. . . ."

Tillægsekstrakt IV to hovedekstrakt A 109–Ad forhold II "Diverse" Bil. 26, pp. 83 ff. We see here that Himmler did not know in advance of Best's appointment (see Appendix on Best) and even opposed the appointment of a new German plenipotentiary.

27. Cf. Best's letter to Himmler of 8/10/42, *ibid.*, Appendix; S.S. man Boysen in Copenhagen wrote to Berger on 11/9/42: "*Gruppenführer* Best has orders to remove the Buhl government and form the Scavenius government legally. Both actions have been carried out in the course of 3 days" (bil. A 70, p. 64).

28. Talk with Grundherr, *ibid.*

29. The conflict assumed prominence from January 1943 on: see *Beretning*, bilag XIII, 2. bind, pp. 787–90; XIV, 5. bind, pp. 510–11. Hanneken already demands here the disbanding of the Danish army. See memorandum of Best from 1/23/48 (bil. A. 68); his relations with Hanneken, telegram No. 277 of 3/13/43 (bil. B. 19, pp. 2–3): "I repeat that according to General von Hanneken's own utterances, he is striving to become supreme military commander in Denmark on the pattern of the military heads in Paris and Brussels." On 5/13 he quotes a coarse remark by Hanneken, *ibid.*, p. 12. The conflict between the two is also one of character: Best himself reported to Berlin on the Danish radio broadcast from London, which voiced a warning against both and made reference to the differences in their characters. The full text is in Himmler Files, Roll 7, Folder 56, abbreviated in *Beretning*, bilag XIII, bind 2, pp. 828–30. See also La Cour, I, p. 352, and telegram No. 750 of 6/21/43 (AA.ST.S.). Hanneken was a brutal type. The Germans themselves sentenced him to eight years of hard labor for embezzlement (La Cour, *ibid.*), but instead of serving his time he was sent to the front. On 4/12/43 an agreement was reached between him and Best regarding their respective spheres of authority, the clauses being quoted in Best's cable No. 743 of 6/18/43, in which he complains of new encroachments by Hanneken: NG–5115; AA.ST.S.

30. Manifestations of this policy were personal contacts and the visit to the crown prince (La Cour, *ibid.*; H. Hansen, pp. 135–36).

31. Frisch, I, pp. 290–91; La Cour, *ibid.* Five days after this speech Best spoke with Luther in Berlin on the problem of the Jews in Denmark. See Chapter II, note 138.

32. Frisch, I, p. 290; *Hvidbog*, II, p. 440.

33. "Die Deutsche Politik . . . ," p. 11.

34. Named after the commander of the volunteer corps who fell on the Eastern front. See Chapter III, THE STRUGGLE AGAINST THE "PURGE." On the corps, see La Cour, I, p. 222, II, p. 475.

35. Frisch, I, p. 305. Typical of the behavior of the Danes in their relations with the Germans was the way in which they raised the question—by the way and without explicitly asking their permission to hold the elections on the fixed date. In a party also attended by Best, Scavenius began to discuss the matter

loudly with a number of ministers while Best stood nearby. As anticipated, Best joined the discussion—and in this way the question was "put before" the Germans (Frisch, I, p. 279).

36. Frisch, I, p. 301. On the election results, See Chapter III, NATIONAL SOCIALISM IN OCCUPIED DENMARK.

37. This process is dealt with by Frisch, I, pp. 311, 319 ff; Møller, *Un Peuple Se Réveille*, p. 103; Leistikow, *Foreign Affairs*, January 1943, pp. 345–46. The latter describes the situation according to his own lights and he therefore exaggerates in talking of the people's spirit of resistance in the first years. It is regrettable that his information, highly erroneous as it was, was relied upon by Lemkin and others. From January to August 1943 the number of monthly acts of sabotage rose from 14 to 198. For a list of the incidents month by month, see *Fakta*, II, pp. 1201 ff.

38. See Scavenius, p. 176; Frisch, I, pp. 314–15, II, p. 245.

39. Frisch, I, pp. 291–92.

40. See Frisch, I, p. 320.

41. The same had already occurred on the 9th of August in Esbjerg (*ibid.*, p. 319).

42. See *ibid.*, p. 312. Frisch relies here on the explanation given by Best himself after the war during his cross-examination in the Copenhagen prison. See dokumentarisk tillæg, *ibid.*, p. 400. A more comprehensive survey of Best's view is to be found in the defense statement "Die Deutsche Politik . . . ," pp. 30–34.

43. Letter of Best to Himmler, 4/3/43 (Document Center, Best file). On the affair itself, related to the acquisition of police for Best, see below.

44. Investigation in Copenhagen bil. A 71. In this letter Himmler acknowledges receipt of two of Best's letters, from the 20th and 22nd of December, 1942, a Christmas present of schnapps, and a report. The letter expresses Himmler's approval of Best's actions and promises him full support.

45. NP–1722. Best sent Himmler a copy of his first half-yearly report to the Foreign Ministry. Himmler's reply 5/14/43 refers to Best's letter of 4/3/43 and the report sent on 5/5/43. For Best's visit to Himmler, cf. Chapter II, BEST—IN RENTHE–FINK'S POLITICAL FOOTSTEPS.

46. See Himmler's notes (see note 25) referring to this talk with Hitler mentioned here (Rigsarkiv, Pk. 443, Box 19, Dan. 193).

47. This telegram of Best is not available, but part of it is quoted in a later telegram No. 1287 of 10/21, which shows that the state of emergency plan was at first prepared through agreement between Hanneken and Best. "Sabotagebekämpfung in Dänemark. Abstellung eines Polizeibataillons, 1942–1944." Inl. II 78; Yad Vashem 027/12.

48. Document Center, Best file. It transpires from the letter that Best sent another report in this vein to the Foreign Ministry on 8/21, but this has not yet been traced.

49. Best himself described the incident in his various declarations, particularly in "Die Deutsche Politik . . . ," pp. 36–39, where he also gives new details on the reports of Hanneken to Hitler, which led to the Führer's outburst.

50. Frisch, I, pp. 327; the full text, *ibid.*, dokumentarisk tillæg, pp. 394–95.

51. *Ibid.*, p. 324. It has unfortunately not been possible to acquire the full text of Buhl's speech.

52. The degree of absurdity attained by the legends about the king is illustrated by a story told by M. Ansbacher, now working in Yad Vashem, who heard from Danish Jews in Theresienstadt that the king was under arrest in his palace because he had refused to abandon his Jewish subjects to their fate.

53. See Frisch, III, pp. 7–14.

54. "I beg to inform the government that its authority is suspended, with the assumption of executive power by the German army" (*Hvidbog*, I, p. 174).

55. Frisch, III, *passim.*

56. On evaluation of the policy of negotiation, see the introduction by Mogens Fog in *Hvidbog*, p. 12; Scavenius, p. 198; Frisch, II, p. 246 (Oluf Carlsson: "Socialdemokrati under Besættelsen").

57. Carlsson, *loc. cit.*

58. Hæstrup, *Hemmelig Alliance*, I, pp. 23–97.

59. Frisch, III, *ibid.*

60. From 9/15/43 on, a frenzied correspondence took place between the director-general of the Ministry of Food and his counterpart in the Foreign Ministry regarding the urgent need for renewing the agreement on the sale of Danish agricultural produce to Germany. The figures given in these documents are very instructive. Der Reichsminister für Ernährung und Landwirtschaft B4–950, 9/22/43, AA.ST.S. Vortragsnotiz Nr. 46, gez. Schnurre, 9/23/43 (see note 22). All the documents: AA.ST.S. In the course of the economic negotiations, O. van Scherpenberg, a Foreign Ministry representative in the German delegation, had a long talk with Svenningsen—see Chapter V, DEPORTATION—A PLAN GOES WRONG; O. van Scherpenberg, Ha Pol. 6006/43g II, 9/28/43; Aufzeichnung 10/31/43.

61. Also laid down in advance in the Best-Hanneken plan (see note 47).

62. Three meetings took place: 9/14/43, 10/2/43, and 10/10/43. Of the meeting on 10/2 it was said that it was much affected by the persecution of the Jews that had taken place that day but whose scope and consequences were as yet unknown

(*Beretning*, bilag VII, bind 1, p. 331). See Mildner's statement on 3/29/46 (PS–2377, p. 4): "Cooperation with the Danish police, an agreement with whom was being worked out, would now stop of itself." On Mildner, see below.

63. See note 9; Mogens Fog, *Danmark Frit*, pp. 34 ff. (written in November 1943); Christmas Møller, *Fakta*, II, p. 1272, 9/19/43; on the divergent conceptions of the police and the resistance movement, see Hæstrup, *Hemmelig Alliance*, I, p. 62.
64. See Frisch, III, p. 49 (chapter on Jewish persecutions).
65. Best's trial, *Beretning*, bilag XIII, bind 2, pp. 190, 206–07, 222–23, 239–40; bilag III, pp. 1373–74.
66. Inl. IIg. 54/8; NG–3923.
67. See below on Duckwitz's activity. Regarding the general view that Best opposed the persecutions, see: La Cour, II, p. 28; *De fem lange Aar*, II, pp. 588 ff; A. Vigen, *Erik Scavenius*, p. 101; Per Møller, *Kanariefuglen*, pp. 186–87 and especially the French edition, p. 147.
68. See Best's statement, *Beretning*, bilag XIII, bind 2, p. 206; Frisch, I, aktstykker, p. 401.
69. The Copenhagen court did not accept Best's excuses and laid down on 9/20/48 that Best initiated the persecutions, although "he tried to limit the consequences as far as possible" (*Beretning*, bilag XIII, bind 1, p. 223). The District Court to which appeal was made annulled the verdict on 7/18/49, thus acquitting Best (*ibid.*, pp. 239–40).
70. Coming back to the verdict of the Copenhagen court, we do not intend to criticize the District Court's decisions; we have reached our conclusion after examining documents, some of which were not available to the court, as will be seen below.
71. IMT XXXVIII, Doc. 901–RF, p. 625.
72. His evidence was heard on 7/31/46; printed in *Beretning*, bilag XIII, bind 3, p. 1394; IMT XX, pp. 135–36.
73. S.D. commander Mildner was sent to Copenhagen to head the special police battalions dispatched there in September. For his duties, see below. The statement of evidence of 6/22/45– Eichmann trial T/585; the extracts relevant to this study were raised in the cross-examination of Ribbentrop, *Beretning*, as in note 72, p. 1387; IMT X, p. 397. The same subject is dealt with in his third statement on 3/29/46–see note 62; second statement, see below, note 75.
74. IMT XLI, pp. 164–67.
75. *Ibid.*, para. 6, p. 166. Already in Mildner's second statement of 11/16/45–PS–2375 (English translation in NCA V, p. 2)– there are no longer any accusations against Ribbentrop. See also IMT XVIII, p. 405; the third statement of 3/29/46 (PS–2377), see note 62. Cf. also IMT XI, pp. 226–27, 254–55.

76. *Beretning,* as in note 65, pp. 206–07. For all evidence and memoranda of Best on persecution of the Jews, see below, note 106.
77. See Duckwitz's evidence in Copenhagen (NG–5208), and his memoirs (Yad Vashem 027/14).
78. IMT XX, p. 153.
79. IMT XII, p. 177, 311/2: "If more evidence is required to prove that falsehood is a constant and invariable companion of crime among the Hitlerites, the false testimonies of . . . Best and others can serve as convincing illustrations. These 'witnesses' in their effort to whitewash the criminal organizations, of which they were the leading members, reached the height of absurdity."
80. Memorandum of Best on the influence of the Foreign Ministry on the situation in Denmark, Copenhagen investigations, bil. A 68; *Fakta,* II, p. 1388; Frisch, I, pp. 312, 326; II, p. 294; Copenhagen evidence 8/31/45–bil. A. 35, p. 19; "Die Deutsche Politik . . . ," p. 41; see also Appendix on Best in this work. Cf. Best's declaration of 4/14/48 (see note 103).
81. Document Center, Best file. Cf. note 48.
82. IMT VI, p. 508.
83. *Beretning,* bilag XIV, bind 1, p. 206; Frisch, I, aktstykker, p. 398 (cross-examination of 8/1/45).
84. "Die Deutsche Politik . . . ," p. 59; memorandum of 1/23/48, p. 3; see also NG–5036. On the position of the HSSPF and Himmler's use of him, see H. Buchheim, "Die Höheren SS-und Polizei-führer," *Vierteljahrsschrift für Zeitgeschichte,* 11. Jhrg., 1963, 4. Heft, Oktober, pp. 362–91. "Skat" is a German card game with three players.
85. Because of the importance of the letter in another connection also, its full text is given here. The exact date does not appear on the copy available, but it was apparently written in the early days of October. It was also Himmler's reply to Best's letters dated 8/22 and 8/30 and others written during September, which will be discussed in Chapter V.

"October 1943
"Field Headquarters

"My dear Best!

"First of all my thanks for your various letters and telegrams. I have followed the general developments in Denmark, which after all have not been extremely good of late. The solution of Clausen joining the *Waffen S.S.* as a doctor I find particularly good. Development of the Schalburg Corps is important. Equally important is the Jewish action. This will raise dust for a time, but all in all will remove the most important saboteurs and agitators. When the state of emergency ends, S.S. *Gruppen-führer* Pancke will be appointed *Höherer S.S.-und Polizei-*

führer. I think it is unnecessary to waste more words but to say that cooperation between you will be highly harmonious, and I am convinced that herewith much will be greatly eased. You must show yourself big enough not to take it amiss that I have not made the HSSPF your subordinate. The organizational form is better this way.

"Yours, H. H."

Tillægsekstrakt nr. 3 til hovedrapport A (Werner Best), bil. A 73, p. 1; Inl. IIg 78, Dänemark, Sabotagebekämpfung in Dänemark, Abstellung eines Polizei-Bataillons von 1942 bis 1944.

86. See note 47.
87. Telegram No. 326 (AA.ST.S.). On 3/25 Berger wrote to Himmler and directed his attention to Hanneken's manipulations (Himmler files, *ibid.*).
88. Telegram of consul Geiger to Wagner and transfer order (Inl. IIg 78); see also NG–4562. In this matter Best got into difficulties through trying to play both games: through Kanstein he approached the chief of police in Germany to make sure of the battalion. Geiger revealed this to Ribbentrop (3/25/43, *ibid.*). Ribbentrop was naturally angry and demanded an explanation from Best, who did his best to find excuses (Rintelen's telegram of 4/2/43, *ibid.*). Ribbentrop's reply, though it contained a sharp rebuke, was nevertheless more positive toward the matter itself (4/6/43, *ibid.*). Ribbentrop demanded to know whether the Danish government would agree to this step. On 4/8/43 Best reported (No. 403, *ibid.*) Scavenius's agreement on the condition that the public would be subjected to certain diversionary tactics. If Best did not distort Scavenius's words, this meant that the latter had approved a dangerous and fateful measure. Thereafter, Ribbentrop agreed to the transfer of the battalion (Geiger's telegram of 4/12/43, *ibid.*). After this experience, Best asked Himmler in his letter of 5/5/43 not to reveal to Ribbentrop that he had received Best's report; see above, notes 24, 43 (NO–1722).
89. Telegram No. 507, 5/3/43, *ibid.*
90. *Ibid.;* NG–5918. The battalion itself arrived in Copenhagen only on 5/13 (telegram No. 590, 5/14/43). See also TWC, Nr. IV, Case 11, Final Brief Against the Defendant, G. A. Steengracht von Moyland, pp. 5, 26.
91. See "Die Deutsche Politik . . . ," p. 39: "The foreign minister of the Reich in the meantime asked him to remain at his post. The point was that the recall of the Reich plenipotentiary would undoubtedly lead to the introduction of a Reich commissar or of military rule. Denmark would thus be removed from German foreign policy and its sovereignty suspended. If, on the other hand, the plenipotentiary—perhaps temporarily

suspended by the military state of emergency—stayed at his post, all the political possibilities would still remain open. Dr. Best yielded to these arguments and returned to Copenhagen on [the] 27th [of] August, 1943."

92. Best's telegrams: No. 995, 996 (8/30); No. 1001 (9/1). Ribbentrop's telegrams: No. 1294 (8/31); 1296 (9/1)—*Beretning,* bilag XIII, bind 2, pp. 922–29.

93. Berichte und Meldungen zur Entwicklung der Lage in Dänemark, Januar 1943 bis September 1944, Inl. II, 352 g.

94. Telegrams No. 989 (8/29), No. 1000 (8/31), in *Beretning,* as in note 92, pp. 916–17, NG–5185; No. 1002 (9/1), NG–5103; No. 1034 (9/8), NG–5106; No. 1039, 9/9, AA.ST.S. Best's attempts to give prominence to his own efficiency were supported by the Foreign Ministry—see memorandum of Deputy Director-General Hencke of 9/2/43 (AA.ST.S.), where he endeavors to show that only Best—in whom the Danes have confidence—is capable of repairing the damage done by Hanneken. The same objectives are clearly present in the letter of the director-general of the Food Ministry, Backe (see note 22).

95. No. 1010, NG–5192; Inl. IIg, 352.

96. Telegram No. 1023, *Beretning,* as in note 90, pp. 930–31.

97. See note 92.

98. Ribbentrop's telegram No. 1294—see note 92.

99. For these complicated negotiations, see Frisch, III, pp. 28–40; La Cour, *Danmarks Historie, 1940–45,* pp. 110–27; Hæstrup, *Til Landets Bedste,* pp. 78–124.

100. The extract from telegram No. 1102 of 9/20 runs as follows: "STEPS SHOULD NOW BE TAKEN IN THE EVENT OF A CONSTITUTIONAL DANISH GOVERNMENT NO LONGER BEING FORMED, WHICH I ASSERT WILL BE THE CASE WHEN . . . AND IF THE DEPORTATION OF JEWS FROM DENMARK IS CARRIED OUT, SINCE IN THE SITUATION THAT WILL ARISE IN DENMARK NO ONE WILL ACCEPT POLITICAL RESPONSIBILITY" (*Beretning,* as in note 90, p. 934). I here differ from Hæstrup's interpretation; he thinks that Best was genuinely interested in having a legal Danish government installed. Cf. *op. cit.,* pp. 93, 126 f.

101. See photocopy on p. 100.

102. NG–3923; *Beretning,* bilag XIII, bind 3, pp. 1373–74; Inl. II. 54/8.

103. "Die Deutsche Politik . . . ," pp. 46–48; declaration of 4/14/48 in Nuremberg, Best trial (Tillægsekstrakt IV til Hovedekstrakt A).

104. Telegrams Nos. 988, 990, 991, 995, 996, 997, 1001 in *Beretning* (as in note 102), *passim.*

105. Of 8/5/46, found among material of Copenhagen trial but without any NG number.

106. All his seven statements of evidence and declarations on the persecution of the Jews: the cross-examinations in Copenhagen: 8/1/45; 8/31/45; 6/28/46 (IMT XLI, pp. 164–67); 7/31/46 (IMT XX, pp. 135–36); 8/23/48, Copenhagen memorandum (bil. 68, pp. 39–40); 4/14/48 (Best trial, as note 103); "Die Deutsche Politik . . . ," pp. 46–48.
107. See talk with Grundherr, Yad Vashem 027/14 and Grundherr's statement on behalf of Best (Til. Extr. IV, bil. 17); and the Appendix on the German Foreign Ministry.
108. In a memorandum of 1/23/48 Best dwells in detail on the question of German Foreign Ministry influence on events in Denmark. Cf. note 80.
109. Declaration of 4/14/48; "Die Deutsche Politik . . . ," p. 47.
110. A copy of this evidence and the documents mentioned in Chapter II were received from the Danish legal authorities. Sonnleithner too was a veteran National Socialist and his career was similar to that of Best. He came from Austria, where he worked in the police from 1929–34 and then joined the Coding Department of the Chancellor's Office. In 1938 he was condemned for treason on behalf of the NSDAP to six years' hard labor. After the annexation of Austria, he worked in the Reich Commissioner's Office in Vienna and from there was transferred to the Foreign Ministry. It may be assumed that he was as good a liar as Best.
111. His name was Dr. Aschenbacher (evidence of Sonnleithner, p. 6).
112. *Ibid.*, p. 3.
113. His name was Dr. Brenner; see declaration of 4/14/48, paragraph 1.
114. Inl. IIg 54/8. Published in *Beretning*, bilag XIII, bind 3, p. 1375; cf. Hilberg, p. 360, note 57.
115. Best seized upon Jodl's evidence at Nuremberg to prove that the decision was made by Himmler and Hitler ("Die Deutsche Politik . . . ," p. 47). Jodl talks of a meeting in which he claims he did not participate (IMT VI, p. 322; XV, p. 311–12; XIX, pp. 35–36). All the material is in *Beretning*, as in note 114, pp. 1389–94. It may be assumed that Jodl meant another meeting on the subject, which took place on 9/21 (see Chapter V, THE STATE OF EMERGENCY AND ITS PROBLEMS). In his evidence of 4/14/48 (paragraph 6), when he still did not know how many documents were available, Best asserted that he never received an official reply to telegram No. 1032 (*ibid.*). But the telegram of 9/17 begins: "WITH REFERENCE TO YOUR TELE-GRAPHIC REPORT 1032 OF 9/8. . . ." (No. 1265, Inl. II 54/8, NG–5121). The document is marked as acknowledged on 9/16. The fact that this telegram was second in the file and the order

of telegrams in the Nuremberg trial led Hilberg in error to think that the telegram of Sonnleithner (note 114) was the first and the decision had been made only on 9/18.

116. Inl. IIg 54/8. This information raises the additional query of how Sonnleithner saw Best's telegram, 1032, for the first time at Nuremberg.

117. *Ibid.*

118. *Ibid.*

119. According to a letter of 3/21/62 from Grundherr to the author: "That all attempts to establish my position have, to my *great* regret, been without result, is strange, to put it mildly, and I and others have our own ideas about this 'disappearance act.'"

120. His evidence, *ibid.*, p. 2.

121. See below, Chapter 5, THE STATE OF EMERGENCY AND ITS PROBLEMS.

122. On the attitude of the army to the persecutions, see below.

123. "Die Deutsche Politik . . . ," p. 43.

124. His diaries, 9/8/43, pp. 388–89. The date itself is interesting!

125. *Ibid.*, p. 442.

126. Document Center, Best file.

127. La Cour states that during the discussion on the future form of government in Denmark, the groups close to National Socialism used the argument that if the Danes did not form a government which they regarded with favor, a German administration under Himmler's inspiration would be set up and this would "introduce the Nuremberg laws, abolish the Freemason lodges, etc." (*Danmarks Historie*, p. 116). It is interesting that in his telegram Best used the same formula, "the Jews and the Freemasons." It is clear that these groups had objectives in Danish policy different from Best. Still, the parallel language may be a coincidence.

128. As late as 9/17 Best requested (in telegram No. 1081, dealing with termination of the state of emergency) a decision regarding his proposals in telegram 1001 (AA.ST.S.).

129. Best announced his arrival in telegram No. 1058 (AA.ST.S.). It is noteworthy that Hoffmann, who was on his way to take office in Paris, was taken out of the train and sent to Denmark, i.e., something unexpected occurred here and arrangements were made in haste—his evidence (NG–5208).

130. Inl. IIg 78. The decision accordingly was made on 9/13—see preceding note.

131. *Hvidbog*, II, p. 56; however, he returned to Kattowitz again and arrived in Copenhagen finally on 9/19—Best reported this in his telegram No. 1097 of 9/20/43. (AA.ST.S.; cf. NG–5106). According to Mildner's evidence, he was appointed on 9/15 (IMT, PS–2375). Cf. notes 62, 73.

132. The telegram form of No. 1001 also contains Grundherr's comment of 9/3: "Being dealt with by higher party: B. Ritter—OKW, Wagner mit RFSS."
133. "Die Deutsche Politik . . . ," pp. 59, 62.
134. Best reported on the arrival of the battalions in telegrams No. 1071, 9/16/43 (AA.ST.S.); No. 1072, 9/16, *ibid.*, NG–3974; No. 1073, 9/16 (Inl. IIg 352); AA.ST.S.; NG–5147; movement order of 9/20 of the security police (Inl. IIg 78); telegram No. 1112, 9/22 (AA.ST.S.); No. 1118, 9/23, *ibid.*; announcement of the security police in Norway, 9/29 (Inl. IIg 78).
135. See Appendix on Best.
136. Kanstein stated under examination in Copenhagen on 4/29/47 that if Best had proposed persecutions, he would certainly not have informed him, Kanstein, since he knew his opposition: "The witness and Best knew that the Jewish problem at that time was a very sensitive one and that Berlin only required a hint from the plenipotentiary to go to work (NG–5208). Karl Heinz Hoffmann similarly claimed, in his evidence at the same place, that Dr. Best was evasive when he, Hoffmann, expressed opposition to the action. Another S.D. man, Hans Wäsche, said on 5/12/47 (in Copenhagen): "The witness does not remember who told him that Best had, for purely political reasons, suggested and demanded the Jewish action in order to strengthen his political position, and that Best was afraid that others in Copenhagen would make such a demand first. The situation was such that the action against the Jews, which was so important a step, was keenly debated by the German leaders and the assertion arose from someone or other that it was Best who had, for the above reasons, demanded the action. . . . The witness explained that he had formed the following theories regarding the motives that had probably impelled Dr. Best to request the action against the Jews: With what had occurred on 8/29/43, Best had seen his policy in Denmark completely destroyed and he himself broke down. He had thought that a consequence of [the] 29th [of] August might be that someone or other would demand action against the Jews, and that he knew who and from where; but if Best himself demanded the action, he could better put his counterstroke into effect."
137. "Die Deutsche Politik . . . ," pp. 41 ff.; "Der Zweifrontkampf vom 29.8.1943–5.5.1945."

CHAPTER V

1. This talk is mentioned both in Frisch, III, p. 50, and La Cour, *Danmarks Historie*, II, p. 136. Both rely on the description by

Duckwitz himself, given under examination in Copenhagen on 5/13/47 (NG–5208) as an appendix; see also his memoirs, Yad Vashem 027/14.

2. The most reliable account is Hedtoft's introduction to Bertelsen's *October 43;* see also Frisch, III, p. 52. Duckwitz's action is mentioned and praised by all who were engaged in the rescue of the Danish Jews. See Chapter II, notes 27 and 143.

3. Evidence: NG–5208. On the connection between Duckwitz and the Danes, see Tage Taaning, "Rigsdagen og Politikerne," *Danmarks Frihedskamp II,* pp. 569, 573; also Frisch, I, p. 326; III, *loc. cit.,* note 1. The meeting was also mentioned by Ekblad in a description of the events sent to the author on 1/22/58– Yad Vashem, 027/13.

4. According to Frisch, *loc. cit.,* he was a friend of Gregor Strasser and for a time worked for Rosenberg.

5. This transpires from Duckwitz in the above sources. Best himself also asserts this in "Die Deutsche Politik . . . ," p. 51, but this evidence should be regarded with suspicion, since Best's main aim is here to justify himself.

6. Memoirs.

7. On the other hand, both Frisch and La Cour (see note 1) are doubtful of the truth of Best's assertion and stress the rivalry between him and Hanneken and the need for him to strengthen his position vis-à-vis the central German authorities.

8. Memoirs.

9. See Chapter IV, BEST'S RESPONSIBILITY. Duckwitz relates that during his visit to Deputy Director Hencke, they were informed by telephone that Ribbentrop had already passed on Best's telegram to Hitler, although he himself was opposed to deportation of the Jews. This is not confirmed by any other source.

10. Declaration of 4/14/48, para. 5; "Die Deutsch Politik . . . ," p. 51. Best, who appeared as a witness in various German courts, even claimed that he himself warned a "prominent Dane," but he mentioned no name.

11. Duckwitz's memoirs, and see Chapter IV, note 115.

12. See NG–5208.

13. On the action of the Swedish government, see Chapter IX.

14. Both Ekblad and Duckwitz confirm this in their personal reports, Yad Vashem, *op. cit.*

15. According to an original, though later erased, comment in the declaration of Höss, the commandant of Auschwitz, Mildner had invented a special method of torture: IMT XXXIII, 3868–PS, p. 278, note.

16. See Appendix on Best and Chapter IV, notes 62, 73, 75.

17. First declaration of 6/22/45.
18. Cf. Chapter IV, note 62. His evidence is confirmed by a memorandum of Grundherr of 9/21, Inl. II, 54/8; Eichmann trial T/579; reprinted in *Beretning*, XIII, bind 3, p. 1378.
19. This transpires from another memorandum of Grundherr dated 9/24: "The commander of the security police and S.D., S.S. *Standartenführer* Dr. Mildner, is flying to Berlin tomorrow to report to the *Reichsführer* S.S." (Inl. IIg 78).
20. See evidence of Kanstein and Hanneken: NG–5208.
21. IMT XXXV, Doc. 547–D, p. 151. The text of the telegram was passed on by Barandon to the Foreign Ministry. Reprinted in *Beretning*, bilag XIII, bind 3, p. 1377.
22. Reitlinger, *The Final Solution*, p. 349.
23. NOKW 356; see Chapter IV, note 115.
24. NOKW *ibid.*; additional explanations below. The discussion begins with telegram No. 1001 on 9/1; see also Nos. 1017, 9/4 (AA.ST.S.); 1023, 9/6 (*Beretning*, bilag XIII, bind 2, p. 931); 1043, 9/10 (AA.ST.S.); 1051, 9/13 (AA.ST.S.); and of course No. 1032.
25. *Beretning*, bilag IV, pp. 383–84.
26. AA.ST.S. and see telephone conversation of 9/22 (NOKW 356), and below, note 40.
27. Best's telegram No. 1081, 9/17 (AA.ST.S.).
28. See No. 1027, 9/16 (Inl. IIg 78). Added is a comment of "B" dated 9/17 that the whole of telegram 1001 was discussed with the OKW and with Himmler. On the same subject, telegram No. 1037 (Inl. II 352); and cf. telegram No. 1080, 9/17 (AA.ST.S.).
29. NG–5121; see Chapter IV, note 115.
30. No. 1094, 9/18/43, *Beretning*, bilag XIII, bind 3, pp. 1375–76.
31. Announcement of OKW, No. 005431/43, quoted in Best's telegram, no number, AA.ST.S.
32. Himmler, personal note, No. 192, 9/20/43: "Report to Führer . . . II. Recruiting in Denmark-Norway." See Chapter IV, note 25.
33. No. 1482, NG–4806; AA.ST.S.
34. See Heiber, *Hitler's Lagebesprechungen*.
35. This would seem to be the meeting referred to by Jodl—see notes 23, 31.
36. Himmler's sharp reaction is borne out by various accounts of his attitude to Best after this period. See declaration of Anton Dunkern, 6/3/48, cross-examination in Copenhagen: tillægsekstrakt IV til Hovedekstrakt A bil. 27.
37. Announcement of OKW, No. 662333/43, in various places: NG–5208; IMT XXXV, p. 152; *Beretning*, bilag XIII, bind 3,

pp. 1378–79. Note that (2) states explicitly that the police battalions were transferred to Denmark to carry out deportation of the Jews.

38. Himmler's notes of that day, 9/22, state (*ibid.*, No. 191): "Talk to Keitel and others: Denmark, prisoners, Jews and HSSPF."

39. Notes from telephone conversation: NOKW–356. Jodl also phoned—due to the urgency of the matter, as he himself said—to headquarters in Denmark, (IMT XV, pp. 311–12).

40. No. 662345/43 (NOKW–356). The same day Best also received, via Wagner (telegram No. 1309) official notification of the army order (Inl. II 54/8).

41. Declaration of Berger at Nuremberg, 4/27/48; examination in Copenhagen—"Diverse," bil. 27; Berger's letter to Himmler, 9/26/43 (Himmler's Files, Roll 7, Folder 56).

42. Best wrote on this matter twice, the first time being on 9/23 in telegram No. 1119 (AA.ST.S.), where he corrects the exaggerated figures and puts the number of the arrested—officers and men—at five thousand. After receipt of new official notices from the army via the Foreign Ministry (OKW 005713/43, 9/27, AA.ST.S.), he sent a long telegram, No. 1156 (AA.ST.S.) on 9/29. Here he describes the reaction of the public and the serious situation created by the action: "SINCE THE MAJORITY OF THE NATIONAL SERVICEMEN ARE FARMERS' SONS, THE DANISH FARMERS, WHO UNTIL NOW HAVE BEEN LITTLE AFFECTED BY EVENTS, WILL NOW FOR THE FIRST TIME BE UPSET AND THIS WILL HAVE AN ADVERSE EFFECT ON AGRICULTURAL PRODUCTION." It should be recalled that at the time negotiations were going on for a new supply agreement between Denmark and Germany (see below, DEPORTATION—A PLAN GOES WRONG.) The views of the army, which were shared by the S.S., were set forth in a long telegram by headquarters in Denmark on 9/25 (IMT XXXV, pp. 154–56).

43. Inl. II, 54/8 (for photocopy, see pp. 162–3).

44. See note 30.

45. Verdict, in *Beretning*, bilag XIII, bind 1, p. 240. See Chapter IV, BEST'S RESPONSIBILITY.

46. In this connection, there is an interesting comment by Berger, in the letter to Himmler mentioned in note 41, on the 4,000 troops: "If we now interfere in this affair, we will in the *last resort have to assume responsibility* and I ask *Reichsführer S.S.* to dissociate himself from the matter" (author's italics).

47. In his notes for the talk with Hitler (see note 32) Himmler also wrote "HSSPF" and it may be assumed that he obtained Hitler's assent to his suggestion on the spot.

48. Ribbentrop presumably knew of Pancke's appointment at that

time, even though we have no such evidence. On 10/2 Ritter wrote to Steengracht on behalf of Ribbentrop: "1. The foreign minister rejects in principle and categorically that the head of a Foreign Ministry mission undertakes an additional function involving the receipt of instructions from another party. . . . Thadden's memorandum that Dr. Best himself be appointed to HSSPF must therefore be finally and decisively rejected" (Inl. IIg 352, Botschafter Ritter Nr. 437). The reference is to a memorandum by Thadden of 9/29 (reprinted in Tillægsekstrakt til Forhild V, pp. 16 ff). On the other hand, at the time the first police battalion was dispatched in May 1943, Ribbentrop laid down that it be subordinate to Best (see Chapter IV, ESTABLISHMENT OF THE POLICE FORCE). Himmler's view is clear from his letter to Best (see Chapter IV, note 85). This letter was written during the state of emergency and possibly before the deportation action (perhaps on 1st or 2nd of October).

49. Inl. II 54/8.
50. Inl. II, *ibid.*; NG–5121.
51. Duckwitz's memoirs, *op. cit.*
52. Hannah Arendt, *Eichmann in Jerusalem*, p. 156, points out that Best traveled to Berlin to insure the transfer of the Jews to Theresienstadt, but she does not quote any source for this assertion.
53. The acts of sabotage providing the pretext occurred on 9/27 in Jutland—see *Fra Passiv til Aktiv Modstand*, p. 214. On the announcement and its relationship to events in Danish eyes, see *ibid.*, pp. 216 ff.
54. No. 1156 (AA.ST.S.).
55. Throughout those days Best constantly urged the German Foreign Ministry to approve the other powers requested in his telegram No. 1001, as may be seen from telegrams No. 1138 and 1139 of 9/27, in which he requests high-ranking officials and the establishment of a special court under his presidency (AA.ST.S.).
56. Microfilms of SKL's reports in the State Archives in Copenhagen: Sp. 8, 6571.
57. *Ibid.*, 6578, 9/29, paras. 3–7. Cf. *ibid.*, 6527/28.
58. Ritter's telegram to Best, No. 1463 of 9/19 (Inl. II 78; NG–5105); Best's reply, No. 1099 of 9/20 (AA.ST.S.) in which Best reports on the army's opposition to his plan.
59. Telegram No. 1163 (NG–5105).
60. NG–5105; Inl. II 54/8.
61. AA.ST.S.; the same day (10/1), Best sent Ribbentrop another explanatory telegram, No. 1181 (Inl. II 54/8).
62. Schnellbrief, Inl. II 54/8; Eichmann Trial, T/580.

63. No. 1144 of 9/28 (NG–5121).
64. Cf. declaration of 4/14/48, para. 6, and also his evidence in Copenhagen on 8/31/45, where he claims that he was merely an "observer" (Hovedrapporter 1A35, pp. 19–20); "Die Deutsche Politik . . . ," p. 51.
65. See evidence of Arthur Henriques, Yad Vashem 027/13, pp. 1–2.
66. Svenningsen's report, NG–5208.
67. See Friediger, *Theresienstadt*, pp. 20–26. See also Frisch, III, pp. 51 ff.
68. Evidence of Josef Fischer, Yad Vashem 027/13, pp. 1–2.
69. See also evidence of Arthur Henriques, pp. 2–3.
70. See Himmler's telegram to Müller (Chapter II, notes 121, 122). See also the big report of January 1942 (Chapter III, THE STRUGGLE AGAINST THE "PURGE"). Renthe-Fink's accompanying letter also contains numbers (p. 39). Cf. the accurate data in Best's possession when he wrote his memorandum of 4/24/43 (Chapter II, BEST–IN RENTHE-FINK'S POLITICAL FOOTSTEPS), and see memorandum of Otto Six dated 10/25, para. 1, in which he states explicitly that Best collected material on the Jews before the outbreak of the crisis (AA.ST.S.). Rabbi Melchior also states that confiscation of the lists was superfluous and brought no practical benefits to the Germans (La Cour, III, p. 360).
71. NG–5208.
72. See Chapter IV, note 129.
73. Telegram No. 1208 of 10/5, para. 5–Inl. II 54/8; Eichmann trial, T/586; memorandum of Six, para. 5 (note 70 above).
74. Statement of 4/14/48, para. 2.
75. Hoffmann's evidence (NG–5208).
76. *Ibid.;* Hermannsen's evidence (*ibid.*); Eichmann trial, cross-examinations, cols. 253, 2661–66.
77. On the functions and character of Günther, see Hilberg, *passim.*
78. Hoffmann's evidence, *ibid.*
79. Evidence, Yad Vashem 027/13.
80. For example: "I received the first warning that something might happen on September 17, 1943, after the Gestapo had searched the community office"; "My two brothers and myself saw how the Germans came and took the librarian, Fischer, from the synagogue during morning prayers, and we later heard that the Germans had looked for lists of members of the community and we could guess what was going to happen"; "We were already warned on the 22nd of September by one of our best friends who was one of the leaders of 'Holger Danske.'" Holger Danske was a Danish underground organization (Yad Vashem, *ibid.*).
81. Telegram No. 1208, 10/5/43, para. 5; see note 73.

82. Chaim Fronberg, "From Denmark to Theresienstadt," *From the Recent Past* (Yiddish), I, pp. 63–64.
83. Cf. Chapter IV, note 67; and see *Fra Aktiv til Passiv Modstand,* report of 9/30, p. 215.
84. P. Møller, *Un Peuple Se Réveille,* p. 149. The name of the bishop is given in the Danish edition, p. 190; and cf. *Hvidbog,* II, p. 96.
85. See introduction to *October 43;* evidence of Henriques (Yad Vashem, *ibid.,* p. 2).
86. Duckwitz's memoirs; his evidence NG–5208; Hvass's evidence, *ibid.*
87. Henriques's evidence, p. 3. Svenningsen himself wrote in his reports on 9/30 (NG–5208): "There have latterly been rumors of an action against the Jews in Denmark. These rumors have been persistent and in the last couple of days have assumed an extremely acute character. On Wednesday, September 29, Jewish circles expressed the conviction that in a few days a deportation of the Danish Jews would take place. In this connection a meeting of the departmental heads was called for 2 P.M. and I reported on the situation before us, emphasizing that the Foreign Ministry had no definite knowledge whatsoever. We had, however, in view of the information available, to assume that the rumors were well-founded. The question of how the departmental heads should act in this situation was closely debated." For more details of this meeting, see Chapter VI, THE HOUR OF CRISIS.
88. No. 1162 of 9/29 (AA.ST.S.).
89. A detailed description of the deliberations is given in Hæstrup's *Til Landets Bedste, passim.* See here, Chapter IV, note 99.
90. No. 1161 of 9/29, *Beretning,* bilag XIII, bind 3, pp. 1379–80. Best explicitly connected this telegram with No. 1156 of the same day, in which he gave a stern warning regarding the transfer of the "farmers' sons" to Germany (see above, notes 54, 55). It may be understood from this that his main intention was to stress once again the damage that would be caused by implementing Himmler's order. Rosting's proposal concerning the Jews is designated by Best as "typical of National Socialist groups in Denmark."
91. Sonnleithner to Thadden "via the director-general," 10/1 (Inl. II 54/8); Best presumably aimed at and anticipated a reply of this sort.
92. The army's version is printed in IMT XXXV, pp. 156–58; source: Rigsarkiv Sp. 11, 14730. Best's version: telegram No. 1176 (NG–3921). There are small differences between the two versions.
93. "Die Deutsche Politik . . . ," p. 46. On p. 52, Best says of the

above telegram, No. 1176: "Hitler was caught off his guard and that same night gave his consent to the release of the Danish soldiers."

94. Statement of 4/14/48, para. 7.

95. Best reported this version on 10/2 at 7 A.M. in telegram No. 1189, para. 4 (NG–3921; Inl. II 54/8).

96. Erling Foss saw in the announcement proof that the release of the troops had been postponed before this in order to connect it with the persecution of the Jews. "No Dane can be deceived in this way, and the affair caused much anger" (*Fra Passiv til Aktiv Modstand*, pp. 217–18). "There was no more insane declaration than this. The accusations against the Jews were obvious lies. However, resistance to the idea of freeing the Danish troops by destroying the Jews was now doubly strong. The bitterness and indignation in the army and navy were profound" (*Hvidbog*, II, p. 99). "This clumsy maneuver fooled no one" (Møller, French version, p. 153). Frisch also expressed his disgust (III, p. 57), although he is generally restrained and moderate in expressing his views.

97. No. 1191 of 10/2, para. 1 (Inl. II 54/8); and cf. Best's statement of 4/14/48, para. 3.

98. An interesting detail in this connection was the announcement of the deputy head of the German Intelligence Services, Sundermann, who explained to foreign journalists at a press conference in Berlin on 10/7 the reasons for the action against the Danish Jews, which resounded throughout the world. He asserted that this was a necessary counteraction against Jewish sabotage, espionage, etc. and this in spite of the good treatment they enjoyed at the hands of the Germans. Publication of this statement was forbidden in Denmark. *Fakta*, II, pp. 1324–25; Adler, *Die Verheimlichte Wahrheit*, p. 320.

99. Telegrams No. 1187 and 1182 of 10/1 (AA.ST.S.). The text of the protest according to Best ran as follows: "THE CHAIRMAN OF ALL THE CENTRAL DANISH ECONOMIC ORGANIZATIONS (EMPLOYERS' ASSOCIATION, TRADE UNIONS, THE INDUSTRIAL BOARD, THE AGRICULTURAL BOARD, PROVINCIAL CHAMBER OF COMMERCE, SHIPOWNERS ASSOCIATION, AND THE WHOLESALERS ASSOCIATION) HAVE ON 9/30/43 SUBMITTED AN ADDRESS TO ME IN CONNECTION WITH THE RUMORS THAT HAVE EMERGED IN THE LAST FEW DAYS REGARDING A GERMAN ACTION AGAINST THE JEWS IN DENMARK, AS FOLLOWS: 'WE FEEL OURSELVES OBLIGED TO POINT OUT THAT—IN THE EVENT OF SUCH AN ACTION TAKING PLACE— IT WILL, IN OUR VIEW, TO A GREAT EXTENT HARM THE EFFORTS BEING MADE FROM OUR SIDE TO CREATE PEACE AND ORDER IN DENMARK. THE JEWS HERE IN DENMARK FORM A PART OF THE COUNTRY'S POPULATION AND A STEP AGAINST THEM WILL AFFECT

THE WHOLE DANISH PEOPLE.' THE ADDRESS REMAINS UNAN-
SWERED."

100. See note 97.

101. This memorandum (AA.ST.S.) forms the continuation of another memorandum of 9/28 which gives details of the size and
importance of Danish supplies for the population of Germany
10 per cent of the meat, butter and oil; 90 per cent of the
fresh fish).

102. He was afterward arrested in connection with the celebrated
tea party following which Miss von Thadden (no relation of
the Foreign Ministry official) was arrested. Cf. Shirer, *The Rise
and Fall of the Third Reich*, p. 1025. The fact that he left the
party saved his life.

103. Letter of 8/20/62 from Scherpenberg to the author, in reply to
a series of questions. The climate of those talks is evident in
the following recollection: "We had been informed a few days
previously by Dr. Best that account should be taken of the
possibility of a large-scale arrest action against citizens of
Jewish origin living in Denmark. Herr Best was very little
pleased with this eventuality, and informed us . . . because he
correctly expected that we for our part could put forward
strong arguments against such an action. In our talks with Herr
Best we also drew up a list of these arguments. . . ." (These
are largely already known to us since they were used by Best
and others involved in the matter.) "These considerations made
a deep impression on Herr Best and he assured us then that
through direct contact with both the headquarters of the
Reichsführer S.S. and the Führer's headquarters, he had tried
to achieve a cancellation or at least a postponement of this
measure. He had at first also met, so he thought, with an
understanding attitude, but then events had occurred which
strengthened the most unreasonable elements. The day immediately before the action he informed us that his efforts had
been in vain."

104. See Svenningsen's report (NG–5208). Scherpenberg presented
his report on this talk to the director of the German Foreign
Ministry, Steengracht (AA.ST.S.). As explained in the letter
above, he informed Best of the talk, but preferred to submit
the report to the Foreign Ministry itself.

105. Evidence of H. Drucker, Yad Vashem 027/13.

106. See also Kanstein's evidence (NG–5208).

107. On 9/30 Best sent a telegram, No. 1170 (AA Pol. VI, 2, No. 6,
JM/2221), as follows: "THE FOREIGN DEPARTMENT OF THE
DANISH POLICE COMMISSIONER HAS INFORMED ME OF A COM-
MUNICATION FROM THE SWEDISH LEGATION OF 9/29/43, WHICH
STATED THAT PROVISIONAL SWEDISH PASSPORTS HAD BEEN ISSUED

TO 11 JEWS, WHO HAD ASKED TO HAVE THEIR SWEDISH CITIZEN-
SHIP RETURNED TO THEM. HOWEVER, IN THE LAST FEW DAYS NOT
11, BUT 45, PROVISIONAL SWEDISH PASSPORTS HAVE BEEN ISSUED
TO JEWS RESIDENT HERE, WHO HAVE APPLIED FOR EXIT VISAS TO
SWEDEN ON THE STRENGTH OF THESE PASSPORTS. I AM DENYING
THIS PERMISSION TO THESE APPLICANTS AND DO NOT INTEND TO
EXEMPT THEM FROM EVACUATION, IF I DO NOT RECEIVE INSTRUC-
TIONS FROM YOU TO THE CONTRARY."

108. *Fra Passiv til Aktiv Modstand,* weekly report of 10/4, p. 217.
Frisch could also find no better description—III, p. 53.

109. Foss, *ibid.,* pp. 219–20; an account originating in the illegal
paper *Frit Danmark* is given in Carlo Christensen, *Under Jorden i Borgergade,* p. 26: "The Nazis dragged them out into the
street and herded them together as if they were animals: old
and sick people, women and children—all were piled on two
trucks and taken to Frihavnen, where they were thrown into
the waiting ships."

110. The telegram was sent at 7:30 P.M.; see note 99. Best exploited
the opportunity to point out once more that rumors on the
persecution of the Jews were rife, particularly after postponement of the soldiers' release on 9/28.

111. Svenningsen's report (NG–5208). The letter runs as follows: "I
have been informed this evening through Herr *Oberstaatsanwalt*
Hoff that the Germans intend tonight to arrest a number of
elements hostile to the Reich. I understand from the announcement that the matter is one of arresting Jews. As I could not
find an opportunity today to discuss this matter with you personally, I would like to send you these lines at the last moment
and ask if there is no possibility that those affected will at
least not be deported. If it is really a matter of immediate deportation, Herr Eivind Larsen and myself are prepared to do
everything to come to an arrangement, whereby the persons
wanted by the Germans will, at the request of the Danes, be
put in confinement in Denmark by our own authorities. I ask
you therefore to propose that a closer examination of such a
solution not be put aside."

112. No. 1188, 1:20 A.M. (AA.ST.S.).

113. No. 1189, see note 95.

114. This is the explanation in telegram No. 1208 of 10/5: see note
73. Hoffmann too stated that no one, neither Hanneken nor
Mildner, wished to be responsible for publication of the ordinance (NG–5208).

115. No. 1194, 10/2, 2:45 P.M. The telegram begins: "REQUEST
FOLLOWING TELEGRAM BE PASSED ON TO REICHSSICHERHEITS-
HAUPTAMT FOR THE INFORMATION OF DEPARTMENTS D IV 4 C
2 AND IV B 4." (Eichmann trial, T/582; NG–3907, Inl. II
54/8; see Eichmann examination, col. 2661 ff.).

116. No. 1193, 10/2, *ibid.* This telegram was also destined for RSHA.
117. A "warning" telegram sent to Best from the Foreign Ministry on 10/4 and signed by Hencke stated: "REICHSSICHERHEITS-HAUPTAMT HAS ANNOUNCED THAT THE JEWISH ACTION LED TO THE SEIZURE OF 284 PERSONS [Köpfen] IN ALL." (Eichmann trial, T/583; NG–3920; Inl. II, *ibid.*; also Friediger, *Theresienstadt*, p. 52).Cf. Best's reply telegram (note 114).
118. Helmuth James Graf von Moltke, a friend of Count von Stauffenberg's, had been arrested in January 1944 and did therefore not participate directly in the attempted coup of 7/20/44.
119. Quoted from a letter by M. B. to the author dated 1/20/60. The author is grateful to Moltke's widow for M. B.'s name. See also Annelore Leber-Freya von Moltke, *Für und Wider*, which includes a letter of Moltke of 10/21/41 in which he writes of mass murders and deportation and torture of Jews (p. 201): "Can I experience this and yet sit by the table in my heated apartment and drink tea? Do I not thus make myself an accessory to the crime? What do I say if I am asked: 'And what did you do at the time?'" It is, however, an exaggeration to say that he was the man whose warning saved the Danish Jews (Zeller, *Geist der Freiheit*, p. 97) or even that he helped many escape through his warning (*A German of the Resistance*, Introduction, p. 21).
120. The telegram was sent simultaneously to the Foreign Ministry, the headquarters of the army in Denmark, and the *Reichsführer* S.S. It was signed by Jodl (OKW/WFST/Qu(N)Nr. 00586/43 gkdos, AA.ST.S.).
121. 1/Skl. B. Nr. 27 635/43 gkdos, Rigsarkiv Sp. 8, 6581.
122. Telegram No. 1214 (NG–5322); see also announcement of cancellation of the state of emergency in the report of the head of the military archives, Goes: "Die Gründe für die Verhängung des militärischen Ausnahmezustandes in Dänemark und seine Durchführung am 29. August 1943." Anlage XXIII. Reprinted in *Beretning*, bilag XIII, bind 2, p. 912, and cf. part of Svenningsen's report, *Beretning*, bilag IV, pp. 324–25.
123. See army telegram of 10/3 (IMT XXXV, Doc. 547–D; NG–5208); in the margin, the recipient wrote a comment on the small number seized: "We couldn't care less!" Naval headquarters in Denmark announced the failure as early as 10/2 (Rigsarkiv Sp. 7, 5424 and daily orders of the same date— *ibid.*, Sp. 9, 7231).
124. Mildner's evidence 6/22/45, Eichmann trial T/585, p. 8; see Chapter IV, note 73. Frisch, III, p. 59.
125. See Thadden's statement in defense of Steengracht (Eichmann trial T/584, TWC, Case XI, p. 2) and his announcements of 10/4 (NG–3920) and of 10/6 (Inl. II geh. 54/8).
126. See examination, col. 251 ff, and meeting 36, 5/11/61, p. 6.

127. Printed in *Life*, Vol. 49 (Nov. 28, 1960), p. 101.
128. Statement of Thadden, as in note 125.
129. On this, see Chapter VII.
130. Hoffmann's evidence (NG–5208).
131. See TWC, Case XI, p. 282. Eichmann stated in the preliminary examinations that he had been a friend of Mildner, col. 946, 1957.
132. See p. 142.
133. Inl. II 54/8.
134. *Life*, as in note 127, p. 110.
135. See notes 70 and 73.
136. Letter of 9/10, see Chapter IV above, p. 144; another letter, of 9/21, deals only with the Schalburg Corps, for which he requests part of the military equipment confiscated from the Danes (*ibid.*).
137. See Chapter IV, note 85.
138. No. 1157 (AA.ST.S.); and cf. Reitlinger, pp. 334–35.
139. He had a talk with Svenningsen on the same day—see below.
140. Much material on the affair may be found in the file mentioned in Chapter IV, note 47. See also Best's telegram No. 1285 of 10/21 (Inl. II 352).
141. Report on the talk and its results: Inl. II 78; see also NG–5455.
142. The text of telegram No. 1524 of 12/11, reads in part: "HE HAS ALSO INFORMED ME [Best] THAT THE FÜHRER ON 12/6/43 DECREED THE FOLLOWING: 'I ORDER THE ESTABLISHMENT OF A COMMAND POST FOR A HIGHER S.S.- AND POLICE-FÜHRER IN DEN-MARK. THE HSSPF WILL BE PLACED AT THE SIDE OF THE REICH PLENIPOTENTIARY AND WILL WORK IN INTIMATE COOPERATION WITH HIM.' "
143. This is borne out by the exchange of personal letters between Ribbentrop and Himmler, copies of which were sent by Wagner to Best on 2/21/44, at Ribbentrop's behest.
144. Frisch, III, p. 59; Svenningsen's report to the parliamentary commission—*Beretning*, bilag IV, p. 325.
145. The German text of the announcement as Best reported it to the Foreign Ministry ran as follows "WITH REFERENCE TO OUR TALK 10/4/43 I CONFIRM THAT IN THE REICH AREA THE FOLLOWING CRITERIA FOR THE TREATMENT OF JEWS ARE VALID: HALF-JEWS ["Mischlinge"] OF LESSER DEGREE ARE NOT AFFECTED BY THE MEASURES IN FORCE AGAINST FULL JEWS. THE SAME IS VALID FOR FULL JEWS MARRIED TO NON-JEWS. WIDER MEASURES THAN IN THE REICH AREA HAVE NOT YET BEEN INTRO-DUCED IN ANY OCCUPIED COUNTRIES" (telegram No. 1323 of 10/28, AA.ST.S.). Best sent the statement to the Foreign Ministry only at this later date following Danish claims for the return from Theresienstadt of Jews deported "in error" (see

Chapter VIII). At the beginning of October he reported neither on this announcement nor on his talk with Svenningsen, and the reason is clear—he had asserted, for Hitler's and Himmler's ears, that the release of the Danish soldiers (in the wake, as it were, of the Jewish deportations) had soothed Danish fears (see above, DEPORTATION—A PLAN GOES WRONG). Cf. Frisch, III, p. 59; La Cour, II, p. 30.

146. On 10/9 and in further talks during that month—see Svenningsen's report, Beretning, bilag IV, p. 325.

147. On the problem of forming a government and Best's true opinion, see pp. 136–7.

148. Best's attempts to clip the army's wings and his pressing complaints on the matter led in the very days of decision to a sharp reaction by Ribbentrop, who demanded that he settle the problem on the spot instead of bringing everything, large and small, for Ribbentrop to settle with the OKW (Inl. II 54/8); Best's reply: Inl. II 78.

149. To a certain extent, Best admits this fact in his defense statement, "Die Deutsche Politik . . ." (pp. 14–15). Thadden relates how surprised Best was when he first learned of Pancke's appointment (statement of evidence of 4/16/46—Tillægsekstrakt til Hovedekstrakt, A, p. 11): "This information of mine came as such a great surprise for the Foreign Ministry departments concerned and for Dr. Best, who was in Berlin at precisely that time, that at first it was met with disbelief."

150. See Anton Dunkern's statement, 6/3/48 (Tillægsekstrakt IV, bil. 9, pp. 36–37).

151. On 12/30 a meeting took place at staff headquarters, with the participation of the central administrative authorities and the leading representatives of the Reich in Denmark. Best appeared armed with full authority on all matters. On the contents of this meeting, where the system of "reprisal murder" (clearingmord) was decided upon, see Frisch, III, pp. 87–89.

152. Characteristic is a comment in the diary of U. von Hassell, who belonged to the German resistance, on 7/10/44: "I was in fact shaken by Grundherr's reports from Denmark. . . . Best, he said, is a very sensible man, but he cannot stand up to the half-diabolical, half-stupid instructions from 'above,' and General Hanneken is a coarse, imbecilic hooligan" (Vom andern Deutschland, Zürich: 1946, p. 362).

CHAPTER VI

1. Government meetings in which the matter was discussed took place on 4/20/40 and 7/15/40. See Beretning, bilag IV, pp. 414, 423.

2. He was himself a refugee. He was released on 5/17/40 due to the efforts of the authorities.
3. Mentioned in *Beretning*, III, Protocols, pp. 363–64.
4. German Foreign Ministry memorandum (Pol Vi, 1742), reprinted in *Beretning*, bilag XIII, bind 3, p. 1263. See Chapter I, p. 20.
5. Federspiel, a lawyer by profession, was one of the central figures of the Danish underground movement; after the war he served as Minister for Special Affairs from 1945 to 1947. *Beretning*, bilag VII, bind 1, pp. 187–88.
6. The shorthand minutes (*ibid.*) are as follows: "In accordance with German demands German Communist refugees were arrested, but the Danish police refused, agreeing to arrest only those who had no means of livelihood in the country and were there illegally."
7. *Beretning*, as in note 5. Renthe-Fink stated in a report of 6/11/42 that a total of 200 refugees were returned to Germany; *Beretning*, bilag XIII, bind 2, p. 575. Information was published three years ago in the Danish press on the tragic fate of a Polish Jew who arrived in Denmark at the end of 1939. Dr. Stefan Glicksman was handed over to the Germans in January 1941 and died three weeks later in Auschwitz (*Politiken*, 3/6/66; *BT*, 4/11/66).
8. *Beretning*, bilag VII, bind 2, pp. 885–86. Information on the Jews is from a letter of Margolinsky to the author dated 1/28/61.
9. Otto Adolf Melchior; Margolinsky, *ibid.*
10. *Beretning*, as in note 5.
11. Michael Sapir, "Copenhagen on the Day of the Germans' Invasion" (Hebrew), *Davar*, 8/26/40; and see Margolinsky, ". . . landbrugspionerer. . . ." According to Sapir, the visas were obtained with the help of the German consul, Krüger, who was known as a decent man. Margolinsky mentions his activity in the matter in relation to the Danish police. On German control of entry and exit, see *Danmark under Verdenskrig*, III, pp. 50–52; *Fakta*, I, pp. 292–93, 311.
12. Margolinsky, *ibid.*
13. Inl. II A/B 46/2, Judenauswanderung, JM/2252, 1941–1943. Cf. Eichmann trial. This seems to be one of the earliest evidences of the definitely reversed German policy concerning emigration, which took place in connection with the implementation of the "final solution."
14. Lachmann's evidence, pp. 2–3, Yad Vashem 027/13; also Henriques's evidence, p. 1. Their statements are borne out by Svenningsen's report on the same talk (NG–5208; according to

Svenningsen, the meeting took place on 9/25, according to Lachmann on 9/24): "Herr Lachmann raised the question of expatriation of Jews living here. This concerned Danish Jews as well as German emigrants. Until now the [leaders of] Jewish community had advised both Danish and foreign Jews against leaving the country. Would it be correct to continue with this policy? I replied that a question of illegal expatriation might arise and that in my opinion the leaders of the Jewish community should continue to exercise caution in deviating from the present stand. If it should suddenly happen that a stream of Jewish refugees left the country, it was my opinion that the danger of measures against the Jews who rejected illegal methods would increase."

15. "Erindringer fra møder med Niels Bohr"—see Chapter I, note 41, and Erling Foss, *Fra Passiv til Aktiv Modstand,* extract on Niels Bohr, p. 284.

16. David Melchior's evidence; cf. Lachmann, note 14.

17. David Melchior's evidence. Lachmann, however, asserts that some of the papers were hidden, at least at night, but no further proof of this is available.

18. Margolinsky relates (in ". . . landbrugspionerer . . . ," p. 6) that the community bore the expenses "but some time after the war this money was paid back to it," i.e., by the Jewish Agency.

19. Rabbi Melchior, "Razziaen paa Jøderne og Flugten til Sverige," La Cour, III, pp. 357–68. In his memoirs (*A Rabbi Remembers,* Lyle Stuart, New York, 1968) Dr. Melchior also ascribes the rescue of the Jews to the careful policy of the Jewish community's leadership (p. 158).

20. Lachmann's evidence on himself; see note 14.

21. Evidence, Yad Vashem, 027/13.

22. The fisherman who smuggled Christmas Møller out in May 1942 was on 7/17/42 sentenced by a Danish court to six years' imprisonment and his helper to three years': *Fakta,* I, p. 304; Chr. Søndergaard, *I tyske Lænker,* p. 217.

23. A note of Grundherr on a talk with the Swedish foreign minister, Sandler, on 1/28/39, i.e., shortly after "Crystal Night," stated: "Herr Sandler then gave assurances that it was not the intention of the Swedish government to set up an *emigrant center* in Stockholm. Sweden naturally had no 'need of emigrant intellectuals' (authors, journalists, etc.), but the situation was otherwise with, for example, non-Aryan skilled workers from Czechoslovakia" (Riga 133/4 Politische Beziehungen zwischen Deutschland und Skandinavien, JM/2342). It should be noted that Sandler was one of the most vigorous opponents of nazism

in Sweden, and in the course of the above talk Grundherr complained of his public comments on this question. See also Chapter IX below.

24. Evidence of Federspiel and Gyberg, Yad Vashem 027/13.
25. *Gaa til Modstand*, pp. 48–54; and his evidence, Yad Vashem (Yod–636/17).
26. Margolinsky, ". . . landbrugspionerer . . . ," p. 7, and letter to author of 1/9/60; Yaari's evidence, *ibid.*
27. Margolinsky, *ibid.*, and report of Adler-Rudel, "A Chronicle of Rescue Efforts," Year Book of The Leo Baeck Institute, XI, London, 1966, p. 224.
28. Supplement to Margolinsky's ". . . landbrugspionerer. . . ."
29. David Melchior's evidence and supplement on the synagogue watch; Lachmann's evidence; and *Beretning*, bilag VII, bind 2, p. 1438; bilag XIII, bind 2, pp. 676–77, 679.
30. David Melchior's evidence and special supplement on the Jewish youth of the period.
31. Evidence of Henriques and Lachmann and report of the secretary of the community, Arthur Henriques. Yad Vashem, 027/13.
32. Margolinsky, ". . . landbrugspionerer . . ."; Flender, pp. 51–52.
33. Dr. Melchior's article (see note 19), and interview with journalist published in *BT* on 10/2/45, where he also tells of the visit of Mrs. Bardfeld. David Melchior had also been in touch with her and asked her to be on the alert (his evidence).
34. NG–5208.
35. Report of secretary of the community; see p. 137 on problem of government in Denmark.
36. According to Oluf Pedersen, *Den Politiske Modstand*, pp. 201–02, a discussion on the subject took place in the already-illegal Council of Nine on 10/4/43. Here the proposal that the departmental heads should resign was rejected.
37. Report of secretary of the community, Arthur Henriques.
38. These deliberations were dealt with at length in Hæstrup, *Til Landets Bedste*, pp. 128–174. More extensive source material was at his disposal. The basic facts remain the same, though there is a difference in evaluation.
39. The report of secretary of the community, Arthur Henriques, and the report of C. B. Henriques himself are not identical on this point. The Danish Foreign Ministry was not inclined to clarify the matter.
40. Erling Foss. *Fra Passiv til Aktiv Modstand*, p. 216.
41. Erling Foss, *loc. cit.*; *Hvidbog*, I, pp. 195–97; Frisch, III, p. 51.
42. Summaries of Danish Foreign Ministry and the report of the meeting held on 9/29, as published, *Kilder*, p. 126 (translation is based on the latter). For more details of the discussion, see Hæstrup, as note 38, especially pp. 152–53; 158–162.

43. Report of secretary of the community.
44. Hæstrup, *ibid.*, p. 160.
45. Announcements of the Danish police.
46. David Sompolinsky is the "David" in Bertelsen's *October 43*. He is now the head of the Department of Physiology at Assaf Harofeh Hospital in Israel and professor at Tel Aviv's university. He gave detailed evidence of the events of those days in which he took an active part (Yad Vashem 027/13); he relates that already on 10/1 he received permission from the municipal old-age home to lodge and hide old Jews there, but he did not succeed in giving the necessary monetary guarantee required, since he found no one able or willing to place these sums at his disposal—he thought he would obtain them from community funds. On the same problem, cf. Bertelsen, *ibid.*, pp. 39–40.
47. Police announcement. How they fled is unknown.
48. The cashier of the community relates in his evidence (Yad Vashem 027/13) that when he learned the news on the morning of the 29th he paid the officials of the community their salaries, "though this was two days before they were due," since he was aware that everyone was now in need of money. It would seem that the man, who was then over seventy, did this on his own initiative.
49. Margolinsky, ". . . landbrugspionerer . . ." and "Undersøgelser."
50. His evidence; see note 46.
51. According to Rabbi Melchior, there were some 150 at prayer; see Flender, foreword.
52. Evidence of Mogens Staffeldt, Yad Vashem 027/13. His brother was a member of the Freedom Council and it was from him that he heard the bad news as early as 9/29. See also *Hvidbog*, *ibid.*, p. 95; and Yad Vashem 027/13.
53. David Melchior's evidence; evidence of Harald Melchior, to whom Svenningsen finally said that it was best to take flight; Henriques relates on this point that Svenningsen himself asked him to warn a Jew whom Svenningsen had told on the morning of 9/29 that there was no need to leave.
54. Dr. Melchior, La Cour, *ibid.*, p. 362; David Melchior's evidence. In a number of cases people left as a result of the warnings given between 9/20 and 9/26. When some of them saw that nothing had happened they returned to the city, and thus had to flee a second time (various statements of evidence, Yad Vashem 027/13).
55. Yad Vashem 027/13.
56. In the last few days before and up to the very eve of the persecutions, groups of Jews and others attempting to flee to Sweden were seized in various places. They were arrested,

some by the Germans and some by the Danish police, "for illegal departure from the country" (police notice).

CHAPTER VII

1. Erling Foss, *Fra Passiv til Aktiv Modstand*, p. 6 (hereafter "Foss").
2. *Op. cit.*, III, p. 57.
3. *Hvidbog*, II, p. 99; Hæstrup, *Hemmelig Alliance* (hereafter "Hæstrup, Alliance"), I, p. 97.
4. Bjørn B. Thomsen in *Danske lægememoirer*, p. 53.
5. Erling Foss, *Paa eget ansvar*, pp. 56–57; *Danske lægememoirer*, *loc. cit.*, as follows: " 'What would you do if a saboteur asked you for shelter?' The answer was nearly always, 'It hurts me to have to say that I would not help.' "
6. Quoted by Hæstrup in *Hemmelig Alliance*, I, p. 54; see also H. Lefèvre, *Mændene i Danmarks Frihedsraad*, p. 39.
7. Hæstrup, Alliance, pp. 226–27, 237; see also notes of author's talk with Frode Jakobsen, Yad Vashem 027/13, and cf. Chapter IV, THE POLICY OF NEGOTIATION AND ITS BREAKDOWN IN AUGUST 1943.
8. Hæstrup, Alliance, I, p. 39.
9. Mogens Fog, *Danmark Frit*, p. 28.
10. A philologist by profession, he only entered politics in the wake of his underground activity.
11. Reported by Frode Jakobsen in the large manuscript (hereafter "Jakobsen Ms.") in which he summarized after the war his experiences in the underground movement. The author is grateful for having had the opportunity of perusing this work. Jakobsen made sure that the group contained a liaison officer for each of the four main parties (Jakobsen Ms., p. 19).
12. Interview with Jakobsen—see note 7, and Jakobsen Ms., p. 21.
13. Jakobsen Ms., p. 27.
14. Interview (see note 7) and Jakobsen Ms., p. 33.
15. Jakobsen Ms., p. 37.
16. *Fakta*, II, p. 1305.
17. Frisch, II, p. 361; Jakobsen Ms.
18. Frisch, II, p. 364; interview with Jakobsen (note 7).
19. See Hæstrup, I, pp. 228–35. On the basis of a bibliography of the illegal press (Buschardt, Fabricius, Tonesen, *Besættelsestidens illegale blade og bøger*) Hæstrup quotes the following figures for the number of such papers appearing: 1940–2; 1941 –30; 1942–76; 1943––227; 1944–363. Circulation rose from 1200 in 1940 to 10,935,000 in 1945. In 1943 this jumped from 301,000 to 2,600,000. Most of the papers were mimeographed

sheets. It should be recalled that Denmark then had 4 million inhabitants.

20. Frisch, I, appendix, pp. 366–67. Hæstrup claims (I, p. 69) that this was the last expression of opposition by the Social Democratic leaders to the resistance movement, and that thereafter they gave it their support; in fact, however, the breach prevailed until the summer of 1944 at least, though the Social Democrats entered the underground ranks at a steadily growing rate (Frisch, II, pp. 247–48).

21. Mogens Fog wrote in November 1943 an incisive analysis of the political situation (*Danmark Frit*, pp. 34–36), but his observations were very one-sided. Frisch, II, p. 20, points out that the parties played an increasingly marked double game (see also Hæstrup, I, p. 69): "The truth is that the game played during the occupation was a double one. The attacking force was the resistance movement. . . . In defense [was] the less temperamental and more traditional Denmark, which warded off the German attack."

22. Frisch, III, pp. 40 ff.

23. Hæstrup, I, p. 48.

24. *Fakta*, I, p. 225.

25. Hæstrup, Alliance, I, p. 55.

26. *Ibid.*, pp. 62, 67, 144–45; see also *Hvidbog*, II, p. 335.

27. *Fakta*, I, p. 235; *Hvidbog*, II, p. 183; Erling Foss gave, in his bulletin of 10/6, the text of the statement to London (Foss, pp. 222–23). The struggle of the council for recognition by the Allies as the representatives of Denmark does not fall within the scope of this work.

28. *Den Hvide Brigade*, p. 186.

29. Frisch, III, pp. 57–58.

30. *Fakta*, II, p. 1324. The editors of Fakta presume that there were a good many more than the forty protests registered.

31. Se *De fem lange Aar*, II, pp. 585–86; Oluf Pedersen, p. 201.

32. *Beretning*, bilag VII, bind 3, p. 1552; Oluf Pedersen, p. 202.

33. Frisch (see note 29).

34. *Fakta*, II, p. 1391.

35. Harald Nielsen, *Europas Ødelæggelse*, note on p. 103. This book is a collection of articles, many of which were written in 1943.

36. Foss, p. 222.

37. His evidence, p. 10.

38. Foss, pp. 218, 223.

39. Local police notice. According to this, students also threatened to strike at first, and here too lessons were canceled for a week.

40. *De fem lange Aar*, II, pp. 597–98.

41. Report from Stockholm printed in *Hatsofeh* (*Hebrew Daily*, Tel

Aviv), 6/4/43. Munk, priest, poet, writer, was one of the leading figures in spiritual resistance. He was considered so dangerous by the Germans that he became one of the first targets of "reprisal murder." Cf. Chapter V, note 151.

42. *Ibid.*
43. *Fakta,* I, p. 75.
44. Frisch, II, p. 360.
45. See p. 87.
46. Bishop Fuglsang-Damgaard, "Kirken og Jødeforfølgelserne," *De fem lange Aar,* p. 104.
47. See Chapter VI, p. 207.
48. As note 46, p. 105; La Cour, I, p. 497; see also Svenningsen's report (NG–5208) and the summaries of the meetings of the departmental heads.
49. Published in *International Christian Press and Information Service,* Geneva, October 1943, No. 37.
50. Foss, p. 218.
51. Jean Marcus, "How We Were Rescued," *From the Recent Past,* I (Yiddish), p. 62.
52. *Lægememoirer,* pp. 78–82. Bertelsen in *October 43* (p. 33), though he is talking about a later stage, gives three urgent needs: to find the fishermen and the boats, to find the money, and to recruit additional helpers.
53. Evidence, Yad Vashem 027/13.
54. Frisch, II, p. 247.
55. Recounted, for instance, by the secretary of the community, Arthur Henriques, who was warned both by the Industrial Board and the Workers' Educational Association (his evidence, pp. 4–5, Yad Vashem 027/13).
56. Information on the warnings may be found both in the answers to Barfoed's questionnaire and in other statements of evidence. The statistics from 54 statements may thus be divided as follows: 9 did not need the warning and fled of their own accord; 5 were warned at their work; 15 were warned by friends and acquaintances, 15 by politicians, trade unions, etc., and about 10 by Jewish friends and relatives. These details are not fully accurate since, as stated, most people were warned several times and from various sources.
57. Evidence, Yad Vashem.
58. *Et dansk Handelshus gennem 6 generationer,* 1961, pp. 39–40.
59. See Chapter X.
60. Gersfelt, *Saadan narrede vi Gestapo,* p. 16.
61. Valdemar Koppel's evidence; evidence from one of the provincial towns (pp. 32–35). See also David Melchior's evidence at the Eichmann trial, Session 35 (5/10/61).
62. Sparring-Petersen, *Danmarks Ufredsaar,* pp. 17–18; *Den Hvide Brigade,* p. 201.

63. Both wrote articles in *Den Hvide Brigade* and the description below is based largely on these (*ibid.*, pp. 175–217).
64. *Ibid.*, p. 187.
65. *Ibid.*, pp. 190–92.
66. *Ibid.*, p. 193.
67. For a typical example of such a description see the hospital action as told by Flender in *Rescue in Denmark* (pp. 116–28).
68. See, for example, *From the Recent Past*, p. 60.
69. *October 43*, pp. 12, 43, and *passim*.
70. La Cour, III, p. 392.
71. Jakobsen Ms., p. 152; Staffeldt's evidence (Yad Vashem 027/13); and cf. Flender, pp. 103–15.
72. See p. 216.
73. See Christen, *Under Jorden*, pp. 10, 57.
74. *I tyske Lænker*, p. 207; Gersfelt, pp. 8–9; P. Møller, *Un Peuple Se Réveille*, pp. 156–57.
75. See p. 127.
76. Evidence, Yad Vashem.
77. Police reports; see also German report on basis of material confiscated at the time of the disbanding of the Danish police on 9/19/44 and the removal of most of its members to a concentration camp in Germany: *Beretning*, bilag VII, bind 1, pp. 902 ff.
78. *Danmark under Verdenskrig*, III, p. 163.
79. Hæstrup, II, p. 83.
80. See Federspiel, "Modstandsbevægelsens finansiering," *Danmarks Frihedskamp*, II, pp. 773–81.
81. See above, p. 225.
82. Hæstrup, *Kontakt med England*, pp. 223–24.
83. Jakobsen Ms., pp. 94–95.
84. *Gaa til Modstand*, pp. 68–75.
85. See Chapter III, p. 105.
86. As note 84, p. 72.
87. Evidence, Yad Vashem 027/13. Flender uses the same source in his chapter entitled "The Bourgeois Housewife" (pp. 129–44).
88. Sompolinsky's evidence, p. 6, Yad Vashem 027/13.
89. Cf. p. 204.
90. His non-Jewish wife and fifteen-year-old daughter remained in Denmark. Mrs. Berendson participated in rescue work until she and her daughter were forced to flee. Berendson's evidence was published as *Verbannung, Aufzeichungen deutscher Schriftseller*, Wegner, 1964; Mrs. Berendson's evidence: Wiener Library; her daughter's: Yad Vashem.
91. *Fakta*, II, p. 856.
92. *Med Gestapo i Kølvandet*. The following extracts are taken from pages 1, 7–8, 13–14, 16–19, 23, 26–27, 32, and 84. Flender

also used this material after talks with Kiær (pp. 157–60). In this chapter he combined various events which will be dealt with separately here.

93. Kiær continued his activities until he was seized by the Germans on 5/12/44. He states that he made the crossing to Denmark 172 times. He brought some 1400 persons from Denmark to Sweden and some 300, mainly intelligence agents, from Sweden to Denmark. His sufferings in Danish prisons and German concentration camps belong to the story of the Danish resistance movement. With other survivors, he was returned to Denmark before the end of the war. On the establishment of the routes, see Chapter IX.

94. As note 60, p. 37.

95. Evidence, Yad Vashem.

96. Evidence, Yad Vashem.

97. See Dr. Melchior, La Cour, III, pp. 366–67; Valdemar Koppel's evidence. The part relevant to this study is reprinted in *Kilder*, pp. 128–29; *From the Recent Past*, I, p. 62; Møller, p. 157; *I tyske Lænker*, pp. 211, 217, 219.

98. Dr. Melchior, *ibid.;* see also Bertelsen, p. 42, who relates that the Danes undertook the sale of furniture and other possessions.

99. See, for example, Bertelsen, p. 35; evidence of lawyer N. A. who served as treasurer of the underground movement (Yad Vashem 027/13).

100. Frisch, II, p. 251; III, p. 56. Cf. also note 87.

101. *Den Hvide Brigade*, pp. 197–98.

102. Evidence, Yad Vashem.

103. Gersfelt, pp. 42–44; see also lawyer's evidence as in note 99, p. 41.

104. See Bertelsen, Chapter 3; Frisch, as note 100; Torben Meyer in *Gjentofte Kommune under Besættelsen*, p. 204. Various statements of evidence, Yad Vashem.

105. *Lægememoirer*, p. 80.

106. See, for example, Dr. Melchior's interview in *BT*, 10/2/45.

107. *Undersøgelser, passim.*

108. These are the 48 pieces of evidence of Barfoed and 8 additional accounts—all in Yad Vashem 027/13.

109. Sompolinsky relates that during preparation for flight lists of reliable taxi drivers were at first drawn up, though it soon became clear that it was easier to write down the unreliable ones.

110. Gersfelt, pp. 37 ff.

111. *I tyske Lænker*, p. 212; Møller, pp. 155–56; Bertelsen, p. 88; Gersfelt, p. 22.

112. Drucker's evidence, pp. 38–39, Yad Vashem 027/13; the German consul in the German port of Malmö reported on 10/12/43 (Inl. IIg 54/8) that six German soldiers had participated in the

rescue of the Jews by disguising themselves as fishermen and had afterward remained in Sweden.

113. On 9/30, naval headquarters in Denmark reported on "the flight of numerous military and civil persons to Sweden as a result of the breakdown of the Danish watch on the Sound and the coast guard service" (Rigsarkiv, Sp. 9. 7222).

114. Copenhagen police report, 10/12/43. However, Dr. Melchior points out that many apartments were ruined (La Cour, III, p. 366).

115. Told about, for example, in Koppel's evidence, pp. 30–31, and in *Hvidbog*, I, p. 196. The degree to which the Germans were aware of what was going on is also clear from the story of the community chairman, Henriques, who refused to leave his hiding place in the hospital and flee to Sweden until Best had been asked in Henriques's name whether the deportation order applied to him also. Only after receipt of an affirmative reply did he agree to tread the path of all the Jews (his evidence). Visas were also given prior to the night of persecutions, and Duckwitz was among those active in their attainment (his memoirs).

116. *Danmark under Verdenskrig*, III, pp. 165–66. For the legal procedure and verdicts, see *Fakta*, I, pp. 293, 311. *Beretning*, bilag VII, bind 1 as note 129, p. 481; Borchsenius, *Udlændighedens Dage*, pp. 41–42. Koppel relates in his evidence that after arrest he was taken to the central prison in Copenhagen, where he was allowed to keep all his money, but he (who was aged seventy-six) and others were beaten by the Germans. He was later released from the camp at Horserød (evidence, pp. 13–16).

117. Telegram No. 1282, Stockholm (Inl. IIg 54/8).

118. Koppel's evidence, p. 22; see also Ralph Oppenhejm's book.

119. Police reports; Gersfelt, pp. 30–35; Kiær, pp. 8–12; *I tyske Lænker*, pp. 220–31; *Gaa til Modstand*, pp. 72–73; *Jødeforfølgelserne og Gilleleje*; various statements of evidence, Yad Vashem.

120. Telegrams No. 1219 and 1225 (AA.ST.S.).

121. Telegram No. 1238 of 10/11/43 (AA.ST.S.; NG–5815).

122. *Næsgaardbogen*, 1945, pp. 60–68.

123. Police commissioner's report of 10/1/43, 10:40 P.M.

124. Police commissioner's report of 10/2/43, 12:15 P.M.; these precise reports enable us to trace arrests carried out by the Germans.

125. His evidence, p. 7.

126. Bertelsen, p. 57.

127. An outstanding example is given by Bertelsen in his account of how one of the members of his group succeeded in removing Bertelsen's wife from a Gestapo cell into which she had been

thrown after her husband had been obliged to disappear (pp. 112–33).

128. These figures are based on police reports (cf. also *Beretning*, bilag VII, bind 1, p. 353). Among those who were released from Horserød was the king's physician, Professor Erik Warburg. In January 1944 an unsuccessful attempt on his life took place (as part of the *clearing-mord* system which the Germans introduced in their fight against "liquidation" of their people by the Resistance). Among those seized while attempting flight was eighty-four-year old Hanna Adler (Niels Bohr's aunt), a former headmistress and renowned educator. She was released after a petition was submitted to the German authorities and signed by senior officials of the Ministry of Education, the mayor of Copenhagen, the rector of the university and other public figures, and some four hundred of her former pupils. She received a "permit" signed by Svenningsen and remained openly and officially in Denmark throughout the war. She was not a member of the Jewish community or of any religious body. The petition stated, *inter alia:* "We address this petition not only out of our great sympathy and admiration for the personality of Mrs. Adler but also out of recognition that Mrs. Adler's life's work was one of such a character that the *whole of Danish society* is exceptionally indebted to her. . . . It is a fact that the deportation of Mrs. Adler would result in a *shock* for a large number of Danes. The fate of Mrs. Adler should not in fact be regarded as a blow struck at the Jews but at a large section of Danish citizens." *Hanna Adler og hendes Skole,* pp. 166–68.

129. Dr. Melchior, La Cour, III, p. 366; Drucker's and other evidence; see also Gersfelt, p. 13.

130. *Hvidbog,* II, pp. 97–98. Frode Jakobsen relates the tragic story of two of his friends, an elderly refugee couple who committed suicide in the woods.

131. Koppel's evidence, *et al.*

132. The story appears in several places, the most reliable being in police reports; Møller, p. 158.

133. La Cour, III, pp. 428–29.

134. *I tyske Lænker,* p. 212; Gersfelt, pp. 14, 41. Among the horrible stories is one told by the mother of twin baby girls, eighteen months old. The babies were muffled so they would make no noise and reached Sweden almost dead, but attempts to save them were successful—Inge Jensen, Yad Vashem 027/13, and Flender, pp. 200–02.

135. Foss, p. 220.

136. Thaulow, p. 335.

137. *I tyske Lænker,* p. 216; I. R.'s evidence; Algreen-Petersen, *Christian, illegale Bote, passim.*

138. Gersfelt, p. 28; *I tyske Lænker,* p. 222; Bertelsen in particular describes his meeting with the Jewish public, which revealed a new world to him (*passim*).
139. Bertelsen, p. 12.
140. Quoted by Bertelsen, pp. 131–32.
141. Jakobsen Ms., pp. 94–95.
142. *Danmarks Ufredsaar,* p. 110.

CHAPTER VIII

1. A. Møller, *Hvidbog,* I, p. 235.
2. Cf. Chapter II, p. 46.
3. Frisch, II, pp. 177 ff.; *Beretning,* bilag VIII, pp. 76–104.
4. Photocopy of the law, Yad Vashem 027/8–9; all the details on activities on behalf of Jewish property are taken from *Københavns Kommune, Beretning for Aarene 1940–1955,* pp. 253–54. A comprehensive description of the activities of the Ministry of Social Welfare in the period under review has been given by its then director-general, H. H. Koch: "Træk af Social-ministeriets Arbejde under Besættelsen," in *Central-administrationen 1848–1949,* pp. 64–86 (hereafter "Koch").
5. These figures are token from a survey of Danish prisoners in the concentration camps and prisons in *Hvidbog,* II, pp. 105–10, but they should not be regarded as accurate in all respects Together with the data of the Danish government appear those of an illegal list compiled in Stockholm during the war. The latter numbers are often larger than the official ones.
6. His evidence, Yad Vashem 027/13.
7. *Ibid.,* p. 19.
8. The senior Oppenhejm later also fulfilled a function in Theresienstadt. His wife had been among the sponsors of the scheme to bring children to Denmark as part of Youth Aliya. See Ralph Oppenhejm, *The Door of Death.*
9. Koppel's evidence, pp. 25–26; Chapter VII, note 128.
10. The main source is Rabbi Friediger's *Theresienstadt* (see *ibid.,* 31). See also Ralph Oppenhejm, *The Door of Death* and H. G. Adler, *Theresienstadt 1941–1945* and *Die Verheimlichte Wahrheit, Theresienstädter Dokumente* (hereafter "Adler, Sources"). See also Erich Kulka, "Five Escapes from Auschwitz and Their Echo" (Hebrew), *Moreshet,* Vol. II, No. 3, pp. 23–38, which (especially in the first section) throws new light on a number of events (hereafter "Kulka").
11. *Danske i tyske Koncentrationslejre,* pp. 175 ff. and *Rapport fra Stutthof* (Chapter V, "Jøderne i Swinemünde"), p. 24.
12. Margolinsky, *Undersøgelser;* Adler, *Theresienstadt,* pp. 40–42, 298. Cf. also *Hvidbog,* as in note 5, and the memorandum of

the Danish government to the Nuremberg Trials (IMT 901–RF).

13. Two Jews appear as such in a list of 77 Danes, most of them Communists, who were deported to a concentration camp on 1/20/44 (*Beretning*, bilag VII, bind 1, p. 353; bind 3, pp. 1593–94).

14. For example, Sompolinsky's evidence; Friediger, p. 31; evidence on packets from Sweden, archives of the Stockholm Jewish community.

15. Tennenbaum, "Red Cross to the Rescue," *YVS Bulletin*, October 1959; and mainly, correspondence of the German Red Cross, Foreign Relations Department, JM/1700/4 (see Kulka), and Adler, *Theresienstadt*, note 229a.

16. Inl. II A/B 63/2 (Yad Vashem 027/10). The contents of this file were not included in the material submitted at the Eichmann trial.

17. The following description is based mainly on the article written by Professor Ege for the Red Cross journal, *Samaritan*, to mark the twentieth anniversary of the events of October 1943, and also on Koch (see note 4); cf. also Frisch, II, p. 364.

18. Instructions of the police commissioner to all stations on 11/13/43. Until the visit to Theresienstadt in the summer of 1944, postal services, when permitted, were organized through the social welfare departments of the local authorities and later by the Red Cross. Cf. Koch, p. 67.

19. See p. 175.

20. Koch, as in note 4.

21. The addresses outside Copenhagen bear witness to the help of the farmers and market gardeners with whom the agricultural pioneers and Youth Aliya children had lived and worked. The cards of many of the latter were marked X or FL (*Freds Liga*, i.e., Women's League for Peace and Freedom), which in 1939–40 had brought Youth Aliya children to Denmark.

22. Cilla Cohn, autobiographical novel, p. 137.

23. For details see *ibid.*, pp. 70–71, and Leni Yahil, "Scandinavian Countries to the Rescue of Concentration Camp Prisoners," Yad Vashem Studies, Vol. VI, 1967, pp. 181–220 (hereafter Yahil, *Rescue*).

24. Friediger, pp. 88–89.

25. Oppenhejm, La Cour, III, p. 373.

26. *Theresienstadt*, p. 306.

27. Ze'ev Shek was born in Czechoslovakia and was twenty-three when he was taken to Theresienstadt. He was one of the leaders of Hechalutz. The youth movements were illegally active in the ghetto, and Shek and his colleagues managed to collect documentary material (see Adler, *Theresienstadt*, pp. 703–04). He was among those sent to Auschwitz in the fall of

1944. He is today one of the senior officials of the Israeli Foreign Ministry. The quotations are from Shek's evidence given to the author (Yad Vashem 027/13).

28. Note of Hencke, 10/8/43, in file of the director-general (AA. ST.S.). Corresponding material from the files of the Danish Foreign Ministry used in Hæstrup, Til Landets Beste, pp. 185, 191.

29. Inl. IIg, 54/8. The next day, 10/8, the Danish minister, Mohr, presented Hencke with an additional copy of this same memorandum. Hencke sent this material on to Inland II together with the comment that in his opinion on this case foreign policy considerations necessitated fulfillment of the assurances given.

30. Ibid. The name of the woman, Klara Schultz, appears in Ege's card index; her two daughters were afterward among those released, in spite of everything. See below.

31. AA.ST.S.

32. See Chapter VII, note 128.

33. Inl. II 54/8.

34. Ibid., signed by Wagner.

35. Ibid. The same document appears again with Wagner's signature on 10/20/43.

36. Ibid. Although Ribbentrop replied on the 15th, Best and the RSHA were only informed on the 20th (see also note 35). The cause of this delay is not clear, but it should be recalled that in the meantime the internal discussions on the failure of the action against the Danish Jews had been going on. The subject, among others, was discussed at a meeting between Thadden and Müller on 10/16 (see p. 190), and presumably the matter of returning the deportees was also raised. On 10/18 Best sent the well-known telegram, No. 1272, in which he admitted that the allegations that the Jews had engaged in sabotage and espionage had been propounded "to justify the ends" (cf. Hilberg, p. 363). The telegram is reprinted in Beretning, bilag XIII, bind 3, p. 1380.

37. Letter of the Danish chargé d'affaires (Inl. II AB, 63/2). All the material was passed on to the RSHA "for examination."

38. This memorandum was sent to the RSHA on 11/2.

39. As note 33. This document is reproduced in L. Yahil: "Danish Jews in Theresienstadt," Yalkut Moreshet (Hebrew), July 1965, pp. 15–16.

40. Cf. Chapter V, note 145. The information about the above letter of Best came as a surprise to the German authorities, and from a marginal comment by Grundherr it transpires that he telephoned to Best on 10/26 concerning the matter; the latter promised to send the written assurance by telegram. Having no choice, he did this on 10/28.

41. Memorandum of Thadden, on Wagner's instructions, to Steen-

gracht (AA.ST.S.). The reply was given to Wagner through Steengracht (Inl. IIg, 54/8).

42. Inl. II 54/8. According to the description given here, the main object of Eichmann's journey to Copenhagen was to clarify the questions at issue and regulate them for future reference. The material quoted here would indicate that the instigator of the trip was not Eichmann but Müller.

43. *Ibid.* The two telegrams were sent in two different ways: the first by the most secret code (deciphered by man) and the second by ordinary code (deciphered by machine—"G"—Schreiber).

44. *Ibid.;* Eichmann trial, T/587.

45. *Ibid.;* T/588. We learn of the discussion between Inland II and Eichmann from the comments inscribed in the margin of Best's telegram form of 11/3 (the so-called *Arbeitsexemplar*). The replies of Eichmann also appear there. On the discussion with the Red Cross, see also correspondence at Yad Vashem JM/1700/4; cf. notes 10 and 15; details in note 56 below.

46. The Germans thoroughly investigated the matter, as is clear from Dr. Friediger's statement that he was questioned on the whereabouts of Mrs. Texière (*Theresienstadt,* p. 53). The report of her deportation to Theresienstadt was spread by the Swedish press, apparently following stories that even misled the Danish underground movement. Dr. Melchior relates in his memoirs (p. 175) that she was taken to another old-age home in Copenhagen. Thadden reported on 11/13 that the Danish chargé d'affaires had told him, "to his surprise," that the information about the deportation of the old lady "was apparently incorrect" (Inl. II 54/8). During police cross-examination before his trial, Eichmann claimed that he had never heard of the affair (Vol. III, col. 2655). All in all, at the trial he only remembered—or pretended to remember—very vague and general things about Denmark, such as "it was not worthwhile," that there was much correspondence on the subject with the Foreign Ministry, and that "he thought they had had to return the Jews from Theresienstadt." Even the evidence about his trip to Copenhagen brought forth no clear statement.

47. This seems to be the case in view of indications in certain documents, though no official written announcement has been traced. It may be, however, that such a note does exist in the archives of the Danish Foreign Ministry. Also Hæstrup in the mentioned book gives no clear indication.

48. Two documents from 11/11/43 (Inl. II A/B 63/2).

49. Inl. II A/B 63/2. At the beginning of the letter, which is addressed to Eichmann, is written: "With reference to the talks on this matter with *Sturmbannführer* Günther." The suggestion

to release a few people at once may therefore have been put forward during this meeting.

50. Note to Hencke via Grundherr (Inl. II A/B 63/2).

51. Hencke's report of the talk, *Beretning*, bilag XIII, bind 3, p. 1402, para, 3; and Adler, *Theresienstadt*, note 441.

52. Inl. II A/B 63/2 and cf. note 30.

53. *Ibid.*

54. The treatment of these cases forms a significant part of the contents of file A/B 63/2. In the case of Dr. Isak Edelmann, it transpires that he was brought to Sachsenhausen (after an unsuccessful late attempt at escape on 12/18/43), and his camp number is given. Correspondence on him covers 4/13/44 to 12/8/44. In the case of Axel Metz (in Professor Ege's card index) inquiries are made as to whether he is still alive. The correspondence is from 8/2/44 to 9/4/44, at which time it is announced that he died on 3/13/44. Correspondence to clarify the whereabouts of six old people, which began on 4/19/44, continues until 10/23/44. In the Gestapo's reply from Prague on 5/25 the addresses of four out of six deportees are given while two are reported dead, one in February and one in March. The Danes now (6/15) requested formal information on these deaths, together with information as to what happened to the legacy. Thadden discussed this matter with the Gestapo in Prague during the visit of the Danish commission, but they refused to deal with it. Eventually, the death certificates were handed over by the RSHA in Berlin. It should be noted that the Red Cross also dealt with inquiries of this nature. However, an order was given in Günther's name that replies should only be given if they were positive. Unanswered inquiries were to be regarded as null and void (note on a meeting of 3/4/43 in the correspondence of the Red Cross—see note 15).

55. Cf. statement of Erdmannsdorff, p. 292 and note 16; also *Hvidbog*, I, p. 236.

56. This telegram of Best, No. 1430, is reprinted in *Beretning*, bilag XIII, bind 3, p. 1381; quoted from here by Adler, *Theresienstadt*, note 41; the telegram itself is in Inl. II A/B 63/2. The telegram from the Danish Red Cross to the German Red Cross, Foreign Relations Department, was sent on 10/15; the reply was given on 11/8, after Eichmann's visit to Copenhagen (correspondence of the German Red Cross, Foreign Relations Department, as note 15). The reply of the German Red Cross is printed in Adler, *ibid.*, note 227; cf. also note 45.

57. Inl. II A/B 63/2.

58. This is one of the few documents in this connection signed by Eichmann himself. Printed in Yahil, *Theresienstadt*, p. 73. See Kulka, pp. 23–26.

59. As note 57. During his visit to Hencke on 1/5 the Danish minister also raised the question of the visit to Theresienstadt (para. 5 of note); cf. note 51.
60. Letter dated February 25 (as note 57).
61. Best's telegram, 3/27, as note 57.
62. Best's telegram, 4/4, as note 57.
63. As note 45.
64. Hæstrup, *Til Landets Beste*, p. 191.
65. PS–2377. Cf. Chapter IV, notes 73, 75.
66. This information was given by Hvass, then Danish ambassador to Germany, to the late Dr. Saul Esh, who talked with him on 7/3/62 regarding his visit to Theresienstadt, after the author had failed to meet him for various technical reasons. At the same time, Dr. Esh also saw Hvass's reports.
67. Notes of Hencke on the talk (as note 57), reprinted in *Beretning*, as note 56, and quoted by Adler, *Theresienstadt*, note 41. According to Hvass, he also visited the German Foreign Ministry a number of times on this question.
68. As note 57. This letter does not leave any doubt that Mildner did in fact deal with the matter. Around June 13 Mildner, as he said in his statement, was sent to Theresienstadt to examine the state of the camp. The Swedes mentioned here and elsewhere did not take part in the visit. On 5/15 Mildner wrote to the Red Cross in reply to its letters of 3/14 and 4/26 on the subject (see note 45 above).
69. Note of Thadden to Wagner on June 7. This memorandum is a sort of summary of the negotiations and is of interest for a number of reasons. See below (file as in note 57).
70. As above, notes 45 and 57. The letters were apparently signed by Müller himself, since Mildner was in Theresienstadt on that day.
71. All the documents, see note 57. They include a letter of the Red Cross to the Foreign Ministry on 6/16.
72. Report of Hvass. See Adler, *Theresienstadt*, pp. 159–81, note 108, and Henningsen's report, quoted in *ibid.*, note 98; Rossel's report is given in Adler, Sources, pp. 312–16. The author has also seen Henningsen's report and has made notes from it.
73. This lecture was, obviously, first approved by the German censor, and the facts and figures in it were adjusted to German specifications; see Adler, *Theresienstadt*, pp. 171–72.
74. Henningsen's report.
75. Henningsen's report here and there contains an inserted question mark as an expression of doubt following assertions or explanations given to the visitors. He also writes brief comments, for example: "It is claimed that they get 2,400 calories a day" or "They say there are no lice" or "They claim there are

no new cases of tuberculosis." The report stresses that the parcels are an important factor in nutrition, and there are other hints which may be read between the lines. However, it does not seem that Dr. Henningsen saw through the deception in all its aspects.

76. *Op. cit.*, p. 43. She even relates how the head of the family, a pious and learned Jew, was forced that day to sit in his room and study the Talmud.

77. See note 69 above.

78. During the period of renovations the following rhyme was found on the wall surrounding the camp: "Aussen rein/Und innen Schwein/So wie unser Murmelstein" (Outside shine/And inside swine/Just like our Murmelstein). Cf. also Adler, *Theresienstadt*, Introduction, pp. 21–22. Sharp criticism is also leveled by Ze'ev Shek (see above, note 27).

79. See Adler, *Theresienstadt*, pp. 161–62; Kulka, see note 10.

80. From Dr. Esh's report on his talk with Hvass (see note 66).

81.
                                    "Dr. Max Friediger,
                                    "Seestrasse 28.
                                    "Theresienstadt 26/6 1944.

"To Messrs. Frants Hvass and Juel Henningsen:
"Dear Sirs,
      "As the representative of the Danish Jews in the Council of Elders here, I thank you cordially for your esteemed visit. Through it the realization that all at home are thinking of us has been strengthened, and we were happy to have had fresh greetings from home.
      "You were able to see that we are in good health, and of course the supplement of foodstuffs from Denmark every third week that we have talked about contributes much to this.
      "We have had much pleasure from the parcels of the Danish Red Cross. It is a good idea to address parcels of every type as the Danish Red Cross does—in addition to the addressee's name to add c/o Gemeindeältester der dänischen Juden, and even my name. We would also be happy to receive toilet articles.
      "We look forward very much to the books you have promised us. It is best that you send them by parcel post.
      "We hope to see you here again in the very near future.
                                    "Sincerely yours,
                                    "Dr. Max Friediger"
A postcard written two weeks after the above is reprinted in Adler, Sources, p. 317.

82. Adler, *Theresienstadt*, p. 179; Oppenhejm, as in note 8.

83. Ze'ev Shek tells in his evidence that "the children even made fun of them [the S.S.] . . . in the presence of the visiting com-

mission, such as clapping hands and shouting 'Schon wieder Sardinen' [sardines again]" in mock reference to what they had been taught by the Germans to say (i.e., to create the impression that sardines were a regular part of their diet). The S.S. men were unable to react in the presence of the visitors.

84. From E. H. Boehm, *We Survived (A People Stands Before Its God)*, pp. 293–94.

85. In his reply Thadden said that he would "when the opportunity arose, use the photographs Rossel had given him to show them to people abroad, should they talk of the horrors, as it were, of Theresienstadt." Adler's assumption (Sources, pp. 358–59) that the pictures were those taken by Rossel is correct. Thadden passed them on to Steengracht on 7/22/44 (see note 57). One of the photos shows healthy-looking and well-dressed children. Oppenhejm says of this picture that these children had arrived from France only a few days previously (La Cour, III, p. 377). The photographs are appended to file Inl. II A/B 63/2 in the German Foreign Ministry, and there are copies in Yad Vashem.

86. Telegram No. 917 (Pol. VI 2, No. 6), Hvass said this to Dr. Esh, who showed him the telegram.

87. Ege's card index contained 488 cards.

88. Günther reduces the number of names from 481 to 479 (two people appear in the list twice). A comparison of Günther's figures and those of other reliable sources is as follows:

		Günther	Margolinsky and other reliable sources
Jews of Danish nationality		295	358
Refugees		135	106
		430	464
Already deceased		23	about 40
		407	
Günther also subtracts:			
Jews not of Danish origin	26		
Persons not in Theresienstadt	10		
Persons not finally identified	13		
	49	49	
Number of internees		358	424

In this way Günther reduced the total from 479 to 358. The figures of Margolinsky (424 internees) and of Hvass (427) are, however, more or less identical.

89. Friediger, *Theresienstadt*, p. 83.
90. *Beretning*, bilag XI, p. 59.
91. Talk with Dr. Esh (see note 66).
92. A reaction of this type found expression in the discussion which broke out after the visit between the Council of Elders and Dr. Friediger. He requested that those Danish Jews who had not been transferred to better quarters on the eve of the visit now be given such quarters. Epstein and his supporters refused to do this, and even in a letter Dr. Friediger wrote to Dr. Henningsen after the war (where he criticized certain aspects of the latter's report) he spoke with bitterness of this squabble.
93. Ze'ev Shek says in his evidence: "I remember that on the eve of the visit we, the Hechalutz people, spoke of the possibility of taking advantage of the visit to filter out to the world the fact of the transportations to Auschwitz. What really happened during the visit I cannot say, as I did not participate. One of our people, however, the engineer Zucker [a Czech Jewish leader and one of the Council of Elders] related afterward that he expressed comments, and urged others to do likewise, which would draw the attention of the visitors to the true state of affairs. He said that when they passed by the house called 'The Sluice,' it was explained that it was called so because 'hier schleusst man die Menschen herein und heraus' (here people are sluiced in and out). The visitors may not have understood the allusions. I also know that attempts were made to smuggle letters into the pockets of the visitors [at the Youth House called No. 414]."
94. They wrote a report on this—which showed great courage (printed in Adler, Sources, pp. 304–07).
95. During these very days the struggle between the Danish resistance movement and the Germans, which had become increasingly bitter throughout 1944, reached its peak in Copenhagen. On 6/22—the day before the visit—resistance fighters blew up a large factory in Copenhagen which worked for the Germans. As a result of this action there were sharp reprisals from both sides, and these led at the end of the month to a general strike in the capital, known as "the people's strike." It was accompanied by acts of terror by both sides, the erection of barricades, the stoppage of water, gas, and electricity by the Germans, and so forth. Among others, it was again Duckwitz who managed to mediate and restore calm.
96. See note 36. A small number of non-Jewish Danish women and children were deported to Germany (mainly, it would appear, to Stutthof), but this was nevertheless an unusual occurrence.
97. Koch, pp. 71 ff; *Hvidbog*, I, pp. 236 ff.; Frisch, II, pp. 79–81.
98. Before the war he had been Norwegian minister in Warsaw,

from which he escaped to Stockholm. On this whole affair, see Yahil, *Rescue, passim.*

99. *Ibid.*

100. Frisch, as note 97, and III, pp. 266–67; Koch, as note 97.

101. Quoted from *Theresienstadt,* pp. 135–40.

102. Dr. Holm served in Berlin from February to May 1945. His name does not appear in Koch's article, but the story is related there in detail, reference being made to "a Danish doctor" (pp. 81–82).

103. A detailed description of the journey to and from Theresienstadt is given in Aake Svenson, *De Vita Bussarna,* which surveys all the rescue operations of the Swedish Red Cross.

104. Only that day, apparently, did Svenningsen inform his colleagues officially of the release (*Hvidbog,* I, p. 239).

105. *Op. cit.,* p. 174. Receptions of this type were also the lot of many captives returning home from Neuengamme.

106. This is Margolinsky's figure. Rabbi Friediger gives 423 (p. 138) and Svenson, 424 *(op. cit.).*

107. According to unpublished material of Margolinsky. Dr. Friediger himself says in his book that he and his colleague Axel Margolinsky at first kept a precise card index and other material, but the fear of German search finally impelled them to burn everything (p. 131). Adler states that there were fifty-two dead (p. 45).

108. See Chapter VII, p. 276.

109. *Ved 150 Aars-Dagen* . . . , p. 209.

110. His evidence, Yad Vashem 027/13.

CHAPTER IX

1. See Chapter VI, p. 203.

2. In a speech given in the Swedish town of Lund on 3/8/37, the Danish prime minister, Stauning, described a Scandinavian defense pact as utopian and asked if Sweden intended to make Denmark "its watchdog in the south." Cf. Toynbee, *Survey of International Affairs, 1939–1946,* "The War and the Neutrals," Part I, "Neutrals and Non-Belligerent Allies: Sweden," p. 171. A detailed description of the period may be found in Herbert Tingsten, *The Debate on the Foreign Policy of Sweden, 1918–1939.* A short but clear presentation of the problem is given in William L. Shirer, *The Challenge of Scandinavia,* Chapter III: Sweden. Other literature, mainly Swedish, includes Erik Lönnroth, *Den Svenska Utrikespolitikens Historia 1919–1939; Svensk Utrikespolitik Under 1900-Tallet;* Aake Thulstrup, *Svensk Utrikespolitik Under Andra Världskriget.* See also general bibliography at the end of this book.

3. Tingsten, *op. cit.*, p. 227.

4. See note 1 to Chapter II. Sweden, however, tried unsuccessfully to obtain the approval of England, France, and even Russia to the joint fortification (with Finland) of its important strategic island Aaland in the Baltic Sea.

5. See Toynbee, *op. cit.*, p. 174. Sweden restricted freedom of the press to some extent by means of a special law enacted by the Riksdag in 1940, whereby a paper could be confiscated for security reasons. The law was applied mainly to papers which expressed open and sharp criticism of Germany. It was abolished after the war.

6. See Toynbee, *loc. cit.*, and Shirer, p. 119.

7. Cf. Thulstrup, *op. cit.*, pp. 41–42.

8. Thulstrup, *ibid.*, pp. 7, 59. Shirer was even more outspoken (*ibid.*, p. 22): "Just how neutral Sweden had really been, we have seen. Certainly she had followed a policy of naked opportunism, of cold-blooded national self-interest, of the stern will to survive under terrorizing German pressure."

9. On the problem of the refugees in Sweden, see the already quoted article by Hugo Valentin, "Rescue Activities in Scandinavia," *passim.*

10. See note 23 to Chapter VI.

11. Valentin, *op. cit.*

12. Symptomatic of the period and Jewish apprehensions over Swedish policy is Ragnar Josephson's book *Den Dubbla Loyaliteten (The Double Loyalty).*

13. With the active support of the Stockholm Jewish community a survey was carried out in 1958–59 by two students under the author's supervision. The work was commissioned by Yad Vashem, and the results may be found in its archives. The survey is the source of the above information.

14. Special investigations of this matter were carried out in Sweden after the war, the most important being that of the Royal Commission which in 1954 examined complaints against the head of the administration of refugee affairs, Paulsson.

15. Ture Nerman sums up his activities during the war in the third volume of his memoirs—named, after his periodical, *Trots Allt!* It includes a survey of the period from his point of view. Nerman also established a publishing firm which issued anti-Nazi books and booklets; these were sold in Sweden by the thousands, and some of them were translated by the Danish resistance movement. Among the better-known were the writings of Professor Israel Holmgren.

16. Segerstedt, perhaps one of the truly great European democrats of the thirties and forties, died in March 1945 and was not privileged to witness the fall of the Third Reich. Two collec-

tions of his more than one thousand articles from those years, many of them leading ones from his paper, have been published under the titles *I Dag (Today)* and *Mänskligt (Humanity)*. His first article after Hitler's rise to power (published on 2/3/33) led to a telegram of protest from Goering to the paper on the "dirty expressions" used (*I Dag*, pp. 5–10). From then until his last article on 3/15/45 Segerstedt did not cease to castigate all totalitarian methods. In addition to his firm attitude, his profound faith in man, and his cultural mission, plus his clear, strong style, he was remarkable for his quick political understanding and the depth of his analysis. On 10/25/41, when Hitler stood at the peak of his success, Segerstedt began his leading article with the words: "The time will come when it will be said that the war was decided on the day that Hitler crossed the Russian frontier." It is to be regretted that his articles have not yet found a translator.

17. Thulstrup, *op. cit.*, p. 48; Shirer, *op. cit.*, p. 121; *Utrikespolitik*, p. 68.

18. Cf. Chapter IV, p. 122. The decision was at first secret and was published only at the end of July.

19. Hæstrup, *Alliance*, I, p. 215. In *Paa eget Ansvar* (p. 25) Erling Foss states: "Any description of Denmark's relationship to the Allies, in particular to England, during the war, must begin and end with Ebbe Munck." During his years in Stockholm he collected documents (presented to the Danish State Archives after the war) which are one of the most comprehensive and reliable sources of the history of the Danish underground. They also include Munck's diary (excerpts JM/1967). He is today a high official in the Danish Foreign Ministry.

20. From Munck's article "Forbindelsen med vore allierede," *Hvidbog*, II, p. 146.

21. For the work of the Stockholm center, see Erik Seidenfaden, "Dansk informations-og pressevirksomhed i Sverige," and Erling Foss, "Frihedsraadets repræsentation i Stockholm," both in *Hvidbog*, II; also Ebbe Munck, "Forbindelsen til de allierede regeringer" in La Cour, III, and his "Efterretningstjenesten" in the collection *Danmarks Frihedskamp*, issued by him and by Børge Outze.

22. See Chapter VII, note 128.

23. See p. 18.

24. Renthe-Fink states that at the request of Weizsäcker he emphasized to Kanstein that he was interested in no harm coming to Bohr and asked that he be informed as to whether the Danish National Socialists were plotting any such step. In addition, he told Clausen that he held him responsible for any interference with Bohr by his followers. During his term of

office he heard of no intentions to arrest Niels Bohr (Memo B; cf. Chapter II, note 27). As to Best, Weizsäcker stated on his behalf in his declaration of 5/13/48: "I took an interest at that time in the fate of the atomic physicist Professor Niels Bohr, who was of Jewish blood and therefore threatened by the Third Reich. Best efficiently and successfully held his protecting hand over him and his institute" (Tillægs Extr. IV, bilag 16, p. 59).

25. Ebbe Munck's diary, as note 19.

26. Cf. p. 201

27. This and many other points of information found here were given personally by Professor Bohr in an interview with the author on 7/26/58. The signed résumé of the talk is in Yad Vashem archives (027/13). In a letter of 7/15/58 to the author, Professor Bohr stated: "In its present shape, it [the summary] gives an account of historical facts which one is fully justified in filing." On this occasion he also debunked the various legendary stories spread about his flight.

28. Talk with Ebbe Munck, as in note 25.

29. His evidence, as in note 27.

30. Information provided by courtesy of the Swedish Foreign Ministry (JM/1215–1219).

31. This is not confirmed by any other source, but it is not impossible that some Jews entertained thoughts of this kind. Cf. Dardell's memoirs, *Lyckliga och Stormiga Aar*, *passim*.

32. Cf. p. 151.

33. As note 30.

34. AA.ST.S.; NG–4093, 5118, 5121; Hilberg, p. 361.

35. Bohr's evidence (see note 27).

36. Swedish Foreign Ministry telegram to Richert (see note 30).

37. On Hurwitz's flight see p. 247.

38. Ebbe Munck's archives.

39. AA.ST.S. Cf. L. Yahil, *Rescue*.

40. Presseabteilung AA, P XII b Sonderdienst politischer Nachrichten–Inl. IIg 54/8.

41. The German news agency DNB and the German radio reported this faithfully to the home intelligence service (Inl. IIg 54/8).

42. The announcements were reported in the British press, for example, between October 4 and 13. Some newspapers returned to the item several times: *Daily Herald:* 10/5, 10/7; *Daily Telegraph:* 10/4, 10/6, 10/12; *News Chronicle:* 10/7, 10/11; *The Times:* 10/4, 10/7, 10/13. The reports contained false figures, mainly on the number of deportees, the ships sunk by the Danes, the departmental heads who resigned, the number of Gestapo agents taking part in the action, the leading Nazis who came to expedite the operation—Daluege and Himmler himself

are mentioned—and of course the stories on the Danish king. *The News Chronicle*, however, reported on 10/11 that more than five thousand refugees had arrived in Sweden (a nearly correct figure) and also expressed the view that the Germans were allowing the Jews to escape. It may be said that on the whole, in the situation then prevailing, correct information was more dangerous than legends. The radio (10/3) and a newspaper (*The Scotsman* on 10/4) even announced that Niels Bohr had arrived in Stockholm. Cf. Andrew Sharf, *The British Press and Jews Under Nazi Rule*, 1964, *passim*.

43. For example, *The Economist* and *The Yorkshire Post*, both of 10/9.

44. See note 41; telegrams of 10/4, 10/8, 10/9, 10/10 (AA.ST.S. Inl. IIg 54/8). The German consul in Malmö also found it necessary on 10/12 to report on the stream of Jewish refugees who had "conquered" the coastal towns, on the great help given to them, on castigation of the Germans which had increased greatly in the circumstances; but he does not forget to mention the complaints made of the behavior of the refugees (Inl. II A/B 63/2; Inl. IIg 54/8).

45. Sven Hedin, for instance, who wrote in the Swedish paper *Social-Demokraten* on 10/3 that what had occurred in Denmark was regrettable. Another friend of the Germans, the jurist Professor Olivecrona, also expressed reservations and wrote in *Aftonbladet* on 10/8 that no sensible person would be convinced that the deportation of the Danish Jews was necessary for the German prosecution of the war.

46. Several papers quoted the derogatory expression applied to the Swedes—"Swine in dinner jackets"—*Newsweek* of 10/18, for example. See also Chapter V, note 98.

47. His telegrams of 10/4, 10/5, 10/6, 10/7 (Inl. II 54/8 g).

48. One of the important Finnish statesmen and long-time premier after the war; later speaker of the Finnish Parliament. Leading article in *Iltasanomat* (Blücher on 10/7, as in note 47).

49. The two papers that reacted most strongly were *Davar* on 10/4 and 10/8 and *Hatsofeh* on 10/4, 10/5, 10/15, 11/7, 11/8, 11/18, and 11/12.

50. The report appears in Philipson's diary. See note 61 below and the information of the Swedish Foreign Ministry mentioned in note 30.

51. Swedish Foreign Ministry. Cf. L. Yahil, *Rescue*.

52. Letter to Christmas Møller of 10/12 (see note 38).

53. Among those active during those years (apart from the then chairman of the Zionist Federation, Hugo Valentin) mention should be made of Mr. Arnheim and Mr. Köpniwsky, who were successive secretaries of the Stockholm community, and

the veterinary surgeon Emil Glück, brother-in-law of Slor of Copenhagen, who set up the agricultural training scheme in Sweden. The entry visas obtained by him came to be known as "the Glück quota." Cf. Chapter I, p. 22.

54. The Bermuda Conference was concerned with the refugee problem and was called by Britain and the United States from April 19–30, 1943. Jewish organizations, collectively and singly, laid proposals to save European Jewry before the conference. In the words of Mark Wischnitzer (*To Dwell in Safety*, p. 246): "The proceedings of the Bermuda Conference were shrouded in mystery. Its decisions were kept secret, and the communiqué issued at the end of the sessions declared vaguely that the two governments had studied the problems of refugee aid. But the immediate practical results were nil." It is generally assumed that the idea of UNRRA was first raised at this conference. Cf. A. D. Morse, *While Six Million Died*, London, 1968, *passim*.

55. The data given below are based on a number of documents in the private collection of Mr. Adler-Rudel, now directer of the Jerusalem branch of the Leo Baeck Institute, who kindly showed them and lent them to the author and in addition presented oral information.

56. Cf. S. Adler-Rudel, *A Chronicle of Rescue Efforts*, Year Book of The Leo Baeck Institute, XI.

57. See p. 204.

58. There were at first various formal problems but it was finally bought by the Jewish attorney R. Goldfarb.

59. Semmy Samson, originally from Copenhagen and now in Tel Aviv. Hollander is now the chairman of the Swedish Zionist Federation.

60. This is the same Norbert Masur who in April 1945 went to meet Himmler (see Yahil, *Rescue*). He took part in the dispatch of Raoul Vallenberg to Hungary in the spring of 1944. He is today honorary Swedish consul in Tel Aviv. He and Hollander, at the author's request, wrote a statement of evidence on the "Beginning of cooperation between Swedish Jews and the Danish resistance movement with regard to the flight of the Jews in October 1943" (Yad Vashem 027/13), and the following description is partly based on this material.

61. According to entries in Philipson's diary from 10/3 to 10/13. The diary is part of his private archives on his period of activity in the illegal transport organization. He presented this material in its entirety to Yad Vashem (027/1–7). A large section of it parallels the material in the archives of the Danish-Swedish Refugee Service and in Ebbe Munck's documents in the Danish State Archives.

62. Thus also in Hollander's and Masur's evidence.
63. Most of Leif Hendil's material is included in the archives of the Danish-Swedish Refugee Service. He published privately a booklet entitled *Den aabne Dør til den frie Verden,* the contents of which he announced in a meeting honoring the work of his route held in Copenhagen on 11/30/45. The booklet contains extremely interesting material. Another important source is his article "De illegale transporter til søs" in *Danmarks Frihedskamp,* II, pp. 653–73. Hendil died in 1963. The author was privileged to have met him on several occasions, during which he gave his permission for the archives of the Refugee Service to be examined for the purposes of the present work.
64. As in any rationing system a black market also existed but purchases, as is customary in such cases, were extremely expensive.
65. Some excerpts, chosen more or less at random from Philipson's correspondence: On 6/14/44 he writes to an acquaintance in the Board of Industry: "Dear Friend, I am once more obliged to bother you with my boats and take the liberty of requesting a license for a number of paints. Since I am not yet in possession of all the details, I have assumed that it is possible to ask for the paint for all the boats on one license, but if you think that the applications should be made for each boat separately, please let me know and I will send particulars." Only three days later, on 6/17, he writes to Hendil: "I send you herewith the permit for linseed oil and oil paint I received today from the Board of Industry." In another letter of 6/29, typical of many, he states: "Dear Mr. Hendil, I enclose herewith purchasing permits No. 17909–17911 for a total of 2000 liters of Motil 25. Kindly acknowledge their receipt. According to what I have heard in the Transport Bureau we have a good chance of obtaining a 100 kilos of lubricating oil, and I will write about this again as soon as I can."
66. From the "items for discussion in the meeting of 10/9/43" (Refugee Service and Philipson archives).
67. Letter of Hendil to Munck dated 10/11, paragraph 9.
68. Published in Hendil's article in *Danmarks Frihedskamp,* II, pp. 656–57. The date is here given in error as 10/11.
69. Report No. 4 in the Refugee Service archives.
70. The patrols are mentioned in a memorandum to Günther and appear thereafter at the beginning of each report on the work.
71. Letter to Munck of 10/15. Negotiations began immediately after Hendil's assumption of duties, but he did not wish to complete them until he had received official approval. Also participating was Masur, who had visited Malmö in the meantime.
72. Philipson's archives.
73. The events described below appear in various sources: each

of the three fishermen wrote a report following the incident, and these three documents are filed in the archives of the Service. The incident is also mentioned in Munck's diary and letters.

74. Munck to Philipson on 12/16.

75. Munck's archives. The motives for Marx's daring journey are not clear. He was perhaps interested in joining the British army or in reaching Palestine. In any event, he left behind him considerable debts, and these caused complicated problems to the officials of the Service and to Hechalutz, as transpires from Philipson's correspondence. Both he and Hendil showed extreme consideration for Marx.

76. At the end of January 1944 (Philipson's letter to Hendil dated 1/31/44).

77. He was accused of not acting according to instructions; he also went to Foreign Minister Günther, without the knowledge of the organization, in order to present his own version of the incident (letters of Hendil to Philipson on 12/18 and to Munck on 12/19; Munck's diary 12/18; Hendil's letter of dismissal 12/21/43).

78. Their evidence.

79. In this memorandum (dated 12/18/43) the people saved by transferal to Sweden are described (archives of Philipson and the Refugee Service).

80. Munck's diary entry of 12/19: "Visit from Helweg, as he has to meet Günther tomorrow. We decided that he should explain to His Excellency that the line is also of importance for the Swedes—and that new permission is therefore necessary."

81. Munck's diary, 12/20. At the same time he relates that nineteen persons had that day been successfully brought over on the "northern route."

82. The summary was written in Copenhagen on the same day (1/11/44) by a member of the resistance movement who took part in the meeting. Hendil gives an account in his letter to Philipson of 1/15/44. The document itself is filed in the Refugee Service archives.

83. Aage Heinberg, "Danske flygtninge i Sverige," La Cour, III, p. 414.

84. A comprehensive account of the illegal transportation system is now in preparation in Sweden.

85. *Den aabne Dør*, p. 20. Hendil's line was only surpassed by the Speditør line, which transported two thousand souls. This organization too emerged from the Jewish rescue operation. According to the booklet *Rapport*, the organizers of this line gave top priority to problems of security, and indeed no mishaps occurred to it nor were any of its participants captured (evi-

dence of the line's founder, Scoldy, and his description of the emergence of the organization through help to the Jews, Yad Vashem 027/13).

86. Refugee Service archives, published in *Kilder*, pp. 134–38 (the date is there erroneously given as 11/18/44).

87. A comprehensive report on the operation, written by "Tom" himself as the introduction to a book which he was prevented from completing, was published in the paper of the veteran freedom fighters (*Frihedskampens Veteraner*, No. 26, January 1966).

88. Refugee Service. The report of the week of October 17–23 shows, for instance, expenses amounting to 5,000 Swedish kronor, while the cash reserves were only 10,000. Also available are the financial reports of the *Julius* which show, for example, an outlay of 1008.50 Swedish kronor for the week of November 14–20, including wages to three persons of 450 kronor; expenses for twenty-one sailing hours (two trips to Denmark and back and one journey to the dockyard), 378 kronor; and miscellaneous expenses incurred by the craft, 180.50 kronor.

89. Philipson's archives. This summary is unsigned but may have been the joint work of Philipson and Hendil. The document is written in Swedish.

90. According to memorandum of 1/18/44 (see note 86), "a little more than 200 Swedish kronor."

91. The program was first laid down in a letter from Hendil to Munck; report No. 15 of 11/6/43.

92. "Kontakt med Sverige." See the schema on p. 348 taken from the same article, which is one of the most important written on the illegal transport organization. Arne Sejr himself led the the students' intelligence service (*Studenternes Efterretningstjeneste*) and when he was forced to flee to Sweden in the summer of 1944, he set up a line similar to Hendil's on both sides of the Sound.

93. Based on the above memorandum (note 86); about 15,000 kronor were paid into this fund up to the middle of January 1944.

94. Philipson's archives.

95. Refugee Service archives.

96. Report No. 28.

97. Hendil's letter to Philipson of 1/15/44 and to a member of the service, Kraft, of 1/24/44. Munck noted in his diary on 12/15 that together with Hendil and another associate from the illegal route he visited Henriques to discuss the exchange of Danish kroner for Swedish kronor. Henriques promised also to talk to Hurwitz about a subsidy from the Refugee Office for the transportation service. On this occasion Munck noted: "Henriques, who, besides, belongs to the decent Jews. . . ."

98. Hendil's letter to Kraft, as in the foregoing note, and Kraft's letter to Hendil of 1/26.
99. Cf. notes 79, 86, 89.
100. This assertion was only correct in isolated instances. As shown in Chapter VII, it was in fact the flight of the Jews which opened up financial sources not previously existing to the underground movement.
101. This approach is discussed further in the next section of this chapter.
102. On 2/8. Hendil wrote to Philipson that "we are nearing the estimated 250,000 Swedish kronor" (Philipson's archives). Summing up the appeal Hendil wrote to Henriques: "We are taking this opportunity of thanking you for your willingness to help and support us. Without your help it would have been much more difficult to implement the appeal successfully."
103. *Den aabne Dør*, p. 11.
104. By an agreement signed on January 17, 1945, by Hendil, Polack, and K. Sørensen (the line's representative on the Danish side) new standing orders were laid down with regard to the transfer of money, power of attorney, etc. (Refugee Service archives). In addition, Minister Kruse also demanded a thorough investigation of the currency exchange transactions of the service, as there were rumors and complaints against Hendil in this respect.
105. Report at a meeting, November 30, 1945, *Den aabne Dør*, p. 50; in his article in *Danmarks Frihedskamp*, II, Hendil estimated the contribution as 1.2 million kronor and the total expenditure for the whole system of routes as 3 million.
106. Mainly the Danish Help Service (see p. 346), whose principal task was the transportation of weapons—English and Swedish—to Jutland. The Hendil route fund also supported the new line set up between Helsingnor and Helsingborg after Kiær's seizure by the Gestapo (see Chapter VII, note 93).
107. These figures and the details below are from *Den aabne Dør*.
108. Swedish Foreign Ministry (dossier HP 21 Ad). The name of the head of the legal section was Gösta Engzell. Many of the attempts of the Ministry during this period to save people by granting them Swedish citizenship and the legal activities involved therein were due to him. See Yahil, *Rescue*.
109. The daily number of refugees was as follows: October 4, 440; October 5, 550; October 6, 710; October 7, 700; October 8, 1100; October 9, 1400; October 10, 410; October 11, 200; October 12, 200; October 13, 330; October 14, 260; October 15, 170; October 16, 180. Cf. Per Møller and Knud Secher, *De danske flygtninge i Sverige*, p. 108.
110. Evidence, Yad Vashem 027/13.
111. Møller-Secher, *op. cit.*, pp. 50–56.
112. On negotiations on this point between the Danish minister and

the Swedish authorities, see *ibid.*, pp. 57–65. Hæstrup claims that the first office was set up on the initiative of the military, who wanted to use it for recruiting refugees to military service (*Alliance*, I, p. 90). On this recruitment, see below.

113. Hurwitz, "Om flygtningeadministrationens oprettelse," *Jødisk Samfund*, April 1955.

114. For example, letters to Christmas Møller of 10/22, 10/25, and 11/26, diary of the latter date and of 1/18.

115. Møller-Secher, *op. cit.*; correspondence between Christmas Møller and Henrik Kauffmann dated 1/24/44 and 3/4/44; and cf. Kauffmann's article in *Jewish Ledger* (see Chapter II, note 86).

116. According to Møller-Secher, in his article (note 113), Hurwitz talks of 18 million.

117. As note 113 and in "De danske flygtninge i Sverige" (*Politiken's Kronik*, 5/23/45).

118. Article of the secretary of the Stockholm community, Mr. Köpniwsky, "Da broder hjælp broder i nöden," *Jødisk Samfund*, April 1955, pp. 6–9, and Møller-Secher, *op. cit.* Among others who rendered outstanding help to the refugees and to the underground was Karl Bermann of Malmö. See also Møller-Secher and *Den aabne Dør*, p. 21.

119. In a report written on 11/16/44 for Adler-Rudel and privately filed.

120. Rabbi Melchior in Møller-Secher, pp. 194–96, and Margolinsky in his report. One woman also states in evidence that she went to such a religious camp but left again in view of the unsatisfactory arrangements. She later worked in the Refugee Office in Stockholm, where she spent, in her own words, "two very comfortable years."

121. The exact figures according to Margolinsky's survey: 7906 Jews and non-Jewish relatives, 9114 non-Jews—a total of 17,020. However, apart from the refugees in the card index, a certain number of nonregistered Danes were in Sweden. Their number is difficult to estimate but was apparently small.

122. As note 119.

123. Ebbe Munck writes in his diary on 11/26/43 about a talk with Hurwitz. Among other things, Munck writes: "He refuted the accusations of a 'Jewish office' and pointed out that only 50 per cent of the personnel were Jews; the others were officers and police, whom it was difficult to account for, as they had special assignments." On 1/18/44 he wrote to Christmas Møller: "Professor Hurwitz and his big Refugee Office work exceptionally well, in my opinion." He then mentions that at first, at the beginning of November, there had been some difficulties, but that now grants and subsidies were already being paid out, professional organizations set up, etc. "Criticism of

the large number of officials, which in the very nature of things consists mostly of Jews, has by now quieted down, and work goes ahead with excellent results and energetically all along the line, and good relations have also been established with the Swedish authorities."

124. Møller-Secher, *op. cit.*, p. 108.

125. His memorandum, as note 119.

126. "Hvor mange var vi i Sverige," *Jødisk Samfund*, April 1955, pp. 20–21. He asserts here that the number of Jews of military age in Sweden was only 626, as against 4,783 non-Jews. These figures are based on his statistical research work (p. 5, Table 7).

127. In an article by one of the volunteers (Leo Israel, "Da brigaden kom hjem," *Jødisk Samfund*) he states that in one or two companies it was difficult to raise the ten men required for a Jewish religious service. See also *Den Danske Brigade*, p. 34. The engineer H. Marcus, who had himself volunteered for the brigade in May 1944, received from the chairman of the Danish Brigade Association a list of all the volunteers. Here, as with all other lists of the Refugee Office, volunteers were not registered by religious affiliation. Marcus, however, identified the Jews by name, adding those among the non-Jews who were known to be of Jewish descent. He counted a total of 749 such names, Jews and non-Jews (according to their religion), of whom 392 were over thirty at the time and 357 between the ages of eighteen and thirty. Of the 7,220 Jewish refugees, including those of Jewish descent, 1,376 were refugees from Germany who, being stateless, were ineligible to serve in the brigade. Of the 5,844 Danish Jews, there were only the said 626 men of military age (that is, 14.1 per cent), whereas the eligible group among the 9,114 non-Jewish Danes numbered 4,773 (or 52.3 per cent). Of the 626 men of military age, 357 (59.5 per cent) did volunteer. The number of Jews aged between thirty and forty-nine was 1,311 (compared with a corresponding non-Jewish group of 1,469). I assume that of these, the 392 mentioned above (30 per cent) were recruited. How many of these volunteers of military age and above were still members of the community and how many were only of Jewish descent is impossible to state. The fact that the latter were in Sweden would seem to corroborate that most of them regarded themselves as belonging to the Jewish group, or at least as being in danger.

128. See the statements quoted above, pp. 351–2 and note 97. Margolinsky in his report also points out that the ratio of numbers in the "police" camps led to anti-Jewish remarks. He says that there was nevertheless a friendly atmosphere in the camps themselves. A particularly bad impression was made on the Danish public by the case of lawyer R., one of the leaders of the

community, who was accused of embezzlement while still absent from Denmark. It should be said in his favor that he did return to the country to stand trial. See Frisch, III, p. 109, where this action is praised, and Munck's diary, entry of 12/20/43. It transpires that he was assured that he would not be handed over to the Germans if he returned—and this promise was kept.

129. Evidence, Yad Vashem 027/13.
130. Margolinsky as note 119.
131. A special chapter is devoted to this aspect in Møller and Secher's book, and Margolinsky also comments on it in his account.
132. Margolinsky points out in his article (see note 126) that it was the Jews, of all people, who objected to his statistical analysis of the Jewish population and comparison with other Danes.
133. His book, *Udlændigheds Dage*, pp. 23–24, 66 ff., 127 ff.
134. He published his memoirs in 1964: H. Hurwitz, *En Sabotørs Erindringer*.
135. Mogens Nathan in *Jødisk Samfund*, May 1955.
136. M. Nathan, *op. cit.*

CHAPTER X

1. The king now accepted the resignation of the Scavenius government submitted to him on August 28, 1943 (see p. 126). The members of the new government who played a part in events described in this book were, in addition to Premier Buhl, the politicians, Ole Bjørn Kraft (Defense), H. C. Hansen (Finance), H. Hedtoft (Labor and Social Affairs), Knud Kristensen (Interior), and the men of the resistance movement: Christmas Møller (Foreign Affairs), Mogens Fog (Special Affairs), Frode Jakobsen (Without Portfolio), and Henrik Kauffmann (Without Portfolio).
2. Some 15,000 persons were arrested (la Cour, III, pp. 940–41).
3. The discussion is treated in detail in Frisch, III, pp. 335–52. On the subject of "settlement of justice" (as the judical process on occupation period activities was called) see in particular: Olaf Forchhammer and Carl Gad, *Fakta og myter omkring retsopgøret*, 1948.
4. H. Hedtoft expressed the thanks to Sweden, especially for its help to the underground, in a broadcast published in the paper *Social-Demokraten* on 5/14/45 under the heading TAK TIL SVERIGE.
5. Hendil's published accounts were somewhat exaggerated. He repeatedly emphasized that all the accounts were examined by the legation accountant (cf. Chapter IX, note 104). Obviously he also wished to sell the boats.
6. The fourteen volumes of reports of the commissions of inquiry,

with all their appendixes and stenographic minutes (*Beretning*), are not merely a certificate of honor to the Danish people but also a veritable treasure-house for the student of history. For a description of the structure of the work, see the author's bibliography in "Denmark Under the Occupation," *WLB*, XVI, No. 4. The first commission was appointed on 6/15/45 and the last on 10/25/50.

7. A report on the work of the Central Committee was written by one of its active members, C. V. Andersen, and published in *Jødisk Samfund* on 4/5/46. See also articles by Magna Hartvig in the Israeli daily *Ha'aretz* on 10/3/46 and 6/27/47. Magna Hartvig was a Danish journalist who emigrated to Israel after the war and settled in kibbutz Dafane, where she died in 1962.

8. See also p. 287.

9. Andersen (see note 7). Margolinsky (*Jødisk Samfund*, April 1955) points out that 90 to 95 per cent of the inmates of these temporary camps were Jews. See also Dr. Melchior, interview in *BT* on 10/2/45 and "Jødiske problemer," *Frit Danmark*, 4. Aarg., Nr. 13, 8/3/45.

10. Rabbi Melchior, interview, *ibid.* It should also be remembered that according to his assertion many people were forced to sell their possessions in order to cover the high cost of their transportation (see interview mentioned in note 9 and Chapter VII, note 102).

11. The letter to the Ministry of Justice includes accurate statistical data.

12. A copy of the letter is in the author's possession. See also Margolinsky, as in note 9, and Melchior, "Jødiske problemer," as in note 9.

13. Thus also David Melchior in his evidence (Yad Vashem 027/13).

14. Strong expression of these feelings was given by Frode Jakobsen in a speech to the association of Jewish youth movements on the first anniversary of the liberation. The speech was published in *Jødisk Samfund* on 5/20/46.

15. *Frit Danmark*, 4. Aarg. Nr. 40, 2/15/46.

16. *Jødisk Samfund*, 8/9/46.

17. Apart from Rabbi Melchior's two articles (see notes 9 and 15) there appeared in *Frit Danmark* another article by him on 1/25/46 ("Zionisme og Palæstina") and in *Dansk Ungdom* on 4/12/46 the article "De danske jøder i besættelsestiden" (dealing mainly with Jewish persecution and rescue). Other articles were, for example: Pastor W. Larsen, "Europas syndebuk," *Indre Missions Tidende*, Aarg. 93, Nr. 51/2, 1946; Professor Axel Torm, "Jøderne under krigen og nu," *Ungdoms Arbejderen*, 29. Aarg., Nr. 8/9, Oct.–Nov. 1946 (which states—p. 136—that that part of nazism called anti-Semitism was still present in many who denied any attachment to nazism; the professor's

conclusion, however, is that Jews should adopt Christianity, and he blames Zionism for approximating Nazi ideas); R. Prenter, "Nogle træk of antisemitismens historie og teori," *Det tredje Standpunkt*, 7.–8. Aarg., November 1945; S. T. (a pseudonym), "Tilbage fra Babylon," *Finanstidende*, 32. Aarg., Nr. 12/3, 12/18/46 (this deals with the refugee problem in Zionism and with the Palestine problem); an anonymous article, "Jøder," *Vejen Frem*, 11. Aarg., Nr. 26, 7/28/45 (this article was supposed to have been published on 9/8/43 but was then forbidden by the censor).

18. Cf. Chapter II. THE OCCUPATION AND ITS CHARACTERISTICS.
19. See pp. 341–2.
20. Letter dated 9/21/44, Philipson's archives.
21. *Ekstrabladet*, 8/20/45, p. 5; this was when Melchior's first article appeared (see note 19).
22. Of special note are: O. Gelsted, *Flygtninge i Husaby*; T. L. Meyer, *Flugten over Øresund*; P. Welner, *Ved Øresunds Bredder*.
23. Magna Hartvig, *Ha'aretz*, 6/27/47 (see note 7).
24. This was demanded by one of the resistance men also active in illegal transportation activities, a Dr. Christensen, in the paper *Information* at the end of 1945. It was also mentioned by Melchior in his *Jødisk Samfund* article of 10/15/46, where he discussed the striving for complete assimilation.
25. Zionism forms the subject of a number of the articles mentioned in note 17, and Palestine becomes the main topic in *Jødisk Samfund*.
26. P. Welner, "Krigen mod Jøderne," *Kronik*, Nov. 1946. A description of the events in Denmark against the general background of Jewish persecution in Europe and the Palestine problem may also be found in T. L. Meyer, *Krigens største tragedie—jødeforfølgelserne*, Gjentofte Kommune.
27. Leading article by Rabbi Melchior in *Jødisk Samfund* on the first anniversary of liberation.
28. Evidence (Yad Vashem 027/13). Ten out of fifty persons who gave evidence stated categorically that they based their utterances on notes or diaries. There are expressions of gratitude by Karl Lachmann, Valdemar Koppel, and others.
29. T. L. Meyer, *op. cit.*, pp. 202–03.

Notes to Appendix II

1. Best under cross-examination in Copenhagen, August 31, 1945: Hovedrapport, bil. A 35, pp. 3 ff. Autobiography of Best in S.

Aronson, *Heydrich und die Anfänge des SD und der Gestapo*, (1931–1935), Freie Universitaet, Berlin, 1967, pp. 190–198.

2. In his evidence (see note 1) he described this document as "personal" and as having been written to counteract unemployment. See also Aronson, *ibid.*, pp. 198–201, with quotations from the document and Best's comment.

3. On this period and its importance for the consolidation of the Nazi regime, see Kogon, *Der SS-Staat*, pp. 20–33; Bracher, Sauer, and Schultz, *Die nationalsozialistische Machtergreifung*, pp. 530–44; H. Bucheim, *Anatomie des SS Staates*, Walterverlag, Olten, 1965, p. 44. On his transfer after differences of opinion with the *S.S. Gauleiter* in Hessen, see Best's evidence in Copenhagen, as note 1, pp. 3, 7, *et al.*, Aronson, *ibid.*, pp. 203 ff., 258–59.

4. Werner Best, *Die Deutsche Polizei*, Forschungen zum Staats-und Verwaltungsrecht, published by Reinhard Höhn, Reihe A, Bd. V, 2nd edition, L. G. Wittich Verlag, Darmstadt, 1941. Werner Best, "Die Politische Polizei im Dritten Reich," in *Deutsches Verwaltungsrecht*, pp. 417 ff.; *Völkische Beobachter*, 1/22/36 (IMT 1956–PS). See also quotations from his articles in PS–2232, NCA II, p. 258, and PS–1852, NCA IV, p. 490; Buchheim, *op. cit.*, pp. 48 *et al.*, 52 ff., 62; Aronson *ibid.*, pp. 314–317.

5. Hillscher, pp. 286 ff., quoted in Aronson, *ibid.*, p. 203. Best's status during this period may be partly gauged from the following letter:

"Chief of Security Police
"Berlin
"1st September 1939–8651/39

"To:
(a) Reichsführer–SS
(b) Chef der Ordnungspolizei, General Daluege
(c) SS–Gruppenführer Wolff
(d) SS–Brigadeführer Dr. Best
(e) SS–Oberführer Müller
(f) SS–Oberführer Webe
(g) Major Staudinger
(h) SS–Brigadeführer Albert
(i) SS–Brigadeführer Jost
(j) SS–Standartenführer Dr. Six
(k) SS–Oberführer Bork
(l) Reich Ministry of the Interior, Oberregierungsrat Jacobi.

During my temporary absence from Berlin in connection with Action Poland I designated department head, SS-Brigadeführer, ministerial deputy director, Dr. Best as my representative in my capacity as chief of Security Police and Reichsführer-SS of

Security Headquarters. Inquiries should be addressed to him as follows: Der Chef der Sicherheitspolizei, Berlin S.W. 11, Prinz-Albrecht-Strasse 8.

"[signed] Heydrich
"SS-Gruppenführe"

6. On the conflict between Best and his superiors see also Buchheim, *ibid.*, pp. 76 ff., 180, 198, 287; Aronson, *ibid.*, p. 317.

7. The correspondence known to us as relating to this matter contains the following letters: Wolff to Best, 11/5/41; Best to Wolff, 11/15/41; Best to Heydrich, 4/5/42; telegram from Heydrich to Wolff, 4/14/42; Wolff to Heydrich, 4/14/42; Best to Heydrich, 4/15/42; Best to Wolff, 5/6/42; Best to Heydrich, 5/7/42; Heydrich to Best, 5/12/42; and Best to Wolff, 5/13/42.

8. See the articles by Nachman Blumenthal, "On the Nazi Vocabulary," Yad Vashem Studies I, pp. 69 ff.; and by Shaul Esh, "Words and Their Meaning," Yad Vashem Studies V, pp. 133–167.

9. Dr. Best asserted (Copenhagen cross-examination, as in note 1, pp. 3 ff.) that he had acquired his ideas on nations and their mission from Fichte. An interesting result of this inner struggle was a memorandum, "Völkische Neuordnung Westeuropas zur Sicherung des Reiches," which he wrote in November 1941 and sent to various leading Nazis. For his own reading list, see Aronson, *ibid.*, p. 193; cf. p. 197.

10. Buchheim, *ibid.*, pp. 281–82; Aronson, *ibid.*, p. 195.

11. "I would be very interested in occupying myself with the colonial question, since I have still not given up the idea of ruling and and developing a colony one day": April 5, 1942 (Document Center).

12. Poliakov, *Das Dritte Reich und die Juden*, p. 414; *idem*, *Das Dritte Reich und seine Diener*, p. 320; Tennenbaum, pp. 269 ff.; Billig, *Le Commissariat*, I, pp. 26, 63, 60–63, and II, p. 17; Monneray, *La Persécution*, pp. 48 ff., 83, 89 ff., 134 ff. and 137 ff.; Center LXXV, pp. 72, 81; Kempner, *Eichmann*, pp. 345–57; IMT XXXVIII, pp. 387 ff.; Hilberg, p. 390.

13. Bertelsen, in his book, quotes a letter of June 22, 1942, from Best to the S.S. commanders. The extract runs as follows: "The Jewish question is the explosive we use to blow up the fortresses where liberalism's last snipers have ensconced themselves. The nations which give up their Jews give up therewith their former special form of existence, which was based on misunderstood ideals of freedom. It is only then that they can conquer their place in the struggle for a new world" (pp. 228 ff. in the English edition; the date is erroneously given as June 22, 1944). Neither Bertelsen nor the author have succeeded in tracing the original document.

Biographical details on Best may also be found in Bracher, *Die*

Auflösung der Weimarer Republik, pp. 432, 434, 540; *Degener's Wer ist's,* Berlin, 1935; E. Eyk, *Geschichte der Weimarer Republik,* pp. 417 ff.; Görlitz and Quint, *Adolf Hitler,* pp. 329 ff.; *Internationales Biographisches Archiv* (Munzinger Archiv), 1959; Poliakov and Wulff, *Das Dritte Reich und seine Denker,* pp. 479, 499, 501; Best, *Lebenslauf,* 1937, Document Center; JMT XX, pp. 137, 141; XX, p. 265; XXIX pp. 15–26.

Note added to paperback edition (1983):

The only principal description and analysis of the Germans' handling of the Jewish question in Denmark in the year following the Wannsee Conference differing from that presented here is presented by Christopher Browning in his instructive book *The Final Solution and the German Foreign Office,* New York - London, 1978, pp. 250f., n. 70. He argues that the reluctant policy towards the Jews in Denmark was not decisively influenced by Renthe-Fink but was mainly based on Luther's own judgment. He ignores, however, my main argument, to wit, that it was the clear stand of the Danish authorities and the population which convinced the Germans at that time that it was not worthwhile to instigate the Danes by implementation of the "final solution." I never argued that this was achieved by Renthe-Fink "leading Luther around by the nose." Many more officials were involved in the policy making. Especially in the fall of 1942 the political situation in Denmark was so complex (as can be seen on pp. 68–75) that Luther's abstention from acting against the Jews has to be attributed to the coincidence of many factors. As stated on p. 71, he wrote to Rademacher on September 9: ". . .we must at once deal with the Jewish problem in Denmark and solve it radically. . . . Our interests demand that it be 'either—or'." Apparently, for many reasons, he chose later the 'or', following Renthe-Fink's suggestion to impose on the Jews only some not very important economic restrictions.

BIBLIOGRAPHY

Bibliography

The bibliography is divided into the following sections: general and Danish bibliographical literature; documentary literature, including published documentary material (as distinct from the documentary material in archives); and general literature on the period, its events, its problems, and persons discussed in this book. In some instances the general material also includes works devoted to the Danish problem in particular (for example, the works of H. G. Adler). This category also contains other Scandinavian literature, mainly Swedish, relevant to our subject. The category "Denmark Under the Occupation" includes mainly Danish works and a number of books, articles, etc. that refer to Denmark in general during that period or to the rescue of the Jews in particular. The remaining two categories are concerned with the history of the Jews in Denmark and with Danish anti-Semitism. The works given here are generally those used in this study. Titles and names of authors have been anglicized. The chapter notes refer to them in abbreviated form; full bibliographical details are to be found in the relevant section of the lists given below.

BIBLIOGRAPHICAL LITERATURE

Bruun, H., ed. Dansk Historisk Bibliografi, H. Hagerups Forlag, Kbhn., 1956.
Burchardt, L.; Fabritius, A.; Toemasen, H. Besaettelsestidens Illegale Blade og Boeger, 1940–1945, Det Kongelige Bibliothek, Kohn., 1954.

Danmark Under Besaettelsen, Litteraturliste No. 23, Udgivet af Dansk Bibliografisk Kontor, 1961.

Kilder til Besaettelsestidens Historie, Fortid og Nutid, Bd. XXII Hefte 2, Kbhn., 1963, p. 1–76.

Robinson, J.; Friedman, Ph. Guide to Jewish History Under Nazi Impact, New York, 1960.

Wiener Library, Catalogue Series No. 1, 2nd ed., London, 1960.

Yahil, Leni. Denmark Under the Occupation: A Survey of Danish Literature, The Wiener Library, Bulletin, Vol. XVI, No. 4, October 1962.

DOCUMENTARY LITERATURE

Alkil, N., ed. Besaettelsestidens Fakta, Dokumentarisk Haandbog, J. H. Schultz Forlag, Kbhn., 1945–46.

Barfoed, J.; Kruchow, E. Denmark Under 2. Verdenskrig Kilder og Tekster, 2 vols., Gyldendal, Kbhn., 1959.

Beretning til Folketinget, Afgivet af den af Tinget Under 19. Dec. 1945 Nedsatte Kommission i Henhold til Grundlovens § 45, Bd. I–Bd. XV, J. H. Schultz A/S, Universitets-Bogtrykkeri, Kbhn., 1945–1958.

Best-Sagen, G. E. C. Gads, Kbhn., 1950.

Foss, E. Fra Passiv til Aktiv Modstand, Gyldendal, Kbhn., 1946.

Haestrup, J. Kilder til Modstandsbevaegelsens Historie, Gyldendal, Kbhn., 1962.

Heiler, H., ed. Hitlers Lagebesprechungen, Quellen und Darstellungen zur Zeitgeschichte, Bd. 10, Deutsche Verlags-Anstalt, Stuttgart, 1962.

International Military Tribunal (IMT), Nuremberg 1947–49, 42 vols.

Nazi Conspiracy and Aggression (NCA), United States Government Printing Office, Washington, 1946, 11 vol.

Trials of War Criminals, case 1–12(TWC), United States Government Printing Office, Washington, 1949–53.

BOOKS AND ARTICLES ON GENERAL AND SCANDINAVIAN SUBJECTS

Adler, H. G. Danish Jewry Under German Occupation, The Wiener Library, Bulletin Vol. IX, 1–2, January–April 1955.

——— Die Verheimlichte Wahrheit, Theresienstaedter Dokumente, I. C. B. Mohr. Tuebingen, 1958.

——— Theresienstadt 1941–1945, I. C. B. Mohr, Tuebingen, 1960.

Anderson, I. A History of Sweden, Weidenfeld & Nicolson, London, 1957.

Arendt, Hannah. The Origins of Totalitarianism, Meridian Books, New York, 1960.

——— Eichmann in Jerusalem, The Viking Press, New York, 1963.

Arneson, B. A. The Democratic Monarchies of Scandinavia, D. van Nostrand Company, Inc., Toronto, New York, London, 1949.

Best, W. Wird Geschossen, Die Wahrheit Ueber das Boxheimer Dokument, Selbstverlag, Mainz, 1932.

———— "Die Politische Polizei im Dritten Reich," in: Deutsches Verwaltungsrecht, 417 ff. (H. Frank, ed.), 1937.

———— "Die Deutsche Polizei," Forschungen zum Staats- und Verwaltungsrecht, Hrsg. von Reinhard Hoehn, Reihe A Bd. V, 2. Aufl., L. C. Wittich-Verlag, Darmstadt, 1941.

Billig, J. Le Commissariat Général aux Questions Juives (1941–1944), Tome I–II, Editions du Centre, Paris, 1955.

Bluecher, W. von. Gesandter Zwischen Dikatur und Demokratie, Limes Verlag, Wiesbaden, 1951.

———— Wege und Irrwege der Diplomatie, Limes Verlag, Wiesbaden, 1953.

Boehm, E. We Survived, Yale University Press. New Haven, 1949.

Bracher, K. D. Die Aufloesung der Weimarer Republic, Ring-Verlag, Stuttgart u. Duesseldorf, 1957.

Bracher; Sauer; Schulz. Die Nationalsozialistische Machtergreifung. Westdeutscher Verlag, Koeln und Opladen, 1960.

Derry, T. K. The Campaign in Norway, Her Majesty's Stationery Office, London, 1952.

Friedmann, P. The Jewish Badge and the Yellow Star in the Nazi Era, Historia Judaica, Vol. XVII, No. 1, April 1955.

———— Their Brothers' Keepers, Crown Publishers, New York, 1957.

A German of the Resistance, The lost letters of Count Helmuth James von Moltke, Geoffrey Cumberlege, Oxford University Press, London, 1947.

Gilbert, G. M. Nuremberg Diary. The New American Library, New York, 1961.

Hansen, P. Contemporary Danish Politicians, "Danes of the Present and Past," Det Danske Selskab, Kbhn., 1949.

Hassell, U. von. Vom Andern Deutschland, Atlantic Verlag, Zurich, 1948.

Hilberg, R. The Destruction of the European Jews, Quadrangle Books, Chicago, 1961.

Hubatsch, W. Die Deutsche Besetzung von Daenemark und Norwegen 1940, Musterschmidt, Goettingen, 1952.

———— Die Deutsche Berufsdiplomatie im Kriege (Um die Daenische Souveraenitaet 1940–1943), Aussenpolitik, Ztsch. f. internationale Fragen, Jhrg. 6, 1955, p. 170–180.

Kempner, R. M. W. Eichmann und Komplizen, Europa Verlag, Zurich, 1961.

Kogon, E. Der SS-Staat, Europaeische Verlagsanstalt, Stuttgart-Zurich, 1959.

Kolb, E. Bergen-Belsen, Geschichte des 'Aufenthaltslagers,' 1943–

1945, Verlag fuer Literatur und Zeitgeschichte, Hannover, 1962.

Kordt, E. Wahn und Wirklichkeit, Union Deutsche Verlagsgesellschaft, Stuttgart, 1948.

—————— Nicht aus den Akten, Union Deutsche Verlagsgesellschaft, Stuttgart, 1950.

Krabbe, L. Histoire de Danemark, des Origines jusqu'à 1945, Ejnar Munksgaard, Copenhagen, C. Klincksieck, Paris, 1950.

Lanwers, J. A., ed. Scandinavian Democracy: Development of Democratic Thought and Institutions in Denmark, Norway and Sweden, Copenhagen, 1958.

Leber, A.; Moltke, F. von. Fuer und Wider, Entscheidungen in Deutschland 1918–1945, Mosaik Verlag-Annelore Leber, Berlin, Frankfurt/M., 1961.

Lemkin, R. Axis Rule in Occupied Europe, Carnegie Endowment for International Peace, Washington, 1944.

Lochner, Louis P., ed. Goebbels Tagebuecher, aus den Jahren 1942–1945, Atlantis Verlag, Zuerich, 1948.

Loennroth, E. Den Svenska Utrikespolitikens Historia, V, 1919–1939, Norstedts, Stockholm, 1959.

Monneray, H. La Persécution des Juifs en France et dans les Autres Pays de l'Ouest, Editions du Centre, Paris, 1947.

Muenz, M. Die Verantwortlichkeit fuer die Judenverfolgungen im Ausland Waehrend der Nationalsozialistischen Herrschaft, typ. J. W. Goethe-Universitaet, Frankfurt/M., 1958.

Nerman, T. Trots Allt! Kooperativa Foerbundets Bokfoerlag, Stockholm, 1954.

Poliakov, L. L'Etoile Jaune, Editions du Centre, Paris, 1949.

Poliakov, L.; Wulf, J. Das Dritte Reich und die Juden, Dokumente und Aufsaetze, Verlags GmbH, Grunewald, 1955.

—————— Das Dritte Reich und seine Diener, Dokumente, Verlags GmbH, Grunewald, 1956.

—————— Das Dritte Reich und seine Denker, Verlags GmbH, Grunewald, 1959.

Reitlinger, G. The Final Solution, Vallentine, Mitchell & Co., London, 1953.

Rost, N. Les Juifs sous l'Occupation Allemande dans les Pays Scandinaves, Paris, 1949.

Rothfels, H. Die Deutsche Opposition Gegen Hitler, eine Wuerdigung, Fischer Buecherei, Frankfurt/M., 1958.

Royal Institute of International Affairs, Administration of Countries Under German Control, 1941; Europe Under Hitler in Prospect and Practice, 1941; The Bulletin of International News, Vol. XVIII, No. 2, 1941; The Scandinavian States and Finland, London, New York, 1951; Survey of International Affairs

1939–1946. (A. Toynbee and M. Veronica, ed.), Oxford University Press, London: Vol. 4, Hitler's Europe, 1954; Vol. 9, The War and the Neutrals, 1956.

Sabile, J. Comment Furent Sauvés les Juifs du Danemark, Le Monde Juif, 4e Année, No. 24–26, Octobre–Décembre 1949.

———— Lueurs dans la Tourmente, Episodes de la Lutte pour la Défense des Juifs Persécutés en Europe du Nord pendant la Guerre de Hitler, Editions du Centre, Paris, 1956.

Sandblad, H. GHT och Hitlerregimen, Goeteborgs Handelstidnings Foerlag, 1960.

Seabury, P. The Wilhelmstrasse: A Study of German Diplomats Under the Nazi Regime, University of California Press, Berkeley and Los Angeles, 1954.

Segerstedt, T. "I Dag," Norstedts, Stockholm, 1945.

———— "Maenskligt," Norstedts, Stockholm, 1948.

Seth, R., The Undaunted: The Story of Resistance in Western Europe, Muller, London, 1956.

Sherman, F. M. ed. Democracy in Denmark, National Home Library Association, Washington, D.C., 1936.

Shirer, W. L., The Challenge of Scandinavia, Robert Hale, London, 1956.

———— The Rise and Fall of the Third Reich, Simon & Schuster, New York, 1960.

Svensk Utrikespolitik Under 1900 Talet, Utrikespolitika Institutet Stockholm, 1958.

Thulstrup, A. Svensk Utrikespolitik Under Andra Vaerldskriget, Albert Bonniers Foerlag, Stockholm, 1950.

Tingsten, H. The Debate on the Foreign Policy of Sweden, Oxford University Press, London, 1949.

Utrikesdepartement (Sweden), Foerspelet till det Tyska Angreppet Paa Danmark och Norge, Amtstycken Utgivna af Kungl. UD, Stockholm, 1947.

———— 1945 Aars Svenska Hjaelpexpedition till Tyskland, Foerspel och Foerhandlingar, Amtstycken Utgivna af Kungl. UD, Stockholm, 1956.

Valentin, H. Antisemitenspiegel, Verlag Dr. Heinrich Glanz, Wien, 1937.

———— Rescue Activities in Scandinavia, YIVO Annual of Jewish Social Science, New York, 1953, pp. 224–251.

Weizsaecker, E. von. Erinnerungen, Paul List Verlag, Muenchen, 1950.

Zander, F. H. Die Verbreitung der Juden in der Welt, Robert Kaemmerer Verlag, Berlin, 1937.

Zeller, E. Geist der Freiheit, Der 20. Juli 1944, Verlag Hermann Rim, Muenchen, 1954.

DENMARK UNDER THE OCCUPATION

Algreen-Petersen, C. Christian, Illegaler Bote, I–III, mim.

Aschenfeldt-Frederiksen. Joedeforfoelgelserne og Gilleleje, "Fra det Gamle Gilleleje," 1946.

Bernadotte, F. Slutet, T. A. Norstedt, Foerlag, Stockholm, 1945.

——— Mennesker jeg Moedte, Gyldendalske Boghandel, Kbhn., 1948.

Bertelsen, A. October 1943, Jydsk Centraltrykkeris Forlag, Aarhus, 1947.

——— October 43, G. P. Putnam's Sons, New York, 1954.

——— October 43, Ner-Tamid Verlag, Muenchen, 1960.

Besaettelsens Hvem-Hvad-Hvor, Politikens Forlag, Kbhn., 1965.

Bindsloev, F. L. Pressen Under Besaettelsen, Universitetsforlaget i Aarhus, 1960.

Borchsenius, P. Udlaendigheds Dage, Steen Hasselbachs Forlag, Kbhn. 1946.

Brix, K.; Hansen, E. Dansk Nazisme Under Besaettelsen, Schultz Forlag, Kbhn., 1948.

Broendsted, J.; Gedde, K. De Fem Lange Aar, I–III, Nordisk Forlag, Kbhn., 1946–47.

Buchardt, L.; Fabritius A.; Ruge, M.; Toennesen, H., ed. Den Illegale Presse 1940–1945: En Antologi, Gyldendal, Kbhn., 1965.

Cholewa, Sulamith. The Danish Jews in Theresienstadt, YIVO Bletter, Vol. 30, No. 2, p. 310.

Christensen, C. Under Jorden i Borgergade, Nyt Nordisk Forlag, Arnold Busck, Kbhn., 1954.

Cohn, Cilla. En Joedisk Families Saga, Nyt Nordisk Forlag, Arnold Busck, Kbhn., 1960.

Danske Laegememoirer, Nyt Nordisk Forlag, Arnold Busck, Kbhn., 1945.

Dardel, G. von. Lyckliga och Stormiga Aar, Wahlstroem & Widstrand, Stockholm, 1953.

Det Stod Ikke i Avisen, Stiftstidendes Forlag, Aalborg, 1945.

Ebbesen, N. (Heinberg, Aage). En Konung, Natur och Kultur, Stockholm, 1942.

——— Danmark Saeger NEJ, Danmarks Fortsatta Oede, Natur och Kultur, Stockholm, 1943.

Flender, H. Rescue in Denmark, Simon & Schuster, New York, 1963.

Fog, M. Danmark Frit 1942–1946, Thaning & Appel, Kbhn., 1947.

Forchhammer, O.; Gad, C. Fakta of Myter, Omkring Retsopgoeret, C. A. Reitzels Forlag, 1948.

Fosmark, J., ed. Danske i Tyske Koncentrationslejre, Nordisk Forlag, Kbhn., 1945.

Foss, E. Paa Eget Ansvar 1944–45, Gyldendal, Kbhn., 1958.

Friediger, M. Theresienstadt, J. Fr. Clausens Forlag, Kbhn., 1946.

Frisch, H. Danmark Besat og Befriet, I–III, Forlaget Fremad, Kbhn., 1945–1948.

————Taenkt of Talt Under Krigen, Forlaget Fremad, Kbhn., 1945.
Friis, A., ed. Danmark Under Verdenskrig og Besaettelse, I–IV, A. C. Normans Forlag, Odense, 1946–48.
Frit Danmarks Hvidbog, Besaettelsestiden i Dokumenter og Kommentarer, I–II, Thaning & Appel, Kbhn., 1945–46.
Gelsted, O. Flygtninge i Husaby, Atheneum, Kbhn., 1945.
Gersfelt, J. Saadan Narrende vi Gestapo, Gyldendal, Kbhn., 1945.
Gudme, S. Denmark: Hitler's "Model Protectorate," Victor Gollancz, London, 1942.
Hansen, H. Besaettelsens Fem Onde Aar, Kandrup & Wunsch, Kbhn., 1945.
Hendil, L. B. Den Aabne Doer, Dansk-Svensk Flytningetjenestes Virksomhed i Malmoe, Privattryk, Kbhn., 1946.
Horwitz, H.; Rasmussen, K. En Sabotoers Erindringer, Forlaget Fremad, Kbhn., 1964.
Haestrup, J. Kontakt med England, Thaning & Appel, Kbhn., 1959.
———— Hemmelig Alliance, Hovedtraek af den Danske Modstandsorganisations Udviking 1943–1945, I–II, Thaning & Appel, Kbhn., 1959.
———— From Occupied to Ally: Danish Resistance Movement, 1940–45, The Press and Information Dept., Ministry of Foreign Affairs, Copenhagen, 1963.
———— Die Daenisch-Deutschen Beziehungen von 1933–1945, Deutschland und der Norden 1933–1945, Internationales Jahrbuch fuer Geschichtsunterricht 1961–62, Albert Limbach Verlag, Braunschweig.
———— Exposé, European Resistance Movements, 1939–1945, I–II, Pergamon Press, Oxford, London, New York, Paris, 1960–1964.
Jacobsen, E. T. Paa en Urias Post, Folmer Christensens Forlag, Kbhn., 1946.
Kauffmann, H. Denmark and the Jews, "Jewish Ledger," Springfield, Mass., 11/12/43.
Kiaer, E. Med Gestapo i Koelvandet, J. Frimodts Forlag, Kbhn., 1945.
Kjerulf; Jensen, K.; Trier Moerch, E. Saadan Kom de Hjem. Ejnar Munksgaards Forlag, Kbhn., 1945.
Koch, H. Dagen og Vejen, Dansk Ungdomssamvirke, Westermann, Kbhn., 1942.
La Cour, V. Danmark under Besaettelsen, Westermann, Kbhn., 1945–46, I–III.
———— Paa Vej Mod Katastrofen, P. Haase, Kbhn., 1945–49, I–III.
———— Danmarks Historie, 1900–1945, I–II, Berlingske Forlag, Kbhn., 1950.
Lampe, D. The Savage Canary: The Story of Resistance in Denmark, Cassel & Co., London, 1957.
Lazar, S. Ruhm dir Daenemark (Historisches Poem), Oriole Press, Berkeley Heights, New Jersey, 1960.

Lefèvre, H. Maendene i Danmarks Frihedsraad, Wilhelm Priors Forlag, Kbhn., 1945.

Leistikow, G. Denmark Under the Nazi Heel, Foreign Affairs, Vol. 21, No. 2 (January 1943), pp. 340–53.

Lembourn, H. J., ed. Gaa til Modstand, Der Schoenbergske Forlag, Kbhn., 1961.

Masur, N. En Jude Talar med Himmler, Albert Bonniers Foerlag, Stockholm, 1945.

Meyer, T. L. Flugten over Oeresund, Jespersen og Pio Forlag, Kbhn., 1945.

———— Krigens stoerste Tragedie—Joedeforfoelgelserne 1943, Gjentofte Kommune under Besaettelsen 1940–1945, Hellerup, 1947.

Moeller, P. Un Peuple Se Réveille, Marguerat, Lausanne, 1944.

———— Kanarienfuglen og Hitler, Povl Branners Forlag, Kbhn., 1945.

Moeller, P.; Secher, K. De Danske Flygtninge i Sverige, Nordisk Forlag, Stockholm, 1945.

Munck, Ebbe; Outze, Børge, ed. Danmark Frihedskamp, I–II, Bogforlaget Nutiden, Kbhn., 1949.

Nielsen, M. Undervejs til Livet, Gyldendalske Boghandel, Nordisk Forlag, Kbhn., 1948.

———— Rapport fra Stutthof, Gyldendalske Boghandel, Nordisk Forlag, Kbhn., 1948.

———— Faengselsdage og Fangennaetter, Tiden, Kbhn., 1949.

Nissen, S. H.; Poulsen, H. Paa Dansk Frihedsgrund, Gyldendal, Kbhn., 1963.

Olesen, A. Fra Utrykte Kilder, A. Olesèn Forlag, Aabenraa, 1951.

———— Forspillet til Danmarks Kamploese Besaettelse 9. April 1940, A. Olesens Forlag, Aabenraa, 1953.

Oppenhejm, R. Det Skulde Saa Vaere: Marianne Petits Dagbog fra Theresienstadt, H. Hirschsprung, Kbhn., 1945.

———— The Door of Death, London, 1948.

Outze, B., ed. Denmark During the German Occupation, The Scandinavian Publishing Co., Allan C. Christensen, Copenhagen, London, Chicago, 1946.

Pedersen, O. Den Politiske Modstand Under Besaettelsen, Gyldendalske Boghandel, Nordisk Forlag, Kbhn., 1946.

Refslund, C.; Schmidt, M., ed. Fem Aar, Indtryk og Oplevelser, H. Hagerups Forlag-Slesvigsk Forlag, Kbhn., 1946.

Sandbaek, H., ed. Den Danske Kirke Under Besaettelsen, H. Hirschsprungs Forlag, Kbhn., 1945.

Scavenius E. Forhandlingspolitiken Under Besaettelsen, Steen Hasselbachs Forlag, Kbhn., 1948.

Soendergaard, C. I Tiske Laenker, Povl Branners Forlag, Kbhn., 1945.

Sparring-Petersen, G. Med Gestapo i Haelene, Nyt Nordisk Forlag, Arnold Busck, Kbhn., 1945.

————, ed. Danmark Ufredsaar, Arnold Busck, Kbhn., 1947.

Svendstorp, A., ed. Den Hvide Brigade, Carl Allers Bogforlag, Kbhn.,
1946.

Svenson, A. De Hvide Busser, Der Schoenbergske Forlag, Kbhn.,
1945.

Thaulow, T. Konge og Folk Gennem Braendingen 1937–1945, H.
Hagerup, Kbhn., 1945.

Torn, A. Joederne Under Krigen, Israelsmissionens Bogforlag, Kbhn.,
1945.

Vigen, A. Erik Scavenius, En Dansk Uderrigspolitiks Hoved Person
og Syndebuk, Arne Frost-Hansens Forlag, Kbhn., 1958.

Welner, P. Krigen mod Joederne, R. Wangel, Kbhn., 1946.

———— Ved Oeresunds Bredder, Thaning & Appel, Kbhn., 1953.

THE HISTORY OF THE JEWS IN DENMARK
(other books and articles are given in the notes to Chapter I)

Balslev, B. De Danske Joeders Historie, O. Lohse, Kbhn., 1932.

Cohen, A. D. De Mosaiske Troesbekjenderes Stilling i Danmark Forhen og Nu, Odense 1837.

Fischer, J. Joederne i Koebenhaven i det 17de Aarhundrede, Joedisk
Almanach (Joseph M. Goldschmidt, ed.), Kbhn., 1906.

Grossmann, V. Joederne i Koebenhavn, Kbhn., 1918.

Gudme, P. Joedeproblemeti Danmark, Gyldendal, Kbhn., 1935.

Hartvig, M. Joederne i Danmark i Tiden 1600–1800, K. E. C. Gads
Forlag, Kbhn., 1951.

Joergensen, H. C. Joederne i Danmark Omkring 1931, Nationaloeko-
nomisk Tidsskrift, 1934.

Margolinsky, J. Statiskiske Undersoegelser over Alders—og Koens-
fordelingen Blandt Flygtninge fra Danmark i Sverige, Stockholm, 1945, mim.

———— Judarna i Danmark, Judisk Kroenika, Stockholm, Februari–
Mars 1946.

———— Joediske Blade i Danmark, Joedisk Samfund, Januar–Marts
1954.

———— Abraham Gotfred de Meza og Hans Familie, Joedisk Samfund,
Januar 1955.

———— Gravpladserne Paa Mosaisk Nordre Kirkegaard i Moellegade
1693–1953, Kbhn., 1956, mim.

———— De joediske Provinskirkegaarde—Historik Overblik, Udvalg af
Gravskrifter, Uddrag af De Joediske Kirkegaarde i Danske
Provinsbyer, Kbhn., 1957, mim.

———— Minder fra Joedekirkegaarden i Moellegade, Historiske Med-
delser om Koebenhavn, 4, Raekke, V, Bd. 3–4, 1957.

————, *ed.* Chevra Kaddischa, Udgivet af Bestyrelsen for det Fore-
nede Israelitiske Begraevelseskab, Kbhn., 1958.

—— Les Juifs au Danemark, Programme du Congrès de la B'nai B'rith, Paris, Août 1962.

—— Danmark Loge, Udgivet in Anledning af 50 Aars Jubilaeet, Kbhn., 1962.

Margolinsky, J.; Meyer, P., ed. Ved 150 Aars-dagen for Anordningen af 29. Marts 1914, Udgivet af Det mosaiske Troessamfund og Danmark Logen, Kbhn., 1961.

Moritzen, J. Denmark's Jews, Contemporary Jewish Record, Vol. III, May–June 1940 (American Jewish Committee).

Nathansen, H. Georg Brandes, Et Portraet, A. Busck, Kbhn., 1929.

—— Jude oder Europaeer: Portrait von Georg Brandes, Ruetten & Loening, Frankfurt/M., 1931.

Nathanson, M. L. Historisk Fremstilling af Joerdernes Forhold og Stilling i Danmark, Kbhn., 1860.

Salomon, J. Bidrag til Dansk–Joedisk Historie, 1820–45, Y. L. Lybeckens Forlag, Kbhn., 1918.

Salomon J.; Fischer, J. Mindeskrift i Anledning af Hundredaarsdagen for Anordningen af 29. Marts 1814, Udgivet af Danmark Loge UOBB, Kbhn., 1914.

—— Tillaeg til Arkivalia XIX i Mindeskrift.

Trap, C. Russiske Joeder i Koebenhavn efter Folketaellingen 1921, Joedisk Tidsskrift, Wilhelm Trydes Forlag, Kbhn., 1922.

Wilhelm, K. Jewish Communities in Scandinavia, Leo Baeck Year Book, East and West Library, London, 1958, pp. 313–322.

DANISH ANTI-SEMITIC LITERATURE

Andersen, A. Verdensanskuelse, National-Socialistiske Studiekredse, Eget, 1934.

Andersen, J. Joederne i Danmark, Den Ny Tid's Forlag, Kbhn., 1940.

Brunde, H. Danskerne og de Andre, Bernh. Meyers Boghandel, Kbhn., 1920.

Christensen, L. Det Tredie Ting, Dansk Bogkreds, Kbhn., 1943, I–II.

Fausboell, V. En Anklaget Anklager, Groenbechs Forlag, Kbhn., 1946.

Hagensen, A. Den Joediske Periode 1864–1900, E. Jespersens Forlag, Kbhn.

Nielsen, H. Joeden, Filisteren of Holsteneren, H. Aschehong, Kbhn., 1917.

—— Europas Fremtid, To Aktuelle Afhandlinger, Eget Forlag, Kbhn., 1942.

—— Europas Oedelaeggelse, Eget Forlag, Kbhn., 1944.

—— Mordokaj og Haman: En Studie, Eget Forlag, Kbhn., 1945.

Nilus, S. Zions Vises Protokoller, Andersen, A. H., Den Ny Tid's Forlag, Kbhn., 1940.

BIBLIOGRAPHIC ENTRIES ADDED TO PAPERBACK EDITION (1983)

Borchsenius, P. Historien om de danske Joeder, Fremad, 1968.
Browning, Ch. The Final Solution and the German Foreign Office, Holmes & Meier Publishers, New York, London, 1978.
Haestrup, J. . . . Til Landets Beste, I, Gyldendal, Kbhn., 1966.
—— Dengang i Danmark, Joedisk ungdom pa traek, Odense Universitets-forlag, 1982 (about to appear in English in USA).
Thomsen, E. Deutsche Besatzungspolitik in Dänemark, Bertelsmann Universitäts-verlag, Düsseldorf, 1971.
Tortzen, Ch. Gilleleje Oktober 1943 - under joedernes flugt for nazismen, Fremad, 1970.

Index

This index is based upon the original Hebrew model which was set up by my son Jonathan, who fell in the Six Day War, and his wife Miriam.—L.Y.